Past and Present Publi

An island for itself

The medieval southern Italian economy is commonly interpreted as having been dependent on foreign trade; and this dependence is held in turn to have caused economic backwardness in the Italian south. This study of late medieval Sicily develops a critique of theories of dependence through trade, and a new interpretation of the late medieval economy. The book thus addresses current debates on the origins of modern Italian economic dualism, and on the transition from feudalism to capitalism in early modern Europe.

The book argues that economic development during this period was shaped largely by regional political and institutional structures which regulated access to markets. Contrary to the view that medieval peasants invariably pursued subsistence strategies, it is suggested that the rate of peasant involvement in the market depended on historically variable institutions; as these institutions changed, rates of commercialization would also change, with major consequences for a society's long-term economic development. Following the Black Death, many institutional and social constraints on commercialization were relaxed throughout western Europe as a result of social conflict and demographic change. Peasants became more commercialized; economic growth occurred through regional integration and specialization. The Sicilian economy also expanded and became increasingly export-oriented, although only a small proportion of its output was shipped abroad before 1500. Late medieval Sicily is thus shown to have been neither underdeveloped nor dependent on foreign manufactures and trade.

Past and Present Publications

General Editor: PAUL SLACK, *Exeter College, Oxford*

Past and Present Publications comprise books similar in character to the articles in the journal *Past and Present*. Whether the volumes in the series are collections of essays – some previously published, others new studies – or monographs, they encompass a wide variety of scholarly and original works primarily concerned with social, economic and cultural changes, and their causes and consequences. They will appeal to both specialists and non-specialists and will endeavour to communicate the results of historical and allied research in readable and lively form.

For a list of titles in Past and Present Publications, see end of book.

An island for itself

Economic development and social change in late medieval Sicily

STEPHAN R. EPSTEIN
Research Fellow, Trinity College, Cambridge

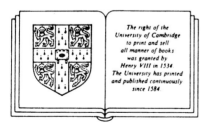

The right of the
University of Cambridge
to print and sell
all manner of books
was granted by
Henry VIII in 1534
The University has printed
and published continuously
since 1584.

CAMBRIDGE UNIVERSITY PRESS
Cambridge   New York   Port Chester
Melbourne   Sydney

PUBLISHED BY THE PRESS SYNDICATE OF THE UNIVERSITY OF CAMBRIDGE
The Pitt Building, Trumpington Street, Cambridge, United Kingdom

CAMBRIDGE UNIVERSITY PRESS
The Edinburgh Building, Cambridge CB2 2RU, UK
40 West 20th Street, New York NY 10011-4211, USA
477 Williamstown Road, Port Melbourne, VIC 3207, Australia
Ruiz de Alarcón 13, 28014 Madrid, Spain
Dock House, The Waterfront, Cape Town 8001, South Africa

http://www.cambridge.org

First published 1992
First paperback edition 2003

A catalogue record for this book is available from the British Library

Library of Congress Cataloguing in Publication data
Epstein, Stephan R., 1960–
An island for itself. Economic development and social
change in late medieval Sicily / Stephan R. Epstein.
        p.   cm. – (Past and present publications)
Includes bibliographical references and index.
ISBN 0 521 38518 0
1. Sicily (Italy) – Commerce – History.   2. Sicily (Italy) – Economic
conditions.   3. Sicily (Italy) – Social conditions.   4. Sicily
(Italy) – History.   5. Sicily (Italy) – Politics and
government – 1282–1870.   I. Title.
HF417.S54E67   1992
380.1'0945'80902–dc20   91-16257   CIP

ISBN 0 521 38518 0   hardback
ISBN 0 521 52507 1   paperback

To R. A. and M. W. E.

Contents

List of maps		*page* x
List of tables		xi
Acknowledgments		xiii
Abbreviations		xiv
Currency and measurements		xvi
Chronology		xvii
1	Introduction. The historiography and the sources	1
2	Regional geographic and demographic differentiation	25
3	Market structures and regional specialization	75
4	Sicily and its regions. Economic growth and specialization	162
5	Sicily and its regions. Eastern val Demone and the southern mainland	240
6	Foreign trade and the domestic economy	268
7	Income distribution, social conflict and the Sicilian state	314
8	A further question: the origins of Sicilian underdevelopment	402
	Bibliography	413
	Index	447

Maps

2.1 Geographic divisions of Sicily   *page* 28
2.2 Val di Mazara   30–1
2.3 Val di Noto   34–5
2.4 Val Demone   38–9
2.5 Sicily   41
3.1 Toll franchises, 1199–1499   104
3.2 Fairs, 1223–1499   114
4.1 Specialized wine production   177
4.2 Cloth manufacturing 1350–1500   192
4.3 Sugar manufacturing 1400–1500   213
4.4 Mines and mining 1400–1500   233

Tables

2.1 The population of Sicily, 1277–1497   *page* 42
2.2 Estimated hearths by *vallo*, 1277–1501   51
2.3 Demographic variations (per cent), 1277–1501   58
2.4 Tax allocation to the demesne (per cent of total),
    1374–6 to 1497   61
2.5 Provisions for in- and out-migration, 1300–1499   64
2.6 Resettlement licences (*licentia populandi*), 1400–1499   66
2.7 The ten largest Sicilian towns (estimated taxed hearths),
    1277–1497   71
3.1 Toll franchises, 1199–1499   98
3.2 Fairs, 1223–1499   108
3.3 Toll franchises and fairs, 1199–1499   119
3.4 Official grain prices (*mete*) in Palermo and Catania,
    1400–1499 (*tarì/salma*)   148
3.5 Frequency distributions of Sicilian communities,
    1277–1497   153
3.6 Settlement hierarchies by *vallo*, 1277–1497   155
4.1 The *fodrum* of 1283   172
4.2 New butcher's shops (*plancae*) and mills, 1400–1499   175
4.3 *Bactinderia* and *paratoria*, 1300–1499   193
4.4 Saltworks, 1300–1499   224
6.1 Terms of trade between wheat (Catania) and foreign
    cloth (Palermo), 1400–1459   287
6.2 Foreign cloth imports to Palermo, 1407–8 to 1496–7   298
6.3 Sicilian trade with Genoa, 1376–1377   301
6.4 Main shipping destinations from Palermo, 1298–1459   305
6.5 Chartering merchants and ships departing·from Palermo,
    1298–1459   310
7.1 Sales of feudal land, 1300–1509   344

7.2 Causes of social conflict in the demesne and the
    Camera reginale, 1392–1499   361

Acknowledgments

In the course of my work I have made many friends and incurred many debts of kindness. Criticism and encouragement have come from David Abulafia, Rita Astuti, Franco D'Angelo, Vincenzo D'Alessandro, John Hatcher, Rodney Hilton, Philip Jones, Sheilagh Ogilvie, Zvi Razi, Marina Scarlata, Peter Spufford, Nick Stargardt and Chris Wickham. Professor Henri Bresc generously provided me with material on the foreign grain trade. Pietro Corrao and Igor Mineo have endured many hours of strenuous discussion; Maria Teresa Ferrer has been unfailingly hospitable at the Departamento de Estudios Medievales (CSIC) in Barcelona; and Santina Sambito has been untiringly helpful in answering my requests for information and material from the Archivio di Stato in Palermo. My thanks go also to Rachel Neaman of Cambridge University Press, for the care and attention with which she copy-edited the final manuscript.

I was able to pursue research in Italian and Spanish archives thanks to generous financial aid from the University of Cambridge, the British School at Rome and the British Academy. Trinity College, Cambridge, has been especially supportive during my years as a graduate and a Research Fellow, and has provided an ideal intellectual setting for writing this book.

Abbreviations

ABP	Archivio Comunale di Palermo, Atti bandi e provviste
ACFUP	*Acta Curie Felicis Urbis Panormi*
AESC	*Annales. Economies. Sociétés. Civilisations*
ASI	*Archivio storico italiano*
ASM	*Archivio storico messinese*
ASS	*Archivio storico siciliano*
ASSO	*Archivio storico per la Sicilia orientale*
BCSFLS	*Bollettino del Centro di studi filologici e linguistici siciliani*
C	Archivo de la Corona de Aragón (Barcelona), Cancilleria, Registros
CR	Archivio di Stato di Palermo, Conservatoria di Registro
CEHE	*Cambridge Economic History of Europe*
CRS	Archivio di Stato di Palermo, Corporazioni religiose soppresse
CS	Archivo del Reino de Valencia (Valencia), Real, Camarae Siciliae et Valentiae, Reginale dominae Mariae
DSSS	*Documenti per servire alla storia di Sicilia*
EcHR	*Economic history review*
ES	*Economia e storia*
JEH	*Journal of economic history*
JJ	Archivo Historico de Protocolos (Barcelona), Jaume Just, leg. 1
LV	Archivio di Stato di Palermo, Tribunale del Real Patrimonio, Lettere viceregie e dispacci patrimoniali

MEFRM	*Mélanges de l'Ecole française de Rome. Moyen âge–temps modernes*
NC	Archivio di Stato di Catania, Notai I versamento
NCorl	Archivio di Stato di Palermo, Notai di Corleone
NM	Archivio di Stato di Messina, Notai
NN	Archivio di Stato di Siracusa, sezione di Noto, Notai
NR	Archivio di Stato di Catania, Notai di Randazzo
NS	Archivio di Stato di Siracusa, Notai I porta
PR	Archivio di Stato di Palermo, Protonotaro del Regno
QS	*Quaderni storici*
RC	Archivio di Stato di Palermo, Cancelleria
RCA	R. Filangieri, *I registri della cancelleria angioina ricostruiti con la collaborazione degli archivisti napoletani* (Naples, 1950 to date)
RR.II.SS	*Rerum Italicarum Scriptores*
RSI	*Rivista storica italiana*
TRP	Archivio di Stato di Palermo, Tribunale del Real Patrimonio
TRP n.p.	Archivio di Stato di Palermo, Tribunale del Real Patrimonio, numero provvisorio
UM	H. Bresc, *Un monde méditerranéen. Economie et société en Sicile, 1300–1450* (Rome, 1986)

Currency and measurements

The basic money of account in medieval Sicily was the gold *onza*, which was, however, never actually coined. One *onza* included thirty *tarì*; 1 *tarì* was worth twenty *grani* and one *grano* was equivalent to six *denari*. Thus 1 *onza* = 30 *tarì* = 600 *grani* = 3,600 *denari*. In references to sums of money, each full stop distinguishes monetary subdivisions. Thus 2.2.15.1 *onze* stands for two *onze*, two *tarì*, fifteen *grani* and one *denaro*; 2.3.4 *tarì* stands for two *tarì*, three *grani* and four *denari*.

Grain, legumes and some other agricultural products were measured in *salme*. In Sicily, west of the river Salso, the *salma* corresponded to c.2.75 hl; to the east of the river Salso the *salma* was twenty per cent larger, c.3.3 hl. The *tratta*, the duty paid to the crown for one exported *salma* of wheat (or for two *salme* of barley and legumes), was correspondingly higher in eastern Sicily than in the west. The smaller *salma* (also known as *salma generale* or *legale*) is the measurement most commonly referred to and I have followed custom.

The *cantaro*, equivalent to 79.35 kg, was the most common measure of weight, and was divided into 100 *rotoli*. The Sicilian pound (*libbra*), which was used, for example, to weigh silk, was equivalent to 0.317 kg. Cloth was measured in *canne*; one *canna* was approximately 2.06 m long.

Chronology

1250	Frederick II of Hohenstaufen dies
1262	Peter, future king of Aragon, marries Constance, daughter of Manfred of Hohenstaufen
1265–6	Charles I of Anjou receives the kingdom of Sicily from the pope
1276	Peter III is crowned king of Aragon
1282	Revolt of the Vespers: the Sicilians rise against the Angevins. Peter III of Aragon lands in Trapani. The Angevins are expelled from Sicily
1283	Combined Sicilian and Aragonese forces occupy Calabria
1285	Peter III dies; he is succeeded by his sons James (in Sicily) and Alfonso (in Aragon)
1286	James is crowned king of Sicily
1291	Alfonso III of Aragon dies; he is succeeded by James (II), who leaves his younger brother Federico in Sicily as his regent
1295	Treaty of Anagni between James II of Aragon, Charles II of Anjou, king of Naples, and Philip IV of France. James renounces his claims over Sicily in favour of Charles
1296	Parliament of Catania. Federico III is acclaimed king of Sicily
1302	Treaty of Caltabellotta between Sicily and Naples. Federico III adopts the title 'king of Trinacria', and agrees that Sicily will return to the Angevins at his death
1312	Anti-Guelph alliance between Federico III and emperor Henry VII

1313	Federico invades Calabria, but is repulsed
1314	Angevin attack on Sicily, followed by a fourteen-month truce
1316–17	Angevin expeditions against Sicily
1321	Sicily is set under papal interdict
1322	Pietro II is raised by his father, Federico III, to the Sicilian throne as co-regent
1325–7	Angevin expeditions against Sicily
1335	Angevin expedition against Sicily, assisted by the Sicilian magnate, Giovanni Chiaromonte, count of Modica
1337	Federico III dies; he is succeeded by Pietro II
1337–8	Magnate revolts in Sicily; new Angevin expedition
1340	Banning of the Palizzi magnates from Sicily
1341–2	Angevin expedition against Sicily; Milazzo surrenders
1342	Pietro II dies; he is succeeded by Ludovico, a minor. Duke Giovanni, Ludovico's uncle, becomes regent
1345	Angevin expedition against Sicily
1347	Peace between Sicily and Naples
1347	Genoese ships from the Crimea bring the bubonic plague to Messina
1348	Duke Giovanni dies; the magnate factions vie for control of King Ludovico
1354	The Angevins conquer Milazzo and land in Palermo to popular acclaim
1355	King Ludovico dies; he is succeeded by Federico IV, a minor
1356	The Angevins enter Messina
1357	Major Angevin defeat in Aci
1362	Peace of Piazza between the main magnate factions
1364	The Angevins lose Milazzo and Messina
1372	Final peace treaty between Sicily and Naples; the papal interdict is repealed
1377	Federico IV dies; his heir, Maria, is put under the guardianship of Artale Alagona, the leading

	magnate in eastern Sicily who resides in Catania. The kingdom of Sicily is officially shared out among four magnate 'vicars'
1379–81	Queen Maria is kidnapped and taken to Sardinia
1388	Maria is taken to Catalonia
1390	Maria marries Martin the Younger (Martino of Sicily), son of Martin, duke of Montblanc
1391	The four vicars and other magnates meet in Castronovo and vow to resist any attempt by the Aragonese to reconquer Sicily
1392–5	Martin, duke of Montblanc and his son, King Martino (I) of Sicily, invade and conquer Sicily
1395	Martin of Montblanc becomes king of Catalonia–Aragon
1397	Parliament in Catania
1398	Palermo surrenders to the Aragonese; the last magnate rebellions in Sicily are defeated Parliament in Syracuse
1402	Queen Maria dies
1403	Martino I of Sicily marries Blanche of Navarre
1409	Martino dies heirless; he is succeeded by his father, Martin I of Aragon. Blanche of Navarre is made regent of Sicily
1411	Martin of Aragon dies heirless; Blanche maintains her office as regent. A rebellion by Bernardo Cabrera, *maestro giustiziere*, leads to civil war in Sicily
1412	Ferdinand I of Castile is elected in Caspe by representatives from Aragon, Catalonia and Valencia to succeed Martin of Aragon
1416	Ferdinand I dies; he is succeeded by his son, Alfonso V of Aragon
1421	Alfonso briefly visits Sicily on his way to Naples
1423	Alfonso is adopted by Queen Jeanne II of Naples; he tries to establish his authority in the kingdom of Naples, but is forced to retreat
1435	Jeanne II dies; heir designate of the kingdom of Naples is René of Anjou. Alfonso launches his *amprisa* to conquer the southern mainland
1442–3	Alfonso conquers Naples and takes up residence there

1444–5	Revolt of Antonio Centelles, count of Collesano, against Alfonso
1453	Constantinople falls to the Turks
1458	Alfonso V of Aragon dies; he is succeeded by his brother, Juan II. The kingdom of Naples is separated from the crown of Aragon and goes to Alfonso's illegitimate son, Ferrante
1459–60	Political crisis over Charles of Viana's succession to the throne of Navarre; his father, King Juan II of Aragon, opposes the succession
1462	Civil war breaks out in Catalonia
1469	Ferdinand of Aragon, son of King Juan II, marries Isabella of Castile
1472	End of the Catalan civil war
1479	Juan II dies; he is succeeded by Ferdinand
1480–1	The Turks occupy Otranto on the southern mainland and begin raiding the Sicilian coasts
1486	With the Sentence of Guadalupe, which allows the peasants to redeem their freedom, Ferdinand puts an end to the *remença* problem in Catalonia
1492	Expulsion of the Jews from Ferdinand's reigns
1494–5	Charles VIII of France invades Italy and reaches Naples, but is forced to retreat
1499–1504	Spanish–French wars for control over Naples; the French are defeated. The kingdom of Naples is incorporated into the Spanish empire
1511	A revolt in Palermo is suppressed with aristocratic aid
1514	Ferdinand II attempts unsuccessfully to revoke feudal titles
1516	Ferdinand II dies; he is succeeded by Charles II (from 1519 Charles V)
1516–23	Series of feudal conspiracies and revolts

1. *Introduction. The historiography and the sources*

A problem that has haunted the Italian nation since its inception is that of the origins and causes of the current economic and social disparities between North and South. For a long time it has been assumed that the answer to the problem – known as the *questione meridionale*, the southern question – could be found in the Middle Ages. There is, indeed, a general consensus that the economy of southern Italy or *Mezzogiorno* (which includes Sicily and Sardinia and borders on central Tuscany to the north) was permanently overtaken by that of central and northern Italy at some point during the high or late Middle Ages.

In this book I suggest a very different interpretation. Taking late medieval Sicily as my example, I argue that the region showed considerable economic, demographic and social dynamism, and that it provides an important test-case for a more general theory of economic development in late medieval Europe as a whole. Contrary to prevailing views that the period was one of economic stagnation or contraction, I suggest that the main result of the late medieval social and economic crisis was to increase regional specialization and integration, which in turn provided the base for the demographic and economic upsurge of the late fifteenth century. However, opportunities for specialization were not pursued in identical fashion throughout late medieval Europe. Each regional 'path to development' was shaped by that region's specific constellation of social institutions defining access to markets and trade. Institutional structures might be more or less flexible, more or less conducive to long-term economic growth. As a result of the crisis, therefore, economic specialization *between* regions also increased, although to a far lesser degree. The late medieval European economy, I suggest, must be examined comparatively by studying the

1

relations between regional institutional structures, and economic development and growth.

Before addressing these problems more closely, however, we must briefly examine the historiographical tradition within which the debate on southern Italian backwardness is set. Some awareness of the debate's general thrust is necessary, if only because readers unversed in the historiography might otherwise find some of what I shall say either self-evident or obscure. In addition, although the debate is shaped by national historiographical and political traditions, its thrust goes far deeper. The *Mezzogiorno* provides a testing-ground for some of the most recent and widely-held theories about the origins and development of capitalism, which state that large parts of medieval and early modern Europe – southern Italy, parts of Spain and much of eastern Europe – were blocked in their development by 'colonial' exploitation through international trade.[1]

The main current approaches to the origins of the *questione meridionale* can be traced back to the nineteenth and early twentieth centuries.[2] The first approach, which might be termed geo-historical, denied that southern Italy had ever had a golden period: the area had *always* lagged behind its neighbours. The reasons for such backwardness were geographic, climatic and sometimes racial; they were either immutable, or responded only extremely slowly to change.

A second approach concentrated on the impact of political developments and social institutions on long-term social and economic performance. According to one version, decline in the South began with the Norman conquest in the tenth and eleventh centuries. The Normans introduced feudal relations in political and social life, and

---

[1] For recent statements on this theme see C. M. Cipolla, *Il fiorino e il quattrino: la politica monetaria a Firenze nel 1300*, p. 14; A. Furió ed., *Valéncia, un mercat medieval*, pp. 7–23; J. Edwards, '"Development" and "underdevelopment" in the western Mediterranean: The case of Córdoba and its region in the late fifteenth and early sixteenth centuries'; M. Balard ed., *Etat et colonisation au Moyen Age et à la Renaissance*; R. H. Britnell, 'England and northern Italy in the early fourteenth century: the economic contrasts'; A. Guarducci ed., *Sviluppo e sottosviluppo in Europa e fuori d'Europa dal secolo XIII alla Rivoluzione industriale*. Theories of 'colonialism' are also commonly applied to eastern Europe, in particular Poland; see W. Kula, *An economic theory of the feudal system. Towards a model of the Polish economy 1500–1800*. See also below, chapter 8.

[2] G. Galasso, 'Considerazioni intorno alla storia del Mezzogiorno in Italia', is the best overview of the debate.

adopted a strongly anti-urban policy. They were therefore responsible for the destruction of a budding bourgeoisie which was developing in cities like Amalfi, Salerno, Naples and elsewhere along the lines of the northern Italian communes.[3] A German historian, Alfred Doren, stressing the importance of *regional* institutions for economic growth, argued in a similar way that the main reason for the South's economic stagnation was its lack of independent city-states.[4] Monarchy, he thought, had transformed the southern, feudal countryside into a centralized, bureaucratic state; instead of developing their own independent ('autarchic') territories as in northern Italy, southern cities 'were fitted into the wider territory of the state as members of a single organism, and as a rule enjoyed very limited autarchy'.[5] Doren was thus suggesting that politically and institutionally independent cities were necessary for long-term economic development. But although the role of the communes in northern Italian economic development is nearly a historiographical axiom, Doren's hypothesis about the role of towns in southern Italy has never been seriously tested;[6] I shall do so in chapter 3.

A different and more influential politico-institutional view was expressed by the philosopher and historian Benedetto Croce in 1925. Croce argued that a political event – known as the Sicilian Vespers of 1282 – 'marked the beginning of much trouble and little greatness'.[7] Between the late eleventh century and 1282, southern Italy and Sicily were unified under the same crown: first under the Normans, later under the German Hohenstaufen, and finally, between 1266 and 1282, under a cadet branch of the French Angevins. In April 1282, a popular uprising expelled the Angevins from Sicily. In their stead the Sicilians called on Peter III, king of Aragon and count of Barcelona, to establish an independent monarchy (Peter's claims to the Sicilian throne were based on his marriage to Constance, the granddaughter of Frederick II). War with the Angevins was inevitable. The new kingdom of Sicily and what became the kingdom of Naples (but was still named kingdom of Sicily until

---

[3] Galasso, 'Le città campane nell'alto medioevo', pp. 134–5; S. Tramontana, 'La monarchia normanna e sveva', pp. 593–6.
[4] A. Doren, *Storia economica dell'Italia nel Medio Evo*, pp. 361–82.
[5] *Ibid.*, pp. 213–14.
[6] S. R. Epstein, 'Cities, regions and the late medieval crisis: Sicily and Tuscany compared', 12–15.
[7] B. Croce, *History of the Kingdom of Naples*, pp. 15–16.

1458) warred intermittently until the mid-fifteenth century. The two
kingdoms were briefly reunited under the crown of Aragon between
1442 and 1458; final unity came only after the Spanish victory
against the French in 1506.

Croce believed that political separation between Sicily and the
mainland following the Vespers had disastrous long-term consequences. The separation sapped the financial and military energies
of what, united, was the wealthiest monarchy in western Europe at
the time. Instead of expanding towards the Levant against the
Arabs, the Anjou spent their kingdom's resources trying to recon-
quer Sicily from the Aragonese. In addition, the separation of Sicily
from the mainland prevented different southern regions from
specializing and complementing each other's deficiencies: after
1282, grain-deficient areas in southern Italy could no longer rely on
Sicilian supplies.[8] Although the expulsion of the Anjou from Sicily
opened the door to later Spanish claims to southern Italy, which had
the merit of reuniting the South under one rule, the benefits of
foreign rule ended at this point.

A third approach to southern Italian backwardness emphasizes
the economic impact of long-distance trade between the North and
the *Mezzogiorno*. The empirical base for this view was provided by
a medievalist, Georges Yver, in a book published in 1903 on the
kingdom of Naples under Charles I and Charles II of Anjou.[9] Yver,
who was only incidentally concerned with current debates on the
questione meridionale, wished to demonstrate the beneficial effects
of Angevin rule in the South. In fact, he initiated one of the main
tenets of current views of southern Italian underdevelopment,
namely the dominance of foreign trade and foreign merchants over
the southern economy. The main exponent of this 'commercialist'
view, however, was Gino Luzzatto, who believed that exchange and
economic 'complementarity' between the North and the *Mezzogiorno* was the main source of southern Italian economic change
before industrialization. Until quite recently, Luzzatto's implied
assumption that Italy was commercially unified before the nineteenth century has been accepted by most historians.

[8] M. de Boüard, 'Problèmes de subsistances dans un état médiéval: le marché et les
prix des céréales au royaume angevin de Sicile (1266–1282)'. This argument seems
to have applied primarily to the southern mainland: Sicily at the time does not
seem to have imported much from the mainland.
[9] G. Yver, *Le commerce et les marchands dans l'Italie méridionale au XIIIe et au
XIVe siècle*.

Luzzatto began by drawing a sharp contrast between predominantly 'agricultural' and predominantly 'industrial' regions. Southern Italy was always 'agricultural', whereas many regions in central and northern Italy were 'industrial'. Because southerners did not engage in foreign trade and lacked the northern Italian entrepreneurial spirit, the South became 'dependent' on northern Italy for its manufacturing, and was forced to specialize in agricultural staples for export. Furthermore, whereas northern exports indicated a strong 'industrial' base, southern surpluses were the result of underpopulation and low living standards. 'Dependence' was not, however, restricted to the *Mezzogiorno*. It existed in any region where there was no great commercial and industrial city. Even 'marginal' regions of northern and central Italy – Piedmont, the Romagna, the Marche and Umbria – became 'dependent' on foreign credit and trade.[10]

Although there have been few new theories advanced to explain the *questione* since Luzzatto's time, there has been one major methodological innovation. This has involved grafting Luzzatto's analysis onto the new stem of development economics which emerged after World War II in the wake of decolonization.[11] In the context of our debate, the most influential theory of 'underdevelopment' has been that of economic dualism. Despite the fact that the theory has no rigorous and generally accepted definition,[12] it is usually employed with two distinct meanings. Economic dualism is often used to denote economic relations between two distinct territories, relations that are also sometimes described as 'complementary'. But the theory of economic dualism is more usually applied to a single territory whose economy is divided into two sectors. The manufacturing (or 'advanced') sector, which is very small, works according to profit-maximizing rules; the agricultural (or 'backward') sector, which includes the majority of the population, operates according to a 'paternalist and quasi-feudalist regime', and the marginal productivity of labour is significantly lower

---

[10] G. Luzzatto, *Storia economica dell'età moderna e contemporanea*, I, pp. 103–15; Luzzatto, *Breve storia economica dell'Italia medievale. Dalla caduta dell'Impero romano al principio del Cinquecento*, pp. 202–9.

[11] A review of the themes and literature of development economics can be found in A. O. Hirschmann, 'The rise and decline of development economics'; I. M. D. Little, *Economic development. Theory, policy and international relations*.

[12] R. Hodson and R. L. Kaufman, 'Economic dualism: a critical review', 727.

than in manufacturing. The 'backward' sector in a dual economy is
poorly, or not at all, commercialized. In addition, there is 'factor
immobility' (of either capital or labour or both) between the two
sectors: for institutional or cultural reasons, capital is not invested
in agriculture and labour does not move freely between agriculture
and manufacturing.[13] An important but often overlooked consequence of the latter assumption is to rule out capital accumulation
and productivity increases in the agricultural ('backward') sector.

One reason why the concept of a 'dual economy' has been so
successful among historians lies in its close parallels with the influential view of the role of towns and long-distance trade for pre-
industrial, and particularly medieval, economic development. According to this view (whose exponents include Adam Smith, Max
Weber and Henri Pirenne), medieval economic and social change
originated with long-distance merchants, whose 'capitalist', pro-
gressive outlook distinguished them from contemporary
'traditional' and stable-state societies. Merchants mobilized large
volumes of capital and achieved high profits; they were especially
well endowed with entrepreneurial skills; their mobility and profit
motivation inclined them towards cultural and technical innovation. Long-distance traders were thus in a unique position to
promote economic growth. In this dualist scheme, town–country
relations are viewed in similar terms, towns being external to the
backward, feudal, agrarian economy to which they convey economic dynamism. Peasants are thus purely subsistence-oriented, and
enter into trade relations only through external pressure or
inducement.[14]

Most recent interpretations of the medieval southern Italian
economy have taken a dualist approach. The first to do so was Philip
Jones,[15] who combined it with a theory of 'colonial' dependence

[13] R. Kanbur and J. McIntosh, 'Dual economies'. The model of dualism in a single
economy was first outlined by W. A. Lewis, 'Economic development with unlimited supplies of labour'.

[14] A. Smith, *An inquiry into the nature and causes of the wealth of nations*, Book 3,
chapter 4; M. Weber, *Economy and society*, II, chapter 16; H. Pirenne, *Medieval
cities, their origins, and the revival of trade*. For critiques of this scheme see
J. Merrington, 'Town and country in the transition to capitalism'; R. Brenner,
'The origins of capitalist development: a critique of neo-Smithian Marxism'. I
discuss peasant economic strategies in chapters 3 and 4 below.

[15] P. Jones, 'Medieval agrarian society in its prime: Italy', p. 348; Jones, 'Economia
e società nell'Italia medievale: la leggenda della borghesia', p. 205.

based on long-distance trade. While stressing that dualism was mainly due to geographical factors,[16] Jones has more recently included some traditional institutional elements – the absence of urban 'freedom', the predominance of aristocratic landowners over a commercial and manufacturing 'bourgeosie' – to explain medieval southern backwardness.[17] 'Dependence' arose because competition from foreign industry either destroyed or inhibited the growth of domestic manufactures in the South; as a result, the local economy began to specialize in the production of agricultural staples for export.

'Only in the primary sector – the export of foodstuffs and primary materials – the South, characteristically, *like all underdeveloped regions*, contributed appreciably to international exchange', writes Jones in an echo of Luzzatto. He continues,

during the Middle Ages, *as later*, 'colonialism' in some form was inherent in the process of economic expansion, at least insofar as this was based on international trade. According to this wider point of view, there was nothing special in the relationship that developed between the North and the *Mezzogiorno*. It was instead, once again, a prototype or model. Similar contrasts and similar links between developed and underdeveloped areas took place in the whole of Europe (just as, later, in the whole world), under the differentiating influence of economic expansion . . . In economic terms, actually, as also socially and politically, the 'North' and *Mezzogiorno* were something more than mere geographic expressions: they symbolized relations which were present, more or less openly, in the whole peninsula.[18]

This passage summarizes three central features of current theories of the origins of the *questione*. First, the South's economy developed under the stimulus and constraints of agricultural exports. Second, agricultural exports are the hallmark of a 'colonized' economy, particularly when manufactured goods are imported in exchange. And finally, 'medieval Italy offered the perfect prototype

---

[16] Jones, 'Medieval agrarian society', pp. 340–2; Jones, 'Economia e società', pp. 204, 215; R. Romano, 'La storia economica. Dal secolo XIV al Settecento', pp. 1813–15.
[17] Jones, 'Economia e società', pp. 232–3. See also J. H. Pryor, 'Foreign policy and economic policy: the Angevins of Sicily and the economic decline of southern Italy, 1266–1343'.
[18] Jones, 'Economia e società', pp. 205, 206 (my italics).

of a 'dual' or 'bisectoral' economy: one part was backward, the other was advanced'.[19] As claimed previously by Luzzatto, this relationship existed throughout Italy, between different regions and individual cities. Even in the most advanced, mercantile urban economies – of which perhaps less than a dozen existed – an extensive 'backward' sector could be found.[20]

The first of these features is the point of departure for most medieval and early modern historians of southern Italy,[21] and I discuss it at length in the body of this book. The second point would seem to derive from the first, apparently because agriculture is assumed to be *always* less productive than manufacturing. In fact, there are no *a priori* reasons for deciding whether this is the case, or even whether agriculture will be more or less capital-intensive than manufacturing at a particular level of technological development.[22]

The third point – that a situation of economic dualism existed both between North and South and within the most developed northern Italian urban economies – is the most problematic, because it applies the concept of 'dualism' indiscriminately to both *territorial* and *sectoral* differences. There are problems with both senses of dualism in the context of the *questione*.

Although the concept of geographical dualism is even more vague than that of sectoral dualism, it does imply stable, long-term and organic relations of 'complementarity' between two distinct territories, relations that shape each economy through competitive forces. Economic 'complementarity' thus presupposes the existence of a unified market. Emilio Sereni and Luciano Cafagna have, however, shown that a unified market in Italy did not exist before the 1870s. At most there existed commercial relations between single regions, or between single northern cities and single southern

---

[19] *Ibid.*, p. 205.

[20] *Ibid.*, p. 214.

[21] For Sicily see, for example, I. Peri, 'Economia agricola e crisi nella Sicilia medioevale. Interpretazioni e prospettive storiografiche', pp. 96, 98–9; V. D'Alessandro, 'Città e campagna in Sicilia nell'età angioino-aragonese', pp. 202–3; C. Trasselli, *Storia dello zucchero siciliano*, p. 14; O. Cancila, *Impresa redditi mercato nella Sicilia moderna*, pp. vii–viii, 263. For the kingdom of Naples see A. Grohmann, *Le fiere del Regno di Napoli in età aragonese*, pp. 262–8; A. Leone, *Profili economici della Campania aragonese*, pp. 49–51, 63, 73.

[22] In the period 1761–1830, for example, English agriculture was more capital-intensive than industry (G. N. von Tunzelmann, 'Technical progress', p. 159).

regions. Moreover, these relations were restricted to only a few products (grain, wine, silk) and were fairly easily interrupted.[23] The concept of geographical dualism applied in this way can be criticized further. To draw a contrast between what were actually 'mere geographic expressions', North and South, presupposes a lack of significant regional economic variation within the *Mezzogiorno*. Medievalists are at pains to differentiate between and within the regions of central and northern Italy, but they often view southern Italy – stretching from Lazio to Sicily, from Sardinia to the Puglie – as being comparatively undifferentiated, and thus as having few opportunities for specialization for the internal (southern Italian) market.[24] Little attention has been given to one of the most significant developments of the late medieval European economy, regional specialization and growth; these are discussed in chapters 3–5.

The concept of sectoral dualism raises different problems. Its main assumptions – the existence of 'surplus labour', the lack of commercialization, and the presence of economically oppressive institutions in the 'backward' sector – have never been seriously tested for any medieval Italian region. Partly because of this, the definition of what constituted the 'advanced' medieval sectors is deduced arbitrarily from dualist assumptions; for example, Jones posits that the luxury textile industries of certain northern Italian communes were more 'developed' than the cheaper manufacturing industries producing for domestic markets.[25] This issue is discussed in more detail in chapters 5 and 6.

There are two major problems with the way the dualist model has been used by historians. First, although the dualist model was devised to explain economic *growth*, historians have tended to use it to describe conditions of permanent economic *stagnation*. Second, the dualist model itself fails to specify the institutional transformations whereby a dual, asymmetrical economy turns into

[23] E. Sereni, 'Mercato nazionale e accumulazione capitalistica nell'Unità italiana'; L. Cafagna, *Dualismo e sviluppo nella storia d'Italia*, pp. 183–220; A. Del Monte and A. Giannola, *Il Mezzogiorno nell'economia italiana*, pp. 392–6. See also below, chapter 8.
[24] See, however, Yver, *Commerce*, pp. 396–8; Grohmann, *Fiere*; R. Comba, 'Le origini medievali dell'assetto insediativo moderno nelle campagne italiane', pp. 393–404. For the early modern period see A. Lepre, *Storia del Mezzogiorno d'Italia*, I, pp. 19–46.
[25] Jones, 'La storia economica', pp. 1480–92.

an integrated one. The model does not account for economic *development* and institutional change.[26] The assumption of institutional stasis or equilibrium is to say the least problematic, for it clearly does not apply to human societies over long stretches of time, and it produces inappropriate generalizations about the character of institutions. To state, for example, that serfdom and indebtedness produce dualistic distortions in labour markets without considering the wider context in which these institutions are set, makes it impossible to explain why apparently similar institutions can lead to very different outcomes, not excluding economic development – the contrast between medieval England and early modern Poland is a classic example.

More recently, work on medieval southern Italian economies has tended to focus on the mechanisms of *exchange* which are supposed to have caused 'colonized' and 'colonizing' areas to emerge. In 1977, David Abulafia published a book whose title, *The Two Italies*, made clear reference to the dualist approach developed by Jones. Abulafia addressed the question of the 'origins' of southern backwardness by examining Genoese, and to a lesser extent Venetian, twelfth-century commercial contracts involving Sicily and southern Italy. He argued that by *c*.1180, northern Italian (Genoese) merchants had established a powerful commercial network based on the exchange of high-value cloths from northern Europe for grain, cotton and other agricultural goods from Sicily and the southern mainland.[27]

In this work, Abulafia payed little attention to domestic conditions in the South, or to the volume of foreign trade relative to domestic output. His emphasis on long-distance trade also led him to solve the problem of the relation between political action and economic development by according a determining influence to the political and fiscal choices of the Norman kings. In later work, Abulafia has addressed domestic conditions in the South more closely, reaffirming his earlier view that Norman policies to a large extent gave shape to the southern Italian economy, and that Italy as a whole was structured dualistically on the exchange of southern

---

[26] Kanbur and McIntosh, 'Dual economies', p. 119.
[27] D. S. H. Abulafia, *The two Italies: economic relations between the Norman Kingdom of Sicily and the northern communes*.

unprocessed raw materials for northern manufacturing and financial services.[28] Abulafia's analysis was extended to later periods by two French historians, Maurice Aymard and Henri Bresc, who together have done most in recent years to establish the relevance for the economic development of Italy, and in particular Sicily, of theories of underdevelopment. Although Aymard has worked mainly on the early modern period, his work has major implications for medieval historians. Aymard began with a simple theory of economic dualism in which Sicily played the role of both a 'backward' and a 'colonial' country.[29] More recently, he has sought to adapt to the Italian case Witold Kula's model for early modern Poland.[30] By integrating these views with Immanuel Wallerstein's 'dependency theory', he has produced a model of Sicilian and southern Italian underdevelopment within a more general theory of Italy's transition from the feudal to the capitalist mode of production.[31]

Like Luzzatto and Jones, Aymard's main theoretical premise is that 'the inequalities of Italy's development form a whole, the coherence of which must be explained'.[32] Within this whole, the South was dominated by the northern 'commercial and manufacturing metropoles of the "developed quadrangle"' (Venice, Milan, Genoa and Florence); economic domination by the North permanently blocked the South's development.[33]

By defining capitalist development in terms of interregional commercial exploitation, however, Aymard is led into a number of inconsistencies. The most significant of these concerns the nature of the integration of Italy's national market which (as we have seen) Sereni and Cafagna argue was of no real significance before the 1870s. On the one hand, Aymard is led by his premises to emphasize

28 *Ibid.*, 'Conclusion'; Abulafia, 'Southern Italy and the Florentine economy, 1265–1370'; Abulafia, 'The crown and the economy under Roger II and his successors'.
29 M. Aymard, 'Production, commerce et consommation des draps de laine du XIIe au XVIIe siècle (Prato, 10–16 avril 1970)'; Aymard, 'Amministrazione feudale e trasformazioni strutturali tra '500 e '700', 22.
30 Kula, *Economic theory*; Aymard, 'Amministrazione feudale'; Aymard, 'Il commercio dei grani nella Sicilia del '500'.
31 Aymard, 'La transizione dal feudalesimo al capitalismo'; I. Wallerstein, *The modern world-system*.
32 Aymard, 'Transizione', pp. 1177, 1183–5.
33 *Ibid.*, pp. 1143, 1145, 1147, 1158, 1169–70, 1179, 1182, 1189. See also Kula, 'Il sottosviluppo economico in una prospettiva storica'.

the unity of the 'national' market and the regional division of labour.[34] On the other hand, he confuses regional division of labour (specialization) with interregional dualism ('developed' versus 'underdeveloped' regions).[35] He writes of a structure of juxtaposed *regional* markets,[36] claiming that regional markets were economically more significant than interregional trade,[37] hinting at the 'speculative' and irregular nature of such trade, particularly of grain,[38] and mentioning in passing that a national market did not in fact exist.[39] The role played by interregional trade for development in the North is never spelled out – a considerable weakness (common to most dualist approaches), since theories of 'dependence' necessarily apply to both parties involved.[40]

Aymard's assumption of the crucial role of interregional trade for pre-industrial Italian development collapses as soon as he confronts the relatively paltry volume of trade involved. By defining capitalism as trade on markets, Aymard cannot explain the apparent capitalist *regression*, the severe *contraction* in interregional trade which occurred in Italy from the late sixteenth century,[41] and the subsequent 'seventeenth-century crisis'. Finally, just as Aymard is unable to shed light on the original process of transition to dependence (the most he can say about the emergence of regional inequalities is that it occurred some time between the twelfth and the sixteenth centuries),[42] his structural theory of dependence is incapable of explaining the process of transition to capitalism.[43]

On this front, Henri Bresc has more to say. Bresc's important study of Sicilian 'economy and society' between *c.*1300 and *c.*1450, the result of two decades of research, is set firmly within the French tradition of the regional *thèse*. It is a 'total history', that wishes to uncover 'the medieval roots of modern Sicily ... of the obsessive

[34] Aymard, 'Transizione', pp. 1145, 1147, 1158, 1179, 1182.
[35] *Ibid.*, pp. 1169–70.
[36] *Ibid.*, pp. 1145, 1172.
[37] *Ibid.*, pp. 1183–5, 1186, 1188.
[38] *Ibid.*, p. 1163.
[39] *Ibid.*, p. 1175; see p. 1161 for the cloth market.
[40] *Ibid.*, p. 1147 and n. 2.
[41] *Ibid.*, pp. 1180, 1183–5, 1186.
[42] *Ibid.*, pp. 1145, 1158.
[43] *Ibid.*, p. 1187.

presence of the prestige and values of an urban aristocracy which
rested on the "fief", in other words the *latifondo*'.[44]
Bresc's work is the first study of its kind of a southern Italian
region, and is also the most consistent attempt to apply current
theories of underdevelopment, 'colonialism' and 'dependency' to a
medieval European region. Bresc's answer to the question of Sicilian underdevelopment raises, more clearly than any of his predecessors, issues concerning the relationship between political,
institutional and long-term economic change, which are central to
the historiography of the *Mezzogiorno*.
Bresc argues that, as a result of Norman economic and fiscal
policies, Sicily began slowly to specialize in grain monoculture for
export.[45] The Muslim rebellion of the 1230s and 1240s and its defeat
by Frederick II marked 'the triumph of an extensive, speculative
economy and of grain monoculture for export' over agricultural and
industrial differentiation based on Muslim technology.[46] This outcome was due to the 'capacity of the Sicilian ruling classes to
develop an organically conceived latifundium', and found parallels
in other Mediterranean countries subjected to 'colonial feudalism'.[47] A further, more crucial break in Sicilian history occurred
with the uprising of the Vespers of 1282. The Vespers definitively
entrenched the island's role as a purveyor of grain to the western
Mediterranean in 'unequal' exchange for manufactured goods
(mainly cloth) it no longer produced.[48] Not only was Sicily forced to
increase grain exports to pay for its military defence against Angevin attack from the southern mainland; the country also lost
any opportunities to engage in fruitful trade with the southern mainland and to exploit economic complementarities for specialization.
Benedetto Croce's dictum that the Vespers sounded southern
Italy's death knell is thereby confirmed.[49]
After 1300, Bresc states, 'the lack of vast changes and the cyclical
character of developments justify a static approach to an economy

[44] *UM*, p. 1. See the review by E. I. Mineo, 'Nazione, periferia, sottosviluppo. La Sicilia medievale di Henri Bresc'.
[45] H. Bresc, 'Reti di scambio locale e interregionale nell'Italia dell'alto Medioevo', p. 157.
[46] *UM*, p. 16. See below, chapter 4.
[47] *UM*, pp. 18, 20–1.
[48] This view was first developed by Carmelo Trasselli; see Epstein, 'The textile industry and the foreign cloth trade in late medieval Sicily (1300–1500): a "colonial relationship"?', 141–2.
[49] *UM*, pp. 576, 917; see Croce, *History*, pp. 15–16.

and society that are blocked, the eternal return of the prestiges and values of a world which after the end of domestic mercantile society was unable to produce an entrepreneurial environment'.[50] Bresc thus combines two only apparently conflicting intellectual traditions. On the one hand, we find Croce's preoccupation with the political and intellectual élite, interpreting southern Italian history as the outcome of ruling-class choice. On the other hand, we have the structuralist theory of Third World economic 'dependency' as elaborated by Samir Amin, André Gunder Frank and Immanuel Wallerstein. The two approaches have this in common, that they both dispense with social conflict and domestic institutions. As Bresc states approvingly,

> [for dependency theorists] the articulation between modes of production, between centre and periphery, was the result of a universal law. The violent capture, simultaneously, of the centres of decision-making, of consumption and production of an archaic economy ... condemned the periphery to long-term backwardness, now renamed dependence.[51]

Bresc's uneasy combination of extreme voluntarism – whereby Sicilian economic structures emerged from deliberate choices by the feudal aristocracy, which imposed its economic and cultural values on the 'Sicilian people' – with equally extreme structural determinism, means that he is effectively prevented from addressing the relation between political and economic change.

In this context, one can also object to Bresc's use of the documentary evidence. Because Bresc assumes from the start that no significant change occurred in Sicily's domestic economy, he presents his evidence *en bloc* for the entire period 1300–1450 with little regard for change over time. Evolution and change is allowed only for sectors linked to foreign markets.[52]

To a certain degree, Bresc's arguments depend on his choice of written sources. His reliance on notarial records for most of the economic analysis is particularly problematic. Although in recent decades the use by historians of the western Mediterranean of private, mainly notarial documents has caused a veritable method-

[50] *UM*, p. 21.
[51] *UM*, p. 3. See S. Amin, *Unequal exchange*; A. G. Frank, *Capitalism and under-development in Latin America. Historical studies of Chile and Brazil*; Wallerstein, *The modern world-system*; J. G. Palma, 'Dependency'.
[52] *UM*, chapters 6, 8–11.

ological revolution and vastly widened the field and techniques of research, some methodological problems of relevance for economic and social history have often been overlooked.

The traditional problem of documentary transmission and of how representative surviving records are is particularly severe in the case of notarial registers, because contracts were customarily drawn up on paper and were thus easily destroyed. Yet this is a minor difficulty compared to that of the *content* of notarial records. Individuals went to a notary to record, in a legally binding way, transactions whose outcome was deferred to some point in the future: the transmission of wealth in wills, *post mortem* inventories and dowries, labour and tenurial relations (self-administered property does not of course appear). Last but not least, notaries recorded commercial transactions involving large payments, or in which one of the parties was foreign and had to be able to enforce legal claims; in fact, the two conditions often coincided.

Notarial contracts are thus biased towards certain kinds of deferred transaction, which as far as commercial relations are concerned tend to overrepresent high-value, often foreign-based, trade over everyday local exchange. Most day-to-day transactions, many informal work relations, and most patterns of livelihood were only recorded by chance and have left few written traces.[53] Yet, the sheer abundance of notarial records for parts of late medieval Europe has sometimes led historians to assume that transactions that went unrecorded did not exist. Bresc, who bases much of his work on an extensive sampling of the notarial registers of Palermo, Sicily's main commercial emporium which particularly dominated the foreign cloth market (see chapter 6), has adopted precisely this assumption, and has consequently greatly overestimated the importance of foreign trade.[54]

Because notarial registers tended to record transactions that were either strictly local or those of foreign merchants, they are a poor basis for constructing a regional picture. Of the few hundred notarial registers that survive for Sicily from the fourteenth and fifteenth centuries, most concern western Sicily and in particular Palermo. Consequently, Bresc's reliance on this type of document has given him a view of the regional economy which is to a large

---

[53] J. Bernard, 'Trade and finance in the Middle Ages 900–1500', p. 302.
[54] Further criticisms of these sources in P. Brezzi and E. Lee, *Private acts of the late Middle Ages. Sources of social history*, pp. xxi, xxiii, 101–2.

degree restricted to western Sicily and Palermo. This is a matter of
some importance. On the one hand, it raises serious doubts about
the accuracy of the many statistical tables Bresc provides.[55] On the
other hand, Bresc's picture of the regional economy emerges much
distorted. The west was the most underpopulated part of the island,
far more oriented than the east to grain production for the domestic
and international markets, and with poorly developed manufacturing. By contrast, far from being 'underdeveloped', as Bresc suggests,[56] eastern Sicily was (as we will see in chapters 2, 4 and 5) the
most dynamic area of the island throughout the later Middle Ages.

This brief outline of current views of the medieval southern Italian
economy suggests that some modern theories of underdevelopment
and 'dependency' have been applied in ways that are imprecise and
ultimately misleading. Concepts like 'dualism' or 'dependence' are
used with little analytical rigour; value-laden terms like 'backward',
'traditional', 'colonial' or 'dependent' are applied rhetorically to
what was in fact a mere geographical expression, the *Mezzogiorno*.
    Largely because of the traditional emphasis on the role of long-
distance trade for the economy of the *Mezzogiorno*, medieval
southern Italian *regional* economic structures, and relations between domestic and foreign markets have aroused less interest. One
of the arguments of this book is that the economic and social
development of late medieval western European regions was

---

[55] Evidence for cheese exports, for example, shows that these statistics can be very
    unreliable. By restricting himself to Palermitan notarial records, Bresc consis-
    tently underestimates cheese exports and misrepresents their regional distri-
    bution. See *UM*, p. 562, Table 143, quoting total cheese exports in 1370–9 of 6,853
    cantara, barely seventy per cent of what Genoa alone imported over only seven
    months in 1376–7; exports quoted by Bresc for the entire fourteenth century are
    only twice what Genoa imported in 1376–7 (below, Table 6.3). *UM*, Table 143,
    suggests that from *c.*1420 onwards, approximately fifty per cent of Sicilian cheese
    exports were shipped from Palermo. On the other hand, in 1407–8 (the only year
    for which precise figures survive), Palermo's quota of the export market was only
    4.7 per cent; evidence of livestock distribution in the fifteenth century also
    suggests that eastern Sicily produced a considerably higher proportion of cheese
    than Bresc allows (below, chapter 4). In 1458–9, for example, two Genoese
    merchants exported 930 *cantara* of cheese from the port of Licata which, accord-
    ing to Bresc, was not trading in that period (CR 847, unnumbered fo.; *UM*, Table
    143). Bresc's own figures are inconsistent. *UM*, Table 143, records exports in
    1400–9 of 4,565 *cantara*, whereas *UM*, p. 558, Table 140, records exports in
    September 1407–September 1408 of 4,518 *cantara*.
[56] *UM*, pp. 561, 566.

largely, although not exclusively, the outcome of domestic differentiation and specialization; and that changes in the structure of long-distance trade, which saw a slow but decisive shift towards cheaper, bulk commodities, meant that such trade played an increasing role in internal regional development. At the same time, I suggest that it was the character of regional social institutions that determined the outcome of the late medieval crisis.

For various reasons, late medieval Sicily provides a good test-case for this hypothesis. It was politically and institutionally distinct, even when it came under the aegis of the crown of Aragon in 1412; it had a sufficiently large territory to be economically self-contained, but at the same time it traded intensively with the entire western Mediterranean and beyond; its long coasts provided good potential conditions for the emergence of a well-integrated domestic market. Yet Sicily was neither unusual nor unique; one of the purposes of this study is precisely to dispel the idea of Sicilian, and by extension southern Italian, peculiarity, and to suggest that my findings for Sicily can be generalized to apply to other European regions in this period. To do so involves, on the one hand, an examination of regional specificities and differences *within* the *Mezzogiorno*; on the other hand, the drawing of broader comparisons with other Italian and European regions.

Such an approach, however, faces considerable methodological problems due primarily to the character of the sources. Historians' neglect of domestic developments is not simply the outcome of *a priori* choice. Foreign trade is generally far better documented than domestic transactions, 'largely because the former was taxed through customs duties and therefore some record of it was kept'.[57] Because of the importance of foreign trade for medieval Sicily, and because of the precocious development of a system of excise on external trade under the Normans and Frederick II, the relative importance of this trade for the Sicilian economy has been particularly exaggerated. As with the use of Sicily's notarial records, this error of perspective overemphasizes the importance of trade with the exterior.

As for sources concerned with domestic conditions, there is a considerable quantitative imbalance between the documentation produced by central administration and that produced by or within

[57] T. S. Willan, *The inland trade. Studies in English internal trade in the sixteenth and seventeenth centuries*, p. 50.

local ecclesiastical, feudal or urban jurisdictions. With the exception of some notable ecclesiastical archives (*tabulari*) that can provide valuable information on local communities, particularly for the fourteenth century,[58] both private and public documentation at the local level is remarkably scarce. Notarial records, as remarked above, survive mainly for Palermo and for a few other western Sicilian communities (Monte San Giuliano, Trapani, Termini, Corleone); the first surviving records from eastern Sicilian notaries date from the mid-fifteenth century (Catania, Syracuse, Noto, Randazzo, Messina). Urban administrative records exist only for Palermo, and from the late fifteenth century for Messina. As for seigneurial administrations, two accounts are known for the fourteenth century,[59] a few more for the fifteenth, but short of some unexpected discovery their number is unlikely to increase very much further.

The reasons for these huge gaps in the local documentation, particularly for the fourteenth century, are not hard to understand. On the one hand, Sicily has had its share of natural and man-made disasters which have sometimes irreparably damaged or destroyed the records of its past. Political upheaval has contributed to the drastic selection of the sources; there is no reason to believe that the lack of feudal administrative records for the fourteenth century was due to a lack of record keeping. The losses were almost certainly caused by the near annihilation of the fourteenth-century aristocracy after the Aragonese restoration of the 1390s, and to the institutional rupture this provoked. Most other official documentation (both urban and feudal) which we can suppose was produced during the second half of the fourteenth century, when the great magnates usurped royal authority, was presumably destroyed after the Aragonese landing in 1392.

On the other hand, the paucity of local documentation during the fourteenth, and to a lesser degree the fifteenth, century was probably the result of weakly developed and informal urban administrative structures before 1400, which I shall discuss in chapter 7. Up to then only the metropoles – Palermo, maybe Messina – seem to

[58] See Peri, 'Rinaldo di Giovanni Lombardo "habitator terrae Policii"'.
[59] E. Mazzarese Fardella ed., *Il Tabulario Belmonte*, pp. 38–46; A. Giuffrida, 'Il libro dei conti dell'Abate Angelo Senisio (1372–1381)'; G. M. Rinaldi ed., *Il 'Caternu' dell'Abate Angelo Senisio*.

have had a sufficiently structured public life to warrant keeping records of current administration. During the 1390s, a major shift in the documentation occurred as a result of contemporary political and institutional developments, whose main result for our purposes was the appearance of an almost completely new kind of document – the community petition to the crown for privileges or settlement of disputes, including accounts of local needs and social structures – which survives in the hundreds, and provides the single most important source for fifteenth-century Sicilian society.[60]

Because of the scarcity and uneven distribution of local sources, therefore, a comprehensive study of Sicily as a *region* must rely rather heavily on documentation produced for, or by, the central offices of the state. Local documentation tends to overrepresent western as against eastern Sicily, and this has resulted in the past in a biased picture of the island as a whole. For a more accurate portrait, we must draw on records which, by contrast with local documentation, have not been sifted by time to privilege one area of Sicily over another. More detailed local analyses, furthermore, depend for their understanding on a general framework of interpretation which they cannot alone provide. Finally, central records – preserved in the Archivio di Stato in Palermo and in the Archivo de la Corona de Aragón in Barcelona, and which include local petitions, royal inquests, concessions of regalian rights, administrative records of the royal demesne's tax offices – are, particularly for the fifteenth century, more numerous than the entire local public and private documentation combined. The reason for this is the administrative and bureaucratic reforms inaugurated by the Catalan–Aragonese monarchy during the 1390s, which vastly increased the extension and complexity of central administration and is only now beginning to attract historians' interest.[61]

It may at first glance seem curious to suggest that one pay greater attention to some of the more traditional forms of documentation generated by institutions (royal edicts, local statutes and petitions) for the study of economic and social history, which is often on the level of local peasant production. These documents' failings are

60 Epstein, 'Governo centrale e comunità locali nella Sicilia tardo-medievale: le fonti capitolari'.
61 A. Baviera Albanese, 'L'istituzione dell'ufficio di Conservatoria del Real Patrimonio e gli organi finanziari del Regno di Sicilia nel secolo XV (Contributo alla storia delle magistrature siciliane)'; P. Corrao, *Governare un regno. Potere, società e istituzioni in Sicilia fra Trecento e Quattrocento*.

well known: they reflect ideal or desired rather than actual conditions; they cover narrow interests with the mantle of the general will; they portray stasis rather than change. Yet a rigorous use of these sources can illuminate individual and group aspirations and goals, and the institutions which help mould society. More than any other, these sources document the relation between institutional, and social and economic change. In general, the traditional dichotomy drawn between norms and the 'real' world underestimates the importance of institutions and norms for the development of markets and the economy. Ordinances and petitions express, in more or less mediated form, social pressures and demands; at the same time, the norms they embody or request reinforce old constraints, establish new ones, and slowly change the structure of the 'real' economy.

One common theme running through the historiography on the Italian *Mezzogiorno* is the powerful influence of political events on economic development. We saw the most trenchant view of these relations expressed by Benedetto Croce.[62] Ernesto Pontieri and Henri Bresc have also argued that the Vespers destroyed any opportunity for economic integration between Sicily and the southern mainland.[63] Others, like David Abulafia, have emphasized the ability of ruling élite groups to shape domestic economic and agrarian structures for their own purposes. By contrast, Alfred Doren was more interested in the role that domestic, particularly urban, institutions played in economic development. Doren's approach is the most akin to the recent interest among economists and economic historians in the role of institutions in economic development and growth.[64]

An institutional analysis dwells necessarily on long-term change, if only because social institutions tend to evolve very slowly and gradually. While not entirely avoiding a discussion of conjunctural change, this book is mainly concerned with long-term economic development for two reasons. The first is that there exist few adequate time-series to follow short-term developments in any

---

[62] Croce, *History*, pp. 15–16; p. 59 on the economic consequences of Sicily's separation from the mainland.

[63] E. Pontieri, *Alfonso il Magnanimo re di Napoli 1433–1458*, pp. 11–63: Bresc, 'La formazione del popolo siciliano', pp. 253–6; *UM*, pp. 576, 917.

[64] See, for example, G. M. Hodgson, *Economics and institutions. A manifesto for a modern institutional economics*.

detail, and there is still a lack of local studies of late medieval agrarian or social history outside the largest cities (Palermo, Messina and Catania). The second reason is my concern with the interplay between institutional and political change, and the process and dynamics of economic growth in the long run.

Taking late medieval Sicily as a test-case, I develop two related but distinct arguments. On the one hand, I reinterpret the late medieval European socio-economic crisis by integrating the main current explanations, the neo-Malthusian and the Marxist – recently summarized in the so-called 'Brenner debate'[65] – and emphasizing the effects of regional institutional structures. On the other hand, I develop a critique of prevailing views of southern Italian economic history that is also relevant to other 'backward' parts of pre-industrial Europe. These two arguments' main unifying feature is the concept of markets as historical and dynamic institutions.

Economic development and growth is an evolutionary process in which social institutions play a crucial role in shaping individual practice and economic action. Markets, in turn, are complex sets of 'social institutions in which a large number of commodity exchanges of a specific type regularly take place, and to some extent are facilitated and structured by those institutions'.[66] Markets are also means of appropriating surpluses, of redistributing gains from production and trade. A market is thus both an enabling and a constraining structure, and the balance between these opposite forces (which varies over time) will to a large extent shape a producer's economic strategies. Markets are thus complex entities whose emergence, reproduction and evolution cannot be taken for granted, but has to be explained. This task is as much that of the political, institutional and social, as of the economic historian.[67]

[65] T. H. Aston and C. H. E. Philpin eds., *The Brenner debate. Agrarian class structure and economic development in pre-industrial Europe.*

[66] In turn, a social institution is 'a social organization which, through the operation of tradition, custom or legal constraint, tends to create durable and routinized patterns of behaviour'; see Hodgson, *Economics and institutions*, pp. 10, 174.

[67] My approach is thus at odds with the economic reductionism of the 'new institutional economics' school. For a critique of this approach see, for example, A. J. Field, 'The problem with neoclassical institutional economics: A critique with special reference to the North/Thomas model of pre-1500 Europe'; see also D. C. North, 'Transaction costs in history'.

The study of market structures is crucial for at least two reasons. First, it provides the economic historian with an organizing principle for a holistic (although not necessarily homologizing) approach to the past. The 'set of social institutions' which define a market include nearly every aspect of social life: property relations, technology, political and legal institutions, demographic factors, ideology, and resource and locational endowments, whose effect is mediated by those social institutions themselves.

Second, because economic development occurs as a result of exchange and competition in markets, it is primarily market structures that determine the character and rate of economic development in a society. By contrast, since property relations are only one (albeit crucial) determinant of market structures, one may not deduce the course of economic development from a (reified) structure of property relations alone.[68] To take an example that will be discussed more extensively below, one cannot infer a peasant smallholder's economic strategies from his ability to subsist on his own land (and his duty to pay rent to a feudal or other landlord); rather, his economic strategies will depend on how his access to markets is structured.

If one assumes that within the same social formation[69] there exists a *plurality* of institutions supporting a range of different market structures (for example, of modes of distribution and appropriation of surplus through trade), certain important consequences follow. First, a society's economic development will be shaped by the *interaction* of a range of different patterns of commercial activity. This might explain why, for example, economic development took such different courses in different parts of early modern East–Central Europe despite the deep integration into international

---

[68] As argued in Brenner, 'The agrarian roots of European capitalism'; Brenner, 'Economic backwardness in eastern Europe in light of developments in the West'. Brenner draws a stark contrast between the feudal economy, in which competitive markets are said not to exist at all (causing a structural tendency towards 'stagnation and involution'), and the capitalist economy, driven entirely by market competition. The approach I advocate here dispenses with the need for such a baldly dualist (and empirically untenable) model.

[69] The concept of social formation as containing a plurality of modes of production was first developed by Lenin. It was rediscovered by E. Balibar in L. Althusser and E. Balibar, *Reading Capital*. See also Sereni, 'Da Marx a Lenin: la categoria di "formazione economico-sociale"', and the debate in *Critica marxista*, 9 (1971); G. A. Cohen, *Karl Marx's theory of history. A defence*, pp. 77–9, 85–6.

trade networks of the area as a whole.[70] Second, the relative *efficiency* of the same market structure, shaped by the balance between its enabling and constraining aspects, may vary at different levels of economic development; in other words, institutional patterns supportive of economic growth vary with the degree of development of the productive forces. An example of this second statement can be seen in the medieval European independent city-state with strong monopolies over local trade. Until the fourteenth century, the market structures associated with such towns produced the highest rates of economic growth that medieval Europe had yet known. Later, as the scale of market efficiency increased to a regional dimension, many monopolistic city-states were left behind.[71] Another example seems to be that of early modern Sicily, whose economic decline appears to have set in when it was no longer able to gain access to institutionally supported supra-regional markets (see chapter 8).

These two points dispense with a normative view of the effects of specific institutions on markets, and thus with a prescription of the types of market most (or least) conducive to economic growth. They also dispense with a teleological view of pre-capitalist economic history as a mere anticipation or preparation to the Industrial Revolution, which does little justice to the spectrum of choices past societies faced and pursued to reproduce and expand their economic base. Just as there were many different kinds of pre-industrial market, there was never a *single* path to pre-industrial growth and development. Many paths led to dead ends or false promises; the glare of retrospective history has made them invisible. For them to be uncovered is a matter for careful theoretical and empirical reconstruction.

This book charts the process of economic development and growth in late medieval Sicily through regional specialization and integration. The main part (chapters 2–5) develops this theme for the domestic market. I begin in chapter 2 by identifying late medieval Sicily's three main sub-regions on the basis of topographic, settlement and demographic features; I then employ long-term

---

[70] See D. Chirot, 'Causes and consequences of backwardness', p. 8: 'Why has contact with the West and with Western markets sometimes stimulated economic progress in backward regions, and why has it sometimes had the opposite effect?'

[71] Merrington, 'Town and country', p. 183; Epstein, 'Cities, regions'.

population trends to follow changes in the territorial patterning of the regional economy. Chapter 3 consists of two parts. The first part develops a theoretical model of the late medieval economic crisis; the second part examines the evolution of market structures and the institutional context in which regional trade and specialization occurred. Chapter 4 examines changes in the structure and geographical distribution of production, and addresses the question of whether late medieval Sicily was characterized by *sectoral* dualism. Chapter 5 is a case-study of the market and productive structures of the smallest of the three sub-regions identified in chapter 2, val Demone, in particular of the area under the direct influence of Messina which included southern Calabria. In chapter 6, by contrast, I examine Sicily's foreign trade structure and test various underdevelopment theories (including that of *territorial* dualism) by assessing export volumes, the balance of trade, and the significance of foreign trade for regional development. Chapter 7 examines the relations between economic and socio-institutional change, looking in particular at the effects of shifts in income distribution on political and institutional power, and on the transition from a 'feudal' to a quasi-absolutist state.

Because I refer throughout this book to the impact of political and institutional developments on the economy, and to the effect of social and economic processes on social institutions, I have provided a brief chronology of the main fourteenth- and fifteenth-century political events to which I shall refer in the book. In order to avoid confusion over proper names, I have Anglicized all names of rulers, popes and Italian and Hispanic countries. The only exceptions are Alfonso V and Juan II of Aragon – who are better known as such than by their English name – and all Sicilian names, including those of the independent Sicilian sovereigns, which I have rendered in Italian.

2. Regional geographic and demographic differentiation

A basic feature of the Italian countryside is its extreme regional and local geographic variation. This diversity is not restricted to central and northern Italy. Sardinia, Lazio, Calabria or Abruzzi, for example, have little in common except their (differently structured) current economic misfortunes; and the same can be said of Sicily.

Although the question of late medieval regional differentiation and specialization is developed more fully in chapter 3, two elements of this hypothesis must be briefly anticipated here. In the first place, I argue that a major consequence for western Europe of the late medieval demographic and social crisis was that comparative advantages in available natural and human resources became increasingly effective, and that, possibly for the first time in the Middle Ages, regional commercial integration became a very powerful engine of economic growth. Secondly, I take the demographic growth rate as a rough index of economic expansion *in the long run*, on the assumption that any given society has a certain relationship between population and resources (mediated by its institutions), and that when resources increase, so too, after a certain time-lag, does population. The calibration between population and resources in a society can, of course, be allowed to change – as I argue in chapter 3, this occurred in most of western Europe between the mid-fourteenth and the mid-to-late fifteenth centuries[1] – but it will do so either rather slowly or as a result of a series of severe exogenous shocks (I believe the latter is what occurred in the later Middle Ages). I assume, therefore, that once the population began to recover, and *in the aggregate*, there was a positive correlation between demographic growth rates and regional wealth. The correlation between population density and

[1] For examples in later periods see P. P. Viazzo, *Upland communities. Environment, population and social structure in the Alps since the sixteenth century*, chapter 10.

wealth is clearly much weaker in periods of demographic decline (when mortality and epidemics, rather than fertility and the availability of resources, played the main role in population change), for the incidence of epidemics is tied inextricably to many other structural features and chance events of the past which are for the most part still unknown.[2]

The purpose of this chapter is to briefly analyse Sicily's natural and demographic resources, and to delineate major sub-regional demographic differentiation. Despite their intrinsic interest and importance I do not discuss small-scale environments, for one of the purposes of this study is to establish a general framework for more detailed local analysis – which will in turn, of course, inevitably modify the framework itself.[3] Given the tendency among historians to write about 'Sicily' as an undifferentiated landmass, or to dismiss most of eastern Sicily as an insignificant exception to a dominant economic model based on a few decontextualized features of the west of the island,[4] it is useful as a first approximation to dwell on large-scale geographical differences and on how they developed 'a dovetailed system of agricultural production'[5] and manufacturing. In the second part of the chapter, I discuss population movements within Sicily's three main sub-regions, laying the ground for the analysis in subsequent chapters of long-term economic change and specialization.

TERRITORIAL DIFFERENTIATION: THE 'VALLI'

Sicily, which extends over 25,434km² not including its small outlying islands, is the largest Mediterranean island. It can be divided into four geographic (sub-)regions, not including the great volcanic mass of Etna.[6]

The first of these regions, sometimes called the *Appennino Siculo*, is a mountain range strung along the northern coast from Messina in the east to the river Torto near Termini in the west. Rising from an average of 1,100–1,200m in the east to nearly 2,000m

---

[2] R. S. Schofield, 'Geographical distribution of wealth in England 1334–1649', 489.
[3] See C. Wickham, *The mountains and the city. The Tuscan Appennines in the early Middle Ages*, 'General Introduction'.
[4] *UM*, pp. 566–8; Aymard, 'Il commercio dei grani', with comments by G. Giarrizzo; Trasselli, 'Villaggi deserti in Sicilia', 249–52.
[5] J. Thirsk, 'The farming regions of England', p. 3.
[6] F. Milone, *L'Italia nell'economia delle sue regioni*, pp. 958–73; Milone, *Sicilia. La natura e l'uomo*, pp. 11–18.

in the west, the mountains are bordered by a narrow strip of land jutting into the sea. Very little arable exists here except for a small territory near the town of Milazzo. No major city has ever developed along these narrow rock shelves, with the notable exception of Messina (see chapter 5). While these mountains form one continuous chain and can be considered a region unto themselves, they divide into three geologically distinct complexes running from east to west: the Peloritani, the Nebrodi or Caronie, and the Madonie. Already in the late Middle Ages these mountains were the most densely forested areas in Sicily. Although Sicily's water-table has probably sunk since the Middle Ages,[7] this mountainous area has preserved its water supplies better than the rest of the island.

The Peloritani are formed mainly of gneiss and dark clay schists. They terminate somewhere between Novara and Francavilla, and are the only mountains in Sicily to contain iron ore, as well as some gold and silver. The Nebrodi, formed mostly of sandstone on the summits and of shaly clays further down, are lower, more undulating, and less craggy and steep than the Peloritani. They connect with the Madonie, the highest group of mountains after Etna, near Gangi (1,120m). The Madonie are calcareous; their watercourses disappear in the ground to reappear lower down as springs. In contrast to the Peloritani, which in the later Middle Ages were covered mainly with conifers, and on their lower reaches, with chestnuts and deciduous forests, beeches probably predominated on the Madonie. The Madonie end at the watershed of two rivers, the Torto and the Platani (also known as the Belice). The latter runs south-south-west to nearby Agrigento.

West of these two rivers lies our second region, a vast expanse of clayey, sandy and tufaceous hills, sloping slightly to the south and south-west. The main peaks tend to follow the northern coast, from Termini to the Conca d'Oro surrounding Palermo, to the hump of the Capo San Vito and the isolated peak on which Monte San Giuliano (modern Erice) rests. In the interior, the only mountains of some height are a southern outgrowth of the Madonie, skirted by the Platani and Belice Sinistro rivers, and culminating in Monte di Cammarata (1,579m). Although the area was probably never heavily wooded except on the outcrops of the Madonie behind

---

[7] J. Johns, *The Muslims of Norman Sicily, c.1060–c.1194*, p. 3 and n. 11, p. 195; M. Finley, *Ancient Sicily*, p. 5; below, chapter 3, n. 70. Less than four per cent (1,000km²) of contemporary Sicily is wooded (Milone, *L'Italia*, p. 965).

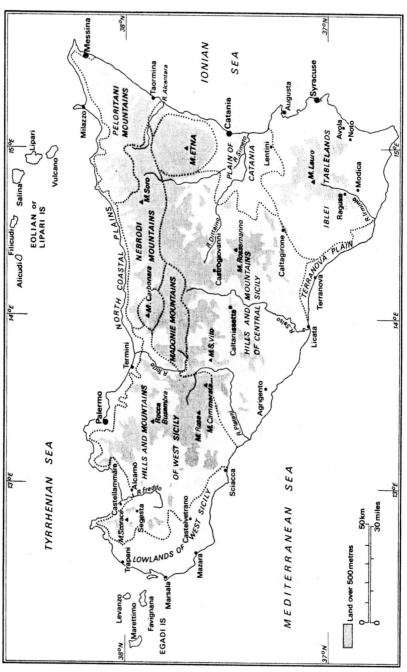

Map 2.1 Geographic divisions of Sicily

Termini, woodland and thick scrub still existed in the late twelfth century,[8] and probably expanded during the period of demographic decline in the fourteenth and early fifteenth centuries. The lack of high mountains has always restricted average rainfall in the area, but rain may have been more plentiful during the Middle Ages than it is today after centuries of deforestation.[9]

In comparison with the eastern and north-eastern parts of the island, this western sub-region has had a greater number of large cities, most of which are also major ports. Besides Palermo we find Trapani, Sciacca, Mazara, Marsala, Alcamo and Termini, which lie on some of the few alluvial and emerged plains; in the interior, Corleone was a major centre in the late thirteenth century.

This second major geographic area blends naturally into the third, today the most desolate and uninhabited region of the island. Its centre, the real heartland of grain-growing Sicily, is bordered to the west by the river Belice and to the east by the river Salso. The Salso has traditionally divided the island into two, often administratively separate areas, described as the 'hither' (*citra*, usually eastern) and 'nether' (*ultra*, or western) sides of the river. Two main geological formations are found in this region: chalky and sandy clays, often with deposits of rock salt; and chalk together with smallish surface deposits of crystallized sulphur, which began to be mined extensively from the early fifteenth century. The soil is such that once they have been uprooted, trees and bushes grow again with great difficulty. There are no large plains, but neither are there any real mountains – the hilly, undulating landscape slopes gently to the south, where it is cut off abruptly by the sea. The main city in this area is Agrigento, the foremost grain exporter of late medieval and early modern times. This area is bordered to the north by Castrogiovanni (modern Enna), and to the west by Piazza. These two towns lie along the main division between western and eastern Sicily, the watershed between the African Mediterranean and the Ionian Sea.

Our fourth area lies to the south and south-east of this watershed. Near Castrogiovanni and Piazza it features major chalk and sulphur deposits, mostly covered by more recent Pliocene marine deposits. To the south-east of these towns the land slopes down through rugged and deeply eroded hills towards Syracuse, Ragusa and the Iblei mountains. These form Sicily's third main mountain range;

---

[8] Johns, *Muslims*, pp. 191–4.
[9] Above, n. 7.

Map 2.2   Val di Mazara

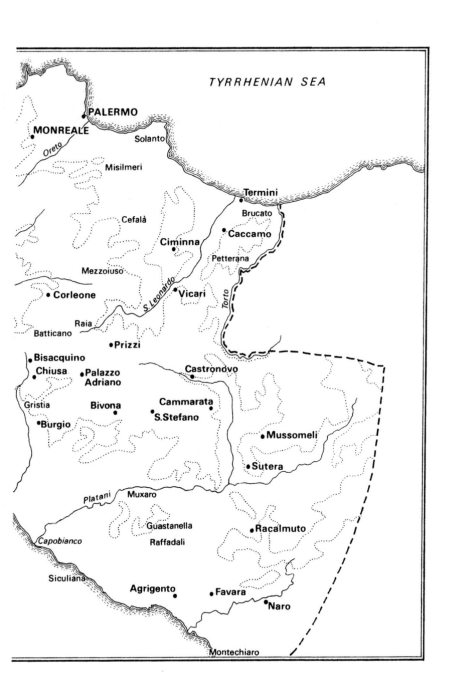

TYRRHENIAN SEA

PALERMO
MONREALE
Oreto
Solanto
Misilmeri
Termini
Cefalà
Brucato
Ciminna
Caccamo
Petterana
Mezzoiuso
Corleone
S. Leonardo
Vicari
Torto
Raia
Batticano
Prizzi
Bisacquino
Chiusa
Palazzo
Adriano
Castronovo
Gristia
Bivona
Cammarata
S.Stefano
Burgio
Mussomeli
Sutera
Platani
Muxaro
Guastanella
Racalmuto
Capobianco
Raffadali
Siciliana
Agrigento
Favara
Naro
Montechiaro

rainfall is higher here than in central Sicily. The soil includes ancient lava deposits, terraces of calcareous sandstone similar to those of western and central Sicily, and, towards Modica, flatlands of yellowish-white limestone providing excellent building material. The soil is generally fertile, and its lightness and permeability are ideal for arboriculture. The only large Sicilian plain is a northern extension of this region, bounded by the great mass of Etna which separates it from the Peloritani. The plain, which covers over 430km², is one of the most fertile soils in Sicily. The only major city in this area is Catania. Geological and geographical evidence thus points to a division of Sicily into four principal regions. Of these, the third in order of description, corresponding to central, grain-growing Sicily, is the least well defined and easily blends into the second, western, and fourth, south-eastern, areas. The geographical and administrative boundaries tend to coincide if we adopt the traditional division of late medieval and early modern Sicily into three *valli* (sing., *vallo*).[10]

Val di Mazara, west of the Salso and Imera rivers, which included all of the second and part of the third geographic region mentioned above, was by far the largest *vallo*, extending over 10,237km². Val di Noto, south of Castrogiovanni and Etna, which consisted of the remaining part of the third geographic region, all of the fourth region, and the plain of Catania, covered 8,499km² altogether. Val Demone, which included most of the northern mountain ranges as far as Termini, as well as the area north and north-west of the base of Etna, was the smallest of the three *valli*, extending over only 6,728km².[11]

The *valli* seem quite soon to have marked the boundaries of

---

[10] Milone, *Sicilia*, pp. 347–58. Until the late fourteenth century, the *vallo* was merely a small territorial unit administered by a justiciar, and the main administrative division was that between *citra* and *ultra Salsum*. See I. Carini ed., *De rebus Regni Siciliae (9 settembre 1282–26 agosto 1283). Appendice ai documenti inediti estratti dall'Archivio della Corona d'Aragona*, nos. 21, 74, 81; R. Gregorio ed., *Bibliotheca scriptorum qui res in Sicilia gestas sub Aragonum imperio retulere*, I, pp. 486–99. The three *valli* became Sicily's main administrative and fiscal subdivisions during the early fifteenth century, but their borders were probably not definitively stabilized before the sixteenth-century censuses (V. Epifanio, *I valli della Sicilia nel Medioevo e la loro importanza nella vita dello Stato*, p. 35). Communities assigned to the 'wrong' *vallo* in RC 76, fo. 109 (1440); C 3482, fos. 79–82 (1461); RC 195, fos. 103–9v (1496).

[11] Figures in K. J. Beloch, *Bevölkerungsgeschichte Italiens, I. Grundlagen. Die Bevölkerung Siziliens und des Königreichs Neapel*, pp. 153–4. The total adds up to 25,464km², 30km² more than what is now considered the correct figure.

distinct social and economic sub-regions; differences between them were well established by the late thirteenth century, and were reflected in patterns of agricultural production and in urban structures, as we shall see in chapters 3 and 4. The origins of the administrative subdivision into three *valli* are unknown, but may lie in the three stages of the Muslim conquest: the west in 827–*c*.841, the south-east in *c*.841–*c*.859 and the north-east in *c*.843–*c*.902. Under Muslim rule these three areas included different proportions of distinct ethnic groups. The west was mostly Muslim, while the south-east was settled equally by Muslims and Greeks, and the north-east by a Greek majority.[12] Under the Normans, these ethnic or religious differences tended to correspond to the distribution of serfdom (villeins were mostly Muslims). Conversely, the distribution of peasant freeholding tended to overlap with Christian settlement, a pattern often reinforced by subsequent immigration from central and northern Italy.[13] We shall see below that the unequal geographic distribution of peasant freehold had important consequences for late medieval social and economic developments.

THE POPULATION (1277–1501)

In common with many medieval population estimates, those for medieval Sicily have been strongly disputed. Early estimates, based on often undocumented inferences from evidence for the early modern period, have been significantly lowered, largely through Carmelo Trasselli's research.[14] Trasselli's revisions, however, describe nearly unchanging population levels between the late thirteenth and the mid-fifteenth centuries, and Henri Bresc has concluded on these grounds that the Sicilian economy in that period was 'immobile'.[15] Others have suggested far higher population figures for the late thirteenth century, without drawing out the full implications of this revision.[16]

[12] M. Amari, *Storia dei Musulmani di Sicilia*, I, pp. 606–10.
[13] Peri, 'La questione delle colonie "lombarde" in Sicilia', 253–80.
[14] Trasselli, 'Ricerche su la popolazione di Sicilia nel secolo XV', 213–71; Trasselli, 'Sulla popolazione di Palermo nei secoli XIII–XIV', 329–44; Johns, *Muslims*, pp. 167–8; F. D'Angelo, 'Terra e uomini della Sicilia medievale (secoli XI–XIII)'; Bresc, 'L'habitat médiéval en Sicile (1100–1450)'; *UM*, pp. 59–77.
[15] *UM*, pp. 60–102.
[16] Peri, *Uomini città e campagne*, pp. 244–5. My own interpretation differs both in method and results.

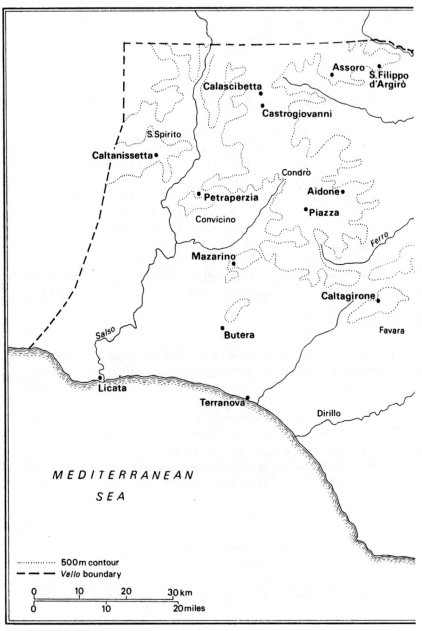

Map 2.3 Val di Noto

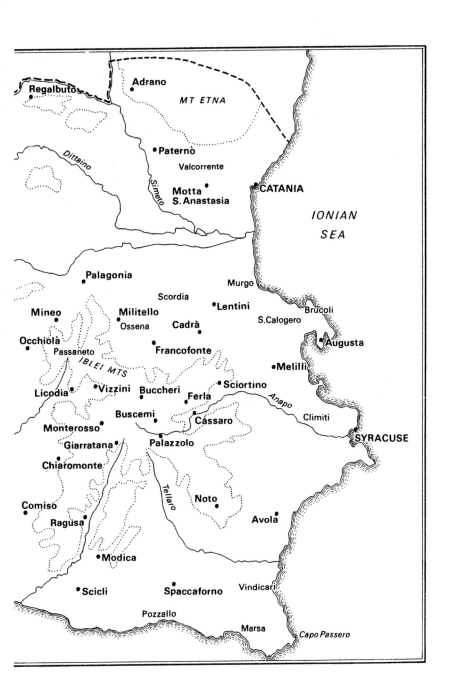

Regalbuto
Adrano
MT ETNA
Dittaino
Paternò
Valcorrente
Simeto
Motta
S. Anastasia
CATANIA
IONIAN
SEA
Palagonia
Murgo
Scordia
Lentini
Brucoli
Mineo
Militello
S. Calogero
Ossena
Cadrà
Occhiòlà
Passaneto
Francofonte
Augusta
IBLEI MTS
Melilli
Licòdia
Vizzini
Buccheri
Ferla
Sciortino
Anapo
Buscemi
Càssaro
Climiti
Monterosso
Giarratana
Palazzolo
SYRACUSE
Chiaromonte
Tellaro
Noto
Comiso
Avola
Ragusa
Modica
Scicli
Spaccaforno
Vindicari
Pozzallo
Marsa
Capo Passero

The main cause of these disputes is the interpretation to be given to some late thirteenth-century hearth taxes. The destruction of the Angevin archives in Naples makes it very hard to study fiscal administration in Sicily for the period 1266–82; in particular, there is no direct evidence of the average hearth tax that was paid.[17] By contrast, the fourteenth and fifteenth centuries are documented by a number of fiscal returns which, when integrated with other indirect evidence, can be used with caution to establish approximate population sizes and demographic trends.

I propose to re-examine these figures and question Bresc's most recent interpretation of those relating to the late thirteenth century. The result will show that the population fluctuated far more widely than is currently assumed, and that demographic trends in late medieval Sicily followed quite closely contemporary developments elsewhere in western Europe. I also discuss changes in demographic distribution between *valli*, on the basis of the assumptions spelt out at the beginning of this chapter about the relationship between demographic growth rates and available resources. I conclude by briefly examining changes in demographic distribution between coastal areas and the interior, and between different urban centres, for what they can tell us about changes in the distribution of rsources in our period. The consequences of these analyses and revisions for interpreting social and economic change in this period will be apparent in the course of the following chapters.

The main demographic sources for the period preceding the Black Death are two tax returns of 1277 and 1283.[18] Both were allocations rather than assessments; in other words, Sicily was set a total tax return, which was then shared out between different communities. Although we do not know the criteria by which this allocation was made, the fact that the full allocation was not returned suggests that local quotas were assigned on the basis of an assessment of demographic numbers and wealth. In 1277, a total of 15,000 *onze* was allocated, 7,500 to the justiciary of Sicily *citra Salsum* (east of the

---

[17] L. Cadier, *Essai sur l'administration du royaume de Sicile sous Charles Ier et Charles II d'Anjou*; R. Trifone, *La legislazione angioina*; G. Di Martino, 'Il sistema tributario degli Aragonesi in Sicilia (1282–1516)'; W. A. Percy Jr., 'The revenues of the Kingdom of Sicily under Charles I of Anjou 1266–1285 and their relationship to the Vespers'; Percy, 'The earliest revolution against the "modern state": direct taxation in medieval Sicily and the Vespers'.

[18] Peri, *Uomini città e campagne*, pp. 244–5, lists tax returns for 1271–8.

river Salso), and 7,500 to that of Sicily *ultra*. In fact, only 14,647.12 *onze* were returned.[19] In 1283, Peter III of Aragon demanded 20,000 *onze*, 12,000 from Sicily *citra*, and 8,000 from Sicily *ultra Salsum*, but only the returns for the latter survive.[20] The main difference between previous Angevin hearth taxes and the Aragonese tax was not the size of the tax itself (Angevins had occasionally demanded even higher sums), but the fact that the load was distributed so unequally between eastern and western Sicily; in previous Angevin taxations, the quota had always been divided equally between the two justiciaries.[21] Thus, while the difference between the two taxes does not necessarily reflect an increase in population, the levy of 1283 does appear to take into account for the first time a major shift of relative population density from western to eastern Sicily, signalling some important long-term changes in the island's demographic and settlement patterns.[22]

Whereas the *subsidium* of 1283 is more accurate than that of 1277, which may have been based on earlier assessments, the latter is the only complete allocation to survive for this period. Consequently, the allocation of 1277 is mainly useful for purposes of comparison with later estimates of total population, whereas the data for 1283 are useful for examining population distribution patterns, which can then be compared with fourteenth- and fifteenth-century data.

I base my revision of current estimates of the late thirteenth-century population on two mutually supporting elements. In the

---

19 The allocation of 1277 was published by C. Minieri Riccio, *Notizie storiche tratte da 62 registri angioini dell'Archivio di Stato di Napoli*, pp. 218–20, corrected by Beloch, *Bevölkerungsgeschichte Italiens*, p. 159.

20 Carini ed., *De rebus*, no. 394.

21 Percy, 'Earliest revolution'.

22 Beloch, *Bevölkerungsgeschichte Italiens*, pp. 91–2, argues instead that in 1277, 'the tax quota for each hearth was thus higher in the one province than in the other'. This is hard to believe, particularly since the tax burden had begun to shift from western to eastern Sicily already before 1250; under Frederick II, western Sicily tended to pay three to four times *more* than the eastern half (Percy, 'Earliest revolution'). While the earlier imbalance might indicate that Frederick II taxed the strong western Muslim population more heavily than he taxed Christians, this would not conflict with the hypothesis that the Muslim repression and deportation in the latter part of Frederick's reign shifted the demographic balance in favour of eastern Sicily (Peri, *Uomini città e campagne*, chapters 11–12). The Angevins must have recognized that such a change had occurred, for they began to levy the same quota from the two parts of Sicily soon after their conquest.

Map 2.4   Val Demone

Capo d'Orlando · Piraino · Gioiosa · Tindari · Milazzo · Bavuso · Faro · Calvaruso · Saponara · MESSINA · Condrò · S.Filippo · Monforte · Rametta · Salvatore · S.Angelo · PATTI · Oliveri · Nasari · S.Lucia · Sicaminò · Capri · Naso · Ficarrà · Martini · Librizzi · Furnari · Castroreale · S.Marco · Mirto · Castania · Sinagra · Raccuia · S.Pietro · Tripi · PELORITANI MTS · Itala · Alcara · Ucria · Novara · Fiumedinisi · Ali · Longi · Tortorici · Montalbàno · Mandanici · Pagliara · Militello · Galati · Casalvecchio · Savoca · Alcàntara · Roccella · Limina · Forza d'Agrò · Francavilla · Motta · MTS · Randazzo · Castiglione · Camastra · Taormina · Maniaci · Linguaglossa · Cesarò · Maletta · Calatabiano · Bolo · Bronte · Fiumefreddo · Mascali

IONIAN

SEA

Acireale

first place, I adopt an average quota of three *tarì* per hearth, rather than six *tarì* as Bresc and others have recently done.[23] I do this on the basis not of direct proof, which is unavailable, but of significant circumstantial evidence. Secondly, I revise population estimates for the 1280s on the basis of the evidence of substantial population losses after the mid-fourteenth century. I return to this evidence below.

The circumstantial evidence for assuming an average quota of three *tarì* per hearth is as follows. To begin with, we can assume that the average official quota in 1277 and 1283 was similar, although in 1283 the tax may have been exacted more efficiently. Evidence for other hearth taxes (*collette*) exacted in the same period shows that the annual hearth tax under the Angevins approximated to three *tarì*, both in Sicily and on the mainland.[24] The allocations of 1277 and 1283, which are both multiples of three, suggest this also. In addition, when Martino I of Sicily re-established the hearth tax in October 1398, chancellory records showed this had been set at 3.15 *tarì* (that is, half an *augustale*) by former sovereigns; Martino reduced this further to three *tarì*. In later years, the mean hearth tax would vary between two and three *tarì*.[25] Since no major fiscal reform was apparently undertaken before the mid-fifteenth century, it seems plausible that the late fourteenth- and fifteenth-century quotas harked back to a long tradition.

Assuming an average allocation of three *tarì* per hearth, the 1283 returns account for approximately 180,000 taxable hearths (allowing for a ten per cent higher average hearth quota for Palermo and Messina, the wealthiest cities in the kingdom), to which must be added a further ten to fifteen per cent to account for tax exempt individuals (ecclesiastics, feudal aristocracy, poor and transients)

---

[23] Beloch, *Bevölkerungsgeschichte Italiens*, p. 92; D'Angelo, 'Terre e uomini', 72; *UM*, p. 60.

[24] For a long time it was believed that the annual Angevin *subventio generalis* was one *augustale* (7.10 *tarì*) per hearth (Amari, *La guerra del Vespro siciliano*, p. 53 n. 4; Cadier, *Essai*, p. 32; Percy, 'Revenues', p. 62); in fact, this amount was only requested in case of war. See P. Egidi, 'Ricerche sulla popolazione dell'Italia meridionale nei secoli XIII e XIV', pp. 736–8, and Peri, *Uomini città e campagne*, pp. 246 and 324 n. 7 for hearth rates of 2 to 3.5.3 *tarì* in Sicily and Calabria.

[25] F. Testa ed., *Capitula Regni Siciliae*, I, p. 133 (1398). See also RC 25, fos. 45–6 (1396); RC 39, fos. 305v–6v (1401); RC 38, fo. 262v (1401); RC 40, fo. 56 (1403); *UM*, p. 72.

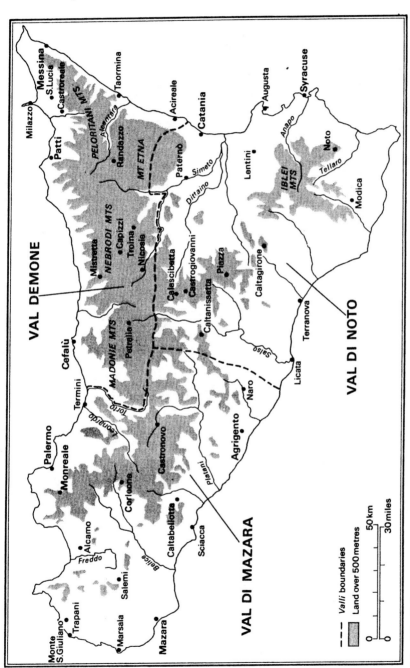

Map 2.5 Sicily

Table 2.1. The population of Sicily, 1277–1497

Val Di Mazara

	1277 (1)	1277 (2)	1374–6 (3)	1439 (1)	1439 (2)	1464 (1)	1464 (2)	1478 (1)	1478 (2)	1497 (1)	1497 (2)
Palermo	2,201.12.-	22,014	4,082	200.-.-	3,000	186.5.-	4,468	325.-.-[a]	5,109[b]	500.-.-	7,500
Agrigento	200.-.-	2,000	1,560	50.-.-	750	86.15.-	2,076	108.-.-	2,160	181.-.-	2,715
Trapani	680.18.-	6,806	2,608	80.-.-	1,200	96.3.7	2,306	132.-.-	2,640	220.-.-	3,300
Monte San Giuliano	160.-.-	1,600	838	40.-.-	600	38.13.7	923	49.5.-	983	79.-.-	1,185
Sciacca	162.-.-	1,620	1,028	120.-.-[a]	1,800	76.26.13	1,846	96.-.-	1,920	160.-.-	2,400
Termini	80.-.-	800	280	15.-.-	225	11.16	277	15.4.-	303	34.-.-	510
Polizzi	240.-.-	2,400	—	80.-.-[a]	1,200	86.15.-	2,076	128.-.-	2,560	161.-.-	2,415
Corleone	660.-.-	6,600	1,136	50.-.-	750	67.8.7	1,615	88.6.-	1,764	143.-.-	2,145
Marsala	390.18.-	3,906	663	40.-.-[a]	600	24.-.16	577	34.-.-	680	56.-.-	840
Salemi	250.-.-	2,500	579	60.-.-	900	57.20.-	1,384	50.12.-	1,008	86.-.-	1,290
Licata	152.-.-	1,520	456	60.-.-	900	48.1.14	1,162	63.-.-	1,260	100.-.-	1,500
Sutera	101.-.-	1,010	170	20.-.-	300	11.16	277	14.12.-	288	26.-.-	390
Naro	111.-.-	1,110	946	50.-.-	750	48.1.14	1,153	60.-.-	1,200	103.-.-	1,545
Castronovo	263.-.-	2,630	720	40.-.-	600	18.26.10	454	31.15.-	630	50.-.-	750
Chiusa			120	15.-.-	225	11.10.-	272	18.27.-	378	30.-.-	450
Sclafani	43.-.-	430	108 }	27.-.-	405	15.3.-	362	21.21.-	434	36.-.-[d]	540
Caltavuturo	180.-.-	1,800	257 }	30.-.-	450	22.20.-	544	37.24.-	756	60.-.-	900
Cammarata	143.-.-	1,430	51	4.-.-	60	-.23.-	18	1.12.-	28	2.-.-	30
Favara	2.-.-	20	175	12.-.-	180	7.16.10	181	9.18.-	192	16.-.-	240
Mussomeli			206	6.-.-	90	1.16.-	37	2.15.-	50	4.-.-	60
Vicari	101.-.-	1,010	514	46.25.12	704 }						
Caltabellotta	120.18.-	1,206	400	28.3.8	422 }	71.15.-	1,716	126.-.-	2,520	140.-.-[d]	2,100
Giuliana	4.-.-	40	472	24.11.-	366						
Bivona	38.-.-	380		6.-.-	90	3.23.10	91	6.9.-	126	60.-.-	900
Sambuca		}	137	2.-.-	30	-.23.-	18	1.7.10	25	10.-.-	150
Partanna			—	5.-.-	75	3.2.10	74	5.-.-	100	8.-.-	120
Burgio	12.-.-	120	36	3.-.-	45	1.16.-	37	2.18.-	52	8.-.-	120
Gibellina		—	48							4.-.-	60

Prizzi	10.–.–	100	86	4.–.–	60	1.16.–	37	2.18.–	52	6.–.–	90
Castelvetrano	60.18.–	606	—	25.–.–	375	18.26.10	454	31.15.–	630	50.–.–	750
Carini	25.–.–	250	56	3.–.–	45	–.23.–	18	1.9.–	26	2.–.–	30
Monreale	37.6.–	372	223	15.–.–	225	9.2.10	218	15.3.–	302	24.–.–	360
Santo Stefano			67	1.–.–	15	–.23.–	18	1.7.10	25	2.–.–	30
Racalmuto	2.–.–	20	136	5.–.–	75	3.2.–	73	5.–.–	100	9.10.–	140
Ciminna	10.–.–	100	343	20.–.–	300	11.10.–	272	18.27.–	378	30.–.–	450
Mazara	300.–.–	3,000	300	40.–.–[a]	600	30.6.–	725	70.–.–	1,400	101.–.15	1,515
Alcamo	70.–.–	700	651							45.–.–	675
Calatafimi	110.–.–	1,100	335							18.–.–	270
Castellammare			54			43.–.–	1,032	37.24.–	756		
Adragna	4.–.–	40									
Troccoli	16.–.–	160									
Muxaro			82								
Guastanella			34								
Santo Spirito			12								
Pietra d'Amico			20								
Bisacquino	20.–.–	200									
Palazzo Adriano	5.–.–	50									
Raia	5.–.–	50	48								
Patellaro											
Brucato	2.–.–	20									
Montemaggiore	2.–.–	20									
Donacby	4.–>	40									
Modica	5.–.–	50								474.18.–[d]	7,119
Cefalà (Chitala)				5.–.–	75					10.–.–	150
Total	6,983.–.–	69,830	20,037	1,208.10	18,125	1,115.26.18	26,782	1,611.9.–	32,226	2,574.10.15	38,615

Table 2.1. (cont.)

Val di Noto

	1277		1374-6	1439		1464		1478		1497	
	(1)	(2)	(3)	(1)	(2)	(1)	(2)	(1)	(2)	(1)	(2)
Catania	212.12.-	2,124[g]	—	100.-.-	1,500	86.15.-	2,076	112.10.10	2,247	190.-.-	2,850
Piazza	170.-.-	1,700	1,542	100.-.-	1,500	96.3.7	2,306	128.-.-	2,560	207.-.-	3,105
Caltagirone	200.18.-	2,006[g]	800	100.-.-	1,500	105.21.13	3,806	153.-.-	3,060	234.15.-	3,518
Calascibetta	—	—	515	29.-.-	435	22.3.4	530	29.-.-	580	48.-.-	720
Noto	91.18.-	916	1,372	100.-.-	1,500	105.21.13	3,806	128.-.-	2,560	206.-.-	3,090
Castrogiovanni	211.-.-	2,110	1,050	80.-.-	1,200	80.22.-	1,938	103.24.-	2,076	183.-.-	2,745
Caltanissetta	15.-.-	150	660	40.-.-	600	28.21.-	689	47.26.-	957	76.-.-[d]	1,140
Sortino	15.-.-	150	332	30.-.-	450	22.19.10	544	25.6.-	504	40.-.-	600
Avola	11.-.-	110	—	25.-.-	375	18.26.10	454	31.15.-	630	50.-.-	750
Mazarino	—	—	103	9.-.-	135	4.16.10	109	12.18.-	252	20.-.-	300
Assoro (Asaro)	11.-.-	110	200	25.-.-	375	17.11.10	411	29.-.-	580	46.-.-	690
Buscemi	25.-.-	250	—	10.-.-	150	7.16.10	181	12.18.-	252	20.-.-	300
Ferla (Ferula)	36.-.-	360	22	25.-.-	375	15.5.-	364	25.6.-	504	40.-.-	600
Occhiolà (Grammichele)	—	—	—	1.24.-	27	-.23.-	18	1.9.-	26	2.-.-	30
Militello	—	—	350	20.-.-	300	20.12.-	490	34.-.-	680	55.-.-	825
Terranova (Eraclea)	442.24.-	4,428	830	5.-.-	75	3.2.-	73	3.24.-	76	8.-.-	120
Paternò	128.6.-	1,282	—	20.-.-	300	18.11.-	440	28.18.-	572	46.-.-	690
Adrano	4.-.-	40	103	10.-.-	150	6.24.-	163	11.24.-	236	18.-.-[d]	270
Buccheri	41.-.-	410	216	8.-.-	120	6.2.10	146	10.2.-	201	16.-.-	240
Petraperzia	5.-.-	50	61	5.-.-	75	1.15.-	36	2.17.-	51	7.-.-	105
Palazzolo	2.-.-	20	26	20.-.-	300	20.11.11	490	34.-.-	680	54.-.-	810
Francofonte	—	—	—	8.-.-	120	6.2.10	146	—	—	12.-.-	180
Cadrà (Chadara)	—	—	—	2.-.-	30	—	—	—	—	—	—
Butera	152.6.-	1,522	193	10.-.-	150	6.2.10	146	7.18.-	152	12.-.-	180
Aidone	10.-.-	100	17	12.-.-	180	4.16.10	109	7.18.-	152	15.-.-	225
Ispica (Spaccaforno)	—	—	32	[f]		1.16.-	37	7.17.-	151	4.-.-	60
Chiaromonte (Gulfi)	—	—	200	[f]		5.15.-	132	2.3.-[f]	42	—	—
Palagonia	—	—	55	2.-.-[f]	30	1.16.-	37	2.12.-	48	4.-.-	60
Giarratana	51.18.-	516	90	—	—	3.24.10	91	6.-.-	120	9.14.-	142
Licodia	11.-.-	110	—	10.26.-	164	6.2.10	146	10.-.-	200	16.-.-	240.

	1277		1374-6	1439		1464		1478		1497	
	(1)	(2)	(3)	(1)	(2)	(1)	(2)	(1)	(2)	(1)	(2)
Syracuse	161.18.-	1,616	1,755	100.-.-	1,500	302.-.-	7,248	497.10.-	9,950	839.-.-	12,585
Francavilla	60.-.-	600	1,000	15.-.-	225						
Lentini	101.18.-	1,016[b]	771	60.-.-	900						
Mineo	103.-.-	1,030	341	40.-.-	600						
Vizzini			250	25.-.-	375						
Augusta	71.-.-	710	45[i]	15.-.-	225	7.-.-	168	7.17.-	151	12.-.-	180
Melilli			52	4.-.-	60	1.16.-	37	2.18.-	52	4.-.-	60
Regalbuto (Racalbuto)				9.26.10	148	7.16.10	190	12.18.-	252	26.-.-	390
Comiso						1.-.-	24	1.8.-	25	2.-.-	30
Ragusa (Bicino)	161.-.-	1,610	677								
Scicli	61.18.-	616	292								
Modica	31.-.-	310	620	200.-.-	3,000[j]	173.-.-	4,152	340.-.-	6,800[k]	474.18.-[d]	7,119
Caccamo	110.-.-	1,100	583								
Monterosso (Lupino)	3.-.-	30	137							10.12.-	156
Cassaro			20								
Dirillo	6.-.-	60	54								
Regiovanni	3.-.-	30									
Total	2,723.6.-	27,232	15,366	1,274.16.10	19,119	1,288.14.18	30,924	1,931.26.10	38,639	3,006.29.-	45,104

Val Demone

	1277		1374-6	1439		1464		1478		1497	
	(1)	(2)	(3)	(1)	(2)	(1)	(2)	(1)	(2)	(1)	(2)
Messina	1,330.-.-	13,300		200.-.-	3,000	144.5.-	3,460	280.-.-	5,600	420.-.-	6,300
Nicosia	131.-.-	1,310	1,250	80.-.-	1,200	76.26.14	1,846	126.-.-	2,520	200.-.-	3,000
Randazzo	401.-.-	4,010[g]	1,100	80.-.-	1,200	81.20.17	1,961	108.-.-	2,160	182.-.-	2,730
Troina	16.-.-	160	512	40.-.-	600	24.-.16	577	27.21.-	554	44.-.-	660
Santa Lucia	40.-.-	400		20.-.-	300	14.12.10	346	22.-.-	440	31.-.-	465
Milazzo	200.-.-	2,000		6.-.-	90	7.20.13	185	15.-.-	300	16.-.-	240
Castroreale				60.-.-	900	57.20.-	1,384	65.-.-	1,300	112.-.-	1,680
Cefalù	220.-.-	2,200	300	10.-.-	150	7.20.13	185	9.-.-	180	14.-.-	210
Capizzi	51.-.-	510				11.16.-	277	15.3.-	302	24.-.-	360
Mistretta	131.-.-	1,310[h]				19.6.13	461	25.3.-	502	42.-.-	630
Patti	161.-.-	1,610		25.-.-[h]	375	24.-.10	577	26.6.-	524	42.-.-	630

Table 2.1. (cont.)

Val Demone

	1277 (1)	1277 (2)	1374-6 (3)	1439 (1)	1439 (2)	1464 (1)	1464 (2)	1478 (1)	1478 (2)	1497 (1)	1497 (2)
Taormina	111.12.-	1,114	—	28.-.-	420	19.6.14	461			57.-.-	855
Calidoro	—	—	—	4.-.-	60	1.27.14	46				
Mongiuffi	—	—	—	3.-.-	45	1.27.14	46	36.18.-	732		
Caggi	—	—	—	4.-.-	60	1.27.14	46				
Granitì	—	—	—	3.-.-	45	1.27.14	46				
Mola				4.-.-	60	1.27.14	46			4.-.-	60
Aci	36.18.-	366	—	20.-.-	300	12.2.10	290	20.5.-	403	32.-.-	480
Rametta	91.-.-	910	—	12.-.-[h]	180	5.23.-	138	7.-.-	140	16.15.-	248
Venetico			—	—	—	1.27.14	46	1.12.-	28		
Geraci	50.-.-	500	—	120.-.-	1,800[i]					240.-.-[m]	3,600
Gangi	102.-.-	1,020	359								
Castelbuono (Ypsigro)	10.-.-	100		n							
San Mauro	16.-.-	160		n		92.28.-	2,231	151.6.-	3,024		
Castelluccio (Castel di Lucio)	4.-.-	40	40								
Tusa			300[p]								
Pollina	15.-.-	150									
Collesano	40.-.-	400		40.-.-[d]	600	31.6.-	749	50.12.-	1,008	60.-.-[d]	900
Petralia Soprana	6.-.-	60	310	40.-.-	600[e]						
Petralia Sottana	5.-.-	50	292								
Caronia	10.-.-	100	40	5.-.-	75						
Castiglione	91.-.-	910		30.-.-	450	18.26.10	454	31.15.-	630	25.11.-	380
Naso	91.-.-	910		20.-.-	300	18.26.-	452	31.15.-	630	50.-.-	750
Motta Sant'Anastasia (Motta di Catania)			65	5.-.-	75	1.16.-	37	2.17.-	51	4.-.-	60
Gagliano				40.-.-[q]	600	7.1.10	169	9.18.-	192	16.-.-	240
Longi				4.-.-	60	3.2.-	73	5.-.-	100	8.-.-	120
Ucria	56.-.-	560		16.-.-	240	7.16.10	190	12.18.-	252	20.-.-	300
Pettineo				8.-.-	120	4.-.-	96	6.9.-	126	10.-.-	150
Calatabiano	31.-.-	310		15.-.-	225	3.2.-	73	4.29.-	99	8.-.-	120
Valcorrente	10.-.-	100		3.-.-	45	-.24.-	19	1.7.10	25	2.-.-	30

	A	B	C	D	E	F	G	H	I	J	K
Limina				7.-.-	105	3.23.10	91	6.-.-	120	10.-.-	150
Scaletta				5.-.-	75	3.23.10	91	4.-.-	80	10.-.-	150
Castania				10.-.-	150	7.16.10	190	12.18.-	252	20.-.-	300
Montalbano	10.-.-		100	15.-.-	225	6.1.10	145	10.2.-	201	16.-.-	240
Gratteri	41.-.-		410	15.-.-	225	6.2.10	146	12.18.-	252	20.-.-	300
Cerami	66.-.-	172	660	12.-.-	180	6.2.10	146	8.24.-	176	14.-.-	210
Monforte	46.-.-		460	6.-.-	90	11.11.-	272		201	30.-.-	450
San Pietro	26.-.-		260	10.-.-	150	6.1.10	145	10.2.-	378	16.-.-	240
Mascali				2.-.-	30						
San Pietro di Nocino				4.-.-	60						
Condrò	2.15.-		25	3.-.-	45	4.16.-	109	18.27.-	152	5.18.-	84
Militello	12.-.-		120	10.-.-	150	27.23.-	666	7.18.-	1,260	12.-.-	180
Tortorici	61.-.-		610	60.-.-	900	4.16.10	109	63.-.-	152	100.-.-	1,500
San Fratello	122.-.-		1,220	10.-.-	150	1.16.-	37	7.18.-	51	12.-.-	180
Rocella	36.-.-		360	5.-.-	75	7.16.10	181	2.17.-	240	5.-.-	75
Fiumedinisi				12.-.-	180	9.2.-	217	12.-.-	302	20.-.-	300
Isnello	24.-.-		240	16.-.-	240	6.2.10	146	15.3.-	200	24.-.-	360
Linguaglossa	12.-.-		120	10.-.-	150	4.16.10	109	10.-.-	144	16.-.-	240
Tripi				6.-.-	90	4.16.-	109	7.6.-	152	12.-.-	180
Raccuia	26.-.-		260	8.-.-	120	7.16.10	181	7.18.-	252	12.-.-	180
Novara	80.-.-		800	15.-.-	225	3.23.10	91	12.18.-	126	25.-.-	375
Motta Camastra	16.-.-		160	6.-.-	90	7.16.10	181	6.9.-	240	10.-.-	150
Agrò				12.-.-	180	13.18.-	326	12.-.-	453	20.-.-	300
San Marco (county)		188		34.-.-	510	9.2.-	217	22.20.-	303	36.-.-	540
San Marco (casali)	51.-.-		510			26.13.10		15.4.-		24.-.-	360
Ficarra	41.-.-		410	28.-.-	420		635	44.3.-	882	40.-.-	600
Galati	4.-.-		40							20.-.-	300
Piraino											
Saponara										12.-.-	
Bavuso											180
Calvaruso (Calabruso)	26.-.-		260	8.-.-	120	4.16.10	109	7.18.-	152		
Cesarò				10.-.-	150	4.16.10	109	7.18.-	152	12.-.-	180
Gioiosa Guardia				10.-.-	150	7.16.10	190	12.18.-	252	20.-.-	300
Salvatore				15.-.-	225	9.2.-	217	15.3.-	302		
Librizzi	26.-.-		260	9.-.-	135	4.16.10	109	7.18.-	152	12.-.-	180
Locadi				3.-.-	45	1.16.-	37	2.12.-	48	3.-.-	45
Antillo				1.-.-	15	-.23.-	18	1.6.-	24		
Casalvecchio				6.-.-	90	3.23.-	90	6.-.-	120	10.-.-	150
Savoca				25.-.-	375	15.3.-	362	24.-.-	480	40.-.-	600

Table 2.1. (cont.)

Val di Mazara

	1277		1374-6	1439		1464		1478		1497	
	(1)	(2)	(3)	(1)	(2)	(1)	(2)	(1)	(2)	(1)	(2)
Pagiara	—	—	—	3.-.-	45	1.16.-	37	2.12.-	48	4.-.-	60
Sant'Angelo di Brolo	31.-.-	310	—	20.-.-	300	12.26.-	308	15.3.-	302	24.-.-	360
Lisico	4.-.-	40	—	—	—	—	—	—	—	—	—
Bronte	—	—	—	3.-.-	45	1.16.-	37	2.15.-	50	7.-.-	105
Mandanici	—	—	—	10.-.-	150	5.8.-	125	8.12.-	168	10.-.-	150
Itaià	—	—	—	5.-.-	75	3.24.-	91	6.-.-	120	—	—
Alì	—	—	—	15.-.-	225	11.12.-	274	18.-.-	360	30.-.-	450
Sinagra	21.-.-	210	—	12.-.-	180	9.2.10	218	14.12.-	288	24.-.-	360
Martini	3.15.-	35	—	3.-.-	45	1.15.10	36	2.18.-	52	4.-.-	60
Alcara	70.-.-	700	—	15.-.-	225	9.25.-	236	16.24.-	336	20.-.-	300
San Filippo d'Argirò	57.-.-	570	627	25.-.-	375	—	—	—	—	—	—
Protonotaro	3.-.-	30	—	—	—	—	—	—	—	—	—
Reitano	—	—	300	— [a]	—	—	—	4.-.-	80	6.-.-	90
Motta d'Affermo (Sparto)	1.-.-	10	—	—	—	—	—	—	—	—	—
Casal del Vescovo	1.-.-	10	—	—	—	—	—	—	—	—	—
Anfusum	—	—	—	—	—	—	—	—	—	—	—
Galo, Resico, Gadara, Cattafi, Papacudi	52.-.-	520	—	—	—	—	—	—	—	—	—
Garufi, San Martino, Cacalimata Grecine, Sant'Andrea dell'Arcivescovo	72.-.-	720	—	—	—	—	—	—	—	—	—
Sicaminò	1.-.-	10	—	—	—	—	—	—	—	—	—
Oliveri	15.-.-	150	—	—	—	—	—	—	—	—	—
Bolo	4.-.-	40	—	—	—	—	—	—	—	—	—
Fiumefreddo	4.-.-	40	44	—	—	—	—	—	—	—	—
Sperlinga	26.-.-	260	—	— [v]	—	—	—	—	—	—	—
Mirto with casali	61.-.-	610	—	—	—	—	—	—	—	—	—
Zuppardino	41.-.-	410	—	—	—	—	—	—	—	—	—
Calegra	4.-.-	40	—	—	—	—	—	—	—	—	—
Casal di messer Nicola	10.-.-	100	—	—	—	—	—	—	—	—	—

	(1)	(2)		(3)		(1)		(3)	(1)	(2)
Anca	8.–.–	80	–	–	–	–	–	–	–	–
Matana	3.–.–	30	–	–	–	–	–	–	–	–
Mugana	80.–.–	800	–	–	–	–	–	–	–	–
San Salvatore Ficalia	8.–.–	80	–	15.–.–	225	–	–	–	–	–
Casale San Giorgio									24.–.–	360
Nasari	2.–.–	20	–	–	–	–	–	–	–	–
Casale Giovanni Baroni	2.–.–	20	–	–	–	–	–	–	–	–
San Filippo del Piano	20.–.–	200	–	–	–	–	–	–	–	–
Total	4,781.–.–	47,810	5,859	1,479.–.–	22,185	1,004.4.18	24.100	1,593.25.10	31,877	2,471.14.–	37,072

a Includes Jews.
b See R. Starrabba, 'Censimento della popolazione di Palermo fatto nel 1479'.
c Includes Salaparuta.
d Includes the whole county.
e Racalmuto is allocated twenty-eight onze over three years (ten onze in 1496–7).
f See Modica (val di Noto).
g See n. 19.
h Includes its casali.
i Includes Altavilla (val di Noto).
j Includes Alcamo and Calatafimi (val di Mazara), Spaccaforno, Giarratana and Chiaromonte (val di Noto).
k Includes Chiaromonte (val di Noto).
l Includes the whole marquisate.
m Includes Castelluccio, Tusa, Pollina, Collesano and Motta d'Affermo, the latter assessed for four onze (val Demone).
n See the two Petralie (val Demone).
o Includes Pettineo (val Demone).
p Includes Castelbuono and San Mauro (val Demone).
q Includes the whole viscounty.
r See Tusa (val Demone).
s Includes Mirto and Capri (val Demone).
t Includes Leoga (val Demone).
u See Mistretta (val Demone).
v See San Marco (val Demone).

Here, and in all subsequent tables, a dash denotes unavailable data, while a blank space occurs after a bracket that combines data for various localities.
Sources: See this chapter, nn. 19, 47, 56, 67.
(1) Tax allocation (in onze, tari and denari).
(2) Estimated hearths.
(3) Assessed hearths.

(see Tables 2.1 and 2.2).[26] At a mean hearth size of four to five people (which is the average size found in the fifteenth century),[27] population in the third quarter of the thirteenth century was 800,000–1,000,000. A similar estimate based on the returns of 1277 gives a population of 650,000–850,000. Assuming that the Aragonese in 1283 were more efficient or ruthless than the Angevins in 1277, and levied a higher tax, I have tentatively adopted a figure of 850,000 inhabitants. This estimate would give Sicily a population density of 33.4 inhabitants per km² at this time, setting it on a par with Lombardy, the Veneto and the Parisian basin in the same period.[28]

Other sources provide indirect evidence on the size of the thirteenth-century population. The first of these is an Aragonese tax (*fodrum*) of 1282–3 on agricultural output.[29] Although it is not known on what basis the tax was levied, in 1395–6 Martino tried to raise a similar *fodrum* in eastern Sicily corresponding to five per cent of agricultural output (of wheat, barley, legumes, wine, cheese, hemp and flax).[30] As with direct taxes, one can reasonably suppose that Martino, having reconquered the island in the name of a dynasty which harked back to Peter III of Aragon, would be anxious to legitimate his authority by re-enacting his ancestor's deeds, particularly since there is no evidence that any *fodra* had been raised between 1282–3 and 1395. Consequently I assume that the quota of the 1282–3 *fodrum* was also five per cent of agricultural output.

Peter III collected 17,210 *salme* of wheat and 23,240 *salme* of barley in 1282–3. If returns correspond to five per cent of domestic output net of seed, Sicily was producing no less than 350,000 *salme* of wheat and 470,000 *salme* of barley, not including lesser grains like

---

[26] In 1442, 24.3 per cent of the hearths in the Cassaro quarter of Palermo were too poor to be taxed (Peri, *Restaurazione e pacifico stato in Sicilia, 1377–1501*, p. 78). I have adopted a lower exemption rate than this, on the assumption that the proportion of indigent poor would be higher in a metropolis like Palermo than elsewhere.

[27] Peri, *Restaurazione*, p. 79; Beloch, *Bevölkerungsgeschichte Italiens*, p. 99. See also F. Cozzetto, *Mezzogiorno e demografia nel XV secolo*, p. 5; D. Herlihy, 'Demography', p. 146.

[28] J. C. Russell, *Medieval regions and their cities*, p. 235.

[29] Carini ed., *De rebus*, nos. 15, 122, 173; summarized by D'Angelo, 'Terra e uomini', 82–4.

[30] RC 24, fos. 160rv, 170, 174v–5, 176v, 182v–3v; RC 27, fos. 27rv, 45v–6, 68v–9. See also *UM*, pp. 127–8, 155–6.

Table 2.2 *Estimated hearths by vallo, 1277–1501*

	1277		1374–6[a]		1439[b]		1464		1478		1497		1501	
	N	per cent	N	per cent	N	per cent	N	per cent	N	per cent	N	per cent	N	per cent
val di Mazara	69,830	48.2	21,037	33.0	18,125–24,167	30.5	26,782	32.4	32,226	31.4	38,615	31.9	38,895	32.2
val di Noto	27,232	18.8	18,156	28.4	19,119–25,492	32.2	30,924	38.4	38,639	37.6	45,104	37.3	42,380[c]	35.0
val Demone	47,810	33.0	24,655	38.6	22,185–29,580	37.3	24,100	29.2	31,877	31.0	37,072	30.8	39,589	32.8
Total	144,872	100.0	63,848	100.0	59,429–79,239	100.0	81,806	100.0	102,742	100.0	120,791	100.0	120,864	100.0

[a] Includes extrapolations from average regional losses.
[b] Estimates differ according to the mean hearth quota (2 or 1.10 *tarì*) that is adopted.
[c] Malta excluded (see Beloch, *Bevölkerungsgeschichte Italiens*, p. 99).
Sources: As for Table 2.1.

spelt, millet and even hemp, which were also consumed. However, a large number of communities (including Palermo and Messina) which had been allocated taxes in 1277, were apparently not required to contribute to the *fodrum* of 1282–3.[31] A number of these communities were under feudal lordship; most were situated in val Demone close to Messina, and included large towns like Santa Lucia, Milazzo and Monforte, noted for supplying large grain surpluses to Messina (see chapters 3 and 5). Others, like Taormina, Novara, Calatabiano, Rametta and San Filippo (to name but the largest) could undoubtedly have contributed wine or livestock if not grain.

These omissions, together with those of Palermo and Messina, suggest that only communities possessing a substantial surplus were asked to contribute, and that neither of the two metropoles, nor Messina's direct area of supply, were taxed for reasons of political convenience. Considering also that the Aragonese had no established administrative records to work from, returns to this tax must have underestimated actual output considerably. If the error margin had been only one per cent (so that, let us say, four per cent instead of five per cent of output was raised) – a most conservative estimate, since nearly ten per cent of the population outside Palermo and Messina was not even taxed – total output in 1283 would have been something over 1 million *salme* of grain. Once we account for exports (which in 1283 were very small) and barley for fodder, we are left with enough to feed a population of a little less than 1 million (average individual consumption being one *salma* per year).[32]

These assessments might be questioned on the grounds that they would result in overestimating the size of Palermo (more than 20,000 hearths) and Messina (*c.*12,500 hearths) and setting them among the largest cities in western Europe at the time. One must, however, consider that tax allocations referred not simply to a legally recognized community (*università*), but included the surrounding

---

31 Excluding Palermo and Messina, communities omitted from the *fodrum* of 1283 accounted for 2.4 (val di Mazara), 2.5 (val di Noto) and 23.2 per cent (val Demone) of tax allocations in 1277; omissions in 1283 were 9.3 per cent of total allocations in 1277.

32 Grain exports in Carini ed., *De rebus*, nos. 8, 20, 35, 38, 48, 50, 140, 208, 243, 476, App. 63. For per capita consumption see RC 132, fos. 62v–3v (1474); N. Torrisi, 'Aspetti della crisi granaria siciliana nel secolo XVI'; Cancila, *Baroni e popolo*, p. 51.

territory or *districtus*, which was often scattered with smaller open settlements (*casali*) and hamlets.[33] Since Messina and Palermo possessed very large *districtus*, a significant proportion of any tax allocation would have burdened families living outside the city walls. How large a proportion of their assessed populations was this? Assuming that a tax allocation similar to that for Sicily applied also to the mainland, some data for Naples – a city of comparable size and importance to Messina and Palermo – may provide an answer to the question. In 1277, Naples and its *casali* were taxed for 770 *onze*; a year later the city *without* its hinterland numbered *c*.4,000–4,500 hearths.[34] In other words, since the mean hearth allocation on the mainland was approximately three *tarì*,[35] Naples' hinterland must have numbered 3,000–3,500 hearths. If one were to assume a similar distribution of inhabitants between city and district for Palermo and Messina, strictly urban hearths would have been respectively 11,500 and 7,100. The city of Palermo would have had 50,000 inhabitants,[36] and Messina approximately 30,000. These figures would seem to be a reasonable estimate of the two cities' standing in the late thirteenth-century European urban hierarchy.

The latter estimate for Messina is borne out by the fact that in 1281, Messina was allowed to import up to 30,000 *salme* of wheat from the rest of Sicily over a period of twelve months, apparently because its usual sources of supply were lacking.[37] This amount of grain was enough to feed 30,000 people for a whole year, and thus sets the lower limit to the city's size. Such imports were presumably not its only sources of supply at the time, for besides strictly local production, grain from Calabria and the plain of Milazzo was easily to hand (see chapters 3 and 5).

I argued in this chapter's introduction that changes in population distribution can be used to alert us to underlying changes in social

---

33 Carini ed., *De rebus*, nos. 33, 83; Percy, 'Revenues', p. 60. See below, chapter 3, for the *districtus*. For this reason it is nearly impossible to trace all settlements from tax lists, and even from other surviving written records which tend to refer to the *università* as a whole; see M. Gaudioso, *La questione demaniale in Catania e nei 'casali' del Bosco etneo. Il Vescovo-barone*, p. 91.

34 Beloch, *Bevölkerungsgeschichte Italiens*, pp. 118–19, 169–70.

35 Above, n. 24.

36 Extrapolating backwards from Palermo's population in 1374–6 (see below) on the basis of average population losses for val di Mazara between 1277 and 1374–6 (see Table 2.3), gives a figure for 1277 of just under 13,400 hearths.

37 Minieri Riccio, 'Il regno di Carlo I d'Angiò dal 2 gennaio 1273 al 31 dicembre 1283', 3.

and economic structures. As we shall see further below, one of the most significant features of the late medieval demographic crisis was to provoke a major redistribution of population from western to eastern Sicily, which in turn had considerable repercussions on economic structures. This process of redistribution would seem to have begun already during the second half of the thirteenth century, for in 1283 the Aragonese reduced western Sicily's tax quota from fifty per cent (as it was under the Angevins) to forty per cent of the total. Assuming that the distribution of 1283 was based on updated information, and that the Angevin tax of 1277 was also based on a correct, though possibly outdated, evaluation of the population, changes in allocation could reflect long-term demographic effects of the Muslim repression earlier in the century, effects which were felt most keenly in western Sicily.

In the late thirteenth century, settlement patterns in the three *valli* already varied considerably; these differences persisted, or may have become more intense during the subsequent demographic crises. The 1277 tax lists forty-one major settlements for val di Mazara, thirty-one for val di Noto, and seventy-six for val Demone. The 1283 returns record forty-five communities for val di Mazara. Average community size in 1277 was 1,703 tax hearths in val di Mazara (1,195 not counting Palermo), 878 tax hearths in val di Noto, and 629 tax hearths in val Demone (460 excluding Messina).

Val di Mazara was characterized by its small number of very large towns and cities, surrounded by vast, possibly already thinly settled, hinterlands. In val di Noto the largest city was Terranova (known today as Gela), with over 15,000 inhabitants; Catania, Caltagirone and Castrogiovanni each had 10,000 or a little less. According to the 1277 tax rolls, the population density of val di Noto was the lowest in Sicily, just over three hearths per km^2. In val Demone only Nicosia, Milazzo and Cefalù – which last would dwindle by the fifteenth century to little more than a large village – numbered 10,000 inhabitants; Randazzo was the largest regional centre next to Messina with 20,000–25,000 inhabitants. If Messina and these larger towns are excluded, each taxable community had a mean size of 370 hearths. Towns in val Demone were thus far smaller and more thickly scattered than elsewhere, whereas population density in the *vallo* was the highest in Sicily.[38]

---

[38] Aymard and Bresc, 'Problemi di storia dell'insediamento nella Sicilia medievale e moderna, 1100–1800', 945–76; Bresc and D'Angelo, 'Structure et évolution de

In conclusion, my revision of the population figures gives late thirteenth-century Sicily a population of approximately 850,000. The country would thus have been densely settled by contemporary European standards. Sicily's largest cities, Palermo and Messina, had 50,000 and 30,000 inhabitants respectively: a respectable size which could not, however, compare with the great metropoles like Venice, Milan, Florence, Paris and London. By the late thirteenth century, one also begins to perceive a shift in demographic distribution from western to eastern Sicily. It is not clear, however, to what extent these changes affected urban networks. According to the Angevin allocation of 1277, eight of the ten largest Sicilian cities were situated in val di Mazara; a century later, the proportion had dropped to four out of ten (see Table 2.7).

As I suggested above, the size of the thirteenth-century population can also be inferred from circumstantial evidence for the decades following the Black Death of 1347–8.

Demographic stagnation or even decline seems to have begun some time before 1347, perhaps already during the last quarter of the thirteenth century. This is implied by the distribution of settlement desertions over time. Desertions were generally most intense between 1280 and 1340, especially after 1320 (when the intensity of Angevin military attack was declining).[39] Palermo suffered particularly severely because of the war with Naples, which cut it off from resources from the mainland.[40] Most losses, however, were the result of the Black Death. The bubonic plague was carried to Europe from the Crimea on a Genoese ship which stopped over in

l'habitat dans la région de Termini Imerese (XIIe–XVe siècles)', 361–402; Bresc, 'L'habitat médiéval'; *UM*, pp. 59–77.

[39] Bresc, 'L'habitat médiéval', 190. Some new, usually fortified, settlements were founded during the fourteenth century. Chiusa Sclafani was founded by Matteo Sclafani in *c*.1320 (*Guida d'Italia. Sicilia*, p. 284); Francofonte was founded by Artale Alagona (D'Alessandro, *Politica e società nella Sicilia aragonese*, p. 33); Gioiosa Guardia was founded by Vinciguerra Aragona in 1366 (S. Giambruno and L. Genuardi eds., *Capitoli inediti delle città demaniali di Sicilia approvati sino al 1458, I. Alcamo-Malta*, p. 245). See RC 2, fo. 142v (*ante* 1 September 1340): curial rights to be paid by immigrants to newly founded or deserted settlements. On the economic difficulties of 1320–40 see below, chapter 7.

[40] Trasselli, 'Sulla popolazione', 329–44; Bresc, 'Les jardins de Palerme (1290–1460)', 99. Corrao ed., *Registri di lettere ed atti (1328–1333)*, no. 69: the revenues of Palermo's *secrezia* are farmed out for 5,700 *onze* in 1329; by contrast, between 1400 and 1439, average *secrezia* income was 4,000 *onze*, despite intervening tax increases (*UM*, p. 842). See below, chapter 7.

Messina in 1347. The effects of the plague were exacerbated by a further epidemic of 1366, and by local and general dearth in 1347–8 and 1349–50, throughout the 1350s and in 1373–5.[41] Endemic civil warfare during the 1350s and early 1360s, while not increasing mortality very significantly, probably delayed the setting up of new households and the recovery of fertility.

One of the most astonishing aspects of the plague is the paucity of literary or other documentary traces it left behind. Michele da Piazza, the only chronicler of the events following the arrival of the Genoese ships in Messina, did not dwell long on them, and described the plague's progress only as far west as Trapani.[42] An anonymous eschatological poem omitted the plague from the litany of ills afflicting Sicily in the 1350s and 1360s.[43]

While the paucity of narrative sources is compounded by the scarcity of other written records for the period,[44] the extent of the demographic collapse can be established indirectly. In the first place, between 1300 and 1392, over sixty per cent of Sicily's aristocratic families disappeared. This phenomenon was due to social and economic besides demographic factors, but the latter also played a significant role.[45] Secondly, wage increases after the Black Death are consistent with very high population losses, particularly since the population had probably already declined somewhat between the late thirteenth century and the onset of the plague in 1347. Between 1323–47 and the last decade of the fourteenth century, nominal agricultural and building wages in and around Palermo increased two to three times; deflating for monetary devaluation, real wages increased approximately 80–120 per cent.[46]

Circumstantial evidence of demographic losses supports con-

[41] *UM*, p. 129; Peri, *Uomini, città e campagne*, pp. 160, 214–15, 226; M. da Piazza, *Cronaca*, I, chapters 114, 116; G. Cosentino ed., *Codice diplomatico di Federico III d'Aragona, re di Sicilia, 1355–77*, no. 624; B. Lagumina and G. Lagumina eds., *Codice diplomatico dei Giudei di Sicilia*, I, no. 65 (1374); RC 5, fo. 26 (1374); RC 13, fos. 37v–8 (1374); RC 14, fo. 44 (1374); RC 15, fo. 45rv (1375).
[42] da Piazza, *Cronaca*, I, chapter 29.
[43] S. V. Bozzo, '*Quaedam profetia*. Una poesia siciliana del XIV secolo'; G. Cusimano and F. Giunta eds., *Prospetto dei documenti in volgare siciliano del sec. XIV*.
[44] An exception is the permission, granted to the baron of Scaletta in val Demone, to confiscate the property of subjects who were leaving Scaletta *en masse* (RC 5, fo. 226v).
[45] *UM*, p. 672; see below, chapter 7, n. 38.
[46] G. Bresc-Bautier and Bresc, '*Maramma*. I mestieri della costruzione nella Sicilia medievale', p. 148; see below, chapter 4.

clusions based on a comparison of my population estimates for the late thirteenth century and evidence from fiscal data for the 1370s. These data, based on a tax raised between 1374 and 1376 to pay for the Avignon papacy's struggle against the Visconti of Milan in the context of peace moves between Sicily and Naples, are the most accurate demographic record for medieval Sicily we have, for it is the only one for which numbers of paying hearths in each assessed locality survive.[47] The tax quota, initially set at one *tarì* per person over ten years of age, had to be modified in the face of popular resistance: Sicilians were said to be unimpressed by Pope Gregory XI's offer to repeal Sicily's religious interdict, which dated back to the early fourteenth century. The poll tax was changed into a hearth tax; hearths payed three, two and one *tarì* according to wealth.[48] Papal envoys visited communities personally to collect the dues, so major discrepancies between actual and declared figures should have been noticed and corrected.[49]

Returns are nearly complete for val di Mazara[50] and val di Noto.[51] For val di Noto the most significant missing data are Catania's, which had surpassed Messina as Sicily's second largest city in this period (see chapters 3 and 5). Judging from a separate tax (*subvencio*) of 1373; in which Catania was assessed for 200 *onze*, the city was nearly unique in having actually *increased* its population since the late thirteenth century. By the 1370s it had, at a conservative estimate, 3,000–3,500 hearths.[52]

More serious problems arise for val Demone, for which only

[47] J. Glénisson, 'Documenti dell'Archivio Vaticano relativi alla collettoria di Sicilia (1372–1375)', 229–30. Accounts are published in *ibid.*, 249–60, and P. Sella ed., *Rationes Decimarum Italiae nei secoli XIII e XIV. Sicilia*, pp. 123–36 (incorrectly dated 1366). They were first used for demographic purposes by L. Gambi, 'La popolazione della Sicilia fra il 1374 e il 1376'. Like other tax rolls, they do not report all existing settlements; see Gaudioso, *Questione*, pp. 115–16.

[48] Glénisson, 'Documenti', 244–6, 251.

[49] *Ibid.*, 253. Nonetheless, major underestimates or exemptions seem to have occurred. Castrogiovanni was assessed for 1,050 hearths in 1374–6, but numbered about 3,000 hearths in 1392 (I. La Lumia, *Studi di storia siciliana*, II, p. 390).

[50] Polizzi, Cammarata and Castelvetrano are missing.

[51] Catania, Avola, Buscemi, Ferla, Petraperzia, Giarratana and Francavilla are missing.

[52] The *subvencio* of 1373 is listed in RC 12, fos. 144–5. Trapani, assessed for 120 *onze* in 1373, declared 2,608 tax hearths in 1374–6. Piazza, Agrigento and Syracuse, assessed for 100 *onze* each in 1373, declared 1,542, 1,560 and 1,755 tax hearths respectively in 1374–6. The 1373 *subvencio* seems, therefore, to be based on a mean hearth quota of 1.10 *tarì*; on this basis, Catania would have numbered 4,000 tax-paying hearths in 1373.

Table 2.3 *Demographic variations (per cent), 1277–1501*

	1277	1374–6	1439[a]	1464[a]	1478	1497	1501
val di Mazara	—	−69.9	−13.8 to +14.9	+10.8 to +47.8	+20.3	+19.8	+21.4
val di Noto	—	−33.3	+3.4 to +40.4	+21.3 to +61.7	+25.0	+16.7	−6.0
val Demone	—	−51.6	−10.0 to +20.0	−18.5 to +8.6	+32.3	+16.7	+29.2
Total	—	−55.9	−6.9 to +24.1	+3.2 to +37.7	+25.6	+17.6	+13.7

[a] Variations differ according to the population estimate for 1439 (see Table 2.2).
Sources: As for Table 2.1.

sixteen returns are known. Messina, Patti, and the towns and villages in the Milazzo plain in particular are missing.[53] Extrapolating the size of individual settlements from general trends estimated from such a narrow range of figures is problematic. For example, such a calculation would give Messina about 3,700 hearths, not many fewer than Palermo, and quite certainly too many in view of the city's severe economic decline after 1350 (see chapter 5). On the other hand, extrapolated trends for the *vallo* as a whole are probably less imprecise, and they suggest an average regional loss of little over half the population compared to a century earlier.

Known and extrapolated figures suggest, therefore, that between 1283 and 1374–6, Sicily lost approximately sixty per cent of its population, declining from *c.*200,000 to *c.*77,000 hearths (the latter figure includes the tax exempt), from 850,000 to less than 350,000 inhabitants.

Population losses were very unevenly distributed between *valli*. Between *c.*1277[54] and 1374–6, val di Mazara lost nearly seventy per cent of its population, val di Noto thirty per cent, and val Demone more than forty-eight per cent (see Table 2.3). From having about forty per cent of the total population in 1283, val di Mazara dropped to just thirty-three per cent in 1374–6; its population density became the lowest of the three *valli*. Val di Noto's share rose from less than a fifth in 1277, to roughly one third of the population in the 1370s, if we include Catania's estimated growth; equally significantly, four

53 Glénisson, 'Documenti', 236–7.
54 I take the Angevin tax of 1277 as the basis of comparison; we saw above that this allocation probably drew on previous compilations.

(compared to none in 1277) of the ten largest towns were now located in this *vallo*. Val Demone's share of total population may have increased to a little over one third,[55] but it remained scarcely urbanized, with still only two of the top ten cities within its boundaries.

For nearly sixty years after the 1370s, no *general* hearth taxes appear to have been successfully levied. The first sovereign to do so was Alfonso V in 1434, but the most reliable surviving tax records for demographic purposes date from 1439. This is because complaints of underestimation in 1434 probably led to more accurate later assessments.[56]

Compared to the *colletta* of 1434, based on the average rate of three *tarì* per hearth re-established in 1398, the tax of 1439 was probably based on a mean hearth quota closer to one and a half to two *tarì*. This hypothesis is based on the following considerations. In 1286 James II of Aragon set a ceiling of 5,000–15,000 *onze* on direct taxes, which remained in force until the late 1470s.[57] By the early fifteenth century, the accepted limit on direct taxation was approximately 5,000 *onze*, which set a ceiling of 50,000 hearths paying three *tarì* each; as a matter of fact, the tax ceiling for the laity was lower, for part of the 5,000 *onze* was paid by the Church. In 1434, for example, Christian communities paid only 4,230.4 *onze* (Jewish communities were taxed separately), the equivalent of 42,301 tax hearths. As a result of the constitutional agreement of 1286, therefore, any kind of demographic increase – whether actual increase or because of more accurate assessments – necessarily reduced the average quota paid by each hearth.[58]

Because of these principles, total population in 1434 was seriously underestimated. Trapani was assessed at 1,000 hearths, whereas it was said to number 2,000; Castelvetrano was assessed for

[55] Extrapolation from the available data gives val Demone 38.3 per cent of the population, but this figure underestimates Messina's decline (see below, chapter 5).
[56] Cosentino, 'I ruoli degli anni 1434, 1442 e 1443 relativi a' fuochi di Sicilia', pp. 570–91; *UM*, pp. 72–3. The tax of 1439 (CR 851, fos. 587–90, 592–601, 602–4, 605–8v) is examined in *UM*, pp. 73–7.
[57] A. Flandina ed., *Il codice Filangeri e il codice Speciale: privilegi inediti della città di Palermo*, pp. 66–7.
[58] In 1450–1, however, a tax of 25,000 florins (5,000 *onze*) actually returned 30,123 florins (*UM*, p. 851).

140 hearths, although 'it [had] many more hearths'.[59] It seems reasonable to assume that, as a result of complaints in 1434, allocations in 1439 were based on more accurate – in other words, generally higher – assessments than in 1434. On the other hand, tax receipts in 1439 were considerably *lower* than in 1434 (3,961.26.10 *onze* compared to 4,230.4 *onze*). The only explanation for this apparent conflict in the evidence is that later allocations were made on the basis of a lower mean hearth quota.

This quota can have been no more, and was possibly less, than two *tarì*. At a rate of two *tarì*, Trapani would have been allocated 1,200 tax hearths instead of the 1,000 tax hearths of 1434; a rate of 1.10 *tarì* would give the city 1,600 tax hearths. In 1439 it was described as having 1,800 households (*masunate*), which presumably included the tax exempt.[60]

According to whether we adopt a coefficient of 1.10 *tarì* or 2 *tarì*, taxable hearths in Sicily as a whole numbered either 58,000 or 78,000; the actual figure was probably somewhere in between. Population in 1439 was therefore either approximately the same size as in the 1370s, or about one fifth larger. In any case, by the 1430s, population had probably recovered from its nadir, which Bresc has situated at around 1400.[61]

The patterns of distribution between *valli* in 1439 did not differ significantly from those in the 1370s, suggesting that the intervening period had seen the consolidation of fourteenth-century changes rather than further upheaval. Val di Mazara may have continued its relative decline, but at a far slower rate than previously. Val Demone maintained, but did not improve, its position of regional primacy. By contrast, it is val di Noto, which now accounted for over thirty per cent of tax-hearths, that is revealed as having best withstood the century-long demographic crisis, nearly doubling its share of total population since the late thirteenth century and overtaking val di Mazara in the process.

Population trends for the second half of the fifteenth century are quite well known, thanks to the *terminus ad quem* provided by a census of 1501 when *c.*120,000 tax-paying hearths were counted.

---

[59] Cosentino, 'Ruoli', 573.
[60] RC 74, fos. 261v–2. In 1427, Trapani was said to have 1,200 tax-exempt hearths (RC 59, fo. 48rv).
[61] *UM*, pp. 70–1.

Table 2.4 *Tax allocation to the demesne (per cent of total), 1374–6 to 1497*

	1374–6[a]	1439	1464	1478	1497
val di Mazara	75.0	71.6	75.2	72.2	71.8
val di Noto	36.4	39.9	38.6	33.9	35.5
val Demone	44.1	39.1	50.3	47.9	48.5
Total	50.6	49.3	54.2	50.2	51.2

[a] Includes extrapolations from average regional losses.
Sources: As for Table 2.1.

Between 1440 and 1460, the population began to increase very rapidly, nearly doubling in about half a century, and continuing to rise at a fast rate until the late sixteenth century.[62] Uncertainty as to when expansion began is due, on the one hand, to the uncertain size of the population in 1439, and on the other, to a lack of reliable figures before 1478, when the population had been increasing steadily for years. The average annual rate of increase, measuring net gains of births over deaths and of in- over out-migration over the whole period 1439–1501, was 0.7–1.2 per cent.

The real demographic take-off probably began around mid-century. After 1450, the price of grain, which had fluctuated wildly during the early fifteenth century, began a steady upward trend (see Table 3.4). Local petitions for privileges to attract immigrants or to stem emigration, which were common in the 1430s and 1440s, slacked off thereafter (see Table 2.5). Conflict over individuals' rights to leave fiefs without losing their property also declined.[63] New settlements were founded, which, in contrast with earlier attempts,[64] successfully attracted immigrants from Sicily and

[62] Aymard, 'Une croissance sélective: la population sicilienne aux XVIe–XVIIe siècles'; Aymard, 'In Sicilia: sviluppo demografico e sue differenziazioni geografiche, 1500–1800'.
[63] R. Starrabba ed., *Lettere e documenti relativi a un periodo del vicariato della regina Bianca in Sicilia (1411–1412)*, no. 90 (Regalbuto, 1411); RC 35, fo. 133rv (Marsala, 1399); C. Giardina ed., *Capitoli e privilegi di Messina*, p. 218 (Messina, 1434); C 2824, fo. 57 (Isnello, 1434); C 2826, fos. 177v–8 (Milazzo, 1435); C 2846, fos. 21v–2 (Aci, 1443); RC 106, fos. 226–8 (Milazzo, 1457).
[64] There were also attempts to resettle villages in order to control peasant activities and mobility. See RC 56, fo. 65 (Castania, 1425); C 2821, fo. 311rv (Santo Stefano, 1433); C 2821, fos. 126v–7, and RC 75, fos. 444v–5 (Regalbuto, 1433 and 1440); C 2865, fos. 30v–1 (Palagonia, 1450); CR 70, fo. 85rv (Limina, 1487).

abroad (see Table 2.6). Some of these colonies were settled by immigrant Albanians fleeing the Turks; Trasselli has estimated their number at 8,000–10,000 individuals.[65] The rising number of government licences to build new mills testifies to the rapidly increasing population. Forty licences were granted after 1450, twenty-seven of them after 1475, compared to only fifteen in 1400–49.[66] From the late 1460s, the number of grants of fiscal immunity to the fathers of twelve or more children also increased very markedly. Eleven grants were made in 1450–74, and forty-nine in 1475–99, as against only four concessions before 1450. Most licences (twenty after 1450) and concessions of fiscal immunity (twenty-one after 1475) were given to inhabitants of val di Mazara, suggesting that this area, the worst hit by the demographic crisis, was also recovering most rapidly.

Demographic growth after the mid-fifteenth century can be measured from three tax allocations (of 1464, 1478 and 1497) and a general census (of 1501).[67] The first allocation was based on a

---

[65] Trasselli, 'Ricerche su la popolazione', 252.

[66] Grants and licences are recorded in CR, Mercedes.

[67] Allocations for 1464 and 1478 are published by Trasselli, 'Ricerche su la popolazione'. The previously unknown *donativo* of 1497 is listed in CR 78, fos. 43–6v. The mean hearth quota adopted for 1497, two *tarì*, is based on internal evidence and on a comparison with the census of 1501. At a rate of two *tarì* in 1497, Palermo, Catania and Messina would have been assessed for 7,500, 2,850 and 6,300 hearths respectively; these figures accord with the assessments of 1501 (respectively 8,000, 2,789 and 5,700 hearths). For a brief period in the 1450s, tax allocations on feudal lands were related in part to baronial incomes. Under pressure from the ecclesiastical and demesne branches of parliament, it was decided in 1456 that barons would pay one fifth of the *donativi* from their personal incomes (Genuardi, *Il parlamento siciliano*, pp. clxix-clxx). In April 1457, however, Alfonso reduced the barons' quota to one tenth, the other tenth being added to their subjects' allocation (C 2879, fo. 75rv; C 2870, fos. 155–6; RC 80, fo. 93rv); after his death the issue was dropped. As a result, returns after 1458 were based on real assessments of feudal communities' sizes; see, for example, C 3487, fos. 152v–3 (1472). Changes in the distribution of tax allocations between the demesne and feudal lands during the fifteenth century (see Table 2.4) also suggest that changes in demographic distribution between the two sectors were taken into account. Data for 1501 are published by Trasselli, 'Ricerche su la popolazione', 220–3, and Beloch, *Bevölkerungsgeschichte Italiens*, pp. 99, 159–60; see also E. Cecchi, 'Censimenti siciliani tra Cinque e Seicento nell'Archivio di Stato di Firenze', p. 215. A comparison of the census of 1501 with the tax of 1497 shows that, although in 1501 assessments for Palermo, Messina and Catania were listed separately, they were also included in each *vallo*'s total assessment. The total number of hearths in 1501 was thus 120,864, and not 137,362 or 137,371 as in Beloch, *Bevölkerungsgeschichte Italiens*, p. 99, and Trasselli, 'Ricerche su la popolazione', 221.

'voluntary tax' (*donativo*) of 25,000 Aragonese florins (5,000 *onze*) voted by parliament in aid of Juan II in the Catalan civil war. Demesne and feudal communities were allocated 3,408.27.4 *onze* (fourteen per cent less than in 1439),[68] but total population had risen to about 80,000 households, an increase of up to fifteen per cent compared to 1439, and of roughly thirty per cent compared to the 1370s. Recovery from the demographic crisis was unequally distributed among the *valli*. Val Demone recovered more slowly than the others. In 1464, this region's population was the smallest of the three, although it still had the highest density of inhabitants per km². While performing better than the region as a whole, Messina had grown more slowly than either Palermo (+11.7–48.9 per cent) or Catania (+3.8–38.4 per cent).[69] The reason for this might have been the separation of Sicily from the mainland at Alfonso's death in 1458, which partly weakened Messina's position as the main link between the two kingdoms (see chapters 5 and 7).

Palermo, with 4,500 tax-paying hearths, had once again become the largest Sicilian city. Although below general and regional rates of increase, Palermo's growth from 12,000–15,000 to 25,000 inhabitants in a quarter of a century was nonetheless remarkable. It was largely the result of Palermo's becoming the regional capital and main seat of government, and of Sicily's political and institutional reorientation towards Spain and away from Naples after 1458. These conditions enabled Palermo to attract immigrants by providing food at stable, non-market prices (see chapter 3).

Catania, which had suffered a huge set-back in the early fifteenth century when it lost political hegemony over eastern Sicily, recovered much more slowly than val di Noto as a whole. Despite its title of 'third sister' of the two regional metropoles, Palermo and

---

[68] *Ibid.*, 264, suggests a mean hearth quota of 1.10 *tarì* or 1.16 *tarì*. Either figure would produce a population size for 1464 either roughly similar or lower than that for 1439, particularly in val Demone. These results do not accord with other circumstantial evidence, which suggests that from the 1450s the population began to increase quite rapidly. I have adopted instead a mean hearth quota of 1.5 *tarì* for two reasons. First, allocations in 1464 are multiples of this figure. Second, this hearth quota would give Catania 2,076 tax hearths, which accords with evidence that the city had c. 8400 inhabitants in 1460 (M. Ginatempo and L. Sandri, *L'Italia delle città. Il popolamento urbano tra Medioevo e Rinascimento (secoli XIII–XVI)*, p. 261).

[69] The range of estimated increases depends on which population estimate (58,000 or 78,000 hearths) one adopts for 1439.

Table 2.5 Provisions for in- and out-migration, 1300–1499

Date	Locality	Provision	Documentary sources
1334	Palermo	privileges for immigrants from Corleone	De Vio ed., *Privilegia*, pp. 138–9
1342–75	Scaletta	emigrants' property confiscated	RC 5, fo. 226v
1399	Marsala, Sicily	right to migrate to demesnial towns upheld	RC 35, fo. 133rv
	Terranova	privileges for immigrants	RC 29, fos. 144–5v; RC 37, fos. 217–18
1400	Cefalù	privileges for immigrants	RC 17, fo. 37v
1402	Palermo	immigration from Corleone	RC 39, fo. 267
1403	Palermo	immigration from Corleone	RC 40, fo. 59
1404	Terranova	privileges for immigrants	RC 41, fos. 221–2
1405	Terranova	privileges for immigrants	RC 43, fo. 58
1407	Augusta	penalties for emigrants (to Catania, Syracuse, Lentini)	RC 44–5, fos. 109–10
	Randazzo	privileges for immigrants	RC 46, fos. 293v–4, 413v–15v
	Monte San Giuliano	penalties for emigrants, privileges for immigrants	RC 46, fos. 370v–1v
1413	Lentini	privileges for immigrants	Starrabba ed., *Lettere Bianca*, pp. 221–2
1420	Sciacca	privileges for immigrants	PR 21, fos. 89v–90v
1427	Agrigento	provisions against emigration	RC 59, fo. 48rv
1428	Augusta	provisions against emigration	CR 11, fos. 206–9
1431	Agrigento	provisions against emigration	RC 65, fo. 240
1434	Agrigento	privileges for immigration and against emigration to fiefs	C 2823, fos. 132–3
	Messina	privileges for immigrants from fiefs	Giardina ed., *Capitoli*, no. 83
	Piazza	privileges for immigrants	RC 70, fos. 69v–70
1435	Milazzo	privileges for immigrants from fiefs	C 2826, fos. 177v–8
	Marsala	provisions against emigrants	RC 70, fos. 235v–6
1443	Terranova	privileges for emigrants	C 2840, fos. 219v–20
	Terranova	penalties for emigrants	RC 80, fos. 263v–4
	Agrigento	privileges for immigrants	RC 79, fos. 81–2
	Aci	penalties for emigrants to Catania	C 2846, fos. 21v–2
1444	Patti	provisions for immigrants	RC 79, fos. 179v–82; RC 81, fos. 485v–8

Year	Place	Subject	Source
1446	Terranova	privileges for immigrants	C 2854, fo. 151rv
1447	Catania	privileges for immigrants	Amico e Statella, *Catana illustrata*, II, p. 327
1448	Augusta	re-population	C 2860, fo. 132rv
1452	Augusta	privileges against depopulation	C 2898, fos. 10v–11
	Polizzi	privileges for immigrants from fiefs	C 2871, fos. 119v–21
1457	Milazzo	privileges for immigrants from fiefs	RC 106, fos. 226–8
	Ferla	provision against emigrants	C 2880, fos. 89v–90
1459	Terranova	privileges for immigrants	C 3473, fos. 121–2
1460	Palermo	provisions for immigration from fiefs	C 3474, fos. 76v–80; De Vio ed., *Privilegia*, pp. 341–50
1465	Favara, Tano	privileges for immigrants	C 3485, fos. 56v–7
1467	Polizzi	emigration to fiefs	RC 118, fos. 164v–6; RC 119, fos. 100–1v
1468	Polizzi	depopulation	CR 47, fos. 1–1bisv
1470	Marsala	provisions against depopulation	CR 50, fos. 230–30ter
1481–90	Terranova	privileges for immigrants	CR 73, fos. 377–8v
1482	Piazza	provisions against emigration to fiefs	RC 149, fos. 55v–6v, 233v–4, 282–6, 293v–5, 430rv; RC 151, fos. 51–2v; CR 63, fo. 16rv
1483–4	Corleone	privileges for immigrants	CR 66, fos. 219, 221rv
1488	Agrigento	provisions against fleeing debtors	RC 171, fos. 172–5v

Table 2.6 *Resettlement licences (*licentia populandi*), 1400–1499*

Locality	Date	Documentary sources
Castelluccio	1421–2, 1433	Garufi, 'Patti agrari e comuni feudali', 104; C 2821, fo. 311rv
Siculiana	1422–5	CR 13, fos. 442–3
Cefalà	1431	D'Alessandro, 'Città e campagna', pp. 208–9
Savoca	1438	C 2829, fos. 201v–2
Contessa Entellina	1448	La Mantia ed., *Capitoli colonie greco-albanesi*, pp. xiii–xiv
Maletta, Maniaci	1449	CR 21, fos. 362–4; C 2863, fo. 32
Conte Ranieri (near Corleone)	1452	C 2871, fos. 131–2v; CR 33, fos. 391–3v; C 2872, fo. 115
Tano (near Castrogiovanni)	1458–63	C 3472, fo. 155rv; LV 78, fos. 105v–6v; CR 42, fos. 299–300
Yandicaturi	1468	CR 48, fos. 169–9bis
Pidadachi, Bandadini	1469	CR 48, fo. 65rv
San Todaro	1479	Trasselli, *Da Ferdinando*, p. 85
Palazzo Adriano	1482	La Mantia ed., *Capitoli colonie greco-albanesi*, pp. xiii–xiv
Lombardo (near Noto)	1485	Littara, *De rebus netinis*, p. 128; RC 164, fos. 109–11v
Limina	1487	CR 70, fo. 85rv
Biancavilla, Piana dei Greci	1488	La Mantia ed., *Capitoli colonie greco-albanesi*, pp. xiii–xiv
Merco, Anidogli (near Monreale)	1488	CR 72, fo. 49rv
Migaido (near Tusa)	1488	Cancila, *Baroni e popolo*, pp. 14–15
Montemaggiore	c.1490	Trasselli, *Da Ferdinando*, p. 85
Villafranca (near Caltabellotta)	1499	CR 81, fos. 76–7

Messina, at the turn of the sixteenth century, Catania was still only the tenth largest city in the island (see Table 2.7).[70]

Despite Catania's relative decline, val di Noto continued to be the most demographically dynamic of the three *valli*. By 1464, the region actually had a larger population than in 1277 (val di Mazara and val Demone, by comparison, had half or less of their thirteenth-century population), and it had the largest population of the three *valli*. In comparison with the late thirteenth century, its share of the total had more than doubled. The fastest-growing areas were mostly outside royal control. The population of the vast county of Modica (which included Ragusa, Caccamo, Comiso, Scicli and

[70] By 1548, Catania was the third largest Sicilian city, with 20,000–24,000 inhabitants (Beloch, *Bevölkerungsgeschichte Italiens*, pp. 159–61). On Catania's difficulties in the fifteenth century see below, chapter 5.

Monterosso) grew by four to thirty-eight per cent; the *Camera reginale*,[71] which included Syracuse, Lentini, Vizzini, Francavilla and Mineo, increased by forty-five to ninety per cent. The largest increases, however, took place in two demesne towns of the interior, Caltagirone and Noto, which more than doubled the number of tax hearths between 1277 and 1464.

Population appears to have increased particularly rapidly between 1464 and 1478 (or else previous fiscal under-assessments were corrected). By 1478, Sicily numbered *c.*120,000 hearths (500,000 inhabitants) including the tax exempt.[72] The fastest-growing area now became val Demone. The population of Messina and its immediate environs, in particular, expanded very rapidly from 3,500 to 5,600 hearths, possibly as a result of its new role as the main silk market in the western Mediterranean; the increase was nonetheless considerably smaller than that of Palermo. The smallest of the top ten cities, Nicosia, had more than 2,500 tax-paying hearths; Agrigento in val di Mazara, Catania and Castrogiovanni in val di Noto, and Randazzo in val Demone were assessed for more than 2,000 taxable hearths each (see Table 2.7). With the exception of Syracuse, Noto and Lentini, which belonged to the *Camera reginale*, all the main Sicilian cities belonged to the royal demesne.

The last quarter of the fifteenth century saw a significant decline in the rate of demographic increase (from 1.64 per cent in 1464–78[73] to 0.8 per cent in 1478–1501), and a less distorted distribution of gains among the *valli*. By 1501, when the first census was made,

---

[71] The territory of the *Camera reginale* was probably established in the early fourteenth century by Federico III as the queen's main apanage. It had near-independent status and was administered by the queen's officials; it was abolished in 1536. See E. De Benedictis, *Della Camera delle regine siciliane*; V. Giménez Chornet, 'Gobierno y control de los oficiales de la Camara de Sicilia (1424–1458)'; M. L. Ribes Valiente, 'La renta de la reina María en la ciudad de Siracusa (1456–1457)'.

[72] Trasselli, 'Ricerche su la popolazione', 264–8, estimates the mean hearth quota for 1478 by dividing Palermo's total allocation by the city's population (which is known for that year), wrongly assuming that Jews paid the same as Christians. An average quota of 1.10 *tarì* for a Christian hearth accords better with evidence that Jews were taxed more heavily than Christians (RC 104, fos. 434v–7v, and CR 38, fos. 128–8quater (1457); C 3472, fos. 187v–9 (1459)). A population of 5,000 for Naro in 1473 (RC 131, fo. 151v) accords with an estimate of 1,200 tax hearths paying an average 1.10 *tarì* in 1478.

[73] Such a high rate of increase was not unusual for Mediterranean regions in this period. E. Baratier, *La démographie provençale du XIIIe siècle au XVI siècle. Avec chiffres de comparaison pour le XVIIIe siècle*, pp. 86, 88–9, 90–4: average increase of 1.74 per cent per annum for Provence in 1471–1540 (my calculations).

Sicily numbered *c.*140,000 hearths including exemptions. For the first time in two centuries, val di Noto showed signs of relative stagnation. Between 1497 and 1501, population actually decreased, possibly as a result of the epidemics of 1495–7 and 1500–1.[74] The end of the fifteenth century, however, seems in many ways a turning point for this area's development. For reasons which are still unknown, the population of val di Noto – which had resisted decline most strongly and had recovered faster than other *valli* – grew most slowly during the sixteenth and seventeenth centuries.[75]

Val Demone was the only *vallo* whose population increased significantly between 1497 and 1501, suggesting that the rapid increase in silk, wine, oil and fruit production was transforming its poorly endowed territory into the most complex and intensively organized economy of the whole island (see chapters 4 and 5).

Although on the whole the population of eastern Sicily recovered fastest after the mid-fifteenth century, val di Mazara was not bypassed by recovery. This was aided by immigration from the mainland, for most new settlements in this period occurred in the emptier territories of western Sicily. By the turn of the sixteenth century, when the long cycle of demographic depression was finally overcome and decades of strong economic growth lay ahead, the population of val di Mazara had stabilized around a third of the total, roughly the same proportion as in the 1370s. Whatever the reasons for val di Mazara's particularly intense losses compared to eastern Sicily during the thirteenth and fourteenth centuries, this area was also slow to recover its former demographic importance. Of the many reasons for this failure, one stands out and will be discussed in the coming chapters: val di Mazara's increasing specialization as a region producing grain extensively and at a low labour intensity for the domestic and international markets.[76]

E. Le Roy Ladurie, *Les paysans de Languedoc*, I, pp. 190–1: 1.09 per cent increase per annum for some Languedocian communities in 1500–60 (my calculations). See also G. Bois, *The crisis of feudalism. Economic society in eastern Normandy c.1300–1550*, chapter 2, for annual rates of increase of 1.9–2 per cent.

[74] For 1495–7 (when epidemics are known for val di Mazara only: Sciacca, Palermo, Termini, Naro), see CR 875, fos. 263–4, 286–7, 288–9v, 330rv; CR 877, fo. 130rv; TRP Atti 56, fos. 171rv, 270v–1; RC 194, fos. 101v–2. For 1500–1 see Peri, *Restaurazione*, p. 69 n. 6.

[75] Aymard, 'In Sicilia', 430.

[76] In the sixteenth and seventeenth centuries, by contrast, val di Mazara showed the highest rates of demographic growth (*ibid.*, 430, 434).

Most of this chapter so far has analysed the redistribution of population between *valli*, on the assumption that aggregate and long-term changes in demographic distribution and growth rates reflect changes in social and economic structures. Changes in population distribution between coastal areas and the interior, and between different urban centres, are equally useful indicators of changes in the territorial distribution of resources.

Whereas in 1277, the twenty-three largest settlements within 10km of the coast[77] included more than fifty per cent of the population, by the late fourteenth century the proportion of coastal dwellers had dropped to less than forty per cent, and by 1439 it was down to 34.2 per cent. In 1464, the proportion had risen again to just over forty per cent, where it remained until the end of the fifteenth century.

What caused these changes? Some communities – like Cefalù and Milazzo on the northern coast, Mazara and Trapani in the west, and especially Terranova in the south – suffered huge losses during the fourteenth century because of military harassment, first by the Angevins and later by North African pirates.[78] Even so, while warfare was clearly a contributory factor, major, generalized changes in population patterns were not the result of fitful and rather ineffectual military activities. Rather, demographic distribution reflects with notable accuracy (though with a slight time-lag) contemporary changes in regional market structures.

The decline in the proportion of coastal dwellers was caused by a process of fragmentation of the domestic market (discussed in chapter 3), which reduced the ability of the grain-scarce eastern areas to supply themselves by sea from the west. As a result of these developments and of heavy population losses, which lowered population pressure on land, towns became more inward-looking and relied more heavily on local sources of supply. These changes also explain why, in the period 1374–1439, middle- and middle-to-smaller-sized centres survived the demographic slump better than the larger cities. By 1439, when the proportion of coastal dwellers

---

[77] Palermo, Agrigento, Trapani, Monte San Giuliano, Sciacca, Termini, Marsala, Licata, Alcamo and Mazara in val di Mazara; Messina, Santa Lucia, Milazzo, Cefalù, Patti, Taormina and Aci in val Demone; Catania, Terranova, Noto, Syracuse, Lentini and Augusta in val di Noto.

[78] Starrabba, 'Documenti relativi a un episodio delle guerre tra le fazioni latina e catalana ai tempi di Re Ludovico d'Aragona', 172 (1400).

may have reached its lowest ebb, market fragmentation was already being reversed. The tax allocation of 1464 shows that population in the coastal areas was increasing more rapidly than in the interior. Conditions, however, did not simply revert to what they were in the thirteenth century. On the one hand, the regional economy had become more integrated than it had ever previously been; on the other, the lower proportion of coastal dwellers in the late fifteenth century than in 1277 suggests that by 1500, towns did not need to rely as much as before on supplies transported by sea.[79]

Changes in the distribution of urban populations in the later Middle Ages are of special interest because of the peculiarity of Sicilian urban structures. A feature distinguishing late medieval Sicily from central and northern Italian regions is that, in the course of two centuries, only three cities – Palermo, Messina and Trapani – were stable among the top ten (see Table 2.7).[80] Only after 1374 were three additional centres consistently among the largest: Piazza, Noto and Syracuse, and, more briefly, Catania. As with relative demographic distribution between *valli*, the most important changes in urban ranking occurred between the late thirteenth and the late fourteenth centuries, with a pronounced shift in urban concentration from western and central to eastern Sicily. Whereas in the late thirteenth century, seven out of the ten largest cities were situated in val di Mazara, two centuries later the proportion had dropped to two out of ten, and val di Mazara's role as the most urbanized area had been taken up by val di Noto, where six of the ten largest cities were situated.

These violent fluctuations in urban ranking imply either a great geographical mobility of the population,[81] or extraordinary differences in rates of natural increase among urban populations, or very effective short-term lobbying by towns to reduce their tax allocations. Since there are no grounds for believing that there were extreme differences and changes in rates of natural increase, nor is there any evidence of significant tax lobbying, the main cause of

---

[79] Nonetheless, population remained heavily concentrated along the coasts throughout the modern era (Milone, *L'Italia*, p. 985).

[80] Epstein, 'Cities, regions', 22–8; Ginatempo and Sandri, *L'Italia delle città*, pp. 163–7.

[81] *UM*, p. 76; A. Varvaro, *Lingua e storia in Sicilia*, p. 219. See also R. Comba, 'Emigrare nel Medioevo. Aspetti economico-sociali della mobilità geografica nei secoli XI–XVI'.

Table 2.7 *The ten largest Sicilian towns (estimated taxed hearths),*
1277–1497

	1277	1374–6	1439[a]	1464	1478	1497
Palermo (M)	22,014	4,082	3,000–4,000	4,468	6,500[b]	7,500
Messina (D)	13,300	[3,000]	3,000–4,000	3,460	5,600	6,300
Trapani (M)	6,806	2,608	1,200–1,600	2,306	2,640	3,300
Corleone (M)	6,600	1,136	—	—	—	—
Terranova (M)	4,428	—	—	—	—	—
Randazzo (D)	4,010	—	—	—	—	—
Marsala (M)	3,906	—	—	—	—	—
Mazara (M)	3,000	—	—	—	—	—
Castronovo (M)	2,630	—	—	—	—	—
Salemi (M)	2,500	—	—	—	—	—
Piazza (N)	—	1,542	1,500–2,000	2,306	2,560	3,105
Catania (N)	—	[4,000]	1,500–2,000	2,076	—	2,850
Noto (N)	—	1,372	1,500–2,000	2,537	2,560	3,090
Nicosia (D)	—	1,250	1,200–1,600	—	2,520	3,000
Syracuse (N)	—	1,755	1,500–2,000	[3,000]	[4,100]	[5,190]
Agrigento (M)	—	1,560	—	2,076	—	—
Caltagirone (N)	—	—	1,500–2,000	2,537	3,060	3,518
Sciacca (M)	—	—	1,800–2,400	—	—	—
Polizzi (M)	—	—	—	2,076	2,560	—
Lentini (N)	—	—	—	—	[2,600]	[3,290]
Total	69,194	22,305	17,700–23,600	26,842	34,700	41,143
Rate of urbanization[c]	47.8	34.9	29.8	32.8	33.8	34.1

[a] Randazzo, Castrogiovanni and Polizzi are also assessed for 1,200 hearths.
[b] Estimated from R. Starrabba, 'Censimento della popolazione di Palermo fatto nel 1479'.
[c] Percentage of total population.
[ ] = estimates.
M = val di Mazara; N = val di Noto; D = val Demone.
Sources: As for Table 2.1.

fluctuations in urban ranking seems to have been individual mobility.

This can be traced to at least two main sources, both of which reduced the costs of migration considerably. The first was the scarcity, except in val Demone, of peasant allodial property; in general, the demise of serfdom in the thirteenth century did not endow the majority of the peasantry with much land in freehold.[82]

---

[82] L. Sorrenti, *Il patrimonio fondiario in Sicilia. Gestione delle terre e contratti agrari nei secoli XII–XV*, chapter 2; see below, chapter 7.

The second reason for mobility was connected with the rather weak institutional powers of towns over their rural hinterlands, which limited the towns' abilities to command economic resources over long periods of time and attract and retain immigrants. I discuss this issue further in chapter 3.

Late medieval Sicily also had an unusually high level of urbanization. If we take the ten largest towns at any one time as the base for calculating the rate of urbanization, we find that the smallest of these, at any date, had no fewer than 1,100 hearths (5,000–6,500 inhabitants including exemptions).[83] On this basis, at no time during the later Middle Ages (with the exception of the 1430s) did less than thirty per cent of the Sicilian population live in such centres. Sicilian rates of urbanization were on a par with the southern Low Countries, and possibly higher than the Italian mean in this period.[84] As we shall see further below, Sicily was able to sustain such a large non-agricultural population thanks to a highly productive system of agriculture and an efficient means of distribution.

CONCLUSIONS

Demographic fluctuations in late medieval Sicily differed less from general European trends than has been recently argued. As elsewhere in Europe, population losses – which probably began in the early fourteenth century and continued into the first decades of the fifteenth – were severe. Towards 1282, Sicily numbered approximately 200,000 hearths (850,000 inhabitants); a century later, the population had dropped to about forty per cent of this figure. Decline probably continued, but at a slower rate, the nadir being reached soon after 1400. By 1439, the population had recovered slightly and was back to, or slightly above, what it had been in 1374–6 (65,000–70,000 tax hearths). The turning-point, however, occurred during the 1450s, and in the course of the next four

---

[83] I have compensated for the fact that a proportion of these hearths was rural by taking only the largest ten towns as the basis of calculation, thereby excluding at every point in time a number of settlements which, on criteria of size, passed the urban threshold. This threshold (expressed in hearths) was 1,400 in 1277; 900 in 1374–6 and 1439; 1,100 in 1464; 1,200 in 1478; and 1,400 in 1497. For the method of calculating the urban threshold see Herlihy and C. Klapisch Zuber, *Tuscans and their families. A study of the Florentine Catasto of 1427*, pp. 53–5.

[84] E. Ennen, *Die europäische Stadt des Mittelalters*, p. 30; P. Bairoch, J. Batou and P. Chèvre, *La population des villes européennes de 800 à 1850*, p. 259.

decades the population doubled, at a mean annual rate of increase of 1.4 per cent. A substantial but unmeasurable proportion of this increase was the result of immigration from the southern mainland, from northern Italy and from present-day Albania; this influx testifies not only to the low density of habitation in the island, but also to the region's economic potential. By 1501, Sicily numbered some 550,000–600,000 inhabitants.

The demographic crisis changed the geographic distribution of the population in at least three ways. First, it resulted in a major redistribution from west to east, with val di Noto in particular (which, in the late thirteenth century, was the most thinly populated *vallo*) gaining at the expense of val di Mazara (which, by the fifteenth century, was established as the most sparsely settled region). Despite its huge population losses during the fourteenth and fifteenth centuries, and despite also its mountainous terrain and lack of arable land, val Demone remained the most densely settled *vallo* up to the eighteenth century. In turn, different rates of population growth were shaped by the availability of natural resources in the different *valli*, as described in the first part of this chapter (see also chapters 4 and 5).

The considerable changes in population distribution between the interior and the coastal areas were primarily the result of institutional forces. During the fourteenth century, the proportion of coastal dwellers dropped sharply, in part as a result of Angevin and North African skirmishes, but in greater measure because of structural changes in the regional market. Markets became more localized; the advantages of coastal settlements over the interior for food supply dwindled. The increasing integration of the regional market during the fifteenth century did not, however, merely re-establish conditions prevailing before the fourteenth-century crisis to the benefit of the coastal areas. Inhabitants of the interior benefited also from Sicily's increasing commercial integration. On the one hand, a larger proportion of the population lived in the interior compared to the thirteenth century; on the other hand, evidence of dearth in the interior became increasingly less common (see chapter 3).

A third kind of demographic redistribution occurred between urban centres. At one level, the threshold separating urban from non-urban settlements changed quite significantly, in connection both with demographic fluctuations, and with changes in the structure of the domestic market.[85] Within this process, however, patterns of change differed according to the institutional resources each centre could command. Thus the hardest hit by the fourteenth-century epidemics were the former metropoles, Palermo and Messina, and some of the western and south-western ports (Mazara, Trapani, Marsala, Licata, Terranova), because of the contraction of foreign markets and because of political, institutional and economic changes on the domestic scene. The most notable development during the fourteenth century (significant also for being one of the few instances of demographic growth in the period) is that of Catania, whose spectacular expansion (followed by an equally rapid decline after 1400) was primarily the result of the same forces which spelled the decline of Palermo and Messina (see chapters 3 and 5). In general, however, urban ranking by size was very unstable. The demographic instability of Sicilian towns was the result of very high individual mobility and of weak urban institutions regulating access to administrative and economic resources, which allowed (or imposed) greater competition between centres (see chapter 7). Despite the fact that a more stable urban hierarchy began to develop in the fifteenth century, Sicily was still characterized by the lack of a single metropolis exerting regional hegemony, and by a relative fluidity of urban ranking.

[85] Above, n. 83; below, chapter 3.

3. Market structures and regional specialization

I argue in this book that the late medieval economic crisis in western Europe promoted regional integration and specialization.[1] In the final part of chapter 2, I briefly discussed the effect of some late medieval institutional changes on the distribution of the Sicilian population, on the assumption that the latter reflected fairly accurately how regional institutions distributed resources. In so doing, I was viewing the population as a body of consumers. In order to examine the hypothesis of increasing regional specialization, however, it is necessary to view the economy as a collectivity of producers. I suggested at the outset of chapter 2 that producers responded to changes in late medieval society by taking increasing advantage of the environmental and demographic resources at their disposal; the purpose of that chapter was to examine the patterning of those resources. The extent to which comparative advantages *could* be exploited, however, depended to a considerable degree on the nature of the markets which producers 'had access to. The structure of these markets, hence the nature of the institutional *opportunities* for specialization through trade, is the problem I analyse below. In this and the next two chapters, I discuss market integration and specialization within Sicily itself; I examine specialization between Sicily and other regions in chapter 6.

[1] See, for example, J. Langdon, 'Agricultural equipment'; G. Astill and A. Grant, 'The medieval countryside: Efficiency, progress and change'; Britnell, *Growth and decline in Colchester, 1300–1525*, esp. pp. 131–2, 246; M. Bailey, *A marginal economy? East Anglian Breckland in the later Middle Ages*; D. Nicholas, *The metamorphosis of a medieval city. Ghent in the age of the Arteveldes, 1302–1390*; W. P. Blockmans, 'Stadt, Region und Staat: ein Dreiecksverhältnis. Der Kasus der Niederlande im 15. Jahrhundert'; T. Scott, *Freiburg and the Breisgau. Town-country relations in the age of Reformation and the Peasants' War*; T. Scott, 'Economic conflict and co-operation on the Upper Rhine, 1450–1600'; E. Fournial, *Les villes et l'économie d'échange en Forez aux XIIIe et XIVe siècles*. A modified version of this Introduction appears in Epstein, 'Cities, regions', 1–12.

INTRODUCTION: SPECIALIZATION AND ECONOMIC GROWTH

Why did regional integration in late medieval Europe increase? It is commonly argued that a massive loss of population, such as occurred after the mid-fourteenth century, would generally favour, assuming declining marginal returns and other conditions discussed below, the conversion of 'marginal' land less adapted to staple crops to more appropriate purposes, which often signified more intensive cultivation.[2] However, it has more seldom been remarked that this process could potentially lead to a gradual increase in specialization of agriculture and, by a feedback process, of manufacture.[3]

Two kinds of margin existed in periods of rising population pressure.[4] The intensive margin was what faced the individual producer or community, bringing under cultivation poorer soils close enough to habitation not to warrant resettlement. The extensive margin, by contrast, distinguished between the relative fertility of larger geographical areas. Increasing demand for food led to areas less suitable for producing grain and other staples being settled and adopting such crops.

As population pressure declined, labour, particularly on the environmental margin for grain production, either abandoned the area altogether or was freed for other activities. In the latter case, rising disparities in production costs might allow peasants in 'marginal' areas to specialize in non-staple crops, in animal husbandry, or in petty crafts and industries, and trade them for staples from better suited arable areas.[5] Evidence of increasing market

---

[2] W. Abel, *Agricultural fluctuations in Europe. From the thirteenth to the twentieth centuries*, pp. 70–9; M. M. Postan, *The medieval economy and society. An economic history of Britain in the Middle Ages*, pp. 63–79; B. Slicher van Bath, *The agrarian history of western Europe: AD 500–1850*, pp. 142–4; G. Duby, *Rural economy and country life in the medieval West*, pp. 308–11.

[3] Slicher van Bath, *Agrarian history*, p. 13; Slicher van Bath, 'Les problèmes fondamentaux de la société pré-industrielle en Europe occidentale. Une orientation et une programme', 38–9.

[4] Bailey, 'The concept of the margin in the medieval English economy'; Bailey, *Marginal economy?*, chapter 1.

[5] I assume here that peasant households devoted a large proportion of their labour time to non-agricultural (manufacturing, processing and distributing) activities, often called 'Z goods' after S. Hymer and S. Resnick, 'A model of an agrarian economy with nonagricultural activities'. A rural economy would thus possess considerable opportunities for increasing output merely through *organizational* change, by shifting to more specialized forms of agriculture and manufacture at unchanging levels of technology.

integration indicates that the kind of specialization taking place during the later Middle Ages tended to exploit shifts in the extensive margin of cultivation between differently endowed areas, rather than the intensive margin within a community, although the latter also occurred.

Changes at the margin through rapid depopulation, however, were neither a necessary nor a sufficient condition for specialization to occur. At least two crucial and interrelated factors affected specialization more directly. The first of these was the redistribution of incomes which depopulation provoked in most western European regions to the benefit of peasants, wage-earners and artisans. Changes in income distribution only marginally affect the output of food grains because of the low elasticity of demand for these products; conversely, such changes can have considerable effects on demand for manufactured goods and higher-quality foodstuffs. I suggest that during the late Middle Ages, the redistribution of incomes led to a considerable increase in demand for more and better non-staple foodstuffs and cheap manufactured goods, especially cloth, which in turn provided the main stimulus for specialization of agriculture and manufacturing. The process of income redistribution, however, did not occur simply as a result of shifts in the supply and demand of land and labour. It was shaped and directed by two further factors: the institutions which different groups in society could deploy and, if possible, modify so as to reallocate resources for their own benefit; and the nature of production relations between peasants and landowners, and between manufacturers and their employees.[6]

For specialization to occur it was necessary for demand, hence trade, to increase at a local, but more especially at a regional, level (in other words, for market size to increase). In theory, however, demographic decline could have the opposite effect on both specialization and trade. If one assumes that peasants were subsistence-oriented and resorted to trade only under compulsion, the logical conclusion is that they would tend to abandon through migration those areas unsuited to cereal cultivation, settle in more fertile territories, but eschew any opportunities for economic diversification. Michael Postan, for example, argued that the improved conditions of the peasantry after the Black Death led to a *retreat* of

[6] Brenner, 'Agrarian roots'; Bois, *Crisis of feudalism.*

the burgeoning middle-ranking peasantry into subsistence: trade and markets were *weakened* by major depopulation.[7] He assumed that peasants (and to a lesser extent wage labourers) did not direct their rising incomes to increase consumption or exploit expanding economic opportunities, but were stuck in a cultural framework of 'self-subsistence' with unchanging consumption preferences. Some Marxist historians have followed Postan in assuming a subsistent peasantry, arguing that peasants were totally risk-averse and that, therefore, where possible, they avoided trade and markets. Peasants became involved in local, regional and extra-regional markets either because outside forces (taxation or feudal and merchant exploitation) compelled them to trade, or because their preferences inexplicably shifted from subsistence to 'profit maximization'.[8]

Miskimin, on the other hand, has argued that the rise in the price of manufactured compared to agricultural goods (the 'price scissors') between 1350 and 1400 was the result of 'hedonistic consumption patterns' which caused a massive bleeding of financial resources from the countryside to the towns that ultimately stabilized urban prices by lowering rural demand.[9] Miskimin assumes that stagnant agricultural prices from 1350 to 1400 are a sign of overproduction and narrower markets. He disregards the spread of rural and semi-rural manufacturing which would have stemmed some of the flow of wealth to towns following changes in terms of trade. He also disregards the possibility that the closing of the price scissors after 1400 reflects the slow adaptation of structures of supply to the changes in consumption patterns from agricultural to manufactured goods, rather than a reduction of rural demand; Miskimin's theory appears to assume another form of peasant irrationality, opposite to Postan's 'subsistence-maximization', namely the peasantry's inability to stop spending at a loss.

[7] Postan, 'The fifteenth century', p. 41; Postan, 'The trade of medieval Europe: the North', pp. 164–5; Postan, *Medieval economy*, pp. 140–1; see Bailey, 'Concept of the margin', 7–13.

[8] Brenner, 'The social basis of economic development'; Brenner, 'Bourgeois revolution and transition to capitalism'; P. Kriedte, H. Medick and J. Schlumbohm, *Industrialization before industrialization. Rural industry in the genesis of capitalism*, esp. chapter 3. These arguments are akin to those of the 'peasant moral economy' school; see S. L. Popkin, *The rational peasant. The political economy of rural society in Vietnam*, pp. 10–17.

[9] H. A. Miskimin, *The economy of early Renaissance Europe, 1300–1460*, pp. 86–92; Miskimin, 'Monetary movements and market structure. Forces for contraction in fourteenth- and fifteenth-century England', 490.

Contrary to what these theories predict, there is increasing evidence for much of rural Europe both of rising consumption, and of expanding (often country-based) manufacturing and commercialization following the Black Death, a phenomenon which did not cease (and was often strengthened) after 1400. In late medieval Europe, external coercive forces were by and large in retreat, but peasants were nonetheless diversifying production and regional trade was increasing; at the same time, there is evidence that in some regions subsistence patterns persisted or were even reinforced. To explain both types of evidence without postulating peasant irrationality, we must examine more closely the various institutions which constrained and enabled peasants in their relations with the market, on the assumption that their behaviour can be explained as a 'rational' response to such constraints.[10]

Different property rights would provide different incentive structures for peasants to commercialize. In addition, the structure of the market (the power of feudal lords or urban institutions to set excise barriers to trade, for example) could affect the terms of trade between agricultural and manufactured products, thereby setting further constraints on peasant commodity production.[11] Specialization was bound by the market structures peculiar to each region; ultimately it was the relative flexibility of these social and institutional structures which oriented long-term regional development by providing incentives to production and trade, and by allowing for a significant increase in demand for more specialized commodities by the majority of the population.

Peasant economic 'rationality' is fully consistent with the common assumption that, for economies with low per capita income, population movements follow changes in the volume of available resources. A consequence of this assumption is that changes in income distribution do not affect the economy in the long run: after a short time-lag, the population will readapt itself to the existing volume of resources, leaving per capita consumption

---

[10] P. Bardhan, 'Alternative approaches to the theory of institutions in economic development'; J. E. Stiglitz, 'Rational peasants, efficient institutions, and a theory of rural organization: Methodological remarks for development economics'.

[11] See below (on urbanization) and chapter 6 (on terms of trade); E. J. Nell, 'Economic relationships in the decline of feudalism: an examination of economic interdependence and social change'.

unchanged.[12] The later Middle Ages, however, are distinctive in that, for at least a century in western Europe, the population did *not* expand in response to a growth in personal income among the lower-to-middle strata. The reasons for this lag of a century or more between the first devastations caused by the Black Death and the beginning of demographic recovery are notoriously obscure. Explanations range from the epidemiological and socio-structural[13] to the socio-economic[14] and the behaviourist;[15] no consensus view has yet emerged. Whichever factors were at work, however, the secular delay between demographic decline and recovery was crucial for promoting the structural changes in the economy which were the basis for the great European expansion of the sixteenth century.

The simple model presented above combines the rising demand for cheap commodities by the middle and lower sections of the population as an effect of a major redistribution of incomes, with the opportunity to exploit shifts in the extensive agricultural margin induced by a declining or stagnant population. In this view, economic change was induced by a *shift* in comparative advantages caused by depopulation. Specialization could not become a self-sustaining process, however, unless institutional constraints on trade were sufficiently flexible not to interrupt the feedback of specialization into the economy.

Institutional constraints are best analysed at a regional level, for two reasons. Firstly, town–country relations, which crucially affected the course of late medieval economic development, were most effective at a regional rather than supra-regional level; these

[12] This assumption underlies K. G. Persson, *Pre-industrial economic growth. Social organization and technological progress in Europe.*
[13] Brenner, 'Agrarian roots', pp. 267–73, suggests that demographic stagnation was a result of a combination of recurrent epidemics and heightened feudal exploitation. The second part of the explanation, however, is hard to reconcile with the fact that population began recovering several decades earlier in France than in England, where seigneurial and state pressure seem to have been weaker. See J. Hatcher, *Plague, population and the English economy 1348–1530*, pp. 63–7; A. Higounet-Nadal, 'Le relèvement', pp. 371–3.
[14] P. J. Goldberg, 'Female migration to towns in the later Middle Ages', and C. Dyer, *Standards of living*, p. 146, have suggested that increasing opportunities for female employment in a labour-scarce economy might have lowered the rate of nuptiality or increased the age of female marriage, thus causing a decrease in natality (see, however, Hatcher, *Plague*, pp. 55–6).
[15] I. S. W. Blanchard, 'Labour productivity and work psychology in the English mining industry 1400–1600'; Persson, 'Consumption, labour and leisure in the late Middle Ages'.

relations will be discussed in detail below. Secondly, the region is where the strongest and most integrated political and administrative organization took shape during the late Middle Ages; this is true even in England, whose central government was the most powerful and the oldest in medieval Europe.[16] Specialization through trade could take place most effectively within such institutionally homogeneous areas, because at this level, institutional distortions of prices (tariffs) were weakest and their impact on transport costs could be most easily reduced; information on differences in (real) production costs was more widely available to individual producers and traders. Information costs associated with pricing were also lower within one region than between many.[17]

For Italy, the relationship between the formation of regional or territorial states and long-term economic development has begun to be explored, but there is a tendency to view the territorial state as a neutral container in which the welfare goal of optimum resource allocation operated through unfettered competition and economic 'rationalization'.[18] Clearly, however, one must take account of those institutions (the state, urban jurisdiction, the structure of property rights and markets) which actively influenced, constrained and sometimes directed the allocation of resources within society. Only thus can one understand long-term economic development and explain regional divergences between northern and southern Italy, and between different parts of Europe.

Besides its influence on the allocation of resources through taxation and direct economic intervention, the state could significantly affect allocation by influencing the structure and size of the market. In an economy constrained by higher transfer and transaction costs on trade in low-value, bulky commodities by land over long distances, political intervention could be crucial for the survival and growth of trade, and hence for specialization. Transport costs overland were, of course, very high; in addition, a number of tariffs were customarily levied which could make the cost of moving a cheap commodity over great distances or across political frontiers economically unprofitable. Compared to the technological con-

[16] See R. H. Hilton, *A medieval society. The West Midlands at the end of the thirteenth century*; M. J. Bennett, *Community, class and careerism. Cheshire and Lancashire society in the age of Sir Gawain and the Green Knight*.
[17] North, 'Location theory and regional economic growth', 245.
[18] Epstein, 'Cities, regions', 11–12.

straits affecting land (and water) transport, however, which were very high and in the short term inflexible, institutional constraints within a politically-defined region could be changed more easily under social and economic pressure. One must therefore look mainly to regional differences and variations in institutional, rather than technical, constraints in order to assess the impact of transaction costs on economic development in this period.

Exemption from tolls could only be obtained from public authority. Except where a powerful monarchy could enforce a reduction of customs throughout the kingdom, however, sovereigns tended to devolve trade regulation to local or regional authorities. Within territorial states like Tuscany or Lombardy, such cost-reducing privileges could only be employed within the region itself.[19] During the fourteenth and fifteenth centuries, Sicily too had the status of, or was treated as, a politically distinct region, and tariff reductions or exemptions applied only within it.

For the reasons just outlined, my definition of the economic region is straightforwardly political. While economic influences and relations clearly did not stop at political frontiers in our period, transit dues weighed especially heavily on the prices, hence the nature, of goods which crossed those borders. In addition, and in contrast with other Italian and Spanish regions,[20] in Sicily there is little evidence of smuggling; the sheer distance and difficulties of communication between most of Sicily and the Italian, Spanish or African coasts make it highly unlikely that a significant part of the export trade occurred outside the crown's knowledge and taxing capacities. Presumably, also, where cross-frontier trade became important for local populations, they or the state would have tried to regularize trade through the usual institutional channels. In the absence of such official agreements, we can assume that volumes of cross-border trade were not very significant.

To demonstrate the importance of politics for trade I can quote the only significant exception, namely relations between Messina and its Sicilian hinterland, and southern Calabria around Reggio, relations crucial to the economic welfare of both areas. When the southern Italian kingdoms were split after Alfonso's death in 1458,

---

[19] L. Frangioni, *Milano e le sue strade. Costi di trasporto e vie di commercio dei prodotti milanesi alla fine del Trecento.*
[20] Epstein, 'Cities, regions', 16 n. 33; A. MacKay, *Money, prices and politics in fifteenth-century Castile*, p. 10.

all previous trading agreements and tariff exemptions between Sicily and Naples were rescinded, with the exception of those between Sicily and southern Calabria: local economic interests were too powerful to bow to the political and fiscal pressures of the state (see chapter 5).

An area of state influence which affected both local trade and urbanization was the relationship between town and countryside. Although medieval urbanization was usually conditional on an exploitative relationship with the rural economy,[21] the link between specific institutional constellations, different market structures and patterns of urbanization, together with the structure and consequences for development of this relationship, have been hardly investigated. In the final part of this chapter I apply some recent developments in central place theory to examine changes in the organization of urban markets.

For the most part, I intentionally ignore smaller-scale or shorter-distance market relations.[22] As I mentioned earlier, the main documentary sources for these relations, notarial contracts, are lacking for most of the period and areas I examine. Although this problem can be partly circumvented, I have not done so at much length for two reasons. There is, firstly, the danger already referred to of relying excessively on notarial contracts which exclude a vast proportion of economic activities and transactions (the volume, if not the exact nature of these activities, is more readily analysed via urbanization). Such contracts provide no information on the institutional context in which transactions took place, a context which must be known to interpret the notarial records correctly. Secondly, while briefly discussing changes in short-range town–country relations, I emphasize infra-regional specialization and trade and the development of a *regional* market in the later Middle Ages, because this appears to be the most significant economic process at work and one which can be most easily compared with contemporary developments in the rest of western Europe.

Because it was easier to reduce transaction costs for trade in cheap, bulk commodities for mass consumption within, rather than between, territorial states, developments *internal* to regions were more significant than those *between* regions. As a result, late medieval specialization was mainly the outcome not of long-distance

[21] A. B. Hibbert, 'The economic policies of towns'.
[22] See Dyer, 'The consumer and the market in the later middle ages'.

trade in predominantly high-value commodities, but of the operation and interaction of differences in natural and social endowments within regions themselves.

What are the implications of this model compared to the dualistic models commonly used in analysing Italian economic development? In the model outlined above I assume, first, that competition through comparative advantage and labour mobility was enhanced by the fourteenth-century demographic crisis; and second, that the regional institutions which shaped and guided these developments could and did vary as a result of changing socio-economic conditions. Both assumptions are incompatible with the usual definition of a dual economy. On the one hand, as will be recalled, this definition *excludes* the normal operation of competitive markets; it precludes the free movement of capital and labour between agriculture and manufacture; and it assumes that agriculture is not commercialized. On the other hand, the dualist model is based on an assumption of institutional equilibrium or stasis; it fails to specify the conditions of institutional *change* which either establish or break dualist equilibrium.

Having laid the theoretical groundwork we can now proceed to see which model better explains the economic development of late medieval Sicily. I shall do this in two stages. Having argued that the outcome of the late medieval economic crisis depended crucially on the institutional constellation which regulated access to markets, in the rest of this chapter we shall examine the relationship between politico-institutional and economic change, particularly the development of an integrated regional market and the impact of modifications in institutional constraints on trade. As I stated above, the purpose of this chapter is therefore largely to assess changing *opportunities* for economic growth and specialization. The second stage in my argument is developed in the following chapter, in which I examine *actual* changes in late medieval Sicily's productive structures.

The remaining part of this chapter is divided into four parts. Firstly, I examine the effect of political developments on market structures. Then, I review deliberate state intervention in the economy. Thirdly, I analyse the effect of economic change on urban institutions. And finally, I examine the circulation of goods and people and its effect on urbanization.

SOCIAL AND ECONOMIC CONSEQUENCES OF WAR

Late medieval Sicily's political history is dominated by the War of the Vespers. The conflict, which began in 1282 and was concluded only in 1442 with Alfonso V of Aragon's conquest of Naples, is the longest of late medieval Europe. Like the Hundred Years War, however, hostilities were frequently interrupted, and years of peace far outnumbered those of warfare.

Unlike the Anglo-French conflict in the Hundred Years War, war between Sicily and the Angevins of Naples was waged mainly by sea and through destructive coastal forays. With the treaty of Caltabellotta (1302), the two parties agreed to give up most of their positions in enemy territory: the Angevins in eastern Sicily, the Sicilians throughout southern Calabria.[23] Robert of Anjou organized a number of brief campaigns in western Sicily in 1314, 1316, 1325–7, 1333, 1335 and 1338 and around Milazzo in 1341–3, but at his death in January 1343, nothing of lasting import had been achieved. Even during the Angevin invasion of 1356, which resulted in the occupation of Messina and other parts of eastern Sicily for a number of years, Angevin attacks were usually localized and rarely lasted long.[24] The peace of 1372 ratified the political and military stalemate between the two parties; subsequent attacks (in the 1430s and 1440s) were launched from Sicily against the mainland by a combination of Iberian and local forces.

Besides long-term hostilities with Naples, Sicily witnessed two other long periods of warfare, both indirectly deriving from the island's submission to Aragonese rule in 1282. The first was the period of civil war between magnate families, which lasted approximately from 1348 to 1362; the second was the reconquest of Sicily by Catalan and Aragonese forces in 1392–8. Sicily thus experienced war mainly during three periods in the 'long fourteenth century': 1282–1302, 1348–62 and 1392–8; that is, for over forty years in total. During the fifteenth century, by contrast, Sicily was untouched by warfare, except for a period of civil strife in 1410–12.

War affects the economy mainly in three ways. First, there is the direct impact of warfare itself, the destruction of men and capital. Second, there are the indirect effects of a protracted war effort in

[23] R. Muntaner, *Crònica*, chapter 198.
[24] D'Alessandro, *Politica e società*, p. 191.

terms of resources foregone or diverted through taxation. Finally, there is the problem of markets foreclosed, the effects of being unable to trade in enemy territory, and of rising transaction costs in one's own country and by sea.

On the first count, it is now generally agreed that even the most brutal late medieval military campaigns in Europe had no very lasting economic effects. As a result of low capital outlay, economic recovery was rapid; military campaigns did not involve very large armies (thus they also did not divert much labour away from productive activities), and were short, localized and not always destructive; and warfare was only one element in a mixture of pestilence and economic and social dislocation which characterized the period.[25]

In fourteenth-century Sicily, the most lasting direct impact of warfare was probably on settlement patterns. Angevin attacks along the coastline destroyed minor localities like the castle of Brucato;[26] Angevin forays and the mid-fourteenth-century civil war contributed to the relocation of settlements from scattered, undefended *casali* to larger walled towns.[27] Even so, warfare was not the principle cause of settlement desertions. Settlement patterns tend generally to change very slowly and over long periods of time. A process of resettlement was unfolding at least from the early thirteenth century (possibly as a result of the destruction by Frederick II of the Muslim communities in val di Noto and vai di Mazara), and contributed to the demographic decline which may have begun in the last quarter of the thirteenth century.[28] Warfare may have given further impetus to resettlement, but it was neither the latter's initiating nor primary cause. Desertions and resettlement were concentrated in the west and south of Sicily. In val Demone, which bore the brunt of Angevin attacks in the mid-fourteenth century and was not exempt from seigneurial conflict, scattered *casali* tended to survive. There is thus no reason to believe that the direct

---

25 Peri, 'Rinaldo di Giovanni Lombardo', p. 466. Similar arguments have been advanced for the effects of the Hundred Years War. See R. Boutrouche, 'The devastation of rural areas during the Hundred Years War and the agricultural recovery of France'; C. T. Allmand, *The Hundred Years War. England and France at war c.1300–c.1450*, chapter 5; P. Contamine, 'La guerre de Cent ans en France: une approche économique'; R. W. Kaeuper, *War, justice and public order. England and France in the later Middle Ages*, pp. 80–9.
26 J. M. Pesez ed., *Brucato. Histoire et archéologie d'un habitat médiéval en Sicile*.
27 *UM*, p. 791; Bresc, 'L'habitat médiéval', pp. 186–97.
28 *Ibid*.

impact of warfare in Sicily was very different from elsewhere in late medieval Europe.[29] I discuss the second aspect of the economic impact of war, taxation, in more detail in chapter 7. On the whole, and contrary to experiences in France and England,[30] the effects of war finance were apparently not felt very keenly in Sicily except during the 1440s and 1450s, as the scanty evidence of popular resistance to royal demands indirectly suggests. Although weak opposition might be due more simply to the ease of tax evasion, especially during the second half of the fourteenth century when royal power was disintegrating, a more basic reason for the lack of popular resistance lay in the structure of Sicilian royal finances. Like wool for the English king, one of the Sicilian monarchy's two financial mainstays at time of war and peace was the grain trade; the second mainstay was the royal demesne. These two sources of tax revenue were on the whole sufficient to preserve Sicily's political independence for more than a century; consequently, direct taxation during the fourteenth century does not seem to have been very harsh.

Finally, did war have a significant impact on markets and on opportunities to trade? Since Benedetto Croce's condemnation of the Vespers, it has been wrongly assumed that as a result of political partition, economic relations were severed as well. During the late Middle Ages, the main ties between Sicily and the mainland were those linking Messina and eastern val Demone to southern Calabria. These ties were never fully broken. Messina's decline in the late fourteenth century was less the result of political separation from the mainland than of domestic developments, namely the division of Sicily under seignieurial rule and the displacement of political power in eastern Sicily to Catania, and possibly of economic changes in southern Calabria.[31] At a regional level, Messina's losses were offset by Catania's gains. Warfare may have temporarily weakened Messina's influence over southern Calabria in the

---

[29] Michele da Piazza's description of the civil war is often quoted as evidence of Sicilian decline. Da Piazza, however, mixed rhetorical and eschatological fancy with witnessed fact which, for lack of independent witnesses is very hard to unravel; his narrative, moreover, is restricted to the region around Catania, the epicentre of the civil war. See Peri, *Il villanaggio in Sicilia*, p. 116 n. 24; da Piazza, *Cronaca*, pp. 14–15. Tramontana, *Michele da Piazza e il potere baronale in Sicilia*, makes few allowances for the source's limitations.

[30] Kaeuper, *War, justice and public order*, pp. 32–117.

[31] E. Pontieri, *La Calabria a metà del secolo XV e la rivolta di Antonio Centelles*.

fourteenth century; political partition, by contrast, was not necessarily the cause of economic decline. When the two southern Italian kingdoms were divided again after 1458, Messina suffered only briefly as a result (see chapter 5).

The effects of warfare on the domestic market were more significant. This was not, however, because of the material damages war inflicted, but rather as a result of the political and institutional disintegration, and consequently the fragmentation of the regional market, that war helped provoke.

Sicily's territorial partition after 1350 into an unstable equilibrium between four feudal factions was the result of a serious structural weakness within the monarchy. This weakness allowed the aristocracy successfully to undermine the state.[32] The young Federico, crowned in 1296 on the basis of a policy of independence from Naples and Rome and from his brother, King James of Aragon, was hostage from his accession to the class that was his main support. The defence of the realm against the Angevin military and ecclesiastical offensive was possible only in exchange for a virtual free hand for the feudal aristocracy. Attempts to counter this situation by strengthening the demesne were unsuccessful, as we shall see in chapter 7.

Federico's successors, possibly weaker and facing the gathering storm of the demographic crisis, could not hold the country together. The plague of 1347–8, when the regent Duke Giovanni of Aragon died, marked a political turning point. After Giovanni's death and the return of the exiled Palizzi magnates from Pisa, most of western Sicily came under the control of the 'Latin' faction, which included the Palizzi, Chiaromonte and Ventimiglia consortia and their allies. South-eastern Sicily, centring on Catania and controlled by the 'Catalan' royal justiciar – the highest state officer – Blasco Alagona, was where the royal heir, Ludovico, usually resided and therefore bore the brunt of conflicts for his control.[33]

As a result of this political instability, the quite limited integration which had existed for the most developed regional food markets in the late thirteenth century began to break down. Messina and Palermo tightened their control over local sources of food supply, and the island as a whole rapidly segmented into sub-

---

[32] D'Alessandro, *Politica e società*, pp. 39, 44–5, 48, 50–3.
[33] For political events in this period see *ibid.*, pp. 81–108; La Lumia, *I quattro Vicari. Studi di storia siciliana del XIV secolo*; *UM*, pp. 823–31.

regional markets, each controlled by one or more of the main feudal families. In October 1352, about a year before the Chiaromonte faction initiated overt contact with the Angevins for the conquest of Sicily,[34] a formal truce was drawn up between them and the Palizzi on the one hand, and Blasco Alagona and the Sclafani family on the other. An agreement to stabilize the political *status quo* was reached, formally 'until our lord king [Federico IV] comes of age', and marriage alliances were drawn up.[35] Given the inherent instability of a situation in which one party still hoped to win the game by playing the Angevin card, it was perhaps inevitable that this truce should last less than a year.

Following the failure of the Chiaromonte–Angevin alliance to conquer Sicily in the late 1350s, the main aristocratic families – Alagona, Chiaromonte and Ventimiglia – met in 1362 to draw up a formal peace treaty and take stock of the existing balance of forces. Sicily was divided into spheres of influence, the usurpation of the lands, rights and revenues of the demesne was formally sanctioned, and two curial offices were instituted, one for the eastern and the other for the western half of the island. The division of Sicily into four separate regions, each under a *vicarius*, after Federico's death in 1377 was the logical outcome of a situation that had existed *de facto* for a quarter of a century.[36]

Political fragmentation and the crisis of royal authority was reflected in the breakdown of the monetary system, especially that regulating the small specie used in petty transactions. A few years after Federico III's death, there were already signs of monetary instability: inhabitants of Palermo asked in 1340 to pay a wine tithe to the archbishop of Monreale in kind rather than in money, despite the contemporary devaluation of billon.[37] Debasement continued in the early 1350s, when the Chiaromonte and Palizzi began coining

---

34 da Piazza, *Cronaca*, I, chapter 80; E. G. Léonard, *Histoire de Jeanne Ire reine de Naples comtesse de Provence (1343–1382)*. *La jeunesse de la reine Jeanne*, III, chapter 2. King Ludovico banished the Chiaromonte and Palizzi families in November 1353 (da Piazza, *Cronaca*, I, chapter 70).

35 *Ibid.*, I, chapters 58–9.

36 D'Alessandro, *Politica e società*, pp. 110–11.

37 M. De Vio ed., *Privilegia felicis et fidelissimae urbis Panormitanae selecta aliquot ad civitatis decus et commodum spectantia*, p. 153. In 1333, the *denaro* was devalued by 32.5 per cent, from 40 to 36 *denari*, and from 10 to 7.5 silver sterlings per *libbra* (RC 4, fos. 76v–8). Trasselli, *Note per la storia dei banchi in Sicilia nel XIV secolo*, pp. 46–7, states, however, that the weight of the silver *carlino* increased.

their own money in Messina.[38] An extraordinary usurpation of traditional royal rights, made even before the Chiaromonte's Angevin alliance to conquer Sicily, this move may have been connected with the truce of 1352 between the warring Sicilian factions. In 1354, Giacomo Chiaromonte, lord of Nicosia, minted his own petty coinage (*denari parvuli*). He called them *jacobini* because, as he stated, 'the name must be in accordance with the thing'.[39]

The breakdown thereafter of the monetary system was rapid and unchecked. In a letter of 1363 to Francesco Ventimiglia describing former times, the king wrote that 'if anything was lacking, magnates coined new money'.[40] Six kinds of aristocratic billon are known from this period and were currently used; other coinages in Messina and Catania under purely formal royal auspices are also recorded. Messina may have continued to coin 'Sicilian' money even under Angevin rule in the late 1350s.[41] What may have been foreign counterfeit gold coins were circulating at the same time. The tax returns of 1374–6 report a large number of 'bad florins', recalling an

---

[38] The *terminus a quo* is the nomination in early 1351 of the master of the mint in Messina (E. Li Gotti, *Volgare nostro siculo. Crestomazia di testi siciliani del secolo XIV*, pp. 71–6). G. Pipitone Federico, in 'Il testamento di Manfredi Chiaromonte', p. 329, and *I Chiaromonti di Sicilia. Appunti e documenti*, p. 10, claims that Manfredi Chiaromonte minted coins in Messina with the coats of arms of the Chiaromonte and the Palizzi; Manfredi died in 1353. Trasselli, *Note banchi XIV secolo*, pp. 33–4, records some ordinances, issued in Palermo in March–April 1351, that may refer to the new situation.

[39] da Piazza, *Cronaca*, I, chapter 87.

[40] Gregorio, *Considerazioni sopra la storia di Sicilia dai tempi normanni sino ai presenti*, V, chapter 1 n. 29.

[41] For billon see E. Gabrici, 'Tessere mercantili delle famiglie Chiaromonte e Palizzi', p. 7; Trasselli, *Note banchi XIV secolo*, pp. 51–2; RC 13, fos. 159–60 (13 December 1375, 19 January 1376; the second document is published by R. Volpes, *Delle coniazioni non ufficiali, in Sicilia, durante il Regno di Federico III 'il semplice'*, pp. 8–9: Guglielmo Peralta, count of Caltabellotta, can coin a large amount of silver he holds in Sciacca). Gabrici, followed by Romano and U. Tucci, 'Premessa', p. xxix, argues that the coins were used as tokens. For mintings in Messina in 1364–73 and 1376 see Trasselli, *Note banchi XIV secolo*, pp. 47–50, 52; for coinages under the Angevins see Giardina ed., *Capitoli*, no. 40 (1357). For minting in Catania see Cosentino ed., *Codice diplomatico*, no. 409 (1356); D. Schiavo, *Memorie per servire alla storia letteraria di Sicilia*, I, pp. 30–2 (1375); RC 13, fos. 159–60 (1375); La Lumia ed., *Estratti di un processo per lite feudale del secolo XV concernenti gli ultimi anni del regno di Federico III e la minorità della regina Maria*, pp. 167, 170, 175, 177, 179, 181, 183; R. Spahr, 'Di un denaro inedito battuto nella zecca di Catania durante il regno di Maria d'Aragona (1377–1401)', 76–80; Trasselli, *Note banchi XIV secolo*, p. 51 n. 112. Minting in Palermo: Volpes, 'Delle coniazioni', 10–12; M. Bonanno, 'Denaro inedito della città di Palermo di epoca chiaramontana (seconda metà del XIV secolo)'.

earlier description of Catania, crowded with foreign mercenaries, where florins had replaced local money and prices had risen accordingly.[42] The creation of local mints by territorial lords after the mid-fourteenth century was merely one aspect of the more general phenomenon of feudal usurpation of royal rights and revenues discussed further in chapter 7. Seigneurial mints served at least two purposes. They provided a powerful source of legitimation of usurped authority, and they were a convenient way of profiting further from the resources arising out of the magnates' seizure of public power. The breakdown of the exchange system increased the difficulties of trading between areas under different lordship. Federico IV referred to this problem in a letter of 1375 to Guglielmo Peralta. The proliferation of local mints was causing great confusion among the people, he wrote, especially in the matter of small coinage for the pettier sorts of transactions.[43] The returns of the papal tax of 1374–6 provide ample testimony to the havoc local mints were wreaking, especially among the poorer sections of the population.[44] Hoarding may also have increased as a result.[45] After Federico's death in 1377, Palermo issued a set of provisions that dealt with the monetary disorders 'caused by certain powerful men of this kingdom'. The city's *denari*, officially coined in 1379 at the latest,

---

[42] da Piazza, *Cronaca*, I, chapter 36; II, chapter 16. The capture by Artale Alagona of Simone Chiaromonte's treasure in 1355 may have enabled Artale to mint gold coins (*ibid.*, I, chapter 114). See also Trasselli, *Note banchi XIV secolo*, p. 43; Trasselli, *Appunti di metrologia e numismatica siciliana per la scuola di Paleografia dell'Archivio di Stato di Palermo*, p. 24. The 'counterfeit' florins could have been minted in Naples in the late 1340s by Louis of Hungary (F. C. Lane and R. C. Mueller, *Money and banking in medieval and Renaissance Venice, I. Coins and moneys of account*, pp. 375–6), or more likely, given Catania's Catalan links, by Peter IV of Aragon in Perpignan (P. Spufford, *Money and its use in medieval Europe*, p. 288 n. 2).

[43] RC 13, fos. 159–60 ('denari minuti'). See also Volpes, *Delle coniazioni*, pp. 10–12.

[44] Sella ed., *Rationes Decimarum. Sicilia*, pp. 124–9, 131–4.

[45] Large numbers of hoards were discovered during the fifteenth century. Trasselli, *Note per la storia dei banchi in Sicilia nel XV secolo*, I, pp. 53–6; *UM*, pp. 222–4; R. Dentici Buccellato, 'Miniere siciliane nel XV secolo: una realtà o una speranza?', 120 n. 21; see E. Benito Ruano, 'Búsqueda de tesoros en la España medieval'. See also PR 21, fo. 64v (1419); CR 851, fos. 665rv, 667 (1439?); C 2853, fos. 131v–2 (1446); C 2856, fos. 31v–2 (1446); C 2884, fos. 77v–8 (1455); RC 116, fo. 168 (1465). Medieval Sicily's positive balance of payments probably caused bullion hoarding in some periods (below, chapter 6).

were now circulated, and *denari* from outside Palermo were forbidden.[46]

The reference to 'bad' locally minted florins implies that gold and silver coins did not escape debasement. Since such coins were employed for major transactions and especially for foreign trade, the partition of the regional market must have been even further institutionalized. Although, as we shall see, economic integration had not progressed very far before the magnates took over the country, any progress that had been made was reversed, and further integration was stifled for half a century.

Wider political alliances defined sub-regional distribution of shares in international trade. Until Federico IV's death in 1377, Sicily was roughly divided into an eastern zone, formally named 'Catalan' and loyal to the king under the lordship of the Alagona, and a western zone under the control of the 'Latin' Chiaromonte and Ventimiglia. The ambiguity of these tags can be seen, however, in the lack of interest Federico (or rather his 'protector' Artale Alagona) showed for the offers of military aid that the king's sister Eleanor, Queen of Catalonia–Aragon, repeatedly made;[47] allegiance to the 'Catalan' cause did not go so far as to give up Sicilian and personal independence.

Although the distinction between 'Latins' and 'Catalans' was basically an ethnic tag to a political problem, it was not, however, an entirely empty denotation. The political alliances implied by the 'Latin' and 'Catalan' denominations led to the creation of spheres of influence of the two main merchant communities active in the island, the Genoese and the Catalan. Probably as a result of this, the power of Florentine and Pisan merchants was much weakened after the mid-fourteenth century.[48] The chronicler Michele da Piazza describes the monopoly that Catalan (especially Majorcan) merchants exerted over the foreign cloth trade in Catania, which the

---

[46] P. Palumbo, 'Nuove testimonianze del siciliano trecentesco', 243; Trasselli, *Note banchi XIV secolo*, p. 53.

[47] Léonard, *Histoire de Jeanne Ire*, III, pp. 630–3, 662–3.

[48] For Tuscans see *UM*, pp. 409–13, 476; M. Tangheroni, *Politica, commercio e agricoltura a Pisa nel Trecento*, pp. 106–7; G. Petralia, *Banchieri e famiglie mercantili nel Mediterraneo aragonese. L'emigrazione dei pisani in Sicilia nel Quattrocento*; *Mostra documentaria sui rapporti fra il Regno di Sicilia e la Repubblica di Genova (Sec. XII–XVI)*, nos. 15, 17–19, 21–3, 25. For Genoese–Catalan conflict in Sicily in the 1330s and 1340s see Corrao ed., *Registri*, no. 146; F. C. Casula ed., *Carte reali diplomatiche di Alfonso III il Benigno, re d'Aragona, riguardanti l'Italia*, nos. 107, 164, 493, 526–7.

local citizens tried to break by calling on Genoese Guelph merchants.[49] People would later recall that Artale Alagona 'showed great honour to Catalans when they visited him, and Catalan merchants were well treated'.[50] Catalan merchants may also have obtained privileges to export grain from eastern Sicily.[51]

The Genoese took over the western markets, principally Palermo; da Piazza refers obscurely to territorial grants to them by one of the 'Latin' counts, Matteo Palizzi, but nothing further is known of these concessions.[52] The Genoese were clearly identified with the Chiaromonte regime in Palermo, which explains why the merchants were attacked and robbed during a major rebellion there against Manfredi Chiaromonte in 1351.[53] Between 1360 and 1400, the Palermo cloth market, which then only included the city and parts of western Sicily, was monopolized by the Genoese.[54] Towards 1360, Flemish cloth – entirely in the hands of Genoese merchants – took over the Palermo market, partly at the expense of Italian cloth; Catalan woollens virtually disappeared, despite being somewhat cheaper. The few Catalan cloths sold in Palermo passed through the hands of the Genoese, who either deliberately excluded this merchandise[55] or found it hard to obtain from enemy country.

The extent of the Genoese monopoly over Palermo's cloth market in this period is revealed by contrast with the upsurge of imports of Catalan cloth to Palermo in the early fifteenth century, when the Catalan share of the market rose from less than ten per cent to nearly seventy per cent in a few years.[56] The flood of Catalan cloth on the Palermo and Sicilian market after the Aragonese reconquest was thus the consequence not of a 'colonial' or 'expansionist' policy by the crown of Aragon, but of the breaking of the Genoese monopoly over Palermo's market.

---

[49] da Piazza, *Cronaca*, II, chapter 51. For Majorcan trade with eastern Sicily see L. D'Arienzo ed., *Carte reali diplomatiche di Pietro IV il Cerimonioso, re d'Aragona, riguardanti l'Italia*, no. 170 (1342).

[50] La Lumia ed., *Estratti*, pp. 27, 33.

[51] Léonard, *Histoire de Jeanne Ire*, III, pp. 630–3; E. Pispisa, *Messina nel Trecento. Politica economia società*, p. 173.

[52] da Piazza, *Cronaca*, I, chapter 63; F. Giunta, *Aragonesi e Catalani nel Mediterraneo*, I, p. 62; Pispisa, *Messina*, p. 106.

[53] da Piazza, *Cronaca*, I, chapter 51.

[54] Bresc, 'La draperie catalane au miroir sicilien, 1300–1460', 108–10; below, chapter 6.

[55] *Ibid.*, 119–22.

[56] *Ibid.*, 109, Table 1.

Like the foreign cloth trade, political alliance with Genoa or Catalonia seems to have affected the trade in salt from Sardinia. As a result, this trade, which was in the hands of the Catalans, was probably interrupted with Palermo after 1379, the year King Federico IV's only daughter and heiress to the throne, Maria, was taken to Sardinia and thence to Catalonia, leaving Sicily fully in the hands of the barons; salt trade with Trapani and Messina, on the other hand, continued without discernible change.[57]

Despite difficulties in trading between different parts of Sicily after 1350, sub-regional barriers were not insuperable, particularly after the peace treaty of 1372 with Angevin Naples which stabilized political power within Sicily. We saw that the burghers of Catania were able, on occasion, to call on Genoese merchants to break the Catalan monopoly over the foreign cloth market. Most ships from Sicily whose loads were recorded in Genoa's customs returns of 1376–7 came from Palermo, but a few stored merchandise from Catania and Messina.[58] A Genoese merchant settled in Catania around 1370.[59] Artale Alagona offered Maria in marriage to Gian Galeazzo Visconti, co-ruler in Lombardy, causing consternation throughout the courts of Europe, and particularly in Aragon at the prospect of Lombardy and Sicily being unified once again under the same ruler.[60] The former 'Catalan' Alagona then proposed an alliance to Genoa against the Catalans.[61] During the late 1380s, the agents of the Tuscan merchant Francesco di Marco Datini traded in both eastern and western Sicily.[62]

In conclusion, evidence of the direct, material impact of war on the population and economy of Sicily agrees with the general view that late medieval warfare did not have very devastating effects. War-

[57] C. Manca, *Aspetti dell'espansione economica catalano-aragonese nel Mediterraneo occidentale. Il commercio internazionale del sale*, pp. 144–5, 231–9.

[58] From Catania: J. Day ed., *Les douanes de Gênes, 1376–1377*, I, pp. 324 (wine, cheese), 357 (skins), 532; II, p. 874. From Messina: *ibid.*, I, pp. 292, 300, 312, 351, 377, 431, 471, 472 (cotton shipments). See also C. Ciano, 'A bordo della nave di Giovanni Carrocci nel viaggio da Porto Pisano a Palermo (1388–1389)', 174: a ship travelling from Porto Pisano to Palermo with stopovers in Tropea and Messina.

[59] La Lumia ed., *Estratti*, pp. 27–8.

[60] D. M. Bueno de Mesquita, *Giangaleazzo Visconti duke of Milan (1351–1402). A study in the political career of an Italian despot*, pp. 22–4.

[61] La Lumia ed., *Estratti*, p. 153.

[62] Grohmann, 'Prime indagini sull'organizzazione fieristica siciliana nel Medio Evo e nell'Età Moderna, con particolare riferimento alla fiera di Sciacca', 313, 320–2.

fare may have contributed to, but was not the main cause of, changes in settlement patterns in western and southern Sicily. War taxation was relatively light, largely because the crown could resort to indirect taxes on the demesne and the grain trade to finance the realm's defence. The most significant effect of war was on the institutional organization of the domestic market after the mid-fourteenth century. As a result of the partitioning of Sicily under feudal lordship, Catania took over Messina's dominant role in eastern Sicily; domestic trade was disrupted or made more costly for lack of a common coinage; international trade was distributed along political demarcations, allowing near sub-regional monopolies by Genoese and Catalan merchants. Evidence of commercial activity after 1400, discussed below, suggests that the disruption of markets after 1350 may have delayed economic growth. By contrast, the political partition of Sicily from the mainland after 1282 did not interrupt trade across the Straits of Messina, and was not the main cause of Messina's decline between 1350 and 1400.

MARKET STRUCTURES AND THE STATE

Most economic actions by late medieval states were motivated by short- or medium-term financial needs. Monopolies were granted or repealed, industries established, and patent rights conceded for the same reason, namely as sources of revenue.[63] Even where governments or individual sovereigns appear to have pursued more wide-ranging policies aimed at generating economic growth, one cannot assume that such policies were successful, consistently implemented, or even attainable within existing social, economic and institutional constraints.

In this section I discuss deliberate government actions which resulted, or were intended to result, in a more integrated regional market: actions which affected trade rather than production. I also briefly examine the hypothesis, first formulated by Mario Del Treppo, that Alfonso V successfully established a Mediterranean 'common market' in the mid-fifteenth century, within the lands of the crown of Aragon and under Catalan hegemony.[64]

---

[63] E. Miller, 'The economic policies of governments. France and England', pp. 338–40.
[64] M. Del Treppo, *I mercanti catalani e l'espansione della Corona d'Aragona nel secolo XV*, pp. 600–5; Del Treppo, *Il Regno aragonese*, pp. 94–9; Grohmann, *Fiere*, chapter 7.

The state could affect the economy more by acting on the institutional framework of production and circulation than through direct intervention on production. Douglass North and Robert Thomas have argued that, during the early modern period, the state could achieve greatest welfare benefits by reducing transaction costs in trade. However, the state's short-term fiscal needs were such that it was rarely able to achieve such reductions; monopolies in production and taxes on trade survived despite their economic inefficiency. The only exception to these powerful constraints on trade were the great international fairs.[65]

North's and Thomas's conclusion is an example of a more widespread underestimate of the changes in structure and organization of European trade which occurred between the mid-fourteenth and the sixteenth centuries, and which were connected with contemporary changes in the structure of European states. I will discuss three of these changes, whose main effect was to reduce rising information-gathering, bargaining, and transport costs for trade of cheap, bulky and sometimes perishable goods: the reduction of tolls on domestic trade; the diffusion of local and regional fairs; and the unification of local measurements. These institutional innovations were introduced by states in response to merchant and community pressure to lower transaction costs at a time when these costs were rising rapidly. These increases were due, first and foremost, to the emergence of the more integrated and specialized regional markets described above, and, secondly and subsidiarily, to higher rates of indirect taxation imposed by the state itself.

Changes in market institutions were undertaken under state influence, but the success of these changes depended on the strength of the coalitions supporting or resisting innovation. The easiest and commonest solution to the need to reduce transaction costs was the local and regional fair. New fairs raised little opposition, except occasionally from nearby communities which feared that their own existing fair would be damaged. Fairs, which were demanded by local communities to increase trade and were promoted by feudal lords to enhance their excise income, also usually cost a government nothing and tended in the long run to increase state revenue. On the other hand, potentially wider-ranging solutions to the problem of rising transaction costs, namely a reduction of, or outright exemp-

[65] North and R. P. Thomas, *The rise of the western world*, chapter 8.

tion from, trade tariffs to the benefit of a community and the establishment of common regional or national measurements, were more difficult to enforce, for they raised conflicts of interest which the state was rarely, if at all, willing to resolve in favour of institutional innovation. Thus, although all of these solutions to the increasing constraints on trade (toll exemptions, trade fairs and measurement standardization) were tried in late medieval Sicily, existing social and institutional forces allowed only some of these measures to be fully successful.

These developments – achieved under the impulse of local communities, occasionally delayed by governmental opposition – are significant, not so much because they marked a new institutional departure, but because existing institutional means of reducing transaction costs were adopted on an unprecedented scale. Because they occurred mainly after the mid-fourteenth century, they also lend support to the hypothesis that the later Middle Ages was a period in which trade became increasingly more complex and specialized.

There are two points to be made about the first institutional innovation I discuss, namely toll franchises (exemptions from the royal *gabella di dogana*, see Table 3.1). First, franchises conflicted with the monarchy's short-term needs, for the crown relied on indirect taxes on trade for maintaining garrisons and local officials and for granting political rewards.[66] Communities petitioning for a franchise were well aware of this problem, and would therefore point out that toll franchises stimulated trade and thus led to increased indirect tax revenues for the crown.[67] Second (with some exceptions I discuss below), franchises were restricted to the home market.[68]

Because toll franchises raised such sensitive financial issues with the crown, for a long time exemptions were an act intended purely to mark or foster political or military loyalty. While not lessening the importance of exemptions for promoting trade, this fact does help explain the chronology of grants. The feature was effective already in the first concessions to Messina and Palermo, in 1199 and

---

[66] PR 21, fos. 89v–90v (1420); C 2838, fo. 78 (1441); CR 29, fos. 135–7v (1447); C 2867, fo. 16 (1450); CR 47, fos. 6–6bis, 167–7bis (1468); CR 47, fo. 149, and RC 128, fo. 370 (1473).

[67] RC 109, fos. 146–8 (1460).

[68] See also De Vio ed., *Privilegia*, pp. 381–2 (1470).

Table 3.1. Toll franchises, 1199–1499

Grantee	First grant and confirmations	Franchise area	Documentary sources
Aci	1424	Sicily (for wine)	CR 11, fo. 197
Agrigento	1367, 1433, 1499	Sicily	CR 84, fos. 66–7
Aidone	1397	Piazza	RC 28, fo. 93rv; RC 31, fos. 99v–100
Alcamo	1331	Sicily (D)	Di Giovanni, *Capitoli di Alcamo*, p. 47
Augusta	1396, 1407	Sicily (D)	RC 25, fos. 166v–7; RC 44–5, fos. 109–10
Caltagirone	1432	Sicily (D)	RC 66, fo. 296; C 2821, fo. 64v; RC 67, fo. 97rv; PR 33, fo. 24rv; CR 16, fos. 127–8; RC 68, fos. 30, 34v; C 2821, fo. 77v
	1440	Noto	RC75, fos. 84v–5v
	1484	Palermo	TRP Atti 37, fo. 165v
Capizzi	1448	Sicily (D)	CR 29, fos. 98–102; C 2859, fos. 72–3v
	1468	Sicily (D)	RC 121, fos. 335–6; CR 47, fos. 167–7bis
Castrogiovanni	1420–1	Sicily (refused)	PR 23, fos. 212–13v
	1445	Sicily (D+CR)	RC 83, fos. 452–7v, 508
	1460, 1469, 1478,		Testa ed., *Capitula*, I, p. 461; CR 48, fos. 5–5ter; CR 60, fos. 15–16; RC 139, fos. 220v–1; RC 175, fos. 313v–15v; CR 73, fos. 77–9
	1490		CR 71, fos. 18–18sexties; RC 78, fos. 163v–70; CR 71, fos. 19–19bis
Castronovo	1491	Sicily	Amico e Statella, *Catana illustrata*, II, pp. 228–33
Catania	1362	Sicily (D+CR)	*Ibid.*, pp. 262–5
	1403	*Camera reginale*	CR 77, fos. 13–14; TRP Atti 50, fos. 114v–15
	1495	Caltagirone	RC 34, fos. 141v–2
Cefalù	1390, 1398	?	CR 29, fos. 135–7v; C 2857, fo. 168
Corleone	1447 (refused)	Sicily (D)	RC 109, fos. 146–8 (obtains franchise in Palermo)
	1460 (refused)	Sicily (D)	RC 121, fo. 189v
	1468	Sicily (D)	RC 31, fo. 27v
Francavilla	1396–7	?	C 2831, fo. 84rv (response unknown)
	1438	local	Pisano Baudo, *Storia di Lentini*, II, pp. 208–9, 233
Lentini	1349, 1392	Sicily (D)	Starrabba ed., *Lettere Bianca*, pp. 226–9
	1414	Sicily (D)	CS 1, fos. 178–83 (request for confirmation; response unknown)
	1431	*Camera reginale*	

Place	Date	Region	Reference
Licata	1392 (refused)	Sicily	RC 21, fos. 36v–7v
	1421–2 (refused)	Sicily	PR 23, fos. 216–18v (request for confirmation; response unknown)
	1450	Sicily	C 2867, fos. 15–20v (response unknown)
	1468	Palermo	RC 121, fo. 332rv; CR 47, fos. 148–8bis (has franchise (?) in Messina, Syracuse, Mazara, Trapani, Cefalù, Malta)
Marsala	1473	Palermo	RC 128, fo. 370; CR 47, fo. 149 (franchise limited to six onze)
Mazara	1316	Sicily	CR 840, unnum. fo.
	1318	Sicily	RC 2, fos. 86v–8v; Testa ed., De vita Federici II, pp. 276–8
	1440	Sicily	C 2836, fos. 71v–2
	1443 (refused)	Sicily	RC 79, fos. 213–18; C 2845, fo. 57v
Messina	1199	Sicily	Giardina ed., Capitoli, no. 11
	1296, 1316, 1368, 1410, 1423, 1440, 1459, 1465		Ibid., nos. 32, 42, 60, 81, 93, 100; RC 2, fos. 108v–9v; C 2810, fos. 10–11; CR 26, fos. 39–40v; C 2831, fos. 240–1; C 3478, fos. 122–8
	1495	bishopric of Catania	TRP Atti 50, fo. 115v
	1495	kingdom of Naples	Giardina ed., Capitoli, no. 104
	1392	communities with franchises in Milazzo	Piaggia, Illustrazione di Milazzo, pp. 118–21, n. 2
Milazzo	1457	Palermo	RC 106, fos. 226–8 (request for confirmation)
	1469		CR 50, fo. 234rv
	1479, 1481		RC 150, fos. 184v–5v; CR 62, fos. 61–3
Mistretta	1448 (refused)	Sicily (D)	CR 29, fos. 80–4v
	1468 (refused)		RC 121, fos. 299v–301; CR 47, fos. 4–4bis
	1499		RC 200, fos. 347v–8
Monte San Giuliano	1314	Sicily	Testa ed., De vita Federici II, p. 274
Naro	1393	Sicily (D?)	RC 19, fos. 44v–5
Nicosia	1398	Sicily	RC 34, fos. 77–9v
	1421 (refused)	Sicily (D)	PR 23, fos. 227–8, Barbato ed., Per la storia di Nicosia, p. 122
	1468		RC 121, fo. 193rv; CR 47, fos. 16–16bis
	1474		CR 56, fos. 123–4bis; C 3487, fos. 237–8v

Table 3.1. *(cont.)*

Grantee	First grant and Confirmations	Franchise area	Documentary sources
Noto	1393	Sicily (D)	RC 19, fos. 134–5
	1401, 1402, 1423, 1424, 1427, 1440		RC 39, fo. 163rv; RC 54, fos. 408v–9; C 2810, fo. 40; Littara, *De rebus netinis*, pp. 95, 109, 113
Palermo	1200	gates of Palermo	De Vio ed., *Privilegia*, pp. 10–11; RC 2, fos. 66–7
	1221, 1253, 1258		De Vio ed., *Privilegia*, pp. 14–15, 20–2; RC 2, fos. 67v–9
	1299	Sicily	De Vio ed., *Privilegia*, pp. 24–9; RC 2, fo. 69rv
	1305, 1421, 1446		De Vio ed., *Privilegia*, pp. 29–38, 379–81; PR 24, fo. 507
	1451, 1470		RC 125, fos. 142–3; CR 50, fos. 72–2bis
	1316, 1325	Calatafimi	De Vio ed., *Privilegia*, pp. 69–70, 86–7
	1438 (refused)	kingdom of Naples	RC 74, fos. 123–4; C 2830, fo. 230rv
	1470	Mazarino	De Vio ed., *Privilegia*, pp. 381–2
	1484	Caltagirone	TRP Atti 37, fo. 165v (reciprocal confirmation)
Pantelleria	1430	Sicily	C 2816, fo. 40rv
Patti	1432	Sicily (D?)	RC 68, fos. 54v–5
	1463	Palermo	RC 112, fos. 234–7, Sciacca ed., *Patti*, p. 310 (response unknown)
Piazza	1375	Sicily (D)	RC 9, fos. 131rv, 158v
	1391, 1392, 1396, 1421–2, 1434		RC 25, fos. 23–4; PR 23, fos. 214–15; C 2824, fos. 96v–7v; CR 12, fos. 97–9; C 2891, fos. 143–4; C 2826, fos. 9v–10
Polizzi	1442	Sicily, Palermo	RC 79, fo. 117; RC 80, fos. 332v–4v; C 2822, fos. 22–4
	1450	Palermo	C 2864, fos. 23v–4; RC 85, fos. 445v–7v; CR 31, fos. 173–4v
Randazzo	1299	Randazzo, Taormina, Messina	RC 2, fo. 104rv; Testa ed., *De vita Federici II*, p. 255
	1414		RC 48, fos. 272v–3
	1421	Sicily	PR 23, fos. 223–6v
	1439	Sicily *citra Salsum?*	RC 74, fo. 391v (response unknown)
	1470	communities with franchises in Randazzo	RC 125, fos. 249v–50; CR 50, fo. 246rv (franchise previously restricted to the district of Messina)

Place	Date(s)	Region	Reference
Salemi	1464–6	Sicily	C 3484, fo. 171rv; RC 116, fos. 156–7v; RC 116, fos. 643v–4
Sciacca	1302, 1317, 1402	Sicily	RC 1, fo. 39; RC 2, fo. 73rv; Testa ed., *De vita Federici II*, pp. 262, 278–9; RC 2, fos. 85v–6, 106v–7; RC 39, fo. 268rv
Sortino	1468	Naro	RC 120, fos. 323v–4; CR 47, fo. 42rv
Syracuse	1396	Sicily (D)	RC 25, fo. 163rv
	1282	Messina	Gallo, *Annali di Messina*, II, pp. 131–2
	1299	Sicily	RC 2, fos. 73v–5; Testa ed., *De vita Federici II*, pp. 244–5
	1484	Malta	CR 68, fo. 72rv
Taormina	1368	Sicily	RC 11, fos. 96v–7
	1392, 1485		RC 20, fo. 141v; CR 67, fos. 103–3ter; RC 154, fos. 450–4v
Termini	1338	Sicily (D)	Bozzo, 'Un diploma di re Pietro II'
Trapani	1315	Sicily	RC 2, fos. 84v–5; Testa ed., *De vita Federici II*, pp. 272–3
	1484	Alcamo	RC 154, fo. 131rv; CR 67, fos. 71–1bis
Tripi	1371	Sicily	RC 20, fo. 60
Troina	1398	Sicily (D)	RC 35, fos. 101v–2v; RC 37, fos. 94v–6
	1403		RC 40, fos. 55v–6
	1429		RC 61, fo. 55
Vizzini	1468	Capizzi, Mistretta	RC 121, fos. 328–9v (response unknown)
	1396	Sicily (D)	RC 31, fo. 48rv
	1397		RC 32, fo. 73v

D = demesne   CR = *Camera reginale.*

1200 respectively, which occurred at the height of a political crisis caused by the landing of Markward von Anweiler in western Sicily in late 1199 to challenge the pope's authority on the island. No other cities were granted the same favour for nearly a century until, in 1282, Alaimo da Lentini, captain of eastern Sicily during the first phase of the Vespers, gave exemption to Syracuse in Messina in reward for military aid; some years later Syracuse was declared toll-free throughout the demesne.

The only other town exempted before the turn of the century was Randazzo, but its franchise was restricted to Messina, Taormina and Randazzo itself. By Federico III's death in 1337, Marsala, Mazara, Monte San Giuliano, Sciacca and Trapani had all been granted similar charters. These towns are all situated in western Sicily, which came under heaviest Angevin attack during the first two decades of the century. Between 1337 and Federico IV's accession to majority in 1362, only Termini was exempted, probably for similar reasons. Most other concessions before 1392 occurred between 1362 and 1375, and with the exception of Agrigento, they were mostly granted to towns in the eastern half of Sicily which were still formally loyal to king Federico IV or to the faction that controlled him (Messina, Catania, Piazza, Taormina and Tripi). At a time when central authority was disintegrating under feudal attack, it is anyhow doubtful that the privileges were of much use. Once Agrigento fell under the sway of the Chiaromonte, for example, previously abolished tolls were reintroduced.[69] Messina consequently asked, on the basis of a forged privilege, for exemption in feudal lands in 1368. We must wonder who could have enforced such rights.

For a variety of reasons, the Aragonese reconquest of 1392–8 marked a first watershed for the diffusion of toll franchises. King Martino's reasons for granting them were once again mainly political, as a token of gratitude and recompense for loyalty to the new sovereign's cause. This is especially evident in the case of small feudal communities which had rebelled against their lords, such as Francavilla, Sortino, Troina and Vizzini. *Demands* for franchises, on the other hand, were motivated by the restoration of a central authority able to enforce such privileges, and by commercial growth during the preceding half-century.

---

[69] RC 39, fos. 71–2 (1401).

The spate of charter confirmations between 1392 and 1415, including one for Lentini in 1414, possibly on the strength of a forged privilege, shows the extent to which franchises had fallen into disuse. More than ten new privileges were also granted in the same period, some to small communities like Cefalù and the feudal communities mentioned previously, which were all (except for Cefalù) to be enfeoffed again later and lose their exemptions. Most newly beneficed towns were situated in the east, especially in val di Noto (which had best resisted demographic decline during the fourteenth century), and like earlier grantees lay on or near the sea where they could most easily enjoy trading improvements; regional and sub-regional trade was still concentrated along the easily navigable coasts and rivers.[70]

After 1415, when the political instability which had marked Sicily for so long finally came to an end, franchises assumed a more markedly economic and less political character. They were given to all remaining large demesne towns, mostly in the interior; most were granted by Alfonso, a sometime believer in freedom of trade, so as to foster the grain trade. Yet Alfonso was no paladin of the free market, nor did he possess clear proto-mercantilist views, as his signature under three of the four known rejections also shows.

By the end of the fifteenth century, the government had, nonetheless, granted over forty cities and towns some form of toll exemption. In several cases, an exemption would be refused on one occasion and granted subsequently. Mistretta was exempted in 1448, was refused confirmation in 1468, and had its privilege renewed thirty years later. In 1448, the lessee of the *gabella di dogana* in Milazzo successfully argued that Randazzo's privilege would forfeit him too much income. Palermo faced a far more serious defeat in 1438, a few years before Alfonso's conquest of Naples, when a request for franchise on the mainland was turned down.

I mentioned above that toll franchises were restricted to the home market. In fact, since the crown lacked jurisdiction over feudal levies, exemptions were restricted to members of the royal demesne and to Syracuse and other towns in the queen's apanage in val di Noto, the *Camera reginale*. As a result, if a demesne community

---

[70] Some of the larger Sicilian rivers could still be navigated by medium-sized boats in the fifteenth century. See C 3492, fos. 51v–2 (1477) for the river Platani; NC 14926, fos. 145rv, 170rv, 189 (1499), and NC 6241, fos. 3–4 (1506) for the river Simeto.

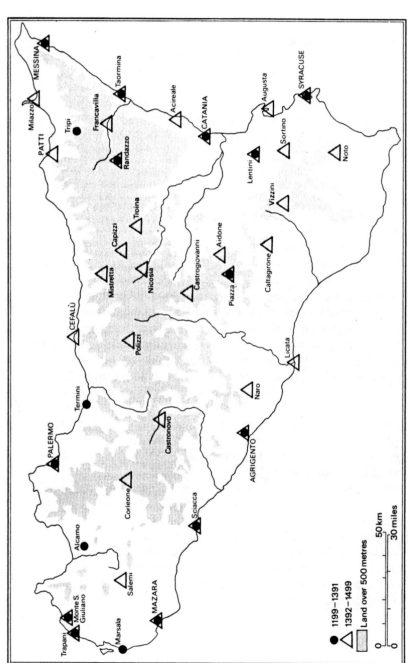

Map 3.1 Toll franchises, 1199–1499

MESSINA

Milazzo
PATTI
Tripi
Francavilla
Taormina
Randazzo
Acireale
CATANIA
Augusta
SYRACUSE
Sortino
Noto
Lentini
Vizzini
Troina
Capizzi
Aidone
Castrogiovanni
Piazza
Mistretta
Nicosia
Caltagirone
CEFALÙ
Polizzi
Licata
Naro
Termini
Castronovo
AGRIGENTO
PALERMO
Corleone
Alcamo
Sciacca
Salemi
Monte S.
Giuliano
MAZARA
Trapani
Marsala

1199–1391
1392–1499
Land over 500 metres

0   50 km
0   30 miles

was alienated or enfeoffed, it lost the franchise for the duration of the alienation. When it returned to the demesne, the privilege was usually reconfirmed. Mistretta and Capizzi, for example, frequently alienated from the demesne during the fifteenth century, were usually granted the franchise again when they were ransomed back. These jurisdictional constraints did not seriously diminish the franchises' economic significance, however, because of the unusual size of the Sicilian demesne. All the largest and commercially active towns belonged to the king's fisc or to the *Camera reginale*, and more than half of Sicily's population lived under royal jurisdiction. Toll franchises established a large trading zone free from much indirect taxation, giving the demesne a considerable comparative advantage over feudal lands. Conversely, competition from the demesne must have exerted pressure on feudal lords to lower their tolls, with beneficial results for the entire country.

Whereas franchises usually applied to the grantee's entire trade with the demesne, they could be restricted to specific products (wine,[71] olive oil,[72] cattle[73]) and towns, probably those with the closest commercial ties with the grantee. Before 1470, Randazzo only had immunity in Randazzo itself and in Messina and Taormina; in 1463, Patti petitioned for exemption specifically in Palermo. In 1495, Catania successfully argued a case to be permitted to export merchandise free of duty from the feudal town of Caltagirone and the *feudo Chamopetra*. In other cases, although general exemptions were granted, the communities would specify the towns where they traded most, providing a reasonable description of their market area in the demesne.[74]

The only exceptions to the rule that franchises be restricted to the Sicilian royal demesne were made by Alfonso, who granted a number of toll exemptions to cities in the kingdom of Naples: Reggio, Scilla and the island of Lipari (which had been under Angevin control since the 1340s) in Calabria, and the trading towns of Gaeta, Ischia and Capua near Naples. By contrast with the commercial privileges enjoyed by Catalan and Genoese merchants,

[71] Table 1: Palermo (1200, 1221, 1253, 1258), Aci (1424).
[72] Table 1: Palermo (1200).
[73] Table 1: Palermo (1253).
[74] CR 47, fos. 148–8bis, and RC 121, fo. 332rv (1468): Licata, citing Messina, Syracuse, Mazara, Trapani, Cefalù and Malta, asks for general exemption but gets it only for Palermo. CR 48, fos. 5–5ter (1469): Castrogiovanni cites trade in Messina, Polizzi, Agrigento, Monte San Giuliano and Corleone; CR 73, fo. 80 (1490): Castrogiovanni trades with Nicosia.

merchants, which restricted customs dues on their high-value goods to three per cent of the price, franchises for the mainland towns were equivalent to those granted to the Sicilian demesne, namely total exemption from tolls applied as fixed, non-proportional taxes on cheap agricultural and manufactured goods.[75] The diverse nature of economic relations between Catalonia–Aragon and Sicily on the one hand, and Sicily and the kingdom of Naples on the other, appears very clearly from these different trading privileges: the former restricted to high-value commodities, the latter based on bulk agricultural and manufactured goods.

To some extent, political motives again lay behind these concessions, especially those to Gaeta, Ischia and Capua, which allowed key military strongholds to be supplied more cheaply during the mainland war. The same reasons explain why the privileges of Scilla and Isola del Giglio, off mainland Tuscany, were not cancelled after Alfonso's death like many of the others.[76] Even so, there is little doubt that franchises were intended mainly to promote trade (mostly exports from Sicily) in iron, steel, salt, pitch, sugar, cattle, cheese, leather, cotton, fish, wine and other cheap goods.[77] As a result, by the mid-fifteenth century Lipari and Reggio were so strongly integrated into the Sicilian economy that no one could think of abolishing their privileges after 1458, when Naples became independent of the crown of Aragon and most trading agreements between Sicily and the mainland were repealed (see chapter 5).

[75] The distinction between the two concessions is clear for Gaeta. After obtaining Messina's privileges, Gaeta also asked for Barcelona's privileges for two Gaetan merchants (CR 17, fos. 121-1ter (1436)). For Gaeta's franchises see CR 12, fo. 49, and CR 13, fo. 102 (1423); RC 55, fos. 274v–6 (1424); CR 16, fo. 80 (1432?); CR 17, fos. 49–50v (1437), 48rv (1443); CR 28, fos. 81–3 (1446); C 2863, fos. 112v–13 (1452); C 2881, fos. 80v–1v (1452). Ischia was granted Lipari's privileges: C 2829, fo. 177rv – CR 17, fos. 62–2bis – CR 34, fos. 115–16v (1437); RC 72, fos. 140v–1 (1438); RC 88, fos. 82–4 – C 2883, fos. 6–7 (1452). RC 95, fos. 98–101v, and CR 35, fos. 22–5 (1453): Ischia is exempted from the *gabella di cantarata* like Capua. Franchises were granted also to the main Sardinian towns, Cagliari (C 2300, fo. 5rv (1396)) and Alghero (C 2843, fo. 15 (1442)), but were little used. See *UM*, p. 310, for the importance of Gaeta and Ischia in southern Italian trade with Sicily.

[76] Isola del Giglio had full toll franchise only in Messina (CR 42, fos. 409, 410).

[77] CR 32, fos. 47–58 (1436, wrongly dated 1446), 46rv (1437): Capua was allowed to buy the first four products toll free in Sicily and the mainland (*Regnum Sicilie citra et ultra Farum*) and to export the other goods from Sicily, also toll free. See also CR 32, fos. 60rv (1437), 62–3v (1438): three Capuan merchants trading in Palermo, Messina and Catania; RC 95, fos. 98–101v (1453): Ischia trades cotton, fish, Greek and 'sweet' wine.

Toll franchises were so important that they were among the first concessions made by Alfonso to major southern cities. The first steps towards a 'common market' under Alfonso's rule were thus taken by the towns themselves, and were not initiated by the king. The repeal after his death in 1458 of privileges to Gaeta, Ischia and Capua, on the contrary, shows that the strongest resistance to economic integration came from the monarchy itself, which gained more in the short term through indirect taxation than by promoting trade in low-value bulk commodities. These political and financial constraints were also expressed in the limited number of privileged towns on the mainland. Alfonso granted franchises to already developed, commercially-oriented communities, rather than to promote interregional trade where none yet existed.

A second way of reducing transaction costs was to grant franchises for new fairs. Historians have tended to underestimate the role and importance of local and regional fairs in the late medieval economy. A widely accepted definition of the medieval fair states that it had to be frequented only by foreign merchants,[78] and fairs are usually interpreted as foci of international trade; where international functions are not immediately apparent, fairs are commonly dismissed as being of little economic significance.[79] Instead, I argue below that, during the fifteenth century, fairs (like toll franchises) were a common institutional response to increasing trade and productive specialization at a *local* and *regional* level.

Records of fairs are more haphazard and harder to interpret than those of toll exemptions (see Table 3.2). Fairs were recorded by the Sicilian royal chancery only when they were enfranchised from royal or feudal excise (*gabella di dogana*). Some fairs might either lack such recognition by the crown, or might have been established some time before obtaining it,[80] but references to such unenfranchised fairs (in notarial records, community petitions, and so on) tend to be unsystematic and may be incomplete. Since fairs were not restricted to demesne communities as toll franchises were, it is also

---

[78] J. Gilissen, 'La notion de la foire à la lumière comparative'; Grohmann, *Fiere*, pp. 27–32.

[79] *La foire*; C. Verlinden, 'Markets and fairs'; Grohmann, *Fiere*, Introduction.

[80] F. Pollacci Nuccio and D. Gnoffo eds., *I due registri di lettere degli anni 1311–12 e 1316–17, il Quaternus peticionum del 1320–21 e il quaderno delle gabelle anteriori al 1312*, p. 63 (1312): fair in Agrigento. Grohmann, 'Prime indagini', 340: fair in Sant'Angelo; *ibid.*, 323: a fair in Sciacca, which existed before 1385, was only officially recognized in 1420.

Table 3.2 *Fairs, 1223–1499*

Locality	Earliest reference	Length (days)	Date and patron saint	Documentary sources
Aci	1422*	15	St Venera	C 2806, fo. 141
Agrigento	1312	15	St Gerland (after Easter)	Pollacci Nuccio and Gnoffo, *I due registri*, p. 63
Alcamo	pre-1368–9	15	Corpus Christi	Di Giovanni ed., *Capitoli di Alcamo*, p. 58
Augusta	1463*	9	Corpus Christi	RC 114, fos. 146v–7v
Bivona	1476*	—	(4 June)	CR 59, fo. 83 (date changed from 2 September)
Calascibetta	1409	—	St Peter (29 June)	*UM*, pp. 365–6
	1426	—	discovery of Holy Cross (3 May)	PR 27, fos. 135v–7 (refused)
Caltagirone	1392*	15	St Francis to St Luke (4–18 October)	RC 20, fos. 58v–9v
Caltanissetta	1337	—	(7–8 May)	*UM*, pp. 365–6
	1426*	15	Holy Spirit (10–24 May)	C 2814, fo. 25v
Castrogiovanni	pre-1420	—	St Peter (29 June)	PR 23, fos. 212–13v, *UM*, pp. 365–6
	1420*	—	first week in August	PR 23, fos. 212–13v (request)
	1434*	—	after St Peter	RC 70, fo. 62rv (date changed)
Castronovo	1491	9	St Peter (29 June)	RC 178, fos. 163v–70
Castroreale	1435*	9	St Mary Magdalene (22 July)	RC 70, fo. 71rv
Catania	1380	—	Blessed Agatha (August)	Anastasi Motta, 'Aspetti dell'economia', p. 12
	1432	—	Blessed Agatha (5 February)	RC 68, fo. 23rv
Corleone	pre-1329	—	St John the Baptist (24 June)	Scarlata, 'Mercati e fiere', p. 482
	1410*	—	St Mark (25 April)	*UM*, pp. 365–6
	1419	—	St Lazarus? (17 December)	*Ibid.*
Ficarra	1450*	8	St Peter *in Vinculis* (1–8 August)	C 2864, fos. 8v–9
Francofonte	1470*	—	St Anthony of Padua (13 June)	RC 125, fo. 181v; CR 50, fo. 187rv

Place	Year	Day	Feast	Reference
Galati	1450*	8	St Anne (1–8 July)	C 2864, fos. 8v–9
Lentini	1287	—	Ascension	Speciale, *Historia sicula*, p. 338
	1456	—	twice a year	CS 10, fo. 28v
	1470*	—	St Anthony of Padua	Gaudioso, 'Per la storia di Lentini', 344
Licata	1475	—	—	RC 135, fos. 225v–6
Licodia	1458*	9	Virgin Mary (8–15 August)	RC 106, fo. 537v
Marsala	1399	17	St John the Baptist (24 June)	RC 34, fos. 273v–4v; RC 37, fos. 89v–90
	1490*	3	Nativity of Blessed Virgin Mary (8 September)	RC 173, fos. 343v–4; CR 73, fo. 483rv
Mazara	1318*	31	Translation of Body of Christ (6 August)	RC 2, fos. 86v–8v; Testa ed., *De vita Federici II*, pp. 276–8
	1438	—	—	Napoli, 'Il Libro Rosso di Mazara', 321
Messina	1294–6*	15	Holy Sepulchre (23 April–7 May)	Scarlata and Sciascia eds., *Documenti*, no. 125; Giardina ed., *Capitoli*, no. 31
	1431	—	complete franchise requested	C 2889, fo. 35
	1436*	25	(24 July–15 August)	Scarlata and Sciascia eds., *Documenti*, no. 76
Militello	1446*	9	St Mary of the Star (6 September)	PR 38, fo. 98rv
Monreale	1410*	11 or 21	Nativity of Blessed Virgin Mary (8 September)	C 2300, fo. 138
Monte San Giuliano	1476	—	Assumption (15 August)	*UM*, pp. 365–6
	1495*	—	Annunciation (25 March)	CR 77, fo. 561rv
Motta Camastra	1435*	9	after St Cataldus (19 January?)	C 2826, fos. 184v–5
Mussomeli	1497*	3	St John the Baptist (24 June)	CR 79, fo. 240
Naso	1254	—	St Marina (18 June)	Sciacca, *Patti*, p. 231
Nicosia	1364	—	(July–August)	*UM*, pp. 365–6
Noto	1408*	17	St James (25 July)	RC 44–5, fo. 301rv
	1427*	17	Pentecost (10 May or 13 June)	C 2814, fo. 142v; Littara, *De rebus netinis*, pp. 97–8 (date changed from July)

Table 3.2 (*cont.*)

Locality	Earliest reference	Length (days)	Date and patron saint	Documentary sources
Palermo	1325?*	17	Nativity of Blessed Virgin Mary (8 September)	Mirto, 'Petrus Secundus', 122
Patti	1348*	31	St Christina (24 July)	Savagnone, 'Capitoli inediti', 101–2
	1499*	11	St Antoninus (May?)	CR 83, fo. 47rv
Piazza	1234*	9	(1 May)	Huillard Bréholles, *Historia diplomatica*, IV, 1, p. 460
	1306	—	(September)	*UM*, pp. 365–6
	1340	—	(26 October–5 November)	*Ibid.*
Polizzi	1382	—	St Pancras? (11–24 May)	Flandina ed., *Statuti di Polizzi*, p. 260
	1413	—	St Gandulf? (17 September)	*UM*, pp. 365–6
	—	—	—	*Ibid.*
Randazzo	1356	—	St John the Baptist (24 June)	Cosentino ed., *Codice diplomatico*, p. 209
	1463		St John the Evangelist (27 December)	Sciacca, *Patti*, p. 313
Regalbuto	1476*	—	Assumption (15 August) (12–20 June)	CR 59, fo. 13rv
	1484*	9	St Bernard? (12–27 August)	RC 152, fo. 247v; CR 65, fo. 39rv
Roccella	1463*	17	vigil of Pentecost	RC 112, fos. 289v–90v; C 3477, fo. 121rv
	1487*	17	St Nicholas of Bari (9 May)	CR 70, fo. 83rv (moved)
Salemi	1340/1*	17	franchise for the fair	Baviera, *Memorie di Salemi*, p. 87, n. 1
	1465	10	Discovery of Holy Cross (3 May)	RC 116, fos. 156–7v
Sant'Andrea (Tripi)	1452*	9	St James (25 July)	C 2872, fos. 108v–9v; CR 34, fos. 197–8v
San Calogero di Augusta	1448*	13		C 2860, fo. 131v–2, *UM*, pp. 365–6
San Filippo di Argirò	1397	9	St Philip	C 2300, fos. 5v–6; CS 4, fos. 10v–11

Place	Date	No.	Festival	Reference
San Fratello	1499*	7	SS Alfio, Filadelfio, Cirino (10 May)	RC 200, fos. 28v–9; CR 83, fo. 387rv
San Pietro Patti	1460*	—	—	C 3474, fos. 96v–7
Savoca	1487*	2	Blessed Virgin Mary of Mercy (18 March), St Lucy (13 December)	CR 72, fo. 385rv
Sciacca	pre-1342, 1385	—	St John the Baptist (24 June)	Scarlata, 'Mercati e fiere', 482; Grohmann, 'Prime indagini', 323
	1420*	—	Ascension	Ibid., 323–31, 335–8; La Mantia ed., Capitoli di Sciacca, pp. 5–11
Scillato	1483*	13	St Hippolytus (13 August)	RC 153, fo. 58rv; CR 65, fo. 227rv
Sutera	1468*	15	Palm Sunday to Easter	RC 121, fos. 337–8v (date changed from Palm Sunday)
Syracuse	1496*	15	St Paulinus (Easter Tuesday)	RC 193, fos. 271v–2v
	1293*	10	Nativity of the Blessed Virgin Mary (8 September)	La Mantia, Antiche consuetudini, p. cxl
Taormina	1487*	7	St Sebastian (9 December?)	CR 72, fo. 35rv
Termini	1223*	—	St Calogerus	Huillard Bréholles, Historia diplomatica, II, p. 377
	1312*	3	St Calogerus	RC 181, fos. 104–5v
	1363*	3	St Calogerus	RC 174, fos. 281–2; RC 181, fos. 104–5v; CR 73, fo. 113rv
Tindari	1490*	3	Visitation of the Blessed Virgin Mary (2 July)	Ibid. (date moved and duration extended three days)
	1406	—	Nativity of the Blessed Virgin Mary (8 September)	RC 46, fos. 183v–5v, UM, pp. 365–6
Tortorici	1402*	9	St Brancaccius	CR 38, fos. 37–8v
Trapani	1302*	—	St George (23 April)	D'Alessandro, 'L'Istoria', 170
	1315*	15	(August)	RC 2, fo. 89rv; Testa ed., De vita Federici II, p. 273
	c. 1380	—	(May?)	UM, pp. 365–6
Tripi	1452*	9	St Fantinus (July)	C 2872, fos. 106v–8; CR 34, fos. 193–4v

Table 3.2 (cont.)

Locality	Earliest reference	Length (days)	Date and patron saint	Documentary sources
Troina	1428*	11	St Philip (24 April–4 May)	PR 24, fo. 66v (1421, first request); PR 30, fos. 52–3v and RC 61, fo. 51 (1428); CR 77, fo. 98rv (1495)

* = first royal concession.

more probable that some went unrecorded or are missed by the historian for other reasons. Finally, one must consider that the state's prerogative to grant fairs was not fully established in Sicily and elsewhere in Europe before the late fourteenth century.[81] For all these reasons, it might be argued that the growing number of fairs in fifteenth-century Sicily is a mirage, provoked on the one hand by a lack of documentary records for earlier periods, and on the other by the increase of state power and ambition to enforce fair franchises. But scepticism of this kind is unwarranted.

In the first place, when an already established fair obtained a franchise from the king, this fact would always be mentioned by the petitioning community to justify and support the request. Since there is no conceivable reason why such a fact should be concealed, we can take silence on this point as reliable evidence that the fair was a new establishment.

Secondly, no fair of any importance would have failed to seek official recognition; whereas a fair franchise may not exactly date a fair's origin, especially before the fifteenth century, it clearly establishes its rise to some commercial distinction. The fact that fifteen of the thirty-eight communities granted a toll exemption from 1195 to 1500 obtained a fair at the same time (as defined in Table 3.3), and eight others obtained them in successive periods, suggests that once a community had reached a certain level of development, it often possessed the wealth and the political influence to demand or purchase trading privileges which would allow it to grow further. Unenfranchised fairs, on the other hand, reflected a need for commercial institutions of lesser importance, which generated as yet insufficient income to make seeking official recognition worthwhile. Although in Sicily the proportion of enfranchised to unrecognized fairs seems to have risen over time, in the late fifteenth century, at least a quarter of new fairs were still established without franchise.

Thirdly, there is little evidence that the state was willing or capable of manipulating existing fairs. In 1408, Martino I declared that he would reorganize the kingdom's fairs in order to stimulate trade, but he lacked the time (he died soon after) and the necessary

---

[81] The fair of Caltagirone existed in 1347 (Bresc, *Economie et société en Sicile, 1300–1450*, p. 918), those of Palermo and Sciacca are known for the 1380s (Grohmann, 'Prime indagini', 320, 323). They were enfranchised by the monarchy in the early fifteenth century.

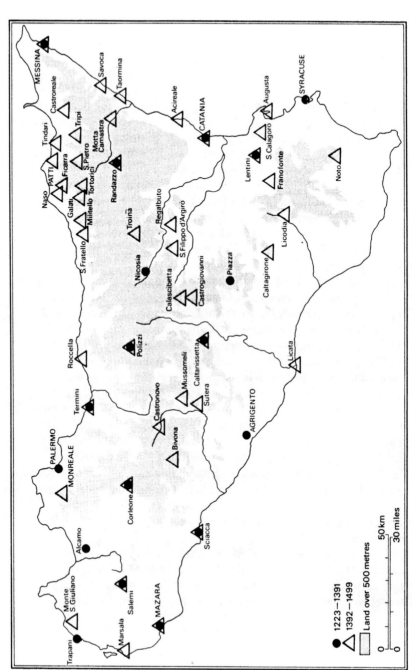

Map 3.2 Fairs, 1223–1499

powers to implement his proposal.[82] All surviving evidence shows that requests for fair franchises came from the communities themselves: they were a privilege to be asked for, not an imposition by the state.

Finally, the spread of fairs in fifteenth-century Sicily was not a unique or even unusual phenomenon; a similar proliferation was taking place throughout late medieval Europe, both east and west.[83]

Even if one accepts that requests for fair franchises did generally refer to new or growing events, one still need not, however, interpret them as I do as a sign of economic and commercial expansion at a *regional* level. It might, for example, be objected that fairs arose in response to rising *taxes* on trade rather than in response to trade itself. It might also be objected that they were an answer to economic depression rather than growth. Finally, it might be argued that such fairs responded primarily to *dirigiste* pressures from government to develop better networks for distributing goods from international trade.

Concerning the first criticism, I mentioned above that a subsidiary cause of the rise in transaction costs after the mid-fourteenth century was the increase in state taxation. Generally, however, these increases affected direct rather than indirect taxes and were highly irregular, coming in response to short-term rises in military expenditure. Irregular tax increases cannot, therefore, have been the main reason for the *gradual* expansion of toll franchises, or for the constant and nearly exponential increase in the number of fairs throughout fifteenth- and sixteenth-century Europe.[84] The latter phenomenon suggests instead that the territorial growth of late medieval states was significant mainly for the political and legal framework it supplied for trade. The state's growing political authority allowed complex fair networks to be established, and meant

---

82 RC 44–5, fo. 301rv (1408): 'presertim suppetit et occurrit nundinas et fora certis annis temporibus in nonnullis civitatis terris et locis sistemare et ordinare, quo possint habilius confluentes undeque de uno in alterum locum eorum mercimonia et res redducere vendere et mercari et gentis gentibus conversari'.

83 General studies of this phenomenon for entire countries are rare. Two excellent examples are Grohmann, *Fiere*, and M. A. Ladero Quesada, 'Las ferias de Castilla. Siglos XII a XV'. For the 'proliferation of fairs' after the mid-fifteenth century see Verlinden, 'Markets and fairs', pp. 150–3.

84 J. N. Ball, *Merchants and merchandise. The expansion of trade in Europe 1500–1630*, pp. 30–2; A. Everitt, 'The marketing of agricultural produce', pp. 532–43. See also above, n. 83.

that the franchises upon which those networks relied could be more effectively enforced. Conversely, the perception that state administration was more effective may well have stimulated local demand for new fairs.

The second objection is based on the fact that new fairs were often requested on the grounds of poverty. These requests were significant, however, because they were made on the assumption that a fair would *improve* a community's situation. A request was made only if it was assumed that trade existed to attract; if this trust was misplaced, the fair rapidly disappeared. While some fairs were short-lived, they were only a small proportion of those that survived, often into the eighteenth century and beyond. Furthermore, as we just saw, new fairs were established throughout Europe in the sixteenth century, when the historiography interprets them, not as a defensive phenomenon, but as a basic feature of a growing economy. In Sicily, for example, the number of new fairs increased markedly after 1460, when population and economy were undoubtedly both growing rapidly.

Concerning the final objection, late medieval Sicilian fairs have been seen as elements of a commercial circuit deliberately organized by the state to distribute foreign goods (mainly cloth) and to collect grain and other agricultural products for export, serving the needs both of the state and of foreign traders.[85] In fact, there is no evidence that a conscious policy in this sense was enacted after Frederick II; we saw that Martino's plans in this sense failed. Furthermore, although a fair franchise, like toll franchises, could be granted to compensate for war damages or even for political expediency, for example to favour one community over another,[86] the government's financial needs seem to have had little or no influence on halting the diffusion of new fairs. On the contrary, the government was well aware that a new fair would benefit the fisc more than a toll exemption, for although trade tolls were not levied during a fair, taxes were levied on merchandise on its way through other towns,[87] on food supplies for people attending the event,[88] and on judicial and other events held during the fair itself. Indeed, since

---

[85] Grohmann, 'Prime indagini'; *UM*, pp. 364–7. For a more balanced view see M. Scarlata, 'Mercati e fiere nella Sicilia aragonese', pp. 477–94.

[86] Grohmann, 'Prime indagini', 329–30; Grohmann, *Fiere*, chapter 7.

[87] *Ibid.*, p. 268.

[88] PR 30, fos. 52–3v (1428); C 2864, fos. 8v–9 (1450); RC 114, fos. 146v–7v (1463); CR 65, fo. 227rv, and RC 153, fo. 58rv (1483).

fairs established in feudal lands could not be taxed by the crown, the latter had an additional incentive to grant franchises in order to maximize income from the sale of new privileges.[89] The state (like local communities) was mainly preoccupied with ensuring that new fairs would not damage existing ones, a first-come first-served policy which was prone to institutional inertia.[90] The proliferation of fairs in Sicily and throughout Europe in the fifteenth and sixteenth centuries cannot thus be explained with reference only to state initiative and international trade.

Most of the new fairs which emerged in this period arose in response to an expansion of trade and specialization within rural economies. They were not by and large distinguished by the presence of foreign merchants; they were periodic events which can be distinguished functionally from simple markets because most transactions were not directed to immediate consumption. Fairs could also involve trade in high-value commodities transported over long distances, but bulk transactions in domestic agricultural and manufactured goods prevailed. These events, therefore, provide crucial indirect evidence of kinds of commercial exchange that have left few direct traces in historical documentation.

Records for local trade are inevitably rather few because evidence for domestic trade at fairs relied on contracts drawn up to ensure future payments or consignments: such contracts were naturally more sporadic than those insuring a foreign merchant against default for costly imports. Even so, it is clear that late medieval Sicilian fairs, including the main 'international' one in Piazza, were mostly local or regional in scope and responded to local and regional needs – like the fair of Scillato, which is said to have served the town of Caltavuturo and the county of Sclafani.[91] Foreign merchandise made up only a fraction of what was ordinarily traded and consumed (see chapter 6). Nicosia was mainly a cattle market, attracting traders from Castrogiovanni, Randazzo and Messina.[92]

---

[89] Grohmann, 'Prime indagini', 331. Also C 3477, fo. 121rv (1463): Roccella; CR 65, fo. 227rv, and RC 153, fo. 58rv (1483): Scillato.

[90] Grohmann, 'Prime indagini', 331. For competing fairs see RC 56, fos. 65v–6 (1425), and RC 70, fo. 62rv (1434); CR 70, fo. 83rv (1487); CR 72, fo. 385rv (1487).

[91] CR 65, fo. 227rv, and RC 153, fo. 58rv (1483).

[92] Above, n. 74, and NR 14, fos. 104–5v (1489). See also A. Barbato ed., *Per la storia di Nicosia nel Medio Evo. Documenti inediti, I (1267–1454)*, p. 123 (1421).

The Randazzo fair too was a major cattle market,[93] but was also an important trading venue for local cloth in val Demone.[94] By the end of the fifteenth century, if not sometime before, the fairs of Patti[95] and Tindari had become important venues for the local cloth trade as well.[96] Tindari's fair also specialized in furs, leather goods and carpets.[97]

Some of the main Sicilian fairs were frequented as an annual circuit by foreign merchants, who would transact in one place and settle accounts at a later event. This practice applied in particular to the main article of international trade, woollen cloth.[98] Although eastern and western Sicilian markets for foreign goods were never fully integrated, they did occasionally overlap. Merchants from Palermo ranged as far as Piazza, Castrogiovanni and Lentini in val di Noto, although they mainly traded in western Sicily. The Tuscan Datini factors (based mainly in Palermo) sold cloth at the fairs of Nicosia, Piazza, Catania and Lentini.[99] Most trade circuits were more localized, however. In eastern Sicily, trade in home and imported goods linked Messina to Catania,[100] Catania to Castrogiovanni[101] and Lentini,[102] Lentini to Randazzo,[103] Randazzo to Tindari,[104] Nicosia to Messina,[105] and Messina to Tindari.[106]

I suggested above that trade franchises can be used as rough indicators of domestic economic trends, mainly because franchises were granted in response to community demands rather than as a result of deliberate state policy. Grants of fairs and toll franchises show analogous changes over time, which reveal common forces

93 Below, n. 103, and NR 14, fo. 135rv (1489): a supplementary toll on cattle and Sicilian cloth.
94 Below, chapter 4. *Orbace*, other woollens and local silk cloth were also sold there (G. C. Sciacca, *Patti e l'amministrazione del Comune nel Medio Evo*, p. 313).
95 CR 83, fo. 47rv (1499): toll on local cloth.
96 NM 7, fo. 190v (1492): advance sale of 230 *canne* of black and white *orbace* to be delivered at the Tindari fair.
97 NM 3, fo. 350 (1446–8).
98 Grohmann, 'Prime indagini', 364–8; *UM*, pp. 500–4. See also Cosentino, 'Un documento in volgare siciliano del 1320', 380.
99 G. Motta, 'Aspetti dell'economia siciliana alla fine del XIV secolo. Da una lettera di Manno d'Albizio a Francesco Datini', p. 522.
100 NM 3, fo. 304v (1446–8): cotton tablecloths.
101 NC 14926, fos. 84v–5v (1499): knives.
102 *Ibid.*, fos. 351, 416v (1500): iron and steel.
103 NM 5, fo. 192rv (1447): cattle.
104 NR 5, fos. 194v, 194v–5 (1456): foreign cloth.
105 NM 6A, fo. 274 (1469), and NM 7, fo. 527v (1492): cattle.
106 NM 7, fos. 190v, 515rv (1492): *orbace* and iron.

Table 3.3 *Toll franchises and fairs, 1199–1499*

	Toll exemptions (1) per cent	Fairs (2) per cent	Fairs (3) per cent
1199–1337	17.3	14.5	15.6
1338–91	8.3	4.8	12.5
1392–1415	20.7	8.1	10.4
1416–58	25.6	29.0	24.0
1459–99	28.1	43.6	37.5
	N=121 100.0	N=62 100.0	N=96 100.0

(1) and (2) = first concessions and confirmations; (3) = first documentary references.
Sources: As for Tables 3.1 and 3.2.

behind both phenomena and similar pressures to improve the collection and distribution of merchandise for the home market. The stronger political influence on grants of toll franchises before 1415 is apparent by comparing percentages in columns 1 and 3 in Table 3.3, particularly for the period 1392–1415, when toll exemptions increased from eight to twenty per cent of the total under the effect of the Aragonese restoration, whereas the number of new fairs continued to decline. Even so, the differences in rates of concession narrowed after 1392. The coefficient of correlation (r) between tolls and all fair attestations, which is a high 0.84 for the whole period, rises to an astonishing 0.96 for 1392–1500.

Assuming, therefore, that both kinds of franchise were made in response to the same general economic conditions, a reading of Table 3.3 indicates an expansive thirteenth century, followed by a long recession – with particular difficulties during the period of political transition at the turn of the fifteenth century – and then accelerating expansion up to 1500. In an even broader perspective, twenty to twenty-five per cent of all franchises were granted between the end of the twelfth and the end of the fourteenth century, and the remaining seventy-five to eighty per cent during the following one hundred years. Especially significant is that thirty-five to forty-five per cent of all franchises were granted between 1392 and 1458, at a time when the economy is usually described as stagnating; expansion from the 1460s is more easily explicable by demographic recovery. Indications as broad as these must be used cautiously, since they gloss over the short- and medium-term economic conjuncture and underrepresent sub-regional differences; they can, however, be used as broad economic indicators for activities such as domestic trade, which cannot otherwise be investigated in much detail.

We saw above that, besides lowering tariffs, the state could reduce rising transaction costs by unifying local weights and measures. Attempts to standardize regional measures began in the late thirteenth century, increased during the fifteenth century, and remained quite frequent after 1500.[107] Before 1509, all efforts were devoted to achieving a unified grain measure, although the tradition that a *salma* of wheat in eastern Sicily was twenty per cent larger than in the west continued to be upheld.[108] These efforts were probably made more in order to lower the costs of exacting export taxes than to help foreign merchants in their trade, but the end result was the same.[109] Contemporary commercial manuals imply that by the fifteenth century, a certain unity had been achieved along the coast and in the grain-exporting hinterlands.[110]

It might seem that the continuing pressure to unify local grain measures would have been directed against the interior, where the influence of international demand was weaker.[111] In fact, standardization was far from established even in the coastal areas.[112] In the early fifteenth century, the merchant Giovanni da Uzzano noted despondently that 'Sicily has many *salme*'.[113] A first attempt to unify grain measures in val di Mazara in accordance with those of Palermo was made in 1471 but clearly failed, since thirty years later

[107] Testa ed., *Capitula*, I, pp. 57 (1296), 215 (1434); II, pp. 281–2 (1582); G. Spata ed., *Capitula R. Siciliae recensioni Francisci Testa addenda*, pp. 68–9 (1509); G. Cesino e Fogletta ed., *Pragmaticarum Regni Siciliae tomus tertius*, pp. 221–4 (1601).
[108] CR 26, fos. 1–5v (1446). Barley was sold using both measures in val di Mazara.
[109] Above, *Currency and measurements*. See, however, RC 5, fo. 147 (1355–77): Noto and Caltagirone are ordered, for the prosperity of trade ('negocia'), to unify their *tummini* with the larger one current in eastern Sicily. The latter was set by the *maestro portulano*, the official in charge of sea trade.
[110] Tucci, 'La Sicilia nei Manuali di mercatura veneziani', pp. 643–4, 646; *UM*, p. 166.
[111] Tucci, 'Sicilia nei Manuali'.
[112] RC 75, fos. 445v–6 (1440).
[113] G. F. Pagnini della Ventura, *Della decima e di varie altre gravezze imposte dal comune di Firenze; della moneta e della mercatura de' Fiorentini sino al secolo XVI*, IV, pp. 164–5: 'Cicilia ae più salme.'

a dispute flared up between Palermo and Agrigento, at the time the main grain-exporter, over the same issue.[114] Market segmentation thus persisted throughout the late Middle Ages. An edict of 1509 was headed 'On the observance of Chapter XXV of King Alfonso [of 1434] on the standardization of measurements.'[115] In 1296, Federico III ordered that the basic unit for Sicily east of the river Salso should be the *salma* of Syracuse; a century and a half later, Alfonso ordered that the common grain measure of val di Noto and val Demone should be the *salma* of Catania.[116]

In general, attempts to standardize measurements were hardest to enforce because of the particularly broad span of interests adversely affected by such moves. Thus, although royal prerogatives in feudal lands included setting weights and measures, these rights were resisted by the aristocracy for fear of a loss of income.[117] Even demesne towns demanded that local measurements be respected,[118] sometimes on the basis of an urban district's prerogatives.[119] As with toll franchises, the structure and needs of the state undermined the provisions it promoted; limits to state intervention were most severe in the matter of standardizing measures, because local interests could exert more influence on this issue than on government tolls. Thus, during the late Middle Ages, neither of the forces that ordinarily increase market integration and act to standardize measurements – trade and a central political authority – was sufficiently strong to achieve anything like a complete unification of the Sicilian market.[120]

While contributing to commercial disunity, however, the heterogeneity of measures was not so much a cause as a consequence of the localized nature of most markets, and supports the argument that short- and medium-range trade had greater impact than long-distance trade. By the end of the Middle Ages,

114 C 3487, fos. 82v–3v (1471); C 3488, fos. 3v–4v (1472); RC 132, fo. 180rv (1475); TRP Atti 58, fos. 198v–200v (1501). Polizzi and Castellammare had different *salme* from nearby Palermo (PR 24, fo. 124rv (1421); LV 83, fo. 21 (1462)).
115 CR 97, fo. 30rv; Spata ed., *Capitula*, pp. 68–9.
116 See V. Cordova, *Le origini della città di Aidone e il suo statuto*, p. 42.
117 Sciacca, *Patti*, pp. 278–9 (Gioiosa Guardia, 1445); RC 128, fos. 309–10v (Sutera, 1472).
118 RC 69, fos. 90v–3 (1434); Sciacca, *Patti*, pp. 278–9 (1445?); RC 152, fo. 152rv (1483).
119 RC 70, fos. 162–3 (Randazzo, 1435); also NR 2, fo. 26v (1445); NR 5, fos. 169–70, 183v (1455–6).
120 Kula, *Les mésures et les hommes*, p. 111.

the combined pressure of the international and domestic grain markets and the state's fiscal needs had resulted in some uniformity of measures for wheat; but the limits of this achievement for overall integration were still to be seen two centuries later. Despite a major edict of 1601,[121] when technicians travelled the island in 1809 with a view towards standardizing measures, they found a bewildering variety for everything except grain, even for legumes, wine and olive oil.[122]

The institutional innovations discussed above can, in conclusion, be interpreted in two mutually supportive ways. On the one hand, they can be viewed as improving *opportunities* for trade, and hence for specialization and economic growth. On the other hand, they can be interpreted as indirect indices of expanding domestic trade during the fifteenth century; this expansion was in turn the effect of major economic changes, examined in the following chapters. Pressure for improved commercial institutions shows, I have argued, that from the late fourteenth century a more complex and more widely integrated economy was evolving. For various reasons, however – the main one being the dissolution of the monarchy after the mid-fourteenth century – markets did not expand in a simple evolutionary way, through ever-widening circles of specialization and integration.

The Aragonese conquest of 1392–8 provided the political and institutional basis for unification of the regional market, because, as I discuss in chapter 7, the new monarchy was better able (compared to its fourteenth-century predecessors) to guarantee freedom of trade against local landholder and community interests. Nonetheless, the government made no deliberate move to foster regional trade before the early 1430s, and even then King Alfonso's provisions imply that his interest in developing a free grain market was instrumental to the state's short-term financial needs; on occasion the crown expressly remitted barons from its provisions.[123] By contrast, far more effort was devoted to regulating the foreign grain trade for fiscal purposes (see chapters 6 and 7).

---

[121] Above, n. 107.
[122] *Codice metrico siculo.* For local measurements see RC 46, fos. 315v–16 (1407); RC 109, fos. 146–8 (1460); NR 15, fos. 326v–7 (1491); NM 7, fo. 190v (1492); NC 6311, fo. 147v (1501).
[123] CR 34, fos. 441–2v (1452): Antonio Peralta, count of Caltabellotta, may ban exports from his lands.

Royal indifference to internal trade and markets continued under Ferdinand II. In the early sixteenth century, the Sicilian parliament petitioned to use 5,000 florins of the annual tax – then in the order of 100,000 florins – to repair the island's bridges, which were needed for trade in victuals and other commodities. The request went unanswered and had to be renewed six years later, when the king was reminded that royal finances depended particularly on grain export revenues, and that for grain to be exported it had to be easily transported to the coast.[124]

This example further supports the conclusion that state intervention on the regional market was largely random and opportunist. With the exception of toll and fair franchises and, to a lesser extent, of interventions on the grain trade, it was also largely ineffective. Government could operate more freely to reduce tolls because it directly controlled the resources involved and did not deprive of means any powerful section of society. Inability to enforce most toll exemptions in feudal lands, however, while exposing the limits to state action did not seriously affect the privileges' impact, since all the largest and wealthiest towns belonged to the royal demesne. Fair franchises, on the other hand, often a source of profit for the state and often requested by the barons themselves, were not hard to obtain. Finally, the partial success in standardizing measures for the foreign grain trade was the result of clearly defined state interests. We shall also see, however, that the state's attempts to improve conditions for the grain trade itself, however, were successful only insofar as they met producers' concerns.

By contrast, when a government grant on trade damaged local privileges or revenues and the local interests were willing to resist royal action, the crown was unable or reluctant to press its case. Crown action was successful only with institutions under its direct influence or when its more powerful subjects could perceive a gain. Ultimately, since even in its most efficient guise the crown normally responded to local demands, its main contribution to the development of a regional market was indirect. The state could provide a unified institutional setting in which trade could operate freely and was subject to clearly defined, non-arbitrary and contained exactions. In this respect, the fifteenth-century Aragonese regime differed markedly from any that had preceded it.

[124] Testa ed., *Capitula*, I, pp. 557–8 (1509), 597 (1515). For roads and transport see Giuffrida, 'Itinerari di viaggi e trasporti'; *UM*, pp. 355–62.

URBAN INSTITUTIONS AND ECONOMIC CHANGE

The discussion of institutional constraints on trade can be concluded by examining urban response to wider economic and political changes. This was directed primarily towards redistributing resources from the countryside to the larger urban communities, and within these mainly to the propertied and administrative classes.

We saw in chapter 1 that among the explanations given for Italian 'dualism' is the lack in the medieval South of 'autarchic' urban markets like those established by independent communes in the North. However, during the thirteenth and fourteenth centuries, Messina and Palermo, followed after mid-century by most other large cities, developed a closer control over their hinterland (*districtus*), in a way vaguely analogous to the earlier establishment of urban *contadi* in central and northern Italy. How far could this analogy be taken? How strong were urban powers over the countryside?

Messina's push to control its rural surroundings began very early, for its poor agricultural hinterland and its good opportunities to trade across the Straits provided strong reasons to control local resources (see chapter 5). Economic and institutional control of the surrounding countryside ensured Messina of regular food supplies, and of access to a market for local and imported manufactured goods and to sources of high-quality agricultural products for export. In the course of the fifteenth century, the district also increasingly became a source of administrative power and income for the Messinese patriciate.

The first territorial concession to Messina may have been that of Randazzo, a large town to the north-west of Etna, in 1199.[125] But although the privilege seems authentic,[126] and was confirmed by the Angevins,[127] it was probably not enforced; jurisdiction over Randazzo was not vindicated when conflict over the boundaries of

---

[125] Giardina ed., *Capitoli*, no. 12.
[126] As against Trasselli, *I privilegi di Messina e di Trapani (1160–1359), con una Appendice sui consolati trapanesi nel secolo XV*, pp. 30–1.
[127] Giardina ed., *Capitoli*, no. 40 (1357).

Messina's district arose in the fifteenth century. Since at this time Randazzo was a regular supplier of timber, one reason for the charter of 1199 can have been to ensure supplies of timber for Messina's shipyards.[128] But integration may have gone much further; Randazzo's toll franchise of 1302, for example, was restricted to Randazzo itself, Taormina and Messina (see Table 3.1).[129] Links between the two towns may have weakened thereafter, but were re-established on a more equal footing in the late fifteenth century when Randazzo, after a long decline, again became a major agricultural, manufacturing and trading centre.[130]

One of the earliest references to a specific urban territory, which may have coincided with the episcopal district, appears in a privilege of 1296, when Federico III (probably on the strength of a Messinese forgery ascribed to Roger II)[131] agreed not to appoint master jurors, who syndicated local administration, in its 'territory and district'.[132] A few years later, the district was extended to include the whole plain of Milazzo; Messina's highest official, the *stratigoto*, was given jurisdiction over the former justiciarates of val Demone, val di Castrogiovanni and val di Milazzo.[133] The concession was motivated by the 'intolerable hunger and famine, the destruction of mills, houses and other goods, the burning of orchards, the cutting down and destruction of vineyards' suffered by Messina at the hands of the Angevins.[134] Yet, the connection between this concession and regular grain supplies from Milazzo is uncertain. The privilege made no mention of the problem of food supplies, except indirectly by referring to dearth. The main motive behind the concession was probably to undermine or destroy the

---

[128] RC 70, fos. 162–3 (1435). For the timber trade in Randazzo see also NR 5, fos. 112v, 220–1, 222v–3, 233rv, 257rv (1456); NR 6, fo. 19rv (1460); NR 10, fos. 10v–11v (1478); NR 15, fo. 383v (1491); NR 59, fo. 7v (1499).

[129] See also RC 2, fos. 104v–5 (1323).

[130] NR 5, fo. 135 (1456); NR 14, fo. 30v (1488).

[131] F. Martino, 'Una ignota pagina del Vespro: la compilazione dei falsi privilegi messinesi'.

[132] Giardina ed., *Capitoli*, no. 31. For a similar privilege for lay and ecclesiastical feudal landholders see Testa, *Capitula*, I, p. 23 (1288?).

[133] Giardina ed., *Capitoli*, no. 33 (1302); Gregorio, *Bibliotheca scriptorum*, II, pp. 437–8; Testa ed., *De vita et rebus gestis Federici II [III] Siciliae regis*, p. 263.

[134] For Angevin occupation of eastern Sicily before 1302 see Muntaner, *Crònica*, chapter 198.

jurisdictional autonomy of smaller communities, which also included the right to ban exports to Messina at times of dearth.[135] Before 1302, Milazzo possessed rights of jurisdiction[136] and a *districtus*, which survived in a weak form into the fifteenth century.[137]

Messina's further attempts to extend its district (which by then included over 200km²)[138] were at best temporarily successful. In 1357, the Angevins extended the district to include, besides Randazzo, about 30km of the coastline beyond Milazzo up to Tindari,[139] but the grant was never reconfirmed.[140] A final, ambitious attempt to expand the district to include Lentini to the south and Patti to the north-west on the basis of some forged privileges was probably made in the 1430s, in response to the opportunity provided by Alfonso's presence in Sicily.[141]

In contrast with all other Sicilian towns, therefore, Messina had established its district already by 1302. Notwithstanding attempts to extend its domain, the city directed most of its efforts thereafter to establishing firmer powers of jurisdiction over existing territory. Nothing is known about this before the mid-fourteenth century, but the dissolution of the monarchy after 1350 must have had disastrous effects on anything achieved previously. Messina doubted its ability to enforce its claims, and local statutes, modified towards the end of the fourteenth century, quoted the pre-1302 limits of the *tenimentum*. When the two Martins landed in 1392, the city was quick to regain control over the village and castle of Monforte, which had

---

[135] 'Quod quolibet de plano Milacii districtus Messane possit extrahere frumentum extra territorium et districtum dicte civitatis contra privilegia banna et deveta antiqua, cuius plani territoria pro maiori parte sunt messanencium, tranquillitatem dicte civitatis plurimum turbantes . . . unde videtur per abominabilem usurpacionem messanensibus de propriis bonis vite alimenta negare' (C 2810, fos. 8v–9v, and RC 54, fo. 506rv (1423?)).

[136] C. Martino, 'La valle di Milazzo fra età angioina e aragonese (Appunti e problemi di topografia e storia dell'insediamento)', 58, quoting C. Garufi, *La Curia stratigoziale*, pp. 20–2.

[137] RC 104, fos. 289–90 (1457).

[138] Beloch, *Bevölkerungsgeschichte Italiens*, I, p. 142.

[139] Giardina ed., *Capitoli*, no. 40.

[140] *Ibid.*, no. 51 (1396); RC 27, fo. 62 (1396); RC 24, fo. 150rv (1397). For a failed attempt to re-exhume the Angevin concession in 1410 see Giardina ed., *Capitoli*, no. 60.

[141] *Ibid.*, nos. 1 (483 *ab U.c.* [*sic*]), 4 (1129), 8 (1194).

been usurped by Blasco Alagona.[142] Motta Camastra,[143] Milazzo, Castroreale, Rametta, Santa Lucia, Taormina and Alì were also reannexed, but Tripi, Novara and Oliveri were lost.[144] The concession to Messina of the power to nominate district captains in 1396, and the extensive criminal jurisdiction given to the *stratigoto* a few years later, were thus major additions to the city's prerogatives.

But when Messina tried later to extend these rights to the district's castellans, petitioning that they be chosen from among its own citizens, Alfonso was unwilling to abandon full control of such a delicate office.[145]

The effect of Messina's new-found powers on the social and economic structure of its district after 1400 can be glimpsed in the frequent protests of its subject communities, and the active resistance of the stronger ones. Milazzo put up the longest struggle, opposing Messina's jurisdiction for nearly half a century and upholding strong rearguard action after that;[146] Taormina also showed some independence.[147] Generally, however, apart from some initial protests against Messina's officials,[148] no evidence of Messina's activities survives besides the city's own record of increasing power

[142] Starrabba ed., *Consuetudini e privilegi della città di Messina sulla fede di un codice del XV secolo posseduto dalla Biblioteca comunale di Palermo*, nos. 48 (1392), 49 (1393). After some uncertainty (RC 37, fos. 193v–4 (1399), Giardina ed. *Capitoli*, no. 53) Monforte was confirmed in fief to Joan Cruilles in 1398 (Testa, *Capitula*, I, p. 130; Mineo, 'Egemonia e radicamento della nobiltà militare catalana in Sicilia dopo il 1392: l'esempio dei Cruilles e dei Santapau', pp. 104–5). In 1400, Messina asked that Monforte return to the demesne together with Tripi and Novara 'per consideracioni dilu bonu trattamentu ki hannu li missinisi meglu in li terri dilu demaniu ki in li terri di li baruni' (RC 38, fos. 61–3v); Martin of Aragon had already written to his son in 1398 to revoke their enfeoffment (Starrabba, 'Documenti riguardanti la Sicilia sotto re Martino I esistenti nell'Archivio della Corona d'Aragona', 153).

[143] RC 24, fo. 156rv (1396).

[144] *Ibid.*; RC 33, fo. 78v (1398); RC 37, fos. 193v–4 (1399), Giardina ed., *Capitoli*, no. 53; *ibid.*, no. 54 (1399).

[145] *Ibid.*, nos. 50 (1396?), 54 (1399), 58 (1404–5), 78 (1437). For an earlier attempt see C 2426, fo. 49v (1413).

[146] For confirmation of Messina's jurisdiction see Giardina ed., *Capitoli*, nos. 63 and 64 (1416). On Milazzo's resistance see PR 22, fos. 272–3v (1413); RC 56, fo. 48 (1425); Giardina ed., *Capitoli*, nos. 71 (1432), 81 (1440); RC 106, fos. 226–8 (1457); C 3472, fos. 161v–2 (1459), Giardina ed., *Capitoli*, no. 90.

[147] C 2819, fos. 154–5 (1433); Giardina ed., *Capitoli*, no. 78 (1437); C 3472, fos. 166–8 (1458); RC 112, fos. 300v–2v (1463); Giardina ed., *Capitoli*, nos. 100 (1465), 106 (1500). Taormina was briefly declared outside Messina's jurisdiction in 1443 (C 2844, fo. 108).

[148] RC 44–5, fo. 334rv (*casale* Santo Stefano, 1408); RC 49, fos. 116–19, and RC 48, fos. 219v–23 (Santa Lucia, 1413–14); RC 51, fos. 39v–40 (Santa Lucia, 1415).

and prerogatives. The *districtuales* had to defend the city in case of danger, and some had to buy their grain from Messina at exorbitant prices.[149] Messina was granted the unusual favour of having jurisdiction over the district's Jewish communities.[150] Perhaps because of mounting land hunger in the late fifteenth century, it also asserted free pasture rights in the district's forests.[151] The inferior rank of the *districtuales* was made quite clear, when Messina asked that *male ablata*, ill-gotten gains confessed to on point of death, be collected throughout the district for ransom from the Saracens of citizens or inhabitants of Messina. The money could be spent for the *districtuales'* ransom only if no Messinese prisoners were available.[152]

Increasing subordination of the hinterland was only partly offset by Messina's consensus-seeking attempts to extend some privileges to the district.[153] In 1459, Messina tried to extend its prerogatives, including possibly its vast commercial franchises, to its entire district. This move seems to have been inspired by the countryside's dissatisfaction at having to bear most of the costs of civil war in Calabria without sharing the possible material gains, but may also be linked with Messina's attempts to gain support for a bid for Sicilian political independence.[154] Paternalistic pleading on behalf of smaller communities helped raise Messina's local standing.[155] Messina also seems to have gained full tax exemption for the city and its district at some point during the fifteenth century.[156]

Although the quest by Messina and Palermo for territorial control seems to follow roughly similar patterns, a closer look reveals major differences, the result of a different geographical setting and socio-economic structure. In contrast to Messina, Palermo had a natural hinterland in the Conca d'Oro, a semi-circle formed by

---

149 Local militias: RC 54, fo. 506rv (1423); C 2862, fo. 161v (1450). Grain supplies: RC 69, fos. 55v–6 (1433); Giardina ed., *Capitoli*, no. 73 (1434).
150 *Ibid.*, no. 73.
151 C 3472, fos. 160v–1 (1459).
152 Giardina ed., *Capitoli*, no. 73 (1434). See S. Fodale, 'Il riscatto dei siciliani "captivi" in Barberia (XIV–XV secolo)'.
153 C 2831, fos. 240–1 (1440).
154 C 3472, fos. 156v–7 (1459). On Messina's support of Charles of Viana's bid for the throne of Sicily see below, chapter 7.
155 Giardina ed., *Capitoli*, nos. 73 (1434), 82 (1443) (Castroreale); PR 21, fo. 65 (Santa Lucia, 1419). RC 127, fos. 382–4 (Santo Stefano, 1472); previously Santo Stefano had protested on its own behalf (C 2854, fo. 63rv, 1445).
156 See below, chapter 7, no. 295.

Solanto in the east through Misilmeri, Monreale, Carini and Sferra-cavallo in the west.[157] Probably for this reason, the city lacked the urge to gain legal authority over its district, which explains why its boundaries were for a long time not fixed.[158] In addition, urban control did not extend to as many sectors of the economy.[159] Palermo's upper classes were encouraged to define the urban territory more accurately, mainly in response to difficulties in ensuring grain supplies after the breakdown of regional markets in the mid-fourteenth century, and in order to defend their share of the wine trade during the fifteenth.

Like Naro,[160] Noto,[161] Polizzi,[162] Taormina[163] and feudal Geraci,[164] most large towns possessed an administrative territory whose origins might lie – as with Messina and Palermo – in Norman or pre-Norman times, but which drew strong impetus from market and political fragmentation after 1350, and the expansion of state administration in the fifteenth century.

Although Catania was annexed to the demesne in 1232, it remained for a long time under partial episcopal control, and final settlement took place only in 1490.[165] In the intervening period, Catania was placed 'in that strange situation . . . of a demesne city lacking a demesne, of a city that while continuing to extend its administrative jurisdiction over its *casali* had no jurisdiction whatsoever over their territories, except for the usual guarantee of "common rights" of "individuals" over pastures and wood-lands'.[166]

157 De Vio ed., *Privilegia*, pp. 203–6 (1433), 231 (1438). In 1489, Palermo set grain prices within a thirty-mile radius (ABP 1488–9, fo. 13v).
158 TRP Atti 53, fos. 114v–15 (1498). In the eighteenth century, the district covered 250km² (Beloch, *Bevölkerungsgeschichte Italiens*, I, p. 134).
159 C 2894, fos. 137v–8 (1447): Palermo forbids the sale of non-local wine 'per barraki o altri loci' in its territory.
160 RC 142, fos. 499v–500 (1480).
161 RC 164, fos. 109–11v (1487).
162 C 2822, fos. 22–4 (1442).
163 PR 18, fos. 396–8v (1416); RC 53, fos. 125v–6, 126v, 128rv (1425); C 2814, fo. 156v (1427); RC 75, fos. 405–8 (1440).
164 RC 174, fo. 409rv (1490).
165 CR 1413, fos. 105–10v; RC 175, fos. 324v–8 (1490). See also G. Scalia, 'Nuove considerazioni storiche e paleografiche sui documenti dell'Archivio capitolare di Catania per il ristabilimento della sede vescovile nel 1091', 50–2; C. Ardizzoni, *Le origini del patrimonio fondiario di Catania, I. Ex feudo Pantano*, pp. 9–10; C 2889, fo. 158 (1433).
166 Gaudioso, *Questione demaniale*, p. 91. On southern Italian urban institutions see F. Calasso, *La legislazione statutaria dell'Italia meridionale*. For Catania's hinter-

Catania's heyday came after the Black Death, when it became the main royal residence and the capital of the 'Catalan' party led by the Alagona family. A clue to the city's influence in this period is the large number of communities in val di Noto and val Demone that adopted its customary laws.[167] Lentini, which came under the Chiaromonte faction's sway in the same period, had earlier adopted Messina's customs, but took up Catania's system of preparing wine for sale.[168] As a result, Catania's *districtus* was possibly the largest in Sicily.[169]

While no equivalent to Messina's privileges exists for Catania, the latter's hold over its district seems more like Messina's than Palermo's. In 1432, Catania stated that Augusta, Cadrà, Francofonte, Motta and Aci belonged to its district, a significant (though highly dubious) statement, at least with respect to the county of Augusta.[170] Aci was certainly under Catania's economic influence; by the mid-fifteenth century, the same could be said of San Filippo, Regalbuto, Assoro, *Callura*, Adrano and Paternò, which in times of scarcity could only export grain to Catania.[171]

Trapani's district first appears fully formed at the end of the fifteenth century. Although Trapani obtained all Messina's privileges, including its extensive commercial franchises, as early as 1315, the city was never able to expand its territory in the way Palermo, Messina and Catania did. The district extended from San Vito lo Capo in the north to the headland of San Todaro facing Marsala's saltpans in the south, including about 50km of

land see da Piazza, *Cronaca*, I, chapter 128, and II, chapter 16; T. Fazello, *Le due deche dell'historia di Sicilia*, p. 82; D. Ventura, *Edilizia urbanistica ed aspetti di vita economica e sociale a Catania nel '400*, pp. 107–22; V. M. Amico e Statella, *Catana illustrata, sive sacra et civilis urbis Catanae historia a prima ejusdem origine in praesens usque deducta ac per annales digesta*, II, pp. 317–25; C 3476, fos. 71v–82 (1460).

167 Aci, Motta, Paternò, Randazzo, Castiglione, Linguaglossa and Vizzini; for Licata see PR 23, fos. 216–18v (1421–2).

168 S. Pisano Baudo, *Storia di Lentini antica e moderna*, II, pp. 197, 232; Starrabba ed., *Lettere e documenti*, pp. 226–9.

169 Beloch, *Bevölkerungsgeschichte Italiens*, I, p. 147: 577km² in the mid-eighteenth century; A. Petino, 'L'arte ed il consolato della seta a Catania nei secoli XIV–XIX', 7 n. 4.

170 RC 67, fo. 102v, continued in RC 68, fo. 23rv (1432).

171 RC 69, fos. 38v–40 (Aci, 1433); NC 6311, fos. 39v–40, 105rv (Paternò, 1500–1); RC 190, fos. 397–8 (Caltagirone, 1495). On grain supplies to Catania see Petino, *Aspetti e momenti di politica granaria a Catania e in Sicilia nel Quattrocento*, p. 33 n. 1. Catania's jurisdiction could be overruled by government; see C 2826, fo. 153rv (1435, grain for Taormina).

salt-producing and grain-exporting coast,[172] and was bordered inland by Monte San Giuliano, Salemi, Castelvetrano and Marsala. Trapani's weakness was apparent in its unceasing confrontation with nearby Monte San Giuliano, which by the fifteenth century had shrunk to a shadow of its former size but remained fiercely independent. Despite Trapani's influence,[173] Monte San Giuliano managed to resist the city's pressure throughout the fifteenth century, even succeeding in opening a new grain port (*caricatore*) in Trapani's district at Bonagia, despite the city's protests.[174] Trapani had previously exploited Monte San Giuliano's lack of an alternative outlet in various ways: by taxing the latter's wine against local custom; by forcing Monte San Giuliano's inhabitants to sell their grain to the city; by forbidding Trapani's butchers to buy animals from them; by imposing a monopoly price on the olive oil they bought in Trapani; and in general by setting up various obstacles in the smaller town's way. During the 1480s and 1490s, Trapani also successfully gained control of some of its neighbour's water resources.[175] Conversely, Monte San Giuliano resisted attempts by Trapani's citizens to buy its land, and tried to usurp rights of usage.[176]

As this discussion suggests, districts developed around most large demesne towns. Syracuse acquired a monopoly over grain and other exports from the gulf dividing it from Augusta to the north in the early fourteenth century;[177] its commercial influence extended inland over the territory of the *Camera reginale* and southwards to Malta.[178] Despite Messina's early claims, by the fifteenth century Randazzo had also established its own district, which adopted the town's measurements and supplied it with food.[179] Randazzo claimed that 'the greater part of *val di Demina*' set the *mete* (the official food prices) in accordance with those of Randazzo.[180] Patti,

172 C 3479, fos. 107–8 (1476).
173 In 1393, Monte San Giuliano was granted all Trapani's privileges (RC 19, fos. 44v–5).
174 C 3479, fos. 102v–3v (1475).
175 RC 41, fo. 175rv (1404); RC 42, fo. 98 (1404); RC 55, fos. 309–11v, 312–13 (1424); RC 154, fos. 410v–11v (1485); RC 180, fos. 343–5 (1492).
176 RC 19, fos. 44v–5 (1393); RC 33, fos. 120v–4v (1399); RC 44–5, fos. 134–5 (1408); RC 59, fos. 129–30 (1428).
177 S. Privitera, *Storia di Siracusa antica e moderna*, II, pp. 498–9; CR 50, fos. 45–6 (1415).
178 Starrabba ed., *Lettere e documenti*, p. 237 (1415).
179 RC 70, fos. 162–3 (1435); RC 118, fos. 57v–74 (1466), V. La Mantia ed., *Consuetudini di Randazzo*, p. 2.
180 RC 70, fos. 162–3 (1435).

which as an episcopal see was considered a *civitas*, obtained the same privileges as Messina in 1392.[181] Its district included Tindari, Librizzi and Gioiosa Guardia, where it levied tolls and even, in the late fifteenth century, compulsory labour services.[182]

In conclusion, therefore, urban control over the countryside intensified throughout Sicily after the mid-fourteenth century in response to two related developments. First, as central government declined and the aristocracy appropriated its resources between c.1340 and 1392, the political role of urban élite groups and of the intermediate, administrative and propertied classes was enhanced. Increasing control over *districti*, most clearly seen for Messina, was an important aspect of the shift in institutional and economic power from the state to local communities. The restoration of the monarchy after 1392, and the expansion of state administration which followed, further strengthened the administrative powers of urban élite groups (see chapter 7).

Second, economic dislocation, in particular the decline of land rents during the fourteenth century, provided a powerful incentive to urban administrators (who were, for the most part, landowners or agricultural entrepreneurs) to exploit and increase institutional powers over the countryside. Direct economic control was applied to protect the wine and grain markets, and at the same time to ensure adequate grain supplies. Even so, as we shall see below, outside of Messina and Palermo urban powers over local grain markets were fairly weak, in part because of state free trade policies, but also because producer interests fluctuated between exploiting local supply monopolies and breaking such monopolies to sell on regional and foreign markets.[183]

That an important purpose of increasing urban powers was to protect local farmers from competition and ensure adequate food supplies is also suggested by the fact that urban powers stopped expanding after the mid-fifteenth century, at the same time as land rents began to increase and structures of grain supply improved. By contrast, urban control was not translated into corporative

---

[181] RC 20, fo. 53rv (1392).
[182] RC 42, fo. 155rv (1404); RC 46, fos. 183v–5v (1406); PR 24, fos. 250v–2 (1425). For labour services granted by the crown on condition that the peasants be paid see RC 128, fo. 291rv (1473); below, chapter 7, nn. 66–9.
[183] T. B. Davies, 'Changes in the structure of the wheat trade in seventeenth-century Sicily and the building of new villages', 380.

legislation for manufacturing, which might discriminate economically against the rural sector; also for political reasons, as we shall see in chapter 7, urban élite groups seem to have effectively prevented strong craft guilds from being established.[184]

The main exception to this generalization was Messina, which by the early fourteenth century had established the basis of authority over a vast hinterland. This territorial expansion was partly caused by food shortages, but the problem only arose because Messina came to occupy a highly strategic position on the Straits as a result of the Norman conquest. We shall see in chapter 5 that the main impulse to control its hinterland came from trade between Sicily and the mainland and with the eastern Mediterranean. Whereas Messina had to fight for new resources and uphold food provisioning through the law, Palermo could rely on safer food supplies and, most of all, on the resources attracted and generated by government presence and administration. Palermo's markets stretched much further than any urban jurisdiction could ever achieve; before its institutional privileges as capital city declined, its 'material constitution' needed little legal backing.

The consequences of the comparative weakness in late medieval Sicily of urban powers over the hinterland were twofold. First and foremost, resources were distributed between urban centres on relatively competitive rather than rent-based criteria. With only a few exceptions, and by contrast with most central and northern Italian urban centres, Sicilian towns could not rely on institutional privilege for food supplies, and hence for population and wealth; I discuss this point further in the following section of this chapter. Second, with the only significant exception of Messina, medieval Sicilian towns were unable, again in contrast to their more northerly neighbours, to accumulate through rural exploitation the necessary resources to establish a strong mercantile base.

REGIONAL MARKETS AND PATTERNS OF URBANIZATION

As mentioned earlier, Italian historians have drawn several points of contrast between urban status in communal Italy and in the South. These differences were the outcome of varying degrees of autonomy from higher political and institutional powers: significant

[184] Leone, 'Lineamenti di una storia delle corporazioni in Sicilia nei secoli XIV–XVII', 91 n. 43, 93.

(but fragile and often short-lived) independence in the Centre–North, subordination to the monarchy in the South. They are often invoked to explain the weakness of southern Italian urban life. It is also common to make a further leap, from urban institutional weakness in the South to an absence of urban sectoral specialization and division of labour. We shall now see, however, that economic backwardness cannot be deduced from the weakness of urban institutions. Although opportunities for urban growth through territorial control were more constrained in Sicily (and in southern Italy) than further north, this does not mean that it was detrimental to the economy as a whole. An equally significant institutional difference between Sicily and northern Italy was that, once economic conditions for a more integrated regional market existed, the monarchy in Sicily was in a better position to establish and uphold the necessary institutional framework than most communes in late medieval northern Italy, which had to establish their territorial states through costly wars.

We have also seen, however, that in Sicily some institutional innovations promoted by the state or by local communities ran counter to regional integration. It is time, therefore, to examine more closely the factors which promoted or hindered specialization and integration, and how they changed over time. Market structures will be investigated by looking at flows of regional trade in three different ways. First, through surveying trade in a staple drink, wine, whose production was widespread and unspecialized; then, through examining trade in the main staple food, grain, whose production was also widespread but became increasingly specialized; and finally, through examining processes of urbanization and changes in the distribution of urban populations over time.

Let us begin by analysing trade in wine. In contrast with their policies toward trade in other staple foods and trade in general, Sicilian governments, especially during the fifteenth century, often upheld the trade monopolies of wine-makers. This single exception to an otherwise cónsistent policy of free trade attests to the power of the wine producers, who included the feudal aristocracy and the urban nobility.[185]

Once again we find Messina obtaining the earliest protection,

---

[185] Bans on other goods in RC 46, fos. 413v–15v (1407); CR 23, fos. 3–8 (1444). See *UM*, p. 744, for anti-monopolistic practices.

from Charles of Anjou in 1272, against outside competition in recognition of the wine trade's importance for the local economy. The privilege was renewed in 1294 to include Messina's district; further measures in the city's favour were passed in the 1350s and 1360s, and again in 1404.[186] Palermo, whose vineyards were also protected by law, was something of an anomaly, because protection was closely connected with the development of the city's *districtus*, and because its privileged political status may have allowed wine producers to lobby more successfully. Palermo's producers generally fought a rearguard battle to protect their market, because the city was never self-sufficient for wine. One of Palermo's first major commercial privileges reduced excise on imported wine to five per cent and exempted all 'imports' – probably from local vineyards – for private consumption.[187] Because of its large population, the presence of the royal court during most of the later Middle Ages, and its different agrarian structures compared with eastern Sicily, Palermo never totally avoided importing wine except perhaps during the worst demographic slump in the fourteenth century.[188] Protectionism against foreign competition, particularly by foreign merchants who had special links with the court, increased during the fifteenth century.[189] The court, however, was as concerned as the merchants to boost wine imports, both for the tax revenues they generated and because of the mounting demand for regional varieties of wine.[190]

In the course of the late fourteenth century, vineyards spread throughout Sicily in response to rising demand and market segmentation (see chapter 4). When the institutional barriers which had favoured this growth were dropped after the Aragonese reconquest, there was widespread concern for the effects the newly unified market would have on local production.[191] The re-establishment of central authority should have improved communication

---

[186] Giardina ed., *Capitoli*, nos. 17, 28, 30, 39, 40 and 56.
[187] De Vio ed., *Privilegia*, pp. 10–11 (1200).
[188] F. G. Savagnone, 'Capitoli inediti della città di Palermo', 101 (1348).
[189] De Vio ed., *Privilegia*, pp. 203–6 (1433), 231 (1438); RC 200, fos. 233–4v (1499). For foreign imports see RC 74, fos. 598v–601 (1439), De Vio ed., *Privilegia*, pp. 247–52; *ibid.*, p. 262 (1440); CR 24, fo. 252 (1445).
[190] RC 76, fos. 175v–84v (1440), 482v–3 (1441). Customs reductions to stimulate imports in CR 859, fo. 81rv (1453); CR 39, fos. 39–40 (1457); LV 71, unnumbered fo. (15 July 1459); LV 93, fo. 317rv (1465).
[191] Provisions for local wine producers: RC 38, fos. 81v–2 (Lentini, 1400); RC 38, fo. 105rv (Trapani, 1400); L. Tirrito ed., *Statuto, capitoli e privilegi della città di*

between sub-regional wine markets and given impetus to specialization and market integration; in fact, specialization did not advance very quickly. Persistent investment in vineyards, when wine
could be had by sea from elsewhere in Sicily, indicates that supply
problems persisted and that the sector was highly profitable, due to
high demand, short-term protectionism and market inefficiencies.[192] Protectionist measures were only breached in favour of
individuals, possibly immigrants, who owned vineyards outside
their place of residence.[193] In some cases, control over the wine
market extended to toll exemptions on trade for consumption
above a specified limit, thereby excluding the poorer members of
the community who were unable to buy large amounts at any one
time.[194] Even successful protectionism in a few localities does not,
however, explain the persistence of a segmented regional market.
An equally important cause of the relative lack of specialization
may have been the difficulty of transporting large quantities of wine
over longer distances by land, which would explain why the main
wine-making towns were strung along the coast.

The structure of the medieval Sicilian wine market thus seems to
have displayed many features of Doren's 'autarchic' communal
markets, and few of the homogeneous, integrated features that I
have argued were more characteristic of late medieval Sicily.
Before drawing any hasty conclusions about the validity of these
two models, however, we must look at the market for the main
staple food, grain.

Changes in the structure of the grain market can be charted on the

Castronuovo di Sicilia, p. 138 (Castronovo, 1401); RC 39, fos. 179v–80 (Castroreale, 1402); RC 49, fos. 86–8 (Milazzo, 1413); RC 49, fo. 183v (Trapani, 1414);
RC 50, fo. 124v (Randazzo, 1415); RC 54, fos. 395v–7, 508 (Agrigento, 1423);
RC 61, fos. 135–6 (Santa Lucia, 1429); RC 61, fos. 94v–5 (Piazza, 1429); RC 74,
fo. 391rv (Randazzo, 1439); CR 23, fos. 3–8 (Castroreale, 1444); Giardina ed.,
Capitoli, no. 86 (Messina, 1450); CR 41, fos. 356–7 (Troina, 1460); C 3484,
fos. 164v–6v (Trapani, 1464); CR 50, fos. 2–2quater (Randazzo, 1470); RC 124,
fo. 325 (Sciacca, 1470); RC 125, fo. 213, and CR 50, fo. 9rv (Catania, 1470);
RC 178, fos. 163v–70 (Castronovo, 1491). The first such provision outside
Messina and Palermo was passed by Alcamo in the mid-fourteenth century
(V. Di Giovanni ed., *Capitoli gabelle e privilegi della città di Alcamo*, p. 63).
[192] Sciacca, *Patti*, pp. 320–1 (*c*.1440).
[193] CR 14, fo. 476rv (Randazzo, 1427); CR 18, fo. 332rv (Randazzo, 1438); C 2826,
fos. 177v–8 (Milazzo, 1435).
[194] RC 67, fo. 102v, and RC 68, fo. 23rv (Catania, 1432); C 3476, fo. 80v (Catania,
1460); C 2845, fo. 58v (Mazara, 1443); C 2857, fo. 168, and CR 29, fos. 135–7v

basis of three independent sources: petitions, laws and other qualitative records reporting or regulating trade; records of local and regional dearth; and urban price series (which are available only for part of the fifteenth century).

Most medium- and long-distance grain freight was done by boat or ship, the fastest and cheapest mode of transport. But although Sicily's long coasts were a major advantage for regional trade, access to low-cost transport was not enough for trade to occur. Neither, however, were laws upholding domestic free trade, the first of which were passed by the Aragonese after 1282. A provision by James II in 1286 was repeated more forcefully by Federico III in 1296. Federico abolished all previous decrees and declared total freedom of trade, both within Sicily and with other countries, of 'wine and other things'; grain was not referred to explicitly.[195] However, both the evidence of toll franchises discussed above and direct evidence of feudal tolls on the grain trade suggest that Federico was unable to enforce the law, either for grain or for other products.[196]

In the late thirteenth and fourteenth centuries, the domestic grain trade was territorially quite restricted. Naturally, most urban supplies came from the surrounding countryside. In 1282, Trapani's catchment area had a radius of about 50km, comprising Marsala, Mazara, Monte San Giuliano and Salemi;[197] in 1399 it was authorized to import victuals from Salemi, Monte San Giuliano and especially Sciacca, a city about 100km away on the south-western coast which was a major collecting point for exporting grain abroad. The greater distance does not, however, indicate any major change in Trapani's supply area, for while 1282 was apparently a normal harvest year, that of 1397–8 was a particularly bad one, and the city had to seek further afield for food and seed for the next year's crop.[198] The nearby town of Mazara, which in 1282 had sent its

(Corleone, 1447); RC 109, fos. 146–8 (Corleone, 1460); CR 875, fo. 327rv (Catania, 1497).

[195] Flandina ed., *Il codice Filangeri e il codice Speciale: privilegi inediti della città di Palermo*, pp. 73–4 (1286); Testa ed., *Capitula*, I, pp. 74–5 (1296).

[196] Testa ed., *De vita Federici II*, pp. 276–8 (1318). Surviving royal *capitula* do not include a ban on feudal tolls, which the crown would have been unable to enforce. RC 34, fo. 290 (1399); C 2890, fo. 150v (1440); CR 71, fos. 18–18sexties (1491), 19–19bis (1500), and RC 178, fos. 163v–70 (1491). See also below, chapter 6.

[197] Carini ed., *De rebus*, no. 20.

[198] RC 33, fos. 120v–4v. See also RC 66, fos. 86v–7v (1431).

quota of the *fodrum* to Trapani, still relied for supplies on its
immediate hinterland a century later.[199]

Developments in the regional grain market during the fourteenth
century can be followed more closely by looking at Messina's supply
structures, for the city's notorious lack of adequate grain supplies
and its constant need for extraordinary provisioning arrangements
produced vast documentation. Since Messina had the best supply
conditions apart from Palermo, their limitations portray the basic
constraints on fourteenth-century Sicily's supply structures as a
whole.

As early as 1160, Messina was permitted to trade victuals in the
kingdom of Sicily, including the southern Italian mainland,[200] probably exchanging wine and fruits for grain. Before the Vespers, in
normal years Messina could rely on supplies from the plain of
Milazzo to the north-west, the plain of Catania and Lentini to the
south, but probably even more from Calabria (see chapter 5).
Disruption of Messina's close political and economic ties with
Calabria after 1282 may have had repercussions for the city's ease of
supply, and was one of the reasons behind the enthusiasm with
which the Aragonese invasion of Calabria after 1282 was greeted in
eastern Sicily.[201] Nonetheless, for a long time after 1282 it was usual
for eastern Sicily to import grain from the mainland, at the same
time as western Sicily exported it abroad. This trade pattern, which
demonstrates how segmented the island's marketplace still was,
also suggests the need to revise figures for grain exports in this
period (see chapter 6).

Even before 1282, however, in bad years Messina could not rely
only on its usual catchment area and had to resort to central and
western Sicily for supply. In January 1281, for example, Charles I
authorized imports of 30,000 *salme* of grain over a period of twelve
months from the ports of Lentini, Terranova, Licata, Termini and
Agrigento.[202] On 15 October 1282, Peter III authorized Messina to
import victuals from Sicily east of the river Salso because of the
dearth caused by Angevin attack. The wheat, barley and legumes
were to feed both men and horses – a reminder that the measure was

[199] RC 34, fo. 290 (1390).
[200] Giardina ed., *Capitoli*, no. 5. See also Peri, *Città e campagna in Sicilia, I.
Dominazione normanna*, II, p. 243.
[201] Carini ed., *De rebus*, no. 395 (1283). See also below, chapter 4.
[202] See above, chapter 2, n. 37.

granted as much for military convenience as out of princely compassion.[203] What was to be a transitory provision was considerably extended a few years later by James II. Messina could import grain from anywhere in Sicily exempt from the export tax (*tratta, ius exiturae*) which was levied on all maritime grain trade.[204] Because evidence for this period is so poor – Messina's relations with southern Calabria and the rest of the mainland are virtually undocumented – we do not know whether between 1282 and the fall of Messina to the Angevins in 1356 the city relied mainly on Sicilian supplies,[205] or whether, after the initial disruption of trade, Messina was able to re-establish links with the mainland. In any case, reliance on Sicilian sources of grain supply did increase considerably.[206]

Termini in the west may have supplied Messina in the first half of the fourteenth century,[207] but the trade probably ended when Palermo came under Chiaromonte control in the late 1340s. Between the onset of the plague in 1347 and Messina's fall to the Angevins in December 1356, the city had to throw its net wider, as far as Sciacca, Malta and Gozo, or resort to waning royal authority.[208] Rural disruption following the plague of 1347–8 and the dearth of 1351–2, 1354–5 and 1355–6 must also have increased Messina's plight.[209]

While Messina did resort to quite distant sources of supply within Sicily after 1282,[210] by the early fourteenth century its main source of supply was the nearby plain of Milazzo.[211] Even so, Milazzo's

203 Giardina ed., *Capitoli*, no. 22.
204 *Ibid.*, no. 28 (1286), where the qualification 'citra [flumen] Salsum' is dropped.
205 La Mantia ed., *Codice diplomatico dei re aragonesi di Sicilia Pietro I, Giacomo, Federico II, Pietro II e Ludovico dalla rivoluzione siciliana del 1282 al 1355. Con note storiche e diplomatiche, I (Anni 1282–1290)*, no. 241; RC 5, fos. 29v–30; da Piazza, *Cronaca*, I, chapters 35, 38.
206 De Vio ed., *Privilegia*, pp. 147–8 (1336); Amico e Statella, *Catana illustrata*, II, pp. 228–33 (1362); RC 13, fo. 199rv (1376?).
207 C. Mirto, 'Petrus Secundus dei gratia rex Siciliae (1337–1342)', 124, App. 2, doc. 6 (1327); La Mantia, 'Su i più antichi capitoli della città di Palermo dal secolo XII al XIV e su le condizioni della città medesima negli anni 1354 al 1392', 406–8 (1349).
208 Cosentino ed., *Codice diplomatico*, nos. 180, 259, 327 (1356).
209 Peri, *Sicilia*, pp. 160 n. 3, 214–15; da Piazza, *Cronaca*, I, chapters 114, 116.
210 A letter 'per curiam galea pro deferendo frumentum in civitatem Messane' cost 7.10 *tarì*, the price of one *salma* of grain (RC 2, fo. 145).
211 B. da Neocastro, *Historia sicula*, chapter 33; Léonard, *Histoire de Jeanne Ire*, III, no. 12.

importance in this sense may have been exaggerated;[212] it may have been more significant for the land Messina's élite owned there.[213]

Only a few weeks after capitulating to the Angevins of Naples in 1356, Messina obtained a privilege which attempted to re-establish conditions prior to its fall. The city could export victuals toll-free throughout the Angevin kingdom and demesne; no grain could be exported east of the river Salso (from val di Noto or val Demone under Angevin control) or from Termini in val di Mazara except to Messina. A further privilege for exports from Calabria was granted a few years later.[214] Allegiance to Naples inevitably strengthened Messina's links with the mainland, although these were never entirely severed except during the harshest years of the Angevin counter-offensive in the early fourteenth century. Yet, between the time of the city's return to Aragonese rule and the 1372 peace treaty between Sicily and Naples, Messina often had to resort to makeshift and unorthodox methods of supply, such as the seizure of ships in southern and western Sicily, sometimes with the active help of the royal fleet.[215] After 1372, relations with Calabria were fully restored.[216]

Messina was very unusual in lacking a close and easily controlled supply of grain; only one other Sicilian city, Palermo, faced similar worries. Palermo was more fortunately situated near major grain growing areas with outlets in Termini, Castellammare, Trapani, Mazara, Sciacca and Agrigento. However, in 1200, increasing size and market rigidities led the city to seek a privilege similar to that granted to Messina in 1160, which enabled Palermo to export grain freely from the whole of Frederick II's realm and in particular from Sicily and Calabria.[217]

By the early fourteenth century, as war and narrower political and administrative functions began to reduce the city's size, Palermo started to look closer to home for grain. Its customary suppliers were Termini and Castellammare.[218] In 1316, after the latter

212 Pispisa, *Messina*, pp. 17–18, 103.
213 *Ibid.*, p. 21 and n. 61; Martino, 'Valle di Milazzo'. See also above, n. 212.
214 Giardina ed., *Capitoli*, nos. 40 (1357), 41 (1363).
215 La Lumia ed., *Estratti*, p. 31 (c.1365); RC 12, fos. 27rv (1369), 51v–2 (1370); RC 6, fos. 132rv, 150v–1v (1370?); RC 8, fos. 68rv, 68v–9 (1370); Bresc, 'The "secrezia" and the royal patrimony in Malta: 1240–1450', p. 132 n. 31 (1371).
216 La Lumia ed., *Estratti*, p. 150 (1377).
217 De Vio ed., *Privilegia*, pp. 10–11.
218 Pollacci Nuccio and Gnoffo, *Due registri*, p. 9 (1311).

had been recovered from the Angevins with Palermo's help, the king granted a monopoly on grain sent to Castellammare, later extended to include Termini.[219] While the privileges were violated on several occasions, they seem never to have completely lapsed.[220] Market segmentation after 1350 meant for Palermo what it did for Messina: restricted opportunities for supply, and greater insecurity in obtaining basic foodstuffs from available sources. The division of Sicily into rival spheres of interest, however, favoured Palermo more than Messina, because Palermo was ruled by the Chiaromonte who also controlled some of the main grain-growing areas in western Sicily.[221]

Conditions changed quite noticeably as a result of the territorial reunification after the Aragonese conquest of 1392–8. The new Iberian regime's first major parliamentary meeting, held in 1398, saw the crown regaining control over the grain trade, which was vital for financial and political reasons.[222] Martino also passed the important decree that no export tax be paid on grain and other victuals traded by sea within Sicily, extending Messina's privilege to the whole island.[223] This decree, aimed at reasserting royal authority over the formerly independent barons, was in fact probably as important as political reunification for establishing a more integrated regional grain market.

No very major changes in the institutions regulating the grain market occurred after 1398. In the early 1430s, Alfonso first tried to stop local bans on grain exports by restricting the amount that could be withheld to domestic needs and to an additional *salma* of grain per hearth.[224] Forestalling was forbidden,[225] and local tolls were abolished.[226] In 1450–1, during a severe dearth, more ordinances

[219] De Vio ed., *Privilegia*, pp. 68–9 (1316), 90–2 (1326). See also Mirto, 'Petrus Secundus', App. 2, doc. 6 (1327), correcting De Vio ed., *Privilegia*, pp. 166–7 (1342).

[220] *Ibid.*, pp. 135 (1332), 147–8 (1336); Savagnone, 'Capitoli inediti', p. 101 (1348); Li Gotti, *Volgare nostro siculo*, pp. 41–4 (1349).

[221] *Ibid.*, pp. 66–70 (1351).

[222] Testa ed., *Capitula*, I, p. 145 (1398).

[223] *Ibid.*, I, p. 155 (1395?).

[224] *Ibid.*, I, pp. 215–16 (1433); see F. P. Di Blasi and A. Di Blasi eds., *Pragmaticae sanctiones Regni Siciliae quas iussu Ferdinandi III Borboni*, I, pp. 47–57 (1434). See also (for the *Camera reginale*) CS 1, fo.178rv (1431); CS 3, fo. 132v (1439). Similar provisions were passed in 1452 (Del Treppo, *Mercanti catalani*, p. 604).

[225] RC 75, fo. 146rv (1432); Testa ed., *Capitula*, I, p. 216 (1433).

[226] In Noto (RC 75, fos. 363–4, 1440).

were passed forbidding all trade bans in favour of producers.[227] Free trade was upheld again a few decades later.[228] But although such intervention may have helped improve domestic trade conditions, it was not the main cause of commercial integration. As we shall see in greater detail below, in fact, regional market integration increased sharply only *after* Alfonso's death in 1458.

The impression provided by the first type of documentary record, that market integration proceeded fairly slowly and fitfully until the mid-fifteenth century, is supported by our second source of evidence, namely reports of harvest and supply deficiencies or overstocking. I have collected information for twenty-six years in the fourteenth century, and sixty-two years in the fifteenth; for the remaining years no evidence is available, and one may assume that they were, by and large, years of normal supply. Evidence for the fourteenth century is scarcer and tends to over-report dearth compared to good harvests, because all the royal administrative documents relating to the grain trade are lost, whereas local reports and chronicles which emphasize distress have survived. In the fourteenth century, there were fifteen years of local deficiency, eight of general scarcity (six of them before 1350); above-average harvests were reported on only three occasions. In the fifteenth century, twenty-five years returned above-average harvests, twenty-three witnessed general scarcity (sixteen of them were years in which exports were temporarily or permanently closed, which may indicate a more serious crisis), and in eighteen years one or more individual localities reported deficiencies.[229]

---

[227] CR 31, fos. 447–8, 453–4; RC 101, fos. 252–3 (passed on 28 September 1450 but only executed on 17 July 1456); RC 85, fos. 306–7v (1451): 'Quam ex frugum aliorumque victualium habundancia tamquam fons et fluvius decurrens nostrum Trinacrie regnum alia mundi climata et regiones stereles et fame quasi extintas alimentis priscis temporibus reparavit et egentes mirum in modico auxilio recreavit'; CR 31, fos. 39–41, 52 (1451); RC 101, fos. 252–3 (1456). See also C 2863, fo. 86rv (1449), and C 2871, fos. 118–19 (1452) for government intervention in local markets.

[228] CR 50, fo. 4, and TRP Atti 28, fo. 203rv (1469).

[229] Good harvests: 1336, 1383, 1388, 1404, 1405, 1407, 1408, 1416, 1417, 1422, 1423, 1427, 1439, 1444, 1445, 1447, 1450, 1461, 1465, 1478, 1479, 1480, 1481, 1482, 1486, 1491, 1492, 1498. General crises (years when ports were closed are marked with an *): 1312, 1322, 1323, 1324, 1340*, 1352, 1375, 1397, 1398, 1400, 1404*, 1413*, 1426*, 1430*, 1431*, 1432*, 1434*, 1435, 1437*, 1438*, 1440*, 1442*, 1449*, 1452*, 1455, 1456*, 1464, 1468, 1469, 1473*, 1483, 1485*. Local crises: 1313, 1316, 1326, 1329, 1335, 1339, 1347, 1349, 1350, 1354, 1355, 1357, 1373, 1374, 1393, 1401, 1404, 1412, 1414, 1417, 1420, 1425, 1426, 1435, 1437, 1441, 1462, 1468, 1472, 1476, 1493, 1494, 1497.

What do these figures tell us? First, the proportion of reports of *local* to reports of *general* crises declined continuously, from 1.67:1 before 1400, to 0.79:1 in 1400–49, to 0.78:1 after 1450. Second, in the fifteenth century, the proportion of reportedly good or bad general harvests declined by roughly thirty per cent after 1450 (thirteen good, fourteen bad in 1400–49; twelve good, nine bad in 1450–99), but reports of lesser, local crises declined by nearly forty per cent (eleven before, seven after 1450). The declining incidence of *local* supply crises during the fifteenth century suggests a steady and accelerating improvement of local distribution structures, and also suggests that political reunification under the Aragonese was a major but far from unique factor for increasing commercial integration. This pattern of gradual improvement contrasts, however, with the pattern of *general* crises, whose number remained stable from 1300 to 1450 and only decreased thereafter, although then rather rapidly. This second pattern accords better with evidence from prices, discussed below, that also shows a marked improvement in commercial integration between different parts of the island after 1450.

General harvest failures in poor agrarian economies are usually blamed on bad weather, and climatic factors are sometimes invoked to explain the fourteenth-century crisis. The problem with this kind of explanation is that it is nearly impossible to test for medieval Europe,[230] and that it assumes a subsistence economy unable to cope with output fluctuations. This assumption underestimates even the simplest economy's capacity to 'use storage to buffer food consumption from output fluctuations'[231] or to resort to outside trade, and at higher levels of development to promote forms of arbitrage and markets for future grain delivery. In fact, not only did all these forms of insurance against risk and output fluctuations exist in Sicily from the early fourteenth century at least, but there is also evidence that they improved considerably during the fifteenth century and especially after the 1450s.

First, grain was stored either in open-air warehouses (in towns, for seasonal consumption) or in ground silos (near ports or outside towns, for periods of up to three years). The latter preserved grain

---

[230] See, for example, J. de Vries, 'Measuring the impact of climate on history: the search for appropriate methodologies'.

[231] M. Ravallion, *Markets and famines*, p. 1; S. Fenoaltea, 'Risk, transaction costs, and the organization of medieval agriculture', 136–41.

most effectively, and were therefore used to carry over surpluses from one year to the next.[232] The number of silos increased first after 1350 as a result of the disruption of trade, and again during the fifteenth century in response to rising domestic and external trade. In the early sixteenth century, state-owned silos appeared for the first time.[233] Second, during the fifteenth century, the government began increasingly to arbitrate between rival claims in the grain market, introducing first local and then regional 'searches' (*cerche*) to establish the level of grain supplies, and allowing the surplus to be sold for domestic consumption or abroad.[234] Finally, a sophisticated agricultural credit market developed, based on the anticipated future price of grain. In *contratti alla meta*, producers were advanced capital at an agreed price per *salma* of wheat, which price (*meta*) was set after the following harvest. This credit market began to develop in the early fifteenth century and was legally sanctioned in 1451.[235] A year later, Alfonso ordered that the *maestro portulano* (the main official in charge of grain exports) or one of his officers arbitrate between merchants and *massari* in setting the *meta*, but this was still only a temporary measure.[236] Although the *meta* was normally set by local communities and was susceptible to collusion[237] and costly bargaining (for the *meta* affected consumers also), the system reduced uncertainty and helped stabilize production, prices and consumption over time.

While the impact of these innovations on consumption fluctuations is hard to measure, there are two good *a priori* reasons to believe that the number of *general* subsistence crises declined after 1450 because of social and institutional, rather than climatic, changes. First, this assumption introduces an intermediate link between output and consumption, whereas climatic models posit a direct correlation; it therefore adopts a more complex and less

[232] This function emerges very clearly from a pragmatic sanction of 26 February 1452, whereby Alfonso forbade storing grain for over a year during supply crises (Del Treppo, *Mercanti catalani*, p. 604). Sicilian storage systems appear to have been more developed than in medieval England; see J. Komlos and R. Landes, 'Anachronistic economics: grain storage in medieval England'.
[233] Bresc, 'Fosses à grain en Sicile (XIIème-XVème siècles)', p. 116.
[234] *UM*, pp. 744–6.
[235] Testa ed., *Capitula*, I, pp. 372–3.
[236] Del Treppo, *Mercanti catalani*, p. 604.
[237] In 1460, the *popolo* of Catania complained that *massari* and merchants colluded in the town council to set the *mete* too high (C 3476, fos. 71v–82).

deterministic view of the correlation itself. Secondly, it recognizes the primary impact of institutions on market structures and of market structures on agricultural production in the medieval economy. The fact that general crises seem to have diminished in much, but not all, of western Europe at the same time suggests that one must search for a common cause behind the decline not in climatic change (which would have been general), but in the growth during the fifteenth century of more effective state and local administrations (which varied across societies).[238]

How serious were provisioning problems in late medieval Sicily? The evidence suggests that there was a remarkably low incidence of dearth for either climatic or institutional causes. First, in the course of one and a half centuries (data for 1350–99 are insufficient) the number of years of serious deficiency, when exports were forbidden, was low: one (possibly) in 1300–49, eight in 1400–49 and three in 1450–99. In England, by comparison, the number of deficient years in the same period was considerably higher: ten years of deficiency in 1300–49, eleven years in 1400–49, and only five in 1450–99.[239]

Second, alleged deficiencies were often not very serious, since scarcity was usually solved simply by closing exports temporarily or, in the most severe cases, for the whole agricultural year. A typical year was 1472–3, when the lack of spring rain raised fears that the harvest would be damaged; by April 1473, the government had decided to forbid further exports to ensure sufficient supplies in the autumn.[240]

Third, the evidence of outright famine is negligible, and food riots were normally sparked off by supply inefficiencies and entitle-

---

[238] For northern Europe in this period see, for example, Dyer, *Standards of living*, chapter 10; H. Neveux, *Vie et déclin d'une structure économique. Les grains du Cambrésis fin du XIVe–début du XVIIe siècle*, p. 106; M.-J. Tits-Dieuaide, *La formation des prix céréaliers en Brabant et en Flandre au XVe siècle*, pp. 251–60. In fifteenth-century Florence, on the other hand, the number of supply crises (defined as a price increase of twenty-five per cent or more over the previous year) remained stable (twelve in 1400–49, eleven in 1450–99) (R. Goldthwaite, 'I prezzi del grano a Firenze dal XIV al XVI secolo', 33–4; my calculations).

[239] Dyer, *Standards of living*, pp. 262–3 (including barley harvests before 1400). Figures for England refer to *national* crises, and probably underestimate the number of *regional* crises; strictly speaking, it is the latter that one should be comparing with the Sicilian data.

[240] CR 55, fo. 67.

ment crises, as in Catania in 1356 and Palermo in 1450,[241] rather than by actual harvest deficiencies.[242] Weak urban intervention during 'crises' indicates, besides a lack of urban powers and the opposition of local producers, that supply was sufficient and distribution was fairly efficient.[243]

Finally, despite a near doubling of the population between 1450 and 1500, and an average increase in grain exports from three to five per cent in c.1400 to thirteen to fifteen per cent in c.1500 of domestic output (see chapter 6), scarcity after 1450 actually diminished. The probability of a disastrous year for the whole island in this period was less than one in fifteen.

Our third source of information on the structure of the regional grain market supports similar conclusions. The information is drawn from two fifteenth-century series of official grain prices (*mete*) set each September in Palermo and Catania (Table 3.4). *Mete* were enforced rather than actual market prices, but, as far as can be ascertained, correlation between the two seems close.[244] In any case, if a discrepancy between the two existed, on average it was probably stable; *mete* should therefore reflect real price *trends* quite accurately.

Although figures are far from complete, particularly for the first half of the century, price trends can be followed from about 1410–19. From 1420–9 to 1460–9 grain prices in Palermo were stable or declined relative to the base index period of 1420–9. During the 1470s, prices rose sharply – by fifty per cent over the previous decade and by more than thirty per cent compared to 1420–9 – but soon stabilized again. Palermo's prices, however, did not apply to the rest of Sicily, as trends in Catania show. There the price nadir seems to have been reached during 1420–9, although figures for this period are too few to be entirely reliable. On the other hand, this conclusion does correspond to other clues that the 1420s and 1430s were periods of economic hardship (see chapter 5). Thereafter

[241] For Catania see da Piazza, *Cronaca*, I, chapter 116; for Palermo see below, n. 245. On entitlement crises see A. Sen, *Poverty and famines. An essay on entitlement and deprivation*; Ravallion, *Markets and famines*, chapters 1–2; L. A. Tilly, 'Food entitlement, famine, and conflict'.

[242] *UM*, p. 85; Dyer, *Standards of living*, p. 271.

[243] *UM*, pp. 744–7. For local trade bans see PR 24, fo. 508 (Palermo, 1421); PR 27, fos. 135v–7 (Calascibetta, 1426); C 2871, fos. 118–19 (Catania, 1452); Flandina ed., *Statuti ordinamenti e capitoli della città di Polizzi*, p. 280 (Polizzi, 1468); RC 137, fos. 60v (Palazzolo, 1476), 159rv (Mistretta, 1476).

[244] Ventura, *Edilizia urbanistica*, p. 146 n. 18.

grain prices rose steadily until the 1440s, and after a slight dip continued to rise until the end of the century. Comparison between the two price indices raises two interesting points. In the first place, it shows that for a long time economic conditions in Palermo could not be taken to apply to other parts of Sicily, at least not without careful consideration. Palermo was the fastest-growing city in Sicily after the mid-fifteenth century, yet the price its inhabitants paid for grain was far more stable than that of Catania, whose population rose much more slowly in the same period. The reason for this was Palermo's more efficient structure of supply, rather than greater proximity to more abundant provision, for the plain of Catania was one of the most fertile and productive grain areas in Sicily, and grain prices were usually lower there than in Palermo (one *salma* of grain in Catania was twenty-five per cent larger than in Palermo). In other words, institutional factors explain why, despite the volume of supply being on average larger in Catania, prices varied far less in Palermo.

In 1450–9, average prices actually dropped in Palermo, while in Catania they rose by seventeen per cent, perhaps as a result of increasing demand and a spate of unsuccessful harvests. By contrast, lower prices in Palermo suggest that the popular uprising of 1450, sparked off by the viceroy's failure to adequately supply the city,[245] had the effect of drawing special attention to the problem for a couple of decades thereafter. Palermo's relatively stable prices, which seem to bear a fairly weak relation to long-term changes in demand, imply that the city was supplied on unusually favourable terms, presumably because of its unique political and economic role. These unusual conditions also explain the fast growth of the population, from 3,000 to 6,500 hearths between 1464 and 1501.

The second point to be made by comparing the two price series, however, slightly modifies the first one, of Palermo's unusual institutional status. If we analyse price trends by half-century periods, we observe that while before 1450 prices in Palermo and Catania are virtually uncorrelated ($r = 0.08$), the coefficient of correlation after 1450 increases to a high 0.82. Whereas the increase may be overestimated because of the lack of data for the first half of the century,

[245] Fazello, *Due deche*, pp. 880–1; Pollacci Nuccio, 'Della sollevazione occorsa in Palermo l'anno 1450. Documenti ricavati dallo Archivio generale del Comune di Palermo'; A. Ryder, *Alfonso the Magnanimous King of Aragon, Naples, and Sicily 1396–1458*, pp. 380–1.

Table 3.4 *Official grain prices (*mete*) in Palermo and Catania, 1400–1499 (*tarì/salma*)*

	1400–9	1410–19	1420–9	1430–9	1440–9
Palermo	7.0 (77.8)	13.0 (144.4)	9.0 (100.0)	6.0 (66.7)	8.5 (94.4)
Catania	—	9.6 (122.5)	7.8 (100.0)	10.0 (127.7)	9.0 (114.9)

	1450–9	1460–9	1470–9	1480–9	1490–9
Palermo	7.5 (83.3)	8.0 (88.9)	12.0 (133.3)	11.1 (123.3)	12.2 (135.6)
Catania	10.5 (134.1)	11.6 (148.1)	12.0 (153.3)	13.3 (170.2)	13.5 (172.4)

Sources: Cancila, 'Le mete dei cereali'; Petino, *Aspetti e momenti.*
Index numbers in ( ).

there is little doubt that a marked increase in correlation did occur. Thus, the increasing integration of the Sicilian grain market after 1450 that is attested to by evidence of dearth, is confirmed by decreasing price variation in the markets of Palermo and Catania. This in turn suggests that Palermo's institutional advantages or peculiarities tended in the course of the fifteenth century to decline.

We can probably take Catania prices as portraying more general trends because institutional and other forces were less unusual than in Palermo. Catania was in the middle-upper range of urban centres; it could control its district quite closely, on occasion by blocking all exports to other parts of Sicily or abroad; it might also, in times of particular need, resort to Calabria or the Puglie for further supplies. In all these features it resembled other medium-sized towns. By contrast, Palermo was the only city besides Messina that could wield enough political power to run counter, at least in the medium-term, to forces of supply and demand. On the other hand, Catania was better supplied from its hinterland than many other towns. In fact, the remarkably high correlation between grain prices in Palermo and Catania after the 1450s may not in fact wholly accurately express *regional* market integration, for integration was more rapid and intense along the coastline than in the interior.

The three kinds of evidence I have used to examine the structure of the late medieval grain market produce remarkably concordant conclusions. Commercial integration did not proceed smoothly and incrementally. In the late thirteenth and early fourteenth centuries, evidence for trade and local dearth suggests that markets were localized and fragmented. After 1282 Messina, which depended to a considerable degree on supra-local supplies, began to buy a larger proportion of its food grains on the Sicilian market, but the city's demand was too small to have a serious impact on regional market structures as a whole. Political fragmentation after the mid-fourteenth century intensified the lack of commercial integration.

By contrast, after the 1390s the Aragonese regime established two prerequisites of integration, namely territorial unity and tax-free trade within Sicily itself. Nonetheless, although the steady decline of localized dearth shows that such institutional changes did help improve Sicily's grain supply networks during the fifteenth century, before the 1450s improvements were fairly slow. The rapid decline in *both* local and general harvest crises after the mid-fifteenth century is particularly striking, because it coincides precisely with a strong demographic upturn. The structure of supply seems to have improved after 1450 for two main reasons. On the one hand, intra-regional *demand* rose very sharply, as val Demone's expanding population turned increasingly towards central and western Sicilian grain supplies instead of returning to pre-1282 conditions when much of its grain had come from the southern mainland. Increasing domestic trade under the effect of demographic growth can be measured from the fact that the proportion of domestic grain shipments relative to total exports rose considerably more (from one to two per cent in 1407–8 to sixty per cent in the 1520s),[246] than did total grain exports relative to total output (from five per cent in *c*.1400 to thirteen to fifteen per cent in *c*.1500). On the other hand, as we saw, the regularity and stability of *production* also improved considerably, as the declining number of general harvest crises

---

[246] In 1407–8, shipments *infra Regnum*, as they were called, accounted for only two per cent of total exports; but this very low figure may be partly due to under-registration (Cancila, *Baroni e popolo nella Sicilia del grano*, p. 15). In 1460–1, after a good harvest, trade *infra Regnum* accounted for 23.3 per cent of total exports (calculations from a transcript of TRP n.p.717 provided by Henri Bresc). Cancila, *Baroni e popolo*, pp. 19–20 argues that in 1450–70, one third of total shipments were *infra Regnum*, but this estimate may be based on assumptions valid only for later periods. In 1500–1, trade *infra Regnum* was twenty-five to thirty-five per cent of total shipments (Aymard, 'Le blé de Sicile, année 1500', pp. 83–4); for domestic trade in the 1520s see Cancila, *Impresa redditi*, p. 258, and Cancila, *Baroni e popolo*, p. 41.

shows. The sharp downturn in the number of bad harvests *despite* rapidly increasing domestic and foreign demand was apparently due to a number of innovations in grain production and storage.

We saw in chapter 2 that late medieval Sicily's rate of urbanization was consistently above thirty per cent. The data I have presented here suggest why this rate could be so high. Taken together with the small number of general harvest failures and the rapid response of producers to rising internal and foreign demand, the rate of urbanization reflects a productive and flexible agricultural system and increasingly efficient capital and product markets capable of shielding the population from outright hunger.

The question of urbanization leads us to the third strand of my analysis of market structures. Throughout the previous discussion I have assumed that institutional structures affected the distribution of resources between town and countryside and between towns themselves. So far we have examined these institutional structures in terms of regional *integration*. In this final section I turn to the effects of these institutions on the flow of resources *between* towns, and consequently on urban networks. I apply some recent developments in central place theory pioneered by Carol Smith, which analyse the effects of institutional power on the 'perfect' distribution of resources among settlements ('central places') posited by the original Lösch–Christaller theory.[247]

As applied here, the theory's main assumptions are as follows. Firstly, for the reasons set out in chapter 2, the geographical framework considered is that of Sicily, subdivided internally along the lines of the three *valli*. (While regional in- or out-migration is not excluded, it is considered subsidiary in determining the size and distribution of a region's population.) Secondly, since both institutional and demographic changes occur quite slowly, their interaction must be examined over a long time-span. Thirdly, population distribution among central places is assumed to reflect the distribution of resources; the wealthier the centre, the larger its population; therefore population distribution patterns will adapt to changes in a centre's access to economic and administrative resources. This third assumption relies on two additional ones: the

---

[247] C. A. Smith, 'Regional economic systems: linking geographical models and socioeconomic problems', with references; A. Lösch, *The economics of location*; W. Christaller, *Central places in southern Germany*.

freedom of movement of persons; and the existence of average regional levels of consumption. Since, in our period, serfdom in Sicily had all but disappeared and peasant allodial property was fairly marginal except in the north-east, institutional constraints on, and costs of, individual mobility were weak. High individual mobiity, and Sicily's fairly strong economic integration, also suggests that information about opportunities outside the local community was not very difficult to obtain. The latter assumptions entail that if the volume of resources a settlement had access to changed, this change would affect in- and out-migration in such a way that average consumption of staple commodities would be the same as elsewhere in the region. In other words, a nearly landless peasant or wage-labourer would not deliberately live in conditions which could be improved by moving to a wealthier settlement.

The third assumption (that distribution of population reflects distribution of resources) enables the historian of pre-industrial societies to reconstruct from data which are often known (the size and distribution of urban populations) processes which are for the most part undocumented (the flow and distribution of administrative and economic resources within a region, that is, consumption). At the same time, one can assess the impact of institutional factors on the distribution of resources by comparing actual urban hierarchies to the original central place model. This predicts that 'perfect' competition between central places results in exact rank–size ordering (where the rank multiplied by the size of the central place is a constant number). Such an approach can be tested against, and integrated with, inferences drawn from qualitative material, such as laws or community petitions, of whose accuracy historians are often justifiably suspicious.

Central place hierarchies will be examined in two ways. First, I shall examine the rank–size distribution of the highest levels of the urban hierarchy, which is where the most significant effects of changes in institutional constraints on resource allocation can be perceived (see Table 3.5). Second, I shall analyse the distribution and hierarchies of *all* settlements in order to avoid the problem of defining an appropriate urban threshold (see Table 3.6).[248]

Messina and Palermo maintained metropolitan status throughout our period, but their regional functions changed considerably over

[248] See de Vries, *European urbanization 1500–1800*, pp. 89–95.

time (see Table 3.5). In the mid-to-late thirteenth century these cities, each with three to four times the population of the third largest town, were typical primate centres which monopolized and concentrated the resources of their tributary areas, leaving the latter relatively poorly endowed and serviced.[249] Palermo and Messina were in practice distinct political capitals whose influence extended in part to the southern mainland. The existence of two metropoles demonstrates the weak integration of the Sicilian marketplace at this time; the two cities grew for political and administrative, rather than economic, reasons and competed weakly for resources.

The political crisis provoked by the War of the Vespers and the civil war significantly modified the urban hierarchy. Palermo and Messina lost their status as the main political and administrative centres in southern Italy, while retaining certain political functions at the level of the *vallo*. The curtailment of the two metropoles' institutional advantages increased opportunities for integration within each *vallo*. Increased competition for resources is reflected in the more balanced distribution of population (the weaker hierarchy) between the main urban centres in the late fourteenth century.[250]

Val di Noto is striking for its *lack* of a city with stable metropolitan ranking before 1500. Terranova (with over 4,000 tax hearths) appeared in this guise in 1277, but by the late fourteenth century, Saracen attacks and the plague had reduced it to little more than a hamlet. Catania took its place during the latter half of the fourteenth century, but by the mid-fifteenth century it had been surpassed by Noto, itself possibly overtaken by Syracuse by 1478. Syracuse may have begun to establish metropolitan status by the end of the fifteenth century, but it was still closely followed by a large number of sizeable towns (Caltagirone, Piazza, Noto and perhaps Lentini with over 3,000 assessed hearths; Catania, Castrogiovanni and perhaps Mineo with over 2,000 assessed hearths), which suggests that its hegemony was very weak.

The explanation for this apparent urban entropy may lie, once

---

[249] Smith, 'Regional economic systems', pp. 30–2. Since Messina's region extended to the opposite side of the Straits, Table 3.6 does not reflect the precise rank–size distribution of settlements within Messina's orbit.
[250] *Ibid.*, pp. 28–30.

Table 3.5 *Frequency distributions of Sicilian communities, 1277–1497*

Tax hearths	1277 M	1277 N	1277 D	1374–6 M	1374–6 N[a]	1374–6 D[b]	1439 M	1439 N	1439 D
0+	14	12	31	16	18	—	11	14	53
200+	4	2	12	7	10	—	7	9	21
400+	1	2	12	5	3	—	3	5	4
600+	2	3	5	3	4	—	7	5	1
800+	1	1	5	2	2	—	2	—	2
1,000+	6	5	5	2	3	—	2	—	3
1,500+	4	4	1	1	2	—	2	5	—
2,000+	4	3	2	1	—	—	—	—	—
3,000+	2	—	—	—	1	—	1	—	1
4,000+	—	1	1	1	—	—	—	—	—
5,000+	2	—	—	—	—	—	—	—	—
10,000+	1	—	1	—	—	—	—	—	—
Total	41	33	75	38	43	—	35	38	85

Tax hearths	1464 M	1464 N	1464 D	1478 M	1478 N	1478 D	1497 M	1497 N	1497 D
0+	11	18	47	11	11	42	11	12	25
200+	6	2	15	9	6	19	5	7	23
400+	4	9	5	—	5	15	3	—	6
600+	1	2	2	6	4	2	3	7	6
800+	1	—	—	1	1	1	3	2	1
1,000+	4	4	1	5	3	2	1	1	—
1,500+	3	2	2	2	4	—	3	—	2
2,000+	3	2	—	3	5	2	5	3	1
3,000+	—	3	1	—	1	—	1	4	1
4,000+	1	—	—	—	1	—	—	—	—
5,000+	—	—	—	1	—	1	1	1	1
10,000+	—	—	—	—	—	—	—	—	—
Total	34	42	73	38	41	84	36	37	66

[a] Includes interpolations for Avola, Buscemi, Ferla, Adrano, Petraperzia, Giarratana and Francavilla, and an estimate for Catania.
[b] Insufficient data.
Sources: For 1277, Minieri Riccio, *Notizie storiche*; Beloch, *Bevölkerungsgeschichte Italiens*, p. 159; for 1374–6, Glénisson, 'Documenti dell'Archivio Vaticano', 249–60; Sella ed., *Rationes Decimarum Italiae. Sicilia*, pp. 123–36; for 1439, CR 851, fos. 597–608v; for 1464 and 1478, Trasselli, 'Ricerche su la popolazione', 213–71; for 1497, CR 78, fos. 43–6v.
M = val di Mazara; N = val di Noto; D = val Demone.

again, with political and institutional rather than purely economic factors. Val di Noto had no stable political or administrative capital. Terranova may have had this function in the latter half of the thirteenth century, but by the late fourteenth century it had been replaced by Catania. When Sicily was reunified after 1392, Catania's importance declined, but no substitute in val di Noto arose. Syracuse's pre-eminence seems to have been the result of its status as capital of the *Camera reginale*, but its political and even economic influence was restricted to the queen's lordship. There was thus little chance of it achieving the strategic and political importance of Messina and Palermo, or of extending its influence over the whole *vallo*.

Table 3.6 reports the coefficient of variation (c) around the mean community size for each *vallo*. The smaller the coefficient, the less hierarchical was the region's urban system (in other words, resources were distributed more equally among towns). The low value of the coefficient for val di Noto points to a relative lack of urban hierarchy in the area. Whereas in val di Mazara and val Demone hierarchy tended to increase in the course of the fifteenth century (the decline of (c) in 1478 may reflect an underestimate of the size of the larger communities), in val di Noto hierarchy seems to have lessened.

The generalized decline of this measure between the late thirteenth century and 1439 testifies to the considerable changes in urban patterns and market structures which occurred in this period. In particular it highlights the reorganization of sub-regional markets in the fourteenth and early fifteenth centuries following the loss of a primate centre in val di Mazara and val Demone. The slow rise of the coefficient during the fifteenth century, by contrast, suggests both a process of consolidation of the gains in urban and market organization and integration within *valli*, and a slow increase in the primate function of Messina and Palermo, particularly of the latter because of its reacquired status as capital.

Despite its increase during the fifteenth century, however, primacy was less extreme than during the late thirteenth century. This was partly because Sicily's political unity with the mainland had been broken, thereby reducing the potential range of attraction of both cities; but it was mainly the effect of the greater integration through specialization of the island's economy over the previous two centuries. In other words, during the later Middle Ages, a more

Table 3.6 *Settlement hierarchies by vallo, 1277–1497*

	1277			1374–6			1439			1464			1478			1497		
	M	N	D	M	Nᵃ	D	M	N	D	M	N	D	M	N	D	M	N	D
x̄	170.3	82.4	63.8	527.3	456.3	—	34.4	32.7	16.5	45.8	42.0	18.7	59.0	55.5	25.2	67.5	68.2	35.3
s	357.4	92.9	161.5	759.8	578.8	—	38.1	42.6	26.9	60.4	54.1	33.1	79.5	66.9	48.2	90.3	84.2	64.4
c	209.9	112.7	253.1	144.1	126.8	—	110.8	130.3	163.0	131.9	128.8	177.0	134.7	120.5	191.3	133.8	123.5	182.4

ᵃ Includes estimates for Avola, Buscemi, Ferla, Adrano, Petraperzia, Giarratana, Francavilla and Catania.

Sources: As for Table 3.5.

M = val di Mazara; N = val di Noto; D = val Demone; x̄ = mean size (hearths); s = standard deviation from the mean; c = coefficient of variation (100s/x). Note that s and x̄ are calculated on the basis of tax allocations, except for 1374–7, where figures refer to numbers of hearths.

integrated, regional urban *network* was being established. Under similar pressures from increasing economic specialization, parallel developments seem to have occurred in other parts of western Europe at the same time.[251] This process established the basis of the larger, supra-regional urban networks that Jan de Vries has identified for the period following 1500.[252]

We saw in chapter 2 that a feature distinguishing Sicily from, probably, most European regions was the rapid change in urban ranking between 1276 and 1501. I suggested that this instability could be traced to two main sources of individual mobility. The first was the general scarcity, except in val Demone, of peasant free property. The second was connected to the weakness of urban control over the countryside. Despite a strengthening of these powers after the mid-fourteenth century, towns were still usually incapable of ensuring the constant food supplies and the corporate monopolies which normally provided medieval European towns with their function and status; at least until the end of the fifteenth century, for example, guilds lacked territorial monopolies. Contrary to most other strongly urbanized regions in this period, grain producers (who coincided usually with the town élite) were interested in opposing local urban monopolies in order to profit most effectively from regional and foreign demand. Sicilian towns also drew little independent income from taxation, which by contrast was a crucial factor for the prosperity of northern communes; at best Sicilian towns could petition the crown for tax exemptions for immigrants. Individual mobility was increased not only by strong 'pull' factors, but also by 'push' factors like war (in the fourteenth century), or indebtedness, as the many moratoria on immigrant debts in the fifteenth century show (see Table 2.5).

Because of their relative institutional weakness and because of forces which upheld freedom in the grain and food markets, Sicilian towns tended to compete for human resources. Resource endowments usually prevailed over political privilege in determining a town's prosperity. Between 1300 and 1500, no single city dominated the rest or enjoyed an outstanding position on account of its institutional functions. Palermo, again the capital after the 1430s, expanded thanks largely to the presence of government and, after the

[251] See, for example, Nicholas, *Metamorphosis of a medieval city*; D. M. Palliser, 'Urban decay revisited', pp. 16–17.
[252] de Vries, *European urbanization*, pp. 253–7.

revolt of 1450, to its privileged food provisioning, but still had to regain full primacy by 1500. Messina, the second largest city, had long enjoyed provisioning privileges because of its vital strategic position on the Straits. Despite their ostensibly metropolitan economic function, however, Messina and Palermo did not wield the same powers of control and exploitation of the *contado* found in northern Italy, nor were they comparable to metropoles like London,[253] Paris,[254] Florence, Milan or Venice.[255]

The rapid changes in size and ranking of Sicilian towns indicate a more fluid and complex structure, characterized by three distinct but interlocking urban systems. In the course of the fifteenth century, areas of overlap, particularly in val di Noto, slowly expanded into a larger integrated region as a result of the general institutional framework provided by the state. Against the inherent protectionism of medieval urban policies, the monarchy ensured the territorial unity that enabled single urban and regional economies to develop in relatively unfettered conditions.[256]

CONCLUSIONS

In the introduction to this chapter I described regional specialization and integration as some of the most significant economic developments in western Europe after the Black Death. I suggested that what are perceived as the main effects of the Black Death, a relocation of labour at the territorial margin and a downwards redistribution of incomes, were insufficient in themselves to initiate significant and long-term economic growth. A third, crucial element for a region's long-term development was provided by institutional and political constraints on local and regional trade. I contrasted this model of economic integration with, on the one hand, current theories of late medieval economic contraction, and, on the other hand, with the theory of economic dualism, which excludes the operation of competitive markets and assumes institutional stasis or equilibrium.

253 F. J. Fisher, 'The development of the London food market, 1540–1640'; Wrigley, 'A simple model of London's importance in changing English society and economy, 1650–1750'; Everitt, 'The marketing'.
254 A. P. Usher, *The history of the grain trade in France 1400–1710*.
255 Ginatempo and Sandri, *L'Italia delle città*.
256 According to L. Gambi, 'I valori storici dei quadri ambientali', p. 55, southern Italian 'backwardness' arose from a *lack* of regional metropoles.

The actual measurement of integration and of its economic gains is 'embarrassingly difficult', as Ann Kussmaul has recently reminded us.[257] In this chapter I have used indirect evidence of commercial and demographic flows and of supply crises to infer changes in the degree of market integration, taking the latter to infer the extent of market competition and gains thereof. I have used evidence of major institutional innovations which reduced transaction costs in production and marketing to make two points.

Firstly, I argued against the stagnationist view of the late medieval economy that these institutional innovations – more and more effective excise reductions, agricultural credit markets and storage and distribution networks – most of which were introduced at the height of the demographic crisis after 1400 and were then extended after the demographic recovery in the mid-fifteenth century, were a response to pressures from a *more*, not a *less*, commercialized society than before the Black Death.

Secondly, by establishing the existence of considerable changes in market structures and integration, I have shown that the dualistic assumption of unchanging institutions and market structures is untenable. By examining the structure of urban networks and the response of grain producers to changes in demand, I have also suggested that in late medieval Sicily, the dualistic axiom of non-communicating and non-competitive markets did not apply. As far as *territorial* dualism between northern and southern Italy is concerned, it appears that the view that the institutional weakness of southern towns was a cause of economic backwardness is misplaced. In the context of an extensive royal demesne in which cost-reducing institutional innovations could be effectively enforced such as that of late medieval Sicily, urban weakness had considerable economic benefits for the country as a whole.

Both in the model of specialization and in the discussion of market institutions and the effects of politics on trade structures, I have emphasized that institutions were merely *enabling* factors. *All* the institutional features identified as being particularly favourable to economic development after the Black Death – weak urban

[257] A. Kussmaul, *A general view of the rural economy of England, 1538–1840*, p. 110, quoting F. Machlup, 'Conceptual and causal relationships in the theory of economic integration in the twentieth century'. Despite the technical difficulties involved, however, Machlup makes a powerful defence of the concept of integration itself.

monopolies, high rates of personal mobility, a large royal demesne, together with the physical advantages of long coasts and ease of sea transport – were in place well before the mid-fourteenth century. Despite this, as we saw, regional market integration before 1350 was extremely weak. Market integration was set in motion by 'real' forces, by the post-Black Death demographic crisis and by the social and economic dislocation the crisis caused.

To some extent, of course, the view I have just outlined is unrealistic, for it takes institutional structures before 1350 as entirely static, something which I have assumed on principle not to be the case. This view is partly a result of beginning my study in the late thirteenth century, and partly a deliberate choice, made to emphasize the different speed and scale of change after 1350 compared to the previous period. But once we adopted 1350 as a conventional year zero, once the first demographic shock had set the process of integration in motion, it is no longer possible to take institutions as given; it is then possible to identify the *reciprocal* links of causation between institutional and economic change.

Thus, demand for trade franchises and fairs was initially a response to the rising volume of regional trade, itself the effect of post-Black Death income redistribution and relocation of labour. For demand to be effective, however, a unified legal, administrative and political framework had to be in place. For half a century after 1350 this framework was lacking, and regional markets, already fairly weakly established, tended to disintegrate further. The reinstatement of a central government in the 1390s was thus crucial for subsequent economic integration and growth.

At the local level, urban control over the countryside increased after the mid-fourteenth century, partly as a result of more general political and economic changes which led the aristocracy and urban élite groups to occupy and strengthen administrative control to integrate their revenues. In the longer term, and in contrast with northern communes, however, control over the rural hinterland was primarily administrative rather than commercial. The reasons for this were twofold. On the one hand, agricultural producers (who constituted urban élite groups) had little interest – in the context of a politically unified regional economy with strong links with foreign markets – in preserving local prerogatives or monopolies over supply. Contrary to most medieval urban governments, Sicilian urban supply policies were more favourable to producers than consumers. On the other hand, the state was also directly interested in upholding free trade (at least for grain), since its main source of revenue from export taxes on agricultural products depended in part on low transport and transaction costs.

Had urban provisioning regularly caused great hardship, the need for social order would have prevailed over the profit motive; when supplies were scarce, urban administrations did not hesitate to impose trade bans. But conditions for free trade policies were very favourable, since Sicily had a highly productive agricultural system and a relatively efficient network of supply based on cheap transport by sea. In this context, an external shock – in our case, a rise in mass demand for non-staple products after the mid-fourteenth century because of the income redistribution caused by the Black Death – could initiate a process of self-sustained growth. Markets expanded under the influence of rising demand and increased agricultural productivity and, to a lesser extent, of state intervention. High agricultural productivity and powerful state and producer interests (the latter also in reaction to improved market conditions) reduced the need and pressures for strong provisioning policies. And high individual mobility together with weak urban control allowed for a more efficient allocation of resources.

By emphasizing improvements in market organization, however, I am not suggesting that there were not many powerful forces which slowed or even stifled those processes. At the lowest level, legally endorsed seigneurial or *de facto* individual monopolies restricted a locality's capacity to dispose of its products. We have already seen a number of examples of seigneurial monopolies; an instance of an individual monopoly is provided by a case in Taormina, a town near Messina which turned to near vine monoculture in the fifteenth century, where the only middleman abused his position in favour of his friends.[258] We also saw how free trade, even among the demesnial *università*, often conflicted with the state's financial needs and, in addition, with the interests of those to whom local fiscal revenues had been granted or farmed out. For this reason, toll exemptions were a politically more relevant concession, and therefore were more often refused, than fair franchises. Demesne communities or toll concessionaries might introduce new taxes on the wine trade, causing the local inhabitants or the surrounding importers to rise in

[258] RC 75, fos. 405–8 (1440).

protest.[259] Toll franchises were also restricted to the demesne, for the crown was unable to compel barons to respect its exemptions.[260] Only larger communities were given more extensive rights, but they were not always capable of backing their claims successfully.[261] More general constraints on market integration were technical (transport problems) or organizational (the slowness of improvements in a demand-led, low-productivity economy).

I suggested above that a major problem with the institutional approach I have adopted in this chapter is that any assessment of market integration is necessarily more evaluative than positive.[262] The institutional approach assumes that gains are to be had from lower transaction costs, but provides no scale on which these costs and gains can be measured. It also assumes, as both cause and effect of institutional change, that specialization and technological innovation will occur, but it makes no prediction as to the nature and rate of change, and therefore as to the aggregate gains in productivity and output that will result. In chapter 2, I took rates of population growth as indirect measures of these aggregate gains, and in this chapter I suggested ways in which Sicilian grain producers were able to cope after 1450 with high rates of domestic population growth and with rising foreign demand by improving credit and capital markets. But specialization and innovation were not restricted to cereal cultivation. In the following chapter I shall examine the changes in structures of production, in the degree of specialization and the technology, which sustained and were shaped by the institutional developments discussed above.

---

259 RC 41, fo. 175rv (1404); RC 42, fo. 98 (1404); CR 14, fos. 572–3 (1428); RC 66, fos. 86v–7v (1431); TRP Atti 58, fos. 163–4 (1500).
260 RC 19, fos. 134–5 (1393); RC 9, fo. 131rv (1375), and RC 25, fos. 23–4 (1396); RC 25, fos. 166v–7 (1396); Di Giovanni ed., *Capitoli di Alcamo*, p. 47 (1398); RC 66, fos. 294–6 (1432); C 2831, fo. 84rv (1438). In 1455, the count of Caltanissetta, Guglielmo Raimondo Moncada, was confirmed the *ius dohane* throughout his lands (C 2875, fos. 90v–1).
261 Palermo: De Vio ed., *Privilegia*, pp. 69–70 (1316), 86–7 (1325); Sciacca: CR 47, fo. 42rv, and RC 120, fos. 323v–4 (1468); Trapani: RC 154, fo. 131rv, and CR 67, fos. 71–1bis (1484); RC 157, fos. 48–9 (1485); RC 172, fos. 266v–8v (1489). See also RC 20, fo. 141v (1392); RC 54, fos. 408v–9, and L. Genuardi, 'Una raccolta di memoriali di re Alfonso il Magnanimo al viceré di Sicilia Nicola Speciale (1423–1428)', 158 (1423); CS 2, fo.151v (1435); RC 75, fos. 84v–5v (1439); C 2835, fos. 40–1 (1439); RC 74, fos. 390v–2v (1439); C 2844, fos. 140v–1 (1444); C 2860, fos. 61v–2 (1447); C 2877, fo. 47rv (1455); CR 68, fo. 72rv (1484); CR 67, fos. 103–3ter, and RC 154, fos. 450–4v (1485).
262 See above, n. 257.

4. *Sicily and its regions. Economic growth and specialization*

In the previous chapter, I argued that the most important result of the late medieval economic crisis was to increase regional integration and specialization, and I suggested that the relative intensity and success of specialization depended critically on the institutions which shaped the access of individuals to markets. A further point of my argument was that the demographic slump caused by the plague provided a strong initial shock, setting processes of specialization in motion that would otherwise not have occurred.

According to Bresc, Sicily was unaffected by these changes. Its small population escaped the Malthusian trap and avoided the problem of diminishing marginal returns to land; agricultural productivity did not decline before 1300 or increase as a result of population losses thereafter. In Bresc's view, the effect of demographic losses (which were in any case quite low) was purely negative, causing a decline of more labour-intensive crops such as cloth fibres and vineyards.[1]

The evidence presented in this chapter shows instead that events in Sicily differed in degree but not in kind from more general western European trends. Chapter 2 showed, by revising demographic estimates, that Sicily lost two thirds (rather than one quarter) of its population between the late thirteenth and early fifteenth centuries. Chapter 3 demonstrated in turn that major changes in the institutional structures of the home market occurred which increased opportunities for integration and specialization. We can now address the question of how, and to what degree, such opportunities were pursued.

[1] *UM*, pp. 21, 87.

AGRICULTURAL STAPLES

Grain

Ever since the Enlightenment criticized the *latifundia*, large-scale farming in Sicily and southern Italy has been given a major share of responsibility for the *Mezzogiorno*'s agricultural 'backwardness'. Latifundism is supposed to have bred many social and economic ills, including landlord absenteeism, low investment, lack of innovation, and peasant poverty and exploitation.[2] So far no convincing explanation exists, however, as to why such backward and inefficient property rights survived apparently unchanged for nearly a millennium.[3] It is *a priori* very unlikely that such an allegedly highly inefficient organization should have endured so long; empirical evidence confirms that this is so.

In fact, despite the use of seemingly 'archaic' tools (oxen and scratch ploughs), both yield ratios and production per hectare in Sicily up to the eighteenth century seem to have been equivalent or higher than in the most advanced northern European countries (England, Flanders, the Netherlands), and substantially better than in northern Italy or the Baltic regions.[4] Whatever Sicilian agriculture's failings during the eighteenth-century 'agricultural revolution' further north, it thus seems that one cannot project such failings unquestioningly onto previous centuries. This chapter suggests reasons why late medieval and early modern Sicilian agriculture achieved such high levels of productivity; I leave to the conclusions of this book speculations as to why agriculture appears subsequently to have stagnated.

The more persistent reasons for Sicily's high agricultural pro-

[2] See V. Giuffrida, 'Latifondi in Sicilia'; D. Mack Smith, 'The latifundia in modern Sicilian history'; G. Giorgetti, *Contadini e proprietari nell'Italia moderna. Rapporti di produzione e contratti agrari dal secolo XVI a oggi*, pp. 72–97, 165–79.

[3] Current explanations (in terms of exploitation, and so on) do not provide adequate theoretical foundations for individual landlord motivation. See below, n. 20 and chapter 8, n. 26.

[4] Aymard, 'Mesures et interprétations de la croissance. Rendements et productivité agricole dans l'Italie moderne'; C. Wilson and G. Parker eds., *An introduction to the sources of European economic history 1500–1800*, pp. 10–11, 85, 121, 197–8.

ductivity were threefold: technical, socio-institutional and organiz-ational. Regarding technology, it is commonly argued that climatic factors posed an insuperable bottleneck to growth for southern Italian or indeed 'Mediterranean' agriculture. Producers were com-pelled to use oxen rather than draught horses because the summers were too dry for barley and fodder crops.[5] This view, often con-trasted with an idealized image of northern European agriculture, rests on the belief that horses were adopted in northern Europe from the early Middle Ages and, in addition, that they were, under every circumstance, the more efficient draught and plough animal.[6] Neither assumption appears to be entirely correct. In medieval England, for example, horses were adopted very slowly: it took several centuries for them to supplant the ox as the commonest draught animal, and then in some regions only. Horses were adopted mainly after economic conditions had changed consider-ably as a result of the late medieval crisis. And in many parts of England, the nature of the soil and terrain gave oxen a premium over horses at least until the sixteenth century.

The northern European agricultural model is in any case inappli-cable to Sicily for climatic and technical reasons. Oxen are more practical for the kind of hilly or stony terrain present in most of Sicily; the only large Sicilian plain near Catania covers less than two per cent of the island. Much of the most fertile arable areas in central and western Sicily, moreover, have heavy, clayey soils to which horses are unsuited. In the later Middle Ages, due to rela-tively low population density and extensive land use, rough pasture (on which oxen fare better than horses) was easily available,[7] and increased after the mid-fourteenth century as the large number of animals used on *masserie* testifies. As a result, in Sicily oxen were cheaper than horses to buy and maintain. Horses cost double the price of oxen from the fifteenth until the end of the sixteenth century, after which prices became even more skewed.[8] The large

[5] Peri, *Villanaggio*, p. 133. For Cancila, *Baroni e popolo*, pp. 98–9, the use of oxen 'is one of the fundamental factors which blocked Sicilian and southern Italian agricultural development'.
[6] See Duby, *Rural economy*, pp. 110–11; Slicher van Bath, *Agrarian history*, pp. 63–4.
[7] Langdon, *Horses, oxen and technological innovation. The use of draught animals in English farming from 1066–1500*, pp. 159–60.
[8] Cancila, *Baroni e popolo*, p. 97.

number of draught animals on *masserie* which pastured on fallow land improved fertility.[9] Sicilian ploughs were light, so there was no need for great draught-power; conversely, deeper ploughing would have left the soil to bake during the summer drought.

A second advantage of Sicilian arable agriculture was socio-institutional, and consisted of the structure of property rights to land. Although by 1300 an active peasant land market was established,[10] peasant smallholding was not very extensive except in val Demone, where the size of the arable was restricted by environmental factors. An overwhelming proportion of arable land was therefore under 'feudal' lordship, both lay and ecclesiastic.[11] This situation was not, however, an insuperable obstacle to agricultural development. From the late thirteenth century, the feudal monopoly over land began to break down. The *de facto* liberalization of the feudal land market originated with the law *Volentes*, promulgated by Federico III in 1296, which legalized the sale of whole fiefs to individuals of 'equal or greater dignity' than the seller.[12] The actual effect of this law – particularly from the mid-fourteenth century, and increasingly during the fifteenth – was to accelerate the circulation and fragmentation of 'feudal' land, at first only among the aristocracy, but increasingly also among urban nobility, merchants and high government officials. In practice, the only barrier to entry into this virtually free land market was set by the availability of capital, since fiefs were expensive and (for reasons of economic efficiency and prestige) were usually not broken up for sale.[13] Non-aristocrats, however, traded mostly in uninhabited, purely agricultural fiefs (see chapter 7).

The third, organizational advantage of Sicilian commercial arable agriculture came from the fact that the high financial barrier to entry into the land market made it easier to organize arable land into very large estates. From the late thirteenth century, fiefs began

---

[9] See below, n. 24.
[10] See, for example, A. Sparti ed., *Il registro del notaio ericino Giovanni Maiorana (1297–1300)*, nos. 2, 4, 5, 7, 11, 12, 13, 15, throughout.
[11] Cancila, 'Distribuzione e gestione della terra nella Sicilia moderna', pp. 153–78.
[12] Interpretations of this law differ. See Gregorio, *Considerazioni*, III, pp. 323ff.; D'Alessandro, *Politica e società*, pp. 56–7; E. Mazzarese Fardella, *I feudi comitali di Sicilia dai Normanni agli Aragonesi*, pp. 66–8; Mineo, 'Forme di successione familiare e di trasmissione patrimoniale nella Sicilia aragonese (secoli XIV–XV)', chapter 3.
[13] Cancila, 'Distribuzione e gestione', p. 158.

to be parcelled out as farms (*masserie*) of fifteen to forty hectares.[14] As we shall see below, the size of the *masserie* seems to have been the result of bargaining between the landlord and the *massaro* based on criteria of commercial profitability. *Masserie*, which were specialized and relatively capital-intensive enterprises, benefited, on the one hand, from the returns to scale associated with extensive farming: higher capital investments because of the indivisiblity of fixed capital (plough and harvesting teams), specialization of tasks, economies in the bulk purchase of variable inputs and, especially, of bulk transport and sale of output. On the other hand, *masserie* were too small to incur most of the diseconomies associated with extensive farming, namely high management and supervision costs, and a limited grasp of ecological conditions over large areas. Management and supervision costs were further reduced by the diffusion during the fifteenth century of leases of *masserie* to *gabelloti*.[15] These were intermediary entrepreneurs who supplied working capital and were responsible for employing and supervising wage labour on the farm, or for sub-leasing to peasants lacking working capital. Finally, *masserie* developed most in the west, centre and south of Sicily, where ecological and geographical characteristics were more homogeneous, a fact which also lowered the potential costs of favouring extensive over intensive use of land and labour.

It could be argued that *masserie* raised average social production costs, because such comparatively capital-intensive, specialized enterprises, which used underdeveloped technology and operated in primitive credit markets, faced greater risks of default. However, *masserie* emerged and spread in the long period of low rents and stagnant domestic and foreign demand after 1350,[16] when tenants held a very strong bargaining position. This implies that *massari* perceived distinct advantages in their arrangement; alternative contracts (in particular emphyteusis) were available which provided tenants with greater long-term security.[17]

Solutions to reduce uncertainty and credit default were also adopted. During the late thirteenth century, a credit system had begun to emerge in which a lender advanced working capital (land, tools, oxen, grain seed and sometimes cash) to a *massaro* in ex-

---

[14] *UM*, pp. 115–16.
[15] *UM*, p. 111.
[16] *UM*, p. 125.
[17] Sorrenti, *Patrimonio fondiario*, pp. 248–74.

change for a share of the following harvest. Lenders seem to have been mostly Sicilians, possibly because risk of default was so high that capital was advanced only in situations where the lender knew the borrower's circumstances intimately and was able to enforce his claims easily.[18] We saw in chapter 3 that, during the first half of the fifteenth century, another, more sophisticated and impersonal credit market was established which did not, however, apparently entirely replace the previous one. In this new system, merchants advanced capital to producers, which was repaid with grain at a price (the *meta*) agreed upon after the following harvest; the *meta* embodied the rate of interest.

Both contemporaries and historians, who have stressed the *massaro*'s indebtedness towards foreign merchant capital, especially as a result of the credit system established in the fifteenth century, view debt as a form of bondage or exploitation.[19] There are two objections to this view. First, the terms of credit (the interest rate) embodied in the *meta* were set by negotiation between the merchants and the *massari*, making it inherently implausible that a 'debt trap' or debt bondage would emerge and perpetuate itself indefinitely.[20] Second, one must view the credit market as emerging in response to, rather than being the cause of, the risk of default by producers. In the long run, a credit market based on anticipated future prices tended to *reduce* such risks by reducing price fluctuations and by allowing producers to respond more flexibly to market conditions, as apparently confirmed by the declining incidence of dearth and overproduction during the fifteenth century discussed in chapter 3.

As the discussion of *masserie* has suggested, Sicilian arable agriculture did not benefit merely from starting advantages. Productivity increased also over time. The high cost of labour caused by the demographic crisis led to the adoption of labour-saving innovations. The highest farm wages increased from 60 *tarì* before 1355

---

[18] Abulafia, 'Il commercio del grano siciliano nel tardo Duecento', pp. 10–11.
[19] *UM*, pp. 108–12; below, chapter 6.
[20] K. Basu, *The less developed economy. A critique of contemporary theory*, pp. 116–19, 137, shows that a 'debt trap' can exist only where the individual lender (landlord) possesses the power to enforce permanent indebtedness by changing the terms of the loan (by raising interest rates, by lowering the tenant's share of output, by setting arbitrary fines, and so on). In Sicily, these conditions seem to be closer to the situation prevailing in the late thirteenth and fourteenth century than to the more impersonal credit market that emerged after 1400.

to 120 *tarì* in 1355–75, and by the turn of the century they had increased further to 160 *tarì*. Maximum farm wages then remained stable until the 1450s. The wages of unspecialized labour increased somewhat less.[21] Commercial agriculture near Palermo faced its worst crisis in 1355–80; as a result, the average size of a *masseria* dropped by nearly sixty per cent. After 1380, average farm sizes increased, but farms were still smaller in the mid-fifteenth century than before 1350.[22] Difficulties in labour supply were still forcing landlords to offer improved conditions to tenants during the early fifteenth century.[23]

Harvesters began to organize into teams doing the rounds among an area's *masserie*.[24] In eastern Sicily, the use of four-wheeled wagons to transport agricultural produce and timber spread during the fifteenth century.[25] The transformation of arable into pasture, which allowed for longer periods of fallow[26] and for a higher ratio of plough animals to land,[27] increased the productivity of land. One can also assume that labour productivity rose in the fifteenth century due to increasing specialization and declining transaction costs. These improvements had two main effects. On the one hand, a larger proportion of the population could be employed part or full time in manufacture and non-staple agricultural production, as we shall see in greater detail shortly. On the other hand, higher productivity enabled the proportion of domestic grain output exported overseas to triple, from about five to about thirteen to fifteen per cent between 1450 and 1500, reaching a level that was possibly unique for medieval and early modern Europe. I examine this second issue in greater detail in chapter 6.

---

[21] Due to currency devaluation, wages expressed in silver increased no more than sixty to seventy per cent in the period 1350–1415. *UM*, p. 121; D'Angelo, 'Il corso della moneta siciliana nel Medioevo', 19–20.

[22] *UM*, p. 115, Table 13.

[23] *UM*, pp. 111, 113.

[24] *UM*, pp. 116–17, 120, 126, 128–30, 880. In the early sixteenth century, the average ox:seed ratio was 1:2.3hl (Cancila, *Baroni e popolo*, p. 98); assuming a traditional sowing density (1.58hl per ha), livestock density was 1:1.45 ha of sown arable. On the improving balance between arable and pasture in southern Italy see Del Treppo, 'Agricoltura e transumanza in Puglia nei secoli XIII–XVI: conflitto o integrazione?'.

[25] NM 6B, fo. 388rv (1469); NC 14926, fos. 394v–5, 420rv, 473 (1500). For carts in western Sicily see *UM*, pp. 117, 356, 357.

[26] According to *UM*, p. 119, fallow ploughing intensified near Palermo after 1350.

[27] See above, n. 24.

Animal husbandry

A well-known consequence of the late medieval crisis was the expansion of pasture and animal husbandry at the expense of arable land. Animal husbandry was one of the most rewarding forms of medieval investment,[28] particularly at a time when vast tracts of land were being abandoned and agricultural wages were rising fast. In Italy, these changes led to the transformation of the Roman Campagna from a grain- into a livestock-exporting region, and to the creation of the *Dogana dei Paschi* and the *Dogana delle pecore* to regulate transhumance respectively in the Sienese Maremma and southern Italy.[29] A change in climate after the mid-fourteenth century towards wetter summers and colder winters may have contributed to these shifts.[30] From the late fifteenth century, however, population pressure reduced the extent of pastures, animal husbandry contracted, and average per capita meat consumption declined sharply.

Developments during the late fourteenth and fifteenth centuries are often seen in simple terms of a reallocation of land from arable to pasture due to lower population pressure. In this view, when population began to increase from the late fifteenth century, pasture was reconverted to arable and conditions returned to the *status quo ante*. By contrast, I suggest that the late medieval cycle of pastoral expansion had a significant *structural* impact on livestock-raising through a process of regional specialization. We saw above, however, Bresc's argument that late medieval Sicily witnessed no shift at all from arable to pasture. Before addressing the question of specialization, therefore, we must follow developments in animal husbandry as a whole.

While evidence that animal husbandry in Sicily expanded after the mid-fourteenth century is still not entirely conclusive, there are strong clues to this effect.[31] There is, first of all, clear proof that arable land was given up to pasture. I have already referred to the difficulties faced by arable farming in western Sicily after 1350, as a

---

[28] Hilton, 'Rent and capital formation in feudal society'.
[29] J. C. Maire-Vigueur, *Les pâturages de l'Eglise et la douane du bétail dans la Province du Patrimonio (XIV–XV siècle)*; G. Pinto, *La Toscana nel tardo medio evo. Ambiente, economia rurale, società*, pp. 53–64; D. Barsanti, *Allevamento e transumanza in Toscana. Pastori, bestiami e pascoli nei secoli XV–XIX*; J. A. Marino, *Pastoral economics in the Kingdom of Naples*.
[30] P. Alexandre, *Le climat en Europe au moyen âge*, pp. 786–9.
[31] Cancila, *Baroni e popolo*, pp. 13–14.

result of which the size of the average *masseria* fell by about two thirds. A large area around Palermo and Termini Imerese, to the north-east of the city, is also known to have shifted from agriculture to pasture in the late fourteenth and early fifteenth centuries.[32] Secondly, the shift to animal husbandry is reflected in the long-term decline in the price of cheese, meat and livestock during periods of political stability after 1350, most notably after *c*.1410 when transition to stable government was fully accomplished. The price of cheese in Palermo fell by about eighty per cent in real terms between 1370 and 1440; meat prices fell slightly less, thirty to fifty per cent in Palermo (1371–1440) and ten to thirty per cent in Catania (1417–50). By contrast, grain prices were stable or only slightly declining.[33]

Like elsewhere in Europe, meat and cheese consumption in Sicily after the mid-fourteenth century increased considerably.[34] Labourers were given large amounts of meat in part payment (2.8kg a week for butchers, 1.4kg a week for *zappaturi*, the orchard and vineyard workers of Palermo), but average consumption was considerably lower, about 20–22kg per person per year. This compares favourably with other Mediterranean regions in the same period.[35] By the early sixteenth century, however, meat consumption had fallen to pre-Black Death levels.[36] Towards 1415, in western Sicily shepherds received *c*. 48kg of cheese in part payment for their services,[37] but average consumption was probably similar to that of meat, *c*. 20kg per year.

[32] *UM*, pp. 106–7; Bresc and D'Angelo, 'Structure et évolution'.
[33] Aymard and Bresc, 'Nourritures et consommation en Sicile entre XIVe et XVIIIe siècle', 552; *UM*, pp. 160, 165; Giuffrida, 'Considerazioni sul consumo della carne a Palermo nei secoli XIV e XV', 590–2. Prices began to rise again after 1450 (Cancila, 'Contratti di conduzione, salari, prezzi nell'agricoltura trapanese del '400').
[34] Abel, *Strukturen und Krisen der spätmittelalterlichen Wirtschaft*, pp. 41–5; L. Stouff, *Ravitaillement et alimentation en Provence aux XIVe et XVe siècles*, pp. 169–74; G. Piccinni, 'Note sull'alimentazione medievale', 608; Dyer, *Standards of living*, pp. 158–9, 199–202.
[35] For Sicilian consumption see Giuffrida, 'Considerazioni', 594–5; Aymard and Bresc, 'Nourritures et consommation', 551; Ventura, *Edilizia urbanistica*, pp. 194–7; Cancila, *Baroni e popolo*, p. 29. For Tuscany see F. Leverotti, 'Il consumo della carne a Massa all'inizio del XV secolo. Prime considerazioni', 237; G. Nigro, *Gli uomini dell'Irco. Indagine sui consumi di carne nel basso Medioevo. Prato alla fine del 1300*, p. 58. For Provence see Stouff, *L'alimentation*, p. 190.
[36] Aymard and Bresc, 'Nourritures et consommation', 553; Cancila, *Baroni e popolo*, p. 99.
[37] *UM*, p. 163.

A third clue to the growth of animal husbandry after the mid-fourteenth century is the considerable expansion of cheese exports in the same period, the evidence for which is discussed in chapter 6. After 1350, in western Sicily a process of 'democratization' of animal husbandry also occurred, whereby an increasing number of people invested in the livestock market, and herds owned by the upper aristocracy, numbering thousands of sheep and cattle, slowly disappeared, to be replaced by a larger number of smaller herds. These changes cannot have been the result of political insecurity, for the higher nobility did not take up animal husbandry again after the civil war ended.[38] A more probable reason for magnate disinvestment was this group's increasing reliance on fiscal and jurisdictional revenues rather than income from the land (see chapter 7).

Although fourteenth-century evidence for these changes in the organization of animal husbandry mainly concerns western Sicily, later evidence for eastern Sicily leads to similar conclusions.[39] High demand and low production costs[40] made for wider profit margins for commercial herds (*mandre*) than for arable *masserie*,[41] and sustained strong upward social mobility among pastoral entrepreneurs.[42] Town élite groups in the interior, especially the petty aristocracy who owned little land or suffered from declining rents, invested heavily in animal husbandry[43] and were much involved in the export trade. A credit market similar to that for grain (*contratti alla meta*) developed for the pastoral sector; a herd's future product was sometimes bartered for foreign cloth or iron.[44]

Having established that livestock raising *did* expand in late medieval Sicily, we can now turn to the question of its territorial distribution. The extent of territorial specialization for animal husbandry

[38] *UM*, pp. 142–5, 149–50. For raids on livestock see RC 3, fos. 60v–1 (1343); da Piazza, *Cronaca*, I, chapters 39, 73, 128.
[39] *UM*, p. 144; Ventura, 'Nella Sicilia del '400: terra e lavoro in alcuni contratti notarili del Catanese', pp. 114, 126, 128; see also below, nn. 47, 50–1.
[40] Shepherds' wages rose by eighty per cent in 1350–65, prior to any major devaluations; subsequent increases mostly affected food and cloth liveries (*UM*, p. 154). Following the civil war, small animal herds were grouped together to save on labour costs (*UM*, p. 144). Wages in the tunny industry rose slightly less than for agricultural activities (*UM*, pp. 268–9).
[41] *UM*, pp. 125–6, 157–8: profits in agriculture varied widely between net loss and 14.5 per cent gain. Net profits in animal husbandry were on average slightly higher (eleven to fifteen per cent) and considerably more stable.
[42] *UM*, p. 152.
[43] *UM*, pp. 149–50.
[44] Petralia, *Banchieri e famiglie*, p. 316; *UM*, pp. 496–7.

172   *An island for itself*

Table 4.1 *The* fodrum *of 1283*

	M per cent	N per cent	D per cent	Total (N)
wheat (*salme*)	65.4	26.8	7.8	17,210
barley (*salme*)	51.0	38.9	10.1	23,240
cattle	46.5	31.6	21.9	5,085
sheep	36.0	42.2	21.8	20,020
pigs	49.7	26.0	24.3	5,235
wine (*salme*)	14.3	57.1	28.6	7,000

Sources: Carini, *De rebus*, nos. 15, pp. 172–3, summarized by D'Angelo, 'Terra e uomini', 82–4. I have corrected the latter's division of communities by *vallo*.
M = val di Mazara; N = val di Noto; D = val Demone.

is particularly striking in this period; as one might expect given the higher elasticity of demand for livestock than for grain, specialization seems to have increased more in animal husbandry than in cereal cultivation. According to the levy in kind (*fodrum*) of 1282–3 (Table 4.1), val di Mazara accounted for 40.1 per cent of total livestock, which accords roughly with its estimated share in population (48.2 per cent in 1276–7, 40 per cent in 1282). Val Demone had little livestock, especially little cattle. Val di Noto was the region most specialized in animal husbandry, due perhaps in part to its good water supply; in 1283 its scant population, less than one fifth of the whole island's, raised nearly two fifths of the livestock. Val di Noto's share was particularly high for sheep. Pigs were less important, particularly in central Sicily around Piazza and Castrogiovanni, areas completely missing from the Aragonese levy.[45] Of course, averages such as these mask striking local differences.[46] The western and south-western val di Mazara seems to have raised only cattle, for example, while the northern flanks of the Nebrodi, which included Patti, sent no sheep whatsoever to Messina.

Over the following century and a half, the distribution of livestock became increasingly unbalanced. As usual, most of our evidence comes from val di Mazara. Here the proportion of sheep declined quite sharply, particularly after 1400, while pigs began to appear around Alcamo and Salemi where there had apparently been none in the late thirteenth century. Western val Demone

[45] In 1477, the inhabitants of Castrogiovanni pastured up to 18,000 sheep and cattle on the nearby lands of Assoro (CR 67, fos. 68–9).
[46] *UM*, pp. 154–6.

around Pollina, Polizzi, Isnello, Geraci, Gangi and Castelbuono, and central and eastern val Demone around Mistretta, Capizzi and Petralia, specialized in transhumant pastoralism.[47] Production in the Nebrodi and Madonie mountains had increased to such an extent that, whereas until 1300 or later, north-eastern val Demone imported part of its supplies from Calabria, by the fifteenth century livestock was moving steadily in the opposite direction (see chapter 5). After 1400, the number of shepherds from the Madonie working near Palermo increased from seven to thirty per cent of the total, marking a major step in the development of a regional labour market.[48]

Livestock, especially cattle, raised in the Nebrodi and Madonie mountains were taken to the great fairs of Randazzo, Nicosia, Lentini and Piazza to be redistributed within Sicily and abroad. In Randazzo pigs were the commonest kind of livestock.[49] Pigs were also common in central val di Noto, marking an important change from the late thirteenth century.[50] The practice of keeping a family pig, common to central and north Italian peasants, may also have begun to spread in Sicily during the fourteenth century, at a time when Muslim traditions were slowly decaying.[51]

These changes were related to contemporary developments in manufacturing and regional trade. The leather industries developed best where access to myrtle for tanning and large cattle herds were most favourable: in western Sicily in Palermo, Alcamo, Trapani, Sciacca,[52] in val di Noto in Catania, Noto, Caltagirone

---

[47] For specialization in the Madonie and Nebrodi see *UM*, p. 141; C 2860, fo. 32 (1447); C 2882, fos. 172–3 (1453); RC 137, fo. 159rv (1476); RC 138, fo. 452v (1478); G. L. Barberi, *Liber de secretiis*, p. 202 (1506).

[48] *UM*, p. 141; Corrao, 'La popolazione fluttuante a Palermo fra '300 e '400: mercanti, marinai, salariati'.

[49] NR 5, fos. 27rv, 36, 47v, 109rv, 222rv (1455–6); NR 6, fos. 21rv, 22rv, 22v–3, 26–7, 31v–2v (1460); NR 15, fos. 85rv, 97v–8 (1490); NR 22, fo. 25rv (1494). For cattle, sheep and horses see NR 2, fo. 21rv (1445); NR 4, fos. 35v, 35v–6, 36v (1453); NR 5, fos. 187v–8 (1456); NR 15, fo. 337rv (1491).

[50] *UM*, pp. 92–3.

[51] Di Giovanni ed., *Capitoli di Alcamo*, p. 60 (pre-1367).

[52] *Ibid.*, pp. 55, 59 (pre-1367); La Mantia ed., *Capitoli inediti della città di Sciacca del secolo XV*, p. 18; Trasselli, 'Il mercato dei panni a Palermo nella prima metà del secolo XV', 332; *UM*, pp. 88, 93, 95; Bresc, '"Disfari et perdiri li fructi et li aglandi": economie e risorse boschive nella Sicilia medievale (XIII–XV secolo)', 951, 953; E. Ashtor, 'The Jews of Trapani in the late Middle Ages', 18–19; C 2861, fos. 131v–2 (1449).

and Lentini;[53] and in val Demone in Messina, Randazzo and Patti.[54] The distribution of sheep-raising in the fifteenth century, on the other hand, is closely correlated with that of wool manufacture discussed below. Perhaps because of increased infra-regional competition, sheep-raising in val di Mazara began to decline after the 1390s. *Caciocavallo*, a hard cheese which became very popular abroad, began to be made in val di Mazara after 1380, but production expanded in earnest only after 1430.[55] Central Sicily, including parts of val di Noto and val Demone, exported cheese and livestock to Palermo.[56]

Far from being '*restricted* to the poor mountain lands and to the *margi* [the swamps]', on the periphery of the periphery, as argued by Bresc,[57] during the late fourteenth and fifteenth centuries animal husbandry *grew* in those allegedly 'marginal' mountain terrains and became an increasingly specialized occupation. Far from being a subsidiary feature of Sicily's 'choice' to favour grain production, for over a century animal husbandry dominated the island's economy by providing meat, cheese, wool and leather to an expanding consumer market.

Once the demographic tide began to turn, however, the interests of the herd owners, made powerful by the population crisis and by changes in consumption patterns, came into conflict with those of agriculturalists. Disputes between agriculturalists and pastoralists were thus not 'purely accidental, local conflicts of interest';[58] it was no accident that conflict flared up in 1330–50 and 1430–60, when the balance between the two sectors was undergoing rapid change.[59] From the mid-fifteenth century, *massari* began to ask to reclaim

[53] Bresc, '"Disfari et perdiri"', 951, 953; R. Zeno, 'Un capitolo di re Martino sull'acatapania catanese', 292 (1400); Ventura, *Edilizia urbanistica*, p. 152; C 2865, fos. 51–2 (1451); CR 73, fos. 83–6 (1489); CR 71, fos. 22–2bisv (1490); NC 14926, fos. 84v–5v, 190–1, 387v, 408 (1499–1500); V. Littara, *De rebus netinis*, p. 20.
[54] Starrabba ed., *Consuetudini di Messina*, p. 226 (late fourteenth century); RC 81, fos. 485v–8v (1444), Sciacca ed., *Patti*, p. 338; NM 3, fo. 329v (?); NM 5, fos. 46v, 86 (1446); NM 6B, fos. 396v–7 (1469); NM 7, fos. 43v–4 (1491); NR 4, fo. 31v (1453); NR 5, fos. 7–8, 142rv, 169v, 238rv, 257v–8 (1455–6); NR 6, fos. 3–4, 10v–11 (1460); NR 14, fos. 172v–3 (1489); NR 15, fos. 414v–15 (1491).
[55] *UM*, p. 163.
[56] *UM*, pp. 161, 164.
[57] *UM*, p. 133 (my italics).
[58] *UM*, p. 137.
[59] *UM*, pp. 136 n. 63, 137 nn. 64, 67; C 2891, fo. 107v (1434); De Vio ed., *Privilegia*, pp. 241–3 (1438); ABP 1488–9, fo. 3rv.

Table 4.2 *New butcher's shops (*plancae) *and mills, 1400–1499*

	plancae				mills			
	M	N	D	Total	M	N	D	Total
1400–24	6	—	6	12	1	3	2	6
1425–49	28	2	2	32	5	2	3	10
1450–74	3	5	9	17	13	6	1	20
1475–99	—	1	3	4	12	9	6	27

Source: CR 1–84.

pasture to arable, in the belief that government support could be enlisted on their side. They proved to be correct, largely because Alfonso had no way of taxing Sicilian pastoral production along the lines of the Castilian *Mesta* or the southern Italian *Dogana delle pecore*, and was therefore keen to promote grain exports that he could tax. In 1451, Palermo's *massari* were allowed to bid first for renting land in the city district, and a year later Alfonso extended the provision to the whole island, stating that too much arable had turned to pasture and had caused grain exports to decline.[60] In 1483, Ferdinand banned enclosed pastures (*chiusure*).[61] The shifting balance between the two sectors is reflected in the sharper rise in the price of animal products than of grain after 1450,[62] as opposed to the fewer number of new butcher's shops (*plancae*) and the rising number of new grain mills established in the same period (see Table 4.2).

Pasture retreated, but things did not return as they had been before 1350. Ian Blanchard has suggested that a network of *regional*

[60] De Vio ed., *Privilegia*, pp. 313–24 (1451); C 2897, fo. 54rv (1452), printed with variations in D. Orlando ed., *Un codice di leggi e diplomi siciliani del Medio Evo*, p. 176.
[61] Giuffrida, 'Latifondi in Sicilia', p. 35. For conflicts between pastoralists and farmers see C 2891, fos. 143–4 (Piazza, 1434); C 2882, fos. 107v–9 (1452); Genuardi, *Terre comuni ed usi civici in Sicilia prima dell'abolizione della feudalità. Studi e documenti*, pp. 97–8 (Patti, 1456); C 2878, fos. 6v–7 (county of Modica, 1456); RC 106, fos. 226–8 (conflicts between Milazzo and Castroreale, 1457); C 3472, fo. 128 (Naro, 1459); Giardina ed., *Capitoli*, nos. 88 (1451), 92 (1459), 100 (1465) (Messina's district); RC 121, fos. 45v–6 (conflicts between the baron of Cerami and Capizzi, 1467); RC 125, fos. 106–8v (1470), and RC 144, fos. 100v–1 (1480) (Polizzi); CR 90, fos. 449–50v (reference to Alfonso's law by Syracuse, 1506); Cancila, *Baroni e popolo*, p. 31 (1490–1520).
[62] *Ibid.*, p. 25; Cancila, 'Contratti di conduzione', 324.

livestock markets developed between 1350 and 1470 as a result of the late medieval retreat from arable land, and of rising demand for meat.[63] Evidence for late medieval Sicily, however, shows that these regional markets were not established on the basis simply of a reallocation in land use from arable to pasture. Had such a reallocation prevailed, the result would have been to increase local self-sufficiency and decrease specialization. Instead, evidence for increasing territorial specialization and regional integration shows that land after the Black Death was mostly being used on the basis of *comparative* criteria of commercial and environmental opportunity. Although late medieval and early modern demographic growth tended to undermine the pastoral base of these regional markets, the market networks themselves did not collapse. As a result, animal husbandry's late medieval cycle of expansion was not entirely reversed.

Wine

Of the various products requested by Peter III in 1282–3 to supply and pay for his army in Messina, wine was the most unevenly distributed. Only six towns (Cefalù, Patti, Aci, Catania, Augusta and Syracuse) contributed wine; all of them were situated on the north-eastern and eastern coast. Messina (which exported wine to Africa and the Levant at the time) was not quoted, no doubt because the Aragonese army was camped there and could be supplied directly. Needless to say, these were not the only wine-producing towns in Sicily; there can have been few villages lacking a narrow ring of vineyards around the houses or scattered among the fields.[64] Contributors to the *fodrum*, however, were the only ones able to provide consistently large surpluses of wine and the expertise for shipping it safely to Messina. Further proof to this effect is provided by Pegolotti's commercial notebook of the early fourteenth century, which mentions only Patti and Messina as exporting wine to Constantinople and, somewhat anachronistically (the city

---

[63] Blanchard, 'The Continental European cattle trades, 1400–1600', 428.

[64] *UM*, pp. 176–9; S. Giambruno ed., *Il Tabulario del monastero di S. Margherita di Polizzi*, nos. 17, 42, 45. For Monte San Giuliano see Sparti, *Registro*, I, nos. 2, 11, 12, 16, 18, 24, 30, throughout (1298); Abulafia, 'Una comunità ebraica della Sicilia occidentale: Erice 1298–1304'.

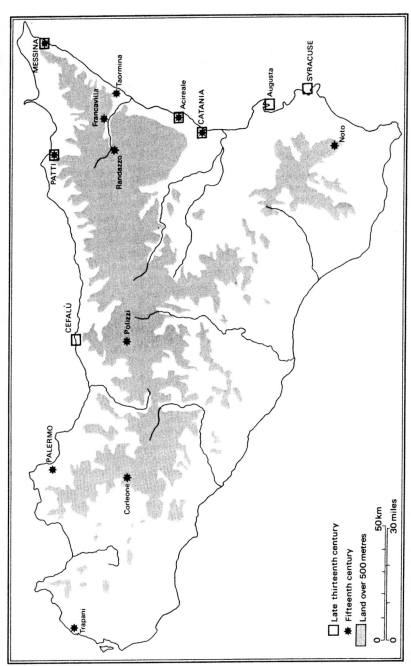

Map 4.1 Specialized wine production

Late thirteenth century
Fifteenth century
Land over 500 metres

50 km
30 miles

MESSINA
Taormina
Francavilla
Acireale
CATANIA
Augusta
SYRACUSE
PATTI
Randazzo
Noto
CEFALÙ
Polizzi
PALERMO
Corleone
Trapani

had fallen to the Mamluks in 1291), to Acre.[65] Syracuse was also exporting to Malta from the late thirteenth century.[66] Rising demand and market fragmentation led to a notable increase in wine production during the late fourteenth century,[67] reflected in the rash of protective measures passed when institutional barriers to trade fell after 1392–8. But although vineyards remained a relatively accessible and widespread form of agricultural investment, property seems to have become more concentrated in aristocratic and patrician hands, especially in the larger cities like Messina, Catania and Palermo;[68] after 1400, taverns were more commonly an upper-class investment.[69]

Increasing output did not rule out specialization. The main producers still included Aci,[70] Catania[71] and Messina,[72] but no longer Patti, Cefalù, Syracuse and Augusta. By the fifteenth century, the latter had been replaced by Noto,[73] Taormina,[74] Randazzo,[75] perhaps Polizzi[76] and, to the west, Trapani.[77] Far more than with grain, most major wine producers were situated on the coast, where they

[65] F. B. Pegolotti, *La pratica della mercatura*, pp. 39, 66. See also Abulafia, 'The merchants of Messina: Levant trade and domestic economy'.

[66] Carini ed., *De rebus*, no. 708 (1283).

[67] *UM*, pp. 185, 820–1.

[68] Sorrenti, *Patrimonio fondiario*, pp. 153, 169 n. 220, 170–4, 182–4, 192; Ventura, 'Nella Sicilia del '400', 117; *UM*, p. 190.

[69] Bresc and Bresc, '"Fondaco" et taverne de la Sicile médiévale', pp. 95–6; *UM*, p. 193; CR 9, fo. 184 (1422); NR 7, fos. 62v–3v (1464); CR 71, fos. 100–100bisv (1493).

[70] RC 4, fo. 200v (1331); da Piazza, *Cronaca*, II, chapter 2 (1357); RC 30, fos. 165v–6v (1398); CR 5, fos. 181–2v (1415); CR 9, fos. 114v–16v (1421); CR 11, fo. 197 (1424); CR 14, fos. 139–41 (1425); Ventura, 'Nella Sicilia del '400', 118.

[71] *UM*, pp. 820–1, Table 189; RC 81, fo. 81rv (1398); RC 30, fos. 169v–70 (1398); CR 34, fos. 35–6; CR 13, fos. 125rv, 127–9v (1425–6); CR 16, fos. 125–6v (1430); CR 20, fo. 317rv (1439); RC 76, fos. 139v–40, 156 (1440); RC 88, fos. 350–1 (1453); CR 47, fo. 25rv (1467); TRP Atti 40, fo. 80v (1486); Ventura, 'Nella Sicilia del '400', 116–24; Sorrenti, *Patrimonio fondiario*, pp. 187, 190–2.

[72] *Ibid.*, pp. 148–54. In the late fourteenth century, the price of wine in Messina was among the lowest in the western Mediterranean (Day, 'Prix agricoles en Méditerranée à la fin du XIVe siècle', 641, 651).

[73] C 2810, fos. 40v–1 (1424); CR 49, fo. 247rv (1475).

[74] da Piazza, *Cronaca*, I, chapter 38 (1348); RC 75, fos. 405–8 (1440); RC 76, fos. 299v–300 (1441); C 3477, fos. 51–2 (1462).

[75] RC 46, fos. 413v–15v (1407); CR 11, fos. 49–50 (1428); NR 2, fos. 14v–16, 19v (1444–5); NR 3, fo. 19 (1446); NR 5, fos. 203rv, 242v, 259–60v (1456); NR 6, fos. 4rv, 15v–17v (1460).

[76] CR 7, fo. 307rv (1410); RC 70, fos. 80v–1 (1434).

[77] Cancila, 'Contratti di conduzione'; Sorrenti, *Patrimonio fondiario*, pp. 176–9, 181–2.

could employ cheap water transport. Sicily began to produce several distinctive qualities of wine[78] which it exported throughout the Mediterranean and to northern Europe.[79] Alfonso in Naples demanded wine from his officials in Corleone, Trapani, Aci and Taormina, 'which we desire for our own palate. Be not remiss for anything in the world', he wrote, 'if you wish to serve us well.'[80] Wines of different ages (some newly pressed, some two to three years old and some 'of the oldest you can find') were sent to the court in Naples from Trapani (Bonagia) and Aci.[81] The main exporter in this period was still Messina, however, which was probably also a collecting point for wine from other parts of Sicily and southern Calabria.[82] Lesser exporters were Francavilla,[83] Patti,[84] Trapani[85] and even, by the fifteenth century, Palermo.[86]

We saw above that, as the main regal or vice-regal seat of residence, Palermo was both a major importer and a producer of wine in its own right. By 1400, new vineyards were competing with new sugar plantations,[87] but the former continued to be planted anyway.[88] Before the mid-fifteenth century, imports to Palermo

---

[78] *Mantonico* or *mantonicato*, both white and red: NM 5, fos. 340, 353 (1448?); NR 8, fos. 33v–4 (1468); NR 14, fo. 54 (1488); NR 15, fo. 22rv (1490); NM 7, fo. 131 (1491) (white *cuctunini*); *UM*, p. 179. *Mamertino*: F. Melis, *I vini italiani nel Medioevo*, p. 23; Fazello, *Due deche*, p. 296. *Vernaccia* or *guarnaccia*: NM 6B, fos. 571v–2 (1470); Trasselli, *Storia dello zucchero siciliano*, p. 108 n. 19; *UM*, p. 180. *Moscatello bianco*: *UM*, p. 180. Wine from Ucria: NR 5, fo. 23v (1455). *Malvasia* of Savoca and Alì in val Demone: Fazello, *Due deche*, pp. 74–5; L. Alberti, *Isole appartenenti alla Italia. Di nuovo ricorrette, et con l'aggionta in più luoghi de diverse cose sino a' nostri tempi adornate*, fos. 38v–9. *Bianco* from Alcamo: Melis, *Vini italiani*, p. 82.
[79] *Ibid.*, pp. 23, 81–2, 103–4, 120, 171, 178.
[80] C 2891, fos. 95v, 187v (1434, 1435): 'lu quali vulimu per nostra bucca et non manki per cosa dilu mundu si ni desiderati serviri'.
[81] CR 39, fo. 81rv (1458); RC 107, fos. 46v–7v (1458).
[82] For transit trade see C 3472, fos. 158v–9 (1459); NM 7, fos. 185rv, 246v–7v, 359 (1492); CR 875, fos. 333–4 (1497). For exports from Messina see NM 5, fos. 28rv (1445?) ('Romania', that is, the Black Sea), 74rv (1446?); CR 869, fo. 162 (1488) (Malta); B. de Pasi, *Tariffa dei pesi*, fo. 115v (1503) (Corfu).
[83] RC 41, fo. 264 (1404).   [84] PR 24, fos. 250v–2 (1425).
[85] CR 877, fo. 139 (1499).
[86] CR 872, fo. 192rv (1493); Alberti, *Isole*, fo. 45v; Tucci, 'La Sicilia nei manuali', 647.
[87] *UM*, pp. 185, 188; Bresc, 'Jardins de Palerme', 95–6 (orchards).
[88] Sorrenti, *Patrimonio fondiario*, pp. 167–9; Giuffrida, '"Lu quarteri di lu Cassaru". Note sul quartiere del Cassaro a Palermo nella prima metà del secolo XV', 453; Trasselli, *Storia dello zucchero*, p. 78; De Vio ed., *Privilegia*, pp. 231 (1438), 358–78 (1466).

came mainly from Calabria and Naples, far less from eastern Sicily.[89] Palermo's imports were viewed with chagrin by the producers of Catania. In 1428, they asked that the surplus of some parts of the island serve the scarcity of others, so that 'money that leaves the kingdom remain therein'. The viceroy retorted laconically that it was 'bad to damage merchant affairs'.[90] As it was, wine exports to the rest of Sicily (mostly from Calabria to Messina) were minimal.[91]

By contrast with grain and livestock production, therefore, evidence for increased specialization in wine production is rather mixed. On the one hand, there is considerable evidence, based in particular on international demand, that the wine industry did become more specialized after 1350, and especially after the Aragonese restoration of the 1390s. On the other hand, there were a number of reasons why the wine sector was more resistant to change than others. First, it was very labour intensive and had low economies of scale in production. Second, entry costs were very low: anyone with a tiny suburban plot could grow some vines. Third, widespread home-based production and the difficulty of storing and transporting wine over long distances kept the market for wine very localized.

Late medieval production of wine for everyday consumption thus did expand, but did not specialize much because gains from special-

---

[89] Bresc, *Economie et société,* p. 1291, records the first imports from val Demone (Alì, Forza d'Agrò) in 1457; see NM 3, fo. 300v, 1446–8: twenty-eight barrels of wine from Messina to Palermo. The Palermo notaries may have dealt mainly in large shipments from abroad; if so, local trade would have to be traced to the ports of origin, for which few registers survive. For foreign wine imports to Palermo see *RCA* XI, no. 141 (Amantea, 1274); Carini ed., *De rebus,* no. 510 (Sorrento, 1283); Starrabba, 'Documenti relativi a un episodio delle guerre tra le fazioni latina e catalana ai tempi di Re Ludovico d'Aragona', 183 (1349); CR 1062, fo. 540rv (Tropea, 1425); CR 11, fo. 355 (Tropea, 1427–8); CR 873, fos. 1–2 (1444): Palermo's wine toll was lowered because most southern Italian wine had been exported to Rome, and because local prices were so low that no merchant would import wine to Palermo. CR 862, fos. 49–50 (1450): imports of *malvasia,* a term usually indicating southern Italian or Greek wine. CR 36, fo. 342rv (Morea, 1453); CR 41, fo. 434rv, and LV 77, fo. 429rv (1461): the toll was lowered to increase imports of *malvasia* from Greece ('lu dictu vinu non essiri latinu'), which a ship's patron would otherwise not unload. LV 80, fo. 330 (*malvasia,* 1462); LV 82, fo. 93v, and LV 83, fo. 250 (1462).

[90] D'Alessandro, 'Vigne e vignaiuoli a Palermo alla fine del Medioevo', p. 101.

[91] NM 5, fos. 427v–8 (1449); NM 6A, fos. 220rv, 229 (1469); Galasso, *Economia e società nella Calabria del Cinquecento,* pp. 153–4; Di Giovanni ed., *Capitoli di Alcamo,* pp. 63–4 (1463).

ization were too low. By contrast, gains from specialization were pursued at the opposite end of the market, by differentiating output to supply higher-quality wines for a newly emerging range of middle- and upper-class domestic and international consumers.

Agricultural staples: conclusion

The late medieval crisis wrought major structural changes in Sicilian agriculture, most of which were the outcome of increasingly complex regional product markets. After the mid-fourteenth century, eastern Sicily specialized to a far greater degree than the west in intensive forms of agriculture. This divergence was probably the result of different pre-existing structures of production and landholding patterns.

A basically arable economy (like that of val di Mazara before the Black Death) tended to be hit harder by the demographic crisis than areas with a more diversified economic base (like val Demone and val di Noto), because demand for grain was less elastic than for other products. As a result, as we shall see, val di Mazara tended increasingly to specialize in land rather than labour-intensive cultivations such as grain, relying for seasonal peaks in labour needs on temporary migrants from the more densely populated val Demone. Territorial specialization and some major institutional innovations raised the productivity of land and labour considerably, tripling the proportion of exports to domestic output between 1450 and 1500.

Livestock production, by contrast, tended to concentrate more in the mountainous north-east, where environmental conditions were harder for grain production and where systems of vertical transhumance could be easily established. Production expanded to such a degree that, by the mid-fifteenth century, val Demone was exporting up to 10,000 cattle each year to the southern mainland (see chapter 5). The livestock industry also sustained new leather and woollen manufactures, both in the west and the east of Sicily, and a considerable volume of cheese exports to northern Italy and Catalonia (see chapter 6). Wine production expanded but specialized to a lesser extent; a more integrated market may have emerged along Sicily's coasts, but there does not seem to have been very intense domestic trade.

Peasant smallholding was far commoner in the east, particularly in val Demone, in comparison with the west. In the kind of conditions prevailing after the Black Death – a combination of high labour costs and rising demand for more labour-intensive crops and manufacturing – small family farms had considerable advantages to specialize over large-scale farms run with wage labour on the model of the western Sicilian *masseria*. Peasant smallholders in 'marginal' regions like val Demone could combine higher intensity of labour and land usage to include double or combined cropping, allowing them to even out seasonal fluctuations in employment and make most effective use of the range of ecological features at their disposal. These peasants could, in other words, diversify *away* from producing agricultural staples. To what extent did they do so?

CLOTH MANUFACTURE

We saw in chapter 1 that the argument for medieval Sicily's 'colonial' or dependent condition hinges crucially on its weak manufacturing base. Cloth manufacture in particular, as the most developed medieval industry, has come under detailed scrutiny. It is commonly argued that, because Sicily was unable to produce quality wool cloth domestically,[92] it was forced to import foreign cloth, which it paid for mainly with grain exports.[93] Sicily thus lacked a home manufacturing base and was forced to specalize in staple exports. In this section I examine domestic cloth production, and connect it with changes in regional agricultural and market structures; I address the problem of foreign trade in chapter 6.[94]

By and large, the medieval international cloth market supplied luxury items to the wealthier sections of the population.[95] Even at

---

[92] Charles I of Anjou expressed worry on this account in 1277 (Yver, *Commerce*, p. 84 n. 1).

[93] Trasselli, 'Sull'esportazione dei cereali dalla Sicilia negli anni 1402–07'; Trasselli, 'Tessuti di lana siciliani a Palermo nel XIV secolo'; Aymard, 'Commerce et consommation des draps en Sicile et en Italie méridionale (XVe–XVIIIe siècles)'; Giuffrida, 'Aspetti e problemi del commercio dei panni in Sicilia dal XIV al XVI secolo'; Aymard, 'Production, commerce et consommation des draps de laine du XIIe au XVIIe siècle (Prato, 10–16 avril 1970)'.

[94] This section is an abridged and modified version of Epstein, 'The textile industry and the foreign cloth trade in late medieval Sicily (1300–1500): a "colonial" relationship?', which includes references to primary sources.

[95] P. Chorley, 'The cloth exports of Flanders and northern France during the thirteenth century: a luxury trade?'.

the lowest end of their price range, these cloths were inaccessible to the vast majority of people. Cloth for export could never command a true mass market.

In his overview of the international cloth market after the Black Death, Miskimin argues (mainly on the evidence of Florence) that a shift towards the production of higher-quality cloth occurred throughout Europe, a 'creative response' to the greater concentration or skewed distribution of wealth and the 'hedonistic consumption pattern' that he argues followed the Black Death.[96] Although Miskimin's scheme seems to apply to some of the better-established exporting industries, the most significant effect of the plague seems to have been to stimulate cheap cloth production (often of non-woollens) on a local and regional scale to supply lower-income consumers. Throughout Italy, rural and semi-rural linen, woollen and fustian clothmaking expanded at a time when the Florentine industry switched to high quality woollen and silk cloth.[97] Genoese tolls on consumption demonstrate the shift in consumption patterns clearly. Between 1341 and 1398, the city's population dropped from 60,000–65,000 to 36,000–40,000 (a loss of about forty per cent), the index of tolls on foreign cloth imports plummeted from one hundred to thirty-nine (minus sixty-one per cent), whereas the index of tolls on local cloth *consumption* actually rose from 100 to 103.[98]

An important characteristic of these changes is their generally rural or semi-rural setting; even the previously mainly urban Florentine industry moved a large part of the simpler manufacturing cycles into the rural hinterland.[99] The shift is commonly seen as a move closer to primary materials, including water to power fulling

[96] Miskimin, 'Monetary movements', esp. 490; Miskimin, *Economy of Renaissance Europe*, pp. 92–100.
[97] M. F. Mazzaoui, *The Italian cotton industry in the later Middle Ages 1100–1600*, pp. 129–38; F. Borlandi, '"Fûtainiers" et fûtaines dans l'Italie du Moyen Age'; J. Heers, *Gênes au XVe siècle. Activité économique et problèmes sociaux*, pp. 227–9; Jones, 'La storia economica. Dalla caduta dell'Impero romano al secolo XIV', pp. 181–3 and n. 14; Romano, 'La storia economica', pp. 1849–53, 1855–6; Comba, 'Produzioni tessili nel Piemonte tardomedievale'; Grohmann, *Fiere*, pp. 85, 87, 137, 173, 211, 297, 414, 427; Leone, *Profili economici della Campania aragonese*, pp. 16–33, 38–43, 47–9; R. Mueller, 'Die wirtschaftliche Lage Italiens im Spätmittelalter'; B. Dini, 'L' industria tessile italiana nel tardo Medioevo'.
[98] Day, *Douanes*, pp. xxviii–xxix.
[99] See, for example, Melis, *Aspetti della vita economica medievale (Studi nell'Archivio Datini di Prato)*; H. Kellenbenz, 'Rural industries in the West from the end of

mills, and towards more accessible, cheaper and less rigidly organized labour.[100] This development enhanced quantity and, perhaps, variability, instead of enforcing high standards of quality, precisely what a nascent mass market then required.[101] It is nearly impossible to assess the overall commercial value of locally marketed cloth because of the generally rural or semi-rural character of production which often eschewed guild organization, because of its integration with peasant subsistence structures, and because of the lack of financial and fiscal records of trade. It can, however, be argued that domestic manufacturing had greater multiplier effects on the economy than export-led industries. In other words, the long-term development and growth of manufacturing was predicated on such popular products and not on luxury or semi-luxury woollen and silk cloths. To what extent did cheaper cloth manufacture expand in late medieval Sicily?

When addressing the question of Sicilian home consumption, historians have taken as their model central and northern European consumption patterns. Recognizing how low cloth imports to Sicily were, Aymard has sought for alternative sources of supply in local woollen production.[102] Others have also searched for what should have been, on the evidence of the small volume of imports, a strong Sicilian woollen industry, finding proof only of manufacture of *orbace*, a heavy, untreated cloth commonly given in part-payment to agricultural labourers.[103] A few medieval manufactures of better-quality wool cloth have recently emerged, but are said paradoxically to demonstrate 'the defeat of Sicily's industrial potentialities' after 1350. This is because they were semi-rural, a rather curious statement given what was occurring elsewhere in Europe at the same time.[104] No other kind of manufacture – of linen, cotton or

the Middle Ages to the eighteenth century'; Fournial, *Villes*, pp. 399–416; H. C. Peyer, 'Wollgewerbe, Viehzucht, Solddienst und Bevölkerungsentwicklung in Stand und Landschaft Freiburg i. Ue. vom 14. bis 16. Jh.'; A. R. Bridbury, *Medieval English clothmaking. An economic survey.* See also above, n. 97.
[100] E. Carus Wilson, 'The woollen industry', pp. 409–14; Carus Wilson, 'Evidences of industrial growth on some fifteenth-century manors'; Thirsk, 'Industries in the countryside'.
[101] Thirsk, *Economic policy and projects. The development of a consumer society in early modern England*; R. Millward, 'The emergence of wage labour in early modern England'.
[102] Aymard, 'Commerce et consommation', 127.
[103] Trasselli, 'Tessuti di lana', 303–4.
[104] *UM*, pp. 195–201.

hemp cloth – has ever been described. Technical knowledge in silk and linen weaving, and dyeing and intensive cultivation of textile plants and fibres, both of which flourished until the early fourteenth century, are said to have later disappeared with dramatic effects on the island's economy, including the definitive establishment of 'unequal' exchange and grain monoculture.[105] But how far does this picture fit the evidence? Let us look in turn at the production and use of each of the main cloth fibres: cotton, flax, hemp and wool.

Raw materials

Cotton was introduced to Sicily by the Muslims. The reasons why cotton spread throughout the western Mediterranean between the ninth and the twelfth centuries were the popularity of cotton textiles among Muslims and their advanced knowledge of the irrigation techniques needed for growing the plant. Thanks to the wide range of cloths it could be used for, cotton came to rival and even to displace the most ancient Mediterranean textile fibre, flax.[106]

Cotton was widespread throughout thirteenth-century Sicily. It was still widely exported in the period 1300–50, mainly to Catalonia but also to Africa and Marseilles. According to Pegolotti's commercial notebook, Sicilian cotton was of poor quality, and Messina and Palermo imported it from Acre and Cyprus. Cotton (perhaps another quality) was later imported to Sicily also from Amalfi.

The plant did not disappear from Sicily after the Black Death, even though the smaller population may have found it more difficult to grow because of its labour intensisty. After 1350, cotton was still grown in the Madonie mountains, on Lipari, on the Terranova plain and near Alcamo. By the fifteenth century, cultivation was located mainly in central and southern Sicily, and particularly in the southeastern val di Noto. Cotton seems to have been grown least in val di Mazara, the area most hard hit by the demographic setbacks, whereas it survived or even prospered in val di Noto, which we saw overcame the population crisis best and also possessed the most favourable soil and climatic conditions (light soil and good watering between Noto and Syracuse).[107]

---

[105] *UM*, p. 167. Amari, *Storia dei Musulmani*, II, p. 512, and III, p. 826, first suggested that 'Muslim' technical and agricultural traditions disappeared after the late thirteenth century.

[106] For cotton see Epstein, 'Textile industry', 150–2.

[107] Intensive irrigation near Noto is mentioned in C 2868, fos. 29–30 (1451).

By 1370 at the latest (but trade was probably already taking place before 1350), Malta and the island of Pantelleria also began exporting cotton to Syracuse (and to Catalonia) in exchange for grain. Catalans bought cotton, probably in eastern Sicily where their political allies held sway, throughout the second half of the fourteenth century. In 1376, over thirty-nine tons of cotton were exported to Genoa, nearly all from Messina, although the fibre may have originally come from Calabria and Lipari; a single ship transported thirty-three tons. The 1382 statutes of Ancona may refer to dyed Sicilian cotton; Marseilles imported Sicilian and Maltese cotton throughout the late fourteenth and fifteenth centuries.

In the early fifteenth century, cotton was sold in south-western Sciacca, in the county of Modica in the south-east and in Aidone in central Sicily. The main consumer was probably Syracuse, which controlled production in Terranova and in the rest of south and south-eastern Sicily, and imported cotton from Malta for local manufacture; Syracuse also exported large quantities to Catalonia. After about 1460, Messina began importing from further abroad than Calabria, which nevertheless probably remained its main source of supply. Sicilian cotton was cultivated throughout the modern period.[108]

Flax was possibly the most common textile fibre in pre-industrial Europe. It has been argued that flax could only be grown in the more temperate, continental climates like that of Lombardy rather than in the South, but a glance at the lists of bed and personal linen in Sicilian inventories shows this not to be the case.[109] Sicilian botanists distinguished up to ten endemic varieties of *Linum usitatissimum*. In reality, flax was far commoner in late medieval Sicily than cotton, but, perhaps because of its wide diffusion and because of not being widely traded, it left few traces in the documents, and has therefore been ignored by historians.

Flax is well attested throughout Sicily under the Normans, but by the late thirteenth century it may have been more common in the east; the tendency towards regional specialization of flax production probably continued until the late fifteenth century. Since flax

---

[108] Mazzaoui, *Italian cotton industry*, pp. 174 n. 77, 177 n. 23, 183 n. 85; F. Cupani, *Hortus catholicus*, pp. 85–6; see also Trasselli, *Storia dello zucchero*, p. 24 n. 6; J. Gussone, *Florae Syculae synopsis*, II, pp. 464–5.

[109] See Epstein, 'Textile industry', 152–3.

exhausts the soil and is thus costly to produce where there is great pressure on the land, the combination of low population pressure and rising demand for clothing which prevailed in Sicily after the mid-fourteenth century provided ideal conditions for expansion. Where flax was abundant, linseed was eaten as a grain substitute and was pressed for oil, but the plant's main purpose was for fibre. In the fifteenth century, flax was produced in Castrogiovanni, Catania, Aci, Aidone, Paternò, Syracuse and the counties of Caltanissetta and Modica in val di Noto; Sciacca, Alcamo, Palazzo Adriano and Palermo in val di Mazara (but it was imported to Mazara itself);[110] and in Randazzo (a major producer) and elsewhere in val Demone. Messina was supplied mostly from Calabria and Naples, but also from val Demone, and exported flax to Genoa, Cagliari and even back to Calabria and other parts of Sicily – sometimes trading it for wheat or less often for cheese. Home production seems, however, to have largely met demand, implying that the plant was more widely grown than it appears. Although, as with cotton, val di Noto was probably the largest producer, flax was also common in val Demone. In late fifteenth-century Messina, as we shall see, local production sustained an export industry in high-quality veils.

In contrast with flax, hemp was mainly used for sacking, sailcloth and rope, but could be mixed with flax to produce a heavier kind of half-linen cloth. Hemp in the form of tow was also used by shipbuilders and so was often needed for the royal arsenals; Alfonso did not hesitate on occasion to ban all trade and export to meet his more pressing needs.

Like cotton and flax, hemp seems to have been grown mainly in val di Noto, near Syracuse, Noto, Catania, Paternò, Lentini and in the county of Modica, particularly in the lands of Ragusa, Scicli and Modica itself.[111] Words for hemp in contemporary Sicilian dialect are found mainly in central and eastern Sicily. In the fifteenth century, sacks for the sugarworks (*trappeti*) near Palermo came from Catania. Hemp was less common in val di Mazara, and I have found no evidence for it in val Demone in this period; it was imported from val di Noto for local use and for re-export. Ropes and naval shrouds were made in Messina for the arsenal and for

---

[110] F. Napoli, 'Il Libro Rosso della città di Mazara. Regesto', 325 (1472).
[111] See Epstein, 'Textile industry', 154.

ports like Trapani. Hemp, in conclusion, seems to have been the least used of all the available cloth fibres.

In medieval northern Europe, wool was nearly as basic a product as grain. In the hotter Mediterranean climates, where woollen clothing was less popular, sheep were more commonly raised for their cheese and meat. As it was, the poor quality of Sicilian wool was common knowledge.[112] Charles I of Anjou attempted to improve the local strain of sheep by importing animals from northern Africa, and while the results of this particular effort are not known, there are sixteenth-century references to wool from Barbary sheep raised in Sicily and three breeds (*siciliana, comisana* and *barbaresca*) are attested. Nonetheless, although there was little domestic or international pressure to increase the quality of local wool in Sicily, this need not have been an insuperable manufacturing constraint, as demonstrated by the fact that the high-quality industries of Florence and Flanders imported wool from Spain and England.

Despite the expansion of animal husbandry after the mid-fourteenth century, and val di Noto's increasing specialization in sheep-breeding, an organized transhumance system such as existed in Spain and central and southern Italy never evolved in Sicily. Sheep-raising seems to have been more integrated into mixed farming and undertaken for meat and cheese rather than wool markets. This could explain why no equivalent of the high-quality Spanish *merino* sheep was bred in Sicily, although the two breeds crossed to obtain *merino* were very similar to the breeds raised in Sicily. A reflection of the lack of interest in high quality wool and the absence of regulated transhumance is the relatively small (and decreasing after 1350) size of the Sicilian flocks, which as we have seen may have inhibited specialized breeding.

Cloth manufactures

As the previous discussion has suggested, the widespread evidence of raw materials is matched by that for cloth manufacture. Sicilian cotton manufacture, for example, is quite well documented.[113] Its popularity is reflected in the large number of Arabic terms employed for particular kinds of cotton cloth. In the fifteenth cen-

---

[112] *Ibid.*, 154–6.
[113] *Ibid.*, 156–7.

tury, the toll (*gabella arcus cuctoni*) on the padding or quilting of cotton doublets, jackets, quilts and coverlets was levied in Messina, Catania, Trapani, Sciacca, Agrigento, Naro, Noto, Caltagirone (under feudal jurisdiction), Castrogiovanni and Palermo. Syracusan *burdo* (a type of fustian used mainly for mattress ticking and curtains) was much in demand throughout Sicily. Randazzo and Marsala also produced a local quality of *burdo*. Some town manufacturers are probably missing from this list, particularly from eastern Sicily for which evidence is more scanty. Nonetheless, one can note that of the dozen distinctive producers, five were situated in val di Mazara, five in val di Noto, while val Demone apparently had only two manufacturing centres, namely Messina and Randazzo. The distribution of manufactures seems to have differed from the distribution of primary materials, which after the mid-fourteenth century came mainly from val di Noto and to a lesser extent from val Demone, whereas they were declining in val di Mazara.

Cotton was used for table and house cloth, for blankets, bedcovers, clothing and garment decoration. Syracuse produced a type of large white blanket with rose-shaped decorations, cloth for mattress ticking and for various kinds of garments. A large number of qualities and designs are recorded for Randazzo. Messina specialized in tablecloths, veils and clothing articles. In 1506, revenues from the *arcus cuctoni* in Messina were far higher than anywhere else (ten *onze* compared to twenty *tarì* and six *tarì* in Trapani and Catania). If the toll was the same as in the early fourteenth century (two *grani* per piece) at least 3,000 pieces (jackets, and so on) were being made there each year.

Fustian production is particularly significant because Sicily did not import large quantities of these cloths, in contrast to the situation in, for example, Catalonia where, by the fifteenth century, fustians and *tele* from Lombardy, Germany, France and even Calabria and Sicily were flooding the market.[114] Fustians may have been imported to Sicily up to the thirteenth century, but from the fifteenth century Sicilian goods were well established and even exported abroad. Manufacture was concentrated mainly in eastern Sicily: in Palermo, where it appeared already in the early fourteenth century, Malta, Patti, Randazzo, Noto and perhaps also in Messina and Catania.

---

[114] C. Carrère, *Barcelone centre économique à l'époque des difficultés 1380–1462*, I, pp. 370–1.

Linen and hemp cloth manufacture is worse documented, probably because it was technically less sophisticated and was therefore more easily practised on a household basis.[115] Dowry lists and *post mortem* inventories are a major documentary source for local cloth production and consumption.[116] They list large quantities of linen shirts, corsets, handkerchiefs, napkins, towels, sheets, cushion and mattress covers, perhaps spun and woven mostly by the bride herself. *Post mortem* inventories in eastern Sicily commonly list spun and sometimes woven flax. There is at least one case in which flax was being put out to peasants to weave, although the quantity of material involved (about 30m) was rather small. Trapani's tolls of 1312 mention linen weavers, who had to pay six *tarì* a year per loom, while looms for other cloth paid five *grani* (only four per cent as much). For fifteenth-century Noto a number of contracts register sales of up to 75m of (linen?) *tela* at a time.

Evidence of production for home consumption, together with evidence of large quantities of linen traded in the fair of Randazzo in the late fifteenth century, suggests that production may have been organized in two distinct ways. Whereas simpler kinds of production may have been carried out within and for the same household, larger and technically more complex work may have involved more specialized labour and was traded on the market. There is evidence of specialized manufacturing of linen bedcovers in Syracuse, Malta, Marsala, Sciacca and Castrogiovanni during the late fourteenth and fifteenth centuries; they were even exported to Florence. The elusiveness of linen manufacture may be due in part to the scarcity of notarial records for eastern Sicily. High-quality linen veils produced in Messina are documented only from the late fifteenth century, but it is possible that evidence only appears at this point in time because veils began then to be widely exported, particularly to Valencia and Barcelona. In the early sixteenth

---

[115] See Epstein, 'Textile industry', 157–60.

[116] See Carini, 'Un testamento del 1376'; C. A. Garufi, 'Ricerche sugli usi nuziali nel Medio Evo in Sicilia'; S. Salomone Marino, 'Le pompe nuziali e il corredo delle donne siciliane nei secoli XIV, XV e XVI'; Salomone Marino, 'Spigolature storiche siciliane dal sec. XIV al sec. XIX'; F. Gabotto, 'Inventari messinesi inediti del Quattrocento'; E. Mauceri, 'Inventari inediti dei secoli XV e XVI (Da atti notarili di Siracusa, Noto, Lentini, Palazzolo Acreide)'; Bresc and S. D. Goitein, 'Un inventaire dotal de juifs siciliens (1479)'. See Heers, 'La mode et les marchés des draps de laine: Gênes et la montagne à la fin du Moyen Age', for the increasing use of linen underwear after 1350.

century, Messina produced large quantities of linen cloth out of imported flax, although again no earlier evidence exists for this manufacture.

Hemp cloth was the poorest and is the least documented. Sacking, sails and rope were too cheap to interest major merchants or involve sums of money sufficiently large to leave much trace in the documents. The largest consumer of hemp was the crown for its arsenals, but in the absence of detailed accounts there is no way of charting production. Because of its arguably common use, hemp cloth may well have been regularly traded, but hemp is mentioned less frequently than flax in *post mortem* inventories and does not seem to have been used much for regular clothing.

During the late fourteenth and fifteenth centuries, production of low- and medium-quality woollens developed in middle-sized, semi-rural towns which had easy access to running water for washing and fulling and to peasant labour (in 1439 more than seventy per cent of the Sicilian population lived in settlements with over 300 hearths).[117] An effect of the contemporary tendency to expand urban jurisidiction over the countryside (see chapter 3) may thus have been to improve access to cheap sources of labour; for the rest, as we shall see, corporate control over labour in cloth manufacture was noticeably weak.

Mills for fulling and stretching wool cloth (*bactinderia* and *paratoria*) and known manufacturing centres mostly coincide (see Table 4.2 and Map 4.2).[118] Industrial machinery was to be found in the area of the Madonie, particularly in and around Polizzi, in the surrounding county of Sclafani, and in the county of Geraci; further east in val Demone, in the plain of Milazzo, in Nicosia, and particularly in Randazzo and its district; and, finally, in val di Noto, near Caltagirone and Lentini, but especially around Noto itself. The only *paratoria* outside the northern mountain ranges and val di Noto were situated in Corleone and Salemi.

Manufacturing was also situated around Ucria and Sinagra near Patti, in Randazzo and Castiglione, all in val Demone. An active trade in wool caps in Messina in the late fifteenth century may indicate local manufacture; Catania also produced *orbace*. The

---

117 Epstein, 'Textile industry', 160–3.
118 These mills were also employed for beating flax and hemp.

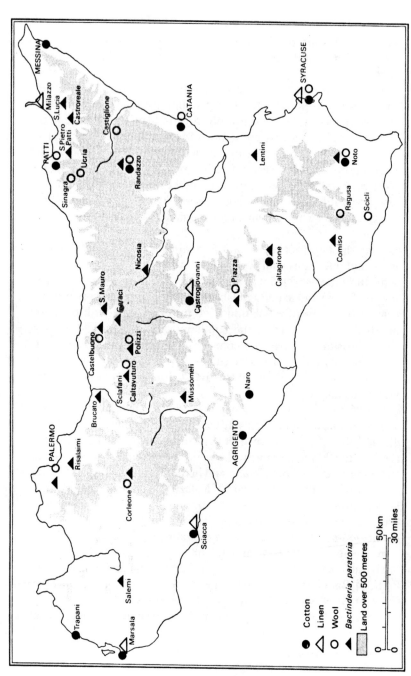

Map 4.2 Cloth manufacturing 1350–1500

MESSINA
Milazzo
S.Lucia
Castroreale
Castiglione
CATANIA
S.Pietro Patti
PATTI
Ucria
Randazzo
Sinagra
Nicosia
S.Mauro
Gangi
Castrogiovanni
Piazza
Castelbuono
Polizzi
Caltagirone
Sclafani
Caltavuturo
Brucato
Mussomeli
Naro
PALERMO
Risalaimi
AGRIGENTO
Corleone
Sciacca
Salemi
Trapani
Marsala

SYRACUSE
Lentini
Noto
Ragusa
Scicli
Comiso

Cotton
Linen
Wool
Bactinderia, paratoria
Land over 500 metres

50 km
30 miles

main wool manufacturing area, however, was situated in the vicinity of Noto and in the county of Modica, particularly around Ragusa and subsequently also in Scicli. By the late sixteenth century, Noto was said to produce 100,000 *braccia* of wool cloth for export each

Table 4.3 Bactinderia *and* paratoria, *1300–1499*

Locality	Date	Documentary sources
Batticano (Corleone)	1452 (PP)	Garufi, 'Patti agrari e comuni feudali', doc. v
Brucato	1472 (BB)	Sorrenti, *Patrimonio fondiario*, pp. 78–80
Caltagirone	1471 (P)	CR 53, fos. 57–8
Castelbuono	1443 (BB)	C 2840, fos. 215v–18v
Castelmanfredi	1451 (BB)	C 2865, fos. 144–50
Castroreale	1453 (P)	Sorrenti, *Patrimonio fondiario*, p. 93, n. 72
Comiso	1468 (PP)	Barberi, *Capibrevi*, II, p. 362
Geraci	1452 (P)	*UM*, p. 892, n. 140
Giardinello (Corleone)	1300–1450 (PP)	Bresc and D'Angelo, 'Structure et évolution', 366
Lentini	1423 (BB)	C 2809, fos. 66–8
Mussomeli	1451 (BB)	C 2865, fos. 144–50
Nicosia	1444 (P)	C 2844, fo. 197
Noto	1438 (PP)	CR 18, fo. 176rv
	1449 (PP)	CR 30, fos. 148–9; C 2863, fo. 30rv
	1456 (PP)	C 2886, fos. 132–3
	1458 (P)	NN 6335, fo. 70v
	1490 (P)	NN 6343, fos. 6v–7
	1493 (PP)	CR 71, fos. 101–1bis
Palermo	1495 (P)	CR 77, fo. 108v
Piazza	1455 (PP)	C 2874, fo. 88v
Polizzi	1303 (BB)	Peri, 'Rinaldo di Giovanni Lombardo', 448
	1347 (BB)	Barberi, *Capibrevi*, III, pp. 476–7
	1452 (BB)	C 2871, fos. 26v–7
	1300–1450 (PP)	Bresc and D'Angelo, 'Structure et évolution', 366
Randazzo	1434 (BB)	C 2823, fos. 58v–9
	1456 (B)	NR 5, fos. 143v–5v, 223v–4
	1469 (P)	CR 48, fo. 123rv
	1471 (BB)	CR 52, fos. 45–5quater
Risalaimi (Misilmeri)	1300–1450 (PP)	Bresc and D'Angelo, 'Structure et évolution', 366
Salemi	1493 (P)	CR 75, fo. 25rv
Santa Lucia	1469 (BB)	CR 50, fos. 60–60bisv
San Pietro Patti	1442 (P)	C 2843, fo. 36v
Sclafani and Caltavuturo	1445 (PP)	C 2849, fos. 188v–9

(P/PP) = one/more *paratorium*; (B/BB) = one/more *bactinderium*.

year.[119] There was probably also an industry in Syracuse. No major manufacturing centres seem to have existed in western Sicily in the fifteenth century.

A widespread view of local woollen production is that it was of the poorest quality, used only by peasants and other poor persons.[120] By the fifteenth century, however, rather better qualities of wool cloth were also being made. In 1474–5 the monastery of San Martino delle Scale, for example, bought three different kinds of black cloth in Ragusa; woollens came also in other colours. Special kinds of *orbace* were made in Randazzo,[121] Castiglione and Catania. A kind of mixed wool and, probably, linen cloth was produced under the generic name of *tela* (but the term referred to a wide variety of textiles, including pure linen and cotton ones). *Tela*, of which Noto was a major manufacturer, also had a modest foreign outlet.

In contrast to lower- and medium-range production, high-quality wool manufacture was never successfully established in Sicily. The two best-known attempts to set up high-quality industries were made in Palermo in the early fourteenth century, first by Federico III, who invited a group of Lombard Umiliati to establish one, and then by a Genoese adventurer, Alafranchino Gallo. Another Genoese made an apparently futile attempt to set up wool production in Messina in 1404 or 1405. Attempts to reintroduce wool manufacturing to Palermo were made in the late fifteenth century, but it is not clear whether they were more than moderately successful, and output was in any case of low quality.[122]

These failures are commonly explained as the result of the poor quality of local wool, of competition by cheaper rural production, or of the low skills of the labour force. In fact, none of these explanations are fully convincing.

The objections to using the low quality of Sicilian wool as an explanation for failed manufacture have been discussed above; in particular, better-quality wool could have been imported from

[119] This industry seems to have emerged in the fifteenth century. See Littara, *De rebus netinis*, pp. 109, 113 (1427, 1440): in Noto 'alio inferunt vel exportant pannos, telas, tergora et similia, quae suis in oppidis sunt operati'.
[120] da Piazza, *Cronaca*, II, chapter 16; Bozzo, '*Quaedam profetia*', 183.
[121] La Mantia ed., *Codice diplomatico*, no. 214 (1290).
[122] Epstein, 'Textile industry', 160–1; RC 190, fo. 303 (1495), cited in A. Baviera Albanese, *In Sicilia nel sec. XVI: verso una rivoluzione industriale?*, p. 74.

abroad had there been local demand for it. In other words, the quality of raw materials did not pose an insuperable obstacle. Nor is local competition a convincing explanation: successful domestic industries produced a different quality of cloth and supplied a different market than did high-quality, export-led industries. Concerning the third constraint, that of technical knowledge, two points can be made. First, Sicily did not lack domestic technical expertise; on the contrary, it possessed at least three distinct traditions of cloth-making. One was north Italian. Between the eleventh and the thirteenth centuries Corleone, Polizzi, Patti, Randazzo, Castrogiovanni and the rest of val di Noto were intensively settled by northern Italians; traces of this immigration survive to this day in local terminology for weaving. Similar considerations apply to the Muslim technical tradition, which left abundant linguistic traces: 54 out of 309 originally Arabic words current in medieval Sicily referred to clothing, dyeing and the cloth trade. The third strand in this complex web was provided by the Jews, whose traditional near-monopoly over dyeing in the Muslim world survived in the newly Christianized culture up to their expulsion from Sicily in 1492–3. Second, there seems no *prima facie* reason why immigration could not supply the requisite technical skills if these were lacking and in demand. The fact that a number of foreign textile workers immigrated to Palermo in the fourteenth and fifteenth centuries shows that the opportunity to import missing skills was available and could be pursued. The question to be answered is not, therefore, whether Sicilians were endowed with an insufficient but fixed bundle of skills, but rather, why, given existing technical endowments and opportunities, were they not taken advantage of?

A more satisfactory explanation of industrial failure can probably be found by looking at two, mutually reinforcing structural elements: first, the nature of foreign competition and market structures; second, the domestic institutional constraints on production.

Medieval high-quality wool manufacture was a typical oligopoly, characterized by the small size of the total market and by economies of scale in production, particularly with respect to the buying of raw materials and finishing processes. Technological barriers to entry were reinforced by the need for an industry to have access to established international commercial networks, because no regional or 'national' market was yet large enough to absorb the whole of an industry's output. These barriers to entry in the industry were raised further after the mid-fourteenth century, because declining population and shrinking upper-class incomes led to a fall in demand for high-quality cloth and to increasing diversification of quality. In such conditions, it was extremely difficult for a new high-quality, export-led manufacturing industry producing for the same market to emerge.[123]

One can assume, in addition, that foreign merchants and local intermediaries had no interest in fostering Sicilian competition, for both parties were keen (in order to keep up a roughly even balance of trade) to maintain and strengthen the link between what they bought (sold), mainly grain, and the only major article they could sell (buy), namely high-quality cloth.[124] Any collusion would have been strengthened after the mid-fourteenth century, when regional grain and cloth markets were shared out between the Genoese and Catalan merchants, both of which had a strong interest in keeping a firm hold over the foreign cloth market (see chapter 3). Finally, political instability and the fragmentation of the domestic market after 1350, which restricted factor mobility, also contributed to the difficulties in establishing a new high-quality industry.

A factor which probably played just as crucial a role as market structure in holding up industrial development in this sector was that of Sicilian urban and corporate structures. Although discussed for the most part in the context of the woollen industry, we shall see that these structures affected the whole of Sicilian domestic industry. Before proceeding, however, it should be noted that, apart from some scattered references to weavers and looms in private inventories, we are in almost total ignorance about the organization of production.

The scanty evidence we do possess suggests that the institutional framework in which Sicilian manufactures operated was rather unusual for late medieval Europe. First and foremost, very few

[123] The role of entry costs for the failure of Sicilian high-quality wool manufacture is suggested by the contrasting case of Sicilian silk manufactured goods for export. Silk manufacture developed successfully in the late fifteenth century when foreign competition was not yet fully established, and foreign markets were expanding fast. Neither the quality of local silk nor available technical skills were superior to those of the wool industry; see below, n. 187. I cannot here address the question of how certain areas, in northern Italy and elsewhere, established a lead in high-quality cloth manufacturing *before* the mid-fourteenth century; one may, however, remark that Sicily's *lack* of high-quality production was the norm rather than the exception in medieval Europe.

[124] Abulafia, *Two Italies*, p. 284, makes a similar point for the twelfth century.

craft organizations for cloth seem to have existed in medieval Sicily. No medieval craft statutes for the industry survive and, with the exception of Palermo in the 1380s and 1430s[125] and Catania in the 1430s,[126] I have found no mention of cloth guilds – despite the fact that weavers' guilds tended usually to develop before those of more specialized artisans. Second, although evidence for putting-out does exist, and master artisans producing *tela* and wool cloth are referred to (though mainly for Noto, Sicily's main cloth-making centre), there is also little direct testimony of involvement of merchant or urban capital in manufacturing. Commercial capital seems to have been involved instead in large-scale trade, and once more most references to this come from Noto.

Given the strong evidence for regional manufacturing, the lack of references to its organization is surprising. On the other hand, although the paucity of surviving records makes any generalization suspect, it is hard to believe that the poor evidence for one of the most characteristic institutions of medieval Europe is due simply to chance documentary survival. The presence among weavers of women, who were normally excluded from corporate organization, is a further clue that production was structured informally.[127]

If the lack of evidence for guilds and for the formal organization of production reflects an actual state of affairs, the reason could lie in the structure of the Sicilian market and in the nature of medieval corporations. These existed to exclude non-participants as much as to enforce and regulate common standards of economic behaviour; in fact, common and rigidly enforced standards were the principal means of exclusion. Corporate monopoly restricted access to the market and (at least in theory) enforced prices to the general disadvantage of consumers.[128] In order to enforce such regulations effectively, guilds and corporations had to have access to urban political authority, either directly or filtered through intermediate powers. In turn, for such authority to be an effective means of corporate enforcement, the town had to have control over the surrounding countryside.

[125] F. Maggiore Perni, *La popolazione di Sicilia e di Palermo dal X al XVIII secolo*, pp. 599–600; *UM*, p. 212, Table 29.

[126] F. Marletta, 'La costituzione e le prime vicende delle maestranze di Catania', 97, 101.

[127] See M. Kowaleski and J. M. Bennett, 'Crafts, gilds, and women in the Middle Ages: Fifty years after Marian K. Dale'.

[128] Kula, *Economic theory*, chapter 3.

We saw above that Sicily lacked a major condition for guilds to emerge, namely strong urban territorial control. If, indeed, a significant proportion of the price increase of manufactured goods in late medieval Europe was the result of intensified urban (guild) monopolies, as I suggest in chapter 6, the actual *decline* in Sicily of the real price of *orbace* after 1350,[129] despite the contemporary doubling of the nominal price of wool and steep wage increases, also suggests a *lack* of producer or commercial monopolies.

In Sicily the functional distinction between town and country was fairly blurred, not least because a large proportion of the peasantry lived within town walls. It is therefore improbable that textile crafts did not emerge because production was so dispersed within small peasant communities that the costs of setting up corporate structures were too high. In fifteenth-century val di Noto, where manufacturing was most developed, eighty per cent of the population lived in communities with more than 300 hearths.[130] A further reason why conditions for guilds in Sicily were unpropitious may have been technological. In pre-industrial Europe, easy-to-master types of production like linen,[131] or industries producing cheap, unstandardized wool cloths, seem often to have lacked guild structures, and these were precisely the industries most present in Sicily. Last but not least, Sicilian urban society before the 1430s seems to have been remarkably unstructured and informal; such informality, reflected in the weakness of cognatic descent structures and of extra-familial ties of neighbourhood and fraternity and enhanced by the very high mobility of the Sicilian population, cannot have provided a propitious setting for the emergence of corporate bonds of solidarity.

On the other hand, in the course of the fifteenth century, artisans in other employment in the larger towns did begin to organize in corporations and to be represented in local government. The possibility that because of the small profit margins involved and the large number of competing producers, the home cloth market was not

[129] The nominal price increased by fifteen to twenty-five per cent between 1299 and 1399 (Trasselli, 'Tessuti di lana', 306–7).
[130] In 1439, 73.3 per cent of the entire Sicilian population lived in communities of over 300 hearths (which did, however, include outlying hamlets). In val Demone this proportion was 50.9 per cent, compared to 87 per cent in val di Mazara and 81.9 per cent in val di Noto.
[131] I. Turnau, 'The organization of the European textile industry from the thirteenth to the eighteenth century', 590–1.

lucrative enough to be worth organizing corporate control, could also explain the lack of artisan requests for restrictive legislation in this period. Fifteenth-century guilds seem to have been primarily involved in promoting access to local power structures for their members rather than in defending their trade (see chapter 7).

Cloth manufacture: conclusions

While detailed records for local manufacturing (particularly of linen) are not available, there is strong circumstantial evidence that it expanded during the late fourteenth and fifteenth centuries in response to rising domestic demand. Evidence for personal consumption from inventories and other sources shows a wide range of products for nearly every level of personal need, including the important matter of colour variety.[132] Evidence for cloth imports shows that they were restricted to high-quality woollens (see chapter 6). Juxtaposing these two sources, we see that Sicilian manufacturing was neither technically primitive nor undeveloped.

In Sicily, as in southern Italy and north Africa, woollens were less popular than linen and cotton cloth.[133] However, wool manufacture was not restricted to *orbace*, and the main cloth-making centre, Noto, developed into a major woollen export industry in the sixteenth century. The lack of high-quality woollen cloth industries was probably due as much to internal institutional features as to foreign competition. Thus, Sicilian wool manufacture developed in a context heavily conditioned by the linen and cotton industries, which commanded a larger share of the market. For technical and social reasons – besides the lack of social integration just discussed, linen and cotton production may have been more deeply integrated into the peasants' household economy than wool production – corporate structures were unnecessary, or too hard to establish, for non-woollen production; this corporate weakness may have affected woollen manufacture also. A probably more significant factor which affected the entire cloth industry was that the cost of enforcing corporate monitoring of output standards was too high in the context of a relatively unspecialized (technically unsophisticated), dispersed, but also rapidly expanding market and a highly

---

[132] Epstein, 'Textile industry', 163–5.
[133] Yver, *Commerce*, pp. 84–95, 104, 189; R. Brunschvig, *La Berbérie orientale sous les Hafsides, des origines à la fin du XVe siècle*, I, pp. 231–2.

200 An island for itself

mobile labour force. The virtual absence of international competition for cheap cloths (the failure of foreign fustians to break into the Sicilian market is particularly revealing) in an expanding home market, reduced (but did not exclude) the desirability of craft monopolies. It may in fact have been the *lack* of standardization that suited consumers best, and insured producers against uncontrollable fluctuation of fashion tied to particular segments of the population.[134]

This would appear to be demonstrated by the fact that in those sectors – primarily the fustian industry – in which these same institutional factors (location of production close to sources of raw material, energy and labour, and apparent lack of corporations) were favourable, Sicilian manufacturing was capable of resisting strong foreign competition.[135]

SILK PRODUCTION AND MANUFACTURE

Early medieval Sicily was famous for its silk manufactured goods which supplied the Muslim and Norman courts and were exported abroad, mostly to Africa;[136] Sicilian Jews are said to have introduced the craft to Lucca.[137] Silk was a 'luxury [product] that had been democratized since the Arab–Norman era'.[138] Before the Black Death, silk was used for veils, scarves and a number of garment decorations; most dowries listed some silk cloth. Widespread use was reflected also in Messina's early sumptuary laws.[139] It has, however, been argued that by the early fifteenth century, only raw silk production survived; manufacturing only reappeared in the late fifteenth century in Messina.[140] This picture has recently

[134] Thirsk, *Economic policy*, pp. 114–17.
[135] Similar conditions applied in Aragon; see Carrère, 'La draperie en Catalogne et en Aragon au XVe siècle'.
[136] Goitein, 'Sicily and southern Italy in the Cairo Geniza documents', 12–14; C. Cahen, 'Douanes et commerce dans les ports méditerranéens de l'Egypte médiéval d'après le *Minhâdj* d'al-Makhzûmi', 229.
[137] Mazzaoui, *Italian cotton industry*, p. 66.
[138] *UM*, p. 198. See also Bresc, 'Reti di scambio locale e interregionale nell'Italia dell'alto Medioevo', p. 166.
[139] Giardina ed., *Capitoli*, no. 18 (1272); see also Testa ed., *Capitula*, I, pp. 88–98 for further legislation of 1309 or 1324.
[140] C. Gallo, 'Il setificio in Sicilia. Saggio storico-politico', p. 225; G. Platania, 'Sulle vicende della sericoltura in Sicilia'; Marletta, 'L'arte della seta a Catania nei sec. XV–XVII'; Petino, 'L'arte ed il consolato'; Trasselli, 'Ricerche sulla seta siciliana (sec. XIV–XVII)'; D'Alessandro, *Politica e società*, p. 222.

been filled in for Palermo, where Bresc has shown that *setaroli* had disappeared by 1360.[141] The crisis in the silk industry is usually explained as a result of the disruption caused by the anti-Angevin war or, in a similar way as with the cloth industry, as due to international competition. The first part of this argument, that before the Vespers Sicily possessed strong, high-quality manufacturing,' defies the surviving evidence. This is simply too scanty to sustain the burden of a Norman or Hohenstaufen 'golden age' for silk manufacture.[142] Until the eleventh century or later, Sicily probably imported most of its raw silk (perhaps from Spain and certainly from Calabria), a fact that does not argue for widespread use of silk cloth.[143] Production may have spread following the Norman conquest and the strengthening of ties between Sicily and Calabria;[144] this hypothesis would account for silk's diffusion in early fourteenth-century Palermo. There is, on the other hand, no proof of any major manufacturing in the island before the Black Death.

If this last point is correct, much of the argument that a decline took place after 1282 or after 1350 collapses. The question instead becomes, why did silk manufacture disappear from Palermo around 1360 and rather suddenly resurface in Messina a century later? There are two problems with an answer which lays responsibility for the crisis with the Vespers and foreign competition.[145] First, around the time when silk manufacturing disappeared in Palermo, intense relations between the city and the kingdom of Naples actually resumed. And second, there is no evidence for silk cloth imports (in other words, outside competition) before the mid-fifteenth century.[146] There is, however, an alternative answer to the question that fits the evidence at our disposal.

Up to the end of the fifteenth century and beyond, eastern val Demone was the main silk-producing area in Sicily. This seems to

---

[141] *UM*, p. 200.
[142] Abulafia, *Two Italies*, pp. 47, 223.
[143] A. Guillou, 'La soie sicilienne au Xe–XIe s.', pp. 285–8; Ashtor, 'Gli ebrei nel commercio mediterraneo nell'Alto Medioevo (sec. X–XI)', pp. 446–9; M. Bettelli Bergamaschi, '*Morarii* e *celsi*: la gelsicoltura in Italia nell'Alto Medioevo', 16, 19–20.
[144] Peri, *Città e campagna*, II, p. 247.
[145] Petino, 'L'arte ed il consolato', 4–5; *UM*, p. 200.
[146] *UM*, p. 491.

belie a narrow connection between silk cultivation and Muslim presence, for the area was only weakly settled by Muslims; it supports instead the hypothesis that manufacturing originated largely on the mainland and spread after the Norman conquest. Messina was supplying other parts of Sicily, including Palermo, with silk well before the Black Death.[147] Genoese merchants exported silk from Messina in 1271,[148] and again probably a century later;[149] Messina may have exported raw silk to Ancona in the late fourteenth century.[150]

Silk manufacture was also better established in eastern Sicily than in the west. Describing Catania's welcome to King Ludovico, Michele da Piazza wrote how everybody wore silk garments and how 'in streets and open spaces silk cloths were hung in the air, such that the sun could not reach the ground'.[151] Making due allowance for his rhetoric, this does not suggest a major crisis in production, particularly since da Piazza did not elsewhere eschew dire descriptions of social and economic decay. His words find confirmation in the fact that King Federico was still buying silk cloth in eastern Sicily, probably in Catania itself, in the 1370s.[152] Other evidence suggests that local manufacturing, already established in the early fourteenth century, was untouched by crisis after the Black Death.[153]

The survival of silk production in eastern Sicily shows that its decline in Palermo was not the result of a *general* slump in the sector, but of the fragmentation of the domestic market after 1350, which interrupted supplies of raw material between eastern and western Sicily. Political reunification brought about a small recovery of silk manufacture in Palermo after 1400, but by then working conditions were difficult and local technical traditions had been lost: two artisans left Sicily for Genoa, and an immigrant from Catanzaro agreed to teach a Jewish woman his art.[154] The mention of a *domus*

[147] *UM*, p. 197 n. 17 (1308).
[148] *RCA*, VI, no. 890.
[149] Day, *Douanes*, pp. 288, 451 (1376).
[150] Ciavarini ed., *Statuti anconitani*, pp. 257–9 (1382).
[151] da Piazza, *Cronaca*, I, chapters 32 (1348), 64 (1354).
[152] RC 4, fo. 241.
[153] Gallo, 'Setificio'; Gaudioso, *La comunità ebraica di Catania nei secoli XIV e XV*, pp. 146–7.
[154] *UM*, pp. 200 n. 37 (1436), 201 n. 42 (1432).

sete in Palermo in 1432,[155] and a vague reference to silk produced in
Mazara in the 1460s,[156] do little to dispel the impression that the
effect of the fourteenth-century political crisis had been to concentrate production and manufacture in the east, where it had always
been strongest anyhow.[157]

Nonetheless, between 1370 and 1460, references to silk production in eastern val Demone are rather scanty. In May 1421, Alfonso
made Antonio de Troia of Messina his master silk weaver, and a few
days later the city's jurors were given the right to nominate a silk
weigher (*ponderator serici*);[158] a 'silk weavers street' (*ruga sitarolis*)
was recorded there in the same period.[159] During the following two
decades, production probably increased. A first reference to
exports dates from 1434,[160] and the shift in the 1430s of Messina's
fair from April to August, when the silk cocoons were ready for
sale, must have been an attempt to respond to the growth of – and to
stimulate – the silk market.[161] In nearby Calabria, Reggio and
Crotone were forced to move back from August to April the dates
of their fairs, in recognition of Messina's regional economic hegemony.[162] As a result of these changes, in the course of the
fifteenth century Messina came to control most of the silk production of north-eastern Sicily and of southern Calabria.[163]

Some idea of the rapidly rising volume of production can be had
from toll returns on raw silk. In early 1440, the toll was pawned to
the Messinese Virgilio de Giordano for 130 *onze*. A year later, the
king wrote to the viceroy that he intended to sell the toll to Antonio
Compagno of Messina for 400 *onze*, having been told that it raised
forty to fifty *onze* a year. Three weeks later, the toll was sold instead
to the Messinese Giovanni de Chirino (Chirini) for 600 *onze*, with a

[155] CR 16, fos. 311–12.
[156] LV 80, fo. 314 (1462).
[157] For a toll on silk exports from Agrigento in 1496 see Gallo, 'Setificio', p. 228.
[158] CR 9, fo. 911; Giardina ed., *Capitoli*, no. 67.
[159] Gabotto, 'Inventari messinesi', 259 (1406).
[160] Carrère, *Barcelone*, I, p. 368.
[161] Giardina ed., *Capitoli*, nos. 76, 78 (1436, 1437).
[162] Grohmann, *Fiere*, pp. 73–4. The date of Reggio's fair changed in 1428, suggesting the *terminus post quem* for Messina's August event.
[163] Pontieri, *Calabria*, pp. 100–1; Del Treppo, *Mercanti catalani*, p. 178. Genoese
importers in the late fifteenth and early sixteenth centuries did, however, distinguish between Calabrian and Sicilian silk (D. Gioffrè, 'Il commercio d'importazione genovese alla luce di registri del dazio 1495–1537', pp. 183, 186).

guaranteed income of eighty *onze*.[164] Since the toll was two *grani* per lb.,[165] this means that no less that 24,000 lbs. (about eight tons) per year was being exported at that time. Production expanded so rapidly that in 1469 the toll was resold to Giovanni de Chirino for 1,000 *onze*. Despite this upward revision, revenues were still greatly underestimated; only two years later the crown could raise the toll's price to 2,000 *onze*. The sale was in perpetuity, which may explain the high bidding, although the crown reserved the right to reclaim the toll.[166] At an eight to ten per cent return, an estimated 48,000–60,000 lbs. of raw silk must have then been traded each year in Messina. Production may have risen to 100,000 lbs. by the early sixteenth century;[167] if so, the value of the silk trade would have been nearly three times that of grain exports (see chapter 6). The trade's importance is also suggested by a request of 1465 by Messina's Jewish community (which was heavily involved in the silk industry) to be exempted from the toll,[168] and by the crown's insistence on resuming the toll in the 1490s with the proceeds of a 100,000 florin tax levied on Sicilian Jews before their expulsion.[169]

From the 1440s at the latest, then, silk was mainly exported abroad.[170] Up to the late 1460s, most of it was probably shipped on the Venetian galleys to Flanders and northern Europe. Towards the end of the century, references to Flanders disappear, and Genoa became Messina's main client.[171] Some silk also passed through Palermo, where the Neapolitan Miraballi competed with Florentine

---

[164] C 2836, fos. 43–6 (1440); RC 75, fos. 448–9 (1440); C 2935, fo. 206 (1441); RC 76, fo. 460rv (1441); C 2838, fo. 178rv (1441); C 2845, fos. 98–101 (1444).

[165] NM 6A, fo. 223rv (1469); CR 75, 6 unnumbered fos. (24 March 1494). The toll may have increased soon after (see below, n. 169).

[166] CR 51, fos. 477rv, 479rv, 481–7v, throughout.

[167] Barberi, *Liber de secretiis*, p. 30, quotes a toll yield of 1,000 *onze* in 1506, which at the current excise rates (see nn. 165, 169) would suggest exports of between 30,000 and 100,000 lbs. See below, chapter 6, n. 83.

[168] Lagumina and Lagumina eds., *Codice dei giudei*, II, pp. 24–5 (1465). For the community's involvement in the silk industry see NM 6A, fo. 212 (1469); NM 6B, fos. 577v, 592v (1470); RC 136, fo. 48rv (1476); NM 7, fo. 322v (1492).

[169] CR 872, fo. 141 (1493); CR 75, 6 unnumbered fos. (24 March 1494). In 1496 the toll, which was to be excluded from sale for twenty years, may have risen temporarily to 1 *tarì* (CR 875, fo. 315).

[170] CR 875, fo. 315 (1496) refers to both domestic and export trade.

[171] NM 10, fo. 535 (1492); Gioffrè, 'Commercio', pp. 183, 187.

merchants.[172] By contrast, there is little evidence that foreigners had much hold on the market in Messina,[173] which was dominated by the local urban nobility.

Silkworms were bred in Aci, Catania, and in the vast southeastern county of Modica, as well as in Messina and its district at least as far west as Castroreale.[174] By the 1460s, Messina's district was deeply involved in the production of silk under the direct control of its nobility.[175] We find a Comito, a Carradore, a Spatafora, a Muleti and two Staiti,[176] and some equally enterprising but less prominent citizens of Messina,[177] buying silk in the countryside and sending it abroad with simple *commenda* contracts. The activities of Marino Campolo, member of a leading Messinese family, are well documented. Like other men of his background,[178] he gave cash, wheat and sometimes wool caps to peasants in the winter in exchange for raw silk delivered the following summer. As with credit markets for grain and cheese production, the silk's anticipated price was corrected on the basis of the price current at delivery.[179] Campolo also put out flax, probably to be woven, possibly for the veils exported to Spain.[180] Many other owners of suburban land also actively participated in the market in mulberry leaves, which they sold to local peasants and occasionally to

---

[172] *UM*, pp. 566 n. 124, 574.
[173] NM 6A, fo. 261rv (7 August 1469): a Cologne merchants buys more than 500 lbs. at nine *tarì* per lb. to be shipped with the Venetian *muda*.
[174] CR 67, fos. 166–6bis (1485): life concession to *nobilis* Nicola de Chiros of 'officis ordinandi locum seu loca patellorum seu manganellorum extrahendi sericum novum'.
[175] Silk-producing localities referred to in NM 5, 6A-B, 7 and 10 (1469–91) are Mandanici, Santo Stefano di Briga, Tremestieri, San Filippo lo Grande, Santa Lucia, Masse, Salice, Marella, Boccetta, Gadara, San Michele, Faro, Castania, Gesso, Bavuso, Monforte. Messina merchants also controlled the silk industry further afield (Sipione, 'Tre documenti', 243–4).
[176] NM 10, fos. 29v–31 (1477): *nobilis* Andrea Comito takes *c.* 1,500 lbs. in *commenda* on a ship to Flanders; NM 10, fo. 36rv (1477): *nobilis* Giovanni Carradore sells 202 lbs. to another Messinese; NM 7, fos. 37v, 522v–3, 534v (1491): *nobilis* Giacomo Spatafora; NM 10, fos. 534v, 535rv (1492): *nobilis* Giovanni Muleti. For the Staiti see below, n. 178.
[177] NM 5, fos. 111v–12 (1446?): *commenda* by Giovanni di Alessandro; NM 6A, fo. 264 (1469): Friar Onofrio de Bufalis gives 32 lbs. in *commenda* for Flanders.
[178] NM 6B, fos. 447v, 465: Giovan Andrea Staiti; fo. 452: *nobilis* Nicola de Bufalis; fo. 480: Pietro Staiti gives money, flax and cloth to an inhabitant of Masse in exchange for the following season's raw silk.
[179] NM 6B, fos. 427, 427v, 428v, 429, 432v, throughout (1469).
[180] NB 6B, fos. 441v, 446–7v, 450, 452, 459v–60, 470rv, 480v (1470).

Calabrian immigrants who supplemented their income by breeding silkworms.[181]

As this discussion suggests, from the mid-fifteenth century Sicilian silk was increasingly produced for foreign markets. Although domestic manufacture was not insignificant, before the late fifteenth century production was mainly restricted to light cloths. Late fifteenth-century inventories show a remarkable diffusion of locally-made silk garments and decorations in val di Noto and val Demone.[182] A petition by the men of Patti referring to 'fustians, silks and *tili*' taken to the fair of Randazzo is a rare reference to local manufacturing;[183] the product's place of origin is also occasionally mentioned.[184] We saw that production in Catania survived the demographic crisis. An attempt was made in the 1470s to concentrate in a single building work done in private homes by both Jewish and Christian masters,[185] perhaps partly in response to competition from Messina,[186] but also probably in order to tax output more easily.

Nonetheless, for a long time the small size of the domestic market, but more especially the poor quality of Sicilian silk,[187] inhibited the growth of more sophisticated production. Under the impact of foreign demand and of changing fashions and tastes among the upper classes, a more specialized manufacturing industry producing velvets was established in Messina in the 1480s.[188] As suggested above, the reason the silk industry was more successful than high-quality wool manufacturing was probably a matter of diverging entry costs, which were substantially lower for the silk industry than for high-quality woollens. This was because the silk industry faced new and rapidly expanding international markets in

---

[181] NM 6A, fos. 41rv, 151v (1468–9); NM 7, fos. 71, 246v, 279 (the buyer is a Calabrian immigrant), 296, 300, 356v–7, 370v, 376v (1491–2).

[182] Mauceri, 'Inventari inediti'.

[183] Sciacca, *Patti*, p. 313 (1463).

[184] Messina: NM 5, fo. 148 (1446); Randazzo: NR 15, fo. 437 (1491); Monte San Giuliano, Trapani: *UM*, pp. 203–4.

[185] CR 80, fos. 51–1quater (1475–97).

[186] Lagumina and Lagumina eds., *Codice dei Giudei*, III, no. 804 (1490).

[187] F. Edler de Roover, 'Andrea Banchi, Florentine silk manufacturer and merchant in the fifteenth century', 237–41; Gioffrè, 'Commercio', p. 186. The poor quality of local raw material seems to explain why, in 1493, two entrepreneurs in Messina asked to import foreign silk for their twenty looms (Cancila, *Baroni e popolo*, p. 85).

[188] Trasselli, 'Ricerche sulla seta', 225, dates the introduction of velvet weaving to 1486; see Cancila, *Impresa redditi*, pp. 261–2; Cancila, *Baroni e popolo*, p. 85.

which, in contrast to the luxury wool industry, neither technical or commercial know-how were yet in the hands of established competitors.

The discussion of silk production throws some light on two issues I referred to earlier when discussing cloth manufacture. On the one hand, it demonstrates the increasing complexity of the rural economy in eastern val Demone, an area where intensive agriculture and specialized manufacture were rapidly combining to overcome the lack of arable land. By the second half of the fifteenth century, when the first relevant notarial records appear, a peculiar agricultural system had begun to develop, which combined into an integrated whole the individual seasonal rotations of the production and transformation of flax (in the high summer and winter), silk (between May and August),[189] wine (in the spring and autumn) and also, by the end of the century, oil[190] (in the early spring and mid-winter).[191]

On the other hand, the preceding discussion helps analyse the process of *emergence* of domestic industry. During the last two decades, rural domestic industry, or 'proto-industry', has become a major area of enquiry for early modern demographic and economic historians. Particular attention has been given to relations between domestic manufacture and population patterns. By contrast, the problem of the origins of domestic industries, which often emerged for the first time in the later Middle Ages, has seldom been addressed, with the result that links between wider social, economic and institutional factors and the emergence of a particular industry at a particular time and place are less well understood.[192] Although these issues cannot be discussed in detail here, we can use the example of the Sicilian silk industry to suggest some points of contrast with current theories of proto-industry, and some further hypotheses about the emergence of the other domestic cloth industries.

---

[189] Fazello, *Due deche*, pp. 28–9, gives a detailed description of the process.
[190] *Ibid.*, p. 296.
[191] A similar pattern emerged in sixteenth-century Calabria (Galasso, *Economia e società*, p. 352).
[192] See, for example, W. Fischer, 'Rural industry and population change'; P. Deyon, 'Fécondité et limites du modèle protoindustriel: premier bilan'; L. A. Clarkson, *Proto-industrialization: the first phase of industrialization?*, chapter 5.

The two main models of proto-industrialization[193] take as their starting point the existence of a population of under-employed peasants living at the subsistence margin in an infertile upland area – in other words, living in a condition of relative Malthusian over-population. Urban entrepreneurs exploit peasant poverty by inducing them to integrate their agricultural revenues with a new export-led domestic industry, which often harnesses pre-existing peasant handicraft skills. The merchants provide tools, sometimes raw materials, and market the output abroad. Domestic industry raises the peasants' subsistence ceiling and thus tends to promote further population growth, which in turn increases demand for agricultural products from neighbouring regions and promotes specialization.

How does the Sicilian silk industry fit this model? First, output from the silk industry began to grow in the 1440s; given that the mulberry trees used to feed the silk-worms take some years to produce sufficient foliage, the first impulse to expand production must have come in the early 1430s, when the population had barely begun to recover from its lowest ebb.[194] Contrary to what the proto-industry models predict, therefore, the industry began to emerge in a period of very *low* population pressure. Second, the industry grew in response to foreign demand mediated by entrepreneurs from Messina, who harnessed to production for foreign markets an activity that had been practised in val Demone for centuries as a marginal form of peasant by-employment. This point, therefore, conforms to the proto-industry models. Third, from about 1470 – thus with a lag of one generation over the initial increase in silk output, and after a period of slow demographic growth compared with other *valli* – val Demone began to experience the most rapid population growth rate in Sicily, sustained by increasing food imports from western Sicily. However, part of this demographic increase seems to have been caused by immigrants attracted by local economic opportunities (see chapter 2).

Thus, the Sicilian silk industry fits the model of proto-industry only in part. Specialization as a result of comparative advantage did

193 F. F. Mendels, 'Proto-industrialization: the first phase of the industrialization process'; Kriedte, Medick and Schlumbohm, *Industrialization before industrialization*.
194 This hypothesis is sustained by the shift around 1428 of Messina's fair from May to August, when the silk was marketed (above, n. 162).

occur, and the population does seem to have increased more rapidly than elsewhere in Sicily parallel to the growth of the silk industry; but it is unclear what proportion of the population increase was caused by endogenous adaptation to the new opportunities provided by silk in contrast to other products like wine, oil and sugar, and what proportion was the result of a net influx of immigrants. The most serious inconsistency with the model, however, concerns the causes for the initial emergence of a domestic industry. The model, we saw, postulates that rural domestic industry was adopted in response to relative overpopulation by peasant societies which pursued traditional subsistence strategies; in other words, that domestic industry emerged as an exogenous input to a subsistent peasant society provided with 'unlimited supplies of labour'.[195] Instead, the Sicilian silk industry emerged in a period of very low population pressure, when land was relatively abundant, rents had sunk to their lowest point for a century, and conditions for peasant smallholders to pursue anti-mercantile subsistence strategies were particularly favourable. The reason peasants did not do so, as I argued in chapter 3, was that they did *not a priori* avoid market relations and commoditization if favourable conditions obtained, as they did in eastern val Demone. The silk industry developed there first because of that area's distinctive constellation of ecological, social and institutional features: a lack of good arable land combined with easy outside food supplies, strong peasant smallholding, widespread technical know-how, and access to international markets via Messina.

The emergence of domestic *cloth* industries in late medieval val Demone and val di Noto can probably be explained by similar features (although little as yet is known of conditions prevailing in val di Noto). I suggested above that, *ceteris paribus*, a relatively differentiated economy based on peasant smallholding such as that of val Demone before the Black Death, could better resist the demographic and economic effects of epidemics than an arable economy like that of western Sicily. An economy combining relatively high population density with a base of peasant smallholders could, in turn, easily adopt and integrate the seasonal cycles of cotton and flax production (which intensified during the winter and spring and slackened in the summer), and the low capital require-

---

[195] Above, chapter 1, n. 13; J. Mokyr, 'Growing-up and the industrial revolution in Europe'.

ments of the cognate industries. In order for such production to be established, however, two further conditions were necessary: a growth in demand for cheap cloth manufacturing, and access to cheap food supplies from neighbouring regions.

This explanation connects peasant smallholding, production of textile raw materials and the emergence of domestic manufacture. It is supported by the fact that, where domestic manufacture was lacking, as in val di Mazara, both other factors were missing also. It is based on the evidence (provided by the example of the silk industry) that peasants pursued economic strategies aimed at expanding, rather than simply reproducing, the resources at their disposal. I take up this point again below in the context of the sugar industry.

SUGAR PRODUCTION AND MANUFACTURE

Together with silk, sugar was late medieval Sicily's main high-quality and labour-intensive export. Because sugar manufacture involved considerable capital expenditure and was heavily taxed, it is also the best documented and studied productive structure in our period. More than silk, however, which was widely used by Sicilians before foreign demand stimulated the export industry in val Demone, sugar manufacture produced primarily for foreign outlets.[196]

Until the fourteenth century, sugar was regarded as an exotic garden plant, and was still found growing as such in many vineyards, orchards and herb gardens in the 1420s. During the early fourteenth century, however, a major change occurred in Palermo towards a more industrial type of sugar production. A moderate expansion of production from *c.*1320 (when sugar was used mostly by local apothecaries) took an upward turn towards 1350 as sugar mills and presses were introduced, possibly as labour-saving devices in the face of demographic decline.[197] By the 1370s, a new structure of production had emerged, combining artisan and patrician capital with the technical expertise of suburban gardeners. This phase, still dominated by artisans, was followed between 1400 and 1430 by a spate of investments by the local urban élite, the feudal aristocracy

---

[196] See Trasselli, 'Lineamenti di una storia dello zucchero siciliano'; Trasselli, *Storia dello zucchero*; Bresc, 'Les jardins'; *UM*, pp. 227–52.

[197] The reasons for these changes are not clear. Sugar mills, initially a simple adaptation of the oil press, began to evolve independently from the early fifteenth century. On the technology of sugar production see Trasselli, *Storia dello zucchero*, pp. xiv–xv, 131, 260 n. 93; Ashtor, 'Levantine sugar industry in the later Middle Ages: a case of technological decline', p. 106; *UM*, pp. 239–40.

and the upper echelons of the expanding state bureaucracy, who were attracted by the new markets for sugar offered by the Aragonese reconquest and by mounting international demand.[198] Sicilian know-how was sufficiently advanced in this period for experts from Palermo to travel to Barcelona to establish sugarworks there.[199] Between 1393 and 1416, cane plantations in Palermo increased tenfold to 162 ha.[200] By the 1430s, upper-class investors had completely taken over the industry, partly because technological development was making the costs of industrial plant too high for smaller investors. An average enterprise cost 220–50 *onze* a year to run, the value of a smallish fief.[201] To this one had to add the initial outlay in machinery, cane and often large engineering projects to convey water to plantations and mills.[202] An aqueduct built in the late fifteenth century by Pietro Campo, baron of Mussomeli, for his plantation in Ficarazzi still survives to remind us of the huge investments needed.[203] In 1452, Pietro Gaetani, an ennobled Pisan, asked to build an aqueduct on his land of Tripi.[204] The three brothers Staiti, who set up an enterprise in Santa Lucia in the late 1460s, built conduits two miles long to convey water to their mills and plantations; the initial outlay on this and other machinery was estimated at 8,000 florins, nearly 1,350 *onze*.[205] Clearly only very high returns could justify such investments. Annual sales in the west averaged 370 *onze* per enterprise,[206] providing fifty per cent profit at an average expenditure of 250 *onze*, compared to nominal returns on land and capital which did not exceed ten per cent.

In the course of the 1430s, production around Palermo faced a first serious crisis. With the exception of a new plantation established in

[198] Egyptian production also appears to have been declining in the late fourteenth century (A. Udovitch, R. Lopez and Miskimin, 'From England to Egypt, 1350–1500', p. 116).

[199] Carrère, *Barcelone*, I, pp. 386–7.

[200] RC 39, fos. 332v–3 (1400); Gregorio, 'Degli zuccheri siciliani', pp. 127, 130; Petralia, *Banchieri*, p. 327 n. 102. A. Lionti ed., *Codice diplomatico di Alfonso il Magnanimo*, no. 169 (1417) reports different figures.

[201] Trasselli, *Storia dello zucchero*, pp. 69–71, 73, 196; *UM*, p. 244.

[202] For technical innovations to irrigate the suburbs of Palermo see Bresc, 'Jardins', 66–7.

[203] Trasselli, *Storia dello zucchero*, pp. 198–200; see also *UM*, p. 235.

[204] CR 32, fo. 128rv. The project may have been abandoned.

[205] M. G. Militi and C. M. Rugolo, 'Per una storia del patriziato cittadino in Messina (Problemi e ricerche sul secolo XV)', 134; CR 48, fos. 63–3bis v (1470); Sorrenti, *Patrimonio fondiario*, p. 159 n. 174.

[206] *UM*, p. 247.

Brucato in 1435, those that had been established along the coast to the north and south of Palermo during the previous decade ceased to operate. Plantations dropped to 103 ha. in 1434–5, sinking to 70 ha. in 1436–7. Recovery was slow, and by 1448–9 cultivation had risen to only 89 ha. The crisis was perhaps the result of bad weather (suggested by the bad grain harvests in the same years), and of a recession in foreign trade; the latter also seems to have affected Messina in those years (see chapter 5). Labour scarcity after an epidemic in 1431 may have been a further contributory factor.[207]

At first, sugar-cane spread rather slowly to other parts of Sicily. The first significant move beyond Palermo's suburbs occurred in the 1430s, in order to avoid heavy taxation[208] and to be closer to sources of running water and of coppice for firing the furnaces.[209] As larger plantations and more complex and capital-intensive industrial structures (*trappeti*) developed, the extreme fragmentation of property and use-rights over watercourses around Palermo became increasingly burdensome and promoted expansion beyond the city's immediate environs to Carini, Ficarazzi, Partinico, Collesano, Bonfornello, Brucato and Vicari. From the 1440s, moreover, Palermo's population began to grow, increasing pressure on land and water, and favouring gardens and vineyards over sugar plantations which were more resource-intensive.[210]

Before the 1440s, cultivation elsewhere – in Trapani or Marsala, Aci and possibly Augusta – was mostly restricted to the orchard cultivation that in Palermo had disappeared nearly half a century before; Syracuse, where the earliest reference to sugar production dates from 1427, was probably the main exception.[211] By the 1440s

---

[207] A labour-saving innovation applied to the grinding mills may have been adopted in 1434 (Trasselli, *Storia dello zucchero*, p. 74; *UM*, p. 240); teams to prepare the cane for grinding appeared after 1436 (*UM*, 243). For trade in Messina see below, chapter 5.

[208] *UM*, p. 233; PR 24, fos. 501–8v (1421); C 2815, fo. 98v (1429).

[209] New springs were discovered (Bresc, 'Jardins', 61).

[210] Trasselli, *Storia dello zucchero*, pp. 156–7.

[211] Trasselli, 'Produzione e commercio dello zucchero in Sicilia dal XIII al XIX secolo', 329 n. 8, and J. Glénisson and Day eds. *Textes et documents d'histoire du Moyen Age, XIVe–XVe siècles*, II, pp. 55–8 for Trapani or Marsala; sugar seems to have disappeared from Marsala around 1430–40 and reappeared in the sixteenth century (Trasselli, *Storia dello zucchero*, p. xiv). Aci: *UM*, p. 232 (1420). Avola: CS 2, fo. 75v (1433). Syracuse: CS 1, fos. 38, 123 (1427, 1430); CS 2, fos. 203v–4 (1437); CS 7, fos. 19v–20 (1447); TRP Atti 10, fo. 72rv (1447); CS 9, fos. 13, 123–4 (1451, 1453). See also Trasselli, *Storia dello zucchero*, pp. 253 n. 39, 314 n. 28; C. M. Arezzo, *De situ insulae Siciliae libellus*, p. 15.

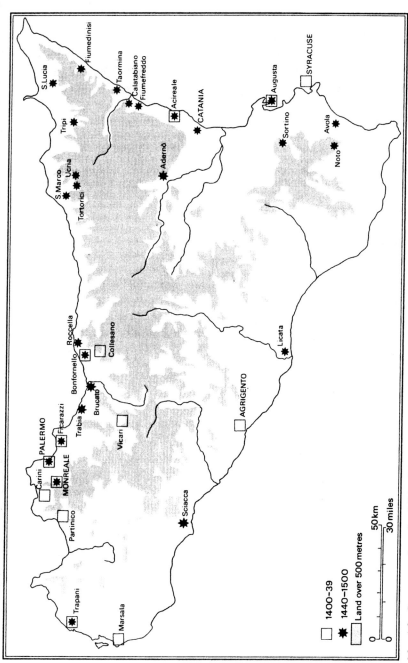

Map 4.3   Sugar manufacturing 1400–1500

Legend:

☐ 1400–39
✴ 1440–1500
▨ Land over 500 metres

Map labels:

S.Lucia
Fiumedinisi
Taormina
Calatabiano
Fiumefreddo
Acireale
CATANIA
Augusta
SYRACUSE
Tripi
Sortino
Avola
Noto
S.Marco
Ucria
Adernò
Tortorici
Roccella
Collesano
Bonfornello
Licata
Brucato
Ficarazzi
AGRIGENTO
PALERMO
Trabia
Vicari
Carini
MONREALE
Partinico
Sciacca
Trapani
Marsala

Scale:
0   50 km
0   30 miles

and 1450s, however, specialized plantations existed in Aci, Augusta, Avola, Noto and possibly Catania in val di Noto;[212] and in Calatabiano, Fiumefreddo, Taormina, Fiumedinisi, Tripi and Santa Lucia in val Demone.[213] The only *trappeti* in val di Mazara outside Palermo's influence were in Sciacca.[214] In 1452, Alfonso ordered the tax on production (*gabella del cannamele*), previously restricted to Palermo, to be levied throughout Sicily, except on the *trappeti* of Calatabiano, Augusta, Avola and Sortino, which were owned by members of the aristocracy. The king was doing them a favour, but was also trying to expand the industry so as to tax it in the future.[215]

Sugar-cane spread to the north- and south-east in the 1440s under the stimulus of rising foreign demand.[216] At first neither capital, water, firewood nor possibly manpower were lacking there; but all of them were needed intensively, and if any one factor was lacking,

[212] Aci: C 2837, fos. 1–3 (1440); C 2838, fo. 129v (1441); C 2843, fos. 27v–9 (1442); *UM*, p. 232 (1442, 1445); C 2852, fos. 80–1 (1445); CR 28, fo. 54 (1446); CR 849, unnumbered fos. (1446–7); C 2858, fo. 139rv (1447); C 2860, fo. 172rv (1448); CR 50, fo. 265rv (1469) and TRP Atti 27, fo. 147rv (1469). Augusta: *UM*, p. 232 (1448); C 2866, fo. 29rv (1450); TRP Atti 12, fos. 44, 46rv (1453); C 3473, fo. 24rv (1459). Avola: CS 2, fo. 75v (1433); *UM*, p. 232 (1443); RC 81, fo. 445rv (1444). Noto: C 2859, fos. 33v–4 (1447). See C 2880, fo. 101 (1457) for a *trappeto* owned by Antonio Caruso in the *Camera reginale*. Catania: C 2865, fos. 1v–2 (1450); C 2869, fo. 147v (1451).
[213] Calatabiano: C 2841, fo. 113rv (1443); *UM*, p. 232 (1444); C 2894, fo. 64 (1445); CR 849, fo. 60rv (1450); C 2869, fo. 138v (1451); C 2883, fo. 176 (1454); Petralia, *Banchieri*, p. 330; CR 41, fos. 302–3v (1460); TRP n.p. 1655, fo. 55rv (1472–3). Fiumefreddo: *UM*, p. 232 (1452); NR 10, fos. 10v–11, 11v (1478); NM 7, fos. 93, 187v–8 (1491–2). Taormina: C 2894, fo. 64 (1445); C 2859, fo. 117rv (1448); CR 849, fo. 60rv (1450); C 2874, fos. 61v–2 (1455); C 2887, fos. 41v–2v (1457); C 3477, fos. 51–2 (1462); NM 6B, fo. 388rv (1469); CR 47, fos. 283–3bis (1476); TRP Atti 35, fos. 83, 87v (1481); NM 7, fo. 436 (1492); CR 103, fos. 253v, 255 (1515); Fazello, *Due deche*, p. 77: 'Il paese di Taormina è abbondantissimo di cannamele.' Fiumedinisi: NM 6A, fo. 115v (1469); NM 6B, fos. 405v–6, 406v (1469), 516v–17 (1470). Tripi: C 2871, fo. 154rv, and CR 32, fo. 128rv (1452); Pietro Gaetani can build an aqueduct in his territory of Sant'Andrea 'ad producendum optimas cannamellas'. Santa Lucia: *UM*, p. 232 (1457); CR 47, fo. 90rv (1467); CR 48, fos. 62–3bis, 63–3bisv (1469, 1470); NM 6A, fos. 218v–19, 268–9, 275 (1469); NM 6B, fos. 504–5 (1470); NM 7, fos. 311v, 428v–9, 432–3, 465, 472v, 478v, 479, 497v, 500v, 551v (1492); CR 74, fo. 133rv (1492). See NM 6A, fo. 94v (1468) for sugar-works in the plain of Milazzo.
[214] I. Scaturro, *Storia della città di Sciacca e dei comuni della contrada saccense fra il Belice e il Platani*, I, p. 641.
[215] C 2896, fo. 112rv. Alfonso maintained the right to revoke the tax benefits.
[216] H. Van der Wee, *The growth of the Antwerp market and the European economy, fourteenth–sixteenth centuries*, III, p. 116; Van der Wee and T. Peeters, 'Un modèle dynamique de croissance interséculaire du commerce mondial (XIe–XVIIe siècles)', 112.

a crisis in sugar production could quickly ensue. The rapid rise and decline of many *trappeti* was partly a result of such deficiencies. Water and firewood were particularly abundant in val Demone, which began to supply Palermo and its environs after 1450 with wood for the furnaces and the barrels for packing refined sugar.[217] After the boom of the 1440s and 1450s, plantations expanded faster and more successfully in val Demone, especially along the eastern coast, than in val di Noto. Avola stagnated after 1443, Tripi disappeared after 1452; Augusta was last mentioned in 1459, Aci in 1469, Calatabiano in 1473. *Trappeti* survived instead in Fiumedinisi (where various takeovers occurred in 1469 and 1470),[218] Fiume-freddo and Santa Lucia (last mentioned in 1492), all situated in val Demone. Taormina exported sugar for a few years after 1470, but production seems to have been already declining.[219] On the other hand, in the 1480s and especially the 1490s, new industries developed near Adrano[220] and Licata,[221] while others recovered near Avola[222] in val di Noto, and in the county of San Marco[223] and Tortorici[224] in val Demone.

Eastern Sicily may have benefited from the deep recession that hit the west once more at the end of the century.[225] The crisis began rather suddenly, for new *trappeti* were still being installed in the early 1490s.[226] It has been explained as a consequence of the lack of firewood, of protracted drought, of soil exhaustion and plant

---

[217] Trasselli, *Storia dello zucchero*, p. 137.

[218] NM 6B, fos. 405v–6v (1469): Andrea and Nicolò Staiti buy out *nobilis* Andrea Gotto; 516v–17 (1470): Angelo Balsamo buys out Lodovico Bonfilio.

[219] TRP n.p. 1655, fo. 55rv (1472–3); TRP n.p. 1653, fo. 54rv (1476–7); TRP n.p. 1651, fos. 49–50v (1486–7); TRP n.p. 1638, fo. 58rv (1493–4).

[220] CR 65, fos. 65–6v (1483): water to be used for an *arbitrium*, a term commonly indicating sugarworks, by Rinaldo Spatafora.

[221] TRP Atti 55, fos. 57v–8 (1498).

[222] NS 1927, fos. 13v, 26v–8v, 71–2v (1498–9).

[223] RC 187, fos. 455–6v (1494).

[224] CR 84, fo. 382rv (1500).

[225] Trasselli, *Storia dello zucchero*, pp. xv–xvii, 206–7, 210, 234–5, 237, 244–6, 268–9, 275, 276; Cancila, *Baroni e popolo*, pp. 71–4; Cancila, *Impresa redditi*, pp. 136–7. For contemporary views on the recession see Barberi, *Liber de secretiis*, p. 15 (1506); Spata ed., *Capitula*, pp. 65–6 (1509); Testa ed., *Capitula*, I, p. 567 (1514). Exports to Genoa declined between 1495 and 1522 (Gioffrè, 'Commercio', p. 187). A brief recession hit Palermo in the 1460s, possibly in connection with a contemporary banking crisis due to the Catalan civil war; see Trasselli, *Storia dello zucchero*, pp. 190, 252 n. 34; C 3478, fos. 29v–30v (1463); CR 46, fos. 497–8v (1467).

[226] CR 870, fo. 79rv (1487); CR 71, fo. 52rv (1491).

disease, of high wages, and of competition from Madeira.[227] None of these elements taken singly or together, however, explains why the crisis was restricted to western Sicily, nor why a strong recovery occurred there after 1550.

Let us refer for the moment to what sugar-makers themselves said about the problem. Between 1460 and 1480, Palermo's producers complained about two things: excessively high taxes on production, and lack of oxen to work the sugar presses. Both complaints referred to issues which were specific to Palermo.

Because of Alfonso's provision of 1452, production (and to some extent exports) outside Palermo were either tax exempt or else evaded taxation;[228] thus, when Gian Luca Barberi described the crown's revenues in 1506, he only referred to the toll levied in and around Palermo. In 1460, Palermo requested that the tax be lowered, and asked again (it had already petitioned for this in 1452) that it be paid at the end of August when producers had just sold their sugar, instead of March when new canes were planted and cash was in short supply. The issue was apparently dropped because of the resistance of the marquis of Geraci, who owned the toll.[229]

In 1477, Palermo's producers asked to ban cattle exports, which they argued damaged grain and sugar production.[230] The latter was a well-founded complaint, for oxen (and sometimes horses) were used to work the sugar mills, and after the mid-fifteenth century they may have also helped to power presses for squeezing the cane.[231] What Palermo's producers did not mention, on the other hand, was that sugar producers in eastern Sicily were in the process of gaining two major technical advantages. First, in this period the east was better stocked with draught oxen than the west (see chapter 5); second, and more significantly, eastern *trappeti* were begin-

---

[227] Trasselli, 'La siccità in Sicilia nel XVI secolo'; Trasselli, *Da Ferdinando il Cattolico a Carlo V. L'esperienza siciliana, 1475–1525*, pp. 31–4; Trasselli, *Storia dello zucchero*, pp. xv–xvii, 244, 246, 276; Verlinden, 'Les débuts de la production et de l'exportation de sucre à Madère. Quel rôle y jouèrent les Italiens?'. Increasingly dense plantations in the fifteenth century may also have caused soil exhaustion (*UM*, pp. 231–2).

[228] *UM*, p. 250.

[229] C 2882, fos. 118v–20v (1452), De Vio ed., *Privilegia*, pp. 327–31; *ibid.*, pp. 341–50, and C 3474, fos. 76v–80v (1460). Sugar was ready by the end of March or May according to its degree of refinement (*UM*, p. 248).

[230] Testa ed., *Capitula*, pp. 392–8. See also below, chapter 5.

[231] For horses see Trasselli, *Storia dello zucchero*, pp. 126–33, 212, 216; *UM*, pp. 238–9; C 2864, fo. 144rv (1451).

ning to replace draught animals with water power to operate grinding mills and perhaps presses.[232] Although local water scarcity (caused by rising demand in a period of increased population pressure in an area that was already poorly served) and competition from Madeira may have contributed to Palermo's difficulties, it would thus appear that the manufacturing crisis after 1490 was mainly the outcome of discriminatory taxation and of a less efficient use of energy sources compared to eastern Sicily.

Producers in eastern Sicily outside Messina's range of influence might face two problems that western *trappeti* close to Palermo could avoid. One was to have access to sufficient capital resources. In fifteenth-century Palermo, investment originated with the feudal aristocracy and the urban nobility, the only groups that could command enough capital and credit to finance such expensive enterprises.[233] In eastern Sicily, by contrast, two distinct investment cycles in sugar production emerged. Until the mid-1450s, *trappeti* were owned nearly exclusively by aristocrats and high government officials: the protonotary Jacobus de Aricio and Peri Aragona in Avola, the Cardona and Platamone families in Aci, the Cruilles in Calatabiano, Pietro Gaetani (an ennobled merchant, originally from Pisa) in Tripi, the royal counsellor Gilbert de Ursa, and the treasurer Jaime Zumbo in Fiumefreddo and Taormina. Vassallo Speciale in Noto, the Bellomo family in Augusta (which disappears from the sources after 1459), the Florentine merchant Pietro Rindelli and his partner Goffredo Rizari, and a Catanese lawyer (Aci, 1441–8), were the only *trappeto* owners who were not aristocrats or government officials. After 1455, except for Guglielmo Raimondo

---

[232] Trasselli, *Storia dello zucchero*, pp. xiv–xv for water-powered mills (with no indication of locality). Sugar mills in Aci: CR 22, fos. 57–60v (1442); CR 28, fo. 54 (1446); C 2860, fo. 172rv (1448). Aqueducts in Tripi: C 2871, fo. 154rv, and CR 32, fo. 128rv (1452). CR 48, fos. 62–2bis (1469): Giovanni, Andrea and Nicola Staiti can build two mills in their 'arbitrio cannamelarum' in Santa Lucia; 63–3bisv (1470): the Staiti 'trassiru l'acqua dilu dictu flumi grandi occidentali [of Santa Lucia] per conducti per loru constructi et murati per spaciu di dui migla pocu plui oi minu undi spisiru grandi quantitati di dinari, et pretera fichiru far unu grandissimu trappito et notabili *et machini di acqua portata per lu dictu conductu et per li dicti conductu machini et trappitu et altri istrumenti necessarii et oportuni* ... hannu spisu appressu octumilia florini, et quistu presenti anni et passatu hannu abiviratu per li dicti conducti machinatu et coctu in lo dictu trappitu appressu quaranta cocti ... et più lu presenti annu intendinu et hannu preparatui plantari plui salmati di terra di cannameli' (my emphasis).

[233] *UM*, pp. 234–6.

Moncada in Augusta (where he took over the Bellomo enterprise together with the Messinese patrician Giovanni Romano), three de Spuches in Taormina in 1472, and Bernabò Gaetani (son of Piero, and only recently ennobled) in Calatabiano in 1478,[234] the urban nobility dominated the industry. Most of the patrician families involved – Saccàno, Staiti, Bonfilio, Gotto, Balsamo and Mirulla – came from Messina, where they had easy access to commercial capital. In this city, sugar manufacture involved people from the same background as investors in silk manufacture and trade.

The second problem was technical, and involved access to adequate trade networks for export. The sugar industry's high capital-intensity and dependence on foreign outlets restricted it to the wealthiest and most commercially active centres of the island. It was probably the distance from good trading outlets rather than financial difficulties that explains the industry's poor results in val di Noto. Since Palermo and Messina controlled a large proportion of Sicily's trading capital and networks already by 1450, and their share probably increased over time, we can understand why by 1500 the whole sugar industry was under the control of these two cities.

Within the scheme of economic dualism outlined in chapter 1, sugar manufacture is seen as an advanced sector surrounded by economic backwardness and traditionalism, 'the greatest effort of Sicilian capitalism'. Less positively, it is viewed as a form of speculative 'colonial' exploitation lacking backward and forward linkages, on the apparent assumption that sugar plantations could only develop under exploitative political and economic conditions.[235]

How accurate are these views? 'Feudal' and patrician entrepreneurs responded to foreign demand by investing large sums of money in a high-risk, capital-intensive industry with long-term returns (the cane took fifteen to twenty-seven months to develop). The industry's large profits reflected not 'speculation', but its high capital expenditure and risk. The industry was an entirely domestic development; control over the production and refining process was never relinquished to foreign capitalists, and profits stayed within Sicily. The industry responded positively to foreign competition through technological innovation, and survived until the late seven-

---

[234] On Bernabò see Pispisa, *Banchieri*, pp. 185–6.
[235] *UM*, pp. 227, 252; Luzzatto, 'Capitalismo coloniale nel Trecento'.

teenth century despite intense competition from Madeira and the Azores.[236]

By the late fifteenth century the original sugar *trappeti* had been transformed by their owners into farms that combined sugar cultivation with vineyards, olive and citrus groves, the raising of livestock and, in some cases, even the working of tunny fish.[237] These developments were made possible by exploiting economies of scale in processing (the sugar presses could be used for olives and grapes) and refining (the spread of bitter oranges was closely linked to the availability of sugar as a sweetener).[238]

An average *trappeto* employed forty to fifty people in the refining process, while cultivation occupied many hundreds. In 1582–3, a *trappeto* in Ficarazzi in western Sicily employed 600 people for about 25,000 working days, an average of forty-two days per person.[239] No comparable figures for any fifteenth-century enterprises are known, but such estimates suggest that these industries were far from being 'isolated nuclei' producing no economic feedback in a dualistic sense.

The sugar industry did not employ people full time, as the Ficarazzi enterprise shows. Most wage-labourers came from the mountainous north, from the Madonie to Palermo, and from the Nebrodi and Peloritani to north-eastern val Demone; however, western industries also drew people from central and south-western Sicily, and even from Calabria.[240] The sugar industry provided

[236] See above n. 207, below, n. 238; also Giuffrida, 'La produzione dello zucchero in un opificio della piana di Carini nella seconda metà del secolo XV'. The aqueducts used for irrigation also demonstrate considerable technical expertise. Sicilian and other western European technology is starkly contrasted with Middle Eastern 'backwardness' by Ashtor, 'Levantine sugar industry', pp. 105–6, 111, 114–15, on the basis of the numerical decline of sugar industries in the Levant; however, this phenomenon, which occurred also in Sicily, probably reflects rising economies of scale due to changing technology and intensification of production (*UM*, p. 231) rather than a decline in output.

[237] Trasselli, *Storia dello zucchero*, pp. 217–18, 240; TRP Atti 14, fo. 55rv (1454); C 3480, fos. 94v–5 (1460).

[238] Trasselli, *Storia dello zucchero*, p. 81; *UM*, p. 247; C 3490, fo. 53rv (1476): the government is warned of the arrival of Guillem Garcia, a merchant of Valencia, who 'segons havem entes ha del.liberat anar en aquiex regne e parar casa en la dita ciutat de Palerm per exercir la mercaderia e fer reffinar sucres, per la qual cosa haia trames aqui totes les heynes e instruments para.l dit reffinament necessaris, lo que fins aci en dit reyne no es stat exercit' (*sic*).

[239] *UM*, pp. 228–32; Trasselli, *Storia dello zucchero*, pp. xxii–xxiii.

[240] *Ibid.*, pp. 72–3, 124–5, 227–8, 238. Messina introduced the sugar industry to Calabria in the late fifteenth century (Pontieri, *Calabria*, pp. 38, 97 n. 1; Tras-

employment for peasants, artisans and mule drivers during otherwise empty periods of the year, or gave them a way of integrating
their income with the high wages supplied.[241] Like silk and olive[242]
production, the sugar industry developed within an increasingly
complex and integrated agricultural and manufacturing system
which saw peasant smallholders in mountainous val Demone exploit seasonal irregularities of employment, and the opportunity to
exchange their produce for grain surpluses from the west to specialize in commercial crops.[243] The case of val Demone shows that
temporary and seasonal emigration did *not* emerge as a result of
cultural or other traits characteristic of Mediterranean mountains,
as argued famously by Fernand Braudel.[244] Nor was it caused by
overpopulation or because a demographic ceiling had been reached,
as has recently been suggested for the central Alps in the later Middle Ages.[245] On the contrary, non-permanent emigration combined
with agricultural and industrial specialization permitted eastern val
Demone's demographic ceiling actually to be *raised* well above the
region's 'natural' carrying capacity.[246] Temporary migration and
specialization seem to have been the cause, rather than the consequence, of val Demone's régime of high demographic pressure.

Contrary also to dualistic assumptions, the sugar industry maintained many intense links with the regional economy; these external
activities may have employed as many people as sugar cultivation
and processing itself. Val di Noto furnished the west with hemp
sacks and occasionally with coppice;[247] the remaining coppice supplies to western Sicilian *trappeti* came from the Madonie and the
Nebrodi, or less commonly from Calabria. Val Demone supplied

selli, *Storia dello zucchero*, p. 22 n. 1). Sugar exports to Calabria in CR 24, fo. 270
(1446); NM 6B, fo. 541 (1470).
[241] The two strategies were not mutually exclusive. For peasant and artisan employment see *UM*, p. 251; Trasselli, *Storia dello zucchero*, p. 124–5, 153 (1434);
Aymard, 'Amministrazione feudale e trasformazioni strutturali tra '500 e '700',
23.
[242] Cancila, *Baroni e popolo*, pp. 82–4.
[243] Peasant smallholding in val Demone was extended in the early modern period
through permanent leaseholds (*metateria perpetua*) on feudal lands (Cancila,
'Distribuzione e gestione', pp. 159–60).
[244] Braudel, *The Mediterranean and the Mediterranean world in the age of Philip II*,
I, p. 35.
[245] J.-F. Bergier, 'Le cycle médiéval: des sociétés féodales aux états territoriaux',
p. 175.
[246] See Viazzo, *Upland communities*, pp. 129, 295.
[247] *UM*, pp. 239, 246.

barrels and wooden parts for the sugar presses.[248] The men of Lipari were particularly active in the coppice trade.[249] Besides the wood-cutters and carpenters this involved, stonemasons, smiths and potters were employed in making and repairing mill stones, iron and copper vats for boiling sugar, iron parts for presses and carts, and clay forms for the sugar. Others were regularly employed to transport coppice and manure by boat or mule[250] and to build the *trappeti*, the aqueducts and the houses where the seasonal labour resided.[251] Potters from Palermo set up their kilns near *trappeti* in order to use the cane's residuals as fuel.[252] Finally, after 1410, the production of sweetmeats, previously imported from the Levant, was established as a major industry in Palermo.[253]

Historians have taken the sugar industry as the best representation of Sicilian economic dualism. The preceding discussion has turned this argument on its head. The example of sugar manufacture demonstrates that dualistic theory is inappropriate both in its sectoral and in its geographical usages. In the first usage, economic dualism postulates that capital and labour do not move freely between the 'advanced' and the 'backward' sectors, and that no linkage between the two sectors exists. In late medieval Sicily, by contrast, we find the allegedly most conservative, 'feudal' sector of society taking the initiative in establishing the sugar industry on a firm financial basis; nor did the urban nobility which invested huge sums after the mid-fifteenth century lack interest in landed, often feudal, property. Labour also moved freely between the sugar industry and other, more 'traditional' occupations, employment in a *trappeto* becoming one further element of a complex strategy of survival which peasant smallholders in the mountainous north-east began to develop during the fifteenth century. And links with other sectors of production were also strong. The theory of dualism in its geographic usage is even less apposite, for it postulates stagnation

---

[248] *UM*, pp. 246, 252; Bresc-Bautier, 'Pour compléter les données de l'archéologie: le rôle du bois dans la maison sicilienne (1350–1450)', pp. 435–9.

[249] C 2891, fo. 186v (1435).

[250] NM 6B, fo. 388rv (Taormina, 1469); NR 10, fos. 10–11v (Randazzo and Fiume-freddo, 1478); NR 15, fos. 134, 135 (Randazzo, 1490); NM 7, fo. 93 (Calata-biano, 1491).

[251] Trasselli, *Storia dello zucchero*, pp. 97, 123–4.

[252] *UM*, p. 245.

[253] Bresc, 'Jardins', 79–80; Trasselli, *Storia dello zucchero*, p. 183; A. A. Ruddock, *Italian merchants and shipping in Southampton, 1270–1600*, p. 75.

and lack of economic initiative in the 'backward' sector, under impulse from the 'advanced' sector. These features can hardly be said to apply to late medieval Sicily. I showed above how rapid was domestic response to rising foreign demand for silk; the example of the sugar industry – an enterprise with a complex and rapidly evolving technology, high capital investment and considerable risk – establishes the same point conclusively. The sugar industry was indeed the greatest, but far from the sole, 'effort of Sicilian capitalism'.

MINING

In the preceding pages I have discussed changes in late medieval Sicily's supply structure in response to changes in patterns of demand, most notably a shift in the domestic market towards better quality and more varied foods and manufacturing, and a shift in the foreign market towards high-quality products like silk and sugar. These changes built on pre-existing elements, intensifying and increasingly commercializing the production of existing goods for wider and more distant markets. Changes in the domestic and foreign markets also affected production of the most 'natural' resources of all, namely minerals, but compared with the other sectors I have discussed the outcome was rather different. Sicily is not particularly well-endowed with mineral resources, except for salt and sulphur. Before the fifteenth century, however, Sicilians were not aware of this fact. The region's paucity of minerals was a late medieval discovery, made because Sicilians responded so enthusiastically to the challenges posed by their new economic environment.

Salt

Salt was Sicily's most abundant mineral resource. By the late Middle Ages, the production and/or distribution of salt, used for preserving meat, fish and animal hides, for cheese-making and for animal husbandry, was under state control throughout Europe.[254] In Sicily, by contrast, the right established by Frederick II to control and tax salt production was abolished by Peter III after 1282.

[254] J. C. Hocquet ed., *Le roi, le marchand et le sel*. See also Hocquet, 'Exploitation et appropriation des salines de la Méditerranée occidentale (1250–1350 env.)'; Manca, *Aspetti*.

Economic growth 223

Regalian rights of discovery were maintained without, however, impairing the concession's significance.[255] The loss of the state monopoly over the salt industry opened the way to extensive alienation of salt mines to private individuals. Between 1274 and 1325, three quarters of existing or new saltworks were enfeoffed, and the process continued in the fourteenth century (Table 4.4). By the fifteenth century, the crown had divested itself of the greater part of its former salt mines. A general inquest of mines, made in 1403 probably in order to reassert royal prerogatives, proved fruitless.[256] The significance of the abolition of regalian rights of ownership becomes clearer if we contrast the situation in Sicily with that prevailing in the kingdom of Naples, where royal prerogatives were never formally renounced. After his conquest, Alfonso V took control of all sources of supply on the southern mainland and forced the population to buy salt at arbitrarily set prices. Later he agreed to furnish each hearth with a fixed amount of salt in exchange for direct taxation, thereby opening up a huge market for Spanish producers.[257] In 1445, Alfonso tried to do the same in Sicily, but failed.[258] Sicily was consequently not burdened by one of the commonest and most resented of pre-industrial monopolies.[259]

Alfonso's failure can be partly explained by the fact that Sicily did not have to rely on foreign salt supplies, which were more easily controlled than domestic ones. Until the mid-fifteenth century, Sicily did import salt, but never in great quantities; half a century later salt was regularly exported to the kingdom of Naples.[260] Sicilian imports from its main foreign supply, Sardinia, between 1346–7 and 1413–14, were less than 20,000 *quartini*, just under fifty-three tons a year. Of Sardinia's main clients in that period,

---

[255] Under Charles I of Anjou, the salt tax accounted for ten per cent of the excise revenues (Percy, 'The indirect taxes of the medieval kingdom of Sicily', 74). While abolishing the salt tax (Dentici Buccellato ed., *Fisco e società*, pp. 44–5), Peter III reasserted regalian rights of discovery in early 1283 (Carini ed., *De rebus*, no. 383). The tax on salt was abolished in Catalonia in the same year.
[256] *UM*, p. 218, n. 93.
[257] Yver, *Commerce*, pp. 31–2; Del Treppo, *Mercanti catalani*, pp. 226, 228–9; Cozzetto, *Mezzogiorno e demografia*, p. 7.
[258] C 2894, fos. 88–9v.
[259] For attempts to establish local monopolies see RC 44–5, fos. 165v–6 (1408); C 2845, fo. 84rv (1444); RC 104, fos. 289–90 (1457); RC 183, fo. 278rv (1492), and RC 195, fos. 103–9v (1496); *UM*, p. 220.
[260] Spata ed., *Capitula*, pp. 66–7 (1509). For earlier exports see Ciano, 'A bordo della nave', 178 (Messina to Tropea, 1388–9); C 2935, fo. 179v (Palermo to the mainland, 1449); CR 36, fo. 326rv (to the mainland, 1452).

Table 4.4 *Saltworks, 1300–1499*

Date	Locality	Documentary sources
1302**	Petralia	Giambruno ed., *Tabulario*, p. 29
1325*	Lentini, Mineo, Nicosia, Marsa, Murro, Vindicari, Trapani	RC 2, fo. 116
c.1330	Terranova	*UM*, p. 219
c.1340	Castrogiovanni	*Ibid.*
1357	Capo Passero	*Ibid.*
1358**	Marsa, Moriella, Ruvetum (Noto)	Littara, *De rebus netinis*, p. 84
1360	Trapani	*UM*, p. 219
1361?	Sutera, Cammarata, *Agrigento*	RC 7, fo. 385rv
1371–1400*	Nicosia	Barbato ed., *Per la storia di Nicosia*, pp. 35, 99–100
1392	Messina (Faro)	*Ibid.*; Starrabba, *Consuetudini di Messina*, pp. 219–20
1396	Castrogiovanni	*UM*, p. 219
1399	*Petralia*	RC 29, fos. 132v–3v
1400, 1426	*Monte Sara* (Sciacca)	CR 13, fo. 446rv
1401	*Marsala*	RC 38, fo. 248v
1401	*Marsala*	CR 4, fos. 362–3
1412	Petralia	CR 12, fo. 16
1413**	Prizzi	*UM*, p. 221
1416**	San Pantaleo (Marsala)	*Ibid.*
1418	*Marsala*	C 2804, fo. 49v
1427**	Noto	C 2814, fo. 156rv
1429	Castrogiovanni	CR 4, fos. 689–90
1434	Castrogiovanni, Petralia	CR 3, fos. 32–6
1434	*Favara*	C 2826, fos. 53v–4; C 2824, fos. 158v–9
1434	*Castrogiovanni, Calascibetta*	C 2826, fos. 36v–7v; C 2825, fo. 69
1436	Sicaminò	*UM*, p. 221
1438	*Mussomeli*	C 2832, fos. 93v–4
1439	*Favara*	C 2835, fo. 48v
1441	Trapani	*UM*, p. 221
1442**	Mussomeli	C 2893, fo. 134
1445**	Castrogiovanni	C 2852, fos. 129v–30v
1445**	Messina	C 2852, fo. 104
1451	*Trapani*	*UM*, p. 221; C 2865, fos. 157–8; C 2868, fo. 68rv
1451	*Marsala*	C 2867, fos. 141v–2
1451	*Trapani, Monte San Giuliano*	*UM*, p. 221; C 2869, fos. 119–20
1451	*Trapani, Monte San Giuliano*	CR 37, fo. 31
1451	*Caltabellotta*	C 2867, fo. 17rvbis
1451	*Mazara*	*UM*, p. 221
1451	*Mazara*	CR 32, fos. 145–6
1451	Augusta	RC 86, fo. 106rv

Table 4.4 cont. *Saltworks, 1300–1499*

Date	Locality	Documentary sources
1452**	Terranova	C 2881, fo. 22rv
1452**	Modica	C 2872, fos. 83v–4
1453	*Melilli*	*UM*, p. 221
1453**	Nicosia	CR 33, fo. 219rv; RC 93, fos. 286v, 305v–6v
1453**	Castrogiovanni	RC 92, fos. 221–4v
1453**	Sutera, Cammarata, *Agrigento*	RC 92, fos. 340v–1v
1453**	Trapani	RC 91, fos. 124–7
1456	*Agrigento, Naro*	*UM*, p. 221
1460	*Raffadali*	LV 74, fos. 259–60
1460	*Nicosia*	C 3476, fo. 166v
1462**	Termini	C 3477, fos. 55v–7v
1469	*San Filippo di Argirò*	C 3479, fos. 34v–5
1469	*San Giovanni Gemini*	C 3487, fo. 12v
1474	*Trapani, Marsala, Monte San Giuliano*	CR 56, fos. 132–3
1474	*Trapani*	CR 56, fos. 164–5
1476	*Castrogiovanni (Pantica)*	CR 56, fos. 154–5
1484	*Messina*	CR 65, fos. 55–6
1487	*Messina*	CR 70, fo. 93rv
1488	*Trapani*	CR 72, fos. 83–4
1490	*Sant'Angelo Muxaro*	CR 71, fos. 147–7bis
1491	*Trapani, Marsala, Monte San Giuliano*	CR 71, fos. 54–4bis
1491	*Trapani*	CR 71, fos. 61–1bis
1494	*Trapani*	RC 189, fos. 405v–7; CR 75, fos. 45–5bis

* = royal saltworks; ** = reference to known saltworks; italicized references = new saltworks.

only Venice imported less. Sardinia exported *c.* 500 tons a year to Catalonia, a bit over 300 tons to the Balearics, and nearly 400 tons yearly to the Ligurian Riviera and Corsica.[261]

More than sixty per cent of Sardinian exports to Sicily were sent to Trapani, in normal times a major producer and exporter in its own right.[262] Shipments were highly irregular, suggesting that they were resorted to in years of bad weather and low local output;

261 Manca, *Aspetti*, pp. 144–5, 231–9.

262 Exports to Venice: Hocquet, *Le sel et la fortune de Venise, II. Voiliers et commerce en Méditerranée 1200–1650*, pp. 368, 500 (1344), 617 (1416); to Naples: C 2891, fo. 124 (1434).

Sardinia may also have produced a different quality of salt.[263] Demand in Trapani was fuelled by its growing tunny and leather industries.

Salt was collected both from mineral deposits and from saltpans along the coast. Rock salt deposits were mostly located in central Sicily where the Madonie and the Nebrodi meet, with small extensions west and east, an area straddling all three *valli*.[264] Most saltpans, on the other hand, lay along the south-west coast between Monte San Giuliano, Trapani and Marsala. By the late fifteenth century, saltpans were being operated by windmills which pumped seawater into basins for evaporation.[265] Other major industrial concentrations were near Agrigento and Naro, between Noto, Syracuse and Augusta, and along the tip of land to the north of Messina. Even so, there was not as yet a very high degree of specialization. With the possible exception of Catania (supplied probably by Augusta and Messina), no major Sicilian city lacked a close source of supply.

There were good reasons why coastal producers, who had access to inexhaustible reserves, faced stiff competition from saltmines in the interior. Rock salt was indispensable for cheese making, and it was probably cheaper to produce than sea salt, at least before windmills were introduced. These two factors explain why coastal cities were sometimes supplied from the interior – Palermo from Cammarata, Catania from Castrogiovanni.[266] In addition, transport costs cut deeply into the final price of such a heavy and bulky commodity; costs were particularly high for landlocked communities distant from the sea.[267]

Can variations in the number and intensity of concessions of *new* mining rights (rather than confirmations of existing rights; see Table 4.4) be used to infer changes in the intensity of demand for salt? We are faced here with a problem similar to that discussed in chapter 3, of using grants of toll franchises and fairs as indicators of changes in the intensity of trade. Since concessions of mining rights were dependent on the monarchy's capacity to enforce its authority,

[263] See Hocquet, *Le sel et la fortune de Venise, I. Production et monopole*, pp. 138–41.
[264] Milone, *L'Italia*, pp. 1022–3.
[265] CR 71, fos. 54–4bis, 61–1bis (1491).
[266] Palermo later diversified its sources of supply; see LV 77, fo. 420 (1461): salt from Monte San Giuliano. For Catania see C 2830, fo. 209 (1438).
[267] Paternò was supplied by Castrogiovanni, which is more distant than the sea coast (NC 6311, fo. 95 (1500)).

changes in the number of concessions might represent changes in the authority of central government rather than in regional demand for salt. The monarchy's weakness during the fourteenth century could thus explain the low number of concessions in that period, for we do not know how many, if any, new enterprises were opened without royal authorization. A number of 'confirmations' of existing mining rights during the fifteenth century may, in fact, have legitimated former usurpations. On the other hand, once a powerful central authority was re-established after 1392, concessions of new mining rights can be taken as a straightforward index of changes in demand for salt. Table 4.4 shows that output increased particularly fast during the 1430s (when five new enterprises were opened) and 1450s (when thirteen new enterprises were opened), but that salt production continued to grow steadily until the end of the fifteenth century. Conditions during the first and second half of the fifteenth century may have differed in one respect, however – namely that, before 1450, output increased mainly in response to rising *per capita* consumption, in contrast with the period after 1450, when supply increased primarily in response to the rise in total population.

Iron

Like salt, the use of iron probably increased during the late Middle Ages in response to changes in agricultural, manufacturing and military technology.[268] By contrast with salt, however, Sicily was poorly endowed with this mineral. The richest veins of iron ore were situated near Fiumedinisi and Alì just south of Messina.[269] However, following some requests in 1402–3 to exploit various ores, including iron, in Fiumedinisi, no more was heard of these mines until 1490.[270] That year a new enterprise was set up by Giovanni Pages, a master artillery-maker, on an eight-year contract with the crown (which retained its regalian rights over metal ore mines). Pages was soon replaced by an artisan from Brescia, whom

[268] R. Sprandel, 'La production de fer au Moyen Age'.
[269] There is little evidence of ore from other parts of Sicily. See NR 5, fos. 9v, 129v–30 (Lipari, 1455–6); Trasselli, 'Miniere siciliane dei secoli XV e XVI', 521 (western Sicily).
[270] RC 39, fo. 125rv (1402), and RC 40, fos. 145–6 (1403), Dentici Buccellato ed., 'Miniere', 136–8.

he had engaged together with a Piedmontese to assist him.[271] Although the two northerners resigned from the project in 1492, leaving the Brescian with a debt of 100 *onze* to the crown,[272] the mines continued to work throughout the sixteenth century.[273]

While there is no direct evidence that iron was mined successfully before 1490,[274] it seems to have been produced near Messina throughout the fifteenth century. References to a toll on ore, iron and steel passing through Messina are common. Although mines existed in Calabria,[275] iron was often exported from Messina to Reggio, and the evidence suggests that local production rather than foreign imports was being shipped.[276] Toll returns must have been quite substantial if seventy *onze* were raised on it in 1460 to help Ferrante of Naples fight rebels in Calabria.[277] Given the importance of the livestock trade between Messina and Calabria (see chapter 5), the fact that Alfonso introduced a new toll on livestock *and* iron leaving Sicily to finance the conquest of Reggio also suggests that the iron trade was a major source of revenue.[278] During the late fifteenth century, Messina remained the main trading centre for eastern val Demone and southern Calabria.[279] The city controlled the mines in Fiumedinisi and Alì, and imported iron from elsewhere

---

[271] TRP Atti 58, fos. 202v–5 (1501). On Brescian mining traditions see E. Baraldi, 'Per un'archeologia dei forni alla bresciana'.

[272] TRP Atti 45, fo. 258rv (1491); CR 71, fos. 292–3ter 193 (1491); TRP Atti 47, fos. 3, 193 (1492). See also Trasselli, 'Miniere siciliane', 516–17, 527–9.

[273] TRP Atti 56, fo. 191 (1499): 100 cantara (7.8 tons) of iron 'spectantes ad ipsam regiam curiam' from the mines. Baviera Albanese, *La Sicilia nel sec. XVI*, pp. 64–6 for the sixteenth century.

[274] Trasselli, 'Miniere siciliane'; Dentici Buccellato, 'Miniere', 125–30.

[275] Pontieri, *Calabria*, pp. 103–5.

[276] C 2845, fos. 189v–90 (1444); C 2897, fos. 50v–1 (1452); C 2896, fo. 136v (1454); C 2886, fo. 4rv (1456); NM 6A, fo. 287 (1469). See Barberi, *Liber de secretiis*, pp. 51–3.

[277] CR 18, fos. 340–3 (1439); CR 23, fo. 227rv (1439–44); LV 75, fo. 23v (1460): fifty *onze* from the toll to pay for forty infantry sent to defend Tropea; CR 41, fo. 322 (1460): twenty *onze* in aid of Reggio. Exports to Calabria were also banned (RC 109, fos. 197–8v (1460)). See also C 3485, fo. 10v (1464).

[278] RC 65, fos. 108–9v (1430) for the toll. Reggio had requested toll exemption in 1425 (RC 57, fos. 66v–8). The same year the *secreto* of Messina sent 50 *cantara* of iron toll free to Reggio to ransom Antonio Soler, *regio fidelis* (CR 1062, fo. 550).

[279] NM 6A, fos. 99v, 190, 254v–5 (1469): sales by *nobilis* Giovanni Mirulla of Messina to men from Tortorici and Castroreale; NM 7, fos. 526v–7 (1492): *honorabilis* Matteo Risignolo of Messina sells iron to a man from Randazzo. See also below, n. 284.

in Sicily to supply local artisans[280] and to re-export it to Calabria. Messina also exported iron further abroad, even to Pisa despite competition from the island of Elba.[281] Venetian galleys loaded some 35,000 lbs of iron on their way to Flanders in 1400.[282] Half a century later, Alfonso asked the viceroy to send him 100 *cantari* of *ferro grosso* to the arsenal in Naples.[283] Iron, probably bought from the Venetians, was sent from Catania and Syracuse to Calabria in exchange for pitch.[284] Trapani shipped iron to Africa.[285]

Evidence for foreign imports of iron during the late Middle Ages is scanty and irregular. In 1328, a load from Pisa was thrown to sea between Palermo and Messina during a storm.[286] In 1376–7, Genoese iron imports were worth only 621 *lire*, compared to total imports in the same period worth 34,469 *lire* 5 *soldi* excluding bullion (see chapter 6). A merchant's letter of 1385 refers to a man from northern Tuscany who boasted about sending large iron shipments to Sicily, but it is hard to say what this meant for a small Apennine merchant.[287] In the period 1381–99, total imports from Valencia, a major supplier, were 6.6 tons;[288] imports from Venice, on the other hand, were no less than 100 tons in the period 1394–1408.[289] Iron was imported to Sicily from Pisa, Genoa, Venice and Biscay, sometimes ready-made as plough-shares, in the fifteenth century.[290] Towards 1500, despite attempts to expand the mines of

[280] Iron chests and caskets (Trasselli, *Mediterraneo*, pp. 248–9).
[281] T. Antoni, 'Costi e prezzi del ferro in Pisa alla fine del Trecento', 100 (1396–9).
[282] Melis, *Aspetti*, I, p. 324.
[283] C 2894, fo. 194rv (1451).
[284] *Ibid.*, fos. 178v–9 (1450) for re-exports. Ventura, *Edilizia urbanistica*, p. 136; CR 850, fos. 113–14 (1447): iron, probably Venetian, sequestered in Catania from a Catalan merchant living in Syracuse; NR 8, fo. 67v (1468): Giorgio Maltese of Syracuse sells 1.78 *cantara* of *virzilluni* iron to two Jews of Randazzo.
[285] Ashtor, 'The Jews in the Mediterranean trade in the fifteenth century', p. 443 (1445).
[286] Corrao ed., *Registri di lettere*, no. 24.
[287] Melis, *Aspetti*, I, p. 156.
[288] R. A. Ilera, 'El comercio valenciano de exportación con Italia y Berbería a finales del siglo XIV', p. 288.
[289] Ventura, 'Sul commercio siciliano di transito nel quadro delle relazioni commerciali di Venezia con le Fiandre (secoli XIV e XV)'.
[290] Petralia, *Banchieri*, pp. 307–8; Trasselli, *Mediterraneo*, pp. 240 and n. 10, 307, 309; Trasselli, *Storia dello zucchero*, p. 187; Heers, *Gênes*, p. 220.

Fiumedinisi, Basque iron shipped to Messina began to flood the Sicilian and southern Calabrian markets.[291]

Alum

Alum was the main astringent used by medieval high-quality wool industries to scour wool. It is found in volcanic soils, which exist in Sicily around Etna and in the nearby Aeolian islands. Although no mining activities are known before the fifteenth century, local resources were not ignored. Alum on Lipari, for example, had been known since ancient times, and in the early thirteenth century the bishop of Patti, whose jurisdiction included the Aeolian islands, owned a *vena aluminis* on the small island of Vulcano.[292] In 1355, some Sicilian alum was exported to Bruges by the Bardi company.[293]

Interest in alum began to increase at the turn of the fifteenth century, possibly in response to the growth of the Sicilian woollen industry. In 1400, Martino granted a licence for mining alum and sulphur near Sciacca,[294] and the two mining licences of 1402 and 1403 mentioned for iron included alum.[295] Half a century later, Alfonso personally entrusted Pietro Mozzicato, of Castrogiovanni, with the task of exploring for alum throughout Sicily. In 1456, Mozzicato discovered a new deposit on Monte Capodarso, between Castrogiovanni and Caltanissetta. He was allowed to mine it for ten years, giving the crown one tenth of the product.[296] In 1459, three other men from Castrogiovanni began work on a new vein discovered in the same area;[297] in 1460, one of the three, together with Mozzicato and two others, were given complete rights over Sicily's alum mines for a ten per cent return.[298]

Alfonso's concession of rights of exploration and mining to Pietro

---

[291] Trasselli, 'Sui Biscaglini in Sicilia tra Quattro e Cinquecento', 152–3; Cancila, *Impresa redditi*, pp. 245–7.

[292] K. A. Kehr, 'Staufische Diplome', no. 3.

[293] *UM*, p. 285 n. 10. Florentines became interested in Sicilian alum once again in the 1460s; see M. Mallett, *The Florentine galleys in the fifteenth century*, pp. 124–5 (but Mallett thinks the alum came from Tolfa); M.-L. Heers, 'Les Génois et le commerce de l'alun à la fin du Moyen Age', 51–2.

[294] RC 17, fos. 99v–100 (1400), cited in *UM*, p. 221.

[295] See above, n. 270.

[296] C 2897, fo. 71v (1453); CR 38, fo. 126rv (1456).

[297] LV 74, fos. 243v–4v.

[298] LV 78, fos. 102v–3v, and CR 42, fos. 444–5 (1460).

Mozzicato in late June of 1453, less than a month after the capture of Constantinople by the Turks, suggests the king's awareness of some of the commercial implications of that event. For nearly two centuries, European industries had been supplied from the eastern mines of the Phocea, of Chio and of Pera, over which Genoa had an absolute monopoly. With the fall of Constantinople, Europeans were abruptly deprived of their main source of supply. For a few years, before the mines of Tolfa in the Roman Campagna were discovered, Europe's luxury woollen industries were in danger of a deep crisis. Alfonso's rapid response to the turn of events may have been hastened by the fact that it was his arch-enemies, the Genoese, who stood to lose most from these developments.

Alfonso did not live to see his foresight borne out by events. By 1458, the Genoese's stocks of alum were giving out; by 1460 they were exhausted. The Genoese reacted by turning to new sources of supply in the west.[299] From early 1461 or possibly before, a Genoese merchant, Damiano Spinola, began to exploit the Sicilian alum mines. At first he worked near Paternò, on the southern slopes of Etna, producing a respectable 820 *cantara* (*c*.64 tons) in the first year.[300] In early 1462, Damiano and Atellino Spinola agreed with the crown to exploit Sicily's known, and as yet undiscovered, resources for three years at an annual rent of 100 *onze*; if they wished, they could later extend the contract another three years for 200 *onze*. The contract was briefly and unsuccessfully disputed by Raimondo de Parisio, a royal secretary. The Spinola (royal procurators both for Alfonso and for Juan) could offer the crucial advantage over de Parisio of having an established trade network at their disposal. In exchange they were granted extensive commercial privileges, including a ban on alum imports from Lipari and a monopoly over Sicilian production.[301] As a result of the strong position on the international market this gave them, the Spinola seem to have ignored the lesser deposits near Paternò, Castrogiovanni and Cac-

[299] J. Delumeau, *L'alun de Rome, XVe–XIXe siècle*, pp. 119–20; Heers, 'Les Génois', 31–2, 51–3.
[300] CR 860, fos. 9, 12v, 78; LV 79, fo. 51v.
[301] LV 80, fos. 278–80 (1462), cited in *UM*, p. 222 n. 106; C 3484, fos. 1–6v (1462): 'nova per tucti lochi di Ponenti per l'alumi di quistu regno'. On the lawsuit with de Parisio see C 3480, fos. 176v–7 (1462)); CR 860, fo. 21; TRP Atti 20, fos. 59v–60v (1463); C 3477, fo. 125v (1463); CR 45, fo. 111rv (1464).

camo because of their inferior quality,[302] and to have concentrated on the mines of Fiumedinisi which were the richest in Sicily.[303]

Sicilian alum appeared abroad for the first time on the Genoese market.[304] In September 1464, Damiano Spinola, who had taken charge of the business, complained that a Catalan merchant had broken the ban on imports, presumably from Lipari, on several occasions.[305] This may have been an excuse, however, for Damiano was also accumulating major debts. In early 1466, he 'departed from [Sicily] an unsaluted guest', leaving behind substantial arrears with the court.[306] The far greater resources of the Tolfa mines near Rome were discovered in 1462 but began sustained production only a couple of years later,[307] and the prospect of having to pay twice the amount of rent over the following three years convinced Spinola to abandon an enterprise that may have been less profitable than he expected. In comparison with the 1,830 tons extracted annually from Tolfa in the same years, Fiumedinisi's production must have seemed quite paltry.[308]

Since the main market for Sicilian alum was abroad, interest in it subsided once Tolfa's far greater resources became known. For a few years after Spinola's departure, mining in Sicily may have been abandoned. In 1470, Nicola di Bonacquisto from Lucca and Giacomo Migari of Messina were allowed to exploit alum and vitriol in val Demone for eight years.[309] This mine was next given in concession in 1496 to Simone de Fide of Castrogiovanni for a ten per cent royalty.[310] Other mines drew little interest after the 1460s; an

---

[302] LV 80, fo. 274rv (1462), cited in *UM*, p. 222 n. 104, for the 'valle alumi in territorio Cactami' discovered by Michele di Luca Zacchi (probably a northern Italian) and his two sons.

[303] Fazello, *Due deche*, p. 74. For mines in Savoca see *ibid.*, p. 29.

[304] Heers, 'Les Génois', 51–2; Heers, *Gênes*, p. 467.

[305] TRP Atti 23, fos. 186v, 187v–8 (1464).

[306] *Ibid.*, fo. 188rv (1464); LV 93, fo. 140 (1466); RC 116, fo. 238rv (1466).

[307] Delumeau, *L'alun de Rome*, pp. 20–1.

[308] In 1466 130 *cantara* were mined on behalf of de Parisio, who died soon after (LV 93, fos. 368v–9; CR 47, fo. 138rv; C 3485, fo. 129rv). Output from Tolfa (annual mean for 1462–6) in Delumeau, *L'alun de Rome*, p. 21.

[309] CR 50, fos. 273–4bis (1470); RC 127, fos. 382–4 (1472). This concession had been preceded by a similar one to Bonacquisto and Giovanni Pela, a silversmith, in 1469 (RC 111, fo. 73).

[310] Royalties were raised to fifteen per cent in 1499; see CR 83, fo. 357rv (referring also to the previous contract of 1496). Simone de Fide may have been a relative of master Lorenzo de Fide, who had taken the mines of Castrogiovanni in concession some twenty-five years before.

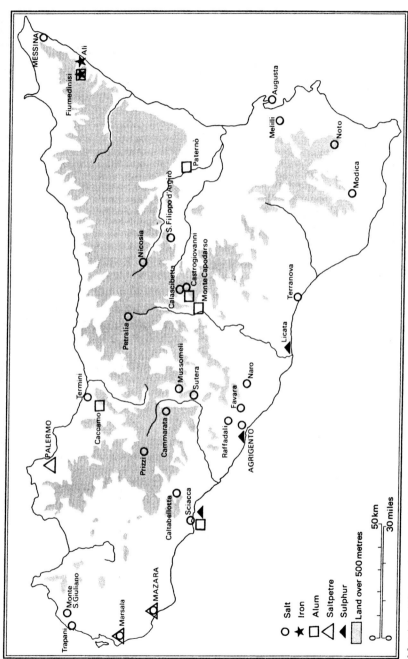

Map 4.4 Mines and mining 1400–1500

Legend:

- ○ Salt
- ★ Iron
- ☐ Alum
- △ Saltpetre
- ▲ Sulphur
- ▨ Land over 500 metres

Scale:
0 — 50 km
0 — 30 miles

Locations:

MESSINA, Ali, Fiumedinisi, Augusta, Melilli, Noto, Paternò, Modica, S.Filippo d'Argirò, Nicosia, Castrogiovanni, Calascibetta, MonteCapodarso, Terranova, Petralia, Licata, Mussomeli, Sutera, Naro, Termini, Favara, Caccamo, Raffadali, PALERMO, AGRIGENTO, Prizzi, Cammarata, Caltabellotta, Sciacca, Monte S.Giuliano, Marsala, Trapani, MAZARA

234   *An island for itself*

attempt to revive those in Castrogiovanni had no lasting results.[311]
While the mines of Fiumedinisi probably continued working for
some time, as the surviving nearby settlement named Allume suggests, Sicily never became a major alum producer.

Saltpetre, sulphur and other minerals

Sicily's only other mineral resources of any significance were saltpetre and sulphur. The development of firearms during the fifteenth
century meant that both minerals were in increasing demand (gun-
powder was made by mixing the two with charcoal); previously they
had been used primarily for medical purposes.[312] Because of their
strategic importance and mainly foreign outlet, however, trade was
under tight governmental control, and our knowledge of the industry derives mainly from government orders and export licences.

Saltpetre was collected in caves during the winter and then refined once or twice.[313] Marsala was the main producer; a mill for
grinding saltpetre existed there in 1498.[314] From Marsala, saltpetre
could be sent for refining to Trapani where it was also stocked for
export.[315] Mazara was another major producer; some saltpetre
came from around Palermo.[316] Messina exported saltpetre to the
mainland or to the Levant, but did not produce any locally.[317]

Until the mid-fifteenth century foreign trade was restricted, and
exports were nearly all to Naples.[318] The situation changed quite
rapidly after Alfonso decided, in 1451, to remove most political

[311] CR 64, fo. 142rv (1483). The concession gave rights of exploration throughout
Sicily, but both concessonaires came from Castrogiovanni.
[312] C 2888, fo. 23 (1420): 100 *cantara* of firepowder for bombards.
[313] *UM*, p. 222.
[314] CR 25, fos. 487–8v (1445); CR 43, fo. 429v (1465–6); LV 98, fo. 25rv (1467);
CR 874, fo. 247rv (1495); CR 78, fo. 428 (1497); RC 200, fos. 199v–200 (1499).
Reference to the mill in RC 198, fos. 304v–5.
[315] C 2804, fo. 108v (1419); LV 73, fo. 251v (1460); LV 93, fos. 166–7 (1466); LV 95,
fo. 251v (1466); LV 94, fo. 36rv (1468); CR 872, fo. 185 (1493).
[316] Mazara: CR 41, fo. 347, and LV 77, fo. 411v (1461); CR 43, fo. 436v (1466–7);
Napoli, 'Libro Rosso', 326 (1479); CR 78, fo. 428 (1497); RC 200, fos. 199v–200
(1499). Exports from Palermo: CR 41, fo. 452 (1461); CR 870, fos. 111, 125
(1487); CR 871, fo. 151 (1492); CR 872, fos. 185, 191, 193 (1493). See also *UM*,
p. 222.
[317] CR 25, fos. 395rv, 396–7 (1444); CR 860, fo. 49, and LV 82, fos. 136v–7 (1461);
CR 869, fo. 162 (1488); CR 875, fo. 290 (1497).
[318] C 2888, fos. 23, 52 (1420–1); CR 25, fos. 487–8v (1445). See C 2827, fos. 16v, 57
(1436) for small exports to Barcelona.

restrictions on trade.[319] The reason for this abrupt change of policy is not clear, but one can surmise that new and competing sources of supply had become available that made the trade-ban worthless. The king himself began to buy far more saltpetre than before, perhaps for his military campaigns in Tuscany,[320] and presented communities of his realm, like Perpignan, with large gifts of saltpetre.[321] In 1454, Aigues-Mortes was allowed to export 100 *cantara* of saltpetre from Palermo.[322] After Alfonso's death, an even more liberal export policy was introduced which seems to have excluded only the government's political enemies.[323] The kingdom of Naples regularly imported saltpetre from Sicily, and exports to Florence, Venice, France and Flanders were also authorized.[324] Demand expanded further from the late 1480s, and by the end of the century over fifty tons were exported every year.[325]

Less is known of sulphur, which together with salt was the most abundant mineral resource in the island, but at that time was less in demand than either salt or saltpetre. Most mining requests were made during the first half of the fifteenth century and were restricted to the south-west (Sciacca, Agrigento, Licata).[326] The only request to exploit sulphur sulphate (vitriol) in val Demone came in 1470 in combination with rights over alum, and seems to have had no lasting results.[327]

Sicily had few other mineral resources. In the early sixteenth cen-

[319] C 2826, fo. 69v (1451). For exports see C 2865, fo. 91 (1451); C 2884, fo. 136v (1455) (to Flanders).
[320] C 2896, fos. 114v–15 (1452): 300 *cantara*; CR 36, fos. 25, 39rv, 41–9v (1453): 400 *cantara*.
[321] RC 85, fos. 372v–3 (1451); C 2868, fo. 110 (1451); C 2896, fo. 87v (1451); RC 86, fo. 185rv (1452).
[322] Trasselli, *Storia dello zucchero*, p. 252 n. 28.
[323] RC 109, fos. 197–8v (1460): exports of saltpetre, iron, *sagictae* and crossbows to Reggio banned because of a revolt in Calabria.
[324] Naples: LV 73, fo. 251v (1460); LV 82, fos. 136v–7, and CR 860, fo. 49 (1461); LV 77, fo. 411v, and CR 41, fo. 347 (1461): 20 *cantara* for the castle of Ischia; CR 877, fo. 173 (1499). Florence: CR 41, fo. 452 (1461): 4.63 *cantara* for a Florentine galley; CR 870, fo. 111 (1487): 200 *cantara* exported by Leonardo Ridolfi, from Florence. See also Mallett, *Florentine galleys*, p. 125. Venice: CR 870, fo. 125 (1487): 200 *cantara* with two Venetian merchants. France: LV 92, fo. 395 (1466): 200 *cantara*. Flanders: CR 871, fo. 151 (1492).
[325] CR 872, fos. 185, 191, 193, 194rv (1493): export licences for 420 *cantara*; CR 875, fos. 275, 290, 291 (1497): licences for 360 *cantara*; CR 877, fos. 131, 133, 140rv, 152, 153, 155, 158, 173 (1498–9): licences for 600 *cantara*.
[326] *UM*, p. 221. See LV 73, fo. 234 (1460): 100 *cantara* from Licata to Messina.
[327] CR 50, fos. 273–4bis.

tury, Tommaso Fazello referred to quarries of porphyry and jasper near Fiumedinisi and Collesano, and of beryl in nearby Gratteri.[328] However, he also falsely claimed the existence of rich silver and gold veins running through the mountains of northern val Demone, recalling similar myths current in the Venetian Terraferma in the same period.[329] What was barely more than a legend[330] was widely believed, however, and upheld popular interest in hidden treasure: requests to search for gold and silver coins and precious metals together were very common.[331] The government granted various mining licences for silver, gold, and even for copper, lead and tin. Notwithstanding any doubts the crown might have had about such requests, it had nothing to lose by granting mining rights and thus never refused.[332] The first requests to mine near Fiumedinisi included alum, iron, silver, copper, lead, tin and 'pulviri di gamillu'[333] In 1438, three noblemen from Messina, Nicola Crisafi, Ludovico Saccàno and Guglielmo Spatafora, stated that silver could easily be found in the city's district.[334] They were soon to be proved wrong.

Mining: conclusions

Most of the evidence of mining dates from the fifteenth century, partly because demand for minerals increased considerably in this period, but also because the state began to stimulate production which might have strategic military value. Yet, although the evidence shows that Sicily was affected by the great European mining

---

[328] Fazello, *Due deche*, pp. 74, 302.

[329] *Ibid.*, pp. 29, 74; Alberti, *Isole*, p. 39; P. Braunstein, 'Les entreprises minières en Vénétie au XVe siècle'.

[330] Trasselli, 'Miniere siciliane', 515: some silver was mined in Fiumedinisi in the eighteenth century.

[331] See above, chapter 3, n. 45.

[332] RC 49, fo. 26 (1413), cited in *UM*, p. 221; Trasselli, *Note banchi XV secolo*, I, p. 53 n. 76 (1435); RC 72, fo. 76rv (1438), Baviera Albanese ed., *In Sicilia*, pp. 171–2; C 2840, fo. 67rv (1441); C 2839, fo. 112rv (1442); RC 78, fos. 192–3v, and Dentici Buccellato, 'Miniere siciliane', 138–41; C 2822, fo. 36 (1442), cited in *UM*, p. 221; CR 850, fos. 137rv, 139rv (two concessions for 1447); RC 104, fo. 234v (1457); CR 44, fo. 112rv (1464); CR 58, fo. 95rv (1474); NR 20, fos. 101–2 (1489); CR 73, fo. 325rv (1489); CR 77, fos. 633–3bis, 634–4bisv, and RC 190, fos. 346–7v (1495), Baviera Albanese ed., *In Sicilia*, p. 53; CR 77, fos. 639–9bis (1495); CR 96, fos. 508–15 (1508).

[333] See above, n. 270.

[334] C 2831, fo. 69v, and RC 72, fo. 198rv, Baviera Albanese ed., *In Sicilia*, pp. 173–5.

boom after 1460,[335] there is little to suggest (except perhaps for the saltpetre industry) that the state played a positive role in this phenomenon. On the contrary, with respect to a strategic product like saltpetre which had mainly foreign outlets, *release* from political restrictions on trade during the 1450s had the most positive effects on production.

In Sicily, both technical and institutional constraints on mining were generally weak. With the exception of iron and possibly alum, all the main minerals could be collected from surface deposits, which reduced production costs considerably. In addition, and in contrast with most other pre-industrial economies, state control over the most important mineral resource, salt, was very weak, which lowered average consumer prices and may have increased industrial flexibility. The Sicilian salt industry did indeed show great dynamism, and by the mid-fifteenth century the country had become self-sufficient and had begun to export salt regularly. By then, the country had also become a net exporter of saltpetre and sulphur.

GENERAL CONCLUSIONS

Two separate but parallel lines of argument have developed in the course of this chapter. First, I have examined the ways in which late medieval Sicily passed through a process of economic growth. And second, I have argued that growth was inextricably linked to a process of specialization.

By stressing *general* change, I have paid little attention to the timing and rates of growth in different sectors of the economy. Rates of expansion in output, productivity and employment, insofar as they can be measured, were far from uniform over time. The main differences in chronology were between the (better documented) export-led sectors and those sectors mainly supplying the home market.

The crucial turning-point for the sugar and silk industries occurred during the 1440s, after which they both expanded remarkably fast. In contrast with the silk industry, however, sugar manufacture (especially in the west) suffered from cyclical crises. This fact can be explained by two characteristics of the industry. Its high capital outlay made it depend, to a far greater degree than other

---

[335] J. U. Nef, 'Mining and metallurgy in medieval civilisation', pp. 469–73.

industries, on still undeveloped capital and credit markets; and the industry's technological complexity made it more open to competition over production costs. Raw silk production, by contrast, required low capital outlay, was technically simple, and faced larger and more rapidly expanding markets than sugar.

The only nearly entirely domestic industry known to have kept pace with, and eventually outstripped, rising home demand was salt mining. Other mining activities either took off more slowly (saltpetre and sulphur) or were unable to grow very far due to poor natural resources (alum and iron). Rates of expansion in cloth manufacture are even less clear. The evidence shows only that, after the mid-fourteenth century, the cloth industry responded positively (both in the quantity and quality of output) to rising demand.

The agricultural balance also changed. The pastoral sector expanded at the expense of the arable as a consequence of demographic retreat; changes, however, were not restricted to these sectors, nor were they simply reversed once the population began to grow again after the 1450s. Agricultural productivity increased not simply as a result of a 'retreat from marginal lands', but also because of major innovations in the organization of production and in rural credit markets. These developments were a result of the way new opportunities, slowly emerging after the mid-fourteenth century, were pursued under the combined pressure of changing demand and commercial competition. Thus, the most significant development in this period occurred in the territorial *distribution* of production, in regional and sub-regional specialization, and in its necessary corollary, market integration. During the half century following the Black Death, however, war (especially in the east) and political fragmentation restricted such structural changes to smaller areas around the main cities and within the boundaries of individual lordships. Incentives to specialization increased markedly only after the reunification of Sicily under the Aragonese, who provided a common and stable institutional framework for exchange to take place.

I argued in chapter 1 that there are good *a priori* theoretical reasons against describing northern Italy and Sicily in terms of a single 'dual economy'. In this chapter, I have tried to show that the concept cannot be applied to medieval Sicily internally either. Two central assumptions of the dualist model are that there exist strong constraints on the mobility of labour between agriculture and manufacturing, and that, for institutional or cultural reasons, capital is not invested in agriculture. One of the main 'feudal' features of 'latifundism', for example, is held to be its traditional, non-commoditized labour relations, which hold up labour mobility. A consequence of these assumptions is that no capital accumulation, and consequently no specialization in the agricultural sector, can occur. What can be said about the first element in this scheme, mobility of labour? We saw in chapter 3 that in late medieval Sicily control over personal mobility had either disappeared or was ineffective. I suggested also (in chapters 2 and 3) that rapid changes in urban hierarchies, and the large number of fifteenth-century petitions concerned with individual migration, indicate a high degree of individual mobility. The crown itself upheld the right to leave feudal territories freely, without losing personal property, against strong baronial opposition (see chapter 7). The Sicilian language, which is far more homogeneous than southern Italian dialects, provides further testimony to strong individual mobility from very early times.[336] One of the main premises for the existence of a 'dual economy' was lacking in Sicily.

The second feature of the dualist model, the immobility of capital between agriculture and manufacturing, is harder to examine because of lack of research on capital formation and individual investment patterns.[337] However, evidence from the sugar industry, which combined high levels of capital investment and a semi-agricultural, semi-manufacturing enterprise, and from the silk industry, which combined peasant agricultural investment and urban credit, suggests that capital was quite easily available and highly mobile. The same conclusion arises from the development during the fifteenth century of a market in agricultural futures (*contratti alla meta*) for the arable and pastoral sectors. The land market itself was fairly well developed (see chapter 7). In other words, late medieval Sicily was provided with relatively sophisticated labour, capital and land markets. This fact invalidates some of the basic assumptions of dualistic theory. It does, by contrast, explain the pattern of Sicilian economic development after the great fourteenth-century epidemics.

[336] Varvaro, *Lingua e storia*, p. 219.
[337] See, however, Mineo, 'Gli Speciale. Nicola viceré e l'affermazione politica della famiglia'.

5. Sicily and its regions. Eastern val Demone and the southern mainland

In the previous chapters I have often referred to some unusual features of north-eastern Sicily (val Demone), and of its *de facto* capital (Messina). I have shown that despite possessing the harshest environmental features of Sicily's three *valli*, val Demone consistently maintained the highest population density in the region, and I have connected this fact with the area's high degree of agricultural and manufacturing specialization. I have also suggested that Messina's status as a city was largely a function of its role as Sicily's foremost gateway to the mainland.

In this chapter I examine these two features in more detail. In the first part of the chapter I look at Messina itself, at the origins of its fortunes in trade, and at its cycles of economic expansion and contraction. The development of Messina is of interest for my more general arguments, for it epitomizes the strengths and weaknesses of purely politico-institutional explanations of economic change. As noted in chapter 1, Benedetto Croce, followed by other historians, argued that the political separation caused by the Vespers of 1282 had disastrous economic effects because it severed all ties between Sicily and the mainland for more than a century and a half.[1] If Messina's fortunes depended largely on trade across the Straits, as I suggest, the city should have suffered a disastrous decline as a result of the Siculo-Angevin war. I argue below that Messina did decline during the fourteenth century, but that both its decline and its recovery after 1400 were only weakly connected with the political and institutional changes brought about by Sicily's separation from the mainland.

By contrast, Messina's growth in the fifteenth century can be

[1] See above, chapter 1, n. 63.

shown to support the wider hypothesis, that regional specialization and trade increased after the Black Death. This theme is pursued more closely in the second part of the chapter, where I discuss the structure of trade across the Straits of Messina. A problem raised in chapter 3 in discussing institutional changes in the market, is that the view that trade increased after the mid-fourteenth century rests necessarily on mainly indirect, institutional evidence, because domestic trade left very few traces. For the same reason, evidence for agricultural and manufacturing specialization for the home market rests to some degree on inferences from aggregate data, such as the food levy of 1283 and the fifteenth-century domestic grain trade. In comparison, foreign trade is fairly well documented because it paid royal excise or incurred higher risks that needed legal, written coverage – and after 1282, trade across the Straits counted as foreign. This fact is of especial interest to us, because as a result of the low cost of boat transport across the narrow channel, and of trade franchises between Messina and Reggio Calabria, cross-channel trade involved the kind of cheap, bulk commodities that would not normally cross state boundaries because transport and excise costs were too high (see chapter 3). For this reason, late medieval cross-channel traffic provides a glimpse of kinds of domestic, regional trade that normally escape our scrutiny. At the same time, it provides further, direct evidence of late medieval val Demone's increasingly commercialized and specialized economy, and supports the critique of dualist arguments.

Val Demone included several distinct but overlapping cultural and ethnic areas. Up to the thirteenth century, when large ethnic influxes came to an end, Greeks characterized the north-east around Messina, the centre was scattered with Latin populations, and the west may have had stronger Muslim penetration. From an economic point of view, val Demone could be divided along rather similar lines. The north-eastern triangle of the Peloritani coincided, in fact if not entirely by right, with Messina's district (see chapter 3). The central Nebrodi, running east to west from Randazzo to Nicosia, also lay largely within Messina's catchment area, but were situated at a sufficient distance, and were powerful enough, to avoid being incorporated into the larger city's district. Nebrodi communities could easily trade with both southern and western Sicily; Randazzo was in contact with Catania as much as with Messina, and attracted merchants from as far away as Palermo. Further west, the Madonie mountains were nearly entirely outside Messina's orbit. They came instead under the influence of Palermo after the latter gained control of the area's main port in Termini in the early fourteenth century.[2] In the course of the fifteenth century, the Madonie became the main source of seasonal labour for western Sicily's fisheries, sugar industries and intensive agriculture (see chapter 4). Here I shall concentrate on val Demone's central and eastern areas, however, partly because they are rather better documented, and partly because they seem more distinctive of the region as a whole. When the humanist Tommaso Fazello described the region in the mid-sixteenth century, he took the north-eastern part as his model:

> This *vallo* is full of the highest mountains, of cliffs, of rolling hills which follow on each other, of great woods and dense thickets, and is set higher up than the other *valli*. Thus it follows that it is poor in wheat and in the other sorts of grain, but most abundant in oil and silk ... Valleys are well tilled and pleasing, and the countryside and farms are excellently worked, and full of the most different things; they have no scarcity of water, indeed water flows abundantly. The hills moreover are covered in Mamertine vineyards, in olive groves and mulberry-trees ... and are densely settled.[3]

During the late Middle Ages, Messina was not merely the largest city in val Demone, it was also (excepting Nicosia and, for a while, Randazzo) the only real city in the area. This was partly the result of geography. In medieval Sicily cities developed mostly along the coasts, where they could be easily supplied from the rural hinterland and the sea. Val Demone's narrow seaboard and lack of good arable terrain meant that the region was particularly dependent on outside supply. In these conditions and with initially low volumes of surplus available for external trade, it was easy for a centre possessing some initial advantages to establish a lead over rival centres that would be increasingly hard for latecomers to challenge. Messina's enviable position on the Straits provided it with just such an initial advantage. This potential for growth was put to the test by political

---

[2] On Termini's hinterland in the Madonie see Bresc and D'Angelo, 'Structure et évolution'.

[3] Fazello, *Due deche*, p. 296.

and commercial conditions which first emerged with the Norman conquest of Sicily.

Messina has been described as 'a Norman phenomenon and a phenomenon of the crusades'.[4] This statement contains two distinct arguments: that the city grew as a result of the unification of Sicily with the mainland after the Norman conquest, and that its wealth derived from traffic between Europe and the Levant. While the first argument is on the whole correct, as we shall see, the second tends to overestimate the importance for Messina's economy of long-distance trade.

What evidence is there of long-distance trade by Messinese? Thanks to her 'active community of entrepreneurs', Messina is described as being an exception to the 'rule' that 'the towns of southern Italy and Sicily performed a passive role as suppliers of raw materials to the merchants of northern Italy and Catalonia from the twelfth century onwards'; it is argued that this was because of Messina's need to pay for food imports with the profits of foreign trade.[5] This view emphasizes the role played by Messina's international merchants in the city's growth. But how significant was foreign trade for the welfare of the city, as opposed to that of individual merchants?

The hypothesis that a strong mercantile community already existed in Messina in the mid-twelfth century rests on the authority of a single privilege granted by William I in 1160. The charter contained two commercial provisions. The most important was the abolition of gate tolls on food imports and exports, whose 'main effect and aim was probably a reduction in the price of food in Messina itself', indicating that the city was beginning to outgrow its local resources. The second provision concerned the reduction of the tax on foreign trade (*drictus dohane*) from ten to three per cent, and was probably requested in imitation of a similar privilege granted to the Genoese a few years before.[6] Neither of these provisions demonstrates the existence of a growing community of international merchants.

A charter of Henry VI forty years later, abolishing all tolls levied

---

[4] Abulafia, *Two Italies*, p. 42; Abulafia, 'Merchants of Messina', 197; Trasselli, *Privilegi*, pp. 12–25.

[5] Abulafia, 'Merchants of Messina'.

[6] Giardina ed., *Capitoli*, no. 5; Abulafia, *Two Italies*, pp. 117–21; Abulafia, 'Merchants of Messina', 198; Trasselli, *Privilegi*, pp. 13, 16.

244   An island for itself

in the port of Messina on the Messinese's own merchandise, but
leaving in place those on merchandise handled by them but owned
by other parties, might indicate that a group of merchants involved
in regional trade was beginning to emerge. The first hard evidence
for 'international' trade by Messinese, however, only appears in the
late thirteenth century, when the city had attained its greatest
medieval extension.[7] Two major commercial privileges granted
immediately after the Vespers seem to confirm a period of commercial growth. In 1283, Messina's merchants were allowed to elect
their own consuls anywhere in Sicily, in the kingdom of Aragon and
elsewhere. In 1286, the merchants were granted a consul in Tunis to
whom all Sicilians were to show obedience. The two privileges were
upheld by the provision that the *dohana maris* toll be paid by the
ship-owners and not by the (Messinese) merchants who made use of
the ships.[8]

The War of the Vespers did not seriously affect Messina's foreign
trade, even with Naples. Until the 1370s, Messina's international
merchants suffered little from domestic political developments;
they seem to have achieved greater importance in local government
than they had ever had during the previous century.[9] However,
Messina was supplied with food by regional rather than international merchants.[10] By the late thirteenth and fourteenth centuries, when conditions in Messina itself begin to be better
documented, we find that the city's international trade was at odds
with Messina's more general circumstances. Messina's long cycle of
demographic growth came to an end just as its community of
internationally-oriented merchants was reaching maturity and expanding its activities. For at least a century, therefore, trends in the
domestic and foreign sectors of the economy moved in opposite
directions; those merchants who are said to have fostered Messina's

---

[7] Giardina ed., *Capitoli*, no. 9 (1197); Abulafia, 'Merchants of Messina'; Pispisa,
   Messina, pp. 11–14; A. Finocchiaro Sartorio, 'Le leggi di Corrado IV', pp. 257,
   261.
[8] La Mantia ed., *Codice diplomatico*, nos. 39 (1283), 107–10 (1285); Giardina ed.,
   Capitoli, nos. 27 (1283), 28 (1286); Trasselli, *Privilegi*, pp. 60–6.
[9] Pispisa, *Messina*, pp. 14, 70–1, 108–13; Abulafia, 'Merchants of Messina', 199–
   212; da Piazza, *Cronaca*, I, chapters 35, 92, 95; *Mostra documentaria*, no. 35;
   Yver, *Commerce*, p. 197; A. Lombardo, 'Un testamento e altri documenti in
   volgare siciliano del secolo XIV a Venezia'.
[10] Pispisa, *Messina*, pp. 11–14.

growth before 1282 were unable thereafter to halt its decline. After 1282, the city's traditional sources of grain supply became less certain, and its economy may have begun to contract (see chapter 3). Probably as early as the mid-fourteenth century, Messina was being surpassed by Catania as the second largest Sicilian city after Palermo.

Even for the period before decline set in, however, it is difficult to argue on the basis of the scanty evidence of Messinese long-distance trading activities, that a population of *c*.30,000 in the 1280s was supported by the profits of a few dozen great merchants, or by the outlet for home products on distant markets that such merchants might provide. I would suggest instead that Messina's mercantile community, the largest and most powerful of its kind in medieval Sicily, arose as a *result* of the city's unusually large number of privileges and monopolies over local resources, which were in turn a response to Messina's poor rural hinterland and its strategic position on the Straits. Messina's economic well-being as a whole depended primarily on the city's role as the main commercial and administrative gateway to the Straits, and on cross-channel trade of livestock, grain, wine, timber and other agricultural and artisan products. Because Messina's wealth and resources depended so much on access to the mainland, which was strongly affected by external political and institutional conditions, its phases of growth and decline reflect, in extreme form, political and institutional changes after 1282 in Sicily as a whole.

Rarely during recorded history can the narrow Straits have been an insuperable barrier. Cross-channel trade was essential for coastal populations from an early date,[11] and already in the early Middle Ages Calabria and north-eastern Sicily were linked by a dense network of Greek monastic institutions.[12] Following the Muslim conquest, many Greek monks fled to Calabria,[13] but some communities may have returned in the wake of the Normans. Several Sicilian ecclesiastical foundations owned property on both sides of

---

[11] Pontieri, *Ricerche sulla crisi della monarchia siciliana nel secolo XIII*, pp. 178–94, esp. pp. 181–7; Pispisa, *Messina*, pp. 21–2.
[12] Guillou, 'Il monachesimo in Italia meridionale e in Sicilia nel Medioevo'; D. Girgensohn, 'Dall'episcopato greco all'episcopato latino nell'Italia meridionale'.
[13] Guillou, 'Monachesimo', pp. 357–8.

the Straits, and had charters exempting them from paying tolls on goods they shipped back and forth.[14]

Before 1282, Messina probably imported most grain supplies from the mainland, for the city was only exempted from export dues on Sicilian grain from 1285.[15] Grain supplies were aided by the fact that, as a result of the Norman conquest, Messina established political and administrative primacy over the southern mainland. Before 1282, for example, the city's mint served both Sicily and southern Calabria. This hegemony allowed Messina to establish itself as the second metropolis of the kingdom of Sicily after Palermo (see chapter 3).

As I remarked previously, there is little doubt that Messina declined after 1282.[16] However, decline seems to have been only indirectly the result of the War of the Vespers itself. Warfare temporarily disrupted, but never fully interrupted, trade with the mainland.[17] Peter III's rapid conquest of most of Calabria in 1282–3 meant that the two regions were not immediately split asunder as a result of the Angevin expulsion from Sicily. For some years conditions were safe enough to draw up regular commercial contracts.[18] The contemporary Bartolomeo da Neocastro was voicing a common view, at least among Sicilians, when he made the men of Reggio address the Messinese as 'citizens of the Faro [Messina's lighthouse], our fathers and lords'.[19] Trade with more distant southern Italian cities like Amalfi was probably temporarily reduced, but Messina had its own consul in Naples in the 1320s.[20]

For roughly four decades after 1282, southern Calabria was either

[14] Garufi ed., *I documenti inediti dell'epoca normanna in Sicilia*, no. 82 (1185), and C 2802, fo. 5rv (1416) (Santa Maria di Valle Josaphat); L.-R. Ménager ed., *Les actes latins de S. Maria di Messina (1103–1250)*, no. 13 (1210), and C 2825, fos. 104v–5 (1435) (Santa Maria di Messina).

[15] See above, chapter 3. For relations with Calabria before the Vespers see G. Romano, 'Messina nel Vespro siciliano e nelle relazioni siculo-angioine de' secoli XIII e XIV fino all'anno 1372'.

[16] Trasselli, *Privilegi*, pp. 33, 36–8, 82–92, 110; E. Pispisa, 'Il problema storico del Vespro'; Pispisa, 'Stratificazione sociale e potere politico a Messina nel Medioevo'.

[17] Varvaro, 'Siciliano antico, siciliano letterario, siciliano moderno', pp. 278–9, argues this on linguistic grounds. For trade immediately after 1282 see Carini ed., *De rebus*, nos. 147, 288, 420, 493, 503, 510, App. 26, 143 (1282–3); La Mantia ed., *Codice diplomatico*, no. 214 (1290).

[18] Carini ed., *De rebus*, no. 320 (1283); Zeno ed., *Documenti*, no. 2 (1287).

[19] da Neocastro, *Historia sicula*, chapter 58.

[20] Yver, *Commerce*, p. 197. If most of the Amalfitan shipping laws (*Tavola amalfitana*), drawn up between 1339 and 1384, are a copy of the laws of Messina's

under Sicilian military control or at peace with the island; Messina's relations with the mainland must have been quite tranquil. Following Emperor Henry VII's revocation of Robert of Anjou's title to the kingdom of Naples, Federico III reopened hostilities on the Calabrian front in 1313 and conquered Reggio; but as a result of the strong Angevin reaction, he was forced to return all conquests to the pope in 1318.[21] Despite these events, and Angevin attacks which resumed in the 1320s and 1330s, trade across the Straits is documented up to the 1350s (we saw in chapter 1 that little documentation of any kind survives for the period between 1360 and 1392).[22]

Messina's capitulation to the Angevins in 1356 further stimulated trade with the kingdom of Naples,[23] and led to some trade privileges with Calabria. One of these allowed Messinese landowners in Calabria to reclaim their usurped rights of ownership.[24] Relations with the mainland returned to full normality only after the final peace treaty of 1372 between Sicily and Naples,[25] but were not enough to bring about Messina's recovery. Some reasons for the city's decline[26] were the fragmentation of Sicily's home market and the shift of Calabrian agriculture to animal husbandry,[27] both of which restricted Messina's sources of grain supply and opportunities for

---

Consolato del mare (Genuardi ed., *Libro dei capitoli*, pp. xlix–xl), this would suggest that commercial relations between the two cities continued in this period.
[21] C. D. Gallo, *Annali della città di Messina capitale del Regno di Sicilia dal giorno di sua fondazione sino a' tempi presenti*, II, pp. 162 (1297), 177 (1313); Epifanio, *Gli angioini di Napoli e la Sicilia dall'inizio del regno di Giovanna I alla pace di Catania*, pp. 64, 72–80, 238, 325; H. Finke ed., *Acta Aragonensia. Quellen zur deutschen, italienischen, französischen, spanischen, zur Kirchen- und Kulturgeschichte aus den diplomatischen Korrespondenz Jaymes II (1291–1327)*, II, no. 446; III, no. 117; M. I. Falcon Perez, 'Un aragonés embajador de Jaime II ante las cortes de Napoles y Sicilia'.
[22] Lionti, 'Un documento relativo a Matteo Palizzi', 99–104; da Piazza, *Cronaca*, I, chapters 35, 100, and II, chapter 8.
[23] R. Bevere, 'Arredi suppellettili utensili d'uso nelle provincie meridionali dal XII al XVI secolo', 636.
[24] Giardina ed., *Capitoli*, nos. 40 (1357), 41 (1363); Starrabba ed., *I diplomi della Cattedrale di Messina, raccolti da A. Amico*, no. 182 (1365).
[25] Cosentino, *Le nozze del re Federico III con la principessa Antonia del Balzo*, p. 80, January 1375; Genuardi, *Libro dei capitoli*, p. xlvi. Relations between Naples and western Sicily had long been good because the Chiaromonte, who controlled most of val di Mazara, were allied to the Angevins.
[26] Pispisa, *Messina*, pp. 120–2, 124–30; RC 11, fos. 144–5 (1368); RC 14, fo. 20 (1374); Starrabba ed., *I diplomi*, no. 204 (1385).
[27] Pontieri, *Calabria*, pp. 31–2.

trade. But the main challenge to Messina's regional hegemony in eastern Sicily had for a long time come from the nearby city of Catania.

Catania was situated at the junction of val di Noto and val Demone. It was assigned to val di Noto in the fifteenth century, making it the *vallo*'s largest city together with Syracuse; but it also exerted a strong pull on south-eastern val Demone, particularly on the area around Etna. A town of no great importance before the mid-fourteenth century, Catania became the capital of the pro-Catalan faction headed by the Alagona family during the civil war of the 1350s and 1360s. Then, as a result of Sicily's political and economic fragmentation, the city became Palermo's counterpart in eastern Sicily, attracting the administrative and commercial resources which had formerly accrued to Messina. As a result, Catania was the only large Sicilian city actually to increase in size after the Black Death. It was due solely to such peculiar political circumstances that Michele da Piazza's chronicle, which was nearly wholly centred on Catania and its surroundings, was able to rise above its parochialism and appear to describe more general, 'national' developments.

Needless to say, these changes provoked strong conflict with Messina. In the early 1350s, relations between the two cities were still peaceful, suggesting that their relative positions had not yet changed to any great extent. Following a truce between feudal factions in 1353, 'every Sicilian began travelling to various places, both by land and by sea, and particularly the people of Messina, who quickly left for Catania to make a profit with their merchandise'.[28] Twenty years later, however, the situation had so far changed that Catania was able to blockade Messina's food supplies effectively. In 1371, for example, Catania set a new tax on exported victuals, to which Messina retaliated with a toll on other goods imported from Catania. A similar attempt was repeated in the early fifteenth century.[29]

These processes of economic and demographic redistribution emerge also from accounts of the *secrezie*, the offices in charge of collecting royal tolls, after the Aragonese invasion of 1392 (income from consumption taxes can be taken as a rough indication of a

[28] da Piazza, *Cronaca*, I, chapter 55.
[29] RC 8, fo. 188rv (1371); Giardina ed., *Capitoli*, no. 58 (1404–5).

community's relative size and wealth). During the first two decades of Aragonese rule, Messina ranked a mere fourth after Palermo, Catania and Syracuse. In 1400–9, Messina's revenues were on average fifty-five per cent lower than those of Catania, while Palermo's surpassed both by a factor of two or three.[30] After the Aragonese conquest and a period of political uncertainty, however, the main court residence moved to Palermo, and very soon Catania began to dwindle to its former, lesser importance. Again, the main clue to the city's rapid decline comes from *secrezie* receipts. We saw above that under the Martins, Catania ranked a clear second after Palermo. By the 1430s, average receipts in Catania had sunk more than sixty per cent to 590 *onze*, whereas commercial activities in Messina – despite a ten per cent decline compared to the 1420s – were more than sixteen per cent higher than in 1400–9.[31] In 1434, the city council described Catania as 'nearly derelict'.[32]

Catania tried to stem decline by asking, first, for all of Palermo's and Messina's prerogatives and franchises, and then, a few years later, for Sicily's first university (*Studium generale*) in the hope of attracting trade.[33] But fifteenth-century Catania never fully recovered from the change of political circumstances.[34] By the mid-fifteenth century it had been surpassed by Noto, itself overtaken by Syracuse by the 1470s. Artisans were leaving Catania for Messina in the late fifteenth century.[35] In 1506, Catania's *gabella tareni* (a toll on imported merchandise) raised little on account of 'the malice of the times and the little trade in the city'.[36]

The fact that Messina's decline was the result of a shift in political power to Catania during the fourteenth century, rather than of the decline in cross-channel trade after 1282 that Croce had posited, is

---

[30] *UM*, p. 842, Table 191.

[31] *Ibid.*

[32] C 2826, fos. 48v–50: 'quasi eam pro derelicta habere videantur'.

[33] RC 67, fo. 102v, and RC 68, fo. 23rv (1432). A similar demand was put forward by the Barcelonese *Busca* to counter the city's decline (C. Batlle, *Barcelona a mediados del siglo XV. Historia de una crisis urbana*, p. 67). On Catania's conditions in this period see Gaudioso, *Questione demaniale*, pp. 118–19 (1436, 1454).

[34] C 3476, fos. 71v–82 (1460): the *popolo* asked that the viceroy establish his court in Catania; the city, which was neither a great port nor much frequented by merchants, was much poorer without it. A new wharf was being built in the same years (Giardina ed., *Capitoli*, no. 97).

[35] Lagumina and Lagumina eds., *Codice dei Giudei*, no. 804 (1490)

[36] Barberi, *Liber de secretiis*, pp. 63–4.

suggested also by the fact that Messina began to recover as soon as the political conditions that had led to Catania's expansion changed. Messina's élite was well aware that its city's strategic and commercial advantages as the foremost gateway to the mainland could be brought to bear most effectively within a unified and independent Sicilian polity. This explains why it offered such a warm welcome to the Aragonese invaders in the 1390s,[37] in contrast with strong resistance in Palermo and Catania, and also why Messina was always most keen to establish an autonomous Sicilian kingdom against Iberian plans to integrate Sicily into a wider empire (see chapter 7).

Besides the damage it inflicted on Catania as Messina's closest rival, the Aragonese conquest was also crucial to Messina's recovery because it re-established Sicily as a unified regional market in relation to the mainland. Easier trade within Sicily itself improved commercial relations with the southern mainland; Messina became once again an emporium servicing the whole of Sicily rather than just its immediate hinterland. Since political relations between Sicily and the kingdom of Naples did not change significantly for at least three decades after the Aragonese conquest of Sicily, it is clear that changes within Sicily itself explain why cross-channel trade rose so considerably after 1400.

Soon after the Aragonese invasion, one sees some first, tentative signs of economic recovery, at least of Messina's mercantile community. In the late 1390s, Messina was allowed to give safe conduct to any foreign merchant in Sicily,[38] and a few years later, after a long lapse, it renewed its consular representation in Amalfi.[39] In 1406, silver was so plentiful that Messina asked for a new coinage.[40] In 1419, the jurors of Catania assigned lodges in the city fair to Genoese and Messinese merchants, apparently the only ones important enough to receive the privilege.[41] Business relations with

---

[37] Giunta, *Aragonesi e Catalani*, I, pp. 192, 196; D'Alessandro, *Politica e società*, p. 127.

[38] Giardina ed., *Capitoli*, no. 52 (1397). See, however, RC 38, fos. 61–3v (1400): 'cun zo sia ki quistu regnu sia poviru ... ki non si fazano colti [hearth taxes] et maxime alu districtu di Missina, li quali su stati affannati per la sua maiestati alu tempu dila guerra et su redducti ki intru tutti non si trova unu dinaru'.

[39] M. Camera, *Memorie storico-diplomatiche dell'antica città e ducato di Amalfi cronologicamente ordinate e continuate sino al secolo XVIII*, I, p. 593; Del Treppo and Leone, *Amalfi medioevale*, p. 195.

[40] Trasselli, *Note banchi XV secolo*, pp. 17–18.

[41] Gaudioso, *Questione demaniale*, p. 19 n. 13.

Calabria also stabilized or improved.[42] Calabrian immigration to Messina intensified.[43] Martin I of Aragon was asked to intercede with Ladislas of Naples to have Ferruleto in Calabria returned to the archbishop of Messina,[44] and was requested to guarantee safe conduct to men from the mainland, just as King Ladislas had granted the citizens of Messina. 'The men of Messina', they stated, 'always have much [trade] going on by sea and in Calabria, while Calabrians trade little.'[45] By the 1430s, as we saw, Messina had recovered its dominant role in eastern Sicily. The city was assessed for 3,000 tax hearths, as many as Palermo and double the number in Catania, and toll revenues were a third greater than Catania's. Evidence of economic activity, as reflected in petitions, increases in the 1430s and co-incides with Alfonso's presence in Sicily, but these documents mostly describe patrician and merchants' needs. Merchants requested trading rights in their competitors' native countries, but also expressed worries that political reprisal by Alfonso against the Genoese might lead to retaliation in Levantine trade against the weaker Messinese.[46] Closer to home, Messina was allowed to sign monthly truces with Calabrians in order to trade.[47] The date of the local fair was moved surreptitiously from May to August, when raw silk was ready for sale; trade during the fair was exempted from a new, value-added tax of 3.3 per cent.[48] The number of forged privileges fabricated in these years to support Messina's claims to pre-eminence in the kingdom, and the many grants of citizenship to foreign merchants,[49] also testify to a more self-confident and

[42] RC 38, fo. 63 (1400).

[43] RC 7, fo. 272v (1394).

[44] Giardina ed., *Capitoli*, no. 60 (1410). RC 49, fos. 116–19 (1413): the viceregents were to ask Ferdinando to intercede with Ladislas in favour of the monastery of San Salvatore di Linguafaro's usurped rights. For the archbishopric's land in Calabria see Starrabba ed., *Diplomi*, nos. 117, 174, 182, 194, 197–8, 229 (1317–1417).

[45] RC 49, fos. 116–19 (1413).

[46] Giardina ed., *Capitoli*, no. 73 (1434).

[47] C 2818, fo. 45v (1431).

[48] The toll exemption was granted in gratitude for Messina's aid in the conquest of Calabria (C 2821, fo. 30, 1432).

[49] Pietro Gaetani, Pisan (CR 15, fos. 309–10v (1430, confirming a privilege of 1418); Petralia, *Banchieri*, pp. 184, 351); Simone da Rasignano (CR 16, fo. 245rv (1431); Petralia, *Banchieri*, p. 351); Battista Agliata, Pisan *campsor* (C 2820, fo. 60v, and CR 10, fo. 152rv (1433); Petralia, *Banchieri*, p. 109); Tuffa di Tommaso, Florentine living in Palermo (CR 16, fos. 303–4, and C 2826, fo. 8rv (1434); Petralia, *Banchieri*, p. 352); Cellino da Settimo and Giovanni Damiani, Pisans (CR 16,

positive outlook, probably connected to expectations about the outcome of Alfonso V's campaigns in the kingdom of Naples. In a period of political and economic transition, signs of growth were inevitably accompanied by some evidence to the contrary. This was particularly true for the 1430s, for Alfonso's war of conquest on the mainland was at its height and coincided with an unusual series of bad harvests.[50] Receipts from Messina's *secrezia* show a ten per cent decline over the previous decade.[51] 'For a number of years', the city government complained in 1434, 'the events and costs of war have caused great damage. It is thus quite

fo. 305rv, and C 2826, fos. 96v–7 (1434); Petralia, *Banchieri*, pp. 175, 254, 351); Onofrio da Calci, Pisan, *secretus* of Syracuse (CR 17, fos. 132–240v [*sic*] (1436); C 2843, fo. 67rv (1442)); Bartolomeo del Tignoso, Pisan (CR 10, fo. 234rv (1436); Petralia, *Banchieri*, pp. 260, 351); Pietro and Bernardo Rindelli, Florentines living in Syracuse (C 2828, fo. 140, and CR 17, fos. 275–6 (1437)); Francesco Morosini, Venetian (CR 18, fos. 320–1 (1439); see Petralia, *Banchieri*, p. 343); Andrea di Lodovico Borromei, from San Miniato (Florence) (C 2834, fos. 99v–100 (1440)); Pere Marquet (C 2842, fos. 133v–4 (1443)); Nicola Rella, Catalan (CR 30, fos. 107–8v (1447)); Giovanni Miraballi, *miles* and merchant of Naples (CR 30, fos. 52–4 (1448; he obtained citizenship rights in Messina, Palermo and Syracuse, but the privilege was soon revoked (fo. 52)); Giacomo and Simone Duro of Messina, who had Venetian citizenship 'ob defensionem ortodoxe fidei cristiane' (CR 60, fos. 222–3, and C 3492, fo. 21rv (1477); CR 75, fo. 87rv (1494)); Pietro de Succarrati (CR 75, fo. 89rv (1479–94)); Nicola de Averna (CR 75, fo. 84rv (1483–94)); Giorgio da Serbia, Venetian (CR 69, fos. 212–13 (1485)); Nicola da Monopoli, *magister* of Scaletta (CR 70, fo. 144rv (1487)); Nicola and Cesare Puleo, *nobiles* (CR 73, fo. 309rv (1487–90)); Marco de Gentili, of Termini (CR 72, fo. 269rv (1488); CR 71, fo. 130rv (1491)); Cataldo Rimasi (CR 73, fo. 191rv (1489); confirmed 1490); Caronetto di Gerardino, a Jewish silk weaver from Catanzaro (CR 73, fos. 215–16v (1489–90)); Faccio, Andrea and Artale Pollicino, *nobiles* (CR 73, fos. 305rv (1489–90)); Nicola de Fessima, *nobilis* (CR 73, fo. 201rv, confirmed 1490; Marco di Frescobaldo, Florentine (CR 75, fo. 52 (1493)); Sebastiano de Panfilia (CR 77, fo. 176rv (1494)); Mariano di Giovanni, *magister* (CR 77, fo. 331rv (1495)); Andrea de Criscimanno, *magister, converso* (CR 77, fo. 337rv (1495)); Bartolomeo de Alexandro, notary (CR 84, fos. 208–9 (1495)); Giovanni de Villardita alias de Modica (CR 80, fo. 80rv (1496–7)); Ambrogio de Nacerio, *nobilis* (CR 79, fo. 94 (1496)); Pietro de Lello, notary (CR 79, fo. 111rv (1497)); Bartolomeo Gioeni, baron of Cammarata (CR 79, fos. 163–3bis (1497)); Pietro de Bonizia (CR 80, fo. 133rv (1498)); Francesco de Brandino, *converso* (CR 84, fo. 232rv (1498)); Andrea, Pietro, Giovanni, Battista and Agostino de Coronato, Genoese (CR 80, fo. 139rv (1498)); Giovan Antonio Barresi, baron of Petraperzia (RC 182, fos. 103v–4 (1499)).

50 CS 2, fo. 141 (1435): economic hardship in the *Camera reginale*. For harvest failures see above, chapter 3, n. 229.

51 *UM*, p. 842, Table 191. Compared to 1420–9, average receipts fell 2.6 per cent in Palermo, 8.7 per cent in Messina and 29.7 per cent in Catania.

incredible that the king's triremes should attack Messina's own ships and capture the citizens and their goods aboard, treating them more like enemies than as friends.' The number of local ships had slumped and the city – or rather its merchants – was 'reduced to misery'. Alfonso's answer makes it clear that inhabitants of the district had been captured, possibly as forced conscripts.[52] The petition included a request for a *Studium*, which was approved but, in contrast with Catania, was pursued no further. Messina also asked Alfonso to intercede in Naples to repeal an order by the duke of Calabria that all his subjects living in Messina return home, at the risk of losing their property.[53]

In 1437, Messina protested to no avail against the choice of Palermo as capital; Messina's first bids for the role went back to the Aragonese invasion, which Messina had welcomed in contrast to Palermo's fierce resistance.[54] When, a few years later, the merchants asked to trade freely 'in every place and part of the wide world, particularly in the Levant and in Calabria', they felt in need of stating that during the previous twenty years (the approximate duration of Alfonso's mainland campaign) trade had been disrupted, causing serious damage to 'merchants and burghers' (*burgisi*). The king consented to the demands, while forbidding all trade in food and iron between Messina and its district and his 'enemies and rebels' in Calabria.[55]

Before Alfonso's triumphal entry into Naples in February 1443, therefore, Messina's prospects in Calabria remained uncertain. In peacetime, trade rights were upheld by both contenders,[56] but as soon as hostilities broke out the situation could change very rapidly: at times Messina's *secrezia* was in charge of the garrison in Reggio

[52] See C 2804, fo. 80 (1419).

[53] C 2820, fos. 129v, 130v (1434); Giardina ed., *Capitoli*, no. 73; see La Mantia, 'L'Università degli Studi di Catania e le pretensioni di Messina e Palermo dal secolo XV al XIX'. The request for a *Studium* was repeated in 1459 (Giardina ed., *Capitoli*, no. 96).

[54] *Ibid.*, nos. 50 (1396?), 60 (1410), 78 (1437). See above, n. 37.

[55] Giardina ed., *Capitoli*, no. 79 (1440). The petition came after Alfonso had forbidden dealings with 'rebel' Calabrians (C 2935, fo. 110v (1440)). The year before, Messina had pointedly reminded him of its crucial role in opposing his enemies in Calabria and had demanded adequate grain supplies (C 2834, fo. 14v).

[56] A charter of 1428 by Louis III of Naples upheld free trade between Reggio and Messina with a fifteen-day safe conduct for merchants in case of war (D. Spanò Bolani, *Storia di Reggio di Calabria*, I, pp. 220–1); for a similar request by Messina, who also demanded a ban on local piracy, see RC 59, fos. 87–8 (1428).

Calabria,[57] at other times all traffic with the 'rebellious' mainland was forbidden.[58] When Reggio fell to Alfonso's enemies in the early 1430s, he tried to conscript soldiers in Messina and its district, arguing that Reggio's recapture would be 'of evident benefit' to them.[59] In 1440, when Calabria rose against the Aragonese, trade was again disrupted, to the dismay of Messina's merchants. Alfonso once again banned trade in foodstuffs and iron.[60] The only other time in the fifteenth century when trade was again disrupted to such an extent, but far more briefly, occurred during a new Calabrian uprising in the early 1460s, when Ferrante of Naples called on the Sicilian government to help defeat the rebels.[61]

Because late medieval Messina stood to lose most from the severing or disruption of relations with the southern mainland, I have used developments there to test two contrasting theories about the effects of the Vespers of 1282. On the one hand, we have Croce's view – that the political partition of Sicily and Naples after 1282, and the Sicilian–Angevin war, sundered all relations between the two countries – which typically overestimates the importance of politico-institutional events for economic development. We have seen that, until records disappear in the 1350s, trade across the Straits of Messina continued apace *despite* the war, in which Messina was often strongly implicated; Messina itself could not have survived had trade collapsed entirely.[62] By contrast, cross-channel

[57] RC 58, fo. 72v (1426). Even after the final conquest of Naples in 1442 Messina was kept in charge of some Calabrian garrisons, like that of Scilla (CR 1, fo. 98v (1452–3)). This arrangement remained in force for a while after Alfonso's death and the division of the two kingdoms (CR 43, fo. 331 (1475)).

[58] C 2889, fos. 60v–1 (1432).

[59] C 2892, fos. 43v–4, 52v–3 (1435).

[60] See above, n. 55; C 2844, fos. 107v–9 (1443). Antonio Spagnolo, a cloth merchant from Messina who had recently set up shop in the county of Sinopoli in Calabria, denounced losses worth 300 *onze* (C 2893, fos. 35v–6 (1440)). The trade ban, renewed a year later (C 2893, fos. 113v–14 (1441)), could be circumvented (RC 76, fo. 412v (1441)).

[61] For Sicilian aid to Naples see LV 74, fo. 255rv (1460); C 3482, fo. 47 (1460); C 3480, fos. 140–1, 143, 167v–8 (1461); LV 77, fos. 374–6 (1461): 'actesa la convicinitat que lo dit reyalme te ab aqueix regne nostre de Sicilia en tant que sinistre algu no poria succehir en lo dit reyalme de Napols . . . que no redundas en grandissimo perill del dit regne nostre de Sicilia'; C 3484, fos. 157v–8 (1464). Evidence of trade in RC 109, fos. 197–8v (1460); CR 858, fo. 131 (1461).

[62] I have emphasized cross-channel trade because that is where commercial relations were strongest. However, in the late fourteenth century there was also intense trade between Palermo and Naples; see *UM*, chapter 8.

trade probably declined after 1360, when the War of the Vespers had nearly entirely abated, and picked up only after 1400, nearly thirty years after Sicily and Naples had signed a peace treaty ending the first, century-long phase of the war. Although Messina's fortunes were affected by the partition of 1282, this was not the main cause of its decline. Messina's wealth was based mainly on its control of trade across the Straits, and on its administrative hegemony over eastern Sicily. During the fourteenth century, both its commercial and its political hegemony were challenged: the first because the fragmentation of Sicily's regional market reduced cross-channel trade, the second because after 1350 Catania took over Messina's role as the eastern capital. These losses were reversed by the Aragonese restoration and, by 1430 at the latest, Messina had eclipsed Catania and re-established herself as the leading city in eastern Sicily. These developments had little to do with political relations with Naples. Indeed, although in the long term Messina gained from Alfonso's conquest of the kingdom of Naples, the enterprise was a mixed blessing, for both the war of conquest and the periodic uprisings in Calabria against Aragonese rule after 1444 tended to disrupt the process of commercial integration that was taking place at the same time.

In particular, the argument that market integration across the Straits became impossible because of political partition falls entirely when one observes that integration began to increase as soon as Sicily was pacified around 1400, rather than after reunification under Alfonso in 1444. During the fifteenth century, both men and goods fed a constant stream of traffic across the Straits.[63] Besides the seasonal labour from Calabria working in Palermo's sugar industries (see chapter 4), a regular flow of southern Italians moved west, stopping temporarily or permanently in Messina. Eastern Sicilian artisans had Calabrian apprentices,[64] while Messina's stocking manufacture seems to have been in the hands of Calabrians.[65] In 1443, Messina asked that all Calabrians, including those living in feudal lands, be allowed to immigrate freely.[66] Move-

[63] See the toll figures for Reggio in 1505–6 published by Galasso, *Economia e società*, pp. 72–3.
[64] NR 4, fos. 29v–30 (1453); NM 7, fo. 423 (1492).
[65] Trasselli, *Da Ferdinando*, p. 319.
[66] Giardina ed., *Capitoli*, no. 82 (1443). For immigrants to Messina see C 2829, fos. 20v–1 (1437); NM 5, fo. 78v (1446?).

ments in the opposite direction occurred mostly at times of dearth
or epidemics.[67] On one occasion inhabitants of Palermo fled to
Messina and Calabria to avoid dearth in western Sicily.[68] Although
the sources are not very informative on conditions prevailing in
Calabria, it does appear from this and other demographic evidence
that immigration from the mainland to Sicily was generally stronger
than in the opposite direction throughout the period.

Most trade across the Straits involved wheat and barley, wine,
salted meat, livestock (cattle and pigs) and horses, timber and
woodwork, leather and iron.[69] Salt was traded in both directions.[70]
Small boats, *tafureae*, *thopae* or *liuti*, regularly plied the channel.[71]
Although before the mid-fifteenth century it was usually Calabria
rather than val Demone that exported grain, or was sufficiently well
supplied to attract Sicilians at times of dearth, Calabria's surpluses
began to dwindle thereafter. Perhaps for the first time in centuries,
in the mid-fifteenth century grain was occasionally exported in the
opposite direction, from val Demone to Calabria.[72] As a result of
this development and of changes within Sicily's domestic market, a
system of triangular exchange emerged, in which Messina figured as
intermediary and final outlet. Merchants from Messina bought
timber in Calabria, transported it to Agrigento and Sciacca in
western Sicily, and there exchanged it for grain for their city.[73] It
was a logical development of Messina's earlier, simpler role as a
commercial intermediary between the southern mainland and the
rest of Sicily.[74]

---

[67] Dearth: RC 121, fos. 309v–10 (1468). Epidemics: C 2869, fos. 10v–11 (1451). In
the spring of 1479, Messina closed trade with Calabria in response to an epidemic
in Naples (TRP Atti 31, unnumbered fo., 27 March 1479); a similar ban was
passed for all of Sicily in 1493 (F. Trinchera ed., *Codice aragonese o sia lettere
regie, ordinamenti ed altri atti governativi de' sovrani aragonesi in Napoli*, II, 1,
no. 283).

[68] C 2891, fos. 14v–15v, 160rv (1434).

[69] RC 57, fos. 66v–8 (1425).

[70] NM 3, fos. 373v–4, 382rv (1446–8); Giardina ed., *Capitoli*, no. 88 (1451).

[71] Messina's *tafureae* were requisitioned for transporting the *infante* Pedro and his
retinue to the mainland in 1437 (C 2890, fo. 75v). A *thopa* in NM 6A, fo. 225
(1469); a *liutum* in NM 7, fo. 135v (1492).

[72] LV 92, fos. 434v–5 (1466).

[73] NM 7, fos. 85, 134v, 424v–5 (1491–2).

[74] A *sagicta* to transport twenty sacks of flax from Calabria to Trapani, loading three
carratas of timber as ballast (NM 6B, fo. 380rv (1469)).

Calabria's main export after grain was timber. Val Demone was still densely wooded, but the mainland's great pine trees and their pitch[75] were in strong demand in both eastern and western Sicily.[76] Beech and chestnut wood was commonly sold to barrel-makers in Messina[77] and Syracuse.[78] Messina's leather industry was supplied with Calabrian myrtle.[79] Calabria also exported some wine, mainly to Palermo but some to eastern Sicily as well,[80] olive oil (before val Demone established its own production),[81] flax[82] and chestnuts.[83] Notarial registers for Messina record a number of *commenda*-like contracts for trade, in or with Calabria, based in Messina; there is also evidence of trade-flows in the opposite direction.[84]

The main item of trade between Sicily and southern Italy in the fifteenth century, however, was livestock. Livestock had been exported to the mainland since at least the late thirteenth century,[85] but the trade's heyday came between the mid-fourteenth and the late fifteenth centuries, in response to the expansion of the pastoral sector and to increased agricultural specialization. Similar regional livestock markets developed throughout western Europe after 1350–70.[86]

The earliest evidence of these changes is to be found in a list of tolls drawn up in the late fourteenth century, which mentions cattle, pigs, rams and goats shipped from Messina to Calabria.[87] One of Messina's first requests to Martino was that he should forbid these exports, especially of 'large animals';[88] in the same period, Palermo, Trapani and Mazara were sending small numbers of sheep

---

[75] Carini ed., *De rebus*, no. 320 (1283); C 2894, fos. 178v–9v (1450); C 2897, fos. 50v–1 (1452).

[76] C 2896, fos. 132v–3 (1454); NM 7, fos. 139, 205v, 276, 307 (1492).

[77] NM 5, fo. 73 (1446?); NM 6A, fos. 73, 144, 225 (1468–9); NM 7, fos. 42v–3, 467v, 503v (1491–2); C. M. Rugolo, 'Maestri bottai in Sicilia nel secolo XV', 207.

[78] NM 7, fos. 282v–3 (1492).

[79] NM 3, fo. 329v (1446–8).

[80] For Messina see NM 5, fos. 427v–8 (1449); for Palermo see above, chapter 3.

[81] NM 7, fo. 291rv (1492); Fazello, *Due deche*, p. 296.

[82] Lionti, 'Un documento'.

[83] NM 7, fo. 135v (1492).

[84] NM 5, fos. 110rv, 189rv, 388, 399 (1446–9); NM 7, fos. 90v (1491); CR 71, fo. 223rv (1491).

[85] *RCA*, XXII, no. 392 (1280); Boüard, 'Problèmes de subsistances', 499.

[86] Blanchard, 'European cattle trades', 428–31; see above, chapter 4.

[87] Starrabba ed., *Consuetudini di Messina*, p. 234.

[88] 'Bestiaria grossa' (Giardina ed., *Capitoli*, no. 48 (1392)).

and oxen to North Africa, Tuscany and the kingdom of Naples.[89] Reunification of the Sicilian market under the Aragonese improved trading conditions, and evidence for trade increases rapidly from the late 1420s.[90] Following the damage to animal stocks in Calabria caused by the rebellion in 1444–5 of Antonio Ventimiglia Centelles, marquis of Crotone and count of Collesano, Messina asked for a three-year franchise on exports.[91] A similar request was made some years later when Centelles rebelled again, this time against Alfonso's successor, Ferrante.[92] Alfonso himself had Sicilian cattle sent to his *masserie* in Puglia, like the Angevins before him.[93]

The tolls on livestock crossing the Straits were very lucrative, which explains why the frequent attempts to abolish them were ineffective.[94] In 1454, the Messinese, Pietro Saccàno, was granted a life pension of 66.20 *onze* per year on the toll's receipts; a few years later, Giacomo Saccàno was granted 1000 ducats (400 *onze*) from the following two years' income as a dowry for his daughter.[95] Toll revenues in these years must, therefore, have been, at a conservative estimate, about 300 *onze* per year.

If we assume that the tolls levied by Messina in the late fourteenth century were the same as the subsequent royal toll (*gabella di passaggio*) (1.19 *tarì* for cattle, 1.1 *tarì* for a calf, 1.10 *tarì* for a pig, at an average of 1.10 *tarì* per animal), approximately 6,000 animals per

---

[89] For Palermo see PR 20, fos. 30v–2v (1418); C 2848, fos. 40–1 (1444). For Trapani and Mazara see C 2820, fos. 101v–2 (1434); C 2845, fo. 58v (1443). Also *UM*, p. 568 n. 135.

[90] CR 15, fo. 634 (1428–9): 200 cows; CR 24, fo. 271 (1446): 200 cows, 50 heifers, and 50 mares and foals for the viceroy of Calabria. CR 24, fos. 280–1 (1447): exports from Lipari. CR 36, fos. 320–1, and CR 1, fo. 98 (1452–3): 1,224 cattle; LV 78, fos. 119v–20v (1461): 698 cattle. LV 93, fos. 301v–2v (1464): 198 cows, 119 calves, 100 pigs and 200 sows. LV 92, fo. 361 (1464): 10 oxen.

[91] Pontieri, *Calabria*, p. 342. See also C 2845, fos. 184–5 (1444): toll franchise of fifty *onze* for a Messinese jurist, Jacobus de Costanzo, to export cattle, sheep and horses to the mainland.

[92] Pontieri, *Calabria*, pp. 33–4.

[93] C 2894, fos. 182v–3v (1450); C 2898, fo. 160 (1455); CR 854, fo. 130 (1455–6), and C 2896, fo. 145rv (1456). See also Del Treppo, 'Agricoltura e transumanza', p. 457; Del Treppo, *Regno aragonese*, p. 154. For exports to Puglia by private individuals see C 2882, fos. 20rv, 91 (1452), and C 2884, fo. 82rv (1455): 1,000 oxen toll free for Francesco Caracciolo; C 2883, fo. 184v (1454): 500 oxen or bullocks toll free for Giovanni de Barbera.

[94] RC 65, fos. 109rv (1430); C 2894, fos. 9, 29 (1443, 1444); CR 19, fos. 249–51 (1450); CR 40, fo. 126rv (1451).

[95] Pietro Saccàno: CR 37, fos. 48–8bis, 49–9bis (1454, 1455), and CR 34, fos. 372–3 (1457); Giacomo Saccàno: CR 34, fos. 321–3 (1457).

annum were crossing the Straits in the 1450s. Since the export tax may, in fact, have been only one *tarì*,[96] trade at its height may have involved 10,000 animals a year. Taking into account Sicily's size, especially the fact that exports came mainly from val di Noto and val Demone, these figures are comparable to early modern shipments from Denmark, Poland and Hungary.[97]

By the 1470s, however, the cattle trade began to tell on Sicilian resources: population was rising rapidly, pasture was contracting, and Sicilians were accustomed to eating large quantities of meat. The first ban on cattle, sheep and pig exports was passed in January 1470, after a drought followed by an epizootic caused a sharp increase in meat prices.[98] The export ban may have been repeated in 1472,[99] but it cannot have lasted long, for in 1476 Palermo again demanded a total ban on cattle exports for three years. As a result of this trade, the petitioners argued, less grain was produced, raising the danger of dearth; declining domestic supplies of meat, cheese and leather lowered state toll revenues; finally, the sugar industry lacked oxen to work the presses.[100] Palermo's request was temporarily successful, but only a year later the duke of Calabria was allowed to export 4,300 cattle, 3,100 of which were to be toll free.[101]

From the early 1480s, the central authorities began to take the issue more seriously. In 1483, King Ferdinand himself led investigations into illegal export grants by the former viceroy, Juan Cardona, to Bartolomeo Cinamo of Capua.[102] More care began to be taken in granting export licences; while the latter appear more regularly in financial registers, their number was in fact

---

[96] C 3490, fos. 34v–5 (1477).
[97] Data summarized in Blanchard, 'European cattle trade', Appendix. Hungary exported on average 50,000 cattle in the early mid-sixteenth century, corresponding to 0.26 head per km²; 10,000 cattle from Sicily correspond to 0.25 head per km².
[98] The price increase was blamed on the export trade (CR 50, fo. 7rv; TRP Atti 28, fo. 207v). The ban was sent to the *secreto* of Messina, to the marquis of Geraci in the Madonie, and to other unnamed Sicilian lords. A few months later, Artale Cardona, lord of Geraci, was accused, together with the captain and *secreto* of Caronia (a town within his jurisdiction), the count of San Marco and the barons of Ficarra and San Fratello, of having illegally exported livestock, particularly cattle, to the mainland (RC 125, fos. 177v–9 (1470)).
[99] RC 127, fos. 382–4 (1472). Exceptions to the ban in C 3487, fos. 162v–3 (1472); CR 55, fos. 147 (1472), 245–6 (1473).
[100] CR 43, fos. 170–3 (1476); for an identical petition, which may simply be wrongly dated to 1477, see De Vio ed., *Privilegia*, pp. 392–8.
[101] C 3490, fos. 34v–5, 36, 47v–8, 52–3, throughout.
[102] CR 65, fos. 1–4v.

260 An island for itself

declining.[103] The largest number of licences for cattle exports (3,665) was granted in 1487–8, followed in 1492–3 by 3,570 and in 1490–1 by 1,500.[104] In 1493, the export tax was increased by 1.10 *tarì*. Less than two years later all grants and franchises were declared void,[105] and exports rapidly dwindled.[106] In the early sixteenth century, there were further attempts to limit inroads into livestock, particularly oxen and bullocks, in order to ensure adequate meat supplies.[107]

Export licences for livestock were issued mainly to feudal lords of the northern watershed of val Demone, particularly of the Nebrodi and the Madonie, and of Calabria, or to high officials.[108] Licences were usually for hundreds of animals at a time, while the smaller-scale (but perhaps busier) trade escapes us nearly completely. The unification of the county of Collesano, which controlled a huge territory in the Madonie above Termini and Cefalù, and the marquisate of Crotone in Calabria, probably also gave a strong boost to trade. On the southern flank of the Nebrodi, around towns like Nicosia and Randazzo, the cattle and, to a lesser extent, the pig, trade was intense.[109] Trade was based on a cash advance invested jointly by two partners or by the receiving partner.[110] Most trade with Calabria, which had its main collecting points at the regional fairs of Nicosia, Randazzo, Lentini and Piazza,[111] was controlled

[103] 150 bullocks in 1482 (CR 867, fo. 126rv; CR 64, fo. 113rv), 180 bullocks and oxen in 1483 (CR 64, fo. 179rv; CR 66, fos. 211rv, 249). In 1482–4, a toll exemption of forty-nine *onze* (for 980 to 1,470 animals) was used (CR 66, fo. 161rv).

[104] CR 869, fos. 133–6, 143, 146–7, 153–7, 159 (1487–8); CR 871, fos. 158–9, 161, 169, 171–5 (1490–1); CR 872, fos. 175, 197, 199–214, 216–17v (1492–3).

[105] R. Raymundettus, *Regni Siciliae Pragmaticarum Sanctionum*, II, pp. 295–6, and *Pragmaticarum Regni Siciliae novissima collectio*, II, pp. 372–3 (1493); CR 75, 15 March 1494. The baron of Assoro was exempted from the ban (RC 191, fos. 101v–2v (1495)).

[106] Barberi, *Liber de secretiis*, p. 30.

[107] Cancila, *Baroni e popolo*, p. 29.

[108] CR 66, fos. 211rv (baron of San Fratello), 249 (baron of Resuttano). In 1487–8 (CR 869, fos. 133–6, 147, 153–4, 156–7), they were given to the barons of Petraperzia, of Muro in Calabria, and of San Fratello; to a royal secretary, Enrico Buxio; to the viceroy of Calabria; to the Venetian consul in Messina, Federico Spatafora; to the counts of Sinopoli, of Adrano, Caltanissetta and Augusta (who was also the *maestro giustiziere*); and to the count of Collesano.

[109] NR 5, fos. 9rv, 186, 245rv (1455–6); NR 15, fos. 160–1 (1490).

[110] NR 5, fo. 37 (1455); NR 6, fo. 9v (1460); NR 8, fo. 12v (1467); NR 20, fos. 14v–15 (1487).

[111] Above, chapter 3. For transactions at these fairs see also NR 4, fo. 32 (1453): Randazzo, Nicosia; NM 7, fo. 527v (1492): Nicosia; NM 5, fo. 192rv (1447): Lentini, Randazzo; NM 5, fo. 397 (1449), TRP Atti 13, fo. 44rv (1454), and

from Messina by local merchants and urban nobility and by men from elsewhere in Sicily and Calabria;[112] however, some trade occurred also in minor ports along the northern coast of val Demone (Patti, Milazzo, Mistretta).[113] Transport boats and landing licences from Calabrian barons were obtained in Messina.[114]

The fifteenth-century trade in cattle and smaller livestock was matched by that in horses and mules. Horses were used mainly for military purposes, and were therefore subject to strict governmental controls. As with other kinds of livestock, trade already occurred under the Angevins. In the late thirteenth century, most exports were from Sicily to the mainland,[115] but imports from Calabria are mentioned in 1286 in Messina's request to build enough boats to transport horses, mules and other animals to and from Catona.[116] After 1300, however, imports seem by and large to have ceased.[117]

Little evidence for trade survives before the Aragonese reconquest.[118] However, the trade must have been already well established before 1392, because five years later exports were forbidden on the grounds that stocks had been depleted.[119] Trade, in any case, soon resumed,[120] not only from Messina but also from western and southern Sicily, particularly from Palermo and Trapani. What was probably still a rather insignificant phenomenon received a huge boost from Alfonso's campaigns in southern Italy, which demanded an uninterrupted supply of thousands of animals. It is nonetheless difficult to estimate exports, for although licences were needed for

C 2886, fos. 145v–6 (1456): Piazza. For a new toll on local cloth and cattle traded at the fair of St John the Baptist in Randazzo, see NR 14, fo. 135rv (1489).

[112] NM 5, fo. 192rv (1447); NR 5, fo. 207 (1456); NM 6A, fos. 50v, 216rv, 221, 221rv (1468–9); NM 6A, fos. 161v–2, and NM 6B, fos. 370–1 (1469); NM 6B, fo. 386bis rv (1469).

[113] Milazzo (CR 867, fo. 126rv); Mistretta (CR 66, fo. 211rv); Patti (CR 66, fo. 241; CR 869, fos. 136, 138).

[114] NM 5, fos. 77rv, 128rv, 183, 187v, 188, 193v (1446–7).

[115] *RCA*, VI, nos. 840, 858, 872, 891, 943 (1270).

[116] *RCA*, V, nos. 192, 195, 214 (1270); Giardina ed., *Capitoli*, no. 28 (1286).

[117] C 2819, fos. 59v–60 (1432): imports from Gozo.

[118] D'Arienzo ed., *Carte reali*, nos. 255–6 (1346): 150 horses for Sardinia.

[119] G. Beccaria, 'Note critiche sul Parlamento di Catania del 1397', 363 (1397).

[120] A. Boscolo, 'Mercanti e traffici in Sicilia e in Sardegna all'epoca di Ferdinando I d'Aragona', p. 274 (1412–17); RC 49, fos. 116–19 (1413); RC 50, fos. 37v–8, 55, 67rv, 206, 211v (1415); C 2801, fos. 88v, 112, 150, 186 (1417–18); C 2803, fos. 103, 126v (1418).

war horses, smaller, less valuable horses could be exported without formal permission.[121]

In 1422 and 1424, the king bought just under 300 horses;[122] by 1426, the viceroy was worried that the drain on stallions would affect the quality of Sicilian breeds, and asked that animals unfit for war be sent back to Sicily.[123] After Alfonso's return to Spain, horses and mules were exported there by the Siculo-Iberian aristocracy, whereas trade with the mainland was apparently forbidden.[124] On Alfonso's return to Italy in 1434, requests for war horses soared,[125] but attempts to ban trade for civilian purposes were ineffective.[126] Between 1434 and 1442, an average 500 horses per year were shipped to Alfonso on the mainland; exports may have been double this figure taking other military and private exports into account. In March 1437, the king demanded 100 animals, and less than a year later he asked for 500 more, all in the moderate price range of three to five *onze*. In August 1439, the *maestro portulano* was told to buy 500 horses for 1,500 *onze*; a year later Alfonso asked for 1,000 horses; in 1441, a shipment of 132 animals was sent to Gaeta. After the end of the war, orders became more generic with no specification of numbers.[127]

Between Alfonso's death and the outbreak of the Catalan civil war in 1462, exports continued apace. Between September 1460 and September 1461, export licences for 395 animals were granted, of which at least 127 passed through Messina.[128] In June 1462, the king ordered that no more victuals and horses be sent to Barcelona; all shipments to him were to be sent to Valencia.[129] Apparently no more export licences were granted until 1470, although there was no

[121] Testa ed., *Capitula*, I, p. 461 (1460); Ryder, *The kingdom of Naples*, p. 359.
[122] C 2888, fos. 88rv, 96rv, 151v.
[123] *Ibid.*, fos. 165, 169v.
[124] Exports to Spain in CR 14, fos. 482, 488, 520, 525 (1426–7); CR 11, fo. 390v (1427). Export ban to the mainland in C 2889, fo. 35 (1431).
[125] C 2891, fo. 145v (1434); C 2892, fo. 20 (1434); Giardina ed., *Capitoli*, no. 73 (1434).
[126] C 2890, fo. 27v (1436); C 2893, fo. 165 (1442): 'cautament e secreta se tinga manera que barons neguns de Calabria no trasguen cavalls' from Sicily.
[127] C 2890, fo. 74v (1437); C 2935, fo. 103 (1438); C 2892, fo. 22quater (1439); C 2835, fos. 41v–2 (1439); C 2935, fo. 127v (1440); RC 76, fo. 522rv (1441); C 2935, fo. 180v (1449); RC 86, fo. 40 (1451). See also *UM*, pp. 567–8, 859.
[128] CR 41, fos. 143rv, 304, 306, 318rv, 324rv, throughout.
[129] C 3482, fo. 11.

evident reason to ban trade with the kingdom of Naples; most subsequent exports were to the Italian mainland.[130] Trade continued but average export numbers declined. From the late 1460s, worries about the depletion of stocks were often voiced, but the excessive number of mules, rather than the export trade, was blamed for this state of affairs. The government tried at first to meet the problem by compelling people who rode mules to keep the same number of horses,[131] and later, perhaps because this measure was proving insufficiently severe, by setting a compulsory reproductive quota.[132] In 1485, in response to the Turkish threat, riding mules[133] and exporting horses from Catania, Messina and Palermo was forbidden (except for persons wishing to aid Ferrante on the mainland).[134] The issue of stock depletion, however, was just a passing worry, and by the late 1480s the provisions were, to all intents and purposes, repealed.[135]

Export restrictions were motivated by domestic military needs, but also reflected the breeds' high reputation abroad.[136] Alfonso presented his brother Juan, king of Navarre, with fifteen Sicilian horses in 1445, and allowed Jacques Cœur, treasurer to the king of France, to export thirty horses toll free a few years later. On three occasions Filippo Maria Visconti, duke of Milan, requested several dozen to be sent to him via Genoa, and the tradition persisted, because Corrado Sforza, brother of Duke Galeazzo Maria Sforza, and later Duke Gian Galeazzo, also had Sicilian horses sent to

[130] In 1460, Juan had agreed to waive the need for export licences; if the law was enforced, many exports would no longer be in the government registers (Testa ed., *Capitula*, I, p. 461).
[131] TRP Atti 28, fos. 208v–9, and CR 48, fo. 1rv (1469). Exceptions were made for Mistretta (CR 50, fo. 169 (1470)) and Cefalù (CR 51, fo. 619 (1471)). The provision provided an excuse for enclosing some common land in Caltagirone, allegedly to breed horses (RC 125, fo. 167rv (1470)).
[132] CR 60, fo. 5 (1478). Exemptions in CR 64, fo. 143 (1483); CR 66, fos. 245, 258rv, 259, 289, 305, 307 (1484).
[133] CR 67, fos. 1–2, 3–4, 7v; CR 69, fos. 1, 11–12.
[134] Export bans in CR 68, fos. 53, 64, 65rv. Exemptions in CR 868, fo. 126 (1486).
[135] Testa ed., *Capitula*, I, p. 527 (1488); CR 73, fo. 8 (1490). For permission to use up to a fourth of one's mares to breed mules see CR 73, fo. 10 (1490).
[136] There were at least two Sicilian breeds (*UM*, p. 881 n. 72). See C 2805, fos. 89–90 (1440, county of Geraci), and RC 131, fos. 66v–7 (1473, Troina) for specialized horse-breeding. The strain may have been strengthened with African imports. See CR 854, fo. 121 (1455–6): three 'cavalli barbariski' exported from Messina for the duke of Calabria.

Milan.[137] Both Ferrante of Naples and the Duke of Calabria were allowed to export twenty-five horses every year, and King Ferdinand the Catholic had his own Sicilian herds.[138]

What do these developments tell us of economic specialization and integration across the Straits of Messina during the late Middle Ages, the second theme of this chapter? I argued in chapter 3 that the toll franchises granted by Alfonso to a number of communities on the mainland must be understood not as traditionally conceived trading privileges, but as instruments for promoting the same trade in cheap, bulky agricultural and manufactured products that they stimulated within Sicily. Such franchises were granted to towns like Reggio, Scilla and Lipari, and to the more distant Gaeta, Capua, Ischia and Isola del Giglio, towns which had already established commercial links with Sicily, especially with Messina and Palermo, and wished to develop them in more favourable conditions. In the case of Scilla and Isola del Giglio, which were spared the abolition of trade franchises following Alfonso's death, military considerations were paramount.[139] Gaeta, Capua and Ischia, whose privileges were sacrificed, continued to trade with Sicily but under less favourable conditions, with the result that such economic integration as had previously emerged may have been weakened.[140]

This kind of interregional integration was thus restricted to a few privileged southern communities, and was based on a fairly small volume of trade. Stable, long-term integration could not be expected to evolve out of a few commercial privileges which depended wholly on changing political circumstances, and which involved comparatively insignificant flows of trade. The nature and limitations of southern Italian ties with Sicily become clearer when we analyse some monetary evidence. In December 1421, Alfonso

[137] C 2855, fo. 43v (1445) (Juan of Navarre); Mollat, *Jacques Cœur ou l'esprit d'entreprise au XVe siècle*, p. 163 (Jacques Cœur); *UM*, p. 568; CR 14, fo. 496rv (1426–7), and CR 24, fos. 254–5, 257rv (1446) (Filippo Maria Visconti); C 3478, fos. 99v–100 (1464), and RC 181, fos. 198–9 (1492) (other orders from Milan).

[138] C 3490, fos. 66rv, 67v, and CR 60, fos. 313rv, 315rv (1477). For Ferdinand's herds see RC 147, fo. 70v (1482); CR 65, fos. 1–4v (1483); CR 68, fos. 1–2v (1484), and CR 868, fo. 99 (1485); RC 176, fo. 131v (1490); RC 181, fo. 202 (1492); Trinchera ed., *Codice aragonese*, II, 1, nos. 119–20 (1492).

[139] LV 71, fos. 6v–7 (1459). For Isola del Giglio see CR 42, fos. 409 (1460), 410 (1461); for Scilla see C 2813, fo. 142v (1427); LV 77, fo. 410rv (1461); RC 158, fos. 425–6v, and CR 69, fos. 411–12 (1486); Epifanio, *Angioini*, p. 76.

[140] This is suggested also by the sharp decline of trade from Amalfi to Sicily after the mid-fifteenth century (Del Treppo and Leone, *Amalfi medioevale*, pp. 189, 219).

broached a project, confirmed in October 1422, to increase trade between Sicily, Calabria and Puglia by coining *tornesi*, a low-value silver coin used on the mainland.[141] The plan was discontinued, partly because Alfonso soon after returned to Spain (where he would remain until 1432), and also because, paradoxically, southern Italy was at the same time flooding Sicily with its own devalued copper coins.[142]

In 1432, envoys from Messina lamented the large quantity of bad billon (*denari di piccoli*) being minted in the city which could not be used for large transactions (particularly to buy victuals) and therefore had little outlet. The envoys were also worried about a new project to coin Neapolitan *tornesi* to use on the mainland, which coincided with the beginning of Alfonso's new military campaign there. Messina probably feared that this project would deplete the city of its remaining silver, and perhaps also that it could open up their market to devalued *carlini* from across the Straits.[143] No more was heard about this project, but after the fall of Naples in 1443, other attempts to unify the Sicilian and Neapolitan monetary systems were made – and regularly failed.[144] In August 1468, Messina had to coin imitation Neapolitan *gigliati* to buy grain on the mainland, for Sicilian currency was not accepted.[145]

Even so, although the failure of these projects confirms how limited economic integration still was between Sicily and the kingdom of Naples as a whole, the substitution of Sicilian billon with bad Calabrian coinage in Messina and (to a lesser extent) in western Sicily, implies that economic links between Sicily and Calabria were very strong indeed. So strong, in fact, that in November 1443 Lope

---

[141] C 2888, fos. 80–1 (1421), 117rv (1422).

[142] Cosentino, 'La zecca di Palermo nel secolo XV e la monetazione dei "denari parvuli" o "pichuli"', p. 203; Trasselli, *Note banchi XV secolo*, pp. 31–2, does not record any mintings in these years.

[143] *Ibid.*, pp. 36–8 and 137–8.

[144] C 2935, fo. 160 (1443); C 2892, fo. 26ter rv (1447); C 2894, fo. 129v (1447): Sicilian *carlini* and *aragonesi* must have the same course as those coined in Naples; C 2896, fos. 86v–7 (1451): the viceroy must pay all the court's current debts, and 'dalli avant faça pesar la moneda axi d'or com de argent per tot lo Regne lo qual pes sia consemblant del pes ab que se pesa en Napols. E perço trametra e se fara venir mossen Francesch Sunyer e faça per aquell sien tramesos los pesos per totes les ciutats et terres del dit Regne'; Trasselli, *Note banchi XV secolo*, pp. 47–8 (1456).

[145] 'Volendovi vui [Messina] subveniri di victuagli dilu Regnu di Napoli non potivino per non si potiri spendiri et curriri la monita di quisto regno in quillo' (CR 864, fo. 115rv (1468)).

Ximen Urrea, viceroy of Sicily, was given the same office for Calabria.[146] By the mid-fifteenth century, economic integration had proceeded so far that after the partition of the two kingdoms in 1458, trade franchises with Sicily could not be revoked for the island of Lipari and Reggio Calabria; the latter, together with its *districtus*, possessed a larger number of Sicilian toll franchises than any Sicilian community except Messina itself.[147] Cross-channel bonds were so strong, and it was so easy to ferry goods across, that the inhabitants of Messina and its district would even occasionally take their pigs to Calabria to graze.[148]

Messina, indeed, has been accurately described as 'primarily . . . the port of southern Calabria'.[149] Its principal role and the reason for its changing status can be found in the link it provided between Sicily and the southern Italian mainland. Messina's spectacular recovery after 1400 shows that recurrent insecurity in Calabria, even war, was not an insuperable obstacle to its welfare, so long as certain political conditions prevailed on the domestic front. These conditions were, primarily, a strong monarchy and, as a secondary condition, that the monarchy should have a strong southern Italian orientation. When these were lacking, as they were during much of the fourteenth century, Messina inevitably suffered. When they were at their optimum, as occurred under Alfonso, the city flourished. Alfonso's death, the separation of the 'two Sicilies' and, most especially, the reorientation of the crown of Aragon's policies by Juan II towards Spanish affairs, seemed to spell once again the city's decline. The Messinese nobility reacted to this danger in 1459–61 with a failed bid for Sicilian autonomy under Charles of Viana, Juan's son (see chapter 7); the effects of this change of Aragonese policy on Messina were reflected in its slower demo-

---

[146] Ryder, 'The evolution of imperial government in Naples under Alfonso V', p. 338.

[147] RC 2, fos. 107rv (1316, Testa ed., *De vita Federici II*, p. 275), 108 (1316); a copy of a late fourteenth-century diploma signed by Enrico Rosso, granting Messina's privileges and a toll franchise throughout Sicily, in RC 5, fos. 240v–1 (1480); RC 57, fos. 66v–8 (1425) confirmed in CR 26, fos. 64–7v, and C 2850, fos. 174v–5v (1445); Pontieri ed., *Calabria*, p. 137 n. 1: toll franchise 'de quibusdam rebus, usui suo necessariis vendendis seu emendis in ipso Regno . . . ferri, frumentorum et ordei ac lignaminum, coraminis, panni, carnium, vini et animalium'; C 2864, fo. 1rv (1450); Spanò Bolani, *Storia di Reggio*, I, pp. 258, 333 (1503).

[148] RC 144, fo. 85 (1480).

[149] Trasselli, *Da Ferdinando*, pp. 324–5.

graphic growth compared to Palermo before the mid-1460s (see Table 2.7). Messina's subsequent rapid growth was not, however, the result of a further change of government policy towards the mainland, but of the development of the wine, sugar, oil and especially silk industries in eastern val Demone and Calabria. These developments reinforced Messina's role as the region's commercial hub, and established it as one of the main ports of trade in the western Mediterranean. They further established val Demone as the most specialized, most outward-looking and least 'marginal' region of late medieval Sicily.

6. *Foreign trade and the domestic economy*

INTRODUCTION

We have seen in the previous chapters that to describe late medieval Sicily as a staple grain exporter, undeveloped but for two industries (sugar and silk) linked to foreign markets, caricatures existing conditions and misrepresents the relative importance of foreign to domestic trade. Nonetheless, while I have argued that the latter was the prime cause of structural changes at the regional level, I do not intend simply to turn arguments about 'dependence' on their head and take refuge in purely 'endogenist' explanations of economic development.

In fact, the theoretical divergences between the 'dualist' and the 'endogenous' models of economic development partly reflect the empirical distinction, which prevailed before the later Middle Ages, between long-distance trade in high-value goods, and shorter-range exchange of low-value, bulk commodities.[1] We saw in chapters 1 and 3 that both the dualist and the 'endogenist' model appear to rest on the assumption of peasant subsistence or of a specific 'peasant

---

[1] The 'endogenist' approach stresses the role of productive forces and the structure of property rights for economic development. In this view, basic pre-industrial, socio-economic change tends to arise within rural society; the main source of change is located in social conflict and dynamism, and in their effects on property rights. I call this view 'endogenist' rather than Marxist, for Marx was not entirely consistent on this point; see Brenner, 'Origins of capitalist development'. 'Endogenists' make little allowance for evolution and change in either domestic or long-distance trade (Kriedte, 'Spätmittelalterliche Agrarkrise oder Krise des Feudalismus?'). This neglect is partly a result of the Sweezy–Dobb debate of the 1950s, which was framed in terms of a stark opposition between 'exogenous' versus 'endogenous' forces of change, and resulted in an 'endogenist' consensus (see Hilton ed., *The transition from feudalism to capitalism*), partly of the Marxian emphasis on commodity production rather than circulation, and partly of widespread assumptions about peasant 'rationality' (see above, chapter 3, n. 8).

economy'. I also suggested that the problems this raises can be solved if one assumes instead that peasants did not avoid commercialization as a matter of principle, but pursued economic strategies shaped by imperfect information and by prevailing institutional constraints on commoditization. With this view, the early medieval distinction between domestic and 'international' commodity markets can be explained as the effect of very high transaction costs restricting long-distance trade to high-value products, rather than as a result of different 'economic rationalities' between the two sectors. Supra-regional trade in bulk goods could develop successfully only if these costs were significantly reduced.

Various late medieval innovations effected just such a reduction. Some can be traced back to the late thirteenth century, but most of them occurred after 1350, when increasing competition in shrinking markets and declining prices of bulk agricultural goods made it imperative to seek out and propagate existing and new technologies to cut long-distance transport costs. Larger ships (cogs, hulks, carracks and great galleys) became more common;[2] maritime insurance was established; and a more sophisticated system of discriminating freight rates was developed.[3] Transaction costs were also reduced (exogenously) as a result of the consolidation of regional and national states. The same forces which had stimulated infra-regional integration thus tended to increase interregional specialization, though more weakly because of the smaller volume of trade involved. While the total volume of interregional trade in mineral and agricultural goods may well have declined between *c*.1350 and *c*.1450, former barriers between markets for bulk and high-value commodities became increasingly blurred or collapsed altogether.

Once differences in transaction costs between external and domestic markets begin to narrow, many assumptions behind the dualistic, 'exogenous' approach can more easily be questioned. One can

---

[2] R. W. Unger, *The ship in the medieval economy 600–1600*, chapter 4; Pryor, *Geography, technology, and war. Studies in the maritime history of the Mediterranean 649–1571*, pp. 39–43; Melis, 'Werner Sombart e i problemi della navigazione nel Medio Evo'.

[3] Edler De Roover, 'Early examples of marine insurance'; Melis, 'Werner Sombart', pp. 119ff.; F. C. Lane, 'Technology and productivity in seaborne transportation', pp. 238–41; J. E. Dotson, 'Stowage factors in medieval shipping'; Kellenbenz, 'Wirtschaft und Gesellschaft Europas 1350–1650', pp. 303–5.

no longer assume that 'capitalist' foreigners and domestic traders were necessarily engaged in different pursuits leading to different outcomes; nor can one take for granted that foreign merchants were interacting with 'traditional', stable-state or subsistent economies, for it becomes increasingly likely that peasants would become involved in production not only for local and regional, but also for supra-regional, markets.

Some of these problems have already been examined in chapter 3, when discussing the emergence of the silk, sugar and cloth industries in eastern Sicily. In this chapter I turn to the main theories of dependency through foreign trade, and confront them with the available empirical evidence. I discuss in turn the main exports (grain, cheese, livestock, tunny, silk and sugar), the main imports (slaves and cloth), and Sicily's balance of trade. I conclude by assessing the importance of these trade flows for the domestic economy.

EXPORTS: GRAIN

Although grain exports were allegedly the 'true axis of the island's exchange economy' during the medieval and early modern periods, the crucial question of what proportion of domestic output was sent abroad has never been clearly established.[4] Since it is a necessary precondition for all dependency theory that the export ratio be very high (however one defines 'high'), I shall examine this point in some detail. The answer will enable us to assess three crucial claims about the trade's impact on domestic markets: first, that the volume and nature of foreign trade was shaped by state policies, at odds with domestic welfare; second, that long-run terms of trade were unfavourable to Sicily; and finally, that foreign commercial domination engendered local dependence. I conclude this section by suggesting an alternative explanation of the sources of agricultural surplus exported abroad, and of the long-term impact of foreign trade on domestic production.

Despite the lack of long series of export figures before the fifteenth century, available data allow us to reconstruct general trends from about 1270. In the late thirteenth century, Sicily exported on average 20,000–30,000 *salme* of wheat a year, with occasional peaks of

---

[4] *UM*, p. 523. Bresc dismisses the question when addressing domestic production (*UM*, pp. 127–8).

40,000 *salme*. Barley exports increased this figure by about twenty-five per cent per year (after 1400 they were insignificant); during the 1270s, therefore, exports of all grains averaged 25,000–35,000 *salme* a year. It is possible that after 1282 the new Aragonese sovereigns were forced by political or economic circumstances to lower customs dues in order to encourage trade,[5] but export figures are fragmentary and unreliable. What does survive for the period 1290–1347 suggests average exports of 40,000 *salme*, rising occasionally to 80,000 *salme*.[6] Considering our evidence that the population was probably declining during the same period (see chapter 2), the proportion of exports to domestic output probably did rise slightly under the Aragonese regime.

Why were customs duties (*tratte*)[7] lowered after 1282? Since the new regime depended to a significant degree on income from *tratte* to finance the anti-Angevin war, it would have seemed more reasonable to maintain or even increase the *tratta* so as to maximize income. However, Sicily's political isolation following the Vespers had narrowed its export markets, and in order simply to maintain their existing share of the foreign markets, exporters had to cut the price of grain: the easiest way to do so was to put pressure on the crown to lower export dues. Since Aragonese political legitimacy hinged to a considerable extent on the reduction or outright abolition of Angevin taxation, it must have been comparatively simple for exporters to accomplish a reduction of the grain *tratta*. We shall see that a similar strategy, but in different political circumstances, was adopted a century later under Alfonso V.

Nearly every previous outlet for Sicilian grain was affected after 1282. No significant trade could continue with southern Italy because of Angevin hostility.[8] Exports to Guelph Genoa were problematic after Federico III's coronation in 1295, which destroyed

5 *UM*, p. 530.
6 Peri, *La Sicilia dopo il Vespro*, pp. 108–9; *UM*, pp. 526, 540.
7 The *tratta* was paid on all cereal and legume exports in the following proportions: 1 *tratta* per *salma* of wheat, ½ *tratta* per *salma* of barley and legumes.
8 See Boüard, 'Problèmes de subsistances' (from the point of view of the mainland); Carini ed., *De rebus*, no. 139 (1282); La Mantia ed., *Codice diplomatico*, no. 214 (1290). Before Federico III's coronation in 1296, some grain was still exported to enemy territory at times of truce. A major law case between the communes of Genoa and Gaeta arose in the winter of 1294 over a shipment of 750 *salme* of Sicilian grain, which had been illegally unloaded in Gaeta from a boat on its way to Genoa (Archivio di Stato di Genova, not. Giovanni de Amandole 58, fos. 39r–47v, 62r–6v; reference provided by David Abulafia and James Mackenzie).

remaining Angevin hopes of recovering Sicily peacefully.[9] Trade
with Guelph Florence was also formally banned (with the minor but
significant exception of the Bardi and Peruzzi companies).[10] Links
with Catalonia, and the Catalan conquests in Greece around 1300,
might have opened up valuable new markets for Sicilian grain,[11]
had those countries not been basically self-sufficient for their food
supplies. The political crisis which followed Federico's coronation
may also have interfered with trade with Catalonia.[12] On the other
hand, Pisa began importing Sicilian wheat as a *result* of the Vespers;
North Africa may have been a good client; and, during the 1330s,
Venice also started supplying itself in Sicily.[13]

We saw in chapter 3 that the war of the Vespers also restricted
sources of grain supply from the mainland for eastern Sicily, in particular Messina and eastern val Demone, causing a partial reorientation of
demand towards the home market; for the crown's purposes the growth
of the domestic grain trade made no difference, for it was still taxed like
exports abroad. The size of this shift is unknown, but although eastern
Sicilian demand was at this time far weaker than it would become in the
late fifteenth century, it must be taken into account when estimating
exportable surpluses. A further, short-term effect of the fragmentation
of the home market and the increase in agricultural productivity after
the mid-fourteenth century may have been to stimulate production in
eastern Sicily, where grain exports seem to have risen from next to
nothing towards 1300 to over forty per cent of total exports during the
1390s.[14]

9 After 1318, the Ghibelline Doria and Spinola families were expelled from Genoa
and established a rival centre of power in Savona; Ghibellines did trade with
Sicily, but their demand was low compared to Genoa's. For Sicilian relations with
the (Guelph?) Genoese in this period see *Mostra documentaria*, nos. 11–13; E.
Déprez and G. Mollat eds., *Lettres closes, patentes et curiales du pape Clément VI
intéressant les pays autre que la France*, no. 1404 (1347); Finke ed., *Acta Aragonensia*, II, nos. 433, 450, 455; III, nos. 79, 80, 190, 201, 248; Giunta and Giuffrida
eds., *Corrispondenza*, pp. 26–30.
10 Corrao ed., *Registri di lettere*, no. 14 (1328); Trasselli, 'Nuovi documenti sui
Peruzzi, Bardi e Acciaiuoli in Sicilia'; Abulafia, 'Southern Italy', 386–7.
11 Trade with Catalonia: La Mantia ed., *Codice diplomatico*, no. 67 (1285); Zeno
ed., *Documenti*, no. 6 (1287); *UM*, p. 526 n. 16. Trade with Greece: B. Krekic,
Dubrovnik (Raguse) et le Levant au moyen âge, no. 106 (1314); on the Catalans in
Greece see N. Cheetham, *Medieval Greece*, chapter 6.
12 Abulafia, 'Catalan merchants and the western Mediterranean, 1236–1300: Studies in the notarial acts of Barcelona and Sicily', 232–42; Tangheroni, *Aspetti del
commercio*, pp. 79–81, 83, 86.
13 Abulafia, 'Southern Italy', 386; Abulafia, 'Venice and the kingdom of Naples in
the last years of Robert the Wise 1332–1343', 193.
14 Part of this increase, however, was due to eastern Sicily being under stronger
Aragonese control in the early phases of the 1390s' war.

Grain exports after 1350 are hard to estimate, but lower domestic and foreign demand following the Black Death must have strongly reduced the volume of trade. The breakdown of the domestic market also affected the export trade adversely. Instead of organizing and co-ordinating trade from Palermo as was previously done, foreign merchants had to deal personally with a number of politically independent local lords, raising bargaining costs and risks of default.[15] Communities were able to count less on imports from elsewhere in Sicily and had to rely more on local resources, which in turn made the estimation and collection of surpluses harder to organize (see chapter 2).

Grain did nonetheless continue to be exported.[16] Indeed, the trade's profits helped convince Catalan, Valencian and Aragonese adventurers to risk the Sicilian expedition in 1392. At first the Martins granted duty-free trade (free *tratte*) quite ruthlessly in reward to their followers. More than 150,000 export licences (including those for domestic shipments) were granted in 1392, nearly 143,000 of which were actually used; the following year, over 80,000 free *tratte* were drawn on Sicilian ports. At this rate, as we shall see, exports accounted for twenty-five to thirty per cent of domestic output. Equivalent proportions would be achieved only once again, when the particularly good harvest of 1406–7 allowed nearly 129,000 *salme* of grain to be exported to finance Martino of Sicily's expedition to Sardinia.[17] In fact, and despite the pressures of war, on average less than 31,000 *salme* of grain were exported annually in the period 1391–2 to 1405–6. Excluding the first two years of invasion (1391–3), when financial needs were exceptionally high, average exports were less than 18,000 *salme*. The policy of 1392–3,

---

[15] Motta, 'Aspetti dell'economia', 524. This disadvantage, however, was compensated for by the merchants' greater monopoly powers over the foreign cloth trade (see above, chapter 3).

[16] For exports to Valencia before 1392 see Archivo Municipal (Valencia), Clavaria, Albarans, I, nos. 1, 9–19 (1367–92); Seguretats, II (1385–91) (references provided by Piero Corrao). Exports to Sardinia in Tangheroni, *Aspetti del commercio*, pp. 109, 111–12, 118, 158. Exports to Majorca are referred to in V. Salavert i Roca, 'El problema estrategico del Mediterráneo occidental y la politica aragonese (siglos XIV y XV)', pp. 213–14 n. 37.

[17] For exports in 1392–1407 see Trasselli, 'Sull'esportazione'; J. P. Cuvillier, 'Noblesse sicilienne, noblesse aragonaise et blé sicilien en 1392–1408'; Corrao, *Governare un regno*, p. 106, n. 96. On the Sardinian expedition during which Martino of Sicily died of malaria see D'Alessandro, *Politica e società*, pp. 206–7; for the harvest of 1406–7 see RC 46, fos. 302v–4, 404–6 (March 1407).

while serving to win the first important military and political victories, was inevitably short-lived, for it was only possible by reducing domestic consumption and grain seed.[18] Economic pillage could last one, at most two, years after which structural constraints on production and the political need to ensure domestic food supplies became once again insuperable.

Exports stagnated until the 1450s. A simple mean of exports for twenty-seven years between 1409–10 and 1460–1 gives a figure just over 25,000 *salme* including domestic shipments. If we exclude the years when exports rose above 60,000 *salme* (1416–17, 1442–3, 1455–6 and 1460–1), average exports drop to 15,500 *salme*.[19] During the 1450s, exports increased slowly, with a few unusually good years (nearly 98,000 *salme* shipped in 1455–6, 92,000 *salme* in 1460–1) in a run of rather bad harvests (1449–52, 1456–7, 1462–3 and 1464–5). By the 1460s, however, average annual exports had risen to 50,000 *salme*, twice the average of the previous half century.[20] By the 1490s, annual exports were 90,000–100,000 *salme*. After reaching a peak of 150,000 *salme* annually in the 1520s,[21] they stabilized around 120,000–150,000 *salme* a year. However, as the domestic population continued to grow, the proportion of exports to output steadily declined.[22]

Nonetheless, as we shall see, although the ratio of grain sent abroad to output increased by a factor of three in fifty years, the share of output shipped from central and western Sicily to the east rose even faster. As a result of demographic growth and institutional changes in the domestic market, the proportion of domestic to total exports increased from about five to ten per cent in the early fifteenth century, to twenty per cent in the 1460s, to twenty-five to thirty-five per cent by 1500, to sixty per cent in the 1530s.[23] Indeed,

[18] See above, chapter 3, n. 229, for local and general harvest crises in the 1390s.
[19] These years are over-represented in the sample. Annual exports are reported by *UM*, pp. 528–9. Bresc's estimate of an average export of 40,000 *salme* (*UM*, p. 527) is far too high.
[20] This estimate is based on extrapolated returns for Licata, Agrigento and Sciacca in 1465–6, 1468–9 and 1469–70, published by Trasselli, *Mediterraneo*, p. 252. These ports accounted for forty-five to fifty per cent or more of grain exports in 1400–59 (*UM*, p. 540).
[21] Cancila, *Baroni e popolo*, pp. 33–4.
[22] For the grain trade in the early modern period see *ibid.*, pp. 33–5; Cancila, *Impresa redditi*, pp. 257–8, 260; H. G. Koenigsberger, *The practice of empire*, pp. 79–80; Aymard, 'Le blé de Sicile', pp. 77, 79, 83–4; Aymard, 'L'approvisionnement des villes de la Méditerranée occidentale (XVIe–XVIIIe siècles)', 179.
[23] See above, chapter 3, n. 246.

if we take domestic trade by sea into account, estimated exports abroad are considerably lowered – to an average 15,000–20,000 *salme* annually between 1400 and 1450, to *c*. 35,000–40,000 *salme* in the 1460s, and to 70,000–80,000 *salme* at the turn of the century. Having established average export figures, we can now provide an estimate of the gross and net proportion of foreign exports to output (E/O). Average grain consumption was one *salma* per person per year.[24] Domestic consumption can therefore be calculated from the population estimates established in chapter 2: 850,000 in 1270–80, 350,000 in 1374–6, 300,000 in *c*. 1400, 350,000 in 1439, 450,000 in 1478, and *c*. 550,000–600,000 in 1501. Grain yields were on average 8–10:1 for wheat, and 10:1 for barley – let us say 8:1.[25]

At the end of the thirteenth century, E/O net of seed averaged 3.4 per cent (assuming average annual exports of 30,000 *salme*). This proportion may have risen to 4.8–7.2 per cent net during 1320–40.[26] Decline in the grain trade after 1350 was followed by a modest recovery, possibly to an E/O of 4.8–6.2 per cent net after 1400. Between 1391–2 and 1405–6, the period for which the most accurate figures survive, E/O averaged 8.3 per cent net, but if exports for 1392–3 (when the Aragonese were stripping Sicily for grain to pay for the invasion) are excluded, E/O drops to five per cent. By the 1460s, E/O had risen to ten per cent, and it continued to increase over the following years, reaching 13–15.4 per cent towards 1500, and possibly 16–17 per cent in 1530–50. This increase was the result of previous gains in agricultural productivity and of declining long-distance shipping costs.[27]

These figures are averages and, as we saw, exports could occasionally be much higher – but the upper limit, an E/O of thirty-three per cent, was reached only once, in 1392, when Sicily was plundered remorselessly to finance its conquest by foreign invaders. Yet averages are what matter in evaluating long-term trends and the developmental role of trade. They show conclusively that in medieval Sicily the foreign grain trade never involved a proportion greater than fifteen per cent of domestic output, and that for most of the later Middle Ages this proportion was below ten per cent.

---

[24] See above, chapter 2, n. 32.
[25] Seed returns in *UM*, pp. 121, 123–5.
[26] Assuming average exports of 40,000–60,000 *salme* and a population of 800,000.
[27] See above, nn. 2–3.

Is it legitimate to infer from these figures that the grain trade gave shape to the entire Sicilian economy, as is so often claimed? We shall see below that at the height of the grain trade, Sicily exported twice to three times the proportion of domestic output of early modern Poland. Poland is often viewed by dependency theorists as epitomizing the pre-industrial, export-dependent country. In this view, demand for grain from international markets caused serfdom to be established during the sixteenth and seventeenth centuries, and is at the root of subsequent economic stagnation.[28] On purely comparative grounds, one might therefore expect the Sicilian grain trade to have had even deeper effects on its economy and institutions.

A claim to this effect has indeed been made. Henri Bresc has argued that Alfonso V, aware of the 'decisive preponderance of foreign demand on price formation in Sicily', was willing to sacrifice general welfare to the needs of foreign merchants and *massari*, who depended on the latters' credit to operate their farms.[29] This statement contains three distinct assertions about the domestic grain market: firstly, the effect of government policies (via the *tratta*); secondly, the impact of foreign demand; and thirdly, the role of foreign credit.

The first point of Bresc's argument seems to be confirmed by two episodes. In the summer of 1422, Alfonso was warned that the harvest was so good (and thus prices so low), that unless export dues were lowered Sicily's *massari* would be ruined. Apparently no action was taken that year, but when the situation repeated itself a year later and warnings were issued directly from the royal council, Alfonso responded by lowering the *tratta*. The petitioners had apparently claimed with success that grain producers depended on foreign demand, and that the government could, by manoeuvring the *tratta*, affect the volume of exports abroad.[30]

Examined more carefully, however, these episodes – which were

---

28 See Chirot ed., *Origins of backwardness*; Mączak, Samsonowicz and Burke eds., *East-central Europe in transition*.

29 *UM*, p. 532.

30 RC 54, fos. 103–6v (November 1422); C 2888, fo. 135rv (June 1423), Genuardi ed., 'Raccolta', pp. 157–8. In 1422, only the landowners and grain merchants of Palermo had complained. For the reduction of the *tratta* to two *tarì* see RC 54, fo. 463 (July 1423), cited in *UM*, p. 532.

in any case very unusual – suggest rather different conclusions. In the 1420s, foreign exports involved no more than five per cent of domestic output; it is thus clear that by stressing the role of foreign credit for the *massari*'s survival, the petitioners merely covered limited, sectional concerns with the mantle of the general interest, and relied on state dependence on the grain trade to gain access to the king's ear. When the request to lower the *tratta* was made only by Palermitans, Alfonso did not see fit to accept it. Only a year later, when the producers' or exporters' lobby was able to mobilize the highest echelons of the state bureaucracy, did the king accept their remonstrances.

It is sometimes argued that the (exporting) state can exploit foreign trade by fixing high and inflexible export tariffs, thereby passing on to producers adverse changes in foreign demand and terms of trade. This did not occur in Sicily, because the government absorbed a considerable proportion of the decline in grain prices at times when supply exceeded demand, as in 1423. Temporary reductions of the *tratta* to stimulate trade were also common.[31] Short-term interventions on rates of excise occurred in the context of a move towards more stable tariffs, a trend initiated by Alfonso in the 1420s and continued by Ferdinand in the 1470s.[32] Between 1420 and 1450, the *tratta* accounted for twenty-one to twenty-three per cent of pre-shipping costs. After 1450, the tariff was unchanged, whereas grain prices rose by thirty to seventy per cent; custom dues

---

[31] RC 46, fos. 302v–4, 404–6 (March 1407); C 2888, fo. 160v (March 1425); C 2894, fos. 37v–8 (September 1444); CR 865, fo. 73 (March 1479); CR 866, fo. 72rv, and CR 867, fos. 65–6 (February 1482); CR 870, fo. 71rv (March 1487); CR 869, fo. 69rv (December 1487); RC 181, fos. 173v–4 (April 1492); CR 877, fo. 107 (January 1499). In May 1451, Alfonso decided to lower the toll to one third of the current price of grain, but the measure lasted little over a year (C 2896, fos. 74v–5). Bresc states (*UM*, p. 532 n. 28) that in 1424, Alfonso had passed a transitory measure reducing the *tratta* in proportion to the price of grain; in fact, the provision (dated 1425) stated that the export tax be reduced by one *tarì*; if the price of grain increased, the *tratta* should also be raised (C 2888, fo. 160v). A permanent sliding scale for the *tratta* was introduced only in the 1530s (Aymard, 'L'approvisionnement des villes', 177).

[32] For Alfonso see Di Martino, 'Sistema tributario', 125; despite short-term changes, the long-term trend was stable. Most evidence for Ferdinand's reign refers to Catania (CR 51, fos. 369–70 (1470); CR 54, fos. 3–4 (1472); RC 133, fo. 55v (1474)). See CR 867, fos. 65–6 (1482) for a statement to the effect that high export taxes reduce trade. Juan tried unsuccessfully to raise tariffs in 1460 (Testa ed., *Capitula*, I, pp. 446–7).

thus declined to fifteen to nineteen per cent of the price before shipping.[33]

The monarchy was willing to keep export tariffs low for at least two reasons. In the first place, the late medieval demographic slump and rising agricultural productivity meant that supply tended to exceed demand; as a result, governments were, like producers, price-takers on the international grain markets. This was a considerable change from the conditions prevailing in the mid- and late thirteenth century, when Charles I of Anjou had levied *tratte* up to three times the value of the grain, thanks to his control of the main grain-exporting regions in the western Mediterranean and to strong foreign demand.[34] Secondly, the Sicilian exporters' lobby included not poor or disorganized peasants, but some of the most powerful feudal and urban landlords of the country, and foreign merchants whose custom the king was normally not prepared to jeopardize. Only Juan's predicament with the civil war in Catalonia, which simultaneously raised his financial needs and lowered his fiscal income, convinced him to attempt an (unsuccessful) tariff increase of 12.5-16.6 per cent, intended to replace some of the feudal tolls formerly granted by Alfonso. Juan's successor, Ferdinand, less needy of cash, had no trouble returning to Alfonso's rates, the rising volume of trade more than compensating for the *tratta*'s marginally declining value.

An evaluation of the effects of government action must distinguish between its short- and long-term effects on production and trade. A corollary of the belief that governments could affect production in the long term, is the argument that they possessed the ability and, on occasion, the will to exploit the domestic economy on a regular basis for their own ends; in other words, to promote grain exports in the face of local dearth. There is in fact no evidence that this ever occurred in medieval Sicily. In 1324–5, 1339–41 and 1344–5, bad years throughout the Mediterranean, Federico III and Pietro II forbade exports despite the fact that Sicily was under sustained Angevin attack and the state must have sorely needed the

---

[33] In 1420–50, the average price of one *salma* of wheat in Palermo was eight to nine *tarì*; the *tratta* averaged three *tarì*, to which a minimum two *tarì* in baronial dues and handling costs had to be added. My estimate is consistent with Alfonso's provision of 1451, that the *tratta* (excluding a recent surtax of one *tarì*) be equal to one third of the current price of one *salma* of grain (C 2896, fos. 74v-5).

[34] Percy, 'Indirect taxes', 75–6.

money for defence.[35] The frequent bans on exports during Alfonso's reign at times of financial stringency prove the same point.[36] The only support quoted by Bresc for Alfonso's alleged ruthlessness in promoting grain exports over domestic needs is a single document.[37] On 31 December 1434, perhaps in response to local requests, the king ordered that a ban on exports set after the previous summer's bad harvest be raised for Lentini, 'because it is well known that various difficulties (*incomoda*), both for our Curia and for the common good of this kingdom, follow from the closing down of victual exports'. As in the 1420s, merchants were said to have stopped advancing money to *massari* who could no longer till the land – 'thus', the king concluded, '*massari* make little or no money *and our Curia loses its tolls*' (my italics). Yet, far from sacrificing local subsistence needs for his own or merchants' benefit, the same day Alfonso also stated that because 'right and just reason decrees that no city's or town's victuals must be taken, even if one pays a just price, if one has not provided beforehand for its inhabitants' needs', enough grain should be left in Lentini to satisfy domestic demands.[38]

Alfonso's unwillingness to put his subjects' subsistence at risk was, on the whole, a matter of political expediency rather than of regal benevolence.[39] It did not stop him from exploiting oppor-

[35] Finke ed., *Acta Aragonensia*, II, no. 455; De Vio ed., *Privilegia*, pp. 158–60; *UM*, p. 530. See also above, chapter 3.
[36] Bans in 1426–7 (CR 14, fo. 432); 1430–1 (CR 16, fo. 655); 1431–2 (C 2889, fo. 20); 1432–3 (C 2818, fos. 182v–3); 1434–5 (C 2891, fo. 87v; C 2892, fos. 33v, 34v); 1437–8 (C 2830, fos. 56v–7, 81rv); 1438–9 (CR 18, fo. 90rv); 1440–1 (C 2893, fo. 52v); 1449–50 (CR 36, fo. 322rv; C 2894, fo. 161rv; CR 862, fo. 33rv); 1452–3 (CR 36, fo. 324rv); 1456–7 (C 2877, fo. 56; RC 104, fo. 144; PR 49, fo. 128rv).
[37] *UM*, p. 532 n. 29.
[38] C 2826, fo. 130 (not fo. 129v as in *UM*, p. 532 n. 29): 'Quia ex prohibicionibus et vetamentis extractionis victualium, tam nostre Curie quam eciam rey publice dicti regni multa incomoda subsequi clare noscitur; mercatores enim, burgenses et divites massariis anticipatas non accomodant pecunias illis necessarias, et massarii ideo non faciunt magnas massarias; et sic ipsi paucum vel nichil lucrantur et nostra curia iura perdit'. C 2826, fo. 129v (same date): 'Equum et consonum racioni censentes quod nulli civitati seu terre debent propria victualia auferri seu capi ecciam cum precio condecenti nisi prius provideatur illius incolae victui necessario . . . super extraccione frumentorum fienda a terra Leontini taliter provideatis quod sufficiens frumentorum quantitas pro victu incolarum eiusdem terre apud terram ipsam omnino remaneat omni mandato in contrarium per quisvis facto cessante'. See also above, n. 36.
[39] In September 1433, Alfonso forbade the export of 1,000 *salme* from Pozzallo in his name in response to 'clamoribus burgensium et incolarum' of the county of Modica (C 2824, fo. 140).

tunities to speculate both on domestic or, more often, foreign markets; but such speculation was of a similar kind to that practised by any merchant of his time, the main difference being that the king's monopoly of political power could sometimes give him temporary control over parts of the domestic grain market.[40] Neither Alfonso nor any other late medieval sovereign ever attempted to monopolize the grain market as a whole, or could have succeeded in doing so. Only episodically, when faced with short-term political and military objectives, did Alfonso resort to trade to integrate scarce or failing revenues. Like Frederick II and Federico III before him, and Juan II and Ferdinand after, Alfonso strove to exploit, rather than control, domestic and foreign markets.[41]

By contrast, Alfonso played an important role in improving the domestic grain market's efficiency. First, his free trade policies and his attempts to check baronial and community speculation on grain reserves were unparalleled in medieval Sicily (see chapter 3). Second, he reorganized the system of concessions of customs revenues from grain exports in order to reduce pressure on the domestic market. We saw above that the invasion of 1392–8 was marked by a general distribution of free *tratte* to the invaders;[42] concessions such as these had been made since the twelfth century, but they were never a major instrument of state-craft as they became after 1391.[43] In the 1390s, however, because of the Aragonese invaders' pressing financial needs, exemptions were granted with no regard for existing resources, so quite soon the number of free *tratte* in circulation became considerably larger than the amount of grain that could actually be exported in any one year. Since these *tratte*

---

[40] *UM*, pp. 554–7 for the royal grain trade and Alfonso's 'cupidité féroce' in exploiting dearth to his advantage. See also C 2888, fo. 160v (1425); CR 15, fos. 639–43 (1428–9); C 2889, fos. 65, 68v–9, 77v–9, 156v (1432–3); C 2891, fo. 101v (1434); C 2826, fo. 141 (1435); C 2890, fos. 78v, 110, 111v–13, 118–21 (1436–7); C 2830, fos. 33rv, 38rv (1437); CR 18, fo. 90rv (1438); C 2935, fo. 102v (1438); C 2892, fos. 9quater, 16vter (1439, 1444); C 2935, fo. 110v (1440); C 2893, fos. 51v–2 (1440); CR 25, fos. 370–1, 410rv (1444–5); CR 850, fos. 116–17, 118–36 (1447); C 2894, fo. 128 (1447); Trasselli, *Storia dello zucchero*, p. 250 n. 23 (1450); Del Treppo, *Mercanti catalani*, pp. 352–6; Ryder, 'Cloth and credit: Aragonese war finance in the mid-fifteenth century', 7 and n. 36.

[41] See CR 41, fos. 495–6v (1461); CR 51, fos. 531, 545 (1470); CR 52, fo. 37rv (1471) for Juan II. CR 869, fos. 89–90 (1488); CR 71, fos. 15, 197–7bis (1490–1); CR 73, fos. 17–18v (1490); TRP Atti 46, unnumbered fo. (1492); CR 874, fos. 149, 175, 218, 223, 224, 227, 228 (1495) for Ferdinand.

[42] Cuvillier, 'Noblesse sicilienne', p. 389.

[43] Bresc, *Economie et société*, p. 1354.

were normally paid by the foreign grain buyers to the crown, a Sicilian recipient of free *tratte* could in theory sell his grain to foreigners at the current price increased by the value of the *tratta*. In practice, the grain seller would sell more competitively by charging a slightly lower price, which gave both him and the buyer a premium over the current selling and buying price respectively. Since before 1450, as we saw, excise accounted for about twenty-one to twenty-three per cent of the price of grain, there was a considerable margin for profit on both the seller's and the buyer's sides. Consequently, a free-handed policy of exemptions also raised the possibility of a conflict between favoured exporters and home consumers.

Possibly because the indiscriminate assignation of free *tratte* exerted excessive pressure on domestic supplies, or possibly because unsuccessful recipients put pressure on the government to provide more reliable alternative sources of income, by the 1420s free *tratte* began to be replaced by grants on actual revenues from duties on grain exports.[44] The result was to shift the focus of conflict over the distribution of resources from the economy as a whole to the government. If the government's income from exports was insufficient to pay all the grants, payment of the latter depended on the recipient's ability to demand compensation from another source of state income.[45]

Bresc's second point about the domestic grain market in Sicily concerns the influence of foreign demand on regional prices, and hence on resource allocation. Given the low proportion of exports to output, this influence could have been strong only if the domestic market were very small or lacked integration, as has been suggested for Poland. Witold Kula has argued that in Poland, the grain trade's real economic impact was far greater than export figures suggest, because so large a share of Polish peasant production was for subsistence ('direct, natural consumption'). In other words, the share of foreign trade in Poland's commercialized economy 'would account for 25–45 per cent of the commodity-product', rather than

---

[44] CR 1062, throughout. A first reform of the *tratta* system in C 2801, fos. 134v–5v, and C 2802, fos. 45v–6 (January 1417); C 2803, fos. 42v–3 (January 1418). See also CR 845, unnumbered fos. (24 September and 29 November 1440); Testa ed., *Capitula*, I, p. 390 (1452); C 2882, fo. 180rv (1453); RC 95, fos. 38–9, 291v–2 (1453); *UM*, p. 885, Table 199.

[45] C 2888, fo. 171rv (1425–6).

for the 5–7 per cent which was the country's grain export to output ratio.[46]

Can Kula's argument be applied to late medieval Sicily? How important was the subsistence economy there? These questions are all the more important, because by *c*.1500, Sicily had a higher export ratio than Poland did a century later; it is indeed conceivable that in the period 1500–20, Sicily achieved higher rates of export than any other European country in the entire medieval or early modern periods.

Aymard and Bresc have, I believe correctly, stressed that Sicilian agriculture, and grain production in particular, were highly commercialized, and conversely that the subsistence sector was very small.[47] This situation was largely the result of two factors: property rights were unfavourable to the subsistence economy; and domestic trade was made easier by access to cheap transport by sea. Aspects of the first point are discussed in chapters 3 and 4, and in summary the argument is as follows. By 1300, serfdom had nearly completely disappeared from Sicily and been replaced by leasehold; the lord's demesne was cultivated with wage labour or was also leased. Arable land was leased in large farms (*masserie*) specialized in producing bread grains for the market. Peasant allodial property was limited, and was concentrated mostly in eastern Sicily, especially in val Demone where grain cultivation faced strong ecological constraints; one would therefore expect the subsistence sector to be strongest in this area. However, the close correlation between population increases in val Demone and rising grain imports there after 1450 indicates the opposite, that peasant smallholders preferred to specialize in more labour-intensive (and more rewarding) activities for the market in exchange for grain, rather than take refuge in subsistence production. This strategy could be pursued because of the possibility of transporting food cheaply by sea, the second main factor enabling a high degree of commercialization to develop. For these reasons, Kula's argument about the Polish situation is inapplicable to Sicily.

[46] Kula, *Economic theory*, pp. 92–3; Kula, *Problemi e metodi di storia economica*, pp. 493–4. Kula calculated this figure by assuming an export rate of ten to fifteen per cent. If we adopt the more conservative estimate of five to seven per cent, exports would account for no more than twelve to twenty per cent of the 'commodity product'.

[47] Aymard, 'L'approvisionnement', 170–1; Bresc, 'Reti di scambio', p. 174; see also above, chapter 4.

We come now to Bresc's third point, namely the importance of foreign credit for Sicilian grain production. We saw in chapters 3 and 4 that from the early fifteenth century, a credit market developed wherein both domestic and foreign merchants advanced operating capital to *massari*. However, since foreign merchants controlled no more than five to ten per cent of domestic output for export, and made very limited investments in local land so as to control grain production directly,[48] it is clear that foreign capital was *not* indispensable for Sicilian agriculture.[49]

As the example of the credit market shows, the actual dynamics of foreign penetration in, and subordination of, the Sicilian economy, are seldom clearly spelled out. The fact, for example, that the *maestro portulano*, the comptroller general of the ports, was usually Genoese (in the fourteenth and early fifteenth centuries) or Catalan (in the fifteenth century), is quoted as evidence of Sicilian subordination. In reality, the official was powerless to alter domestic supply structures and thus to engender 'dependency'; the position seems merely to have combined a governmental sinecure with the advantages to be gained by having an official in charge who had direct knowledge of one or other of Sicily's two main foreign grain customers.[50]

Many foreign merchants with the most substantial investments in the Sicilian economy were, in fact, only nominally foreigners, for investment in the land was most often a prelude – probably a necessary one – to integration into the local urban nobility or into aristocratic society. The most significant example of merchant immigration followed by rapid social integration is that of the Pisan diaspora after the city's fall to Florence in 1406. The Pisan position was directly related to their homeland's political weakness and to Pisa's traditional enmity with Alfonso's main central Italian foe,

---

[48] Evidence for these investments dates from the last quarter of the fifteenth century. See RC 128, fos. 395–6v (Piazza, 1473); CR 71, fos. 18–18sexties, and RC 178, fos. 163v–70 (1491), CR 71, fos. 19–19bis (1500) (reference to *masserie* owned by *furisteri* in Castronovo; the term does not necessarily refer to non-Sicilians); RC 191, fos. 225–8, and CR 77, fos. 599–601 (Sciacca, 1495).

[49] As argued in *UM*, p. 545. There is no evidence that foreign merchants invested in production for the domestic market.

[50] Under Alfonso, the *maestri portulani*, who previously had been mainly Genoese, were invariably Catalan (*UM*, p. 551; D'Alessandro, *Politica e società*, pp. 225–7).

Florence.[51] Pisan merchants constituted the main financial and banking community in fifteenth-century Palermo, and possibly in Sicily as a whole. They contributed substantially to the operation of the most capital-intensive enterprises of the period, the sugar and tunny industries. At the same time, they achieved the highest positions in the state administration, and by the second half of the fifteenth century were on their way to becoming fully-titled members of the Sicilian landed aristocracy. In contrast with the Genoese, Florentine or even Venetian merchants,[52] who, as we shall see, were obstructed by the Sicilian monarchy whenever foreign policy dictated it, Pisans maintained a privileged relationship with the Sicilian crown during most of the fifteenth century.

This discussion has shown that the role of the state and of foreign demand in the domestic grain market have been considerably overestimated. On the one hand, the state was in the short term unwilling, and in the longer term incapable, of affecting the course of output and the volume of foreign trade. On the other hand, neither foreign credit nor foreign demand affected more than a minor proportion of total output. To assume that a larger proportion of foreign trade would have made any difference to Sicilian 'dependence', however, the relation between trade and 'dependence' must be spelt out more clearly. I turn to this question below.

One theory of the 'dependence' engendered by foreign trade concentrates on the use of 'foreign trade as an instrument of national power policies'.[53] 'Dependence' can result from one foreign partner having an overwhelming share of a country's external trade, allowing the former to exert strong influence over the latter's domestic economy and politics. In this theory, therefore, it is assumed that economic power has causal primacy over political power.

In fact, during the Middle Ages, the causal relation between political and economic power in the context of international trade tended to run the opposite way. This was because, among other

[51] Petralia, *Banchieri*, pp. 70–80, 341–58; *UM*, pp. 412–13. The Genoese underwent a similar metamorphosis in the seventeenth century (Aymard, 'Il bilancio di una lunga crisi finanziaria', 999–1010).

[52] For Alfonso's anti-Venetian policies see Ryder, *Alfonso the Magnanimous*, chapter 7; Venetian attacks on Sicily in June 1449 on p. 281. Venice had tried to organize an uprising in Syracuse the year before (C 2868, fos. 30–1). In this period, Syracuse was the main port of call for Venetian galleys bound for North Africa or northern Europe.

[53] Hirschmann, *National power and the structure of foreign trade.*

factors, long-distance trade was particularly vulnerable to political pressure. Since trade volumes were low and competition was very strong, a ruler could forbid trade with a rival nation or merchant community and generally count on the ensuing commercial slack being taken up by other foreign traders. Successful foreign trade also depended on customs privileges, which could be obtained only from friendly governments. International merchants were therefore usually more vulnerable to political pressure and constraints than were governments to economic 'power policies' by foreign mercantile nations. Medieval Sicilian foreign trade reflects these conditions very clearly. Sicilian rulers consistently applied economic pressure for political goals. After 1282, trade with Naples, Florence, Guelph Genoa, and occasionally even Catalonia, was interrupted or reduced. This process was as much the result of Sicily's military and political effort to defend itself as the effect of military and commercial blockades by the Angevins and their allies; it was also, of course, a strategy more easily pursued because of the high level of western Mediterranean demand for wheat before the Black Death, which allowed Sicilian grain exports to continue despite the narrowing of its traditional foreign markets.

After the compromise of Caspe of 1412, when Sicily was annexed to the crown of Aragon, the island became a crucial pawn of Aragonese foreign policy on the Italian mainland.[54] The main foreign power to suffer from these developments was Genoa. After 1420, first in Sicily and later also in Naples, Alfonso drastically reduced Genoese presence as part of a strategy of containment of the duchy of Milan, to which Genoa was allied. Continuing a confrontation which had begun more than a century before, the crown of Aragon and the Genoese waged open or clandestine warfare well into the second half of the fifteenth century. In Sicily, the Genoese were pushed to the margins of most industrial and financial activities, although they maintained a stake in the grain trade.[55] For two decades, the Genoese share of the Sicilian freight

[54] Alfonso's trading policies are discussed by Petralia, *Banchieri*, pp. 340–50 (with bibliographical references).

[55] Heers, *Gênes*, pp. 332–6, 425–6; *UM*, p. 551. Also A. M. Adroer i Tasis, 'Organització d'una armada contra Genova (1458)'; E. Basso, 'La Corona d'Aragona e la dominazione viscontea su Genova (1421–1435)'; G. Olgiati, 'La Repubblica di Genova nella guerra di successione al regno di Napoli (1436–1442)'. See C 2801, fos. 63, 68 (January 1417): three-year truce; C 2888, fo. 160 (March 1425):

market was taken up by Catalan ships, but after 1440, the Catalans seem to have lost out both to the Sicilian and to other regional navies (see Table 6.5). A similar policy of containment was applied by Alfonso against Florence in the late 1440s and 1450s.[56] Even Catalan merchants were penalized in this manner. After 1462, Juan II expelled from all subject-territories, including Sicily, those merchants who had sided with the enemy in the Catalan civil war.[57]

In order to attain its political goals, therefore, the Sicilian government did not spare from economic reprisal any merchant nation with a large stake in the island's market. The only exceptions were the Pisans, whose favoured status in Sicily was a direct consequence of their political weakness and of their condition as refugees from Florentine expansion. Because medieval merchants depended for their trade on friendly relations with foreign governments, their position was structurally weak, and this weakness tended to increase in proportion with the rise of state power. Sicily's rulers exploited this fact whenever it was convenient and possible to do so. The only period when this situation may have been partly reversed was the second half of the fourteenth century, when the fragmentation of political authority and of markets in Sicily may have enabled Catalan and Genoese merchants to strike better bargains in the cloth trade with local lords. But even though, during this period, the Genoese had a near monopoly over Palermo's cloth market, and the Catalans had a similar hold over the cloth market in Catania, there is nothing to suggest that they were able or wished to influence domestic politics. If political dependence through trade

three-year truce; C 2812, fo. 84rv (1425); CR 14, fo. 305rv (11 September 1426): no Genoese trade in Catania; TRP n.p. 67, fos. 7–8: no Genoese trade in Trapani in 1434–5; CR 17, fos. 60–60bis (1437): Catalan merchants are offered the Genoese *loggia* in Palermo; Testa ed., *Capitula*, I, p. 371 (1451); De Vio ed., *Privilegia*, pp. 313–24 (1451). Relations remained tense after Alfonso's death: C 3482, fo. 103v (1461); G. Balbi, 'Le relazioni tra Genova e la Corona d'Aragona dal 1464 al 1478' (1464–78); C 3476, fo. 92rv (1460); C 3474, fo. 79 (1460); CR 60, fos. 245–6 (1477); CR 82, fos. 262–3v (1482); CR 65, fos. 1–4v, 293rv (1483, 1484).
[56] C 2826, fos. 93v–4v (1434); C 2896, fo. 83rv (1451); C 2895, fo. 22vbis (1453); C 2884, fo. 140 (1455); RC 98, fos. 66v–7v (1455), 164rv (1456); C 2878, fos. 16–17v (1456); C 2886, fos. 153v–4 (1457). Conflict did not entirely cease under Juan II: C 3474, fos. 76v–80v (1460), De Vio ed., *Privilegia*, pp. 341–50; C 3488, fo. 108rv (1473).
[57] J. Vicens Vives, *Fernando el Católico, príncipe de Aragón, rey de Sicilia (1458–1478)*, pp. 150–5; Del Treppo, *Mercanti catalani*, p. 186.

Table 6.1 *Terms of trade between wheat (Catania) and foreign cloth (Palermo), 1400–1459*

	1400–29	1430–9	1440–9	1450–9
wheat	8.84 (100)	10.00 (113.1)	9.00 (101.8)	10.50 (118.8)
cloth	2.84 (100)	2.96 (104.2)	3.11 (109.5)	3.81 (134.2)

Sources: As for Tables 3.4 and 6.2.
Prices in *onze* (including decimal values); index numbers in ( ).

was ever an issue, the relationship operated on the whole *against* foreigners, rather than the other way around.

Another influential theory of 'dependency' has suggested that contemporary underdevelopment is the result of a secular decline in the net barter terms of trade (henceforward 'terms of trade') between primary and manufactured products, to the former's disadvantage.[58] Does this theory apply to late medieval Sicily? What can we say about terms of trade between grain and imported cloth, supposedly the key items in Sicily's pattern of 'unequal exchange'?

Terms of trade can be estimated with difficulty and only for part of the fifteenth century (see Table 6.1). The poor quality of the evidence restricts analysis to a few indications on long-term changes, which generally reflect changes in real production costs. Short-period fluctuations, and thus monetary and demand factors, cannot be traced. In addition, the price-index for foreign cloth must be constructed as an average of import prices to Palermo, for we lack adequate price-series for luxury cloth at the point of production; as a result, however, the price-index for cloth primarily reflects consumer preferences in Palermo and Sicily rather than changes in production costs at the source.

No consistent pattern emerges from a comparison of price trends for 1400–59. Grain prices fluctuated considerably around a slightly rising trend, whereas the average price of cloth tended to rise more steadily. It increased less than grain in 1430–9, but rose more strongly in the next two decades. On the other hand, the general price-index means for the two products for 1400–49 are barely

---

[58] J. G. Palma, 'Structuralism'; H. Singer, 'Terms of trade and economic development'. The net barter terms of trade are defined as the ratio over time of export to import prices.

distinguishable, which might suggest that in the longer run, terms of trade were stable.[59]

This conclusion seems to contrast with the well-documented post-Black Death 'price-scissors', whereby the price of manufactured goods increased more (or decreased less) than agricultural prices.[60] The 'price-scissors' has been explained both from the supply side, as reflecting rising manufacturing costs (because epidemics reduced the number of specialized artisans and returns to scale were hard to achieve in most manufacturing industries),[61] and from the demand side, as expressing a higher elasticity of demand for manufactured compared to agricultural products.

Both explanations assume that prices accurately reflect, in the short term, forces of supply and demand, and in the longer term, changes in productivity. This assumption, however, may underestimate the fact that producers and traders of manufactured goods are more often in the position of price-makers than are agriculturalists, who are generally price-takers. For example, changes in relative bargaining power between cloth buyers and sellers, rather than 'real' economic forces, seem to explain why average cloth prices in Palermo dropped so steeply (by nearly forty per cent) after 1400, when the Genoese quasi-monopoly was broken.[62]

The Aragonese conquest reversed the bargaining positions which had prevailed since the mid-fourteenth century, and which had tended to favour the cloth purveyors and grain buyers. On the one hand, the unification of the grain market after 1400 reduced information costs for grain producers. These costs of course declined for buyers also, but foreign grain merchants were deprived of the bargaining opportunities provided by the formerly fragmented grain market. On the other hand, the lowering of information costs for foreign cloth merchants, caused by the increasing concen-

---

[59] I have assigned the index number 100 to the period 1400–19. The mean index figure for 1400–59 is 103.725 for grain, 103.425 for cloth.

[60] Abel, *Agricultural fluctuations*, pp. 51–3; Slicher van Bath, *Agrarian history*, pp. 139–40.

[61] Miskimin, *Economy in Renaissance Europe*, pp. 82–6.

[62] *UM*, p. 482: the average price per *canna* of Florentine cloth dropped from thirty *tarì* in 1380–99 to twenty-four to twenty-six *tarì* in 1400–19. One can note in passing that forms of oligopoly would be expected to be particularly common at the level of town–country relations, which is usually the institutional context from which data reflecting the 'price scissors' are taken.

tration of the regional cloth trade in Palermo, was probably offset by rising competition as local trade monopolies broke down.[63]

There may have been reasons other than changing market structures for why 'international' terms of trade between grain and cloth did not diverge. For example, the technical constraints on cost-reducing investments in manufacturing, quoted by Miskimin to explain the increase in the price of manufactured goods after the Black Death, were weaker for capital-intensive cloth industries producing for foreign markets than for simpler home industries. There are good technical reasons why productivity in high-quality cloth manufacture may have *increased* after the Black Death, in parallel with increased productivity in agriculture; if this was the case, the result would have been to narrow the 'price-scissors' between agriculture and high-quality cloth.

Since cloth prices after 1459 are unknown, comparisons with the price of grain for this period are not possible. There is, however, reason to suggest that terms of trade shifted in favour of wheat. The price of wheat increased steadily after 1450, and by the 1480s was over fifty per cent higher than in 1400–29. In contrast, data for cloth elsewhere in Italy suggest that prices after 1450 were by and large stable.[64] This shift in the terms of trade was mainly the result of the higher rate of increase in the demand for grain compared to luxury cloth under conditions of rising population.[65]

In sum, terms of trade were probably either stable or favourable to grain for the entire fifteenth century. Evidence for earlier periods is lacking, but the situation then may have been less advantageous to Sicily. Greater market fragmentation and, from 1350 to *c*.1400, a decline in foreign demand, may have artificially depressed relative grain prices by increasing the foreign (cloth) merchants' bargaining powers. If this hypothesis is correct, it would imply that terms of trade could, under certain conditions, be set as much by institutional as by 'real' economic factors.

[63] Local monopolies in cloth retailing were abolished by Alfonso in 1452 (Del Treppo, *Mercanti catalani*, p. 605). On bargaining in the medieval economy see Nell, 'Economic relationships'; Persson, *Pre-industrial economic growth*, pp. 36, 40, 43, 51, 54.

[64] H. Hoshino, *L'Arte della Lana in Firenze nel basso Medioevo. Il commercio della lana e il mercato dei panni fiorentini nei secoli XIII–XV*, pp. 290, 293.

[65] Terms of trade for wheat could also improve as a result of the decline of grain tariffs after the 1460s. The reduction would increase Sicily's competitivity on the international grain market, as long as a comparable tariff reduction was not also benefiting Sicily's competitors.

To summarize the argument so far, it is clear that the power of the government and, to a lesser extent, the landholders depended on taxable grain surpluses which were beyond their capacity to control. The state could affect some institutional constraints on trade by manipulating customs dues, but it could not bring into being a non-existent surplus. Landlords could not force a non-servile population to produce grain surpluses against the latter's will,[66] except by increasing rents. The fact that fifteenth-century grain exports began to increase earlier, and far more rapidly, than land rent (see chapter 7) suggests on the contrary that in normal conditions it was producers, rather than landlords, who responded first to new opportunities abroad. Foreign merchants could not engender 'dependence' or affect domestic economic conditions except indirectly by mediating foreign demand; by contrast, the state was often able to turn *foreigners'* dependence into a powerful political weapon against them. But the previous discussion has mainly shown that the issue of foreign trade and 'dependence' has been addressed in a misleading and ultimately sterile fashion. Part of the problem with this approach is that no one has clearly spelled out a theory of 'dependence' with adequate micro-foundations in individual action.

The Sicilian grain trade developed because Sicily's arable farming was more productive and faced lower trade and transport costs than most western Mediterranean regions, and as a result regularly exported larger surpluses than, for example, countries like early modern Poland or England.[67] Some advantages were due to Sicilian institutional and property rights' structures and have been examined in previous chapters. Other advantages lay with Sicily's natural endowments.

First, cereals were cultivated on large, relatively capital-intensive and specialized farms within a highly commercialized and competitive economy. Production benefited from close integration with animal husbandry, which provided cheap and abundant draught oxen and manure. Although it involved only a fraction of total output, foreign trade and international competition also helped

---

[66] As argued by Rugolo, 'L'organizzazione del lavoro nelle campagne siciliane del tardo Medioevo', 57–9.

[67] Brenner, 'Origins of capitalist development', 69–70 and n. 61. Between 1700 and 1750, England exported on average 3 per cent of domestic production, with a peak of 6.8 per cent in 1750 (D. Ormrod, *English grain exports and the structure of agrarian capitalism 1700–1760*, pp. 52–3).

stimulate agricultural innovation by increasing competition among domestic producers.

Second, Sicily had the advantage of relatively low transaction costs. The island's long coast allowed small ports for loading grain (*caricatori*) to be opened easily at the shortest distance from areas of production. The internal transport system based on mule trains was highly specialized and flexible.[68] The development of credit markets and efficient storage networks, the unification of the regional market, and the government's arbitrating role for urban consumer prices (*mete*) and customs dues (*tratte*), contributed to reduce further uncertainty and transaction costs.

Finally, Sicily possessed an endemic species of durum wheat, which had extremely high yields and was especially resilient to storage and sea transport.[69] The grain's advantages were well known. For example, Charles I of Anjou used Sicilian durum wheat on his southern Italian *masserie* because of its especially high yields. In the fourteenth century, attempts were made to introduce a Sicilian variety of wheat into Tuscany, but either because of different soil and climatic conditions or, more probably, because of inefficient selection processes, after a few years Sicilian wheat became indistinguishable from local varieties.[70]

Grain exports were the result neither of a deliberate choice by domestic ruling classes, nor of foreign compulsion or exploitation. It is only because government income depended so heavily on export dues that such a vast documentation on the grain trade was produced, the trade thus appearing more important, and the government's role in promoting it more central, than was ever truly the case.

---

[68] Giuffrida, 'Itinerari di viaggi'.

[69] N. Jasny, *The wheats of classical antiquity*, pp. 23–4, 77, 91. Sicily possessed a large number of varieties of wheat (*Il lavoro contadino nei Nebrodi*, p. 39; *Immagini di lavoro e vita contadina a San Piero Patti*, p. 13; S. Nicosia, 'La coltivazione tradizionale del frumento nei latifondi del "Vallone"', p. 224; Bresc, *Economie et société*, p. 408 n. 41; Cupani, *Hortus catholicus*). D. Sestini, *Descrizione di varj prodotti dell'isola di Sicilia relativi al commercio della medesima con l'estere nazioni*, pp. 3–6, distinguishes three main types: the *forte* (*Triticum durum*), the most widely cultivated and easy to ship; the *roccella* (*russella*) or *majorca*, the best for white bread but rather tender for transport (see, however, Torrisi, 'Aspetti della crisi', 177); *tumminia*, a variety of spring wheat (see da Piazza, *Cronaca*, II, chapter 43).

[70] de Boüard, 'Problèmes de subsistances', 484; Pinto, *Toscana*, pp. 95–6. Comparisons between Sicilian and Apulian grain in Pagnini della Ventura, *Della decima*, IV, pp. 164–5; Trinchera ed., *Codice aragonese*, II, 1, pp. 34–6.

EXPORTS: CHEESE AND LIVESTOCK

In the late thirteenth and early fourteenth centuries, Sicily had exported cheese and salted meat to North Africa, the southern mainland, Pisa and Genoa, but at that time these products were still rather marginal to its balance of trade.[71] After the mid-fourteenth century, however, rising domestic and foreign demand for meat and cheese led to substantial increases in exports. The change in the composition of exports reflects the shift from arable to pastoral agriculture examined above.

By the 1370s, the value of cheese exports was comparable to that of grain, and occasionally it was considerably higher. Between February and May 1376, Genoa alone imported 6,264.2 *cantara*, approximately 488.6 tons of Sicilian cheese, at an estimated price of 15,962 Genoese *lire*; between August and October 1377, it imported 3,198.1 *cantara* worth 8,210 *lire* (see Table 6.3). Assuming similar export patterns in 1376 and 1377, Genoa alone seems to have imported nearly 12,138 *cantara* (*c*. 950 tons) of Sicilian cheese a year in this period, presumably mainly from western Sicily where it had the strongest commercial links.[72] If we rely on Bresc's estimate, that in 1370–9 ninety-seven per cent of (west) Sicilian cheese was sent to Tuscany and Liguria,[73] western Sicilian exports in those two years would have been no less than 2,000 tons (assuming that no cheese was shipped to Tuscany). If grain exports in the 1370s were the same as in the early fifteenth century (*c*.20,000–30,000 *salme*, probably an overestimate), cheese exports in the 1370s would have been worth about twice as much as those of wheat.[74]

The 1370s may have been a particularly favourable period for foreign trade, for in 1407–8 only 4517.99 *cantara* of cheese were

---

[71] Africa: Carini ed., *De rebus*, nos. 489, 522–3, 591 (1283); Pegolotti, *Pratica della mercatura*, p. 134. Naples: *ibid.*, p. 178; Giuffrida, 'Aspetti della presenza genovese nei secoli XIV e XV', pp. 290–1 (1349). Pisa: Zeno ed., *Documenti*, nos. 27, 33 (1298); Pegolotti, *Pratica della mercatura*, p. 205; Giuffrida, 'Aspetti della presenza', pp. 290–1 (1342–9). Genoa: *ibid.*, pp. 290–1 (1342–9); RC 4, fos. 198v–9 (1331).

[72] Figures calculated from Day ed., *Douanes*. Annual cheese imports to Genoa have been estimated by dividing known imports by the number of trading months recorded (seven) and multiplying the result by nine (months), the length of the average trade year in that period.

[73] *UM*, p. 569, Table 147.

[74] *UM*, pp. 132, 165.

exported.[75] Production and trade in eastern Sicily seems to have increased thereafter. Catania alone exported 3,000 *cantara* per annum to Lipari in the 1460s, and this was not an unusual occurrence.[76] The lord of Aci exported large quantities of cheese and hides in the same period;[77] Messina exported cheese at the end of the century.[78] Figures for total exports, however, are unavailable before the end of the fifteenth century. In February and May 1498, the government licensed shipments of 24,560 *cantara* of cheese, and the following year it gave permission for 8,750 *cantara* despite a temporary ban on exports.[79]

Can one assess the proportion of exports to output? The latter can be estimated by assuming that average consumption per head in the early fifteenth century was *c.*20kg (see chapter 4). Annual domestic consumption in 1400–50 would therefore have been *c.*5,000–6,000 tons excluding exports. The proportion of exports to output would have been fourteen to seventeen per cent in 1376–7, and six to seven per cent in 1407–8. Although very scanty, figures for 1498 and 1499 suggest that this proportion increased considerably ably during the fifteenth century. Were one to assume a stable level of personal consumption, the export to output ratio for a population of 500,000 would be about sixteen per cent as in the 1370s. This assumption, however, is nearly certainly wrong, given the rising price of cheese and meat and the evidence of a decline in meat consumption after the mid–fifteenth century (see chapter 4). If cheese consumption had declined at the same rate, the proportion of exports to output can have been no less, and was probably somewhat more, than one fifth every year.

We saw in chapter 5 that the development of the pastoral sector, which sustained the expansion of the cheese industry after the mid-fourteenth century, also established a strong livestock trade from Sicily to the southern mainland. The cattle trade probably peaked towards the mid-fifteenth century, when up to 10,000 animals were exported every year. In contrast with the cheese

[75] *UM*, pp. 164, 558.
[76] CR 864, fo. 123rv, and LV 98, fos. 49v–50 (1468). See also CR 870, fo. 160rv (1487); CR 877, fos. 184, 187, 188rv (1499): licences to export 1,500 *cantara* from Catania.
[77] TRP Atti 27, fo. 147rv (1469).
[78] CR 877, fo. 171 (1499): 200 *cantara*.
[79] CR 876 and 877, throughout, for export licences; CR 876, unnumbered fo. (30 June 1498) for the trade ban.

trade, however, the livestock trade seems to have declined during the second half of the century, although upwards of 3,000 free export licences were still being granted in the 1490s. An even more significant decline probably occurred in the horse trade, which had flourished under Alfonso, who had demanded hundreds of animals each year to furnish his armies.

EXPORTS: TUNNY, SUGAR AND SILK

Silk, sugar and, to a much lesser extent, tunny were the only sectors of the Sicilian economy that depended primarily on foreign markets. The tunny industry, which grew very rapidly after 1350, exported mainly to the kingdom of Naples and to Rome. According to Bresc, the industry's main outlet was abroad, but evidence of exports is too slender compared to the productive capacities of the industry as a whole to be certain.[80] A proportion of the output (though how large is hard to estimate) was undoubtedly sold on the domestic market.[81]

Before the late fifteenth century, the silk and sugar industries faced very small domestic markets. But whereas silk manufacture developed in Messina and elsewhere in Sicily during the late fifteenth and sixteenth centuries, partly in response to home demand,[82] the domestic confectioners' industry seems to have never absorbed more than a fraction of sugar production. The two industries differed mainly, however, in the quality and quantity of labour they employed.

Between 1440 and 1470, silk exports from Messina doubled from 24,000 to 48,000–60,000 lbs; by the end of the century they may have risen to 100,000 lbs.[83] Simply raising the silkworms and reeling the silk would have employed 900 women full time for 100 days (production employed predominantly female and child labour); since the work was normally done on a part–time basis, as many as 4,500 women may have been involved in producing silk at the end of the century. Had the silk also been spun, this would have employed a further 1,650 women full time for 200 days, possibly

[80] *UM*, pp. 266, 568–74.
[81] Giuffrida, 'Considerazioni sul consumo', 585.
[82] Aymard, 'Commerce et consommation', p. 127.
[83] Above, chapter 4, nn. 167, 169. In 1593, exports were just under 400,000 lbs and were still rising (Aymard, 'Commerce et production de la soie sicilienne aux XVIe et XVIIe siècles', Table 5).

10,000 on a less intensive schedule.[84] By comparison, the sugar industry employed far fewer individuals, mainly male, also sometimes on a part-time basis, but with a tighter seasonal work schedule.

Silk production required forms of integration of agricultural practices and rural lifestyles that the sugar and tunny industries never demanded. It prospered where geographic conditions and agrarian structures could combine intensive labour practices and support high population densities. The industry seems initially to have spread by absorbing labour surpluses generated by the sexual division of labour and by the unequal seasonal distribution of agricultural work.[85] We saw in chapter 4 that there is no reason to believe that peasants were in any way constrained to find additional employment in the silk industry by merchants, landlords, the state or even demographic pressure (the industry began to grow in a period of very *low* population pressure). On the contrary, the silk industry seems to have been a rational and flexible response by the peasantry to market forces. Whether, however, the industry transformed socio-economic structures in val Demone, leading to 'proto-industrial' demographic patterns and to the emergence of a rural proletariat, is a problem awaiting further investigation.

Income from these industries, and their contribution to Sicily's balance of payments in the fifteenth century, can be estimated as follows. By *c*.1450, thirty to forty tunny and sugar establishments (*tonnare* and *trappeti*) were in operation. The average annual income of a sugar *trappeto* was 370 *onze*, and of a *tonnara* possibly 400–500 *onze*.[86] Output value was therefore in the range of 23,000–38,000 *onze*. Assuming that fifteen to twenty per cent of tunny and the near totality of sugar was shipped abroad, these industries would have exported goods for *c*.13,000–19,000 *onze* per year. This was significantly less than the value of the silk trade. In 1500, silk shipments from Messina were worth up to 90,000 *onze*, quite dwarfing the revenues of the other export sectors, even allowing for the

---

[84] On female employment see Fazello, *Due deche*, pp. 28–9; work times in J. Brown, *In the shadow of Florence. Provincial society in Renaissance Pescia*, p. 84 and n. 65.

[85] Mendels, 'Seasons and regions in agriculture and industry during the process of industrialisation'.

[86] *UM*, pp. 247, 272.

fact that Messina also operated as southern Calabria's main silk emporium.[87]

IMPORTS: SLAVES AND CLOTH

The main Sicilian imports were slaves and cloth. While Sicily provided a transit route for spices, dyes and other Levantine luxury goods on their way to western Europe (and must have profited from this trade's financial and commercial externalities), domestic demand for these products was not very significant. The same, by and large, can be said for slaves. Only a few hundred seem to have been owned in Sicily at any one time, and ownership was mainly a matter of urban prestige. Slave imports to Palermo, the main source of demand, between 1290 and 1460 were only a few thousand. Less than ten per cent of these were re-exported to the hinterland. Only a few hundred *onze* per year were apparently spent on slaves.[88]

Cloth, therefore, was Sicily's only significant import. We have already seen that much of the argument about Sicilian 'dependence' rests on the assertion that the entire regional economy was structured by the exchange of Sicilian grain for foreign cloth; in fact, however, foreign cloth imports supplied only a minute proportion of domestic demand, and most foreign cloth was bought by middle- and upper-class customers.[89] A simple calculation can give us some idea of the proportion of foreign imports to domestic consumption. The latter can be estimated by assuming that each person annually used two to three *canne* of cloth, sufficient for one set of clothing.[90] A population of 300,000 in the mid-fifteenth century would, therefore, have been using the equivalent of 46,150–69,200 foreign cloths of an average length of thirteen *canne* each every year, about twelve

[87] Price of raw silk: TRP Atti 51, fos. 96v–7 (1495); exports: Barberi, *Liber de secretiis*, p. 30.

[88] *UM*, pp. 439, 460, 469; Verlinden, 'L'esclavage en Sicile au bas moyen âge'; Ventura, 'Aspetti economico-sociali della schiavitù nella Sicilia medievale (1260–1498)'. Slave labour was seldom used in agriculture (RC 49, fos. 45v–7 (1413); CR 36, fo. 466 (1453); C. Avolio, 'La schiavitù in Sicilia nel secolo XVI', 56–7, 61–2, 65, 67; Ventura, 'Aspetti economico-sociali', 128–9).

[89] This point was made in 1613 for southern Italy by Antonio Serra, *Breve trattato delle cause che possono far abbondare li Regni d'oro e d'argento dove non sono miniere con applicazione al Regno di Napoli*, pp. 112–13. For the argument in this section see Epstein, 'Textile industry', 143–6.

[90] *Ibid.*, 143. Inventories and dowries (which admittedly list whole trousseaus) record an extraordinary wealth and variety of clothing, suggesting higher levels of average consumption than I have assumed.

to eighteen times the amount imported in the period (see Table 6.2). Analysis of the data for fifteenth-century cloth imports to Palermo substantiates the claim that foreign imports supplied an élite market. These data are representative of more general patterns of trade, because Palermo was the main cloth importer throughout the later Middle Ages, and a large proportion of its imports was redistributed to the rest of Sicily. Cloth imports to Sciacca, Catania, Syracuse and Messina were of marginal significance compared to Palermo.[91] Palermo's hegemony was broken only during the second half of the fourteenth century when Catania came to control the eastern market. In the fifteenth century, Palermo's internal market area for cloth corresponded to about two thirds of the Sicilian population.[92]

Between 1407–8 and 1438, average annual imports to Palermo were *c*.4,000 cloths. Of these, between 1,600 and 2,000 (let us say 1,800) cloths were re-exported to the interior.[93] If two thirds of the population living there, *c*.180,000 people, shared this amount of cloth, average consumption would have been no more than 25–29cm a year, or one complete dress every two decades. This means that about five per cent of the population could buy a new set of foreign clothing every year. In comparison, Palermo's 30,000 inhabitants bought on average eight times as much. These averages are nonetheless misleading, because they conceal disparities of income and consumption patterns both in Palermo and in the interior. Demand for foreign cloth was more polarized than averages suggest: a minority of the population was buying up to half a cloth a

[91] Barberi, *Liber de secretiis*, throughout; Giardina ed., *Capitoli*, no. 60 (1410). For Messina see CR 875, fos. 311v, 317 (1496). In 1521–39, average annual imports to Messina were 1,865 cloths (Trasselli, *Da Ferdinando*, p. 37 n. 12), compared to 9,000–11,000 in Palermo. A large quantity of cloth sold in 1500 in Catania may have come from Messina (NC 14926, unnumbered fo., and fo. 588 (6 and 15 July 1500)). For Syracuse see C 2893, fo. 85 (1441): 'Item perço com los mercaders catalans que solien habitar en Saragossa eran acostumats anar ab lurs draps a les feries de Catania e altres lochs de vall de Notho, los quals draps venien en gros e les gabelles de la cort del dit senyor ne havian gran util, de alguns anys ença han acostumat los dits mercaders catalans no anar hi ans los mercaders de vall de Notho van comprar los draps a Saragossa, perço com per lo secret de Saragossa los es feta alguna gracia del dret deles gabelles.'

[92] Aymard, 'Commerce et consommation', 129.

[93] Bresc overestimates re-exports to the interior at 2,400 cloths; his own figures, based on notarial records which over-represent re-exports, give an average rate of 52.1 per cent during 1400–50 (*UM*, pp. 500, 505–7).

Table 6.2 *Foreign cloth imports to Palermo, 1407–8 to 1496–7*

	(a)	(b)	(c)	(d)
1407–8	350.–.–.–	10,500.–.–	2.84	3,697
1410–11	144.27.19.–	4,347.28.10	2.84	1,531
1416–17	344.–.–.–ᵉ	10,320.–.–	2.84	3,634
1426–7	600.–.–.–	18,000.–.–	2.84	6,081
1434–5	392.7.4.–	11,767.6.–	2.96	3,975
1435–6	455.–.–.–	13,650.–.–	2.96	4,611
1436–7	402.–.–.–	12,060.–.–	2.96	4,074
1437–8	402.–.–.–	12,060.–.–	2.96	4,074
1438–9	446.–.–.–	13,380.–.–	2.96	4,520
1454–5	447.17.3.–	13,427.4.10	3.81	3,524
1455–6	125.–.–.–ᶠ	3,750.–.–	3.81	984
1462–3	778.–.–.–	23,340.–.–	[3.81]ᵍ	6,126
1463–4	597.27.2.3	17,937.3.15	[3.81]	4,708
1464–5	741.14.18.–	22,244.27.–	[3.81]	5,839
1465–6	622.–.–.–	18,660.–.–	[3.81]	4,898
1466–7	865.12.–.–.–	25,962.–.–	[3.81]	6,814
1467–8	1,309.24.17.–	39,294.25.10	[3.81]	10,314
1468–9	710.9.7.–	21,309.10.10	[3.81]	5,593
1469–70	850.3.11.–	25,503.16.10	[3.81]	6,694
1470–1	782.22.19.–	23,482.28.10	[3.81]	6,164
1472–3	974.2.18.–	29,222.27.–	[3.81]	7,670
1473–4	1,088.–.–.–	32,640.–.–	[3.81]	8,567
1482–3	1,149.2.3.–	34,472.4.10	[3.81]	9,048
1486–7	1,700.1.17.–	51,001.25.10	[3.81]	13,386
1487–8	2,012.9.9.–	60,369.13.10	[3.81]	15,845
1489–90	1,813.2.4.–	54,392.6.–	[3.81]	14,276
1490–1	2,531.3.2.–	75,933.3.–	[3.81]	19,930
1492–3	1,136.22.11.–	34,103.16.10	[3.81]	8,951
1496–7	2,100.22.13.–	63,022.19.10	[3.81]	16,541

(a) Receipts of the *caxia pannorum* (in *onze, tarì, denari, grani*).
(b) Total value of imports (thirty times the revenue of (a); see Sipione, 'Tre documenti', 240; Orlando, *Un codice*, p. 166; Trasselli, 'Il mercato dei panni', 295).
(c) Average price of one cloth (with decimal values).
(d) Estimated number of imported cloths.
ᵉ Only until February 1417.
ᶠ Receipts for September 1455–July 1456.
ᵍ Figures in [ ] refer to the average price of one cloth in 1450–9.
Sources: Trasselli, 'Frumento e panni inglesi', 302–3; *UM*, p. 507; Giuffrida, 'Aspetti e problemi', Table 2; TRP n.p. 121; CR 843, fos. 212–27; CR 854, fos. 5rv, 8; TRP n.p. 2. Where Trasselli and Giuffrida disagree I follow the former.

year, while the vast majority either went without or, if slightly better off, acquired a small article that was kept only for important occasions and was handed down to heirs.

Reliable figures for the value of imports only resume in the 1460s, but since average cloth prices are not known for that period, the volume of imports cannot be reconstructed accurately.[94] If we use 1450–9 prices, imports would have risen to an average 6,300 cloths in the 1460s, and increased further in the early 1470s to 7,470 a year. In 1482–3 to 1496–7, they could have risen to an average of 14,000. If we are to assume that cloth prices increased at the same rate as grain, imports in 1480–99 would have been about 11,500 pieces, just slightly more than in 1500–20 when accurate figures are once again available.

Already in the fourteenth and early fifteenth centuries, there was a tendency for an increasing proportion of imports to stay within Palermo. Between 1400 and 1459, the proportion of cloth in transit to the interior dropped from an average 69.5 per cent during the fourteenth century, to 52.1 per cent. By 1450–9, the proportion had declined to 42.9 per cent.[95] Between 1450 and 1520, re-exports from Palermo lagged behind the rising population; at the same time, imports to Palermo were higher than they had ever been. By 1500–20, only about one quarter of the 9,000–11,000 cloths shipped every year to Palermo was re-exported to the interior.[96] If Palermo still supplied, as it had a century before, two thirds of the island's population, consumption in the interior would have been twenty to thirty per cent lower compared to the early fifteenth century. At the same time, average consumption in Palermo had roughly doubled.

The simplest and most convincing explanation for these contrasting developments is that they reflect a residential move by upper-class customers from the interior towards Palermo, the result of Palermo's increasing attractions as the seat of central government and political power and prestige. This phenomenon corresponds also to changing patterns of urbanization, discussed in chapter 3, which show that Palermo increased its regional primacy after the mid-fifteenth century.

[94]. I have divided the value of imports by the average price for 1450–9, the latest period for which prices are available. Since prices thereafter rose very considerably (Aymard, 'Commerce et consommation', 129), imports after 1459 must be significantly lower than I have estimated.

[95] *UM*, p. 505, Table 122.

[96] Aymard, 'Commerce et consommation', 129.

Although late medieval Sicily's foreign cloth trade has left abundant documentary traces because it was subject to royal excise, and because distributors from Palermo inland drew up notarial contracts to ensure that the cloth would be paid for, evidence of cloth imports is in inverse proportion to the trade's impact on the Sicilian economy as a whole. Foreign cloth was late medieval Sicily's main import, but it was a luxury good and as such was restricted to a narrow, élite market; it supplied approximately one twentieth of domestic consumption. There is little in this to sustain claims about the foreign cloth trade's cardinal role in medieval Sicily's 'dependency' on imports from the North. By contrast, the fact that foreign cloth, which was Sicily's main import, took up such a small share of the domestic market, suggests that an overwhelming proportion of export income was retained and spent locally on domestically produced goods and services.

THE BALANCE OF TRADE

The question of Sicily's balance of trade cannot be resolved conclusively, for we lack significant price compilations and long series of import and export figures. Although the problem can be partly circumvented by considering the balance of trade between Sicily and each of its main commercial partners (Genoa, Catalonia, the kingdom of Naples and North Africa), the result is inevitably rather schematic and conclusions must be based on extrapolations from individual years to far longer periods, on the assumption (which can of course be questioned) that patterns of foreign trade did not change very rapidly in the late medieval economy.

Sicily's trade with Genoa is the best documented, thanks to two surviving registers of a toll on sea trade exacted in Genoa in 1376–7 (see Table 6.3). Even so, the registers are incomplete, and a number of exemptions for goods (grain and salt) and merchant nations (Catalans and Sicilians) make them even less reliable for our purposes.[97] In addition, the document dates from a period in which, for political reasons, Genoese trade was largely restricted to Palermo and western Sicily. Nonetheless, omissions are either statistically random or can be identified quite easily. As to the problem of the markets accessible to Genoa, throughout the late Middle

[97] Day, *Douanes*, pp. 8, 10.

Table 6.3. *Sicilian trade with Genoa, 1376–1377 (in* lire di piccoli *and* soldi genovini)

Exports	1376	per cent	1377	per cent	Total	per cent
cheese	15,927	(52.7)	8,200	(73.4)	24,127	(58.3)
salt meat	949	(3.1)	—		949	(2.2)
lard	12	(0.04)	383	(3.4)	395	(1.0)
sheep fells	405	(1.3)	75	(0.7)	480	(1.2)
hides	101	(0.3)	—		101	(0.2)
cotton	6,156	(20.4)	—		6,156	(14.9)
wool	14	(0.05)	—		14	(0.03)
flax	50	(0.2)	—		50	(0.1)
silk	968	(3.2)	25	(0.2)	993	(2.4)
wine	30	(0.1)	—		30	(0.07)
furs	299	(1.0)	—		299	(0.7)
haberdashery	1,764	(5.8)	1,025	(9.2)	2,789	(6.7)
spices, dyes	551	(1.8)	523	(4.7)	1,074	(2.6)
mica	—		46	(0.4)	46	(0.1)
unspecified	—		393	(3.5)	393	(0.9)
silver	1,257	(4.1)	500	(4.5)	1,757	(4.2)
gold	1,750	(5.8)	—		1,750	(4.2)
Total	30,233	(100)	11,170	(100)	41,403	(100)

Imports	1376	per cent	1377	per cent	Total	per cent
wool cloth	10,941.10[a]	(51.5)	9,671	(41.9)	20,612.10	(46.5)
tela	55	(0.3)	130	(0.6)	185	(0.4)
silk cloth	—		469	(2.0)	469	(1.1)
haberdashery	705	(3.3)	2,048	(8.9)	2,753	(6.2)
sheep fells	100	(0.5)	32	(0.1)	132	(0.3)
hides	535	(2.5)	—		535	(1.2)
spices, dyes	1,325	(6.2)	207	(0.9)[b]	1,532	(3.5)
sugar	219	(1.0)	—		219	(0.5)
honey	1,075	(5.1)	—		1,075	(2.4)
coral	60	(0.3)	—		60	(0.1)
tin	25	(0.1)	660	(2.9)	685	(1.5)
iron	110	(0.5)	511	(2.2)	621	(1.4)
copper	300	(1.4)	—		300	(0.7)
unspecified	4,901	(23.0)	390	(1.7)	5,291	(11.9)
gold	105	(0.5)	8,958	(38.8)	9,063	(20.4)
bullion[c]	812	(3.8)	—		812	(1.8)
Total	21,268.10	(100)	23,076	(100)	44,344.10	(100)

[a] One *lira* = twenty *soldi*.
[b] Includes l.140 of gallnuts.
[c] Unspecified.
Sources: Day, *Douanes.*

Ages, Genoese trade tended to concentrate in any case in western Sicily. The source, therefore, provides a picture that may not be fully reliable in detail, but which is so in broad outline. In 1376–7, (western) Sicily had a trade deficit with Genoa of just under 2,500 Genoese *lire*, approximately 5.8 per cent of the value of its exports to the city. If bullion flows are excluded, however, the situation is reversed, and a positive balance of trade of 3,400 *lire* emerges (about nine per cent of exports excluding bullion flows).[98] These figures do not include grain exports, which must, however, have been considerably reduced due to Genoa's heavy population losses.[99] One can thus state with some confidence that in these years, (western) Sicily's balance of trade with Genoa was entirely in the former's favour.

In fact, even the bullion deficit is probably illusory, for the two flows, in and out of Sicily, seem of an entirely different character. Genoese bullion imports to Sicily included both gold and silver. Since Sicily had a chronic dearth of silver, there are good reasons to believe that silver imports helped balance Genoa's trade deficit with the island. Bullion exports, on the other hand, consisted nearly entirely of African gold, mostly in the form of gold dust. Only one shipment of European coins is recorded, 116 gold florins from Palermo in October 1377.[100] In contrast with bullion imports, therefore, bullion exports seem to have been linked with Genoese traffic with North Africa and the Levant, for which Sicily acted as a major point of transit.[101] If, on these grounds, the balance of trade is revised to exclude bullion exports but to include bullion imports, (western) Sicily's credit towards Genoa increases to nearly 7,500 *lire*, approximately one fifth of the value of its recorded exports.

Recorded Sicilian exports to Genoa in this period consisted mostly of cheese (63.7 per cent, excluding bullion imports) and cotton (16.2 per cent). Cotton came mainly from Messina, which may also have acted as a collecting point for Calabria. Messina

---

[98] In Table 6.3, figures for bullion in the *export* column refer to bullion *imports* by the Genoese to Sicily; those in the *import* column refer to bullion *exports* by the Genoese. This is because I have assumed that bullion flows compensated (in part) for imbalances of trade.

[99] Glénisson and Day eds., *Textes et documents*, I, pp. 76–8 (1375).

[100] Giuffrida, 'Aspetti della presenza', pp. 281ff.; Trasselli, *Note banchi secolo XIV*, pp. 42–4; Spufford, *Money and its use*, p. 288.

[101] Giunta and Giuffrida eds., *Corrispondenza*, pp. 29–30. African gold passed through Sicily *en route* to Genoa in the fifteenth century (Heers, *Gênes*, pp. 66–71).

exported large quantities of silk and of wood and iron caskets (included under haberdashery in Table 6.3). Small quantities of exported spices were in transit from the Levant. The simultaneous export and import of animal hides probably concerned different parts of the island. Sugar, probably from Egypt, still counted among Sicilian imports; a few decades later it became a major Sicilian export. Iron imports were of marginal importance. Wool cloth was Sicily's only major import from Genoa comparable to cheese exports (59.8 per cent of trade exluding bullion). During the fifteenth century, Genoa added no other important article to its trade to Sicily, whereas Sicily began to export to Genoa tunny fish, sugar, silk and an increasing amount of grain in addition to cheese. As a result, Genoa's balance of trade with Sicily constantly deteriorated, until in 1495–1537 exports to Sicily were approximately one quarter the value of imports, *excluding* grain, wine and animal fats.[102]

Sicily's fifteenth-century trade with Barcelona and Catalonia was better balanced. Catalan exports to Sicily consisted mainly of wool cloth, which flooded Palermo's market as soon as the city came under Aragonese control in the late 1390s (see chapter 3). However, Sicilian exports to Catalonia were more varied than to Genoa. Maltese and other local cotton was highly prized in Catalonia, as were sugar, saltpetre, slaves and, to a lesser extent, cheese (Catalans seem to have preferred Sardinian cheese). Catalan imports of Sicilian grain were more significant than during the thirteenth and fourteenth centuries, but always less so for Barcelona (which had closer alternative sources of supply) than for Genoa.[103]

Carrère and Del Treppo have argued that the balance of payments (rather than the balance of trade) favoured Catalonia over Sicily, on the assumption that invisibles such as freight charges and triangular trade with North Africa mostly benefited Catalan merchants.[104] Evidence for western Sicily seems to show that the implied assumption that freight and distribution between the two countries was mainly under Catalan control is by and large cor-

---

[102] Gioffrè, 'Commercio d'importazione', 196.
[103] Carrère, *Barcelone*, II, pp. 634–9; Del Treppo, *Mercanti catalani*, pp. 175–7.
[104] Carrère, *Barcelone*, II, pp. 637–8; Del Treppo, 'Assicurazioni e commercio internazionale a Barcellona nel 1428–1429'; Del Treppo, *Mercanti catalani*, pp. 183–5.

rect;[105] I return below to the question of the size of the Sicilian navy. On the other hand, Catalan profits from trade of Sicilian grain or hides in North Africa, apparently included in Carrère's and Del Treppo's calculations, are irrelevant either to Sicily's balance of trade, or to its balance of payments with Catalonia. Evidence for bullion exports by Catalans, quoted by Del Treppo for the fifteenth century to demonstrate a Sicilian trade deficit, is no more conclusive, since it is unclear whether the bullion originated in profits from Catalan trade with North Africa and the Levant, or from trade with Sicily itself.[106]

The balance of trade between Sicily and the southern mainland is especially hard to assess, for very few figures for trade are available outside Palermo. Qualitative evidence, however, is not hard to come by. In chapter 3, I discussed Alfonso's grants of toll franchises to various southern cities; in chapter 5, I described eastern Sicily's close commercial ties with southern Calabria and Messina's role as the area's metropolis.

In the long term, therefore, trade with the southern mainland (including both the kingdom of Naples and the Roman state) tended to increase. Even western Sicily became more closely integrated with the southern mainland (see Table 6.4). Western Sicilian trade expanded significantly for the first time in the 1360s, when Palermo was cut off from most of Sicily and clung to its Angevin life-line. At the height of Sicilian division in the 1380s, Palermo's ties with the mainland came close to being exclusive. The Catalan–Aragonese conquest reduced, but did not seriously weaken, links between Palermo (which after 1400 regained its former role as western Sicily's main commercial emporium) and the kingdom of Naples. Trade with Rome, particularly in cheese, tunny and sugar, grew quite rapidly after 1400.[107] Alfonso's mainland campaigns also stimulated southern Italian trade. By the 1450s, western Sicily's

[105] *UM*, Tables 41, 45, 49, 51, 54, 57, 59, 61, 64: Sicily's share in freight to Catalonia rose from less than ten per cent in 1400–9 to forty-six per cent in 1440–9 and twenty per cent in 1450–9. See also below, this chapter.

[106] See C 2894, fo. 99v, and C 2856, fos. 63rv, 71v–2 (1446); C 2858, fo. 12 (1447); C 2862, fos. 143v–4 (1449); RC 105, fos. 163v–4 (1457). Specie was sometimes exported from the *Camera reginale*; CS 1, fo. 146v (1431); C 2851, fos. 162v–3 (1447); LV 80, fos. 248–9 (1461). For royal bullion exports see below, chapter 7.

[107] *UM*, p. 569.

Table 6.4 *Main shipping destinations from Palermo, 1298–1459*

	Catalonia per cent	Liguria–Tuscany per cent	Kingdom of Naples per cent	Maghreb per cent	Levant per cent	Other per cent	N
1298–1310	8 (5.3)	76 (50.7)	22 (14.7)	22 (14.7)	5 (3.3)	17 (11.3)	150
1319–39	18 (40.0)	8 (17.8)	2 (4.4)	4 (8.9)	2 (4.4)	11 (24.4)	45
1340–59	6 (5.4)	67 (59.8)	19 (17.0)	5 (4.5)	4 (3.6)	11 (9.8)	112
1360–79	23 (13.0)	80 (45.2)	41 (23.2)	9 (5.1)	6 (3.4)	18 (10.2)	177
1380–99	9 (7.3)	23 (18.5)	81 (65.3)	3 (2.4)	2 (1.6)	6 (4.8)	124
1400–19	13 (25.5)	8 (15.7)	12 (23.5)	—	13 (25.5)	5 (9.8)	51
1420–39	57 (17.2)	33 (9.9)	102 (30.7)	73 (22.0)	38 (11.4)	29 (8.7)	332
1440–59	111 (17.4)	145 (22.7)	156 (24.5)	94 (14.7)	44 (6.9)	88 (13.8)	638
Total	245 (14.8)	440 (26.6)	435 (26.3)	˙210 (12.7)	114 (6.9)	185 (11.2)	1,629

Sources: UM, Tables 42, 46, 48, 52, 55, 62, 65, 69.

trade with the mainland had surpassed its trade with all other countries, and this predominance must have been even greater for eastern Sicily. It therefore comes as no surprise that Alfonso should have exempted the two kingdoms from his otherwise strict rulings against outflows of bullion.[108]

The rising volume of southern Italian trade is particularly significant because it occurred between two areas that are usually perceived as having similar, predominantly agricultural economies.[109] Trade – in grain, wine, oil, timber and cotton from the mainland, and grain, livestock, cheese, fish, sugar, leather and iron from Sicily – took place for the same reasons that led to greater regional integration in this period: specialization as a result of depopulation; and relatively low transfer costs (because of geographical proximity and a common ruler) for low-value bulk commodities. In view of Alfonso's stated policy of developing trade between the Iberian and the southern Italian members of his empire, it is paradoxical that his Neapolitan enterprise seems to have improved ties most with his main other Italian 'agricultural' realm, rather than with Iberian manufacturers and merchants.

Although lower transfer costs enabled stronger commercial relations to develop, major institutional constraints on trade remained in place. As far as most custom dues, money, weights and measures were concerned, Sicily and Naples were different countries; in these areas, trading costs were no lower than those for trade with other countries. Southern Italian market structures in this period must still be studied, but the very small size of the Neapolitan demesne and the far greater powers of its aristocracy compared to Sicily, suggest that markets were less integrated on the mainland than in Sicily (see chapter 8). If, for these reasons, interregional specialization progressed more slowly on the mainland, Sicilian integration with the southern Italian economy could also have been held up, notwithstanding rather favourable political conditions.

The trade franchises granted to southern Italian towns were, by and large, meant to favour southern Italian trade in Sicily rather than vice versa. Palermo, as we saw, was refused a comparable privilege on the mainland. Taken together with Messina's control over southern Calabria, this suggests that the balance of trade in the

---

[108] C 2897, fo. 73rv (1453).
[109] Leone, *Profili economici*, pp. 49–51, 73.

fifteenth century was in Sicily's favour.[110] Further evidence of this imbalance can be found in the attempts to unify the Sicilian and Neapolitan monetary systems discussed in chapter 5. There is little proof, by contrast, that this imbalance was subsequently reversed. How does Alfonso's brief attempt to unify the 'two Sicilies' in a 'common market' with the Iberian parts of his empire fit into the picture of Sicilian trade with Catalonia and Naples? The document in which Alfonso outlined this project in 1451 is said to express a fully formulated and long-standing political and economic strategy.[111] On this reading, the conquest of Naples was a crucial strand in a strategy leading to the economic and political subordination of the Italian *Mezzogiorno* to Catalan–Aragonese imperialism.

This reading of the evidence faces the problem that more than ten years before this declaration, Alfonso had deliberately destroyed his empire's future unity by making his illegitimate son, Ferrante, heir to the kingdom of Naples. Moreover, even if one were to take Alfonso's statement of 1451 as a serious political and economic programme, the fact remains that economic relations between the Iberian and the Italian parts of the Aragonese empire were still too weak, and specialization insufficiently advanced, to sustain a process of integration based on overseas trade which totally excluded outside participants. High transport costs restricted 'common market' trade to exchanging Catalan and Majorcan cloth and salt from Ibiza for a few agricultural products from the *Mezzogiorno* and Sicily. Moreover, the Iberian markets were too narrow to absorb more than a small part of Italian exports, both grain[112] and the more expensive products like sugar, silk, tunny, cheese and wine. The small size of the Catalan and Sicilian domestic markets was one reason why Catalan merchants were unable to take full advantage of the opportunities Alfonso's policies opened up for

[110] Ryder, 'Cloth and credit', 9; Leone, 'Il Regno di Napoli e l'età aragonese', 164; Carrère, *Barcelone*, II, p. 616 n. 8; Grohmann, *Fiere*, p. 117; Del Treppo, *Mercanti catalani*, pp. 196–7.
[111] *Ibid.*, pp. 600–5. Already a few years earlier, the citizens of Majorca had referred to the 'common market' in a petition calling for exemption from a ban on bullion exports from Sicily and the kingdom of Naples: 'entre los altres regnes e terres dela vestra senyoria lo dit Regne de Mallorques principalment es per los artes mercantivols, enter los quals principal es la draperia la qual es mercantivol-ment en los dits Reyalmes [of Sicily and Naples] tramesa' (C 2856, fos. 44v–5, 11 June 1446).
[112] *UM*, p. 551.

them in Sicily.[113] For their part, the Sicilian and Neapolitan upper classes were too sophisticated to be supplied only with cheap Catalan cloth. Finally, as we saw when discussing the problems of establishing full trade franchises in Sicily, a radical policy of economic integration faced a further, unsurmountable contradiction between two exigencies of the state: on the one hand, the political goal of excluding northern Italian and French rivals from profits of trade in the Aragonese lands; on the other, the customs revenue gained by taxing non-Aragonese traders. Because the state could not, for political and economic reasons, set heavy tariffs on members of the 'common market' to compensate for the fall in tax revenue resulting from a total ban on 'foreign' trade, no government could fully pursue an unwavering strategy of integration based on commercial protectionism.

Like trade with the southern mainland, trade with North Africa involved mostly primary goods. Frederick II's exports of grain to Ifriqiya, probably in exchange for the gold used to coin his new *augustales*, are well known.[114] Peter III and James II profited again from the grain trade after the Vespers,[115] and Alfonso V and his successors often capitalized on North African famines. Royal activities expanded in the 1420s and 1430s because of the exclusion of the Genoese from the Sicilian market,[116] but even after the Genoese returned, trade with Africa stayed fairly buoyant. In 1438, Alfonso needed gold to pay troops on the mainland; since the only gold coins available in Sicily were Almohad double dinars, he had these re-minted as false Venetian ducats to be shipped to Naples.[117] In 1488 and 1490, Ferdinand II authorized exports to North Africa and Egypt in exchange for gold and silver needed to defeat the last Moors in Granada.[118]

[113] Bresc, 'Draperie catalane', 123–6.
[114] Abulafia, 'Maometto e Carlomagno: le due aree monetarie italiane dell'oro e dell'argento', pp. 261–2.
[115] Carini ed., *De rebus*, nos. 248, 457, 583–5, 732, 735–8 (1282–3); A. De Stefano and Giunta eds., *Codice diplomatico dei re aragonesi di Sicilia*, nos. 17, 23, 34 (1291).
[116] *UM*, pp. 536–7, 554–5. In 1423, Alfonso referred in a letter to Messina to the strong inflow of gold double dinars thanks to trade with North Africa (Gallo, *Annali di Messina*, pp. 298–9).
[117] RC 72, fos. 98v–9, Trasselli ed., 'Sul debito pubblico in Sicilia sotto Alfonso V d'Aragona', 111–12. See above, n. 116.
[118] See above, n. 41.

Although Sicily, particularly Trapani, imported hides,[119] and although Africa was one of Sicily's main sources of slaves,[120] the balance of trade seems to have been constantly in Sicily's favour. Gold flowed in and through the island by way of direct exchange with North Africa, and of the triangular trade organized by Tuscan, Genoese and Catalan merchants, who used Sicily as a great transit emporium for Western–Levantine trade.[121] Late medieval Sicily was, as a result, one of western Europe's main channels of supply of Black African gold.[122]

Sicily, in conclusion, had a very favourable balance of trade throughout the fifteenth century;[123] the large number of coin hoards discovered during that period suggests that this situation had already prevailed for some time.[124] A rough estimate of the balance of trade between 1450 and 1500 gives the following results. Towards 1450, cloth imports accounted for *c.*18,000 *onze*, including shipments outside Palermo. The main exports included grain (*c.*7,000 *onze* at Catania prices), sugar and tunny (*c.*16,000 *onze*), livestock (10,000 *onze*),[125] silk (possibly 15,000 *onze*) and cheese (2,000–3,000 *onze*). If we assume that lesser exports (cotton, wine, honey, coral and lesser manufactured goods) compensated for minor imports (wine, timber, iron and slaves), the value of exports was then approximately three times that of imports.

This major trade surplus may have narrowed slightly in the course of the late fifteenth century. The expanding grain trade, the growing silk, sugar and mining industries, and the steady flow of livestock into Calabria, were probably unable to match the nearly fivefold increase in the value of cloth imports. Towards 1500, the 87,500 *onze* spent on foreign cloth had to be balanced against exports of

---

[119] CR 850, fo. 118rv (May 1447): Alfonso sent some grain to Tunis in exchange for hides, which his agent then tried unsuccessfully to sell in Trapani; the hides were sent on to Naples or Gaeta 'undi continuamenti si usa tali mercancia'.

[120] *UM*, pp. 439–54.

[121] Del Treppo, *Mercanti catalani*, pp. 181–2; Ashtor, 'The Jews', pp. 444, 445.

[122] Spufford, *Money and its use*, pp. 368–9.

[123] Trasselli, *Note banchi secolo XV*, p. 103; Aymard, 'Commerce et consommation', 128, 134–5; Cancila, *Impresa redditi*, p. 256. C 3472, fos. 158v–9, Giardina ed., *Capitoli*, no. 95 (1459): Venetians buy more than they sell in Messina 'et sic moneta apud dictam civitatem remanebat'.

[124] See above, chapter 3, n. 45.

[125] An ox cost on average 18–24 *tarì* in the 1450s (NR 5, throughout; NR 6, fo. 6). The horse trade declined considerably after Alfonso V's death and the partition of the two kingdoms because of the animals' military uses.

Table 6.5 *Chartering merchants and ships departing from Palermo, 1298–1459 (percentages of the total)*

	Sicily			Catalonia			Genoa			Other			N		
	(A)	(B)	(C)	(A)	(B)	(C)	(A)	(B)	(C)	(A)	(B)	(C)	(A)	(B)	(C)
1298–1310	13.0	3.2	6.5	10.3	41.6	37.4	5.5	28.8	25.9	71.2	26.4	30.2	146	125	139
1319–39	13.6	13.0	19.6	40.9	43.5	39.2	11.4	17.4	15.7	34.1	26.1	25.5	44	46	51
1340–59	12.2	2.2	11.3	13.3	19.6	17.0	51.0	72.5	65.4	23.5	5.8	6.3	98	138	159
1360–79	21.7	9.7	24.4	11.5	21.4	15.7	40.1	53.1	43.1	26.8	15.9	16.8	157	145	197
1380–99	24.4	19.8	22.7	9.2	24.0	20.9	22.7	40.6	40.9	43.7	15.6	15.4	119	96	110
1407–8	31.2	13.4	41.2	30.8	24.4	16.2	36.6	43.7	30.3	1.3	18.5	12.3	224	238	357
1400–19ᵃ	42.3	11.3	28.9	26.5	20.0	15.8	26.2	44.3	35.4	5.0	24.4	19.9	321	566	720
1420–39	35.7	15.9	22.4	38.4	39.0	35.5	6.2	13.3	11.9	19.6	31.8	30.2	336	308	344
1440–59	18.2	15.7	27.7	30.3	24.4	20.9	20.9	10.9	9.1	30.7	49.0	42.2	750	726	865

(A) = chartering merchants; (B) = chartered ships (excluding *barche*); (C) = chartered ships (including *barche*).
ᵃ (A) = 1410–19.
Sources: *UM*, Tables 40–1, 44–5, 47, 49–51, 53–4, 56–61, 63–4.

grain (36,000 *onze*), silk (90,000 *onze*), livestock (9,000 *onze*), sugar and tunny (32,000 *onze*), and cheese and minerals (10,000 *onze*).[126] By the end of the fifteenth century, in other words, imports had risen from approximately one third to one half the value of exports.

A puzzling feature of the Sicilian economy, connected as we saw with the question of its balance of payments (rather than the balance of trade), is the comparative weakness of the regional navy. Although Sicily's naval power improved after the mid-fourteenth century, evidence from western Sicily suggests that external trade was dominated throughout our period by foreign navies, in particular by the Genoese and Catalan fleets (see Table 6.5).[127] Not surprisingly, (western) Sicily dominated the short- and medium-range trade with *barche* (see Table 6.5, column C). But before 1460, it seems to have only occasionally captured more than fifteen per cent of the long-distance freight markets. On the other hand, the (western) Sicilian fleet improved at the same time as the Genoese and Catalan hold on Sicily's market was weakening, due to the emergence of other strong regional navies.

One must nonetheless wonder why, on average, eighty-five to ninety per cent of (western) Sicily's long-distance trade seems to have been carried by foreign ships, despite the fact that Sicily lacked neither the technical capacity nor the primary materials to establish a strong navy. To explain this as the result of a weak domestic merchant class merely begs the question why, despite such a favourable geographic position, Sicilians did not develop stronger trade interests abroad. A full answer would take us too far, to the origins of medieval trading communities, and is an issue still lacking a basis in comparative research. Many successful Mediterranean commercial cities, however, seem to have developed in response to local scarcity. By comparison, Sicily offered too many alternative and easier ways of making a living to provide many such challenges, as the very success of Messina's merchants, in the face of seemingly overwhelming natural odds, would suggest. The fact that the Sicilian navy *expanded* after the mid-fourteenth century, at a time of contracting foreign trade and of stronger international competition

---

[126] I assume that imports to Palermo accounted for eighty per cent of the foreign cloth market, and that the price of livestock, tunny fish and sugar increased by fifty per cent in the period 1450–1500 (Cancila, *Baroni e popolo*, p. 25).

[127] *UM*, pp. 257–61; Melis, 'Werner Sombart', pp. 108–9.

for markets, when barriers to entry into international commercial networks (due to technical and information costs, among others) were rising, also suggests that Sicily's naval and commercial weaknesses were, at least in part, the result of the region's considerable trade surplus and domestic wealth. The decline of the trade surplus after the 1350s may thus have provided the initial stimulus for expanding the domestic navy.

CONCLUSIONS

None of the arguments advanced for Sicilian 'dependency' or underdevelopment resulting from long-distance trade, in grain or otherwise, stands up to critical scrutiny. The foundation of these arguments, the assumption that grain was a staple export, collapses in the face of estimated export ratios which, for most of the period under consideration, were no more than five per cent of domestic output, and only briefly rose to thirteen to fifteen per cent. More significantly, there is no reason to believe that the foreign grain trade had a uniquely determining and/or negative domestic effect. Trade was the result neither of domestic nor of foreign pressure, but of Sicily's lower comparative production and distribution costs. Terms of trade between grain and the main Sicilian import, high-value cloth, were apparently either stable or favourable to grain. On the other hand, although the grain–cloth commercial dichotomy did exist,[128] it was always too weak seriously to affect domestic developments, either agricultural 'monoculture' or de-industrialization.

Even so, late medieval Sicily's foreign links did become stronger and more diversified over time. Initially, structural economic change occurred mainly in response to changes in domestic demand, but during the fifteenth century, the Sicilian economy began to respond increasingly also to foreign demand. The sugar and silk industries produced primarily for foreign markets; the cheese, tunny and mining industries exported a large proportion of their output; large numbers of livestock were shipped across the Straits of Messina until the late fifteenth century; rising agricultural productivity allowed grain exports to increase threefold in proportion to domestic output by the end of the century. As a

128 Aymard, 'Commerce et consommation', 133–6, for the sixteenth century.

result, Sicily had one of the most 'open' economies of late medieval Europe.

Even silk production, however, which of all the sectors producing for foreign markets had the greatest impact on home employment, involved at the outset probably no more than a few thousand people. Its rapid growth cannot alone explain val Demone's success in feeding an increasing proportion of the island's population after 1450, although the silk industry's role in sustaining this area's high population density probably increased as production spread. More generally, sectors producing for foreign markets probably employed, directly and indirectly, no more than one tenth of late medieval Sicily's population at the height of commercial expansion after the mid-fifteenth century.

Two questions have been left unanswered in this discussion, and I pursue them to some extent in chapter 7. First, we have the problem of the disposal of export revenues, and the proportion of those revenues spent upon domestically produced goods and services (including productive investments). While it is customary to view southern Italian grain exporters as squandering their profits on titles of nobility and luxury imports, rather than ploughing back their profits into the domestic economy,[129] the view from Sicily seems less clear-cut. The answer appears to lie in the social groups those profits accrued to, and in the character of those groups' economic behaviour.

The second question concerns the role of foreign trade in the state's survival and growth. Since a substantial part of late medieval state revenue came from tolls on trade within and without the island, trade occupies a central position in official documents of the time. It is on the state that international trade had its most significant impact, although the state itself was unable directly to shape the volume of trade. Before we can fully understand the effects of international trade on the Sicilian economy, therefore, we must examine the structure of the Sicilian state.

[129] Giorgetti, *Contadini e proprietari*, pp. 174–9.

7. *Income distribution, social conflict and the Sicilian state*

Up to this point, I have adopted an institutional approach to economic history which emphasizes the impact of political structures on economic development and growth. In this chapter we shall take the opposite line. Rather than viewing the economy merely as an enabling 'base', whose function it is to supply resources for, or set constraints upon, statecraft and administration, we shall examine how economic development transformed social structures, and how these transformations were given political and institutional shape.

A striking feature of the debate on the late medieval European crisis is the lack of communication between economic and social, and political and institutional historians. This barrier has many sources, most of which are not restricted to our debate. A more specific reason for non-communication, however, may be the two fields' seeming intellectual dissonance over the nature of the crisis. Whereas socio-economic historians emphasize destruction, contraction and decline, politico-institutional historians prefer to stress the innovations that emerged from the crisis, particularly the broader range of social classes and interest groups that found representation within increasingly complex institutional structures.

If one takes the latter as a broad characterization of late medieval state formation, its connections with the model of socio-economic change outlined in previous chapters are immediately apparent. In effect, I have argued that if the late medieval crisis promoted economic specialization and growth in the long run, such growth as occurred was largely the outcome of intense social conflict over the distribution of income and power, a conflict which saw the lower and middle classes prevail in the main over the aristocracy. In arguing this, I have implied that economic change brought into the political arena new social forces, and that these changes resulted in

314

comparable alterations to institutional and political structures. The economic struggle was thus ultimately resolved – given shape and stability – through political change.

In this chapter I trace these developments for Sicily. The argument is structured in three parts. First, I discuss the aristocracy's response to economic, political and institutional change, in its relations both with its rural subjects and with the royal demesne. I then examine urban (demesne) society, the emergence of class and corporate identities, and relations with the state. Finally, I look at the relationship between the state's fiscal policies, income distribution, and political consensus and representation, and at the effects of membership of the crown of Aragon on Sicilian politics, society and institutions.

THE ARISTOCRACY AND ITS SUBJECTS

'The ending of the Middle Ages and the transition to modern times is marked by a crisis in seigneurial revenues.'[1] The problem Marc Bloch stated so trenchantly, the relation between the late medieval decline of seigneurial income and the vast social transformations which heralded the early modern world, is still far from being resolved. On the other hand, it is now firmly established that feudal revenues did tend to decline throughout late medieval Europe.[2]

In Sicily this phenomenon, which began in the 1330s or earlier and lasted for more than a century, was very pronounced. The scale and rapidity of the decline in seigneurial incomes can be estimated by comparing two feudal levies of 1336 and 1343, which assessed total feudal revenue at 20,691 *onze* and 14,405 *onze* respectively (the size of the levy was proportionate to feudal income).[3] Part of this drop – a loss of one fifth in seven years – probably reflects aristocratic pressure on the monarchy to reduce feudal military duties, pressure which may have been more effective after King Federico III's death in 1337. On the other hand, there is evidence that the aristocracy was indeed being affected by the considerable

[1] M. Bloch, *French rural history. An essay on its basic characteristics*, p. 102 (my translation).

[2] General overviews of the literature in J. Topolski, *La nascita del capitalismo in Europa. Crisi economica e accumulazione originaria fra XIV e XVII secolo*, chapter 2; W. Eberhard, 'Die Krise des Spätmittelalters: Versuch einer Zusammenfassung'.

[3] 16,205 *onze* in 1343 if one includes the recently confiscated counties of the Ventimiglia and Antiochia families (*UM*, pp. 670–1, 677).

social and economic upheaval which began in the 1320s. The number of deserted settlements increased markedly between 1320 and 1340, at a time when Sicily was not undergoing major Angevin attacks (see chapters 2–3); then, in the early 1340s, a combination of bad harvests and higher military expenditure provoked widespread debt among the aristocracy.[4] In the early 1320s, income from land rents and direct cultivation on one of the greater magnate estates, that of Francesco Ventimiglia, count of Geraci and Ischia in the Madonie mountains, was less than two thirds of that from rights of lordship. Although Ventimiglia was a shrewd and active landlord who reinvested nearly nine per cent of his annual income in new enterprises (cotton plantations, vineyards, a mill) and made considerable profits, agricultural income was about twenty-five per cent less than annual expenditure on family maintenance and administration alone.[5] In other words, this magnate was able to maintain his standard of living only thanks to seigniorial dues (rights of justice, milling, and so on). We shall see below that conditions among the lesser aristocracy, who owned only unpopulated fiefs, were probably far harder.

Early fifteenth-century data give a more accurate idea of the scale of the decline in rents. Income from the uninhabited *feudo Chamopetra* near Caltagirone, which was 510 *onze* in 1330–1, was only 200 *onze* in 1427–8, a decline of 76.7 per cent, weighting for currency devaluation; income from the *feudi* Femmenino and Veneroso dropped by 89.5 per cent in the same period, from 85.22.10 *onze* in 1321 to 15 *onze* in 1433 and *c*.18 *onze* in 1446.[6] The average price of a fief, which was presumably related to expected income, sank from 180 *onze* in 1300–50 to 139.10 *onze* in 1350–99, and then declined even further to 108 *onze* in 1400–29 (a loss of sixty-four per cent with devaluation).[7] At the same time, the costs of farm labour increased by sixty per cent between the 1330s and the early fifteenth century.[8]

---

[4] *UM*, pp. 792–3.
[5] The accounts are published by Mazzarese Fardella, *Feudi comitali*, pp. 109–16, and are summarized in *UM*, p. 676, Table 170. By comparison, agricultural revenues of the barony of Mussomeli in 1486 accounted for 71.8 per cent of the total (Cancila, *Baroni e popolo*, p. 26).
[6] *UM*, pp. 712, 879.
[7] *UM*, pp. 674, 880 n. 65; the data conflict, but those at p. 880 n. 65 seem more accurate. If the average size of a *feudo* changed over time, land prices would be less reliable as proxy for rent.
[8] See above, chapter 4, n. 21.

The aristocracy could respond to these conditions with a variety of strategies. One was to redistribute land and revenue within the aristocracy itself through warfare. Another was to increase rights of jurisdiction, the significance of which always tended to increase in periods of declining rents. A third strategy was to expand customary sources of income to include revenue from the state. Finally, an aristocrat could become an entrepreneur, although in the long run this was the hardest option of all, for above all, business acumen and capital, rather than military and political coercion, were needed to compete successfully in the market.

During the fourteenth century, the Sicilian aristocracy seems to have reacted to economic hardship mainly by adopting the first three, defensive strategies – in other words, by trying to redistribute power and existing resources to itself, rather than by exploiting new economic opportunities.

From the 1330s until the early 1360s, the greater Sicilian magnate families waged civil war, with effects on institutional and economic life far more serious and long-lasting than the War of the Vespers itself (see chapter 3). Although the violent political and social conflict which erupted in the 1330s was caused primarily by the decline in aristocratic incomes, the shape and extent of the struggle were largely determined by the establishment of the Aragonese dynasty itself in 1282. The roots of the crisis lay in the fact that after 1282–90, the Aragonese found it necessary, in order to stabilize their new regime and defend it against Angevin attack, to re-establish a strong feudal military class, by enfeoffing large parts of the demesne and by creating great territorial complexes under the stewardship of counts.[9] The previous ban on sub-infeudation was relaxed, enabling the greater magnates to establish an independent power-base in their counties.[10] Inevitably, the anti-Angevin war strengthened the barons' hand, particularly because the monarchy's attempts to establish the urban demesne as a political counter-weight to the aristocracy were unsuccessful. The monarchy thus had few means of resisting a 'seignieurial reaction' to declining income when it occurred.

From the 1340s, 'nationalist' feelings with a clear economic bent were increasingly expressed in demands to expel 'Catalans' from

[9] Mazzarese Fardella, *Feudi comitali*, pp. 45, 72; *UM*, pp. 797, 807.
[10] Mazzarese Fardella, 'Osservazioni sul suffeudo in Sicilia', 135–8.

royal offices and lands.[11] Between 1348 and 1350, two aristocratic parties (the 'Latins' and the 'Catalans') were formed. Initially these were *ad hoc* coalitions of aristocratic lineages organized around members of the royal family for reasons of legitimacy and prestige. Slowly, however, and increasingly after the death of King Ludovico in 1355, they became independent warlord factions.

By the early 1350s, there had been a process of drastic selection among the greater magnate families, the first and most brutal phase of which occurred during the crisis of the 1330s and 1340s.[12] A situation was reached in which no single contender, lineage or coalition was in a position to achieve total and definitive victory. Even so, it took the aristocracy many years to realize that no single winner was going to emerge, and that long-term losses from warfare and general insecurity outweighed immediate gains (see chapter 3). Attempts were made to reach a peaceful partition of the country among the surviving magnate houses (Chiaromonte, Ventimiglia, Alagona, Peralta, Moncada, Rosso, Aragona, Sclafani). A first truce, drawn up in 1350, lasted only six months; a second agreement, reached on 9 October 1352, was more successful and lasted a full year; but a further ten years were to pass before a final settlement was reached to divide the country's administration on a power-sharing basis. The existence by the 1360s of three or four feudal 'states', loosely organized around the figure of a count, was thus the outcome of decades of selection through military confrontation.

In comparison with internecine conflict, the second kind of response to economic hardship open to the aristocracy, namely attempts to increase demands on subjects, are less well documented. Although there is no doubt that attempts were made to increase feudal dues, and possibly even to re-establish servile relations,[13]

---

[11] *UM*, pp. 805–6.
[12] By the end of this phase, the counts Maletta, Passaneto, Sclafani, Antiochia, Cisario, Palizzi, Prefoglio, Uberti and Monteliano had disappeared (*UM*, p. 807).
[13] Attempts to increase seigneurial rights are known for the late 1330s; see Gregorio, *Considerazioni*, IV, chapter 4, n. 43 (1338); RC 2, fo. 145v (1340). Contemporary records mainly refer to usurpations of land and property; see Cosentino, *Codice diplomatico*, nos. 338–9, 375 (1355–6); RC 8, fo. 203 (1371); RC 12, fo. 153 (1373); G. Silvestri ed., *Tabulario di S. Filippo di Fragalà e di S. Maria di Maniaci*, no. 23 (1391); RC 21, fos. 36v–7v (1392); RC 20, fo. 60rv (1392); RC 27, fo. 38rv (1395). There is, however, little doubt that after 1350 royal jurisdictional dues were intensified by the victorious aristocracy (Barbato ed., *Per la storia di Nicosia*, p. 69 (1392)).

these were probably hard to enforce in the context of existing property relations and power structures.[14] Serfdom had begun to decline from the mid-thirteenth century, and by the early fourteenth century had disappeared almost entirely.[15] Peasant freehold was largely restricted to val Demone. Peasants had the right to move freely to the royal demesne, an important privilege given the demesne's considerable size (in the fifteenth century it included more than half the population, despite major grants to feudal lords). For all these reasons, it must have been well-nigh impossible to control individual mobility, particularly after the Black Death when declining royal power probably tended to increase feudal competition for subjects and labour.

The zero-sum outcome of warfare, and the difficulty of increasing seigneurial exactions, tended to channel feudal energies into establishing control over the royal demesne itself, particularly because this still included the larger part of Sicily's population and resources. Attacks on royal lordship began in the 1340s, or possibly earlier in Palermo,[16] and were completed over a couple of decades. Their main purpose was to appropriate the demesne's fiscal and judicial resources.[17] The process of usurpation intensified after the death of Ludovico and the succession of Federico IV, still a minor, in October 1355, and coincided with an Angevin invasion from the mainland at the instigation of the Chiaromonte faction. As a result, the magnates took definitive control of the higher offices of the

---

[14] See for similar arguments Hilton, *The decline of serfdom in medieval England*, pp. 56–7; Brenner, 'Agrarian roots'.

[15] Sorrenti, *Patrimonio fondiario*, pp. 10–11, with bibliographical references; bastard forms of labour service are recorded for the late fifteenth and early sixteenth centuries (*ibid.*, pp. 49–50). See also this chapter below.

[16] *UM*, pp. 722–3, 816–17.

[17] Mazzarese Fardella, 'L'aristocrazia siciliana nel secolo XIV e i suoi rapporti con le città demaniali: alla ricerca del potere', p. 184, has suggested that the aristocratic offensive was not meant to capture urban resources but was directed against the demesne as a royal institution. In fact, the aristocracy's political motives were barely distinguishable from the economic ones. The only provision of the treaty of 1362 directly concerned with the king specified that he be left with an annual income of 1,000 *onze*, about one tenth of royal income at that time. As Federico put it in 1356, 'aliqui ex nobilibus regni ipsius, non contentis propriis comitatibus et baroniis ac dignitatibus gubernacione et tenuta civitatum et locorum multorum nostri demanii cum amplissima iurisdictione et percepcione reddituum et proventum eorundem, rapacitate seva vorante quesita' (Cosentino ed., *Codice diplomatico*, no. 222).

kingdom, which conferred legitimacy to their actions and enabled them to nominate judges and notaries in the lands they controlled.[18]

Lordship in the demesne was initially established by force, but usurpers made it common practice to give themselves a semblance of legitimacy by donning the office of castellan or war captain (*capitano di guerra*) of the community.[19] As Federico put it, writing on 18 October 1363 to the magnate Francesco Ventimiglia, 'our kingdom has come to such a pass, that it is of far greater import to be captain of a community than justiciar of a province, *maestro razionale* or treasurer of the crown'. 'Despite having turned twenty-one', he wrote,

despite being a father and being near to making another marriage, we have come to such low esteem that life in our kingdom is like living under a commune, in which we have the smallest share ... A life in peace with lord Artale [Alagona] and with all the other [lords] we accept most gratefully; but what use is the barons' peace to us, if we lack our royal justice and dignity, if our great cities and towns are usurped, if our name is invoked but others enjoy the demesne's fruits, and we live in need and are ashamed of our majesty? This seems a hard life to us, all the more that we are now adult and know the way things stand: yet, if everyone knew their limits [as I do], they would render to Caesar the things that are Caesar's and be content with their baronies and benefices.[20]

After the aristocratic offensive and settlement of 1362, magnate *consortia* took complete possession of demesne income, including export rights on grain,[21] increased existing royal dues, and established new seigneurial rights. In 1340, Pietro II had also granted barons the right to raise one quarter of the royal tax assessment (*colletta*) from their subjects for the marriage of a sister or child, paralleling conditions governing royal rights of taxation. The rise in feudal levies, especially in hearth taxes, was thus a continuation of the upward trend in royal taxation during the anti-Angevin wars,

---

[18] da Piazza, *Cronaca*, I, chapter 58.

[19] D'Alessandro, *Politica e società*, pp. 262, 281–2; Mazzarese Fardella, 'L'aristocrazia', pp. 186–8; *UM*, pp. 801–2, Table 184.

[20] Gregorio, *Considerazioni*, V, chapter 1, n. 29. La Lumia, *Studi di storia*, II, p. 534: former demesnial towns petition Queen Maria for 'Catalan' captains.

[21] Giuffrida ed., *Il cartulario della famiglia Alagona di Sicilia. Documenti 1337–1386*, nos. 49–50, 65, 78, 80, 105; Mazzarese Fardella ed., *Tabulario Belmonte*, nos. 26–8, 30, 36; Gregorio, *Considerazioni*, V, chapter 2, n. 20.

the transformation of extraordinary fiscal practices into ordinary ones.[22]

Communities might try to oppose new exactions by force,[23] but in most cases there was little they could do; appealing to the king was useless, for he lacked the authority to challenge baronial power.[24] Rebellion tended, therefore, to break out after the death of one lord and before a new one was installed.[25] Although rebellion against feudal rule is undocumented for the period 1377–1392 when Sicily no longer had a king and government was formally taken over by four 'vicars' (the heads of the main magnate houses), this does not mean that conflict ceased, let alone that harmonious relations based on fealty and obedience prevailed.[26] Agreements drawn up in this period between barons and communities fixing local custom were the outcome of long-standing conflict between the two sides.[27] The frequent demands after the Aragonese reconquest of 1392 to abolish rights exercised by former 'tyrants' indicate how grievous previous conditions had been.[28]

The civil war had the effect of undermining and in the end destroying the monarchy, and of drastically reducing the number of feudal forces in the field. But the aristocracy was unable to

[22] RC 2, fo. 145rv (1340); Starrabba and Tirrito eds., *Assise e consuetudini della terra di Corleone*, pp. 185–6; Gregorio, *Considerazioni*, V, pp. 54–63.

[23] RC 8, fo. 86 for Francavilla (1376, wrongly dated 1364 by Gregorio, *Considerazioni*, V, chapter 2 n. 16).

[24] See Cosentino ed., *Codice diplomatico*, nos. 222, 483, 624, for revolts in the demesne in 1356–8. In a letter of 1375 to Nicosia, the king was forced to admit his helplessness against Manfredi Chiaromonte's usurpation (Barbato ed., *Per la storia di Nicosia*, pp. 65–7).

[25] RC 16, fo. 29 (Avola, 1375); RC 13, fo. 210 (Nicosia, 1375). See also RC 13, fo. 259v (1371) for San Pietro Patti, which is allowed to take over its former lord, Giovanni Oriolis's, possessions in the town's castle.

[26] See Mazzarese Fardella ed., *Tabulario Belmonte*, no. 43 (1396).

[27] The agreements of 1382 between Polizzi and Francesco Ventimiglia are published in Flandina ed., *Statuti di Polizzi*, pp. 259–62, and Mazzarese Fardella ed., *Tabulario Belmonte*, pp. 109–13; they are examined in Mazzarese Fardella, 'L'aristocrazia', pp. 187–8. A. Guarneri, 'Un diploma di grazie e privilegi municipali concessi nel 1393 dai magnifici conti di Peralta alla città di Calatafimi', is examined by Sorrenti, *Patrimonio fondiario*, pp. 25, 29–31, 100–3.

[28] For 1392 see RC 20, fos. 25rv (Castiglione), 46 (Troina), 55v–6 (Caltavuturo), 171rv (Ferla); Barbato ed., *Per la storia di Nicosia*, pp. 69–70; Gregorio, *Considerazioni*, V, chapter 2, n. 25 (Syracuse). Later requests in RC 37, fos. 39v–41 (Noto, 1396); RC 25, fos. 45–6 (Castiglione, 1396); RC 28, fo. 124rv (Terranova, 1397); RC 32, fos. 192–3v (Sutera, 1398); RC 33, fo. 69rv and RC 34, fos. 222v–3 (Mazara, 1398); RC 35, fos. 261v–2 (Alcamo, 1399); RC 39, fos. 71–2 (Agrigento, 1401).

overcome its main weakness, its lack of political legitimacy, which laid it open to attack from without and fissure from within. The magnates always justified their actions as a temporary devolution of royal power during a sovereign's minority; even during the long period of direct baronial rule after 1377, they upheld the fiction that they were acting as 'vicars' of an absent monarch. When such a monarch reappeared, as did Martino I in 1392, the baronage was ideologically defenceless. On the other hand, the partition of sovereignty among the four 'vicars' in 1377 might have seemed the best solution to the recurrent dangers of internecine conflict. In fact, it did nothing to allay the temptation of asserting personal hegemony for, at regular intervals, one of the 'vicars' would seek foreign support to gain the upper hand on the domestic front.[29]

Because of these weaknesses, the most significant long-standing result of the aristocratic offensive against the demesne was, paradoxically, to strengthen urban institutions and to push urban élite groups onto the political stage. I return to this aspect of the crisis below.

Before examining seigneurial action in the fifteenth century, let us look briefly at how the late fourteenth-century crisis affected the structure and reproduction of the aristocracy as a class. To do so, one must bear in mind that a characteristic feature of the medieval aristocracy was its low rate of demographic survival. Because of the demographic, political and economic characteristics of late medieval society, European noble families and lineages did not survive on average much more than a century.[30] In late medieval Sicily, aristocratic instability was particularly intense because of the frequent changes of the ruling dynasty.[31]

The first revolution in feudal membership occurred following the expulsion of the Angevins in 1282 and the arrival of Peter III of Aragon. From c.1290, the new Aragonese dynasty began to establish a strong feudal aristocracy for purposes of military defence and political and social stability; more than seventy-five per cent of the families known to have enjoyed noble status between 1300 and 1340

29 Giunta, *Aragonesi e Catalani*, I, chapter 3.
30 See G. Delille, *Famille et propriété dans le Royaume de Naples (XVe–XIXe siècle)*, p. 30; E. Perroy, 'Social mobility among the French *noblesse* in the later Middle Ages'; Dyer, *Standards of living*, pp. 47–8.
31 Bresc, 'La feudalizzazione in Sicilia dal vassallaggio al potere baronale', pp. 501–41.

were established after 1282.[32] Aristocratic ranks were further depleted during the fourteenth century by plague, and political and economic upheaval. Domestic disruption probably affected the middle and lower end of the feudal hierarchy particularly badly. In other parts of western Europe in this period, the decline of the seigneurial economy and political upheaval initiated a process of polarization between the upper nobility and the petty aristocracy and knights (*milites*).[33] In Sicily, this process may have occurred in a particularly intense form. Knights, who had increased considerably in number after 1282, began to be excluded from the larger urban administrations (Palermo and Messina) from the early fourteenth century under pressure of royal and urban policy, although they continued to play an important role in local politics for some decades thereafter. After 1350, however, previously active *milites* began to disappear from the higher reaches of power.[34] Between 1350 and 1392, approximately thirty per cent of the petty aristocracy died out or was deprived of its status, to be replaced mostly by upwardly mobile judges and notaries.[35]

The knights' difficulties after the mid-fourteenth century were probably due in part to political factors, for the higher aristocracy, which was trying to establish its own following in the royal towns, had little need for men with few of the judicial, administrative and economic skills needed to rule the new possessions, and whose loyalties tended to lie with the monarchy. But knights were most vulnerable in their pocket, for they possessed only uninhabited fiefs and thus could not fall back on seigneurial dues once rents began to fall; they also held little suburban property, the most profitable of all after the 1350s.[36] Finally, the lack of significant institutional barriers to sales of 'feudal' land meant that knights experiencing hardship tended to be unprotected from the pressures of debt.

[32] *UM*, p. 672. Knights were exempted from direct taxation in 1296 (Testa ed., *Capitula*, I, p. 75).
[33] Bois, 'Noblesse et crise des revenus seigneuriavx eu France aux XIVe et XVe siècles: essai d'interprétation', pp. 226–7; P. De Win, 'The lesser nobility of the Burgundian Netherlands', p. 97.
[34] Pispisa, *Messina nel Trecento*, pp. 23–8, 83–97; *UM*, pp. 722–4; Baviera Albanese, 'Studio introduttivo', pp. xxi–xxix.
[35] *UM*, p. 672.
[36] Pispisa, *Messina nel Trecento*, pp. 92–3, 100, 103–5; Bresc, 'Il feudo nella società siciliana medievale', pp. 22–3; *UM*, p. 672.

The aristocracy underwent further major changes following the Aragonese invasion and conquest of 1392–8.[37] The Aragonese succeeded, thanks to superior military force, skilfully divisive political action *vis-à-vis* the baronage, and appeals to anti-seigneurial resentment which had built up among the élite groups of the usurped royal demesne. All of these features, however, could be activated only because of Martino I's claim to dynastic legitimacy (he had married Maria, daughter of Federico IV, and last descendent of the Siculo-Aragonese cadet line).

Both before and immediately after the invasion, the Martins tried to rally the Sicilian aristocracy to their cause. But the latter's unwillingness to respond soon made it clear that little less than a near-total replacement of the higher aristocracy with new, more accountable individuals would give the restored monarchy its needed stability. In various phases between 1392 and 1410, when Martin the Elder died, he and his son accomplished just such a feat. Only 105 of 240 aristocratic families living in the second half of the fourteenth century survived after 1400; since at the same time the number of tenants-in-chief rose to 420, no more than a fourth of the pre-conquest aristocracy survived through the 1390s.[38]

Even so, the Martins' attempt to implant a new feudal and military structure based on the Catalan, Aragonese and Valencian aristocracy that had participated in the Sicilian expedition, was only partly successful. When the most acute phase of conquest ended in 1396, part of the Iberian forces sold its Sicilian benefices and sailed for Spain. Those who stayed behind began to build a more permanent land-base in Sicily, but in so doing, tended inevitably to provoke conflicts of interest and allegiance with the Iberian branch of their families. In the long run, the difficulties arising from divided patrimonial interests and political allegiances were resolved either by abandoning Sicily and returning to Spain after selling all feudal benefices, or by permanently dividing a family's patrimony between its Sicilian and Iberian branches. As a result, much of what had been confiscated by right of conquest and assigned to the invaders found its way back in a few years into Sicilian hands,[39] whereas those

---

[37] This period is examined by Giunta, *Aragonesi e Catalani*, I, chapters 4–5; D'Alessandro, *Politica e società*, pp. 127–60; *UM*, pp. 831–7; Corrao, *Governare un regno*, Part 1.

[38] *UM*, pp. 672, 868. This compares with a rate of substitution of fifty-five per cent for the entire period between 1495 and 1600 (Cancila, 'Distribuzione e gestione', p. 161).

[39] *UM*, p. 833.

individuals who had decided to settle permanently in the island were quite rapidly integrated into the local aristocracy.[40] The original Aragonese contingent was further weakened after the compromise of Caspe of 1412, which sanctioned the rise to the Aragonese throne of the Castilian house of Trastámara. Under Ferdinand I and Alfonso V of Trastámara, the remaining Siculo-Aragonese aristocracy was politically marginalized, and its role was taken up by a new aristocracy, often of Castilian origins.[41]

There were two reasons why the infusion of new aristocratic blood during the Aragonese restoration was unusual compared to earlier similar events. First, the process included a determined royal policy to break up the great territorial complexes, established during the late thirteenth and fourteenth centuries, which had provided the economic and military base for magnate attacks on the crown. Second, the process coincided with a period of profound economic malaise for the aristocracy as a whole, a result of the near-halving of rents over the preceding half century, and of the loss after 1392–8 of a large proportion of substitute income from the royal demesne. We shall see more clearly below that this, in some ways fortuitous, conjuncture of relatively independent political and economic developments provided the crucial impetus for a structural transformation of a 'feudal' into a quasi-absolutist state.

Landlord conditions changed little and very slowly during the fifteenth century. Low population pressure kept rents depressed until at least the 1450s or 1460s. Between 1430 and 1460, the average price of an uninhabited fief rose by about sixteen per cent,[42] but was still ten per cent less than in 1350–99, and a third less than in the decades preceding the Black Death. Rents began to increase in the same period, at first not very fast or enduringly;[43] further increases during the 1450s[44] were followed by a set-back in the early 1460s.[45]

[40] Mineo, 'Egemonia e radicamento', pp. 108–21, and references therein; Bresc, 'Les Gascons en Sicile 1392–1460'.
[41] Mineo, 'Egemonia e radicamento', pp. 121–2; D'Alessandro, 'Per una storia della società siciliana alla fine del Medioevo: feudatari, patrizi, borghesi'.
[42] *UM*, p. 880 n. 64.
[43] RC 71, fo. 279 (Calatabiano, 1437).
[44] For Palermo see De Vio ed., *Privilegia*, pp. 313–24 (1451), 328 (1453); C 2882, fos. 118v–20v (1452); Cancila, *Baroni e popolo*, pp. 18–19. For Tripi and Chiaromonte (under Pietro Gaetani's lordship) see CR 21, fos. 406–7 (1453); C 2875, fos. 80v–1, and Genuardi, *Terre comuni*, pp. 95–7 (1454).
[45] Cancila, *Baroni e popolo*, p. 19.

In many areas – especially in the interior, where demographic recovery was slower and where coastal and foreign demand for grain still had little impact – rents did not increase significantly before the 1480s or even the 1490s.[46] Starting in the 1480s, barons and communities in the interior (Castelvetrano, Cammarata, Petraperzia, Aidone) drew up agreements defining reciprocal rights and obligations which often established higher levels of rent; this was achieved by reducing the size and raising the rent of the standard holding (*aratato*). Elsewhere, like in Castronovo, communities appealed to the government to uphold customary rents,[47] and resistance to landlord pressure seems for a long time to have been successful. The custom that rents be equivalent to the quantity of sown grain was still upheld, implying that at current returns to seed (8–10:1) landowners were receiving no more than ten to twelve per cent of the harvest. On a *masseria* near Racalmuto in 1490–1, rent accounted for barely five per cent of production costs.[48]

Because of its political and economic weakness, after 1400 the aristocracy – which, as we shall see below, was being more narrowly defined as a class possessing lordship over men, rather than simply possessing a fief in chief from the king – was deprived of two possible responses to economic distress which it had successfully adopted in the fourteenth century: warfare, and usurpation of the royal demesne. Instead, it could confront its economic difficulties by intensifying seigneurial pressure, by gaining a share of tax revenues from the state, or by investing in high-profit enterprises.

The main documentary sources for tracing changes in lords' demands are complaints by subject communities to the king against baronial practices. While the number and intensity of such petitions can be taken to reflect changes in seigneurial demands, patterns of dispute also respond in complex ways to changes in the institutions devised for mediating or resolving conflict. In other words, dispute

---

[46] *Ibid.*, pp. 25–6; Cancila, *Impresa redditi*, pp. 12–13. In Trapani, on the other hand, land rent more than doubled between 1454–61 and 1500 (Cancila, *Baroni e popolo*, p. 32).

[47] RC 165, fo. 191rv (Castelvetrano, 1487); CR 75, fos. 49–9quater (Cammarata, 1494); CR 81, fos. 58–64 (Petraperzia, 1498); RC 178, fos. 163v–70 (Castronovo, 1491), Tirrito ed., *Statuto di Castronuovo*, p. 172; V. Cordova, *Le origini della città di Aidone e il suo statuto*, pp. 51–68 (Aidone, 1495). See also Cancila, *Baroni e popolo*, pp. 32–3; Cancila, *Impresa redditi*, pp. 12–13.

[48] *Ibid.*, pp. 12–19; Cancila, *Baroni e popolo*, pp. 25–33, 43, 122. Rents increased four to fivefold between the late fifteenth and the early seventeenth centuries.

settlement tells us nearly as much about the institutions to which disputants could appeal as it does about the sources of conflict themselves. The intensity of litigation between lord and community in the fifteenth century has thus to be set in the context of changes in the extent of royal jurisdiction.[49]

Two main patterns of conflict can be discerned during the fifteenth century. First, conflict was most intense in two clearly-defined periods, between the early 1430s and the mid-to-late 1450s, and between *c*.1490 and the first decade of the sixteenth century.[50] One third of known fifteenth-century disputes over community and seigneurial rights occurred during the 1490s; another half occurred between 1430 and 1459. Second, disputes were very unevenly distributed. From 1430 to the end of the fifteenth century, two fifths of the disputes over rights of jurisdiction occurred in val Demone; between 1430 and 1459, more disputes occurred in val Demone than in the rest of Sicily combined. Conflict in val di Noto, on the other hand, was particularly intense during the 1490s. Finally, disputes in val di Mazara apparently subsided after the 1450s; although conflict flared up again in the west during the 1490s, it was still less intense than in eastern Sicily.

It is possible that the rate of feudal pressure increased after the early fifteenth century because of the decrease of substitute sources of income from the royal demesne, although before 1413 the problem of seigneurial extortion is hardly referred to in local petitions – suggesting either that the Martins were not paying much attention to the problem, or that the new feudal lords were slow to re-establish their predecessors' rights. From about 1414, by contrast, the government began to voice concern about rising seigneurial dues. This development coincided with the arrival of Ferdinand I's Castilian viceroys,[51] and presumably expressed the new sovereign's wish to establish firm authority over Sicily, comparable to Ferdinand's attempts to support the peasant *remença* uprising in Catalonia. Royal concern for feudal oppression was short lived, however, and the issue was dropped for a decade or more. In the mid-1420s, the viceroy Nicola Speciale wrote to King Alfonso about prospects for resuming former demesne lands from the baronage. He suggested dealing with lords individually, because it would be

---

[49] See R. L. Kagan, 'A golden age of litigation: Castile, 1500–1700'.
[50] For the period after 1500 see Trasselli, *Da Ferdinando*.
[51] RC 48, fo. 219rv (1414).

easier to strike good bargains and because of the 'disapproval (*poca contintiza*) in which the populace holds such lordships, especially because some are unduly oppressive, which royal lordship neither is nor ever tends to be'. Speciale, a baron himself, was worried that the barons' 'unusual and unjust oppressions (*gravicii*)' had brought matters to such a pass that it would be hard to avoid revolts by communities which were formerly part of the royal demesne.[52]

Despite such intense popular disaffection, few further complaints against feudal practices were raised during the 1420s.[53] By contrast, between Alfonso's landing in Sicily in May 1432 and his departure for the mainland in April 1435, such complaints multiplied fourfold.[54] Remembering that no titled sovereign had resided stably in Sicily since 1409, one might argue that the increase in complaints was a result of Alfonso's presence in the country. However, it is also clear – from the great increase in community petitions, for example[55] – that for both political and financial reasons, Alfonso was deliberately promoting himself as the supreme arbiter of conflict in the localities.[56] In either case, Alfonso was responsible for bringing to the surface previously submerged conflicts by providing a larger arena for their resolution.

Conflict was not merely becoming more visible. Alfonso's years of Italian rule (1432–58) also coincided with a period of heightened seigneurial pressure, itself a reaction to the unprecedented military and fiscal demands made by Alfonso's wars on the mainland which threatened to deliver a final blow to the aristocracy's already shaky

[52] The island of Gozo had recently rebelled on these grounds (C 2888, fos. 170v–1 (1425–6)).
[53] PR 24, fo. 505v (1421); C 2809, fos. 137v–8 (1423); RC 56, fos. 65v–6 (1425); RC 53, fo. 126, and PR 24, fos. 250v–2 (1425); CS 1, fo. 70v (1427); RC 61, fos. 67v–9 (1429); C 2818, fo. 45 (1431); CS 1, fo. 178v (1431); C 2817, fo. 184rv (1431).
[54] C 2821, fos. 44v, 221 (1432); C 2820, fo. 1rv (1432); C 2818, fos. 142, 152 (1432); RC 68, fos. 62, 64v–5 (1432); RC 68, fos. 143rv, 187rv, 202v–3, 205rv, 209rv (1433); C 2820, fos. 69v, 77–8v (1433); C 2819, fo. 187 (1433); C 2821, fos. 310v–11 (1433); RC 69, fo. 57rv (1433); CS 2, fo. 111 (1433); C 2825, fos. 36v–7 (1434); C 2821, fo. 348 (1434); C 2891, fos. 127v–8, 134, 143–4, 148v (1434); C 2889, fo. 195rv (1434); CR 32, fos. 43–5 (1434); RC 70, fos. 81v–2 (1434); C 2824, fo. 57 (1434), cited in Bresc, 'Les Gascons en Sicile', p. 91; RC 70, fos. 137v–8, 157 (1435); C 2891, fo. 179v (1435).
[55] Epstein, 'Governo centrale', Table 1.
[56] C 2891, fos. 127v–8, 134, 148v (1434): Tortorici must pay a fine of 300 *onze* to repeal the exile to Malta of thirty men who had risen against their lord, Ruggiero Pollicino, and whose rebellion Alfonso considered to be justified; the baron had been sentenced to death for crimes committed against his vassals (C 2889, fo. 195rv, 1434).

economic foundations. Pressure on the great and petty baronage came in the first place from the costs of war. It was still common for barons to recruit and pay their own retinue, and paying ransom could be financially devastating.[57] In January 1438, for example, Giovanni Ventimiglia, marquis of Geraci and one of the greater Sicilian magnates, declaring that he was no longer able to sustain military expenses on the mainland, asked the king for permission to sell or lease his patrimony, for Alfonso, who was himself facing financial difficulties, was unable to help Ventimiglia otherwise.[58] A second source of financial worry came from the unprecedented growth of state taxation. As royal taxation intensified, local opposition to feudal taxes rapidly increased;[59] conversely, resistance to feudal levies weakened after the 1450s in response to a decline in government taxes.[60] Economic convenience thus explains both the barons' initial opposition to royal taxation, and why Alfonso rarely challenged the legitimacy of the feudal direct tax (*colta*).[61] Occasionally, indeed, the government stepped in to uphold a baron's fiscal prerogatives against resistance from subjects.[62]

The barons' onslaught from the 1430s took place on several fronts. In a letter of 16 March 1452 – although his description could easily apply to earlier periods as well – Alfonso summed up feudal activities thus:

[57] *UM*, p. 889, on the lesser baronage.

[58] C 2830, fos. 151–2v. Two years later, Ventimiglia was granted the village of Roccella in perpetuity together with an annual income of 300 *onze* on export dues from its port (C 2836, fos. 147v–9).

[59] C 2821, fos. 44v, 221, and C 2820, fo. 1v (1432); RC 68, fos. 202v–3 (San Marco, 1433); C 2836, fo. 24bis (Ficarra, 1439); RC 79, fos. 126–9v (Mazara, 1443); RC 81, fo. 75 and PR 35, fo. 193 (Galati, 1443); C 2841, fo. 103v (Sclafani, 1443, cited in *UM*, p. 890 n. 125); C 2846, fos. 94v–7 (county of Caltanissetta, 1444); PR 35, fo. 71v (San Fratello, 1445); PR 39, fo. 146v (San Fratello and Isnello, 1447); C 2862, fo. 81rv (San Pietro Patti, 1448); C 2881, fo. 31 (Naro, 1452); RC 95, fos. 260v–1 (Spaccaforno, 1453); C 2876, fo. 118rv (Tripi, 1455). Direct feudal taxation had been resisted before the 1430s, but only insofar as it was considered too harsh rather than because of the principle itself. In 1427, for example, Ferla in val di Noto forced its lord to lower the yearly direct tax from one hundred to seventy *onze* (PR 29, fo. 89, cited in *UM*, p. 890).

[60] Feudal taxes were an accepted part of agreements for new village foundations in the 1480s (La Mantia ed., *I capitoli delle colonie greco-albanesi di Sicilia dei secoli XV e XVI*, pp. 3, 8).

[61] Alfonso challenged a baron's right to tax without royal authorization on an occasion when the king was raising a new *colletta* himself (C 2836, fo. 24bis (1439)).

[62] C 2841, fo. 103v (Sclafani, 1443, cited in *UM*, p. 890 n. 125); PR 39, fo. 146v (Isnello and San Fratello, 1447).

It has come to the notice of the said lord king that . . . some barons of the said kingdom of Sicily have imposed and demanded without legitimate authority in their lands new dues or tolls (*vectigals o cabelles*) . . . They have demanded an oath of fealty from their vassals without the king's permission . . . They force their vassals to pay dues on livestock brought to pasture outside the baron's fiefs and lands, to pay a *tarì* for every *onza* on the merchandise and goods which said vassals wish to export from the kingdom, to pay a rent (*terratge*) on land tilled outside the said fiefs, and furthermore to pay a tax on each head of livestock raised within these fiefs.[63]

Attempts to reintroduce serfdom, including labour dues (*angherie*) and restrictions of personal mobility, had only limited success. Palagonia and Militello consented in 1444 to provide one day's labour per year for each *aratato*; two years later, the abbot of Sant'Angelo di Brolo managed to reintroduce labour dues in that *casale*.[64] The Graeco-Albanian colony of Mezzoiuso agreed in 1501 to supply a day's labour every year in its lord's vineyard.[65] For the most part, seigneurial demands were successfully resisted. Conscripted peasants often had to be paid, as in Savoca in 1437. The attempt by Perruccio Lanza, baron of Ficarra, to re-establish serfdom was foiled by Ficarra's appeal to the king. Lanza's demands were deemed unjust, partly because he requisitioned transport animals without compensation.[66] In response to local petitions, the government repulsed similar baronial attempts in San Fratello, Galati, Aci and Lisico in val Demone,[67] and in Ferla and Francavilla in val di Noto.[68] Elsewhere the government invigilated agreements between communities and their lords, reducing seigneurial

---

[63] C 2896, fos. 100–1v. A review of feudal possessions and rights in 1453 was partly a response to these challenges to royal authority, which for many years had been ignored due to more pressing political issues. See CR 33, throughout; Peri, *Restaurazione e pacifico stato*, chapter 16, n. 3. In 1457, Alfonso passed various pragmatic laws against baronial abuse, but soon after was granting exemptions; see C 2946, fos. 152v–3v.

[64] *UM*, pp. 891–2.

[65] La Mantia ed., *Capitoli delle colonie*, p. 50.

[66] C 2836, fo. 24bis (1439).

[67] C 2818, fo. 142, and RC 68, fos. 62, 64v–5, 209rv (San Fratello, 1432); RC 81, fo. 75, and PR 35, fo. 193 (Galati, 1443); C 2846, fo. 34rv (Aci, 1443); RC 83, fo. 581 (Lisico, 1445).

[68] RC 68, fos. 143rv, 187rv, 205rv (Ferla, 1433); CS 2, fo. 111 (Francavilla, 1433).

dues or abolishing them altogether.[69] Pressure to reintroduce serfdom was most intense in val Demone, and to a somewhat lesser extent in val di Noto, probably because villainage had survived longer in these areas compared to val di Mazara, where it disappeared as a result of the extermination or forced exile of the Muslim population in the early thirteenth century. Since feudal property was also more fragmented in the east, especially in val Demone, the baronage may have faced more intense economic problems there and have consequently reacted more strongly. For the same reasons suggested for the late fourteenth century, however, serfdom was no longer a feasible solution to the lords' economic problems in the fifteenth.

In some cases, attempts to reintroduce serfdom were intended to challenge peasant rights to leave feudal lands without loss of property. Conflict over the issue tended to flare up in periods of high fiscal pressure (for example, 1434–5, 1443), when moving to the demesne could reduce a family's or an individual's tax load considerably. Whereas the crown always upheld the 'ancient custom' (*antiquissima consuetudo*) of free movement into the demesne, its attitude towards peasant property was more ambiguous. During the 1430s, the crown seems to have allowed barons to impound emigrants' property; twenty years later, Alfonso assented to a request by Milazzo that immigrants from feudal lands be allowed to keep their property there, so long as they paid rent and dues (*onera realia*) on them.[70] Such conflicts were more unusual after the 1450s, reflecting a general decline of disputes over seigneurial rights, and less need to check personal mobility because of population growth.[71]

Under the Martins, rights of high and low justice (*mero e misto imperio*) were alienated to feudal lords only exceptionally. By contrast, the sale of these rights became a central element of

---

[69] For San Marco in val Demone see RC 68, fos. 202v–3 (1433); C 2848, fo. 104v (1445), cited in *UM*, p. 891 n. 134.

[70] Peasant allodial property was strongest in eastern Sicily, which explains why attempts to control labour mobility were most intense in that area. For rights of migration to the demesne see RC 35, fo. 133rv (Marsala, 1399); Giardina ed., *Capitoli*, no. 73 (Messina, 1434). The lord's right to impound emigrants' property was accepted in C 2824, fo. 57 (Isnello, 1434); C 2826, fos. 177v–8 (Milazzo, 1435). The latter rights were requested, implying that the issue was not clear cut, by the baron of Aci in 1443 (C 2846, fos. 21v–2); they were refused in Milazzo in 1457 (RC 106, fos. 226–8). See also Table 2.5.

[71] See above, chapter 2, n. 64.

Alfonso's policy in periods of most severe financial pressure. Sales were most intense prior to, and at the height of, Alfonso's military campaigns, in 1420–5, 1430–4 and 1440–6.[72] The concession of independent rights of justice was one of the aristocracy's most significant achievements under Alfonso; by 1458, the baronage exercised such rights in nearly half their lands.[73] *Mero e misto imperio* was revoked and returned to the crown by Juan II in April 1459, soon after his accession, but pressure against this decision was intense, and in early 1460, many concessions were reconfirmed; they were revoked once more in February 1472.[74] Although the right of appeal to central government had been established,[75] in practice *mero e misto imperio* gave barons undisputed control over their subjects.[76] This explains, for example, why rights of justice were sometimes granted in order to repopulate a fief, presumably by compulsion.[77]

A less violent means of increasing feudal revenue was to enforce local trade monopolies and traditional milling and fulling rights. Attempts to set new feudal dues and tolls were frequent,[78] and were seldom challenged.[79] When the government's decision on these matters is known, however, it often conflicted with subjects' interests.[80] Castronovo denounced the 'various rights and

[72] *UM*, p. 895, Table 201.
[73] *UM*, p. 894. For similar developments on the mainland see Ryder, *Kingdom of Naples*, pp. 50–1.
[74] Barberi, *Capibrevi*, I, p. 44; Gregorio, *Considerazioni*, III, pp. 80–1; C 3474, fo. 103rv (1460); C 3487, fo. 122rv (1472). See also RC 116, fos. 173v–4 (1465): *mero e misto imperio* granted to the city of Noto; C 3486, fos. 44–6 (1467). For grants made after the general revocation of 1472 see CR 59, fo. 227rv (1476); CR 61, fos. 163–5v (1477); CR 63, fos. 221–2v (1483); CR 78, fo. 154rv (1496).
[75] Testa ed., *Capitula*, pp. 159–60 (1398).
[76] C 2862, fo. 81rv (San Pietro Patti, 1448).
[77] RC 65, fo. 42 (Siculiana, 1430); C 2863, fo. 32 (Maletta, 1449). See also above, n. 71.
[78] RC 74, fo. 391 (Randazzo, 1439); RC 79, fos. 126–9v (Mazara, 1443).
[79] See C 2835, fo. 26rv (Randazzo against the baron of Castiglione, 1439); C 2836, fo. 24rv (canons of the cathedral of Messina versus the baron of Ficarra, 1439); RC 75, fos. 400v–1 (1440), and C 2839, fo. 200v (1443) (a Messinese citizen versus the baroness of Saponara); C 2894, fo. 25 (the *secrezia* of Palermo versus the baron of Solanto, 1444).
[80] C 2845, fo. 84rv (monopoly of salt ground in the lord's mill in Cammarata, 1444); C 2849, fos. 188v–9, and C 2846, fo. 232v (near-monopoly of milling and fulling rights in the county of Sclafani, 1445–6); C 2860, fo. 32 (permission to raise a toll on transhumant cattle in Petralia Soprana, 1447); *UM*, pp. 890 n. 892. Later examples in RC 183, fo. 278rv, and RC 195, fos. 103–9v (Nicosia, 1492, 1496); La Mantia and La Mantia eds., *Consuetudini di Santa Maria di Licodia*, p. 6 (late fifteenth century).

exactions' which Gastone Moncada, a *miles*, had begun to levy on trade with Cammarata, threatening 'unpleasantnesses' (*incomoda*) if Castronovo did not return immediately to the demesne. Instead of abolishing the tolls, the government ordered that the income from one of them be used to redeem the town from Moncada.[81] Again, Termini and Mistretta asked to abolish tolls set by their former lord only after their return to the demesne, suggesting that they had previously been unable to challenge the tolls.[82] The crown was also unwilling or unable to grant to communities of the demesne toll franchises which included feudal lands.[83]

One form of commercial monopoly with positive economic effects, on the other hand, was the local fair. The moving force behind a request for a new fair was often a baron, whose main interest in the enterprise was for the income from rights of jurisdiction and trade tolls[84] and the commercial opportunities it provided.[85] Some of the barons most cited for their acts of oppression – Pietro Lanza, baron of Ficarra,[86] and Pietro Gaetani, one of the most successful Pisan immigrants to Sicily and baron of Tripi[87] – also showed special interest in new fairs. Many religious institutions set up new fairs during their patron saint's festival.[88]

Alfonso was willing to resist baronial attack against the demesne's customary rights, including rights of hunting and pasture, of transhumance and toll-free trade, whenever the issue was clear

---

[81] C 2818, fo. 45 (1431). Castronovo was redeemed in 1434 in exchange for 4,000 *salme* of wheat (C 2891, fo. 108), and sold again in 1446 (PR 44, fo. 214).

[82] C 2846, fos. 227v–8v (Termini, 1444); CR 31, fos. 171–2v (Mistretta, 1450).

[83] See above, chapter 3. However, an ecclesiastical request in parliament in November 1452 for the *ius dohane* (a tax on trade) on Church lands was not accepted (C 2882, fos. 123–4).

[84] C 3474, fos. 96v–7v (1460): a tax on wine sold at the fair of San Pietro Patti. See also C 2806, fo. 141 (Aci, 1422); PR 38, fo. 98rv (Militello, 1446); C 2864, fos. 8v–9 (Ficarra and Galati, 1450); C 2872, fos. 106v–8, 108v–9 (Tripi and Sant'Andrea, 1452); RC 112, fos. 289v–90v (Roccella, 1463).

[85] The monastery of Sant'Andrea in Piazza establishes a butcher's shop at the fair in Piazza (C 2884, fo. 19v, 1454); the duke of Calabria wants to open three cloth shops at the fair in Lentini (CS 10, fo. 28v, 1456).

[86] C 2864, fos. 8v–9 (1450).

[87] Petralia, *Banchieri*, pp. 182–7; C 2872, fos. 106v–8, 108v–9 (1452).

[88] C 2300, fos. 5v–6 (monastery of San Filippo di Argirò, 1397); RC 46, fos. 183v–5v (bishopric of Patti, 1406); C 2300, fo. 138 (archbishopric of Monreale, 1410); C 2814, fo. 25v (abbey of Santo Spirito, Caltanissetta, 1426); C 2860, fos. 131v–2 (abbey of San Calogero, Augusta, 1448).

cut.[89] Generally, however, the king took a more cautious stance towards disputes involving demesne communities' rights in unpopulated fiefs – the commonest kind of dispute, but also the hardest to resolve, both parties basing their arguments on unrecorded custom. Such cases were usually referred for further investigation to the Magna Regia Curia, the office in charge of the royal fisc and rights of jurisdiction.[90]

One reason why the government might have been unwilling to uphold popular complaints was that the seigneurial dues being challenged had actually existed for some time. The fact that community action was not always purely defensive is suggested by the demand by some barons for royal aid against subjects who were allegedly breaking custom. This was the only situation apart from rebellion in which barons asked for royal aid, presumably because they felt secure in their rights.[91] Frequent changes of lordship and political upheaval made it easier to challenge feudal powers, but so long as these could be documented they tended to be upheld. Carlo de Gravina, baron of Palagonia, asked in 1449 to reintroduce some tolls which had been suspended many years before by his father because of depopulation. The king decided that if the statement was true, or if such tolls were customarily set in Lentini (whose customs Palagonia followed), Gravina's demands should be accepted.[92]

After 1430, conflict between lords and communities intensified mainly for two reasons. Fiscal pressure by the state and seigneurial demands increased rapidly and almost simultaneously; and for a variety of reasons, Alfonso was more anxious than his forebears to give voice to local requests and protests. But even though feudal action was largely defensive and not in the short term very

---

[89] Noto against the barons of Ragusa, Avola, Palazzolo (RC 46, fos. 405v–6, 1407); Castrogiovanni against local lords (RC 56, fos. 65v–6, 1425); Patti against the baron of Oliveri (RC 53, fo. 126, and PR 24, fos. 250v–2, 1425); Mistretta and Capizzi against barons who raid their transhumant herds (C 2882, fos. 172–3, 1453).

[90] RC 61, fos. 67v–9 (Agrigento, 1429); RC 70, fos. 81v–2 (Polizzi, 1434); C 2891, fos. 143–4 (Piazza, 1434); C 2831, fo. 84rv (Francavilla, 1438); C 2835, fo. 26rv (Randazzo, 1439); RC 75, fo. 395 (Monte San Giuliano, 1440); RC 83, fos. 216v–17v (Gioiosa Guardia, 1444); Giardina ed., *Capitoli*, no. 88 (Messina, 1451); C 2871, fos. 119v–21 (Polizzi, 1452); C 2882, fos. 107v–9 (Piazza, 1452); C 3472, fo. 128 (the baron of Favara against Noto, 1459).

[91] C 2838, fos. 182v–3 (Isnello, 1442); C 2854, fo. 150v (Calatabiano, 1446); C 2860, fo. 32 (Petralia Soprana, 1447).

[92] C 2861, fos. 115v–16.

successful, its cumulative effect had a more positive outcome. Alfonso was compelled by military needs on the mainland to take seriously aristocratic needs and complaints. By curbing and regulating feudal excesses, he legitimized the basis of aristocratic power, the right to levy customary or arbitrary dues, and to exercise low (and sometimes high) justice. In its moment of greatest weakness, the aristocracy was setting the basis of future strength.

After Alfonso's death in 1458, conflict over seigneurial rights did not cease, but for a long time it was much muted.[93] Disputes over feudal taxes are noticeable for their absence;[94] more generally, there were few complaints against new seigneurial dues, tolls and impositions.[95] The muting of conflict may have been partly induced by a royal decree of 1460 which banned assemblies by feudal communities held without the lord's permission,[96] but its main cause was probably a lowering of feudal pressure as a result of rising population.

During the 1490s, disputes over seigneurial and community rights intensified abruptly. Litigation became very popular, and the Magna Regia Curia was flooded with requests to cite barons in court and protect community representatives against reprisal.[97]

---

[93] C 3473, fos. 88–9 (San Pietro di Raccuia, 1459); C 3472, fo. 128 (Favara, 1459); LV 80, fos. 259v–60 (Tortorici, 1461); RC 109, fo. 308rv (Castania, 1461); Sciacca, *Patti*, pp. 308–9, 311–12 (Patti, 1463); RC 125, fos. 249v–50 and CR 50, fo. 246rv (Randazzo, 1470); RC 126, fo. 246 (Regalbuto, 1472); RC 127, fos. 382–4 (Santo Stefano, 1472); Starrabba ed., *Diplomi della Cattedrale di Messina*, no. 295 (Alcara, 1473); RC 128, fos. 301v–3, and CR 54, fos. 107–8 (Agrigento, 1473); RC 137, fos. 188v–9v (San Fratello, 1476); C 3492, fos. 67v–8v (Sutera, 1477); RC 139, fos. 378v–9 (Ucria, 1478); RC 141, fos. 313v–14 (Regalbuto, 1479); *UM*, p. 891 (Gagliano, 1480); CR 69, fos. 51–2, and RC 152, fo. 38rv (San Mauro, 1482–3); RC 157, fos. 74rv, 368v–9v (Caltagirone, 1485); Gaudioso, *Questione demaniale*, pp. 35, 41 (Catania, 1485–8); RC 154, fo. 420v, and RC 160, fos. 540–1, 561v–2v (Castania, 1485–6); RC 171, fo. 461 (Castania, 1488); CR 73, fo. 339rv (Palazzolo, 1489); Gaudioso, *Sicilia feudale. La questione feudale in Francofonte*, pp. 138–9 (Francofonte, 1489).

[94] RC 165, fo. 191rv (Castelvetrano, 1487).

[95] CR 50, fo. 161 (Fiumedinisi, 1469); RC 128, fos. 309–10v (Sutera, 1472); RC 160, fos. 372–3 (Francofonte and Passaneto, 1486).

[96] Testa ed., *Capitula*, I, p. 464 (1460).

[97] CR 73, fos. 439–40, 473rv – RC 175, fos. 435v–7v – RC 178, fos. 155v–6 – RC 187, fo. 266rv (Ferla, 1490–1, 1493); RC 180, fos. 332v–3v – CR 74, fo. 93rv – RC 183, fo. 279rv (Buccheri, 1492); CR 74, fo. 104rv (Novara, 1492); RC 185, fos. 243–4v (Ficarra, 1493); CR 77, fos. 369–70 (Petraperzia, 1494); CR 77, fos. 483–4, 485–6 (Tortorici, 1495); RC 195, fos. 294–5 – CR 79, fos. 227–7bis

Disputes seem to have concerned mainly royal taxes and rights of jurisdiction, issues which for the previous thirty years had nearly disappeared from the records.[98] What caused this sudden change? I mentioned above that anti-seigneurial conflict was more intense in eastern Sicily – in val Demone under Alfonso, in val Demone and val di Noto thirty years later – than in the west. During the 1490s, all disputes around taxation, for example, occurred in val Demone (Ficarra, Geraci, Castania) and val di Noto (Ferla, Buccheri). Trasselli has suggested that the distribution of conflict during the late fifteenth century reflects eastern Sicily's economic dynamism, in particular the rapid development of wine and silk production, compared to val di Mazara where no major economic changes were occurring. In this picture, anti-seigneurial conflict was the result of social mobility, itself the consequence of rapid economic growth.[99]

For all its attractive simplicity, this explanation raises some objections. First, whereas the economy in val di Mazara was not changing as significantly as in eastern Sicily, this *vallo*'s share of total population was stable or slightly increasing during the last quarter of the fifteenth century, suggesting that its economy was not lagging very far behind; in val di Noto, by contrast, the population was growing more slowly than the regional average (see chapter 2). Second, Trasselli's model would predict intense conflict during the 1460s and 1470s, when demographic growth was at its height; but lord–peasant relations appear to have been remarkably peaceful at the time. Finally, his explanation does not account for the fact that conflict of a similar kind in the same areas had been particularly intense during a period of comparative demo-economic stagnation half a century before.

(Castania, 1496–7); RC 192, fos. 230v–2 (Randazzo, 1496); CR 80, fos. 168–8bis (Partanna, 1497); CR 79, fos. 217–17bisv (Ferla, 1497); CR 80, fos. 177–7bis (Galati, 1498); CR 83, fos. 290–1 (Petraperzia, 1498); CR 80, fos. 178–8bis (Buscemi, 1498); CR 83, fos. 371–2, 405–5bis (Cammarata, 1499); CR 83, fo. 349rv – RC 200, fos. 254v–5v (Burgio, 1499); CR 83, fo. 367rv (Gagliano, 1499); RC 182, fos. 151–2 (Gangi, 1499). A few cases were brought against a baron before 1490. See RC 109, fo. 308rv (Castania, 1461); RC 126, fo. 246 (Regalbuto, 1471); RC 139, fos. 378v–9 (Ucria, 1478); RC 154, fo. 420v – RC 160, fos. 561v–2v – RC 171, fo. 461 (Castania, 1485–6, 1488).

[98] RC 175, fos. 435v–7v (Ferla, 1490); RC 180, fos. 332v–3v (Buccheri, 1492); RC 185, fos. 243–4v (Ficarra, 1493); RC 184, fos. 290–1 (Aidone, 1493), 295rv (Geraci, 1493); RC 195, fos. 294–5 (Castania, 1496); CR 79, fos. 217–17bisv (Ferla, 1497).

[99] Trasselli, *Da Ferdinando*, pp. 488–9.

In slightly modified form, the reasons I gave for intensified conflict during the 1430s apply also to the late fifteenth century. From the late 1480s, fiscal demands by the Spanish state began again to grow in response to the increasing Turkish threat; the Turks attacked Malta, Gozo and Pantelleria in 1488.[100] We do not know whether military demands weighed as heavily on the aristocracy as they had half a century before; aristocrats certainly saw the war against the Turks as a profitable enterprise.[101] Higher taxes coincided with an economic slump. Two good harvests, in 1491 and 1492, were followed by a series of bad years.[102] Western Sicily suffered a long period of drought that contributed to the crisis in the sugar industry (see chapter 4). In 1491, the largest Sicilian bank, owned by a former Pisan, Pietro Agliata, failed.[103] In 1492–3, the Jews were expelled, contributing to general disarray, both because this deprived Sicily of many entrepreneurs and artisans, and because the Jews had to pay a 20,000 *onze* fine – a sum the whole of Sicily normally paid as tax in three years – and a 1,000 *onze* 'gift' to the viceroy before leaving, a drain on domestic financial resources which was all the more severe for occurring over such a short time-span.[104]

At the same time, Ferdinand initiated a policy similar to that which he had embarked upon in Spain, based on more active intervention in local administration and a more anti-aristocratic stance. This policy culminated in the early sixteenth century in a review of all feudal rights and titles,[105] but signs of the sovereign's changing attitude appeared from the late 1480s. Thus, for example, the viceroy's office became from 1489 a three-year, non-renewable position so as to make it less open to political manipulation. The promotion of litigation against feudal lords and the protection of local communities, which became so common from the 1490s,[106]

---

[100] Parliament voted a *donativo* of 100,000 Aragonese florins over three years in 1488 (Testa ed., *Capitula*, I, p. 525); for grants of 100,000 Aragonese florins in three years in 1494 and 200,000 Aragonese florins in three years in 1499 see Di Martino, 'Sistema tributario', 113. In 1503, possibly because of the results of the census of 1501, the tax rate rose to 300,000 Aragonese florins in three years (Testa ed., *Capitula*, I, pp. 533–4).

[101] Francesco Ventimiglia practised piracy on the North African coast with two ships (CR 71, fo. 191rv (1491)).

[102] Trasselli, 'Siccità in Sicilia'.

[103] Petralia, *Banchieri*, p. 112.

[104] Peri, *Restaurazione e pacifico stato*, chapter 13.

[105] Barberi, *Liber de secretiis*, Introduction.

[106] Trasselli, *Da Ferdinando*, chapter 8.

were another aspect of these new royal policies, which may have
been adopted under the influence and fear of the last great revolt of
the Catalan peasant *remença* in the 1480s. The rapid increase of
local petitions during the 1490s, is a further indication that conditions for the settlement of disputes were changing both in the
periphery and within central government itself.[107]

Social conflict, therefore, appears to have increased at a time of
economic stagnation, or even contraction, rather than expansion as
Trasselli argued. Nonetheless, Trasselli's explanation stands, insofar as economic hardship followed a long period of growth, which
must have increased social mobility and individual expectations and
contributed to anti-seigneurial resentment. There were, however,
further, possibly more significant, sources of conflict in this period.
Some, which emanated from the state – a strong increase in taxation
and a greater willingness by the government to give vent to local
grievances – do not account for the geographical distribution of
conflict. The latter was probably the result of a peculiar combination of circumstances in eastern Sicily and especially in val Demone: stronger peasant resistance because of the greater strength of
freehold, and more intense seigneurial pressure on subject populations because of aristocratic poverty (fiefs were smaller in the east
and did not include large urban centres as in parts of val di Mazara
and val di Noto).

Another strategy that began to be pursued after the Aragonese
restoration was for the aristocracy to supplement its income with
revenues from the state. This phenomenon was in many ways an
inevitable, though largely unforeseen, development of events after
1350. While feudal occupation of the demesne during the fourteenth century had cushioned the impact of declining revenues by
redistributing royal income among the aristocracy, the Martins,
followed more deliberately by Alfonso, transformed this mechanism into a powerful instrument of state policy and social
stabilization.

Aragonese political strategy during and following the conquest
was eminently 'feudal'. Like their forebears in the 1280s and 1290s,
the Martins' actions were shaped by their need to establish a strong

107 Epstein, 'Governo centrale', Table 1.

and loyal military presence in Sicily. Although the Martins were anxious to curb some of the *de facto* and *de iure* powers, such as extensive rights of sub-infeudation, which their predecessors had alienated to the aristocracy,[108] such actions did not affect the basic thrust of their policy, which was to establish a strong feudal backbone capable of providing military service to the king. The traditionally 'feudal' functions assigned to the new Iberian aristocratic establishment were, for example, expressed in the distinction, prevailing under Martino I, between governmental (political) and administrative personnel: the former were invariably of Iberian origin, the latter generally Sicilian.[109]

The Martins' policy was expressed also in their initial attitude towards the royal demesne. A crucial aspect of the invasion of 1392 had been, of course, the successful recuperation of royal prerogatives and rights over the demesne and over direct and indirect taxation. Not only military garrisons and court expenses had to be paid out of these revenues, but perhaps more importantly, political and military stability depended on a powerful and loyal demesne to balance against the aristocracy. The Aragonese invasion would undoubtedly have failed had the demesne not rallied to the invaders, on the agreement that it would return under royal authority once the conflict was ended. These needs and responsibilities with respect to the demesne, however, had for the first time to be set againt other, equally pressing considerations. Due to the fall in population and rents, a new feudal aristocracy could not be established sufficiently securely on the basis solely of lands and prerogatives of uncontroversial feudal status (that is, on the basis solely of those that had not been usurped during the fourteenth century). In order to strengthen the military foundations of the kingdom, parts of what was *de jure* the demesne had to be granted feudal status,[110] and the Martins made sure that feudal possession of confiscated property was granted full legal title.[111] At the same time, resources from the demesne began to be channelled

---

[108] Mazzarese Fardella, 'Osservazioni sul suffeudo', 153–5.
[109] Corrao, *Governare un regno*, pp. 106–11; Mineo, 'Egemonia e radicamento', pp. 101–3.
[110] *Ibid.*, p. 105.
[111] Testa ed., *Capitula*, I, pp. 160 (1395), 167 (1400); Starrabba, 'Documenti riguardanti la Sicilia', 172–3.

increasingly towards the aristocracy in order to support its faltering income from the land.

These decisions have been interpreted as a sign of royal weakness and of the need to compromise with an overly powerful aristocracy. It is a view that finds support in a letter by Martin of Aragon from Barcelona to his son in Sicily, enjoining him to act with determination to recover all alienated rights in the demesne. The young king answered that such a policy would be 'a most grievous thing . . . nearly unbearable by Sicilians and Catalans alike'. In order to avoid open rebellion, it would seem, the crown was forced to concede prerogatives it would otherwise have reasserted.[112]

At one level this interpretation is correct. There is little doubt that the process of alienation of demesne property and rights worried the monarchy, which tried to stem it insofar as this did not endanger political stability. We shall see below that the problem of balancing the budget against constantly increasing aristocratic and other claims was particularly severe throughout the first half of the fifteenth century. At another level, however, the view that Aragonese concessions signalled the defeat of an otherwise radical policy of royal restoration is deeply misleading.

The economic pressures which had helped provoke civil war and the attack on the monarchy during the mid-fourteenth century had not abated half a century later. Indeed, demographic collapse – the demographic nadir was reached towards 1400–10 – may have increased feudal difficulties at the height of the Aragonese restoration of 1392–1410, and resources from the royal demesne became correspondingly more important to the aristocracy. As Martino I pointed out to his father, had the monarchy applied strict criteria for recovering the demesne, it would have endangered the class upon which its own military and political authority mainly rested. To view royal grants to the aristocracy as dictated by political timidity or weakness diverts attention from the most significant aspect of Aragonese restoration, namely the failure, *despite* both the monarchy's and the aristocracy's aspirations to the contrary, to re-establish a feudal state. Because of this failure, the aristocracy came increasingly to depend on resources channelled to it by the sovereign, and the king's legitimacy and strength came increasingly to depend on his

---

[112] *Ibid.*, 167 (July 1400).

ability to appropriate and redirect such resources to the aristocracy and to other social groups.

This decisive institutional shift from a feudal to a proto-absolutist monarchy was not, therefore, the result of a deliberate royal strategy to subdue the aristocracy by making it functionally dependent on resources allocated by the state. Insofar as such dependence emerged in this period it was unforeseen, a consequence of the fact that in the early fifteenth century, feudal landed income was insufficient for the baronage to fulfil its customary social and military functions. On the other hand, the crown's systematic and unprecedented use of demesne property and income for financial and political purposes was aided by the fact that the new fifteenth-century aristocracy (both Iberian and Sicilian) possessed few political and economic resources besides what it drew from its loyalty to the king. There was little danger of an independent baronage undermining the monarchy from within, as had happened a century earlier.

How did feudal dependence on state revenues actually emerge? Before the 1390s, apanages or grants on royal income had been insignificant. We saw in chapter 6, for example, that free export rights for grain had been granted for centuries, but not until the invasion of 1392–8 did they become a linchpin of government policy. While making basically indiscriminate and unchecked use of *tratte* on grain, however, the new Aragonese regime was initially more cautious as regards other sources of income from the demesne, both from indirect taxation and from local administrative offices.

Writing to his son in Sicily in 1400, Martin of Aragon outlined a model annual budget for the Sicilian government, based on a minimum income of 90,000 Aragonese florins. One third was to be used for the upkeep of the royal court, 10,000 florins for the maintenance of castles and their garrisons, 48,000 florins to pay for 200 foreign and 100 Sicilian soldiers (the core of a permanent army), leaving 2,000 florins for unforeseen expenses. All 'grants, donations and concessions' were to be made on royal income over and above such basic needs, with the exception of grants of income made to Sicilians during the recent war which were to be honoured in all cases; if a person had been given a barony, fief or other piece of property together with a grant of income (annual pensions, tax exemptions and concessions), the latter was to be revoked if it earned less than a third more than the land.[113] Nonetheless, by setting the precedent of using demesne resources to pay off political debt, this apparently rigorous strategy to recover the demesne was doomed to failure. From the 1420s, Alfonso departed from his predecessors' caution. As far as the aristocracy was concerned, this king's financial policies probably benefited it considerably more than those of any other fifteenth-century monarch. Alfonso made two major changes of policy which were particularly favourable to the baronage. First, he seems to have effected a nearly complete transformation of grants of free export rights on grain (*tratte*) into pensions charged on tax revenues from the grain trade.[114] This development lowered transactions costs for individual beneficiaries (who no longer had to search for buyers for their free *tratte*), benefited the population at large (by reducing incentives for the recipients of pensions to export abroad at times of dearth), and shifted onto government the financial burden of finding a substitute source of income if the grain trade slackened. Second, Alfonso made far more extensive use than his predecessors of the demesne itself to finance his activities on the mainland – by pawning or selling rights of justice, offices and entire towns to the aristocracy, higher bureaucracy and civic nobility;[115] by supporting the ransom of these rights so as to sell them off again; by raising loans from the demesne which were not always repaid; and by pawning the proceeds of a particular tax or whole tax offices (*secrezie*). The financial records of his reign are so hopelessly confused that it may never be possible fully to evaluate the volume of resources that he mobilized in this way, but there is little doubt of its very considerable size.[116]

The outcome of this financial strategy, which was in many ways a

[113] *Ibid.*, 167–9 (1400). This budget substituted one of 1398 of 70,000 Aragonese florins, in which the court's apanage was set at 12,000 Aragonese florins (Testa ed., *Capitula*, I, p. 133).
[114] See CR 1062, throughout.
[115] I employ the term 'civic nobility' (for which see Gaudioso, 'Genesi e aspetti della "nobiltà civica" in Catania nel secolo XV') or 'urban aristocracy', rather than 'patriciate', for the reasons adduced by D. Marrara, 'Nobiltà civica e patriziato: una distinzione terminologica nel pensiero di alcuni autori italiani nell'età moderna'.
[116] Alfonso inaugurated this policy in 1420. He wrote to the viceroys that they should solicit loans from 'barons cavallers e gentils homens', giving any kind of state income as surety (C 2888, fo. 15). See *UM*, pp. 856–8, Table 194, for a partial summary of transactions involving the demesne in this period. For communities repeatedly pawned or sold see above, n. 81; C 2831, fos. 26v–7 (1437) and C 2833, fos. 116–24 (1440) (Salemi). Towns were also encouraged to offer

response to the constraints on direct taxation faced by the king, was to transform the state irreversibly into an indispensable source of révenue for the aristocracy, and at the same time to strengthen aristocratic claims to seigneurial and jurisdictional rights over subject communities. The result of this stabilization of aristocratic rights, in turn, was considerably to increase subject exploitation, as reflected in the frequency of revolts by demesne towns against (temporary) lords,[117] or even against the prospect of being enfeoffed,[118] and conversely in the strong aristocratic resistance to returning such property and powers to the crown.[119]

These social and institutional changes had two further results. By contrast with the fourteenth century, aristocratic opposition to the monarchy during the fifteenth century was insignificant. Between the civil war of 1410–12 and 1516–22, there was no major conflict between crown and baronage.[120] Major revolts during the fifteenth century were confined to the demesne – a sign of certain far-reaching changes in social and political structure which I discuss below. The rapid and painless marginalization of much of the newly-established Aragonese aristocracy by Ferdinand I after 1413,[121] also shows how weak the Sicilian aristocracy had become compared to its fourteenth-century forebears. By the early fifteenth century, the aristocracy had lost its economic independence and with it the power to make and unmake kings.

---

money to the king to avoid alienation. See C 2890, fo. 110v (Monte San Giuliano for 150 *onze*, 1437); C 2893, fo. 106 (Trapani for 100 *onze*, 1441). For loans see RC 54, fos. 38, 395v–7, 493v–4, 510rv (1422–3); RC 56, fos. 144–5, and RC 57, fos. 195v–6 (1426); RC 59, fo. 48rv (1427); RC 65, fos. 104–5 (1430); Trasselli, 'Debito pubblico', 81 (1435, 1437); RC 75, fos. 335v–6 (1440). For royal default on debts see Giardina ed., *Capitoli*, nos. 78 (1437), 81 (1440).

[117] RC 49, fos. 165v–8v (Alcamo, 1414); RC 50, fo. 38rv (San Fratello, 1415); RC 55, fos. 467v–8v (county of Modica, 1424); RC 83, fos. 452–7v (Castrogiovanni, 1445); C 2860, fos. 27v–8 (Corleone, 1447); *UM*, p. 894. Even the *Camera reginale* was not spared revolts against the queen's lordship. See *UM*, p. 894, n. 150 (1448); Privitera, *Storia di Siracusa*, II, pp. 125–6 (1459).

[118] C 2888, fos. 168v–9v (Castrogiovanni and Nicosia, 1426); *UM*, p. 893.

[119] RC 68, fo. 165rv (Mazara, 1433); C 2859, fos. 24v–5, 26v–7, and C 2892, fo. 30vter (Capizzi and Mistretta, 1447); C 2859, fos. 114v–15 (San Pietro Patti, 1448).

[120] The only major rebellion was led by Antonio Centelles, marquis of Geraci and Crotone. Significantly, Centelles' revolt occurred in his lands in Calabria rather than in Sicily. See C 2851, fos. 1–3v (1 December 1444), 4–7 (5 January 1445); Pontieri, *Calabria*; below, n. 294.

[121] Above, n. 41.

Table 7.1 *Sales of feudal land, 1300–1509*

	Uninhabited fiefs	Inhabited fiefs
1300–89	24	3
1390–1409	46	13
1410–19	8	—
1420–59	44	16
1460–79	9	6
1480–1509	56	13

Source: UM, p. 874, Table 196.

Moreover, as a result of the aristocracy's increasing dependence on the state, mechanisms of promotion to lesser and higher noble status changed considerably. In the course of the fourteenth century, a feudal land market had slowly been established (see Table 7.1). Access to this market changed over time, from being governed by social status to being simply a matter of having disposable capital (see chapter 4). As a result of this development, and of simultaneous social and political changes, it became increasingly easier for fiefs to be bought with wealth accumulated through administrative office and economic entrepreneurship. Changes in the social origins of the buyers of fiefs reveal these shifts very clearly.[122] Before 1390, seventy-three per cent of fiefs coming on the market were traded between members of the higher or lower aristocracy; fifteen per cent were bought by lawyers and individuals in charge of public administration; and only twelve per cent were bought by merchants or members of the urban oligarchy. After 1390, only forty-two per cent of fiefs were traded among members of the aristocracy; lawyers, judges and public administrators increased their share slightly to about seventeen per cent; merchants retained their share of the market (nine per cent) – but also bought the largest number of *inhabited* fiefs with the exception of the upper aristocracy, probably because they could best command the necessary capital. It was members of the urban oligarchy who took up most of the aristocracy's losses, however, buying nearly thirty-two per cent of the fiefs on sale compared to less than three per cent before 1390.

[122] *UM*, pp. 874–5, Tables 196–7. Table 197 ('Les acheteurs des biens féodaux') provides aggregate figures for two periods only, 1300–90 and 1390–1460, and cannot be compared with Table 196 ('Les aliénations des fiefs (1300–1509)'), which presents (different) figures by decade.

The disappearance of legal barriers to buying feudal property caused the emergence of a new definition of the aristocracy, based on the possession of *inhabited* lands. This new concept was enshrined in the parliament of 1452, where for the first time membership in the *braccio militare*, the feudal arm of parliament, was restricted to the possessors of *feudi nobili* (inhabited fiefs) rather than to all direct vassals of the king as had formerly been the case. Nobility could no longer be achieved by buying an agricultural fief (*feudo piano*), possession of which had previously defined the condition of a knight. The decision of 1452 virtually decreed the end of the *milites* as a distinctive group;[123] their role was taken up by the civic nobility, whose members owned an increasing proportion of *feudi piani*, and who began in the same period to define themselves as *nobiles*. One of the most significant results of the Aragonese reconquest, and of the institutional changes it brought about, was thus to give vent to the pent-up energies and ambitions of urban élite groups and to provide them with new sources of social legitimacy. I return to this issue below.

We saw that another way in which the aristocracy could respond to declining incomes was by investing in the new economic opportunities that arose after the mid-fourteenth century. To what extent was this strategy pursued?

There is evidence suggesting that the aristocracy responded less effectively than other classes to economic change during the latter half of the fourteenth century. Lucia Sorrenti has suggested that the kind of estate management that prevailed until the mid-fifteenth century was similar to that outlined in Francesco Ventimiglia's accounts of the 1320s: a patrimony administered by a head bailiff (*magister procurator*), who leased the land to farmers (*massari*), shepherds (*curatoli*), and wage-labourers.[124] In fact, although this kind of direct administration may have been quite common during the early fourteenth century (and on the larger feudal estates possibly somewhat later), there is little evidence that it was much practised after 1350, and even less for the years after 1400. There was instead an increasing tendency to lease individual *masserie* or

---

[123] In Messina, however, the figure of the *cavaliere* re-surfaces in the 1450s (PR 42, fos. 37v–40 (1450); Giardina ed., *Capitoli*, no. 88 (1451)).

[124] Sorrenti, *Patrimonio fondiario*, pp. 30–1, 36.

entire fiefs to rural or urban entrepreneurs, who either organized cultivation themselves or sub-let the land to others.[125] As occurred elsewhere in Europe, after the 1350s the higher aristocracy in Sicily seems to have abandoned direct estate management; most aristocrats who invested directly in *masserie* were *milites*.[126]

The baronage was probably more interested in raising livestock, which was generally more profitable than grain production and required less active supervision. Even in this sector, however, the aristocracy lost ground after the mid-fourteenth century to more enterprising individuals from other classes. Before 1400, there was also little aristocractic investment in the two other most profitable activities, tunny fishing and the sugar industry in Palermo (see chapter 4). The crisis of the lesser aristocracy in the same period is a further sign of serious economic hardship. Between 1350 and 1400, the higher aristocracy appears to have invested more heavily in suburban orchards and vineyards, in taverns and in urban estates;[127] but viticulture was dominated by urban smallholders and, increasingly in the fifteenth century, by urban noblemen.

For some decades after 1400, perhaps because the return of the demesne under royal authority put greater economic pressure on the aristocracy, we find them taking the initiative in establishing the sugar industry, both in western Sicily outside Palermo[128] and in the east; in val Demone and val di Noto barons dominated the industry until the 1450s (see chapter 4). Declining feudal interest in sugar manufacture after 1460 coincided with the slow recovery of rents and rights of jurisdiction as a result of demographic growth. Taken together with the evidence surveyed above, this suggests that the aristocracy, while not entirely disregarding new economic initiatives, devoted most of its energies to defending or expanding traditional and more recent feudal rights and apanages. It could also, however, use these rights for a positive economic purpose, as is demonstrated by the many new village foundations the aristocracy successfully promoted from the 1460s (see Table 2.6). The long decline of land rents and their very slow recovery during the fifteenth century did little to allay the barons' difficulties. Trasselli has

[125] *UM*, pp. 108–12; Sorrenti, *Patrimonio fondiario*, pp. 50–3, dates this development to after 1450.
[126] *UM*, pp. 109–10, Table 10.
[127] *UM*, pp. 679 (Table 171), 820–1 (Table 189).
[128] *UM*, p. 232, Table 34.

suggested that the baronage faced a severe crisis during the reign of Ferdinand II,[129] and the rapid increase of sales of feudal estates after 1480 seems to bear out this hypothesis (see Table 7.1). However, since rents had begun to increase at the same time, the barons probably enjoyed better overall economic conditions than in earlier periods.

As argued above and in more detail below, fifteenth-century political and institutional developments were generally unfavourable to the aristocracy, reflecting its economic weakness and its lessened role in the political balance of the country. In 1511, an anti-Spanish revolt in Palermo was repressed thanks to aristocratic intervention; in 1514, Ferdinand's attempt to revoke feudal titles was successfully resisted in parliament; in 1515, the aristocracy demanded that *mero e misto imperio* be granted throughout its lands; from Ferdinand's death in 1516 until 1523, there was a series of greater and lesser aristocratic rebellions. All of this amounted to a massive aristocratic reaction to a century of relative decline, a reaction deriving as much from new confidence based on rapid economic improvement as from the perception of the new political opportunities which Charles V's accession entailed.[130]

URBAN SOCIETY

After 1282, James II and especially Federico III had attempted to strengthen the institutional role of demesne towns in Sicily on the Catalan parliamentary model, in order to balance the powers of the aristocracy,[131] establish wider political consensus, and provide additional financial support for the anti-Guelph conflict.[132] This policy had little success. The aristocracy was still economically

---

[129] Trasselli, *Da Ferdinando*, chapter 7.
[130] Baviera Albanese, 'Sulla rivolta del 1516 in Sicilia'; Baviera Albanese, 'La Sicilia tra regime pattizio e assolutismo monarchico agli inizi del secolo XVI'; Trasselli, *Da Ferdinando*, chapters 9–12.
[131] D'Alessandro, *Politica e società*, pp. 37–68; *UM*, pp. 715–17. See also Gaudioso, *Natura giuridica delle autonomie cittadine nel 'Regnum Sicilie'*.
[132] For example, Federico III forbade barons and *milites* from interfering with the election of local demesne officials in 1296 (Testa ed., *Capitula*, p. 75); he repeated the order for Palermo in 1321 (De Vio ed., *Privilegia*, p. 80). Pietro II intervened again in Palermo in 1339 (Corrao, *Governare un regno*, p. 51, n. 43).

independent of royal patronage but was militarily indispensable, for the king did not have the resources to raise a non-feudal, standing army. By contrast, cities were in the short term more susceptible than the aristocracy to the economic effects of prolonged warfare. The monarchy also had little to offer urban élite groups in exchange for their support, besides some further autonomy in local government,[133] toll franchises (see chapter 3), and more extensive usage rights in the demesne itself. Even more significantly, however, urban society before the early fifteenth century (with the possible exception of Messina) seems to have been politically and institutionally unstructured and informal.

The seeming informality, even incoherence of urban social structures in this period – despite a very high rate of urbanization (see chapter 3) – clearly distinguishes late medieval Sicilian society from that of central and northern Italy and of other lands in the western Mediterranean such as Catalonia or Provence. Even in the kingdom of Naples, which shared a common institutional framework with Sicily for over two centuries, a more structured communal life – centred around the social and political conflict between *nobiles* and *popolo* – existed already in the first half of the fourteenth century, nearly a century earlier than in Sicily.[134]

These characteristics of Sicilian urban life have not attracted much attention, however, so I can do little more than speculate on some reasons why they might have prevailed. It is tempting to point to the similarities between late medieval Palermo, with its still fundamentally Muslim urban structure, and contemporary Aleppo and Damascus, which were similarly inchoate and lacked extensive forms of social cohesion or formal ties beyond the few the Mamluk state allowed to survive.[135] By appealing to Muslim influence and tradition, however, we assume that these conditions in early fourteenth-century Palermo had already existed for centuries; and

---

[133] Baviera Albanese, 'Studio introduttivo'; *UM*, p. 716. This increased autonomy is reflected in the large number of urban customary laws (*consuetudines*) drawn up in the early fourteenth century.

[134] Caggese, *Roberto d'Angiò*, I, pp. 273–86; II, pp. 356, 358; Galasso, *Potere e istituzioni in Italia. Dalla caduta dell'Impero romano a oggi*, pp. 53–9. The informality of fourteenth-century urban society is attested to also by Michele da Piazza's *Cronaca* (1336–61), which generally refers to *cives* and *habitatores* rather than to social groups or classes.

[135] I. M. Lapidus, *Muslim cities in the later Middle Ages*.

although Muslim influence cannot be dismissed out of hand, it is also true that we know too little of Sicilian urban society under their rule to make any general statements of this kind. More proximate causes of Sicily's urban informality may have been state action, personal mobility and family structure. Norman, Hohenstaufen and Angevin policies concerning towns were either negligent or eminently dirigiste. Urban institutional independence was viewed with suspicion and was given few chances to establish itself; what emerged was only a neutered form. Political chaos after Frederick II's death, and under Angevin rule in Sicily, enabled the larger towns to formulate claims to greater independence – the Sicilian Vespers, which were initially spearheaded by Palermo and Messina, testify to this – but the Aragonese reconquest nipped these aspirations in the bud.

I have already suggested various reasons why personal mobility was particularly significant in late medieval Sicily: the destruction caused by the anti-Muslim wars in the early thirteenth century; the decay of serfdom which was the most significant corollary of those wars; the weakness of peasant smallholding outside val Demone; and the inflow of migrants from across the Straits of Messina. Palermo was awash in this period with immigrants from other parts of Sicily and abroad.[136] Between 1300 and 1460, on average twenty-five per cent of male wills and five to ten per cent of female wills were drawn up by first-generation immigrants.[137]

Family structure in fourteenth- and early fifteenth-century Sicily seems to have been strictly nuclear, with a tradition of cognatic ('Latin') succession at least as strong as the 'Greek', agnatic tradition. Bonds of locality, fraternity and patronage were extremely weak. In Palermo, families were only rarely associated with specific streets or neighbourhoods.[138] Fixed surnames began to be established, slowly and insecurely, only during the late fourteenth century; even so, clearly identifiable kinship ties

[136] Scarlata, 'Una famiglia della nobiltà siciliana nello spazio urbano e nel territorio tra XIII e XIV secolo'; Scarlata, 'Strutture urbane e habitat a Palermo fra XIII e XIV secolo. Un approccio al tema attraverso la lettura documentaria'; Corrao, 'Popolazione fluttuante'.
[137] *UM*, p. 651, Table 163.
[138] *UM*, pp. 684–97.

between individuals with the same surname can only rarely be identified.[139] Personal mobility, lack of family ties and strong state authority help explain why, with the exception of Messina and Palermo, urban (demesne) society is still largely uncharted.[140] On the one hand, relations between towns and the monarchy were desultory because of urban social and institutional weakness. On the other hand, the two metropoles – which controlled such a large proportion of regional resources before 1350 – are far better documented than any other town. A measure of relative importance is the number of petitions addressed to the monarchy before 1392: ninety-seven by Palermo (before 1350), fifteen by Messina, and only twenty by the rest of the demesne combined.[141]

Social informality in fourteenth-century Palermo is reflected in the town's administrative records, which distinguish only two status groups – the *milites* and the legal experts (*iurisperiti, iuriste*) – within the governing élite. The other members of government can be identified socially and economically as being largely local merchants and entrepreneurs, but they had no consistent distinguishing title to set them off from the rest of the population.[142] Lack of significant class, status or group-identity is suggested also by the considerable freedom of access even to the highest administrative, financial and legal posts that seems to have prevailed in Palermo before the Black Death.[143]

Magnate control after 1350 did not necessarily restrict social mobility. Taking into account the considerable decline in Palermo's population, recruitment to office did not narrow significantly after the Chiaromonte established their lordship in the 1340s: the seventy-nine counsellors from sixty-seven families known for 1350–95 compare well with the 140 counsellors from 110 families known for 1311–49. By contrast, the *identity* of the personnel

---

[139] Mineo, 'Forme di successione familiare e di trasmissione patrimoniale nella Sicilia aragonese (secoli XIV–XV)', esp. chapters 5–6. Because of the weak kinship ties among urban élite groups in this period, one cannot straightforwardly assume that individuals with the same surname were related and measure rates of access to urban office on these grounds (see below, n. 144).

[140] Baviera Albanese, 'Studio introduttivo', pp. xv–xviii; Corrao ed., *Registri di lettere*, 'Introduzione'; *UM*, pp. 652–4; Pispisa, *Messina*; Pispisa, 'Stratificazione sociale'.

[141] Epstein, 'Governo centrale'.

[142] Corrao ed., *Registri di lettere*, pp. xxii, xxiv–xxv; see, however, *UM*, p. 655.

[143] Corrao ed., *Registri di lettere*, 'Introduzione'; *UM*, pp. 722–3.

changed considerably: only fourteen families provided jurors or judges both before and after 1350.[144] The knightly class seems to have suffered most during the period of magnate rule.[145] The quite wide base of recruitment of Palermo's élite in the two periods, together with the very strong loyalty shown by the two 'capitals', Palermo and Catania, towards their lords after the Martins' landing,[146] suggest that at least in the two 'capitals' the new lords acted cautiously, leaving some margin of autonomy to self-government and restricting their actions to administering former royal revenues through the local, legally-trained élite.

Conditions in fourteenth-century Palermo were probably more similar to those in smaller towns than were conditions in Messina, for the presence of central government in the capital was counterbalanced by Palermo's higher rate of immigration. Developments in Messina followed a somewhat different course, largely because of the city's unusual level of commercial development and long-standing legal tradition.[147] On the one hand, a local oligarchy with a mercantile and especially juridical background developed earlier than elsewhere. Already by the early fourteenth century a class of *meliores civium* ('better sort') was emerging to dominate the city's administration. This group allied itself with a family of knightly origins, the Palizzi, which effectively controlled Messina for the first five or six decades of the century. Under the Palizzi's shadow, urban administration was strengthened, while at the same time it weakened its ties with the crown. On the other hand, no significant institutional changes arose as a result of Messina's coming within the orbit of Artale Alagona in Catania after the mid-fourteenth century. Messina seems to have been the only large Sicilian city free of direct seigneurial rule. As a result, the families of the *meliores* or *nobiles*[148] tended to consolidate their hold over the city's resources,

---

[144] *UM*, pp. 722–4. Bresc may have overestimated the degree of family continuity in office before and after the Black Death if he based his assessments on evidence of surnames, for before the early fifteenth century, cognatic ties of kinship were very weak; consequently, a common surname is no proof of kinship relations (see above, n. 139). On Bresc's count, the rate of substitution of political personnel is nearly ninety per cent, of which possibly less than half can be ascribed to demographic losses due to epidemics.

[145] Corrao ed., *Registri di lettere*, pp. xxxiv–xxxv.

[146] Giunta, *Aragonesi e Catalani*, I, pp. 188–207; D'Alessandro, *Politica e società*, pp. 127–55.

[147] Pispisa, *Messina*, chapter 3.

[148] See da Piazza, *Cronaca*, II, chapter 8 for 'nobiles atque populares' in Messina.

particularly over the more profitable suburban properties and the fiefs of impoverished *milites*.

Messina's rather eccentric position within the Sicilian polity, and the strength of its ruling élite, explain why it was the first city to be approached by the Martins in 1390 with offers to side with their cause, and why, in contrast with the two other largest cities, Palermo and Catania, it did side so decisively with the Aragonese.[149] It hoped thereby to gain ascendancy over the whole demesne and to become the capital of the restored kingdom; but whereas the new rulers were willing to pit the demesne against the baronage to gain the upper hand, they were not prepared to see a pole of potential opposition emerge in the cities.

The nearly unanimous reaction of the smaller demesne communities, which in 1392 denounced baronial 'tyrannies' and turned to the Iberian invaders as liberators, suggests that, in their case, feudal lordship during the second half of the fourteenth century had been less respectful of pre-existing social balances. Magnates probably found administrative structures and lines of power and privilege in these towns even more informal and unestablished, and hence more easily controlled and reshaped, than in the greater cities. Michele da Piazza described Manfredi Mohac as ruling Caltagirone 'through a wide net of relatives and in connection with the wealthy and the better sort'.[150] In lesser towns, lordship could be more exacting and less reluctant to reallocate resources against entrenched local interest.

On these grounds, the fourteenth-century urban élite (except in Messina) cannot be identified as a distinct social group. On the one hand, there were the matters of access to urban power and economic success. These were largely defined, though not restricted, through practice of the liberal arts and of trade. However, the constant and substantial turnover of officers, and the rapidly shifting fortunes of families, suggest social and political structures of considerable fluidity, in which wealth and political status were still indeterminate and somewhat independent of each other.

On the other hand, partly as a result of the fluidity of access to economic and political power, urban élite groups possessed as yet no common, binding ideology and self-perception: a civic nobility – a restricted group of families defined by their activities, wealth and

149 Pispisa, *Messina*, pp. 251–3.
150 da Piazza, *Cronaca*, I, chapter 67.

genealogical self-consciousness – was still in the making. During most of the fourteenth century, the urban administrative and commercial élite lacked a clear-cut group or even family identity. This lack was reflected in the strength, before the late fourteenth or early fifteenth century, of cognatic succession. The transition within the civic nobility from cognatic to agnatic descent, and hence to family 'lineages' and dynastic self-consciousness, occurred with the emergence of individuals endowed with sufficient political status and wealth to give them special prominence within their families.

This transition was aided during the second half of the fourteenth century by the magnates, who promoted greater jurisdictional autonomy in the larger cities (see chapter 3), thereby providing new opportunities of social mobility to administrative, financial and judicial personnel. In the shadow of feudal lordship and of its self-imposed political and economic autarky, the grounds were thus being laid for fifteenth-century urban vitality and power. A more structured urban society and more self-conscious urban élite groups were to emerge in response to changes in the structure of the late medieval state.

After the Aragonese invasion, relations between the crown and urban communities were in a state of extreme flux. This was due to the institutional vacuum which followed the monarchy's dissolution after the 1350s, and to the combination of conquest and peacemaking pursued by the Aragonese during the 1390s. But as a result of rapidly increasing administrative and fiscal demands, directed mainly towards the demesne, relations between the latter and the crown soon became the linchpin of the fifteenth-century political equilibrium. The contrast with the fourteenth century, dominated by magnate and baronial territorial factions, could hardly be greater. For much of the fifteenth century, however, relations between central government and local communities in Sicily cannot be depicted in terms of the institutional dichotomies so often drawn for the early modern period – centralism and 'absolutism' *vis-à-vis* local subjection, resistance or 'encapsulation'. Such terms presuppose the existence, not only of relatively antagonistic relations, but also of comparatively stable institutions channelling communication between clearly defined interlocutors, the state and the localities; whereas, up to at least the 1460s, neither the channels of communication nor the main interlocutors were as yet clearly defined.

Changes in relations between monarchy and demesne towns after 1392 are reflected most clearly in the vast increase in local petitions, the result not of an institutional innovation – such petitions had been introduced in 1282 – but of socio-political change.[151] Petitions from the demesne provide the main source for charting relations between the monarchy and the towns from 1392 onwards. Local petitions almost invariably expressed conflicts over access to economic or political resources, often in connection with the expansion of local government, which in turn was responding to rising fiscal demands by the state. Even more than anti-seigneurial complaints, the content and intensity over time of petitions tend to express the content and intensity of relations between central government and local communities, relations defined both by the state's fiscal requests and by the degree of attention which, for different reasons, the crown was willing to pay the demesne.

Relations were thus far from one-sided or clearcut. Like all early modern states, the Sicilian monarchy was as much in need of the financial aid of the localities as the latter were of its privileges, intervention or mediation. The legitimacy itself of regular taxation had yet to be established, and in Sicily this could be done only if the monarchy was capable of establishing a basis of understanding with the urban élite. But in order to do so, the latter had first to be identified. Conversely, before establishing themselves as legitimate, stable and reliable interlocutors of the state, élite groups had to define themselves as such. We saw above that such self-consciousness can only begin to be discerned during the last quarter of the fourteenth century, in a period of notable weakness of central authority. Before the 1420s or 1430s, no clear definition seems to have fully emerged. Full consciousness of urban class and status was achieved, however, at a time when the state was characterized ambiguously both by considerable weakness – the result of fiscal demands which it could not fully enforce – and a surprising degree of strength – the result of satisfactory responses to those demands.

The state's urban counterparts were not primarily defined through deliberate royal intervention. Rather, groups defined along boundaries of class and status emerged during the first half of the fifteenth century as a result, primarily, of conflict over increasing state taxation and administrative benefits, whose dynamics

---

151 Epstein, 'Governo centrale'. Of a total of 741 petitions to the crown before 1499 (excluding Palermo and Messina), only twenty are known for 1282–1391.

were affected only to a small degree by direct relations between local communities and the state.[152] Once established, such groups were able to channel social conflict into pre-ordained courses, and to regulate and restrict access to local government on the basis of corporate membership.

Various new taxes and demesne tolls were introduced or extended by Martino I, who faced a serious fiscal crisis in the early years of his reign;[153] this process was intensified under Alfonso, but with a crucial difference. Instead of setting up new local taxes by government *fiat*, Alfonso made peremptory demands for financial aid and expanded the range of financial and administrative burdens which localities had to bear, leaving it to communities to meet them as best they could and shifting the focus of conflict over allocation to the localities. It became commonplace for communities to raise local taxes for *ad hoc* and often short-term purposes: for meeting the government's financial requests,[154] for financing demands for royal privileges,[155] for repairing the town walls[156] or building a new wharf, as in Catania,[157] or even, increasingly, for buying back (or avoiding the sale of) local offices[158] or the town itself[159] (demesne

[152] The first cases in which collective rather than individual counterparts were identified, however, concerned strictly economic issues, mostly related to wage restrictions; see PR 21, fos. 108–9v (Piazza, 1420).
[153] Corleone, toll on wine retailing in the *feudi* (RC 39, fo. 267, 1402); Patti, toll on meat and wine (RC 42, fo. 155rv, 1404); Noto, toll on houses (RC 41, fo. 235, 1406); Noto, conflicts with local barons over the *ius dohane* (RC 46, fos. 405v–6, 1407); Milazzo, tolls on fish and fishing (RC 46, fos. 315v–16, 1407); Sant'Angelo, toll on meat and wine (C 2809, fo. 79v, 1423).
[154] RC 89, fo. 195rv (Sciacca, 1453).
[155] C 2891, fo. 32rv (Palermo, 1432); C 2821, fo. 187 (Trapani, 1433); C 2823, fo. 164rv – C 2825, fo. 11rv – C 2892, fo. 18 (Trapani, 1434); C 2821, fo. 346rv (Corleone, 1434); RC 74, fo. 419v (Catania, 1439); CR 19, fos. 60–3 (Mistretta, 1449).
[156] C 2816, fo. 187v (Salemi, 1431); C 2820, fos. 28–9 (Palermo, 1433), 56v (Licata, 1433); RC 69, fos. 90v–3 (Patti, 1434), 102v–6v (Sciacca, 1434); C 2823, fo. 125rv (Licata, 1434); C 2825, fo. 56rv (Trapani, 1435); RC 75, fos. 405–8 (Taormina, 1440); PR 18, fo. 66rv (Catania, 1448); C 2875, fo. 74rv (Naro, 1454).
[157] C 2882, fos. 70–1v (Catania, 1452).
[158] C 2819, fos. 17–18 (Taormina, 1431); RC 66, fos. 294–6 (Caltagirone, 1432); RC 79, fo. 136rv (Castrogiovanni, 1433); C 2820, fo. 46 (Agrigento, 1433); C 2820, fos. 158v–9, and RC 69, fos. 107v–8v, 110rv (Sciacca, 1434); C 2890, fos. 73v–4 (Castrogiovanni, Nicosia, 1437); RC 79, fos. 179v–82 (Patti, 1444); C 2852, fos. 63–75v, and C 2848, fos. 153–64 (Polizzi, 1445); RC 104, fos. 52v–6 (Randazzo, 1456); C 3472, fos. 38–9v (Piazza, 1458).
[159] RC 55, fos. 237–8 (Taormina, 1423); C 2821, fos. 318–19, and RC 68, fo. 165rv (Mazara, 1433); C 2891, fos. 111v–12 (Naro, 1434); C 2820, fo. 167 (Sciacca, 1434); C 2891, fos. 108rv (Castronovo, 1434), 115rv (Sutera, 1434); C 2892,

property being usually ransomed by the community concerned, not by the king).

The effects of this kind of taxation on the structures of authority in the localities were far more significant than the consequences of the hearth taxes raised directly by central government. The latter could, of course, be manipulated by local sectional interests, and reports of unjust allocations both to communities and individuals were frequent.[160] But hearth taxes were not amenable to particularly sophisticated manipulation; moreover, they tended to direct taxpayers' resentment against its rightful object, the monarchy, and against the local authorities in charge of allocation. Excise taxes had none of these drawbacks.[161] Furthermore, the resources and opportunities for privilege generated by excise (through tax farming and tax exemptions respectively)[162] created and sustained forms of collusion between the state and dominant local groups and individuals. The state could make temporary taxes permanent;[163] it could grant new tolls on consumption to finance growing local administration;[164] and it could tighten or relax controls over local finances, even when this endangered political stability.[165] This discretionary use of power was a most effective way of establishing political loyalty in conditions of imperfect information and difficult enforcement of the law.

fo. 31v (Licata, 1435); C 2890, fo. 110v (Monte San Giuliano, 1437); C 2831, fos. 26v–7 (Salemi, 1437); C 2893, fo. 106 (Trapani, 1441); C 2822, fo. 19rv, and RC 80, fos. 273v–5v (Polizzi, 1442–3); C 2845, fos. 55–9v, and RC 81, fos. 217v–22v (Mazara, 1443); C 2894, fos. 16–17 (Castrogiovanni, 1444); C 2846, fos. 227v–8v (Termini, 1444); C 2894, fos. 132v–3 (Licata, 1447); C 2894, fo. 141rv, and C 2857, fos. 164v–5v (Corleone, 1447); C 2858, fos. 92v–3, and CR 29, fos. 73–7v (Mistretta, 1447–8); C 2860, fo. 142rv (Marsala, 1448); C 2892, fo. 41v (Mazara, 1448); C 2859, fos. 113v–14 (San Pietro Patti, 1448); C 2864, fo. 155rv (Cefalù, 1451).

160 C 2891, fos. 111v–12 (Naro, 1434); C 2892, fo. 38 (Castroreale, 1435); RC 75, fos. 405–8 (Taormina, 1440); RC 83, fo. 186rv (Castrogiovanni, 1444).

161 Public control over local finances was not taken for granted. Federico Rizari was outraged that the jurors of Catania wished to check his accounts as city treasurer 'in order to remove him from office' (C 2871, fo. 72rv, 1452).

162 RC 61, fos. 67v–9 (Agrigento, 1429); C 2818, fo. 184rv (Catania, 1432); C 2821, fos. 219v–20 (Catania, 1432); RC 70, fos. 162–3 (Randazzo, 1435); RC 75, fos. 177v–81 (Noto, 1439); CR 23, fos. 3–8 (Castroreale, 1442).

163 RC 59, fo. 48rv (Agrigento, tax on the normally tax exempt, 1427).

164 RC 71, fo. 399rv (Taormina, 1436); CR 10, fos. 142–3v, and RC 71, fo. 375v (Troina, 1437); CR 23, fos. 3–8 (Castroreale, 1442); C 2844, fo. 108v, and Giardina ed., *Capitoli*, no. 82 (Messina, 1443).

165 C 2861, fo. 35v (Catania, 1448); PR 42, fo. 81v (Catania, 1450).

Alfonso was fully aware that social stability and political consensus for his military activities depended crucially on relations with the demesne: these he developed to unrivalled intensity and scope.[166] Where Martino had introduced the new rule that the highest urban officials (captain, judges and the *stratigoto* of Messina) be nominated by the king,[167] Alfonso went a step further. By permanently establishing the office of the master juror (*maestro giurato*) who syndicated the communities' administration, including their accounts, he created at one stroke a powerful means of intervention in local affairs.[168]

Groups defined along lines of property and occupation began to form during the first decades of the fifteenth century. But as we saw, a common social or economic background had not been enough for a clear group or class identity to develop previously. A common identity emerged under two related impulses: through conflict over access to local government, conflict which increased considerably during the 1430s and 1440s as Alfonso mobilized all available fiscal resources for his Neapolitan enterprise (see Table 7.2); and as a result of the increased administrative autonomy which the monarchy was forced to concede in exchange for political and financial support.

At the turn of the fifteenth century, urban populations were still described in generic terms, and social distinctions were hardly drawn at all: 'citizens' in Milazzo in 1413,[169] 'people' in Nicosia as late as 1430,[170] and in Caltagirone still in 1432.[171] The sort of people which would later be called the *popolo* were described simply as the 'poor and indigent';[172] the future urban aristocrats

---

[166] Alfonso enacted similar policies in Catalonia (T. N. Bisson, *The medieval Crown of Aragon. A short history*, pp. 145, 157–9), but very different ones on the southern mainland (according to Pontieri, *Calabria*, pp. 76, 79–80; see also Ryder, *Kingdom of Naples*, chapter 10).

[167] Testa ed., *Capitula*, I, pp. 141–2, 157–8.

[168] *UM*, p. 717 n. 56 (1429); Testa ed., *Capitula*, I, p. 221 (1433). The officer rolls in the demesne, which were submitted every year to the government's approval (*ibid.*, I, pp. 157 (1392?), 216–17 (1433)), allow one to follow processes of selection and promotion of local élite groups. During the fourteenth century, royal intervention in local administrative elections had tended to increase, although no formal legislation in this sense was passed (Baviera Albanese, 'Studio introduttivo', pp. xxix–xxxv).

[169] RC 49, fos. 86–8 (*citatini*).   [170] RC 65, fos. 23–4v (*genti*).

[171] RC 66, fo. 205v (*populus*).

[172] RC 20, fo. 50rv (Piazza, 1392) (*pauperes et indigentes*)

were just the 'better sort'.[173] In Salemi in 1418, the distinction
between 'certain noble citizens' and the *popolo* was still indeterminate.[174] Agrigento's requests in the 1420s for *gentilhomini* or
'honourable persons' to be represented in local government were
unusually precise.[175]

The civic nobility was the first status group to develop a self-
conscious identity. The Aragonese restoration and the political
consolidation under Alfonso gave decisive impetus to the emergence of this urban élite, whose wealth and status increasingly
depended on the administration of fiscal and other resources for the
locality and the state.[176] At the familial level, as I remarked above,
this period coincided with the establishment of agnatic descent and
of a clear 'dynastic' self-consciousness. Within the group as a whole,
the expansion of state and urban administration, and of the volume
of resources the group managed, led to the formation during the
first three decades of the fifteenth century of an increasingly strong
identity as a specifically *civic* nobility, whose members began to
describe themselves as *gentilhomini* or *nobiles*.[177] Although a
phenomenon of patrician ennoblement took place also in central
and northern Italy in this period,[178] the process occurred on the
sediment of powerfully, though divisively, structured urban societies. In Sicily that sediment did not exist.

The most distinctive and vocal urban group besides the *nobiles*
was that of the artisans. That artisans should obtain any form of
political representation at all testifies to their increased economic
and social importance. The Normans and Hohenstaufen had
opposed craft guilds on the basis of a general hostility towards urban
autonomy, so it comes as no surprise that guilds first appeared in
Sicily after the breakdown of state authority in the fourteenth
century.[179] Craft guilds are first mentioned as a list of forty-four

173 *UM*, p. 737 n. 190 (Calascibetta, 1397) (*migliori*).
174 PR 20, fo. 39 (*certi citatini nobili*).
175 RC 54, fos. 395v–7 (1423); RC 61, fos. 67v–9 (1429) (*persuni honorati*).
176 Epstein, 'Governo centrale'; Mineo, 'Speciale'. The merchant élites did not
     possess a distinct social identity and tended to identify with the civic nobility.
177 The Messinese *meliores* who occupied the higher administrative posts were
     addressed as *nobilis* already in the fourteenth century (Pispisa, *Messina*,
     pp. 98–9). By contrast, in early fourteenth-century Palermo, the adjective *nobilis*
     was prefixed only to *milites* (Corrao ed., *Registri di lettere*).
178 M. Berengo, 'Patriziato e nobiltà: il caso veronese', 494–5. See above, n. 115.
179 Leone, 'Lineamenti di una storia'.

corporations participating in a religious procession in Palermo in 1385,[180] but the nature of the event and circumstantial evidence about Palermitan government in those years suggest that corporations had as yet no independent political functions; they were more probably being harnessed by the Chiaromonte lords symbolically to parade popular consensus.[181]

The growth of manufacturing in Sicily during the late fourteenth and early fifteenth centuries inevitably increased the wealth and influence of artisans, but for a long time improved economic conditions were not translated into tangible political benefits, such as the right to organize and gain local representation. Artisans achieved some political power corresponding to their social and economic gains only as a result of the upheaval caused by Alfonso's war on the southern Italian mainland – in other words, in a period of relative weakness of central government. The first and most successful artisan challenge to the civic nobility occurred in Catania, where nobiliary government may have been weakened by the deep crisis that had followed the city's loss of political hegemony in eastern Sicily.

The origins of the long struggle between the artisans and *gentilhomini* of Catania lay in the creation by Alfonso in 1435 of twenty-two guilds with the right to elect their own consuls and officials. In the early 1440s, these guilds began to strive for a share in local government, and in 1445 they asked to be represented by their consuls on the city council, where they had an absolute majority for about a year. A few months later the *gentilhomini* accused the artisans of attempted conspiracy (*manipolium*). At that point, Alfonso seems to have sided with the civic nobility.[182]

Following Catania's lead, craft guilds were established in Noto,[183]

---

[180] Maggiore Perni, *Popolazione di Sicilia*, pp. 599–600.

[181] See P. Mainoni, 'I paratici a Milano in età visconteo-sforzesca: problemi e indirizzi di ricerca'.

[182] PR 42, fo. 27 (1435); C 2840, fo. 127rv (1442); PR 37, fo. 154 (1446); C 2854, fos. 183–5v (1446); C 2857, fos. 62–3v, and PR 38, fo. 173 (1446); C 2857, fos. 57v–60v, and PR 42, fo. 30 (1446); PR 38, fos. 196v–8 (1447); PR 42, fos. 48–51v (1448); PR 42, fos. 81v–4v (1450). See also Marletta, 'La costituzione'; P. D'Arrigo, 'Notizie sulla corporazione degli argentieri in Catania'; *UM*, p. 736. In 1460, the *popolo* petitioned successfully to reintroduce guild consuls (C 3476, fos. 71v–82).

[183] C 2841, fo. 10 (1442).

Caltagirone,[184] Patti,[185] Termini,[186] Syracuse, Castrogiovanni, Messina and Mistretta[187] during the 1440s and 1450s. At first, guilds seem to have had mainly political rather than economic functions; hence if political activity declined, guilds weakened also. In Catania and Noto, for example, the appointment of guild consuls had lapsed for some years before being reintroduced in the early 1460s,[188] despite the fact that since Noto was one of the main cloth-making centres in Sicily, one might expect at least cloth guilds to have been well-established. The example of Noto, in fact, suggests that there may have been other reasons, besides opposition by the crown and the local élite, why guilds were so few in late medieval Sicily. I explained the lack of craft guilds in the cloth industries by referring to technological constraints, to the difficulty of establishing territorial monopolies in a region with weak urban institutions, and to the strength of domestic demand which reduced the need for corporate protection (see chapter 4); similar factors may have affected other manufacturing industries. But the preceding discussion of urban society suggests that more general factors were also at work. The very basis of corporate solidarity, trust and stability of membership, was undermined by the weakness of extra-familial ties and by the very high rate of personal mobility.

The chronology of craft-guild demands suggests that the transition to a more stable and hierarchical social order defined along lines of status and occupation gathered pace during the 1440s (see Table 7.2). In this period, a third status group began to emerge alongside the civic nobility and artisans, namely the *popolo* or, more derogatively, the *plebe* – a term that had been used in various contexts on the Italian mainland for centuries. In 1439, the *popolo* challenged the jurors of Messina and offered to commission a galley for King Alfonso to support its demands. The same *popolo* or *plebe* asked in 1450 for adequate political representation in local government, alongside the *gentilhomini* and knights; again it offered a

184 S. Randazzini ed., *Le consuetudini di Caltagirone e i diplomi dei re che le confermarono*, p. 71 (1443).
185 RC 79, fos. 179v–82, and RC 81, fos. 485v–8v (1444).
186 C 2853, fos. 158v–9 (1446).
187 *UM*, p. 212, Table 29.
188 C 3476, fos. 71v–82 (Catania, 1460); C 3484, fo. 175 (Noto, 1464). Guilds in Catania, however, were officially suppressed in 1451 (Petino, *Aspetti di politica granaria*, p. 56).

Table 7.2 *Causes of social conflict in the demesne and the* Camera
reginale, *1392–1499*

Year	Locality	Cause	Documentary sources
1392	Piazza (N)	U	RC 20, fo. 50rv
1398	Trapani (M)	U	RC 34, fos. 100v–1
1399	Messina (D)	RO	RC 17, fo. 47v; Giardina ed., *Capitoli*, no. 55
1400	Randazzo (D)	U	RC 38, fos. 127v–8
1404	Agrigento (M)	U	*UM*, p. 738, Table 181
1406	Marsala (M)	RO	RC 46, fo. 243v
1407	Randazzo (D)	LG	RC 46, fos. 413v–15v
1408	Monte San Giuliano (M)	RO	RC 44–45, fos. 134–5
1410	Nicosia (D)	U	Barbato *Per la storia di Nicosia*, p. 115
1410	Randazzo (D)	LG	*UM*, p. 738, Table 181
1413	Santa Lucia (D)	U	RC 49, fos. 116–19
1413	Milazzo (D)	RO	RC 49, fos. 86–8
1413	San Filippo di Argirò (D)	RO	RC 7, fos. 27v–8
1414	Alcamo (M)	FL	RC 49, fos. 165v–8v
1415	San Filippo di Argirò (D)	U	RC 50, fo. 40v
1415	Licata (M)	RO	RC 51, fo. 46rv
1415	San Fratello (D)	FL	RC 50, fo. 38rv
1416	Monte San Giuliano (M)	RO	RC 51, fo. 105rv
1416	Randazzo (D)	LG	C 2802, fo. 11v
1416	Alcamo (M)	RO	RC 51, fo. 333rv
1417	Augusta (N)	FL	C 2802, fos. 76v–7
1417	Alcamo (M)	U	*UM*, p. 738, Table 181
1421	Messina (D)	RO	C 2888, fos. 72, 88v
1423–4	Noto (N)	FL	Littara, *De rebus netinis*, pp. 105–7
1424	Castroreale (D)	RT	RC 55, fos. 298v–300
1425	Taormina (D)	RT?	PR 24, fos. 253v–4
1426	Castrogiovanni (N), Nicosia (D)	FL	C 2888, fos. 168v–9v
1430	Nicosia (D)	RO	RC 65, fos. 23–4v
1431	Patti (D)	RO	C 2817, fo. 189
1431	Syracuse (N)	RO	CS 2, fos. 4–6v
1432	Caltagirone (M)	RO?	RC 66, fo. 205v
1433	Regalbuto (N)	RO	RC 68, fo. 94rv
1434	Avola (N)	RT	C 2891, fo. 99rv
1434	Nicosia (D)	RO	RC 70, fo. 65rv
1434	Caltagirone (M)	LG	C 2824, fos. 179v–80
1434	Trapani (M)	RT, LG	C 2825, fos. 54–5
1436	Messina (D), Trapani, Sciacca, Agrigento (M)	RT?	C 2890, fos. 19v, 47v–8, 75
1437	Santa Lucia (D)	RO	RC 71, fos. 283v–4
1437	Salemi (M)	RT?	C 2890, fos. 122v–3
1437	Monte San Giuliano (M)	U	C 2890, fo. 89v
1439–40	Messina (D)	LG	C 2893, fo. 8rv; Giardina ed., *Capitoli*, no. 79

Table 7.2 *(cont.)*

Year	Locality	Cause	Documentary sources
1440	Trapani (M)	RO	C 2890, fo. 239; C 2893, fo. 67; C 2935, fos. 203v–4
1440	Agrigento (M)	RO	RC 75, fos. 279v–81
1441	Polizzi (M)	FL	RC 76, fos. 588v–9v
1441	Piazza (N)	RO, RT	RC 76, fos. 416rv, 458–9v, 582rv
1441	Castrogiovanni (N)	U	RC 76, fos. 416v–17v
1441	Messina (D)	RT	C 2893, fo. 66v
1441	Salemi (M)	RO?	C 2893, fo. 67
1443	Polizzi (M)	FL	PR 35, fos. 48v–9
1443	Caltagirone (M)	LG	C 2805, fo. 139v; PR 35, fo. 61
1444	Syracuse (N)	LG	Gallo, *Annali di Messina*, pp. 325–6; Privitera, *Storia di Siracusa*, II, p. 117
1445	Sciacca (M)	FL	CR 25, fo. 479rv
1445	Patti (D)	U	*UM*, p. 738, Table 181
1447	Syracuse (N)	FL?	CS 5, fo. 112v
1448	Syracuse (N)	LG	C 2859, fo. 162v; Privitera, *Storia di Siracusa*, II, pp. 117–21
1448	Lentini (N)	U	C 2859, fo. 162v
1448	Castrogiovanni (N)	U	PR 40, fo. 119
1449	Messina (D)	LG	C 2895, fo. 42; *UM*, p. 738, Table 181
1449	Syracuse (N)	LG	C 2862, fos. 142v–3v
1450	Messina (D)	LG	PR 42, fos. 37v–44v; Giardina ed., *Capitoli*, no. 100
1450	Palermo (M)	LG	see chapter 7, n. 194
1450	Syracuse (N)	FL	C 2865, fos. 23v–5v
1450	Piazza (N)	RT, LG	RC 84, fo. 106rv
1451	Polizzi (M)	RT, LG	RC 84, fo. 325rv
1451	Noto (N)	RO?	C 2897, fo. 50
1451	Scicli (N)	U	RC 84, fos. 362v–4; CR 928, unnumbered fos.
1453	Nicosia (D)	LG	PR 45, fo. 96rv
1454	Noto (N)	RO	C 2874, fos. 17v–18v
1455	Agrigento (M)	RO, LG	PR 46, fo. 302
1455	Taormina (D)	RO	C 2876, fos. 28v–9v
1455	Noto (N)	LG	C 2897, fo. 109rv
1456	Cefalù (M)	LG?	RC 77, fo. 411
1456–7	Paternò (N)	FL, RT?	RC 104, fos. 145v–7; C 2897, fo. 142; PR 51, fos. 250v–2v
1457	Castrogiovanni (N)	LG?	PR 52, fo. 231rv
1458	Trapani (M)	RT	PR 50, fos. 349v–50v
1458	Castrogiovanni (N)	U	PR 52, fo. 231
1459	Syracuse (N)	FL	Privitera, *Storia di Siracusa*, II, pp. 125–6
1459	Buccheri (N)	RO	RC 87, fos. 255v–6
1459	Lentini (N)	RO?	C 3473, fo. 26rv

Table 7.2 (cont.)

Year	Locality	Cause	Documentary sources
1460	Messina (D)	LG	Giardina ed., *Capitoli*, no. 98; C 3480, fos. 133–4; RC 109, fos. 197–8v
1461	Polizzi (M)	U	LV 80, fos. 262v–3
1463	Messina (D)	LG	Gallo, *Annali di Messina*, pp. 367–8
1463–4	Castrogiovanni (N)	RT	C 3490, fos. 53v–4v; LV 93, fo. 100; LV 92, fos. 347v–9, 364rv, 376v–7, 383v–4, 407v
1464	Messina (D)	LG	Trasselli, *La questione sociale in Sicilia*
1465	Piazza (N)	U	LV 93, fos. 109v–10, 345v–6
1472	Messina (D)	LG	RC 127, fos. 382–4
1478	Palermo (M)	RT	Gallo, *Annali di Messina*, pp. 380–4
1483	Castronovo (M)	RT?	RC 149, fos. 354v–5
1484	Monte San Giuliano (M)	LG	RC 155, fos. 178–9
1488	Syracuse (N)	FL	Gervasi, *Siculae sanctiones*, III, p. 92

D = val Demone; M = val di Mazara; N = val di Noto; FL = feudal lordship;
LG = local government; RO = royal official(s); RT = royal taxation;
U = unknown.

considerable sum, 400 *onze*, to obtain the king's ear.[189] In 1443, the 'party of the noble and best' (*pars nobilium et primariorum*) wrote to Alfonso from Caltagirone asking him to repeal two requests previously granted to the *plebea gens*, which forbade giving the captainship to a local citizen and established an annual scrutiny for other offices. The king, who set up a commission to enquire into the matter, betrayed his sympathy for the request and especially for the definition it gave of the parties involved: 'from Creation onwards', Alfonso admitted, 'noblemen have always hated the plebs'.[190]

The fourth and last group to take shape under political and fiscal pressure was that of the *borgesi*, who seem to have been a lesser version of the civic nobility. They included petty retailers, lesser merchants and especially agricultural entrepreneurs. The distinction between *borgesia* and *popolo* expresses to a certain degree the structure of property in land, the term *borgesia* defining what

189 C 2894, fo. 172rv; PR 42, fos. 37v–44v. See below, n. 199.
190 C 2805, fo. 139v.

364 An island for itself

might be called the native yeomanry, the *popolo* including the owners of petty suburban allotments besides the vast numbers of dispossessed rural and urban wage-labourers. The category of peasant smallholders was comparatively so small, and restricted to parts of eastern Sicily, that no specific denotation for it appears to have emerged.

Until the end of the fifteenth century, all major urban conflict was ordered within and around these four groups (see Table 7.2).[191] In 1434, for example, Alfonso decided that a tax to repair the city walls in Sciacca would,be allocated by a committee formed by a *nobilis*, a *borgese* and an artisan (*ministerialis*); the poor (*miserabiles*) were exempted.[192] In Castrogiovanni in 1453, 'a certain party of the *populus*' which identified three distinctive political groupings – the *gentilhomini, menestrali* and *borgesi* – besides the *popolo* itself, petitioned against the *borgesi*.[193] A major uprising in Palermo in 1450, described contemptuously by parliament and Alfonso as a rebellion of the 'plebs' and of 'villeins',[194] in fact involved, besides the *popolo* itself, various *borgesi* and even a few *gentilhomini*.[195]

Whereas the terms *gentilhomo, menestrale* and even *borgese* seem to have had quite clear social and political connotations, the term *popolo* was never clearly defined. The *popolo* was composed, for the most part, of smallholders and landless labourers, but the term was used also as one of opprobrium: any violent, non-institutional form of political struggle was inevitably described as 'tumults of the people',[196] 'fury or impetus of the people'.[197] In this view, the *popolo* was an indefinite mass of 'have-nots', what was left after better-identified and more powerful groups had been

191 The *gentilhomini* of Piazza against the jurors and their allies (C 2874, fos. 80v–9, 1455); agreement between the 'noble' jurors and the *popolo* of Messina (C 2878, fo. 111rv, 1456); the *gentilhomini* of Messina against the *popolo* (C 3480, fo. 133rv, 1460; Giardina ed., *Capitoli*, no. 100, 1465; RC 116, fos. 294v–5, 1466); petition against the 'general assembly' of the *popolo* in Randazzo (PR 68, fos. 136v–7, 1470). In 1460, the term *magnates* is used, possibly for the first time, by the *popolo* of Messina (Giardina ed., *Capitoli*, no. 98).
192 RC 69, fos. 102v–6v.
193 C 2883, fos. 63v–5v.
194 C 2864, fos. 163–5 (ed. from another source by Pollaci Nuccio, 'Della sollevazione', 164–70); Testa ed., *Capitula*, I, p. 362 (1451). The same term was used to describe the *popolo*'s revolt in Messina in the same year (*ibid.*, I, p. 373).
195 De Vio ed., *Privilegia*, p. 313; *UM*, p. 740. In contrast with Messina in this period, the *popolo* lacked political representation in Palermo.
196 'Tumultus populi': RC 77, fo. 411 (Cefalù, 1456); PR 52, fo. 231rv (Castrogiovanni, 1457); LV 92, fos. 364rv, 383v–4, and LV 93, fos. 100, 347v, 348–9, 376v–7, 407v (Castrogiovanni, 1465); LV 93, fos. 109v–10 (Piazza, 1465).
197 'Furia o impetu de poble' (C 3480, fo. 7rv, Palermo, 1458).

subtracted from the body politic. By the late 1450s, in fact, violence
of this kind began to lose even the weak class or sectional connotations it had previously had, and the *popolo* was referred to increasingly seldom as a constituted or identifiable body of persons.
Inchoate, unstructured violence became increasingly the only kind
of action left to the humbler members of the population excluded
from political representation and deprived of the few institutional
channels they had possessed to express dissatisfaction.

This process bears remarkable similarities to that of the progress-
ive 'fragmentation and isolation' described for the Florentine *popolo minuto* in the fifteenth century.[198] In both cases, we find
massive immigration contributing to de-structure previous networks of social solidarity; in both cases there was a determined
effort on the part of urban élite groups to exclude the *popolo* from
power. Differences between the two societies, however, may have
been even more significant. In Florence, social fragmentation followed a period of 'remarkably modern' popular political action,
which culminated in the Ciompi revolt of 1378, and was deliberately
promoted by the Florentine oligarchy through a combination of
legal, policing and resettlement policies. At the present state of our
knowledge, developments in fifteenth-century Sicily seem far more
ambiguous. On the one hand, urban government did not coincide
with the state as it did in Florence. We do not know to what extent
the central government intervened in urban politics through its
control over local officers' elections, but however much its sympa-
thies might have lain with the *nobiles* and other higher status
groups, it could only rarely pursue overtly anti-popular policies.[199]
Indeed, the *popolo* could often appeal to the crown for support,
which the latter was willing to grant if it did not contrast with its
own, wider fiscal and political concerns. The state expressed no
single, overarching policy. It acted in an empirical and *ad hoc*
fashion in response to local demands, and was thus not directly
responsible for the disappearance of the *popolo* as a political force.
On the other hand, although the urban polity which emerged after

[198] S. K. Cohn Jr., *The labouring classes in Renaissance Florence*, p. 127.
[199] An unusual example of anti-popular policy is the revocation in 1466 by the
viceroy Lope Ximen Urrea of a royal decree of 1450 which had given the *popolo*
representation in Messina's government; the viceroy stated that 'officia civitatis
sint penes nobiles' (Tramontana, *Antonello e la sua città*, p. 58). This exclusion,
however, did not last for long, suggesting that the *popolo* of Messina was
sociologically rather different from its namesakes elsewhere.

the 1460s was more hierarchical than it had ever previously been, thus conforming to contemporary developments in northern Italy,[200] the range of social forces that achieved political representation in Sicilian towns may have been far wider; the *nobiles* seem not to have achieved the kind of political hegemony they could generally aspire to further north.

The process of exclusion of the *popolo* from political representation thus went hand in hand with a process of corporate definition. The first efforts during the early 1430s to regulate access to local offices by excluding certain trades[201] were followed a decade later by the more effective policy of defining who *could* accede to office. One of the first *libri mastri*, a roll of men eligible to hold office, appeared in Caltagirone in 1443, apparently as a result of conflict between *gentilhomini* and *popolo* over municipal administration. Caltagirone's example was followed by Patti and Milazzo in 1444, by Agrigento in 1447, and by Catania in the same years.[202] In some cases, like Caltagirone and possibly Agrigento, this was a corporatively inclined innovation meant to reduce political dissent by establishing clear rules of access to power for legitimate groups. In most towns where the *libro mastro* was introduced, however, access was restricted to the civic nobility, which tried to use the roll to enforce political hegemony in periods of crisis. Most rolls of office were drawn up in communities like Patti, Mistretta, Catania and even Agrigento, which were experiencing relative economic decline. In Catania, a roll of nobility was established in the late 1440s only as a defensive measure in response to the guilds' attacks, for in practice local government was already restricted to a small number of families.[203] On the other hand, where economic conditions were more favourable, as in Palermo or Trapani, social mobility was more intense, access to office was relatively easier,[204] and an official *libro mastro* seems not to have existed.

Thus from the mid-1430s, in response to rising fiscal pressure,

---

[200] D. Hay and J. Law, *Italy in the age of the Renaissance 1380–1530*, chapter 3.
[201] For Patti see RC 68, fos. 54v–5 (1432); RC 69, fos. 90v–3 (1434). For Corleone, where bread, vegetable and tunnyfish retailers, innkeepers and butchers were excluded from the highest administrative offices, see RC 69, fos. 127v–8 (1434).
[202] RC 79, fos. 104–8v (Caltagirone, 1443); RC 79, fos. 179v–82 (Patti, 1444). For Milazzo, Agrigento and Catania see *UM*, p. 726; for Catania see also Testa ed., *Capitula*, I, pp. 492 (1459), 495–7 (1470); RC 109, fos. 86–97v (1460).
[203] *UM*, pp. 726–7.   [204] *UM*, pp. 725–9.

Sicilian urban society began to reorganize political conflict around local corporate interests. The short- and long-term consequences for the state were twofold: the state's capacity to mediate and discriminate and, thus, its political legitimacy and its ability to reallocate resources, were enhanced; and the costs of identifying local political interlocutors were considerably reduced.

The process of corporatization of urban society explains why, although popular resistance to royal taxation in the localities was as intense in the 1430s as it had been a decade earlier, by the mid-1430s the king was able to extract resources from his subjects much more effectively. By then, Alfonso could rely on the complicity and consent of corporate groups in demesne towns, most especially the civic nobility, to push through his growing financial demands. These groups, which had evolved largely in response to such requests, were increasingly aware of the benefits to be derived from them. A new political settlement was being reached. Alfonso felt so secure in this that he was willing to sell or pawn to consortia of (often related) citizens the military captaincy of major cities – an office politically so delicate that the Martins had never dared entrust one to a Sicilian.[205]

From the 1430s, state manipulation of local divisions and social stratification became a firmly established practice for resuming demesne offices or property, in the face of strong community resistance to the taxes used to finance such operations.[206] Promoters of these transactions were rewarded with the removal of the previous office incumbents[207] and with local offices or other benefits.[208] In 1448, Giacomo Agnello was rewarded for his efforts to recover Mistretta and Capizzi to the demesne, with the right to fell 20,000 *cantara* (1,600 tons) of timber duty-free in Mistretta's woods, the ownership of a large olive grove, and the fief of Francavilla in Mistretta's district.[209] In 1456, a group of citizens and officers in Castrogiovanni asked to resume a toll and a piece of common land, which had been alienated some years before by the town, offering to loan the necessary capital in various amounts 'according to

[205] RC 69, fos. 107–8v, 110rv (Sciacca, 1434); C 2890, fos. 73v–4 (Castrogiovanni and Nicosia, 1437).
[206] C 2821, fos. 318–19 (Mazara, 1433); C 2891, fo. 108rv (Castronovo, 1434); C 3472, fos. 38–9v (Piazza, 1458).
[207] C 2859, fos. 5v–6v (Corleone, 1447), 75v–6 (Mistretta, 1448).
[208] C 2802, fos. 84rv, 110–11, 114–15 (Alcamo, 1417); C 2896, fo. 70v (Marsala, 1451).
[209] C 2859, fos. 76v–8.

the [petitioners'] dignity of office'. The petitioners demanded a monopoly over local offices for four or six years, adding that the officers' names would be drawn by lot by an 'innocent', 'so it not be thought that this would be done in fraud'. The request was accepted, with the proviso that the officials' names had to be approved by the viceroy or the President of the kingdom.[210] At the same time as urban political and economic conflict was being corporatized on the basis of occupation and wealth, factional conflict along lines of lineage, family or 'party' (*parcialitati*) became institutionalized.[211] The simultaneous development of organized forms of vertical and horizontal conflict was not fortuitous, however, for horizontal conflict tends to emerge when a patron or head of a faction or lineage is able to offer his followers stable and continuous access to local resources. This ability is based in turn on the patron's privileged access to relatively established and secure institutional channels. In other words, factionalism is most effective under conditions of relative institutional stability and constrained social mobility, where present resources can be traded for future political or other support because neither party need fear a rapid change of fortune. When, as seems to have been the case in Sicily before the 1430s, individual or familial power is based mainly or wholly on *economic* success, a success which cannot be translated into more than short-term political recognition, some necessary preconditions for factionalism appear still to be missing.

Juan's political disengagement from Sicily, and the lowering of taxation during his reign, resulted in a sharp decline of major social conflict in both the demesne and feudal lands. By contrast, when anti-seigneurial conflict flared up again under Ferdinand II towards the end of the century, the demesne stayed comparatively quiet. Urban conflict was not lacking,[212] but it rarely involved corporate groups as it had thirty years before.[213] What is more, conflict seldom concerned tax issues;[214] mostly it addressed personal and factional ones, or wage levels.

Towards the end of the fifteenth century, there were new nobiliary attempts to restrict access to local administration, but in

---

[210] RC 77, fos. 278–9v.
[211] C 2802, fo. 11v (Randazzo, 1416); RC 73, fo. 109rv (Castroreale, 1437); RC 74, fos. 390v–2v, and C 2833, fos. 6–7 (Randazzo, 1439); PR 45, fo. 96rv (Nicosia, 1453); RC 121, fo. 281rv (Sciacca, 1468); *UM*, p. 730.
[212] Trasselli, *Da Ferdinando*, chapter 5.
[213] Despite the large number of artisan guilds that obtained official recognition after 1500 (*ibid.*, pp. 277–80).
[214] *Ibid.*, p. 279.

contrast to the mid-fifteenth century they found little governmental support.[215] Unlike the mid-century examples quoted above, which came in response to conflict over the establishment of new urban power structures, these later attempts were purely defensive. The nature and boundaries of status and corporate groups and urban administrative institutions were largely established. Local resources were distributed through recognized channels. Social conflict had largely shifted from the vertical and collective (between class, status or corporate groups) to the horizontal and individual (between factions and individuals). Even during the semi-insurrectional years following Ferdinand's death in 1516, urban struggle seems to have been disorganized and fragmented. Participants were scarcely aware of other than local issues and were unwilling, unlike members of the aristocracy in the same period, to establish a more general programme for political autonomy or to withdraw political consensus from the monarchy. There thus seems to have been little in common between Sicilian non-aristocratic conflict of this period and the organized and politically sophisticated peasant and urban insurrections in Castile and Germany to which they have been compared.[216]

The only significant exception to the general tendency towards less extreme forms of redistributive conflict was connected with control over common land and common rights. Before the 1460s, the main source of conflict over common rights, both within feudal communities and between barons and the demesne, lay in seigneurial rights to tax or regulate access to common land,[217] but a

[215] RC 171, fos. 172–5v (Agrigento, 1488); CR 77, fos. 573–4 (Piazza, 1495); RC 194, fo. 68v–9v (Piazza, 1496); RC 193, fos. 271v–2v (Sutera, 1496).

[216] Trasselli, *Da Ferdinando*, chapter 11; Baviera Albanese, 'Sulla rivolta del 1516'; Baviera Albanese, 'La Sicilia tra regime pattizio'.

[217] See above for conflict between lords and feudal communities. For conflict between demesne lands and the barons, see PR 24, fo. 505v (Palermo, 1421); CS 1, fo. 178v (Lentini, 1431); C 2817, fo. 184rv (Resuttano, 1431); C 2819, fo. 187 (Sant'Angelo, 1433); C 2820, fos. 69v, 77–8v (Catania, 1433); RC 69, fos. 127v–8 (Corleone, 1434); C 2825, fos. 36v–7 (Milazzo, 1434); C 2821, fo. 348 (Calascibetta, 1434); PR 35, fo. 149 (Salemi, 1443); C 2843, fo. 215 (Castroreale, 1444); Genuardi, *Terre comuni*, pp. 88–90 (Lentini, 1445); C 2854, fos. 34v–5 (Mineo, 1445), 150 (Calatabiano, 1446); C 2856, fo. 128rv (Naro, 1446); C 2882, fos. 43v–4 (Noto, Palazzolo, 1452), 63v–5 (Paternò, Licodia, 1452); C 2881, fo. 106rv (Taormina, 1452); C 2883, fos. 155v–6v (Palermo, 1454); C 2876, fo. 84rv (Santo Stefano, 1455); RC 97, fos. 231v–2v (Savoca, 1455); C 2886, fo. 127v (Taormina, 1456); C 2885, fos. 145v–6 (Castroreale, Milazzo, Santa Lucia, 1456); RC 106, fos. 226–8 (Milazzo, 1457); C 2880, fo. 86rv (Taormina, 1457); Genuardi, *Terre comuni*, pp. 99–100 (Favarotta, 1458); Sandri, *Patrimonio fondiario*, pp. 38–9.

provision by King Juan in 1460 in defence of common rights set this kind of dispute to rest.[218] Under Alfonso, when land was plentiful and cheap, it had been quite easy to enfeoff common land without raising major objections.[219] But from the 1470s, as population pressure began to mount, there are increasing references to enclosure, lease, sale or enfeoffment of commons by or to local *nobiles*, in a context usually of latent or open hostility.[220] For the first time, such alienations had to be justified. Some communities argued that sales were a necessary response to financial and tax pressures,[221] as if no other source of revenue had existed; but the real motives for alienation were rather different. In May 1470, for example, four *nobiles* of Castrogiovanni offered to buy back a piece of common land and to pay the town's tax allocation of eighty *onze*, so as to control the land themselves. A request made a few days earlier by the same community to enclose some horse pastures and to cancel a lease of the town's *feudo* Racalseni was probably supported by similar propertied interests or by agricultural entrepreneurs, *borgesi* and *massari*, who lacked the capital to buy the land outright.[222] *Borgesi* and *massari* were, in fact, commonly the moving force behind attempts to buy back communal land.[223] The denunciation by the *borgesi* of Nicosia of 'some powerful people of this land, [who] because of the favours and the wealth they command' had usurped common land, expresses the long struggle between the civic nobility and the higher ranks of the peasantry to establish a private as against a collective monopoly over common land.[224] The civic nobility wished to privatize communal land; the *massari* wanted to keep the land under communal control so as to exclude outsiders and keep rents low.

Let us sum up this chapter's arguments so far. From the early 1430s

---

[218] Testa ed., *Capitula*, I, pp. 448–9.

[219] *UM*, pp. 898–9, Table 202.

[220] C 3479, fos. 100v–2v, and CR 132, fos. 203v–4v (Nicosia, 1475); RC 149, fos. 55v–6v (Piazza, 1482); RC 152, fo. 101rv (Monte San Giuliano, 1483); RC 172, fos. 179v–80 (Milazzo, 1489); RC 189, fos. 206v–7v (Linguaglossa, Castiglione, 1493); RC 187, fos. 266v–7 (Nicosia, 1493).

[221] RC 125, fos. 169v–70 (Castrogiovanni, 1470); CR 66, fo. 286rv, and RC 155, fo. 161rv (1484). ɾ

[222] RC 125, fos. 169v–70; RC 125, fo. 167rv, and CR 50, fos. 8–8bis.

[223] See RC 109, fos. 380–1 (Nicosia, 1461); RC 125, fo. 105 (Nicosia, 1470); CR 51, fos. 413–14 (Mistretta, 1471); RC 142, fo. 261v (Caltagirone, Calascibetta, 1480).

[224] TRP Atti 57, fos. 181–2 (1500).

to the late 1450s, Sicily was swept by great waves of conflict expressing both traditional and new forms of struggle for economic and political resources. The main, unifying cause of the struggles was Alfonso's huge financial effort to conquer the southern mainland, but the structure and content of conflict in the demesne towns differed significantly from that in the feudal countryside. Equally, the intense social and political upheaval within the demesne signalled urban society's new economic and political powers and confidence.

The feudal aristocracy, especially the lower rungs, was in a condition of unprecedented weakness, both economic and political. Economic weakness was caused by the demographic crisis, which had reduced rents to a tenth of what they were a century before and had lowered seigneurial dues as well; and by the loss after the 1390s of substitutive sources of income from the royal demesne. Political weakness arose from the fact that (with the exception of the county of Modica) the fourteenth-century magnate consortia and estates had been dissolved, and two waves of feudal substitution in 1392–8 and 1413–20 had shaken aristocratic continuity, independence and self-confidence to the foundations. The aristocracy responded slowly, but with increasing enthusiasm, to Alfonso's Neapolitan enterprise once its opportunities for success became more apparent. But the practice of war cut deep into greatly reduced incomes. The aristocracy responded to its needs by investing in new economic activities such as sugar *trappeti*, by attempting where possible to increase land rents, but most of all by trying to extract higher seigneurial dues from its subjects. This latter strategy was basically defensive and not, in the social and demographic conditions prevailing before the 1460s, very effective, despite the monarchy's agnosticism or sometimes its active support of feudal rights.

The baronage would adopt this strategy in nearly identical form thirty years later, when economic conditions took a temporary turn for the worse. But although by the late fifteenth century the demographic tide had turned again in the landlords' favour, state policies had also changed. From the late 1480s, Ferdinand began to implement more authoritarian and anti-seigneurial policies, one aspect of which was to give local grievances more voice in royal courts. As a result, local communities became increasingly disputatious, and feudal lords were forced either to retract their demands or to agree to settlements with their subjects.

Conditions in the demesne towns were very different. Fourteenth-century urban society appears to have been unusually unstructured. Social networks were weak; geographical and social mobility was intense; and urban government was in the hands of individuals who lacked the administrative and political resources to establish themselves as a closed élite. At the beginning of the fifteenth century, social relations in the demesne were still fluid, and clear distinctions of class and status were still not fully established. But in the political vacuum that followed the collapse of royal authority after the Black Death, something within this structure had begun to change.

After 1400, a vigorous and dynamic urban society, which included the nucleus of a new financial and administrative class, began to emerge from a long period of economic and political autarky under feudal rule. At first rather slowly, then increasingly rapidly, the urban social landscape was transformed from an informal, even inchoate, structure to a more recognizably hierarchical, 'Renaissance' corporate body. The urban middle and upper classes were the main beneficiaries of what the Aragonese restoration brought in its train: greater political security, unity of the domestic market and toll franchises, and especially the new financial and administrative opportunities provided by a rapidly expanding state structure.

The struggle for control over urban administration and deliberate royal intervention crystallized four urban corporate groups: the civic nobility, which adopted the title of *nobiles*; the rural entrepreneurs (*borgesi* and *massari*); the artisans (*menestrali*); and the *popolo*. The structuring of urban society thus came to a head at a time when the state's intense fiscal pressure was not yet backed by a comparable weight of authority, or supported by adequate institutional props.

Because demesne society was far more urbanized, hence more complex, than communities under feudal lordship, conflicts caused by the growth of state taxation after 1400 were particularly harsh in the demesne. Within the latter, struggle was more intense and took more complex forms in the larger and more thriving communities situated mainly in val di Mazara and especially val di Noto. In val Demone – where demesne communities were numerous but mostly small – social conflict reached a high pitch only in Messina and, to a lesser extent, in Randazzo.

Social polarization and even increasingly formalized social hierarchy seems not to have excluded social mobility within the towns. This was probably increased by the new opportunities provided by economic change and by the expansion of the state. Until the mid-fifteenth century (later periods are still *terra incognita*), access to urban government seems to have been quite open. Urban government can be described as oligarchical insofar as it was occupied by a small number of families at any one time, but those families were still defined empirically through their wealth rather than through acquired or hereditary status, and could disappear as rapidly as they arose as a result of economic failure.

Wealth came from economic diversification and growth – from the sugar, silk, wine and tunny industries, from animal husbandry and mining, from suburban orchards and petty manufacture described in previous chapters. Ultimately, the source of this wealth lay in a massive redistribution of income from land to labour – reflected in sharply declining land rents, strong increases in agricultural and industrial wages,[225] strong and often successful challenges to seigneurial exactions in the countryside and, last but not least, the appearance in the fifteenth century of urban corporate bodies of wage earners.[226] This redistribution fuelled the demand which sustained specialization and growth.

Between *c.*1430 and *c.*1460, the wage-labourers, small peasants and petty retailers who had benefited from these economic changes were able to organize collectively under the name of *popolo*. But the *popolo* was the least clearly defined of the four collective actors

---

[225] See above, chapters 3 and 5. I assume that real wage increases were reflected (to an unknown extent) in a rise in real earnings. Communities frequently tried to restrict wages in the early fifteenth century. See Garufi, 'Patti agrari e comuni feudali di nuova fondazione in Sicilia. Dallo scorcio del secolo XI agli albori del Settecento. Studi storico-diplomatici', 75–81; Tirrito ed., *Statuto di Castronuovo*, p. 142 (1401); Trasselli, *Storia dello zucchero*, p. 84 (Palermo, 1407, 1412, 1424, 1425); PR 21, fo. 108 (Piazza, 1420); PR 24, fo. 120rv (Polizzi, 1421); RC 54, fos. 383v, 386v (Nicosia, 1423); RC 56, fos. 65v–6 (Castrogiovanni, 1425); PR 27, fos. 135v–7 (Calascibetta, 1426); Cordova, *Origini di Aidone*, pp. 43–8 (1427); *UM*, p. 215 (Catania, 1435); De Vio ed., *Privilegia*, pp. 241–3 (Palermo, 1438); RC 79, fos. 81–2, and Giambruno and Genuardi, *Capitoli inediti*, p. 306 (Agrigento, 1443 and 1445). See also CR 48, fos. 158–8bis (Sinagra, 1469); CR 50, fo. 2 (Randazzo, 1470).

[226] 'Vigneri, lavuraturi, urtulani, vaccari' in Catania in 1445; but by 1460, the 'lavuraturi' and 'vaccari' had disappeared (Marletta, 'La costituzione'). 'Lavoratori' and 'ortolani' in Syracuse in 1474 (Privitera, *Storia di Siracusa*, II, pp. 499–500).

to emerge, the most open to social tensions caused by demographic growth and migration, lacking resources to stabilize political consensus and a common identity. After the 1460s, as the demographic tide turned against it, the *popolo* vanished as a political force. Above it, a new political balance was slowly being established on the lines of a corporative allocation of power in the localities, a balance which was forcing opposition by those people lacking direct political representation into fragmented, individualistic and factional forms. The bases of the modern corporatist state had been laid.

THE STATE

Besides the aristocracy and urban society, the third main role in the social processes I have described was played by the state. So far, I have portrayed the state largely as a passive combination of institutions providing an arena for conflict between the aristocracy and demesne society, and within the demesne itself. But the state also played a more active and independent part, and in the process was itself transformed.

By and large, late medieval Sicilian monarchs lacked a deliberate economic policy (see chapter 6). However one judges Frederick II's policies,[227] few of his medieval successors had a similar self-conscious urge to harness trade to their own political ends. Most rulers wished merely to ensure that their financial needs were met by adequate tax revenues. The only exception to this general pattern was Alfonso V, the most 'mercantilist' of Sicilian rulers; his vision of a Mediterranean 'common market' under the aegis of the crown of Aragon is unusual for the political self-awareness it bespeaks. Even so, most of the time Alfonso himself acted in a thoroughly traditional way, harnessing international trade to political rather than economic ends, or devising policies whose sole aim was to increase customs dues. In this guise, he protected the iron and saltpetre industries for military and fiscal purposes; he upheld free trade and tried to unify local measurements to foster taxable grain exports; and he established new fairs to raise tax revenues, but refused toll franchises when financial needs were pressing.

[227] J. M. Powell, 'Medieval monarchy and trade: the economic policy of Emperor Frederick II of Sicily'; E. Maschke, 'Die Wirtschaftspolitik Kaiser Friedrichs II. im Königreichs Sizilien'; Abulafia, *Frederick II. A medieval emperor*, pp. 214–25.

State and urban economic policies in late medieval Sicily may have been weaker than in other monarchies and regional states in the same period.[228] Some common regulatory measures were adopted by Sicilian towns, especially in matters of food supply, but even in this customary sphere of intervention, only sporadic efforts were made and may even have declined over time as market integration increased. Craft guilds were undeveloped. Government regulation of rural credit markets developed mostly in the sixteenth century.[229] The state thus had its greatest impact on social and economic processes through taxation. This may be seen by examining in turn the late medieval state's fiscal and financial policies; their effects on the distribution of financial resources between Sicily and the rest of the Aragonese empire in the fifteenth century; and the question of how the late medieval state was able considerably to increase its tax base while at the same time reinforcing its political stability and legitimacy.

Taxation and financial policy

Royal fiscal and financial policies after 1282 have yet to be examined systematically.[230] What follows is therefore restricted to an outline of the more enduring structural features of the tax policies, and to their most significant transformations and consequences.

I have already mentioned the main structural constraint on late medieval Sicilian royal taxation. In 1286, as part of the political settlement following the Sicilian Vespers of 1282, James II had established constitutional limits on direct taxation based on the Catalan model. Hearth taxes were allowed to be raised for four reasons only: the defence of the realm from invasion or rebellion; the ransom of the sovereign or of his heirs; the knighting of the king, his brothers or heirs; and the marriage of the king's sisters or heirs. In the first two cases, 15,000 *onze* could be raised; in the other two, no more than 5,000 *onze*.[231] Martino I confirmed this settlement in 1403,[232] but in actual fact no more than 5,000 *onze* at a time were

[228] Postan, Rich and Miller eds., *Economic organization and policies*, chapter 6.
[229] Aymard, 'Amministrazione feudale'; Aymard, 'Commercio dei grani'.
[230] See Di Martino, 'Sistema tributario'; Trasselli, 'Debito pubblico'; Trasselli, 'Su le finanze siciliane da Bianca ai Viceré'; Dentici Buccellato ed., *Fisco e società*, 'Introduzione'; *UM*, pp. 792–7, 840–3, 846, 850–4.
[231] See above, chapter 2, n. 57.
[232] Testa ed., *Capitula*, I, pp. 174–5 (1402); Gregorio, *Considerazioni*, V, chapter 5, pp. 57–63.

raised for most of the fifteenth century.[233] This tax ceiling was probably first broken in 1476–7, when parliament voted a 'donation' (*donativo*) of 6,000 *onze*.[234] As a consequence of this constitutional limitation on direct taxation, the state's main source of fiscal revenue was from excise on domestic and foreign trade.

Available evidence suggests that, for about forty years after the Vespers, the intensity of taxation was rather light. In particular, the scanty evidence of taxation between 1296 and 1302, when the crown's needs were at a peak because of the struggle against Naples and the presence in Sicily of a large contingent of Catalan knights and foot-soldiers (*almugaveres*), suggests that feudal levies and trade excise were still sufficient to finance Sicily's defence.

Both direct and indirect taxes began to increase from the late 1320s,[235] but the reason was not a rise in expenditure for, despite some Angevin skirmishes in the 1330s, the worst of the war was by then past. Rather, the main reason for increasing taxes was a considerable decline in fiscal revenue, itself the result of demographic stagnation or decline in Sicily and abroad. A smaller population within Sicily provided lower revenue from domestic excise; the same phenomenon abroad was translated into lower demand for Sicilian grain, and thus a smaller income from export dues. However, the monarchy's tax base was not being narrowed only as a result of declining domestic and foreign population. An equally serious problem was the rapid erosion of the royal demesne itself. From its accession, the new Aragonese dynasty had had to alienate an increasing proportion of demesne rights and property to the feudal aristocracy and to the larger demesne cities in exchange for military and political support.[236] But from the late 1320s and the 1330s, as we saw, the aristocracy began a more deliberate attack on royal resources in response to deteriorating economic and political conditions.

The Sicilian monarchy's plight was not unusual, for the erosion of

---

[233] Testa ed., *Capitula*, I, pp. 174–5.
[234] TRP n.p. 80, Trasselli ed., 'Ricerche su la popolazione'.
[235] *UM*, p. 795, Table 183. Reference was made in 1336 to annual *subvenciones* (Dentici Buccellato ed., *Fisco e società*, pp. 309–10).
[236] Tax exemptions (including toll franchises; see above, chapter 3) must be interpreted in this sense. See Giardina ed., *Capitula*, nos. 34, 40, 42 (Messina, 1302, 1367, 1368); De Vio ed., *Privilegia*, pp. 45–6 (Palermo, 1314); RC 2, fos. 86v–8v (Mazara, 1318); Pisano Baudo, *Storia di Lentini*, II, pp. 202–3, 207–8 (Lentini, 1339, 1349).

the royal demesne is a common feature of many western European monarchies in this period.[237] The roots of the phenomenon were common also: increasing conflict over resources, to which nascent central states, caught up in the spiralling costs of war, were still too weak to oppose much resistance. By raising taxes, on the other hand, the monarchy was in danger of initiating a vicious cycle of 'poverty taxing': it needed to increase taxes in order to maintain stable revenues, but risked depressing the country's production, and thus further reducing taxable resources.

The considerable decline in excise income from the royal demesne can be estimated by comparing revenues in the late 1270s and the 1320s. In 1278–9, total excise income from the demesne was 19,857.4.13 *onze*.[238] Assuming that excise from individual cities was roughly in proportion to their size, tax returns from Palermo can have been no less than 6,300 *onze* (in 1277 the city was allocated 31.8 per cent of the demesne's *colletta*); since Palermo monopolized much of Sicily's foreign trade at the time, excise revenues in the city were probably an even larger proportion of the total. In 1326, by contrast, tolls in Palermo were farmed out for 4,700 *onze*, despite the fact that a number of new tolls had been introduced during the previous decade. In 1327–8, Palermo's excise was farmed out for 5,000 *onze*, and a year later for 5,700 *onze*; the increase reflected expected rises in income from tolls introduced in 1328.[239] Thus, despite a considerable increase in indirect taxation, returns from excise in Palermo seem to have dropped at least a quarter between the 1270s and the 1320s. The decline in domestic excise income increased the importance of taxes on the grain trade,[240] but export

---

237 M. T. Ferrer i Mallol, 'El patrimoni reial i la recuperació del senyorius juris-diccionals en els estats catalano-aragonesos a la fi del segle XIV'; M. Rey, *Le domaine du roi et les finances extraordinaires sous Charles VI (1388–1413)*, pp. 41, 45–51; W. Küchler, 'Länder- und Zentralfinanz des aragonesischen Staaten-bundes im 15. Jahrhundert. Zur Rolle der spanischen und italienischen Länder in der Finanzpolitik der Krone', 38–42; R. Cazelles, *Société politique, noblesse et Couronne sous Jean le Bon et Charles V*, pp. 29–30, 512–15, 560–5; B. P. Wolffe, *The royal demesne in English history: the Crown estate in the governance of the realm from the Conquest to 1509*, pp. 79–84, 112–17, 124–58, 195–201.

238 *RCA*, XXI, no. 327.

239 *UM*, p. 794 n. 119; Dentici Buccellato ed., *Fisco e società*, pp. 40, 46–7, 284–93; Corrao ed., *Registri di lettere*, no. 59.

240 In January 1323, Federico III was forced by local dearth to forbid grain exports, 'quod nobis cessit ad incommodum maximum presertim cum proventus et reditus regni nostri pro maiori parte consistant in iuribus exiturarum [bladi]' (Giunta and Giuffrida eds., *Corrispondenza*, no. 132).

revenues at this time did not exceed 10,000 *onze*,[241] approximately twice the proceeds from Palermo's *secrezia*.

While the first two years of the Iberian reconquest were largely financed with concessions of export rights on grain, the monarchy was also forced to grant large parts of the demesne to its Iberian and Sicilian followers. By doing this before their authority had been fully established, however, we saw that the Martins were in danger of undermining their financial resources and weakening crucial demesne support.[242] The Martins were able to re-establish authority over their demesne because, for the first time, they could rely on powerful political and economic support from the demesne itself.

In the first major parliamentary assembly after the invasion held in Syracuse in 1398, the monarchy re-asserted its monopoly over the grain trade and over regalian rights, and drew up a list of communities which would belong in perpetuity to the demesne.[243] The latter decision was meant, of course, to set a limit to feudal encroachment and to provide the monarchy with an adequate financial base. But by excluding the possibility of future alienations of its land and rights, the monarchy was not so much marking a change of policy *vis-à-vis* fourteenth-century royal practice, as signalling far deeper changes in the political and social framework within which it could manœuvre. Half a century earlier, the demesne had been unable to rally to the king's side and to exert any effective resistance against magnate usurpation; in 1398, by contrast, the new Iberian sovereigns could re-establish a strong financial base *because* of the backing from the demesne's élite groups which had been considerably strengthened by the fourteenth-century political and economic crisis. For a century thereafter, the monarchy's ability to act independently from feudal pressure relied on the possibility of appealing to an alternative urban political base.

Between 1398 and 1420, the monarchy wavered between two

---

[241] Exports were 40,000–80,000 *salme* in the early fourteenth century; the *tratta* was set at three to four *tarì* per *salma*. See above, chapter 6, and *UM*, p. 531.

[242] Corrao, *Governare un regno*, pp. 341–80, is most useful for the period 1392–1420. See also Trasselli, 'Finanze siciliane'; Baviera Albanese, 'L'istituzione dell'ufficio'.

[243] Testa ed., *Capitula*, I, pp. 152–3. A similar provision was passed by Martin of Aragon for Catalonia in 1399 (Ferrer i Mallol, 'El patrimoni reial', 355).

apparently conflicting fiscal and financial policies – between, on the one hand, attempts to introduce financial 'rigour' and stringency for the crown's own needs and, on the other, attempts to maintain the laxity necessary to sustain political consensus in the kingdom. This indecisiveness was expressed in recurrent moves to reform royal finances, particularly when grants on demesne revenues became so excessive as to threaten the upkeep of military garrisons and of the court itself.[244] Attempts at reform were based on the belief that financial chaos was due to the proliferation of new offices charged with tax collection and expenditure, offices which were only rarely if ever scrutinized or challenged. But although technical problems connected with the still-rudimentary development of a central financial administration played a part in this confusion, the root cause of the monarchy's difficulties lay elsewhere. Laxity and periodic appeals to rigour were structural and interdependent aspects of the monarchy's finances in this period.

Royal finances had three main purposes: to maintain the court; to finance the defence of the realm (and, on occasion, foreign wars); and to be distributed to subjects in patronage or for service. Court expenditure was relatively stable, but military and patronage costs tended ineluctably to spiral as the state extended its powers and spheres of activity. In peacetime, the source of expenditure with the strongest capacity for inertial growth was patronage, which expanded in response to increasing social differentiation and to the proliferation of individual and group interests that could claim royal attention. Once established, moreover, patronage was difficult to reverse. It could only be retracted in the event of rebellion, civil war or outside aggression, when the state could reallocate resources with no loss of legitimacy. The boundaries of financial 'rigour' were thus rather narrowly defined.

The Aragonese monarchy faced two potentially conflicting claims to its patronage. On one side was the aristocracy, for which demesne revenues were a necessary supplement to their dwindling incomes from the land. On the other side were the urban élite groups, which demanded an increasing share of revenues from taxation in return for local and national political support. Before

---

[244] Corrao, *Governare un regno*, pp. 341–80.

the 1430s, these claims probably increased faster than available resources, partly because much of demesne trade was being exempted from excise (see chapter 3) and grain exports were stagnant, and partly because the monarchy found it very hard to raise taxes during peacetime. Stagnant tax revenues exacerbated competition between the relatively fixed sources of expenditure (court livings and military defence) and the more elastic share assigned to royal patronage, and explain both the periodic attempts to reduce or at least stabilize state expenditure, and the failure of these efforts.

Taxation did not increase substantially before the 1430s, when Alfonso launched the decade-long war to conquer the kingdom of Naples. Although he had attempted to raise a *colletta* in 1421 and 1423, when organizing his first expedition to Naples, he had encountered such stiff resistance – led in 1421 by the countess of Caltabellotta, whose example was followed by 'many other towns and lands both of the demesne and under feudal lordship'[245] – that he had had to desist. As a result, Alfonso was forced to raise loans among the aristocracy and civic nobility, which he paid with demesne revenue and with taxes on the Church and the Jews.[246] Soon after landing in Sicily in 1433, he tried to raise a hearth tax for his sister Leonor's marriage, but failed once more.[247] Although a new attempt a year later was more successful, Alfonso was unable to raise a regular hearth tax on a yearly basis before 1439.[248]

Alfonso's financial policies have been judged harsh and exploitative,[249] but the evidence hardly supports this view. Although his financial demands were usually high for Sicily, they are far less remarkable when compared with other countries. The late fourteenth and the fifteenth centuries was a period of profound change in financial and fiscal systems throughout western Europe, which in most cases involved intensifying fiscal pressure by the state. In this broader context, Sicily's lack of political or dynastic continuity may actually have delayed developments which elsewhere (in Castile or

---

[245] C 2888, fos. 67v–9v, 70v, 72v–3; C 2811, fo. 95. For 1423 see PR 24, fos. 253v–4; Genuardi, 'Raccolta di memoriali', pp. 158–9.
[246] C 2888, fos. 76v–7; Ryder, *Alfonso the Magnanimous*, p. 90 n. 81; CR 11, fo. 589rv.
[247] RC 67, fo. 96v (1432); C 2889, fos. 82v, 84rv (1432).
[248] *UM*, pp. 852–3, Table 193.
[249] Trasselli, 'Debito pubblico'.

Burgundy, for example) were initiated during the second half of the fourteenth century or even before.[250] In fact, Alfonso seems to have had far greater difficulty in obtaining aid from Sicily than from other lands of the crown of Aragon. On 22 March 1418, when he was still debating whether to embark for Sicily, Alfonso wrote to Palermo, Messina, Catania, Agrigento and Syracuse informing them of a 189,000 florin subsidy voted that same day by the parliament of Valencia.[251] His hint was not taken, and for the following two decades Sicilians remained unforthcoming. Sicily's tax load increased considerably from the mid-1430s (when demesne assets began to be alienated at an increasing rate), but it was still below the level demanded uninterruptedly from a far earlier date from Alfonso's Iberian kingdoms, in particular from Valencia.[252] Also in contrast with the rest of the Aragonese lands, Sicily was not subjected to a state monopoly over salt (see chapter 4).

Alfonso compensated for the Sicilians' resistance to direct taxation by increasing indirect taxes, and by exploiting to an unprecedented degree the demesne's resources. Yet he never considered such measures as anything more than temporary expedients, to be reversed whenever finances allowed. Each wave of alienations (in 1420–5, 1430–4 and 1440–6) was preceded and followed by orders to recover the royal patrimony. As far as one can tell, these orders were carried out quite successfully.[253] In March 1433, the king congratulated officials for their efforts to recover Mazara, Sciacca, Naro, Castronovo and Sutera, but warned them that what these towns were offering as ransom was not enough. A year later, the viceroy was authorized to free communities which wished to buy their way back to the demesne from oaths of obedience to their liege lords. A meeting in Palermo in late September 1434 between the king and demesne representatives (including those temporarily

---

[250] See J. P. Genet and M. Le Mené eds., *Genèse de l'état moderne. Prélèvement et redistribution*.

[251] C 2801, fo. 178.

[252] C. López Rodríguez, 'La estructura de los ingresos de la tesorería general de Alfonso el Magnánimo y la conquista de Italia (1424–47)', p. 331 and Table 8.

[253] C 2804, fo. 26 (1418); C 2888, fos. 170v–1 (1425–6). The fact that nearly twice as many perpetual apanages were granted by Martino than by Alfonso (Corrao, *Governare un regno*, pp. 341–80) also suggests that the latter paid more care to financial detail than he is usually credited for.

under feudal lordship) probably addressed the same issues.[254] In the course of 1434, Troina, Naro, Sutera and Castronovo returned under royal authority.[255] Another successful campaign to buy back demesne rights and property, partly financed with a surtax of one *tarì* on grain exports, was launched in 1443–5.[256] On both occasions, the king's financial exigencies had temporarily changed. The campaign of 1434 was possible because the successful hearth tax of 1433–4 had made the sale of royal patrimony unnecessary. The campaign of 1443–5, by contrast, coincided with the conquest of Naples, which brought about a temporary reduction in military expenditure. Alfonso's statement that 'after his innumerable labours' and the pacification of his kingdom he intended to recover all alienated rights and jurisdictions, rings true.[257]

In return for parliamentary demands to put a stop to alienations,[258] Alfonso levied special taxes to buy back the demesne in 1446–7 (150,000 Aragonese florins over six years) and 1452–3 (200,000 Aragonese florins over twelve years).[259] How much of this money was spent for its official purpose is unclear,[260] but most major alienations – of entire communities or of their tax offices (*secrezie*) – appear to have been recovered before Alfonso's death in 1458.[261] Among the goals of the reconnaissance of feudal rights begun in 1453 was the recovery of usurped rights.[262] Whether in the end Alfonso was, or indeed could be, entirely successful in reclaiming royal resources, however, given the powerful web of interests his previous policy had woven, is a question that awaits further research.

[254] C 2889, fo. 114rv (March 1433); C 2892, fo. 21bis (June 1434); C 2891, fos. 125, 138v (September 1434).

[255] *UM*, p. 856, Table 194. Attempts were also made to recover Mazara (C 2821, fos. 318–19, and RC 68, fo. 165rv, 1433), Sciacca (C 2820, fo. 167, 1434) and Licata (C 2892, fo. 31v, 1435).

[256] C 2935, fos. 155v–6 (1443); CR 847, unnumbered fos. (23 September 1444); C 2894, fos. 52v, 63rv (1445).

[257] C 2859, fo. 79 (1448). Garufi, 'Patti agrari e comuni feudali', doc. 5 (1452): Giacomo Playa, an official of the Magna Regia Curia, may found a new village near Corleone (Conte Ranieri) in reward for his successful efforts to recover demesne rights and property.

[258] Testa ed., *Capitula*, I, pp. 335 (1446), 366 (1451).

[259] *UM*, p. 853, Table 193.

[260] In 1452, Polizzi asked that the money be spent for the purposes it had been voted for (C 2871, fos. 119v–21).

[261] *UM*, pp. 856–8, Table 194. See also C 2896, fo. 70v (1451); C 2897, fo. 97v (1454).

[262] Above, n. 63.

Alfonso's death in 1458 temporarily ended the long period of intense war finance begun in the 1430s. In 1461, Juan II of Aragon agreed to reduce direct taxes in exchange for the demesne's political support in the Catalan civil war. In contrast with Alfonso, Juan could rely on steadily rising income from taxes on domestic trade and especially on exports (grain and silk in particular), and could thus generally avoid disposing of regalian rights and property.[263] However, financial exigencies in Catalonia forced him a few years later to a slight change of policy, and between 1465 and 1469 he authorized the sale of the county of Augusta, Marsala and Aci 'for the preservation of the state and [his] other kingdoms'.[264] At the same time, he considerably increased financial transfers from Sicily to his central treasury. By and large, however, the tax load seems to have decreased greatly compared to the 1440s and 1450s, for in 1462 Juan agreed to abolish the annual *donativi* in exchange for Sicilian complaisance in the Catalan civil war.[265] Juan's policy of non-interference and financial conservatism seems to have been pursued by Ferdinand up to the late 1480s.

The evidence in conclusion suggests that late medieval Sicily was not very heavily taxed except possibly under Alfonso. In order to assess this statement more closely, however, we must examine two further issues: what was late medieval Sicily's share of financial contributions to the crown of Aragon as a whole, and to what purposes were these contributions put.

Taxation and regional resources

For a long time the assumption that the Spanish state exploited its Italian territories through taxation dominated southern Italian historiography. This view has never been challenged for late medieval Sicily; Alfonso's financial 'pillage' of the Sicilian economy to pay for expensive wars on the Italian mainland is a topos of the literature.[266]

---

[263] C 3480, fo. 106v (1460): Juan refuses the proposed sale of Mazara by his nephew, King Ferrante of Naples, to Giovanni Miraballi, a Neapolitan banker.

[264] C 3486, fos. 29–31v (1467), 135v–49, 150rv (1469); TRP Atti 27, fo. 147rv (1469); C 3481, fos. 42–5v (1469), 84–92v (1470). At the same time Juan decided to dispense with Sicilian military aid in Catalonia (Vicens Vives, *Fernando el Católico*, p. 176).

[265] See this chapter below, and n. 290. Juan may have introduced a new tax on trade; see C 3487, fo. 70rv (1471): 'gabella nova tareni unius pro uncia noviter omnibus comitibus et baronibus regni Sicilie concessa'.

[266] Trasselli, 'Debito pubblico'; Trasselli, 'Finanze siciliane'.

Before addressing the question of Sicily's financial contribution to the crown of Aragon as a whole, however, it is necessary to provide an estimate of the volume of resources which the Aragonese sovereigns could dispose of, relative to the size of each of their subject lands, for differences from country to country in the size of the royal patrimony meant that income from the demesne relative to an individual country as a whole could vary considerably. These differences provide not so much a measure of relative state exploitation, as an element that can help explain divergent patterns of growth of the late medieval state.

The relative size of a country's demesne can be evaluated in two ways. On the one hand, it can be measured as the proportion of individuals living under royal, as opposed to feudal, authority. No figures are available for the Iberian kingdoms, but for Italy the picture is clearer. Compared to twenty per cent of the population (*c.*45,000 hearths) living in the southern Italian demesne towards 1450,[267] in Sicily at least half the population (*c.*30,000 hearths) came under direct royal authority in the same period (see Table 2.4). This difference, as we shall see, helps explain not only the monarchy's comparative lack of interest in the demesne towns on the southern mainland before the second half of the fifteenth century, and conversely the importance of crown–demesne relations in Sicily, but also different political and institutional developments in the two lands.

On the other hand, the size of the demesne can be measured in terms of the resources which the monarchy could actually dispose of. By the mid-fifteenth century, the royal demesne was largely pawned or sold off in many of the Aragonese territories, and as a result, the king's financial resources were often very meagre. In fifteenth-century Catalonia, believed to be the wealthiest member of the crown, demesne assets are described as 'liquidated', barely sufficient to cover administrative costs and debt repayment; the monarchy was unable to raise loans for lack of security.[268] As a result, the Barcelonese oligarchy was deprived of a lucrative source of income, and the monarchy lost a powerful means of forging

[267] Estimates are based on the tax returns for 1443 published by Cozzetto, *Mezzogiorno e demografia*, to which 10,000 hearths for Naples and Taranto have been added (*ibid.*, pp. 23–4).
[268] Küchler, 'Länder- und Zentralfinanz', 31, 47–8. See also Ferrer i Mallol, 'El patrimoni reial', 436–48; Ryder, *Alfonso the Magnanimous*, pp. 388–9.

political loyalty. In the kingdom of Naples, the demesne was in less disarray. In 1443, excise returned *c*.100,000–115,000 ducats (30,000–34,500 *onze*);[269] by 1458, income had risen to 155,000 ducats (46,500 *onze*).[270] The only available estimate of demesne revenues in Sicily refers to 1418, when demesne population was *c*.25,000 hearths. Income from the *secrezie* was said to be no more than 12,000–12,500 *onze* per year; the estimate did not include revenues from export dues which, however, at the time were probably not very significant.[271] Sicilian finances were in complete disarray after years of civil war and hand-to-mouth administration, and the estimate was produced in order to stress financial hardship. Towards 1450, therefore, revenues would have been considerably higher, since the demesne's population had risen to 30,000 hearths, and excise on agricultural and manufactured exports had risen to *c*.3,500–4,000 *onze* per year.[272] By 1450, annual excise income from the Sicilian demesne was in the region of 18,000–20,000 *onze*, approximately the same as in the 1270s with a population less than half the size.[273]

Towards 1450, the Sicilian and southern Italian demesnes were financially profitable, for they both provided a considerable surplus over their current administrative expenditure. But although average receipts per demesne hearth from indirect taxation were roughly the same (about twenty *tarì* per demesne hearth on the mainland compared to about eighteen to twenty *tarì* in Sicily), the two countries differed considerably in the intensity of *direct* taxation which applied to the entire population rather than only to the

[269] These figures were allegedly estimated by an ambassador from Ferrara, Borso d'Este, in 1444 (C. Foucard, 'Proposta fatta dalla Corte estense ad Alfonso I re di Napoli'; Del Treppo, *Regno aragonese*, p. 117). D'Este's report was based on a population estimate of 400,000 hearths, subsequently revised to *c*.230,000 hearths (Cozzetto, *Mezzogiorno e demografia*, pp. 23–4). I have corrected d'Este's estimate of excise revenue (200,000 ducats for 400,000 hearths) on the basis of the revised population figures.

[270] Del Treppo, *Regno aragonese*, p. 121. Excise provided 220,881 ducats in 1483 (*ibid.*, pp. 118–19).

[271] Corrao, *Governare un regno*, p. 374.

[272] Average grain exports were 25,000 *salme*, and average excise was 3–4 *tarì* per *salma*; annual revenues from the grain trade alone were therefore 2,500–3,330 *onze*.

[273] Bresc, 'Società e politica in Sicilia', 281 estimates an average annual government income in 1405–43 of 25,000 *onze*, but provides no detailed figures. This estimate presumably includes income from hearth taxes and from the alienation of demesne resources.

386   *An island for itself*

royal demesne. In the kingdom of Naples, every hearth paid one ducat (nine *tarì*) per year as hearth tax and half a ducat (4.10 *tarì*) per year to purchase state salt; in Sicily, the average hearth tax was less than a fifth that amount (1.10–3 *tarì*) and the salt tax did not exist.[274] As a result, in Naples sixty-nine per cent of government revenues came from direct taxation, whereas in Sicily it was a mere twenty per cent. The different fiscal structure in the two countries had some serious consequences. First, due to the smaller size of the demesne on the southern mainland, higher levels of direct taxation there did not in fact provide the crown with proportionately higher levels of income. In other words, although direct taxes were between five and nine times as high on the mainland as they were in Sicily, tax revenue per hearth was less than twenty-five per cent higher because indirect taxes levied in the demesne were so much less profitable.[275] Second, indirect, demesne taxation in Sicily provided its government with considerably more scope than on the mainland for political patronage via fiscal administration and allocation in the localities. Third, during the 1440s and 1450s, between one half and two thirds of royal income in the kingdom of Naples was spent on financing Alfonso's wars in central and northern Italy, in particular on paying his mercenary forces. Thus, a very large proportion of the Neapolitan fiscal resources would appear to have been spent outside the kingdom.[276] By contrast, most tax receipts in Sicily never left the country at all. Most tax returns were redistributed as military or administrative wages and as patronage for the aristocracy, urban élite groups and the expanding government bureaucracy; the rest tended to be spent on supplies for armies or for the court in Naples or Spain.[277] In 1440, for example, the king ordered the viceroy to buy 10,000 *salme* of grain and 1,000 horses with 15,000 ducats Alfonso had previously asked be sent to Naples;[278] in 1425, Alfonso had actually imported cloth and bullion from Valencia to pay his troops in Sicily and on the mainland.[279]

---

274 Del Treppo, *Regno aragonese*, p. 117; above, chapters 2 and 4.
275 In 1458, government income in Naples was 500,000 ducats (150,000 *onze*), approximately 19.10 *tarì* per hearth; income in Sicily was *c*.25,000–30,000 *onze*, *c*.15 *tarì* per hearth.
276 Del Treppo, *Regno aragonese*, pp. 117–19.
277 C 2889, fo. 113rv (1433).
278 C 2935, fos. 127v–8 (1440); only 10,000 ducats had been sent.
279 C 2888, fo. 159v (1425): 8,000 Aragonese florins in cash and 7,000 in cloth.

Differences in fiscal regime between the kingdom of Naples and Sicily show very clearly how the dual character of taxation could affect the development of the late medieval state. As a means of taking away from, and of distributing to, individual and collective interests, taxation tended both to erode and to reinforce the power of the state. Political stability depended to a large degree on finding a correct balance between the extremes of over-taxation and political ineffectuality. Was such a balance struck in Naples and Sicily? In fifteenth-century Naples, the state imposed a high rate of taxation, but benefited little from the opportunities for political patronage taxation provided; in fifteenth-century Sicily, a lower level of taxation could be distributed in politically far more effective ways. This contrast seems to explain much of the countries' different patterns of political conflict in this period, both within and against the state: on the mainland, a succession of concerted, massive peasant and baronial revolts against the monarchy, and foreign invasions assisted by domestic discontent; in Sicily, a period of intense but fragmented demesne-based revolt under Alfonso, followed by over half a century of social and political stability.

A full answer to the question, what was Sicily's financial contribution to the Aragonese empire after annexation in 1413, must await further research on the finances of individual Aragonese lands. Winfried Küchler's work on the finances of the crown of Aragon under Alfonso V and Juan II has, however, established some important preliminary points.[280]

Küchler argues that, while the co-ordination of territorial finances by the central treasury provided considerable impetus for unifying the Aragonese crown, unification was not actually achieved because the necessary institutional, political and technical conditions were lacking. In the first place, because of the administrative confusion and lack of technical expertise caused by the rapid growth of financial exigencies and taxation, the king had only a very rough idea of his territories' financial abilities and solvency, and was thus unable accurately to plan expenditure.[281] As a consequence,

---

[280] Küchler, 'Länder- und Zentralfinanz'; Küchler, *Die Finanzen der Krone Aragon während des 15. Jahrhunderts (Alfons V. und Johann II.)*, chapter 1.

[281] This situation began to change under Charles V, who reversed the balance between domestic and foreign expenditure and intensified the pressure for a more efficient and effective bureaucracy (Küchler, 'Länder- und Zentralfinanz', 89); nonetheless, Sicily's financial administration only came under a single unified authority with Philip II (Trasselli, 'Debito pubblico', 95).

royal demands to transfer money to the central treasury bore little relation to the actual level of the revenue or financial surplus of individual territories, and a country's capacity to contribute to the central treasury seems to have been assessed only very approximately from estimates of its wealth and the size of the available demesne. Secondly, the technical means available for transferring money between different administrations – bullion transfer and bills of exchange – made such operations complicated, risky and expensive. These technical problems were accentuated, in third place, by a lack of continuity, both in the crown's financial needs and in the methods used for meeting them. Most payments to the central treasury were used for military expenditure which varied considerably in intensity and duration, while the transfers themselves were usually demanded at very short notice and never evolved into a stable financial mechanism.

Because of these difficulties, financial transfers abroad never constituted more than a small proportion of a land's total fiscal revenues, and the king preferred to obtain most resources for war and foreign policy from the country in which he was residing. In the crown of Aragon as a whole, expenditure on foreign policy was only a small proportion of expenditure for domestic purposes. Because of these features of the financial system, and because, as we saw above, domestic demands on fiscal resources had a tendency to increase, there was a parallel tendency for national financial administrations to become detached from central authority, policies and needs. These centrifugal forces were so powerful that, from 1475, Juan II was forced to use false bills of exchange to trick local administrations – in particular the Sicilian treasury – into paying into the central treasury money they would otherwise not part with.[282]

Evidence for Sicily confirms that financial transfers – by way of bullion exports or bills of exchange – were fairly infrequent and involved comparatively small sums of money. Available figures show that total transfers within the crown of Aragon were c.52,070 Sicilian *onze* under Alfonso V (1426–58). Transfers increased under Juan II to c.92,817 *onze*, but were still paltry in comparison with

[282] Küchler, 'Länder- und Zentralfinanz', 88–9; Ryder, *Kingdom of Naples*, pp. 170, 191.

total fiscal revenue.[283] For its part, Sicily transferred *c*.27,215 *onze* under Alfonso, and *c*.72,949 *onze* under Juan (58,130 *onze* between 1458 and mid-1466). Sicily's contribution to the central treasury thus rose from 52.3 per cent of total transfers under Alfonso to 78.6 per cent under Juan. These figures have a number of implications. First, Sicily's contribution to the Aragonese central treasury in terms of the volume of monetary transfers was by all accounts the largest of all the Aragonese lands. But such a measure is misleading, for it takes no account of the fact that financial accounts do not record any 'transfers' from countries in which the king resided, despite the fact that the latter were those which generally contributed most to the central treasury. Since no king resided for long or waged war in or from Sicily after 1413, this country's transfers inevitably overestimate its contribution to Aragonese finances as a whole. The second consideration, which slightly qualifies the first, is that the high volume of financial transfers from Sicily could reflect the comparatively large volume of resources (in relation to the size of the country) available to the monarchy in Sicily, a situation of fiscal 'surplus' which could make financial transfers overseas easier to achieve. This leads to a third consideration, that there is little sign that such transfers had any serious impact on the Sicilian economy. Total transfers between 1426 and 1478 involved about four or five years' income from the demesne, probably considerably less than ten per cent of total tax revenues in the same period. The fact that the country's subsidy of Aragonese central finances raised so few complaints,[284] together with the infrequent and easily relaxed bans on bullion exports,[285] suggest that the issue was not considered to be very serious by the local political and commercial élite, which had no compunction on other occasions in addressing strong complaints

[283] Küchler, 'Länder- und Zentralfinanz', 12, underestimates Sicilian transfers, because the central treasury registers he uses record only some of the direct transfers between Naples and Palermo. On the other hand, his data for the Iberian territories are probably quite accurate. I have integrated his figures for Sicily with data from Trasselli, *Note banchi XV secolo*, I, pp. 43 (1434–5), 253 (1458–66); RC 72, fos. 98v–9, 134 (1438); C 2935, fos. 127v–8 (1440); C 2805, fo. 133v (1442); RC 85, fos. 424v–5, and C 2896, fos. 69v, 82 (1451).

[284] Testa ed., *Capitula*, I, pp. 434–5.

[285] C 2935, fo. 160 (1443); C 2935, fos. 166v–7 (1446); C 2894, fos. 96v–100 (1446); C 2856, fos. 41, 63rv, 71v–2 (1446); V. Cusumano, *Storia dei banchi di Sicilia. I banchi pubblici*, I, p. 36 (1460, 1478, 1491–2, 1498–9). Bans were usually declared in connection with government bullion exports or new coinages.

to the Aragonese king. As we shall see below, there is no reason to believe that the Sicilian élite groups willingly acquiesced to being fiscally and financially exploited.

Taxation and political consensus

Indeed, a crucial question, to which I have so far provided only a partial answer, concerns the establishment in the course of the fifteenth century of the state's right to raise taxes on a regular basis. Developments in fifteenth-century Sicily tend to be explained in functionalist or conspiratorial terms as the result of a 'colonial pact', whereby local élite groups traded domestic political autonomy for subordination to Aragonese fiscal needs. But this sort of explanation fails on at least two counts: it neither spells out how such a collective agreement could emerge, nor accords with the considerable evidence for intense feudal and urban *resistance* to royal taxation until the 1430s. A satisfactory interpretation must explain why and how the ruling classes changed their attitude towards taxation and state powers, without resorting to forms of conspiracy theory or positing a unanimous and homogeneous social élite.

One reason why rights of taxation took so long to be established, and then only under pressure from Alfonso's Neapolitan wars, was Sicily's lack of a strong parliamentary tradition.[286] In the Iberian kingdoms of the crown of Aragon, taxes and subsidies were regularly voted in parliament by the feudal, ecclesiastical and urban representatives from the thirteenth or the early fourteenth century; in Sicily, the first parliament to vote a *donativo* on the Iberian model was held in 1446. Iberian parliaments (Cortes, Corts), which had evolved as a concession to the three estates under the pressure of mounting royal financial needs, could be a powerful means of resistance to royal demands. At the same time, parliament gave legitimacy to the contractual model of state relations (*pactismo*), which during the thirteenth and fourteenth centuries became the basis of the Aragonese, and more especially the Catalan, unwritten constitutional settlement. By contrast, piecemeal bargaining for financial aid – to which the monarchy had to resort in Sicily until the late 1430s – could help the king pre-empt concerted resistance by his subjects, but in the long run led to high political and administrative

[286] D'Alessandro, 'Sulle assemblee parlamentari.

costs, prevented financial planning, and was more vulnerable to individual evasion.

Following the Aragonese restoration in the 1390s, and primarily in response to tax demands by the state, the Sicilian parliament began to develop as a forum of political and financial negotiation between the monarchy and the Church, the aristocracy, and representatives of the demesne. The Aragonese had attempted a similar policy in Sicily after 1282, but aristocratic resistance and urban weakness combined with the lack of an established domestic parliamentary model in causing the institution to fail. The first important parliamentary assembly after the Aragonese reconquest, held in Syracuse in 1398, established the basis for later institutional developments: at the same time as the monarchy re-established its rights over the demesne, the demesne marked a first political victory over the feudal aristocracy.

A few more parliaments were convened by Martino, but they were bland affairs, suggesting that the main purpose of the assembly of 1398 had been to re-assert royal authority rather than promote a genuine dialogue with the Sicilian estates. The reasons for the absence of dialogue were complex, and have already been discussed: the still eminently 'feudal' character of the Aragonese reconquest; the crown's comparatively moderate fiscal needs in this period; and the as yet unstructured nature of urban society which made it hard for the demesne to express a unified position in dealing with the king.

With the exception of an assembly held in Messina in 1421, just before Alfonso's first attempt to get possession of Naples, no further parliamentary meetings were held before December 1433. Under Alfonso, parliament took the shape it would maintain for two centuries thereafter. Through parliament, Alfonso established a form of *pactismo* on the Catalan model, whereby the three Sicilian estates consented to direct taxes (called *donativi*, donations) in exchange for chapters or petitions submitted for royal approval (*capitoli del Regno*).

Alfonso cannot have been unaware of the dangers that might arise from a strong parliamentary institution, particularly since in the same period the Catalan Corts were giving voice to powerful opposition. For a parliamentary forum to work according to royal intentions, some essential preliminary conditions were required. In particular, Sicilian élite groups had to recognize and accept the contractual nature of their relationship with the monarchy, and at the same time they had to be relatively stable, predictable interlocutors. Neither condition was fully established in the early 1430s, when Alfonso revived parliament to meet his financial demands. But Alfonso had little alternative. His standing in Sicily was still uncertain; he had come to ask for financial aid, not to exact it. Of the two main alternatives in political and institutional practice and culture available to him at the time – Catalan *pactismo* and Castilian authoritarianism[287] – Alfonso could only adopt the former. For the social and institutional basis for a settlement of this kind to be established, however, needed over a decade of intense political and fiscal pressure by the state, and of struggle in the demesne. The contractual basis of political authority in Sicily was officially accepted and enshrined in parliamentary practice only in 1446, when parliament granted its first *donativo* in exchange for royal privileges and considerable *de facto* political autonomy.

Nonetheless, Alfonso's desire to establish a contractual political consensus cannot explain his success in Sicily, as contemporary civil war and rebellion in the kingdom of Naples and Catalonia so clearly demonstrate. The lack of widespread social conflict and anti-monarchical action in fifteenth-century Sicily was not so much the result of successful royal endeavour, as of the Sicilian upper classes' decision to abide by *pactismo* in their own interests. Why were they willing to restrict themselves to corporatist policies, in contrast with their peers in Naples and Catalonia?

Part of the answer to this question, as I suggested above, lies in the volume of resources the state could redistribute as patronage; all things being equal, the greater the proportion of resources at the state's disposal in relation to the wealth of the country as a whole, the stronger the capacity of the state to command political allegiance. In this respect, we saw how the Sicilian demesne was possibly the largest and wealthiest of the whole crown of Aragon, and how political consensus in the demesne was slowly constructed during the 1430s and 1440s. The Aragonese monarchy's legitimacy was further enhanced by its crucial role in shaping group and class identities in the demesne out of former urban social informality.

The comparatively greater size and wealth of the demesne in Sicily, however, were necessary but not sufficient conditions for a

287 J. N. Hillgarth, *The Spanish kingdoms 1250–1516*, II, pp. 203–5, 247–8.

stable political consensus to emerge. The additional feature which distinguished Sicily from the rest of the crown of Aragon, and which goes far to explain the island's political stability during the fifteenth century, was the fact that in Sicily the demesne's wealth was not overwhelmingly concentrated in a single metropolis, as it was by contrast in Catalonia (in Barcelona) or on the mainland (in Naples). The same factor may also explain why the Sicilian demesne was able to resist more effectively than Catalonia royal policies of alienation under Martino and Alfonso.

The large size of the Sicilian demesne and the lack of hegemony by a single metropolitan centre explain both the strength of the urban élite and its weakness, the emergence of *pactismo* as the state's answer to that strength, and the inability of Sicily's ruling classes to demand more. On the one hand, Sicilian urban élite groups had a far stronger voice in domestic politics than elsewhere, particularly on the southern Italian mainland (where the feudal aristocracy controlled four fifths of the country), and could therefore present a more effective counterweight to aristocratic demands when matters of general importance, such as tax allocations, were at stake. On the other hand, the lack of a single, dominant metropolitan voice meant that competition among towns for political authority and state resources was far harsher in Sicily than in Catalonia and the kingdom of Naples. Because of this competition, most eloquently expressed by the rivalry between Palermo and Messina, the Sicilian civic nobility was unable to unite behind a single banner – as did much of Catalonia in 1462 under Barcelona's leadership – and to exploit more fully its political and economic powers.

A well-known illustration of this stalemate can be found in a series of political events in 1459–61 which, it has been argued, marked Sicily's definitive submission to Iberian domination. Charles of Viana, the son of Juan II of Aragon and his first wife, Blanche of Navarre, was Juan's heir, but also his main political enemy. Charles should have inherited the kingdom of Navarre at his mother's death in 1441, but Blanche had insisted on her deathbed that her son could not succeed without Juan's consent, which the latter had never granted. Charles had a special claim to Sicilian independentist affections from his mother's side, for Blanche was Martino of Sicily's second wife and had stood, as Sicily's viceregent in 1410–12, for political independence from Aragon. After Alfonso V's death in 1458, Charles came to Sicily to revive traditional hopes for political autonomy (the country was still not fully integrated into the crown of Aragon). Parliament, hastily convened in late 1458 or early 1459, decided to send an embassy to King Juan in Spain requesting that Charles be made governor of Sicily. By January 1460, however, when the embassy landed in Barcelona, Charles had renounced all his claims and Sicily's bid for autonomy collapsed. Yet part of Charles' reason for renouncing his claims was the lack of decisiveness of his supporters, especially among Sicilians. Nonetheless Juan's position was still very insecure, and the king responded characteristically. To begin with, he made a number of political concessions to the Sicilian embassy, granting many of Charles' aristocratic followers high and low justice on their lands, and promising the demesne cities not to raise any more taxes during his reign; he followed this a few months later with an act of formal incorporation of Sicily into the crown of Aragon, thus depriving Sicilian demands for political autonomy of any remaining constitutional base.[288]

What has puzzled historians is why the Sicilian ruling classes, most notably the civic nobility, backed Charles of Viana's claims so indecisively, and were in the last resort willing to forgo political independence for what Vicens Vives described as 'a plate of lentils'.[289] Vicens argued that by renouncing Charles, the Sicilian ruling classes gained unprecedented institutional privilege and *de facto* political autonomy. He believed at the same time that this settlement had benefited the aristocracy most, giving the civic nobility by contrast only a few years' respite from taxation. As it was, the grants of *mero e misto imperio* to the aristocracy were revoked in 1472, and the promise not to tax was broken briefly and ineffectually in 1464,[290] and definitively in 1478.

Events become less puzzling, however, if we abandon the assumption that Sicilian élite groups were politically united and had as their highest aspiration 'national independence', and instead look more closely at the composition and motivations of Charles' supporters in the light of Sicily's social and institutional developments in this period. The composition of the embassy sent to deal with

---

288 A narrative of events can be found in Vicens Vives, *Fernando el Católico*, pp. 74–114.
289 *Ibid.*, pp. 90–1. See also Giarrizzo, 'La Sicilia dal Cinquecento all'Unità d'Italia', pp. 103–9.
290 Trasselli, *La 'questione sociale' in Sicilia e la rivolta di Messina del 1464*, pp. 137–41. Exaction of the tax was particularly slow.

Juan shows that the main forces supporting Charles and the bid for political autonomy were to be found among some greater and lesser aristocrats; the main demesne representative was a jurist from Messina, Girolamo Ansalone.[291] The *nobiles* of Palermo, on the other hand, who were far more uncertain and may even have opposed the project, sent a further, independent representative of their own to accompany the official parliamentary embassy to Barcelona in 1460.[292] Palermo's ambiguous role in the affair emerges from the fact that Juan first granted exemption from direct taxation to Palermo alone (on 1 February 1460, a day after *mero e misto imperio* had been granted to members of the aristocracy), and that the concession was made to include all of Sicily only later at the request of Palermo itself.[293] With this one act, Palermo established itself as the demesne's political leader against Messina's more partisan interests. When a second Sicilian embassy set sail for Spain in November 1461, this time to convey a message of loyalty, it included only three men: two government officials and a citizen of Palermo.

Even Charles of Viana's supporters were interested in political autonomy only insofar as it brought them sectoral benefits; regional nationalism could not be further from their minds. We saw that Charles' support came mainly from within the aristocracy, many of whom were probably worried that Juan II's succession and the separation of Naples from the crown of Aragon would push Sicily to the periphery of Aragonese concerns, and that Juan's Iberian interests would weaken, if not wither away, the strong links with Naples without providing much of a substitute. Indeed Juan, who never set foot in either Sicily or Sardinia during his reign, bore out such forebodings. Messina, Charles of Viana's main urban supporter, had somewhat similar worries, for its well-being and political relevance depended to a considerable extent on links with the southern Italian mainland. Messina's élite must have believed that the damage to the city's prosperity coming from partition from Naples after 1458 might be contained or reversed if Sicily were an independent state, for then the country's natural point of reference

---

[291] G. Zurita, *Anales de la Corona de Aragón*, VI, p. 253.
[292] Vicens Vives, *Fernando el Católico*, pp. 87–8. However Zurita, *Anales*, VI, p. 253, states that Palermo sent two representatives: *nobilis* Vassallo Speciale, and Cristoforo de Benedictis, a banker.
[293] De Vio ed., *Privilegia*, pp. 341–50.

would be Naples. An Iberian hegemony within the crown of Aragon risked marginalizing the city to Palermo's benefit.[294] By contrast, Palermo's élite had little to lose from a shift of the Aragonese empire's political fulcrum to Spain, for the city remained Sicily's administrative and financial capital and had also, with Trapani, the closest commercial ties of any city with Catalonia. On the other hand, a more autonomous government might have increased the resources at Palermo's disposal. Both the city's initial irresolution and the final decision to side with Juan are thus explained – the possible advantages of political autonomy being more than offset by the losses resulting from war against Juan. War would have entailed retaining the high rates of taxation established by Alfonso and interrupting all commercial links with Catalonia. Palermo's position gave it greater bargaining power; thus it was Palermo, rather than Messina, that obtained from Juan the tax concessions that could unite the demesne behind the capital. Messina was less anxious to press for reductions, given that it and its district were already tax exempt.[295]

This conflict over Sicilian autonomy is a good illustration of the unstable balance between the feudal aristocracy and the urban noble and administrative classes that had emerged over the previous half century. The aristocracy was, on the whole, favourable to Sicilian political autonomy, or at least equally divided over the issue; urban élite groups – with the significant exception of Messina – were more uncertain, particularly because so much of their recently acquired wealth and status derived from their links with the Aragonese monarchy. This indecisiveness contributed to Charles of Viana's abdication of his claims, which in turn tipped the scales in favour of Palermo, whose representatives seized the opportunity to

294 Zurita, *Anales*, VI, pp. 216, 221–2, suggests that Charles of Viana, who spent most of his time in Sicily residing in Messina, was connected with the southern Italian barons who staged the first major challenge to Ferrante of Naples' succession in 1459. One of the leaders of the uprising was Antonio Centelles Ventimiglia, marquis of Geraci and Crotone, whose lands spanned the Straits of Messina and who had already led a rebellion against Alfonso V in Calabria (above, n. 120). In 1460, the issue of Sicilian independence became the focus of the longer-term struggle between *nobiles* and *populares* for control of Messina's administration. Between 1461 and 1463, Messina was governed by a 'popular', explicitly pro-Aragonese regime, which was overturned by the Aragonese themselves as soon as political conditions in Sicily had become less volatile. Events are described by Trasselli in '*Questione sociale*', pp. 77–103.
295 Giardina ed., *Capitoli*, nos. 4 (1129, probably a forgery), 23 (1283), 34 (1302), 42 (1368).

gain a significant political and financial victory for the demesne and for Palermo as its leader. Thus, contrary to Vives's view, the events of 1459–61 resulted in a victory of Palermo and the demesne against the feudal aristocracy. Sicilian political 'self-determination' was meaningful only insofar as it benefited some sectors in society over others. During these events, Palermo was able to represent the demesne's general interest because this was quite clearly defined, and because aristocratic support for Charles of Viana provided a focus for demesne antagonism. The conflict of interests between Messina and Palermo, on the other hand, shows how inherently weak the demesne was, and how difficult it was for it to reach a unified position. This weakness would become more apparent when no unifying opponent was at hand.[296]

CONCLUSIONS

The picture I have just drawn provides little support for the view, persistently argued for Sicily and increasingly for other parts of Italy as well,[297] that no major changes occurred in late medieval social structure, and that the political, economic and cultural hegemony of the aristocracy persisted unchallenged until the eighteenth century.

Even at the most superficial glance, by the late fifteenth century the aristocracy differed profoundly from its late thirteenth-century forebears. The insurrection of 1282 had established a renewed and powerful aristocracy on the land to provide the backbone of the new Aragonese settlement. This class was economically and politically independent of the monarchy, and possessed near-total control of military force in the kingdom. Increasing economic difficulties from the 1320s and 1330s intensified competition within the aristocracy itself, which soon turned into a sustained attack on the foundations of royal power in the demesne. For nearly half a century thereafter, the aristocracy controlled the demesne towns. However, any attempts to establish a stronger hold over subject populations was foiled by the latter's extreme mobility.

The main effect on the aristocracy of the Aragonese restoration

---

[296] In 1478, a violent conflict opposed Messina and Palermo over capital status. See Starrabba, *Il conte di Prades e la Sicilia (1477–1479)*; G. Arenaprimo, 'Protesta dei messinesi al vicere conte di Prades del 1478'.

[297] *UM*, pp. 863–4, 901, 917, 921–2. For northern Italy see Jones, 'Economia e società', and the review by S. Polica, 'Basso Medioevo e Rinascimento: "rifeudalizzazione" e "transizione"'.

of the 1390s was, on the one hand, a near-wholesale replacement of its upper and middle echelons with Iberian and, increasingly, Sicilian new blood; and on the other hand, the development for the first time of a bond of economic, rather than purely political, dependence on the monarchy. The latter came to be, unwillingly under the Martins and more deliberately under Alfonso, a crucial source of political and economic support for the aristocracy, whose revenue from the land had sunk to a fraction of its early fourteenth-century levels, and which had been deprived by the Aragonese restoration of an alternative source of income in the demesne. The transition from a feudal to a proto-absolutist monarchy thus began as the unintended outcome of the conjuncture of a deep crisis of feudal incomes, and of the Aragonese monarchy's determination to recover most of the royal demesne. Alfonso was the first sovereign to realize that the demesne could be used as a tool to bind the aristocracy and the urban élite to the crown, rather than making them more independent.

During the first half of the fifteenth century, the aristocracy tried to respond to continuing hardship and increasing loss of control over feudal land – a process exacerbated by the financial demands caused by the war on the southern mainland – by increasing its hold over the rural population. Attempts to reintroduce serfdom failed, and other feudal privileges were upheld only in part or were successfully overturned; the *legitimacy* of seigneurial rights, by contrast, was reaffirmed by Alfonso as an integral part of his policy towards Sicily.

By the 1480s, when Ferdinand II began to exercise a more deliberate anti-feudal policy, the economic tide had turned. Ferdinand's actions may have temporarily weakened the aristocracy, but in contrast with the late fourteenth and early fifteenth century, rents were increasing once more and aristocratic confidence was rising. The barons made a show of their new strength in the course of the decade of intermittent rebellion that followed Ferdinand's death and Charles V's succession in 1516. The political crisis of the early sixteenth century resulted once again in a general redistribution of aristocratic fortunes, but it also shifted the internal political balance in the aristocracy's favour.[298] The wheel had apparently come full circle; aristocratic hegemony was once more established. By

[298] Aymard, 'Une famille de l'aristocratie sicilienne aux XVIe et XVIIe siècles: les ducs de Terranova', 30, 35.

contrast with the fourteenth century, however, superiority was not unchallenged; moreover, it rested on a radically different political settlement. Federico III was raised to the throne in 1296 as a guarantor of Sicilian independence and aristocratic lordship, drawing legitimacy and power from a source outside his control. By the sixteenth century, aristocratic rebels might demand more extensive privileges – *mero e misto imperio*, defence of primogeniture against the fragmentation of property, protection against indebtedness – but their relations with the Spanish state, an empire of which Sicily was becoming an increasingly minor part, were based on collaboration and guarded political devolution. It was now the turn for aristocratic demands to be shaped and constrained by forces of empire that could be challenged but not overthrown.[299]

The aristocratic reaction after 1516 came after a century of decline, followed by the slow and gradual recovery of a class, few of whose members could trace their descent further back than 1392. The restriction of aristocratic status to the baronage during the first half of the fifteenth century limited, without fully excluding, a slow but constant insertion of new forces into its ranks. New members generally came from the most dynamic sectors of the civic nobility including the merchant class; some of the better-known individuals originated in the expatriate Pisan community (see chapter 5). While inevitably adopting many of the habits and practices of the baronage, these individuals also brought with them a shrewd and sophisticated appreciation of the value of economic enterprise – an exemplary case being that of Pietro Gaetani, a Pisan immigrant who, on becoming baron of Tripi, combined the establishment of a new sugar *trappeto* and a new fair with a wholly 'feudal' policy of brutality and exploitation towards his subjects.

Changes within the urban (demesne) society mirror developments within the aristocracy. Attempts to portray the movement of the Vespers of 1282 as expressing urban, 'communal' desire for political independence[300] fail to match the scanty evidence of urban political and institutional structure, let alone autonomy, during the century of war which followed. The Catalan–Aragonese 'feudalization' of Sicily after 1282 was a response to Angevin attack, but also to the weakness of the only alternative power-base available to the monarchy, the demesne. This weakness, expressed most vividly

[299] Koenigsberger, *Practice of empire*, pp. 52–3.
[300] *UM*, pp. 709ff.

by the incoherence of urban social structures, led to the subordination of towns to the aristocracy once the monarchy began to decline after the 1340s. In the political vacuum that followed, an urban administrative and judicial élite began to take shape, forming a first tassel of identity around family lineage and unpopulated *feudi* acquired from the lesser aristocracy. Alongside this élite, other groups – agricultural entrepreneurs, artisans, petty suburban landowners and even wage-labourers – buoyed by declining rents, rising wages and more widespread economic change, were also, albeit more slowly, taking shape.

If the fourteenth century was a period of aristocratic hegemony, weakened but as yet unchallenged by the sharp demographic downturn, the fifteenth was the century of the towns. Yet urban society came only slowly to recognize its strength. At first the royal demesne was merely a pawn, albeit a powerful one, of the Aragonese monarchy's strategy to recover its lost resources. But the establishment of the first embryo of a modern state bureaucracy under the Martins and, more crucially, the massive expansion of fiscal and consequently administrative demands by Alfonso, gave all levels of demesne society a chance to press for a bigger share of local political and economic resources. For the first time, the domestic impact of foreign warfare was to strengthen and extend the role of a new, more structured, hierarchical but also self-confident urban polity. The outcome of the demesne's new powers was the political settlement of 1459–61: a victory not so much of Palermo over Messina, but of the demesne over a segment of the aristocracy. A victory of *pactismo*, however, that was far from inevitable, coming as it did from the contradiction between the demesne's great economic powers and (in contrast with the aristocracy) its comparatively weak and fragmented political expression. By contrast with the aristocracy, the demesne could not show a common political front, for it did not possess a common set of interests: the loss of social informality during the 1430s and 1440s brought, in the train of greater strength, the formalized structure of class and group division. These differences emerged most starkly when, after 1516, the towns watched passively as the aristocracy staged its return to the centre of the political stage.[301]

---

[301] At the same time, Koenigsberger has argued (in 'The parliament of Sicily and the Spanish Empire'), that the Sicilian parliament was more effective than parliament in Naples in restraining Spanish taxation in the early modern period.

The state was instrumental to all these developments. While dwelling at greater length on its role as purveyor of military and tax resources to different groups in society, I have also suggested that its nature in this period was to a considerable extent the outcome of a more general distributive crisis, within which the state often played a largely passive role. The Aragonese conquest and restoration would have been inconceivable without the backing of urban society, whose strength in turn derived from a prior redistribution of power and wealth away from the aristocracy and the monarchy. Fiscal pressure and political manipulation by Alfonso helped create a corporate urban society, but corporatism was grounded in social and economic changes over which the king had no influence.

The fifteenth-century state emerged and developed both by promoting social mobility (in the towns) and by stabilizing it (within the aristocracy). This complex balancing act was accomplished in Sicily largely thanks to the good fortune of possessing – by contrast with the kingdom of Naples and Catalonia – a large and wealthy, but politically divided, royal demesne. The effects of this situation on Sicily in the longer term were ambiguous. On the one hand, the population at large benefited for a long time from a light tax load, from domestic peace, and from (albeit limited) integration into the Aragonese and Spanish empires. Bullion exports in the guise of taxes were still a low price to pay. On the other hand, increased regional autonomy would lead in the 1520s and 1530s to a partial overturning of the former urban hegemony. The present state of research makes it impossible to say, however, whether the outcome of this aristocratic reaction was as disastrous as historians in the past have made out.

8. A further question: the origins of Sicilian underdevelopment

This book has offered a critique of theories of dependence through trade in the Middle Ages and has suggested an alternative model for the late medieval economy. In the course of the argument, however, I have raised many questions which cannot, at the present state of our knowledge, be pursued any further. On the one hand, the extent to which the view developed here is applicable to western Europe as a whole can only be tested through further empirical research on other regions; indeed, the institutional approach I have advocated assumes that further analysis of the kind I have pursued here is necessary for further theoretical refinement. Such research may establish that late medieval Sicily achieved an unusual degree of market integration and specialization for the time; but I have provided theoretical grounds for arguing that specialization was a process common to the whole of western Europe, and that regional differences were a matter of (possibly significant) degree. On the other hand, if my critique of current theories of economic dualism and dependency applies to late medieval Sicily, which had one of the most export-oriented economies in Europe at the time, these arguments can be presumed to hold all the more for other, less export-oriented areas in medieval Europe to which similar dualist theories have been applied. Recent work on eastern Europe in the early modern period is also beginning to raise similar questions and suggest comparable answers to mine.[1]

The critique of the dualist paradigm and the depiction of late medieval Sicily (and by implication, also of the kingdom of Naples) as a relatively sophisticated and growing economy do, however, raise the challenge of explaining when, and why, the economies of

[1] See above, chapter 1, nn. 1, 70.

the Italian *Mezzogiorno did* begin to lag behind those of other western European regions, including parts of northern Italy. While it would be premature to venture very far in providing a full answer, some of the arguments developed here suggest new ways of approaching these questions. In these last few pages I take up the challenge and suggest two, inevitably partial, answers: that the critical turning-point in southern Italian fortunes occurred during the so-called 'seventeenth-century crisis'; and that the outcome of this social and economic crisis depended crucially on pre-existing regional and supra-regional market structures. Both points emerge particularly clearly if we contrast economic developments in seventeenth-century Sicily and the kingdom of Naples.

Although most early modern historians assume that the *Mezzogiorno's* structural backwardness dates from the Middle Ages, it is also generally accepted that an important turning-point for the economy occurred during the seventeenth century. There are currently three versions of this view. Some historians, like Rosario Villari, Giuseppe Galasso and more recently Aurelio Lepre,[2] argue that backwardness in the kingdom of Naples was caused primarily by domestic social structures, in particular by the extensive feudal powers in the countryside which stifled social mobility and capital formation (especially in the towns); delayed technological innovation; compressed peasant incomes; and induced social conservatism. The seventeenth-century crisis was caused by the impact on these social and productive structures of the fiscal demands of the Spanish state. The huge increase of Spanish taxation in the first decades of the seventeenth century in connection with the Thirty Years War led to widespread rural and urban uprisings in the late 1640s. The effects of these revolts and of subsequent state and feudal repression were dramatically intensified by a plague epidemic in 1656, which killed more than twenty per cent of the population. The century-long stagnation which followed these epidemics was the outcome of a further 'feudal reaction', a heightening of aristocratic powers which led to an increase in feudal dues (including excise) and rents without any corresponding growth of

[2] R. Villari, *La rivolta antispagnola a Napoli. Le origini (1585–1647)*; Villari, *Ribelli e riformatori dal XVI al XVIII secolo*; Galasso, 'La feudalità napoletana nel secolo XVI'; Lepre, *Storia del Mezzogiorno d'Italia*.

agricultural productivity.[3] As a result, the economy of the kingdom of Naples was outpaced by that of more rapidly developing areas in other parts of Europe.[4]

Although this analysis seems to provide a good description of events in the kingdom of Naples, it is less effective in explaining the outcome of the crisis there. This analytical weakness becomes most apparent if we contrast developments in the kingdom of Naples and in Sicily, for whereas most of the structural and conjunctural factors which are taken to explain economic decline on the southern mainland apply to seventeenth-century Sicily also, the social and economic crisis took a very different course in the two countries.

The second interpretation of *Mezzogiorno* backwardness is that of Maurice Aymard, which I discussed briefly in chapter 1.[5] Aymard accepts that a turning-point in southern Italian fortunes occurred during the seventeenth century, but he differs from the previous position by trying to provide a more general interpretation of the crisis which also includes Sicily. Aymard argues that southern Italian economic stagnation was caused by the breakdown during the seventeenth century of commercial integration with the North; southern relations of dependency were replaced by forced commercial autarky.

Despite my reservations about Aymard's model (see chapter 1), his implicit argument that foreign trade had a positive impact on southern Italian development and that stagnation was caused by the interruption of trade in the seventeenth century can plausibly be applied to early modern Sicily. It is less plausible a model for Neapolitan developments, however, because foreign trade was far less important for the latter's early modern economy as a whole than it was for Sicily in the same period.

The last theory to be discussed has no direct connection with either the debate on the economy of the *Mezzogiorno* or with the debate on the seventeenth-century crisis, for it was developed to explain northern Italy's delayed nineteenth-century industrialization. It is nonetheless very relevant for our purposes. Thus, Emilio Sereni argued that a necessary prerequisite of industrial growth in

---

[3] *Ibid.*, II, pp. 12, 39.
[4] The main contributions to the debate on the 'seventeenth-century crisis' can be found in Aston ed., *Crisis in Europe 1560–1660*; G. Parker and L. M. Smith eds., *The general crisis of the seventeenth century*.
[5] Aymard, 'Transizione'.

the North was a 'national' (supra-regional and excise-free) market with substantial consumer demand, which could provide the base for industrial and agricultural specialization and economies of scale. Sereni demonstrated that such a market did not exist in Italy before the 1870s, and suggested that this fact explained slow industrial development in the North.[6] The same argument was later applied by Renato Zangheri to late medieval and early modern Lombardy. According to Zangheri, fifteenth-century Lombardy's agricultural base was already sufficiently developed to sustain an industrial revolution, had there been sufficiently large (supra-regional) markets to be supplied.[7]

Zangheri's argument can be questioned on empirical grounds,[8] but it has the merit of raising the fundamental question of the role of markets in economic development, which has never been systematically addressed for the kingdom of Naples before the seventeenth-century crisis. This omission, which is probably due to the unvoiced assumption that the economy of the *Mezzogiorno* was too underdeveloped to pursue a course of self-sustained growth, is rather surprising, given that the kingdom of Naples possessed until *Unità* the largest politically unified territory in Italy, and thus had at least the basic institutional prerequisites for establishing a 'national market'.

Why did it not do so? What held up commercial integration? Why was it both possible and rational for the southern Italian aristocracy to react to economic contraction and demographic depression in the mid-seventeenth century by increasing rates of exploitation rather than by promoting economic expansion as it had done in the sixteenth century,[9] and as the Sicilian aristocracy, by contrast, seems to have continued to do in the seventeenth?[10] The answer to these questions seems to differ crucially for the two countries, and combines features of all three preceding interpretations.

If we take demographic trends as proxy for long-term economic performance, the Sicilian and southern Italian economies clearly shared fully in the general sixteenth-century European expansion.

[6] Sereni, 'Mercato nazionale'.
[7] R. Zangheri, 'The historical relationship between agrarian and economic development in Italy'.
[8] See D. Sella, *Crisis and continuity: the economy of Spanish Lombardy in the seventeenth century*, chapter 7.
[9] See Galasso, *Economia e società*; Galasso, 'La feudalità'.
[10] See below, n. 14.

Between 1500 and 1600, population in both countries doubled, from c.550,000 to c.1,100,000 inhabitants in Sicily, and from c.250,000 to c.540,000 hearths in the kingdom of Naples. From the early seventeenth century, however, trends in the two countries began to diverge.

Sicily suffered no major demographic set-back during the seventeenth century; its population remained stable, or increased slightly after the 1650s.[11] By contrast, population in the kingdom of Naples had already declined by 7.4 per cent between 1595 and 1648 before it was struck by the plague in 1656 and lost a further twenty per cent. More significant than pre-plague decline, however, was the length of time it took for the southern Italian population to recover. Recovery took far longer than in other parts of Italy that were also badly hit by the same epidemic. By 1700, population in the kingdom of Naples had increased by little over ten per cent compared to 1656, and it took nearly a century for the population to return to pre-plague size.[12]

These population figures suggest that economic performance in Sicily and the kingdom of Naples diverged considerably during the seventeenth century. These differences, I suggest, were largely due to the fact that the seventeenth-century crisis was unfolding within different market structures.

It is increasingly recognized that one of the most significant effects of the seventeenth-century demographic and economic crisis in western Europe was to provide greater opportunities to increase interregional specialization and integration.[13] This process, which tended to occur within the political boundaries of states because of the lower transaction costs incurred within a unified polity, unfolded along similar lines to those I have described for the later Middle Ages. But whereas in the late fourteenth and fifteenth centuries integration occurred *within* regions, from the late seventeenth century, integration involved *supra-regional* networks; it was thus supported by more complex and territorially extensive

---

[11] Beloch, *Bevölkerungsgeschichte Italiens*, I, p. 152; Aymard, 'In Sicilia: sviluppo demografico'.

[12] Beloch, *Bevölkerungsgeschichte Italiens*, I, p. 215; Lepre, *Storia*, II, pp. 50–1; G. Felloni, 'Italy', pp. 6–7.

[13] See, for example, E. L. Jones, 'Agricultural origins of industry'; De Vries, *The economy of Europe in an age of crisis, 1600–1750*; Kussmaul, *General view*; Sella, *Crisis and continuity*.

patterns of specialization. Because supra-regional market structures, and thus also opportunities for interregional specialization, differed widely across Europe, the result of the seventeenth-century crisis was to establish or accentuate economic divergences between more 'advanced' and more 'backward' territories.

These processes affected Sicily and southern Italy very differently. Sicily's strong demesne and high rate of urbanization, its relatively small size and its long coasts, its openness to foreign trade and its highly productive agriculture, had allowed its economy to achieve an unusual degree of domestic territorial specialization during the later Middle Ages. A small economy like Sicily's, however, could only expand further by specializing for foreign markets. This path was followed after 1500.[14] Val Demone in particular intensified late medieval patterns of development to specialize in high-value-added agricultural products for export; during the sixteenth and early seventeenth centuries, its economy centred increasingly on silk (and to a lesser extent sugar) production for northern Italian and northern European markets.

However, the Sicilian economy's increasingly foreign orientation made it particularly vulnerable to changes in foreign demand. The first area to be hit by such changes was val di Noto, whose trade links with the Levant were badly damaged by the European conflicts with the Ottoman empire after the mid-sixteenth century. From the mid-1620s, val di Noto's population began to decrease. Silk production in val Demone began to contract after 1640 because of northern Italian demographic and industrial decline; sugar production in the same area decreased after 1650 because of American competition. Thereafter, population in val Demone stagnated.

Grain production, increasingly concentrated in val di Mazara, was also affected by changes in foreign markets. Grain exports as a proportion of domestic output reached a peak of sixteen to seventeen per cent in 1530–50, but began to decline thereafter. The volume of grain exports remained fairly stable until the great Mediterranean famine of 1590–1, when northern Italian cities that had traditionally relied on Sicilian supplies began to resort to

---

[14] Aymard, 'Commerce de la soie'; Aymard, 'Il bilancio di una lunga crisi finanziaria'; Davies, 'Structure of the wheat trade'; Davies, 'Village-building in Sicily: an aristocratic remedy for the crisis of the 1590s'; Cancila, 'Commercio estero (sec. XVI–XVIII)'; Cancila, 'L'evoluzione della rendita fondiaria'.

cheaper grain from the Baltic, North Africa and Turkey; traditional grain markets contracted even further as a result of the heavy population losses of northern Italy, and especially Genoa, after 1650.

In the short term, however, val di Mazara suffered little from declining grain exports since, by contrast with other export-oriented sectors, foreign losses were compensated for by domestic gains. The largest number of new village foundations, established by aristocrats to expand wheat cultivation in val di Mazara, occurred between 1595 and 1650 at a time of stagnating or contracting foreign demand for grain. Demographic stagnation or decline in eastern Sicily was matched by continued growth in western and central val di Mazara where, between 1580 and 1680, population grew by as much as twenty to fifty per cent. The population gains in val di Mazara explain why the population of Sicily as a whole continued moderately to increase during the seventeenth century. These gains also suggest that the seventeenth-century crisis in Sicily was due in the first place to a collapse in *foreign demand* rather than to domestic constraints on output.

Val di Mazara's buoyancy was thus insufficient to maintain economic momentum in Sicily as a whole, for eastern Sicily found it far harder to reorient its export-led, highly specialized and labour-intensive agriculture to alternative forms of employment. Eastern Sicily's susceptibility to fluctuations in foreign markets was intensified by three factors. First, the situation I described above, whereby most of the late medieval export trade was in the hands of foreign merchants, apparently did not change significantly after 1500. One may surmise that if Sicilians had themselves marketed a large share of their exports abroad, they might have been able to respond to a decline in Sicily's traditional outlets by seeking markets elsewhere, for example on the southern mainland. Whether outlets in the kingdom of Naples were a viable alternative to northern Italian markets is a question I return to below.

Two other factors which affected responses to declining foreign trade were institutional. On the one hand, Sicily exported mainly agricultural goods, and it is generally more difficult (because capital investments are longer-term and relatively immobile, and labour is often tied to the land) to convert agricultural investments and transform agrarian structures than it is to re-structure industry in response to changes in demand. On the other hand, for reasons that must still be investigated, the early modern silk industry – the only major Sicilian export industry with considerable potential for *manufacturing* growth – never produced a combination of labour- and capital-intensive agriculture, petty manufacture and entrepreneurial talent equivalent to that which sustained Lombard industrialization in the nineteenth century.[15] Consequently, when foreign demand for raw silk collapsed, there was no basis in Sicily on which to establish substitute domestic manufacturing for export.

One could probably compile a list of natural, technical, institutional, social and other constraints which prevented economic re-structuring and the growth of manufacture in late seventeenth-century Sicily. But to do so would divert attention from the crucial fact, that between *c.*1350 and *c.*1650 the Sicilian 'economic model' was highly successful, as both the rising population and the constant trade surplus demonstrate.[16] May it not have been this country's extraordinary economic *success*, rather than simply endogenous and exogenous constraints, that made it harder for Sicily to adapt to rapidly changing economic conditions? For centuries, Sicily enjoyed natural comparative advantages in the Mediterranean economy thanks to its geographical position and to what was, for the time, a highly productive agricultural system. The sixteenth-century European 'price revolution', during which wheat prices tended to rise faster than the rest, must have further improved Sicily's terms of trade.[17] When Sicilian wheat began to be undercut by eastern European and Turkish competition, silk production became the island's main source of export revenue and engine of growth, and former wheat exports were simply diverted to domestic consumption. Even val di Noto's difficulties in the mid-sixteenth century were for a long time compensated by growth in other parts of the island. The crisis of the silk industry after the 1640s caught Sicilians unprepared: their economy had specialized too far to submit to rapid structural transformation. A solution to the crisis in

---

[15] Cafagna, *Dualismo e sviluppo*.
[16] See above, nn. 11, 14.
[17] At the same time, because wages were unable to keep up with food prices, the distribution of income tended to become more distorted (Cancila, *Baroni e popolo*, pp. 193–5). However, this process would have constrained the growth of domestic manufacture only if one assumes, first, that Sicily's domestic market would otherwise have been large enough to sustain long-term industrial development; and second, that no alternative (export) markets were available. I suggest here that both assumptions are open to question.

traditional foreign outlets might have been to search for new markets in the kingdom of Naples: unfortunately, conditions on the southern mainland were unpropitious for such a change. We saw above that, according to population figures, the kingdom of Naples was hit far more seriously than Sicily by the seventeenth-century crisis. By contrast with Sicily, moreover, the crisis on the southern mainland – expressed most vividly by the massive outbreak of popular and peasant anti-feudal revolts in Naples and the provinces in 1647–8 – was the outcome of primarily domestic problems. A comparison with Sicily shows that outside political and economic factors contributed to hardship on the mainland, but did not have a determining impact. Thus, although early modern Sicily had a far more export-oriented economy than did southern Italy as a whole, and suffered similar or stronger external pressures (declining agricultural exports and escalating Spanish taxation to finance the Thirty Years War),[18] its population continued to increase up to the mid- or late seventeenth-century, and there were no major outbreaks of revolt except for that of Messina in 1674–8.

I suggested above that one of the most important *internal* differences between the two countries concerned their market structures. Sicily, I argued, had a highly integrated domestic market and strong links with foreign markets which played an increasingly important part in the country's long-term economic development. The kingdom of Naples had much weaker outside links, which were also restricted to only a few of its regions (Calabria, Puglia, and to a lesser degree Terra di Lavoro and Abruzzi). The country's domestic market, which was territorially very large and physically extremely diverse, provided the kingdom with its main base and potential source of economic development through interregional specialization and integration.

How were opportunities for regional integration pursued on the southern mainland in the early modern period? While there seems little doubt that more integrated regional markets emerged during the fifteenth and sixteenth centuries, a 'national' market in the kingdom distinct from Naples' extensive catchment area did not exist.[19] In the sixteenth century, there was widespread demand for

---

[18] Aymard, 'Bilancio di una crisi'.
[19] L. De Rosa, 'Comunicazioni terrestri e marittime e depressione economica: il caso del Regno di Napoli (secoli XIV–XVIII)'; Grohmann, *Fiere*; Lepre, *Storia*, I, p. 179.

freedom of trade and for toll exemptions within feudal territories;[20] nonetheless, interregional trade and specialization seem not to have advanced very far.[21] This fact helps explain the Spanish government's attempts in the sixteenth century to improve the internal road network, although the policy's main purpose was to improve Naples' network of supply.[22]

Thus, although market integration at a regional level does seem to have increased in the kingdom of Naples after 1500, no equivalent to the toll-free market established in the Sicilian demesne during the fifteenth century could or did develop on the mainland – for the simple reason that in Sicily the royal demesne included all the main cities and over half the population, whereas on the mainland only one fifth of the inhabitants (including the huge Neapolitan metropolis) were under royal authority. In Sicily, lower tolls stimulated trade and opportunities for specialization, and competition from a large, virtually toll-free area may well have also put pressure on feudal lords to lower jurisdictional rights of trade in their territories. On the mainland, stimuli and competitive pressures from toll-free trade were inevitably far weaker as a result of the greater fragmentation of public authority and excise.[23] For the same reason, gains towards greater commercial integration could be rapidly reversed. This is precisely what seems to have occurred in the course of a few years in the 1630s and 1640s, when the Neapolitan aristocracy took advantage of the Spanish state's weakness to stage a violent offensive and extend its rights of jurisdiction over men, production and trade throughout the kingdom. This offensive led to a wave of anti-feudal revolts in 1647–8, which were in turn successfully repressed by the state in alliance with the aristocracy itself.[24]

Thus, just as population pressure was easing only a few years before the 1656 epidemic, conditions for supra-regional integration on the southern mainland – which had tended to improve during the sixteenth century – suddenly became very unfavourable. These

[20] Galasso, *Economia e società*, pp. 85, 93; C. Penuti, 'Il principe e le comunità soggette: il regime fiscale dalle "pattuizioni" al "buongoverno"', p. 91.

[21] Lepre, *Storia*, I, p. 86.

[22] A. Giannetti, 'La strada dalla città al territorio: la riorganizzazione spaziale del Regno di Napoli nel Cinquecento'.

[23] Peasant subsistence was probably considerably more important in the kingdom of Naples than in Sicily. See above, chapter 6 for Sicily; F. Galiani, *Della moneta e altri scritti*, p. 234, for the southern mainland.

[24] Villari, *Rivolta antispagnola*, pp. 166–7.

developments had two important consequences for the outcome of the economic and demographic crisis in the kingdom of Naples. On the one hand, the 'feudal reaction' increased transaction costs just before the sudden lowering of demographic pressure at the margin caused by the plague of 1656 improved opportunities for interregional specialization; in these circumstances, the plague caused a contraction rather than an expansion of the potential domestic market, and a severing or weakening of the links previously established between different regions of the South.[25] On the other hand, the more or less simultaneous increase in barriers to trade throughout the kingdom reduced competitive pressures on the aristocracy itself to respond to the demographic slump of 1656 through economic improvement rather than by increasing levels of exploitation. In this context, it was quite rational for the individual aristocrat to respond to a contraction of trade by increasing levies rather than by raising output.[26] As a result, it took the kingdom of Naples a century to recover from this set-back, a century during which the economies of other regions and countries were able to establish a permanent lead.

We may conclude with a conjecture: had the southern mainland's domestic market been more developed, had demographic losses led as a result to greater interregional specialization rather than to commercial closure and retreat, late seventeenth-century Sicily might have found a solution to its crisis through greater integration with its closest neighbour and historic companion, the kingdom of Naples. Instead, the island partook, less dramatically but with equally long-lasting effects, of Naples' disastrous decline.

[25] Lepre, *Storia*, II, pp. 24, 41–2. For the low level of commercial integration in the eighteenth century see P. Chorley, *Oil silk and Enlightenment. Economic problems in XVIIIth century Naples*, and P. Macry, *Mercato e società nel Regno di Napoli. Commercio del grano e politica economica nel Settecento*.

[26] No individual landlord will rationally eschew innovation under competitive circumstances, for he risks bankruptcy. See Bardhan, 'Marxist ideas in development economics: an evaluation', p. 69; Basu, *Less developed economy*, pp. 111–19, 167–8.

Bibliography

MANUSCRIPT SOURCES

Barcelona, Archivo de la Corona de Aragón
Cancillería, Registros, 2298–300, 2426–30, 2801–99, 2935, 2946–7,
  3472–93
Barcelona, Archivo Historico de Protocolos
  Jaume Just, leg. 1
Catania, Archivio di Stato
  Notai I versamento nos. 6241, 6242, 6311, 14926; Notai di Randazzo nos.
  1–8, 10, 12–15, 20–3, 59
Florence, Archivio di Stato, sezione di Prato
  Carteggio Datini nos. 442, 531, 534–6, 539, 546, 648, 669, 670, 704, 783,
  844, 904, 914, 999, 1003, 1060, 1072, 1075, 1076
Messina, Archivio di Stato
  Notai nos. 3, 5, 6A/B, 7, 10
Palermo, Archivio Comunale
  Atti bandi e provviste *ad annum* 1485–6, 1488–91, 1497–9
Palermo, Archivio di Stato
  Cancelleria 1–199; Corporazioni religiose soppresse S. Martino II fondo,
  118; Protonotaro del Regno 5, 17–24, 27, 30, 33, 35, 38, 42, 45–6, 49–52,
  68; Protonotaro della Camera reginale 1–3; Conservatoria di Registro: (a)
  Mercedes 1–84, 90, 93, 96–8, 103, 107; (b) Computa 840–78, 928;
  Tribunale del Real Patrimonio: (a) Atti 1–59; (b) Lettere viceregie e
  dispacci patrimoniali 71–100; (c) numero provvisorio (n.p.) 2, 3, 62, 63,
  67, 101, 121, 816, 911, 980, 1161, 1556, 1571, 1638–40, 1645–51,
  1653–5, 1678, 1719, 2373; Miscellanea archivistica, II, 571
Syracuse, Archivio di Stato
  Notai I porta, nos. 1927, 10227, 10245
Syracuse, Archivio di Stato, sezione di Noto
  Notai nos. 6332, 6335, 6341, 6343, 6352
Valencia, Archivio del Reino
  Real, Camarae Siciliae et Valentiae, Reginale dominae Mariae 1–23

413

PRINTED SOURCES

Alberti L. *Isole appartenenti alla Italia. Di nuovo ricorrette, et con l'aggionta in più luoghi de diverse cose occorse sino a' nostri tempi adornate*, Venice, 1576.

Amico e Statella V. M. *Catana illustrata, sive sacra et civilis urbis Catanae historia a prima ejusdem origine in praesens usque deducta ac per annales digesta*, 4 vols., Catania, 1740–6.

Arezzo C. M. *De situ insulae Siciliae libellus*, Messina, 1542.

Barbato A. ed. *Per la storia di Nicosia nel Medio Evo. Documenti inediti I (1267–1454)*, Nicosia, 1919.

Barberi G. L. *I capibrevi*, ed. G. Silvestri, *DSSS*, ser. 1, IV, VIII, XIII, Palermo, 1879–88.

Liber de secretiis, ed. E. Mazzarese Fardella, Acta Italica, II, Milan, 1974.

Bozzo S. V. '*Quaedam profetia.* Una poesia siciliana del XIV secolo inedita. Studio paleografico, letterario e storico', *ASS*, new ser. 2 (1877), 41–81, 172–94.

'Un diploma di re Pietro II relativo all'assedio di Termini nel 1338', *ASS*, new ser. 3 (1878), 331–46.

Bresc H. and S. D. Goitein, 'Un inventaire dotal de juifs siciliens (1479)', *Mélanges d'archéologie et d'histoire*, 82 (1970), 903–17.

Camera M. *Memorie storico-diplomatiche dell'antica città e ducato di Amalfi cronologicamente ordinate e continuate sino al secolo XVIII*, 2 vols., Salerno, 1876–81.

Carini I. 'Un testamento del 1376', *ASS*, new ser. 1 (1876), 332–44.

ed. *De rebus Regni Siciliae (9 settembre 1282–26 agosto 1283). Appendice ai documenti inediti estratti dall'Archivio della Corona d'Aragona*, *DSSS*, ser. 1, V, Palermo, 1893.

Casula F. C. ed. *Carte reali diplomatiche di Alfonso III il Benigno, re d'Aragona, riguardanti l'Italia*, Pubblicazioni dell'Istituto di Storia medioevale e moderna dell'Università degli studi di Cagliari, 15, Padua, 1970.

Cesino e Fogletta G. ed. *Pragmaticarum Regni Siciliae tomus tertius*, Palermo, 1700.

Ciavarini C. ed. *Statuti anconitani del mare, del terzenale e della dogana, e patti con diverse nazioni*, Ancona, 1896.

Codice metrico siculo, Catania, 1812.

Cordova V. *Le origini della città di Aidone e il suo statuto*, Rome, 1890.

Corrao P. ed. *Registri di lettere ed atti (1328–1333)*, *ACFUP*, 5, Palermo, 1986.

Cosentino G. 'Un documento in volgare siciliano del 1320', *ASS*, new ser. 9 (1884), 372–81.

ed. *Codice diplomatico di Federico III d'Aragona, re di Sicilia, 1355–77*, *DSSS*, ser. 1, IX, Palermo, 1885.

Cupani F. *Hortus catholicus*, Naples, 1696.

Cusimano G. and F. Giunta eds. *Prospetto dei documenti in volgare siciliano del sec. XIV*, Palermo, 1948.

D'Arienzo L. ed. *Carte reali diplomatiche di Pietro IV il Cerimonioso, re d'Aragona, riguardanti l'Italia*, Pubblicazioni dell'Istituto di Storia medioevale e moderna dell'università degli studi di Cagliari, 14, Padua, 1970.

Day J. ed. *Les douanes de Gênes, 1376–1377*, 2 vols., Ports routes trafics, 17, Paris, 1963.

Dentici Buccellato R. M. ed. *Fisco e società nella Sicilia aragonese. Le pandette delle gabelle regie del XIV secolo, ACFUP*, 2, Palermo, 1983.

De Pasi B. *Tariffa dei pesi e misure*, Venice, 1557.

Déprez E. and G. Mollat eds. *Clément VI (1342–1352): lettres closes, patentes et curiales intéressant les pays autre que la France*, Bibliothèque de l'Ecole française d'Athènes et de Rome, 3rd ser., Paris, 1960–1.

De Stefano A. and F. Giunta eds. *Codice diplomatico dei re aragonesi di Sicilia, DSSS*, ser. 1, XXIV, Palermo, 1956.

De Vio M. ed. *Privilegia felicis et fidelissimae urbis Panormitanae selecta aliquot ad civitatis decus et commodum spectantia*, Palermo, 1706.

Di Blasi F. P. and A. Di Blasi eds. *Pragmaticae sanctiones Regni Siciliae quas iussu Ferdinandi III Borboni*, 2 vols., Palermo, 1791–3.

Di Giovanni V. ed. *Capitoli gabelle e privilegi della città di Alcamo, DSSS*, ser. 2, I, Palermo, 1876.

Fazello T. *Le due deche dell'historia di Sicilia*, Venice, 1573.

Filangieri R. ed. *I registri della cancelleria angioina ricostruiti con la collaborazione degli archivisti napoletani*, Naples, 1950 to date.

Finke H. ed. *Acta Aragonensia. Quellen zur deutschen, italienischen, französischen, spanischen, zur Kirchen- und Kulturgeschichte aus den diplomatischen Korrespondenz Jaymes II. (1291–1327)*, 3 vols., Berlin–Leipzig, 1908–22.

Flandina A. ed. *Statuti ordinamenti e capitoli della città di Polizzi, DSSS*, ser. 2, I, Palermo, 1884.

ed. *Il codice Filangeri e il codice Speciale: privilegi inediti della città di Palermo, DSSS*, ser. 1, XIV, Palermo, 1891.

Foucard C. 'Proposta fatta dalla Corte estense ad Alfonso I re di Napoli', *Archivio storico per le province napoletane*, 2 (1874), 689–752.

Gabotto F. 'Inventari messinesi inediti del Quattrocento', *ASSO*, 3 (1906), 251–76, 479–87; 4 (1907), 154–64, 339–46, 483–90.

Galiani F. *Della moneta e altri scritti*, ed. A. Merola, Milan, 1963.

Gallo C. D. *Annali della città di Messina capitale del Regno di Sicilia dal giorno di sua fondazione sino a' tempi presenti*, 3 vols., Messina, 1758.

Garufi C. A. 'Ricerche sugli usi nuziali nel Medio Evo in Sicilia', *ASS*, new ser. 21 (1896), 209–307.

ed. *I documenti inediti dell'epoca normanna in Sicilia, DSSS*, ser. 1, XVIII, Palermo, 1899.

Genuardi L. *Terre comuni ed usi civici in Sicilia prima dell'abolizione della feudalità. Studi e documenti, DSSS*, ser. 2, VII, Palermo, 1911.

ed. *Il libro dei capitoli della corte del Consolato di mare di Messina*, Palermo, 1924.

'Una raccolta di memoriali di re Alfonso il Magnanimo al viceré di Sicilia

Nicola Speciale (1423–1428)', in *Ad Alessandro Luzio gli Archivi di Stato italiani. Miscellanea di studi storici*, 2 vols., Florence, 1933, I, pp. 151–9.

Gervasi N. *Siculae sanctiones*, 3 vols., Palermo, 1752.

Giambruno S. ed. *Il Tabulario del monastero di S. Margherita di Polizzi*, DSSS, ser. 1, XX, Palermo, 1906.

Giambruno S. and L. Genuardi eds. *Capitoli inediti delle città demaniali di Sicilia approvati sino al 1458, I. Alcamo-Malta*, DSSS ser. 2, X, Palermo, 1918.

Giardina C. ed. *Capitoli e privilegi di Messina*, Memorie e documenti di storia siciliana, ser. 2, I, Palermo, 1937.

Giuffrida A. ed. *Il cartulario della famiglia Alagona di Sicilia. Documenti 1337–1386*, Acta siculo-aragonensia, 1, Palermo, 1978.

Giunta F. and A. Giuffrida eds. *Corrispondenza tra Federico III di Sicilia e Giacomo II d'Aragona*, Acta siculo-aragonensia, 2, Palermo, 1972.

Glénisson J. 'Documenti dell'Archivio Vaticano relativi alla collettoria di Sicilia (1372–1375)', *Rivista di storia della Chiesa in Italia*, 2 (1948), 225–62.

Glénisson J. and J. Day eds. *Textes et documents d'histoire du Moyen Age, XIVe–XVe siècles*, 2 vols., Paris, 1970.

Gregorio R. ed. *Bibliotheca scriptorum qui res in Sicilia gestas sub Aragonum imperio retulere*, 2 vols., Palermo, 1791–2.

Guarneri A. 'Un diploma di grazie e privilegi municipali concessi nel 1393 dai magnifici conti di Peralta alla città di Calatafimi', *ASS*, new ser. 14 (1889), 293–314.

Guida d'Italia. Sicilia, Milan, 1968.

Gussone J. *Florae Siculae synopsis*, 2 vols., Naples, 1842–4.

Huillard Bréholles J. L. A. ed. *Historia diplomatica Friderici secundi*, 11 tomes in 6 vols., Paris, 1852–61.

Kehr K. A. 'Staufische Diplome im Domarchiv zu Patti', *Quellen u. Forschungen aus Italienischen Archiven u. Bibliotheken*, 7 (1904), 171–81.

Lagumina B. and G. Lagumina eds. *Codice diplomatico dei Giudei di Sicilia*, 3 vols., DSSS, ser. 1, VI, XII, XVII, Palermo, 1884–95.

La Lumia I. ed. *Estratti di un processo per lite feudale del secolo XV concernenti gli ultimi anni del regno di Federico III [IV] e la minorità della regina Maria*, DSSS, ser. 1, III, Palermo, 1878.

La Mantia F. ed. *Capitoli inediti della città di Sciacca del secolo XV*, Sciacca, 1908.

La Mantia F. and G. La Mantia eds. *Consuetudini di Santa Maria di Licodia*, Palermo, 1898.

La Mantia G. ed. *I capitoli delle colonie greco-albanesi di Sicilia dei secoli XV e XVI*, Palermo, 1904.

ed. *Codice diplomatico dei re aragonesi di Sicilia Pietro I, Giacomo, Federico II [III], Pietro II e Ludovico dalla rivoluzione siciliana del 1282 al 1355. Con note storiche e diplomatiche I (Anni 1282–1290)*, DSSS, ser. 1, XXIII, Palermo, 1917.

La Mantia V. ed. *Antiche consuetudini delle città di Sicilia*, Palermo, 1900.

ed. *Consuetudini di Randazzo*, Palermo, 1903.

La Rosa, *Le consuetudini di Noto*, Catania, 1903.

Li Gotti E. *Volgare nostro siculo. Crestomazia di testi siciliani del secolo XIV*, Florence, 1951.

Lionti F. 'Un documento relativo a Matteo Palizzi', *ASS*, new ser. 10 (1885), 99–104.

Codice diplomatico di Alfonso il Magnanimo, *DSSS*, ser. 1, XV, Palermo, 1891.

Littara V. *De rebus netinis*, Palermo, 1593.

Lombardo A. 'Un testamento e altri documenti in volgare siciliano del secolo XIV a Venezia', *BCSFLS*, 10 (1969), 46–83.

Madurell Marimón J. M. 'Contabilidad de una compañia mercantil trecentista barcelonesa (1334–1342)', *Anuario de historia del derecho español*, 35 (1965), 421–525; 36 (1966), 457–546.

Marletta F. 'La costituzione e le prime vicende delle maestranze di Catania', *ASSO*, 1 (1904), 354–8; 2 (1905), 88–103, 224–33.

Mauceri E. 'Inventari inediti dei secoli XV e XVI. (Da atti notarili di Siracusa, Noto, Lentini, Palazzolo Acreide)', *ASSO*, 12 (1915), 105–17; 13 (1916), 182–90.

Mazzarese Fardella E. ed. *Il Tabulario Belmonte*, *DSSS*, ser. 1, XXX, Palermo, 1983.

Ménager L.-R. ed. *Les actes latins de S. Maria di Messina (1103–1250)*, Istituto siciliano di studi bizantini e neoellenici, Testi, 9, Palermo, 1963.

Minieri Riccio C. *Notizie storiche tratte da 62 registri angioini dell'Archivio di Stato di Napoli*, Naples, 1877.

'Il regno di Carlo I d'Angiò dal 2 gennaio 1273 al 31 dicembre 1283', *ASI*, 4th ser. 2 (1878), 193–205, 353–64; 3 (1879), 3–22, 161–70.

Mirto C. 'Petrus Secundus dei gratia rex Siciliae (1337–1342)', *ASS*, 4th ser. 2 (1976), 53–126.

Mostra documentaria sui rapporti fra il Regno di Sicilia e la Repubblica di Genova (secoli XII–XVI), Palermo, 1984.

Muntaner R. *Crònica*, in F. Soldevila ed. *Les quatre grans cròniques*, Barcelona, 1971.

Napoli F. 'Il Libro Rosso della città di Mazara. Regesto', *ASS*, new ser. 4 (1950–1), 317–42.

da Neocastro B. *Historia sicula*, ed. G. Paladino, *RR.II.SS.*, XIII, Bologna, 1921.

Orlando D. ed. *Un codice di leggi e diplomi siciliani del Medio Evo che si conserva nella Biblioteca del Comune di Palermo ai segni Qq.H.124*, Palermo, 1857.

Pagnini della Ventura G. F. *Della decima e di varie altre gravezze imposte dal comune di Firenze; della moneta e della mercatura de' Fiorentini sino al secolo XVI*, 4 vols., Lisbon–Lucca, 1765–6.

Palumbo P. 'Nuove testimonianze del siciliano trecentesco', *BCSFLS*, 1 (1953), 233–45.

Pegolotti F. B. *La pratica della mercatura*, ed. A. Evans, Medieval Academy of America Publications, 24, Cambridge, Mass., 1936.

da Piazza M. *Cronaca*, ed. A. Giuffrida, Fonti per la storia di Sicilia, 3, Palermo, 1980.

418   Bibliography

Pipitone Federico G. 'Il testamento di Manfredi Chiaromonte', in *Miscellanea di archeologia, storia e filologia dedicata al Prof. Antonino Salinas*, Palermo, 1907, pp. 328–39.

Pollacci Nuccio F. 'Della sollevazione occorsa in Palermo l'anno 1450. Documenti ricavati dallo Archiviò generale del Comune di Palermo', *Nuove effemeridi siciliane*, 3rd ser. 1 (1875), 149–70.

Pollacci Nuccio F. and Gnoffo D. eds. *I due registri di lettere degli anni 1311–12 e 1316–17, il Quaternus peticionum del 1320–21 e il quaderno delle gabelle anteriori al 1312*, Gli atti della città di Palermo dal 1311 al 1410, I, Palermo, 1892.

Pragmaticarum Regni Siciliae novissima collectio, 2 vols., Palermo, 1636–7.

Randazzini S. ed. *Le consuetudini di Caltagirone e i diplomi dei re che le confermarono*, Caltagirone, 1893.

Raymundettus R. *Regni Siciliae Pragmaticarum Sanctionum*, 2 vols., Venice, 1574.

Rinaldo G. M. ed., *Il 'Caternu' dell'Abate Angelo Senisio*, 2 vols., Collezione di testi siciliani dei secoli XIV e XV, vol. XVIII, Palermo, 1989.

Salomone Marino S. 'Le pompe nuziali e il corredo delle donne siciliane nei secoli XIV, XV e XVI', *ASS*, new ser. 1 (1876), 209–40.

'Spigolature storiche siciliane dal sec. XIV al sec. XIX', *ASS*, new ser. 21 (1896), 363–96.

Savagnone F. G. 'Capitoli inediti della città di Palermo', *ASS*, new ser. 26 (1901), 84–109.

Scarlata M. and L. Sciascia eds. *Documenti sulla luogotenenza di Federico d'Aragona*, Acta siculo-aragonensia, new ser. 2, Palermo, 1978.

Schiavo D. *Memorie per servire alla storia letteraria di Sicilia*, 2 vols., Palermo, 1756.

Sciacca G. C. *Patti e l'amministrazione del Comune nel Medio Evo*, *DSSS*, ser. 2, VI, Palermo, 1907.

Sella P. ed. *Rationes Decimarum Italiae nei secoli XIII e XIV. Sicilia*, Studi e testi, 112, Vatican City, 1944.

Serra A. *Breve trattato delle cause che possono far abbondare li Regni d'oro e d'argento dove non sono miniere con applicazione al Regno di Napoli*, ed. C. Trasselli, Reggio Calabria, 1974.

Sestini D. *Descrizione di varj prodotti dell'isola di Sicilia relativi al commercio della medesima con l'estere nazioni*, Florence, 1788.

Silvestri G. ed. *Tabulario di S. Filippo di Fragalà e di S. Maria di Maniaci*, *DSSS*, ser. 2, XI, Palermo, 1887.

Sipione E. 'Tre documenti trecenteschi', *ASSO*, 4th ser. 21 (1968), 211–52.

Sparti A. ed. *Il registro del notaio ericino Giovanni Maiorana (1297–1300)*, 2 vols., Palermo, 1982.

Spata G. ed. *Capitula R. Siciliae recensioni Francisci Testa addenda*, Palermo, 1865.

Speciale N. *Historia sicula*, in R. Gregorio ed. *Bibliotheca scriptorum*, I, pp. 283–508.

Starrabba R. 'Documenti riguardanti la Sicilia sotto re Martino I esistenti nell'Archivio della Corona d'Aragona', *ASS*, new ser. 1 (1876), 137–76.

ed. *I diplomi della Cattedrale di Messina, raccolti da A. Amico, DSSS,* ser. 1, I, Palermo, 1876–88.

ed. *Lettere e documenti relativi a un periodo del vicariato della regina Bianca in Sicilia (1411–1412), DSSS,* ser. 1, X, Palermo, 1877–8.

'Documenti relativi a un episodio delle guerre tra le fazioni latina e catalana ai tempi di Re Ludovico d'Aragona', *ASS,* new ser. 9 (1884), 157–94.

ed. *Consuetudini e privilegi della città di Messina sulla fede di un codice del XV secolo posseduto dalla Biblioteca comunale di Palermo,* Palermo, 1901.

Starrabba R. and L. Tirrito eds. *Assise e consuetudini della terra di Corleone, DSSS,* ser. 2, II, Palermo, 1880–2.

Testa F[ederico] ed. *De vita et rebus gestis Federici II [III] Siciliae regis,* Palermo, 1775.

Testa F[rancesco] ed. *Capitula Regni Siciliae,* 2 vols., Palermo, 1741–3.

Tirrito L. ed. *Statuto, capitoli e privilegi della città di Castronuovo di Sicilia, DSSS,* ser. 2, II, Palermo, 1877.

Trinchera F. ed. *Codice aragonese o sia lettere regie, ordinamenti ed altri atti governativi de' sovrani aragonesi in Napoli,* 3 vols., Naples, 1866–70.

Zeno R. 'Un capitolo di re Martino sull'acatapania catanese', *ASSO,* 6 (1909), 280–92.

ed. *Documenti per la storia del diritto marittimo nei secoli XIII e XIV,* · Documenti e studi per la storia del commercio e del diritto commerciale, 6, Turin, 1936; repr. Turin, 1970.

Zurita G. *Anales de la Corona de Aragón,* ed. A. Canellas Lopez, 9 vols., Saragossa, 1967–85.

SECONDARY WORKS

Abel W. *Agricultural fluctuations in Europe. From the thirteenth to the twentieth centuries,* Eng. trans. O. Ordish, London, 1980.

Strukturen und Krisen der spätmittelalterlichen Wirtschaft, Stuttgart–New York, 1980.

Abulafia D. S. H. *The two Italies: economic relations between the Norman kingdom of Sicily and the northern communes,* Cambridge, 1977.

'Venice and the kingdom of Naples in the last years of Robert the Wise 1332–1343', *Papers of the British School at Rome,* 48 (1980), 186–204.

'Southern Italy and the Florentine economy, 1265–1370', *EcHR,* 2nd ser. 33 (1981), 377–88.

'Il commercio del grano siciliano nel tardo Duecento', in *XI Congresso di storia della Corona d'Aragona. La società mediterranea all'epoca del Vespro,* Palermo, 1983, pp. 5–22.

'Maometto e Carlomagno: le due aree monetarie italiane dell'oro e dell'argento', in R. Romano and U. Tucci eds. *Storia d'Italia: Annali,* VI, pp. 221–70.

'The crown and the economy under Roger II and his successors', *Dumbarton Oaks Papers,* 37 (1983), 1–14.

'Una comunità ebraica della Sicilia occidentale: Erice 1298–1304', *ASSO*, 80 (1984), 157–90.

'Catalan merchants and the western Mediterranean, 1236–1300: Studies in the notarial acts of Barcelona and Sicily', *Viator*, 16 (1985), 209–42.

'The merchants of Messina: Levant trade and domestic economy', *Papers of the British School at Rome*, 54 (1986), 196–212.

Frederick II. A medieval emperor, London–New York, 1988.

Adroer i Tasis A. M. 'Organització d'una armada contra Genova (1458)', in *Atti e comunicazioni del XIV Congresso di storia della Corona d'Aragona*, I, pp. 3–8.

Alexandre P. *Le climat en Europe au moyen âge*, Paris, 1987.

Allmand C. T. *The Hundred Years War. England and France at war c.1300–c.1450*, Cambridge, 1988.

Althusser L. and E. Balibar, *Reading Capital*, Eng. trans. B. Brewster, London, 1970.

Amari M. *La guerra del Vespro siciliano*, 5th ed., Turin, 1851.

Storia dei Musulmani di Sicilia, 2nd ed. C. A. Nallino, 3 vols., Catania, 1933–9.

Amin S. *Unequal exchange*, Brighton, 1976.

Antoni T. 'Costi e prezzi del ferro in Pisa alla fine del Trecento', *Bollettino storico pisano*, 40–1 (1971–2), 75–105.

Ardizzoni C. *Le origini del patrimonio fondiario di Catania, I. Ex feudo Pantano*, Catania, 1902.

Arenaprimo G. 'Protesta dei messinesi al vicere conte di Prades del 1478', *Atti della Reale Accademia Peloritana*, 11 (1896–7), 169–205.

Ashtor E. 'The Jews in the Mediterranean trade in the fifteenth century', in J. Schneider ed. *Wirtschafstkräfte und Wirtschaftswege, I. Mittelmeer und Kontinent. Festschrift für Hermann Kellenbenz*, Beiträge zur Wirtschaftsgeschichte, IV, Nürnberg, 1978, pp. 441–54.

'Gli ebrei nel commercio mediterraneo nell'Alto Medioevo (sec. X–XI)', in *Gli Ebrei nell'Alto Medioevo*, 2 vols., Settimane di Studio, 26, Spoleto, 1980, pp. 401–64.

'Levantine sugar industry in the later Middle Ages: a case of technological decline', in A. L. Udovitch ed. *The Islamic Middle East 700–1900: Studies in economic and social history*, Princeton, 1981, pp. 91–132.

'The Jews of Trapani in the late Middle Ages', *Studi medievali*, 3rd ser. 25 (1984), 1–30.

Astill G. and A. Grant eds. *The countryside of medieval England*, Oxford, 1988.

'The medieval countryside: Efficiency, progress and change', in Astill and Grant eds. *The countryside*, pp. 213–34.

Aston T. H. ed. *Crisis in Europe 1560–1660*, London, 1965.

Atti e comunicazioni del XIV Congresso di storia della Corona d'Aragona (Sassari–Alghero 19–24 maggio 1990), 5 vols., Cagliari, 1990.

Avolio C. 'La schiavitù in Sicilia nel secolo XVI', *ASS*, new ser. 10 (1885), 45–71.

Aymard M. 'Commerce et production de la soie sicilienne au XVIe et XVIIe siècles', *Mélanges d'archéologie et d'histoire*, 77 (1965), 609–40.

'Une croissance sélective: la population sicilienne aux XVIe–XVIIe siècles', *Mélanges de la Casa de Velazquez*, 4 (1968), 303–27.

'In Sicilia: sviluppo demografico e sue differenziazioni geografiche, 1500–1800', *QS*, 6 (1971), 417–46.

'Production, commerce et consommation des draps de laine du XIIe au XVIIe siècle (Prato, 10–16 avril 1970)', *Revue historique*, 499 (1971), 5–12.

'Il bilancio di una lunga crisi finanziaria', *RSI*, 84 (1972), 988–1021.

'La transizione dal feudalesimo al capitalismo', in R. Romano and C. Vivanti eds. *Storia d'Italia: Annali*, I, pp. 1131–92.

'Une famille de l'aristocratie sicilienne aux XVIe et XVIIe siècles: les ducs de Terranova', *Revue historique*, 96 (1972), 29–65.

'Mesures et interprétations de la croissance. Rendements et productivité agricole dans l'Italie moderne', *AESC*, 28 (1973), 475–98.

'Amministrazione feudale e trasformazioni strutturali tra '500 e '700', *ASSO*, 71 (1975), 17–63.

'Commerce et consommation des draps en Sicile et en Italie méridionale (XVe–XVIIIe siècles)', in M. Spallanzani ed. *Produzione commercio*, pp. 127–39.

'Il commercio dei grani nella Sicilia del '500', *ASSO*, 72 (1976), 7–40.

'L'approvisionnement des villes de la Méditerranée occidentale (XVIe–XVIIIe siècles)', *Flaran*, 5 (1983), 165–85.

'Le blé de Sicile, année 1500', in G. Motta ed. *Studi Trasselli*, pp. 77–98.

Aymard M. and H. Bresc, 'Problemi di storia dell'insediamento nella Sicilia medievale e moderna, 1100–1800', *QS*, 8 (1973), 945–76.

'Nourritures et consommation en Sicile entre XIVe et XVIIIe siècles', *MEFRM*, 87 (1975), 535–81.

Bailey M. *A marginal economy? East Anglian Breckland in the later Middle Ages*, Cambridge, 1989.

'The concept of the margin in the medieval English economy', *EcHR*, 2nd ser. 42 (1989), 1–17.

Bairoch P., J. Batou and P. Chèvre, *La population des villes européennes de 800 à 1850*, Geneva, 1988.

Balard M. ed. *Etat et colonisation au Moyen Age et à la Renaissance*, Lyons, 1989.

Balbi G. 'Le relazioni tra Genova e la Corona d'Aragona dal 1464 al 1478', in *Atti del I Congresso storico Liguria–Catalogna*, Bordighera, 1974, pp. 468–87.

Ball J. N. *Merchants and merchandise. The expansion of trade in Europe 1500–1630*, London, 1977.

Baraldi E. 'Per un'archeologia dei forni alla bresciana', *QS*, 24 (1989), 101–22.

Baratier E. *La démographie provençale du XIIIe siècle au XVI siècle. Avec chiffres de comparaison pour le XVIIIe siècle*, Démographie et sociétés, 5, Paris, 1961.

Bardhan P. 'Marxist ideas in development economics: an evaluation', in J. Roemer ed. *Analytical Marxism*, Cambridge, 1986, pp. 64–78.

'Alternative approaches to the theory of institutions in economic development', in Bardhan ed. *Economic theory*, pp. 3–17.

Bardhan P. ed. *The economic theory of agrarian institutions*, Oxford, 1989.

Barsanti D. *Allevamento e transumanza in Toscana. Pastori, bestiami e pascoli nei secoli XV–XIX*, Florence, 1987.

Basso E. 'La Corona d'Aragona e la dominazione viscontea su Genova (1421–1435)', in *Atti e comunicazioni del XIV Congresso di storia della Corona d'Aragona*, I, Cagliari, 1990, pp. 125–44.

Basu K. *The less developed economy. A critique of contemporary theory*, Oxford, 1984.

Battle C. *Barcelona a mediados del siglo XV. Historia de una crisis urbana*, Barcelona, 1976.

Baviera F. S. *Memorie storiche sulla città di Salemi*, Palermo, 1846.

Baviera Albanese A. 'L'istituzione dell'ufficio di Conservatoria del Real Patrimonio e gli organi finanziari del Regno di Sicilia nel sec. XV (Contributo alla storia delle magistrature siciliane)', *Il Circolo Giuridico* (1958), 3–161.

In Sicilia nel secolo XVI: verso una rivoluzione industriale?, Palermo, 1974.

'Sulla rivolta del 1516 in Sicilia', *Atti dell'Accademia di Scienze Lettere e Arti di Palermo*, 4th ser. 35 (1975–6 [1977]), 425–80.

'La Sicilia tra regime pattizio e assolutismo monarchico agli inizi del secolo XVI', *Studi senesi*, 92 (1980), 189–310.

'Studio introduttivo', in L. Citarda ed. *Registri di lettere (1321–1326). Frammenti, ACFUP*, 3, Palermo, 1984, pp. xv–lxviii.

Beccaria G. 'Note critiche sul Parlamento di Catania del 1397', *ASS*, new ser. 12 (1888), 345–68.

Beloch K. J. *Bevölkerungsgeschichte Italiens, 1. Grundlagen. Die Bevölkerung Siziliens und des Königreichs Neapel*, Berlin–Leipzig, 1937.

Benito Ruano E. 'Búsqueda de tesoros en la España medieval', in *Studi Federigo Melis*, III, pp. 177–92.

Bennett M. J. *Community, class and careerism. Cheshire and Lancashire society in the age of Sir Gawain and the Green Knight*, Cambridge, 1983.

Berengo M. 'Patriziato e nobiltà: il caso veronese', *RSI*, 87 (1975), 493–517.

Bergier J.-F. 'Le cycle médiéval: des sociétés féodales aux états territoriaux', in P. Guichonnet ed. *Histoire et civilisation des Alpes*, 2 vols., Toulouse–Lausanne, 1980, I, pp. 163–204.

Bernard, J. 'Trade and finance in the Middle Ages 900–1500', in C. Cipolla ed. *The Fontana economic history of Europe, 1. The Middle Ages*, London–Glasgow, 1972, pp. 274–338.

Bettelli Bergamaschi M. '*Morarii* e *celsi*: la gelsicoltura in Italia nell'Alto Medioevo', *NRS*, 73 (1989), 1–22.

Bevere R. 'Arredi suppellettili utensili d'uso nelle provincie meridionali dal XII al XVI secolo', *Archivio storico per le province napoletane*, 21 (1896), 626–64.

Bisson T. N. *The medieval Crown of Aragon. A short history*, Oxford, 1986.

Blanchard I. S. W. 'Labour productivity and work psychology in the English mining industry 1400–1600', *EcHR*, 2nd ser. 31 (1978), 1–24.

'The Continental European cattle trades, 1400–1600', *EcHR*, 2nd ser. 39 (1986), 427–60.

Bloch M. *French rural history. An essay on its basic characteristics*, Eng. trans. J. Sondheimer, London, 1966.

Blockmans W. P. 'Stadt, Region und Staat: ein Dreiecksverhältnis. Der Kasus der Niederlande im 15. Jahrhundert', in F. Seibt and W. Eberhard eds. *Europa 1500. Integrationsprozesse im Widerstreit: Staaten, Regionen, Personenverbände, Christenheit*, Stuttgart, 1987, pp. 211–26.

Bois G. 'Noblesse et crise des revenus seigneuriaux en France aux XIVe et XVe siècles: essai d'interprétation', in P. Contamine ed. *La noblesse au Moyen Age XIe–XVe siècles. Essais à la mémoire de Robert Boutrouche*, Paris, 1976, pp. 219–33.

The crisis of feudalism. Economic society in eastern Normandy c.1300–1550, Eng. trans. (translator not cited) Cambridge, 1984.

Bonanno M. 'Denaro inedito della città di Palermo di epoca chiaramontana (seconda metà del XIV secolo)', *Schede medievali*, 6–7 (1984), 92–8.

Borlandi F. '"Fûtainiers" et fûtaines dans l'Italie du Moyen Age', in *Eventail de l'histoire vivante. Hommage à Lucien Febvre*, 2 vols., Paris, 1953, II, pp. 133–40.

Boscolo A. 'Mercanti e traffici in Sicilia e in Sardegna all'epoca di Ferdinando I d'Aragona', in *Studi Federigo Melis*, III, pp. 271–7.

Boüard M. de. 'Problèmes de subsistances dans un état médiéval: le marché et les prix des céréales au royaume angevin de Sicile (1266–1282)', *Annales d'histoire économique et sociale*, 10 (1938), 483–501.

Boutrouche R. 'The devastation of rural areas during the Hundred Years War and the agricultural recovery of France', in P. S. Lewis ed. *The recovery of France in the fifteenth century*, New York–London, 1972, pp. 23–59.

Braudel F. *The Mediterranean and the Mediterranean world in the age of Philip II*, 2 vols., Eng. trans. S. Reynolds, London, 1973.

Braunstein P. 'Les entreprises minières en Vénétie au XVe siècle', *Mélanges d'archéologie et d'histoire*, 77 (1965), 529–608.

Brenner R. 'The origins of capitalist development: a critique of neo-Smithian Marxism', *New Left review*, 104 (1977), 25–92.

'The agrarian roots of European capitalism', in T. H. Aston and C. H. E. Philpin eds. *The Brenner debate. Agrarian class structure and economic development in pre-industrial Europe*, Cambridge, 1985, pp. 213–327.

'The social basis of economic development', in J. Roemer ed. *Analytical Marxism*, Cambridge, 1986, pp. 23–53.

'Economic backwardness in eastern Europe in light of developments in the West', in D. Chirot ed. *Origins of backwardness*, pp. 15–52.

'Bourgeois revolution and transition to capitalism', in A. L. Beier, D. Cannadine and J. M. Rosenheim eds. *The first modern society. Essays in English history in honour of Lawrence Stone*, Cambridge, 1990, pp. 285–303.

Bresc H. 'Pantelleria entre l'Islam et la Chrétienté', *Cahiers de Tunisie*, 19 (1971), 105–27.

'Les jardins de Palerme (1290–1460)', *MEFRM*, 84 (1972), 55–127.

'Società e politica in Sicilia nei secoli XIV e XV', *ASSO*, 70 (1974), 267–304.

'The "secrezia" and the royal patrimony in Malta: 1240–1450', in A. T. Luttrell ed. *Medieval Malta*, pp. 126–62.

'Il feudo nella società siciliana medievale', in S. Di Bella ed. *Economia e storia (Sicilia–Calabria XV–XIX sec.)*, Cosenza, 1976.

'L'habitat médiéval en Sicile (1100–1450)', in *Atti del colloquio di archeologia medievale*, 2 vols., Palermo, 1976, I, pp. 186–97.

'Fosses à grain en Sicile (XIIème–XVème siècles), in M. Gast and F. Sigaut eds. *Les techniques de conservation des grains à long terme*, 2 vols., Paris, 1979, I, pp. 113–21.

'La feudalizzazione in Sicilia dal vassallaggio al potere baronale', in R. Romeo ed. *Storia della Sicilia*, III, pp. 501–41.

Economie et société en Sicile, 1300–1450, 4 vols. University of Paris IV, June 1982.

'"Disfari et perdiri li fructi et li aglandi": economie e risorse boschive nella Sicilia medievale (XIII–XV secoli)', *QS*, 18 (1983), 941–69.

'La draperie catalane au miroir sicilien, 1300–1460', *Acta mediaevalia historica et archaeologica*, 4 (1983), 107–27.

'Reti di scambio locale e interregionale nell'Italia dell'alto Medioevo', in R. Romano and U. Tucci eds. *Storia d'Italia: Annali*, VI, pp. 135–78.

'La formazione del popolo siciliano', in A. Quattordio Moreschini ed. *Tre millenni*, pp. 243–65.

Un monde méditerranéen. Economie et société en Sicile, 1300–1450, 2 vols., Bibliothèque des Ecoles françaises d'Athènes et de Rome, 262, Rome, 1986.

'Les Gascons en Sicile 1392–1460', in *Atti e comunicazioni del XIV Congresso di storia della Corona d'Aragona*, I, Cagliari, 1990, pp. 74–99.

Bresc H. and F. D'Angelo, 'Structure et évolution de l'habitat dans la région de Termini Imerese (XIIe–XVe siècles)', *MEFRM*, 84 (1972), 361–402.

Bresc-Bautier G. 'Pour compléter les données de l'archéologie: le rôle du bois dans la maison sicilienne (1350–1450)', in *Atti del colloquio di archeologia medievale*, 2 vols., Palermo, 1976, II, pp. 435–64.

Bresc [Bautier] G. and H. Bresc, '"Fondaco" et taverne de la Sicile médiévale', in *Hommage à Geneviève Chevrier et Alain Geslan*, Colmar–Strasbourg–Paris, 1975, pp. 95–106.

'Lavoro agricolo e lavoro artigianale nella Sicilia medievale', in *La cultura materiale*, pp. 91–139.

'*Maramma.* I mestieri della costruzione nella Sicilia medievale', in *I mestieri*, pp. 145–84.

Brezzi P. and E. Lee, *Private acts of the late Middle Ages. Sources of social history*, Toronto, 1984.

Bridbury A. R. *Medieval English clothmaking. An economic survey*, London, 1982.

Britnell R. H. *Growth and decline in Colchester, 1300–1525*, Cambridge, 1986.

'England and northern Italy in the early fourteenth century: the economic contrasts', *Transactions of the Royal Historical Society*, 5th ser. 39 (1989), 167–83.

Brown J. C. *In the shadow of Florence. Provincial society in Renaissance Pescia*, Oxford–New York, 1982.

Brunschvig R. *La Berbérie orientale sous les Hafsides, des origines à la fin du XVe siècle*, 2 vols., Paris, 1940.

Bueno de Mesquita D. M. *Giangaleazzo Visconti duke of Milan (1351–1402). A study in the political career of an Italian despot*, Cambridge, 1941.

Cadier L. *Essai sur l'administration du royaume de Sicile sous Charles Ier et Charles II d'Anjou*, Bibliothèque des Écoles françaises d'Athènes et de Rome, 59, Paris, 1891.

Cafagna L. *Dualismo e sviluppo nella storia d'Italia*, Venice, 1989.

Caggese R. *Roberto d'Angiò e i suoi tempi*, 2 vols., Florence, 1922–30.

Cahen C. 'Douanes et commerce dans les ports méditerranéens de l'Egypte médiéval d'après le *Minhadj* d'al-Makhzûmi', *Journal of economic and social history of the Orient*, 7 (1964), 217–314.

Calasso F. *La legislazione statutaria dell'Italia meridionale, I. Le basi storiche: le libertà cittadine dalla fondazione del Regno all'epoca degli statuti*, Biblioteca della Rivista di storia del diritto italiano, 3, Bologna, 1929.

Caldarella A. 'La "burgisia antiqua" in Sicilia', in *Ad Alessandro Luzio gli Archivi di Stato italiani. Miscellanea di studi storici*, 2 vols., Florence, 1933, I, pp. 247–51.

Cancila O. 'Contratti di conduzione, salari, prezzi nell'agricoltura trapanese del '400', *Rivista di storia dell'agricoltura*, 10 (1970), 309–30.

Impresa redditi mercato nella Sicilia moderna, Bari, 1980.

Baroni e popolo nella Sicilia del grano, Palermo, 1983.

'Commercio estero (sec. XVI–XVIII)', in R. Romeo ed. *Storia della Sicilia*, VII, pp. 123–61.

'L'evoluzione della rendita fondiaria', in *ibid.*, pp. 197–216.

'Le mete dei cereali e del vino a Palermo dal 1407 al 1822', in G. Motta ed. *Studi Trasselli*, pp. 157–65.

'Distribuzione e gestione della terra nella Sicilia moderna', in *Contributi per una storia economica della Sicilia*, Palermo, n.d., pp. 153–78.

Carrère C. *Barcelone centre économique à l'époque des difficultés 1380–1462*, 2 vols., Civilisations et sociétés, 5, Paris–La Haye, 1967.

'La draperie en Catalogne et en Aragon au XVe siècle', in M. Spallanzani ed. *Produzione commercio*, pp. 475–507.

Carus Wilson E. 'The woollen industry', in M. Postan and E. Rich eds. *Trade and industry*, pp. 355–428.

'Evidences of industrial growth on some fifteenth-century manors', *EcHR*, 2nd ser. 12 (1959–60), 190–205.

Cazelles R. *Société politique, noblesse et Couronne sous Jean le Bon et Charles V*, Mémoires et documents publiés par la Société de l'Ecole des Chartes, Geneva–Paris, 1982.

Cecchi E. 'Censimenti siciliani tra Cinque e Seicento nell'Archivio di Stato di Firenze', in G. Motta ed. *Studi Trasselli*, pp. 209–41.

Cheetham N. *Medieval Greece*, New Haven–London, 1981.

Chirot D. ed. *The origins of backwardness in eastern Europe. Economics and politics from the Middle Ages until the early twentieth century*, Berkeley–Los Angeles, 1989.

'Causes and consequences of backwardness', in Chirot ed. *Origins of backwardness*, pp. 1–14.

Chorley P. *Oil silk and Enlightenment. Economic problems in XVIIIth century Naples*, Istituto italiano per gli studi storici, 18, Naples, 1965.

'The cloth exports of Flanders and northern France during the thirteenth century: a luxury trade?', *EcHR*, 2nd ser. 40 (1987), 349–79.

Christaller W. *Central places in southern Germany*, Eng. trans. Englewood Cliffs, N.J., 1966.

Ciano C. 'A bordo della nave di Giovanni Carrocci nel viaggio da Porto Pisano a Palermo (1388–1389)', *ES*, 13 (1966), 141–83.

Cipolla C. M. *Il fiorino e il quattrino: la politica monetaria a Firenze nel 1300*, Bologna, 1982.

Clarkson L. A. *Proto-industrialization: the first phase of industrialization?*, London, 1985.

Cohen G. A. *Karl Marx's theory of history. A defence*, Oxford, 1978.

Cohn S. K. Jr. *The labouring classes in Renaissance Florence*, New York, 1980.

Comba R. 'Emigrare nel Medioevo. Aspetti economico-sociali della mobilità geografica nei secoli XI–XVI', in Comba, G. Piccinni and G. Pinto eds. *Strutture familiari*, pp. 45–74.

'Produzioni tessili nel Piemonte tardomedievale', *Bollettino storico-bibliografico subalpino*, 82 (1984), 321–62.

'Le origini medievali dell'assetto insediativo moderno nelle campagne italiane', in C. De Seta ed. *Storia d'Italia: Annali*, VIII, pp. 367–404.

Comba R., G. Piccinni and G. Pinto eds. *Strutture familiari epidemie migrazioni nell'Italia medievale*, Naples, 1984.

Contamine P. 'La guerre de cent ans en France: une approche économique', *Bulletin of the Institute of Historical Research*, 47 (1974), 125–49.

Cordova V. *Le origini della città di Aidone e il suo statuto*, Rome, 1890.

Corrao P. 'La popolazione fluttuante a Palermo fra '300 e '400: mercanti, marinai, salariati', in R. Comba, G. Piccinni and G. Pinto eds. *Strutture familiari*, pp. 435–50.

Governare un regno. Potere, società e istituzioni in Sicilia fra Trecento e Quattrocento, Naples, 1991.

Cosentino G. 'La zecca di Palermo nel secolo XV e la monetazione dei "denari parvuli" o "pichuli"', in *Centenario della nascita di Michele Amari*, 2 vols., Palermo, 1910, I, pp. 189–216.

'I ruoli degli anni 1434, 1442 e 1443 relativi a' fuochi di Sicilia', in *Atti del VII Congresso geografico italiano*, Palermo, 1911, pp. 570–91.

Cozzetto F. *Mezzogiorno e demografia nel XV secolo*, Soveria Mannelli, 1986.

Croce B. *History of the kingdom of Naples*, Eng. trans. F. Frenaye, ed. H. Stuart Hughes, Chicago, 1970.

La cultura materiale in Sicilia, Palermo, [1980].

Cusumano V. *Storia dei banchi di Sicilia. I banchi pubblici*, Rome, 1892.

Cuvillier J. P. 'Noblesse sicilienne, noblesse aragonaise et blé sicilien en 1392–1408', in *IX Congresso di storia della Corona d'Aragona. La Corona d'Aragona e il Mediterraneo: aspetti e problemi comuni da Alfonso il Magnanimo a Ferdinando il Cattolico*, Palermo, 1984, pp. 75–119.

D'Alessandro V. *Politica e società nella Sicilia aragonese*, Palermo, 1963.

'Per una storia della società siciliana alla fine del Medioevo: feudatari, patrizi, borghesi', *ASSO*, 77 (1981), 193–208.

'Vigne e vignaiuoli a Palermo alla fine del Medioevo', in *I mestieri*, pp. 99–107.

'Sulle assemblee parlamentari della Sicilia medievale', *ASSO*, 80 (1984), 5–17.

'L'Istoria di Trapani di Giovan Francesco Pugnatore', *Nuovi quaderni del Meridione*, 89–90 (1985), 165–75.

'Città e campagna in Sicilia nell'età angioino-aragonese', in C. Damiano Fonseca ed. *La Sicilia rupestre nel contesto della civiltà mediterranea*, Galatina, 1986, pp. 199–212.

D'Angelo F. 'Il corso della moneta siciliana nel Medioevo', *Economia e credito*, new ser. 12 (1972), 3–25.

'Terra e uomini della Sicilia medievale (secoli XI–XIII)', *Quaderni medievali*, 6 (1978), 51–94.

D'Arrigo P. 'Notizie sulla corporazione degli argentieri in Catania', *Bollettino storico catanese*, 1–2 (1936–7), 35–48.

Davies T. B. 'Changes in the structure of the wheat trade in seventeenth-century Sicily and the building of new villages', *Journal of European economic history*, 12 (1983), 371–405.

'Village-building in Sicily: an aristocratic remedy for the crisis of the 1590s', in P. Clark ed. *The European crisis of the 1590s. Essays in comparative history*, London, 1985, pp. 191–208.

Day J. 'Prix agricoles en Méditerranée à la fin du XIVe siècle', *AESC*, 16 (1961), 629–56.

'La Sardegna e i suoi dominatori dal secolo XI al secolo XIV', in Day, B. Anatra and L. Scaraffia, *La Sardegna medioevale e moderna*, Storia d'Italia diretta da G. Galasso, X, Turin 1984, pp. 1–187.

Uomini e terre nella Sardegna coloniale. XII–XVIII secolo, Turin, 1987.

De Benedictis E. *Della Camera delle regine siciliane*, Syracuse, 1890.

Delille G. *Famille et propriété dans le Royaume de Naples (XVe–XIXe siècle)*, Bibliothèque des Écoles françaises d'Athènes et de Rome, 259, Rome–Paris, 1985.

428   *Bibliography*

Del Monte A. and A. Giannola, *Il Mezzogiorno nell'economia italiana*, Bologna, 1978.

Del Treppo M. 'Assicurazioni e commercio internazionale a Barcellona nel 1428–1429', *RSI*, 69 (1957), 508–41; 70 (1958), 44–81.

I mercanti catalani e l'espansione della Corona d'Aragona nel secolo XV, Naples, 1972.

'Agricoltura e transumanza in Puglia nei secoli XIII–XVI: conflitto o integrazione?', in A. Guarducci ed. *Agricoltura e trasformazione dell'ambiente*. *Secoli XIII–XVIII*, Istituto Internazionale di Storia Economica 'F. Datini'. Pubblicazioni, 2nd ser. 11, Florence, 1984, pp. 455–60.

Il Regno aragonese, Naples, 1986.

Del Treppo M. and A. Leone, *Amalfi medioevale*, Naples, 1977.

Delumeau J. *L'alun de Rome, XVe–XIXe siècle*, Ports, routes, trafics, 13, Paris, 1962.

Dentici Buccellato R. 'Miniere siciliane nel XV secolo: una realtà o una speranza?', *Ricerche storiche*, 14 (1984), 117–42.

De Rosa L. 'Comunicazioni terrestri e marittime e depressione economica: il caso del Regno di Napoli (secoli XIV–XVIII)', in A. Vannini Marx ed. *Trasporti e sviluppo economico*, pp. 3–21.

De Seta C. ed. *Storia d'Italia: Annali*, VIII, Turin, 1985.

De Win P. 'The lesser nobility of the Burgundian Netherlands', in M. Jones ed. *Gentry and lesser nobility in late medieval Europe*, Gloucester–New York, 1986, pp. 95–118.

Deyon P. 'Fécondité et limites du modèle protoindustriel: premier bilan', *AESC*, 39 (1984), 868–81.

Di Martino G. 'Il sistema tributario degli Aragonesi in Sicilia (1282–1516)', *Archivio storico per la Sicilia*, 4–5 (1938–9), 83–145.

Dini B. 'L'industria tessile italiana nel tardo Medioevo', in S. Gensini ed. *Le Italie del tardo Medioevo*, Pisa, 1990, pp. 321–59.

Doren A. *Storia economica dell'Italia nel Medio Evo*, Ital. trans. G. Luzzatto, Padua, 1936; repr. Bologna, 1965.

Dotson J. E. 'Stowage factors in medieval shipping', in A. Vannini Marx ed. *Trasporti e sviluppo economico*, pp. 273–8.

Duby G. *Rural economy and country life in the medieval West*, Eng. trans. C. Postan, London, 1968.

Dyer C. *Standards of living in the later Middle Ages. Social change in England, c.1200–1520*, Cambridge, 1989.

'The consumer and the market in the later middle ages', *EcHR*, 2nd ser. 42 (1989), 305–27.

Eatwell J., M. Milgate and P. Newman eds. *The new Palgrave. Economic development*, London, 1989.

Eberhard W. 'Die Krise des Spätmittelalters: Versuch einer Zusammenfassung', in Seibt and Eberhard eds. *Europa 1400*, pp. 303–19.

Edler de Roover F. 'Early examples of marine insurance', *JEH*, 5 (1945), 172–87.

'Andrea Banchi, Florentine silk manufacturer and merchant in the fifteenth century', *Studies in medieval and Renaissance history*, 3 (1966), 221–85.

Edwards J. '"Development" and "underdevelopment" in the western Mediterranean: The case of Córdoba and its region in the late fifteenth and early sixteenth centuries', *Mediterranean historical review*, 2 (1987), 3–45.

Egidi P. 'Ricerche sulla popolazione dell'Italia meridionale nei secoli XIII e XIV', in *Miscellanea di studi storici in onore di Giovanni Sforza*, Lucca, 1920, pp. 731–50.

Emmanuel A. *Unequal exchange. A study of the imperialism of trade*, with additional comments by C. Bettelheim, Eng. trans. B. Pearce, London, 1972.

Ennen E. *Die europäische Stadt des Mittelalters*, 3rd edn., Göttingen, 1979.

Epifanio V. *Gli angioini di Napoli e la Sicilia dall'inizio del regno di Giovanna I alla pace di Catania*, Naples, 1936.

I valli della Sicilia nel Medioevo e la loro importanza nella vita dello stato, Naples, 1938.

Epstein S. R. 'The textile industry and the foreign cloth trade in late medieval Sicily (1300–1500): a "colonial relationship"?', *Journal of medieval history*, 15 (1989), 141–83.

'Governo centrale e comunità locali nella Sicilia tardo-medievale: le fonti capitolari', in *Atti e comunicazioni del XIV Congresso di storia della Corona d'Aragona*, V, Cagliari, 1990, pp. 403–38.

'Cities, regions and the late medieval crisis: Sicily and Tuscany compared', *Past and present*, 130 (1991), 3–50.

Everitt A. 'The marketing of agricultural produce', in J. Thirsk ed. *The agrarian history*, IV, pp. 466–592.

Falcon Perez M. I. 'Un aragonés embajador de Jaime II ante las cortes de Napoles y Sicilia', in *Atti e comunicazioni del XIV Congresso di storia della Corona d'Aragona*, V, Cagliari, 1990, pp. 293–312.

Felloni G. 'Italy', in C. Wilson and G. Parker eds. *An introduction to the sources of European economic history*, London, 1977, pp. 1–36.

Fenoaltea S. 'Risk, transaction costs, and the organization of medieval agriculture', *Explorations in economic history*, 13 (1976), 129–52.

Ferrer i Mallol M. T. 'El patrimoni reial i la recuperació del senyorius jurisdiccionals en els estats catalano-aragonesos a la fi del segle XIV', *Anuario de estudios medievales*, 7 (1970–1), 351–491.

Field A. J. 'The problem with neoclassical institutional economics. A critique with special reference to the North/Thomas model of pre-1500 Europe', *Explorations in economic history*, 18 (1981), 174–98.

Finley M. *Ancient Sicily*, 2nd rev. ed., London, 1979.

Finocchiaro Sartorio A. 'Le leggi di Corrado IV', in *Studi storici e giuridici dedicati ed offerti a Federico Ciccaglione*, 2 vols., Catania, 1909, I, pp. 235–61.

Fischer W. 'Rural industry and population change', *Comparative studies in society and history*, 15 (1973), 158–70.

Fisher F. J. 'The development of the London food market, 1540–1640', *EcHR*, 5 (1934–5), 46–64.

430   Bibliography

Fodale S. 'Il riscatto dei siciliani "captivi" in Barberia (XIV–XV secolo)', *Quaderni medievali*, 12 (1981), 61–84.

La foire, Recueils de la Société Jean Bodin, 5, Brussels, 1953.

Fournial E. *Les villes et l'économie d'échange en Forez aux XIIIe et XIVe siècles*, Paris, 1967.

Frangioni L. *Milano e le sue strade. Costi di trasporto e vie di commercio dei prodotti milanesi alla fine del Trecento*, Bologna, 1983.

Frank A. G. *Capitalism and underdevelopment in Latin America. Historical studies of Chile and Brazil*, New York–London, 1967.

Furió A. ed. *Valéncia, un mercat medieval*, Valéncia, 1985.

Gabrici E. 'Tessere mercantili delle famiglie Chiaromonte e Palizzi', *Giglio di Roccia*, new ser. 9 (1957), 6–7.

Galasso G. *Potere e istituzioni in Italia. Dalla caduta dell'Impero romano a oggi*, Turin, 1974.

Economia e società nella Calabria del Cinquecento, Milan, 1975.

Mezzogiorno medievale e moderno, Turin, 1975.

'Considerazioni intorno alla storia del Mezzogiorno in Italia', in Galasso, *Mezzogiorno medievale*, pp. 15–59.

'Le città campane nell'alto medioevo', in Galasso, *Mezzogiorno medievale*, pp. 61–135.

'La feudalità napoletana nel secolo XVI', in E. Fasano Guarini ed. *Potere e società negli stati regionali italiani del '500 e '600*, Bologna, 1978, pp. 241–57.

Gallo C. 'Il setificio in Sicilia. Saggio storico-politico', in *Nuova raccolta di opuscoli di autori siciliani*, I, Palermo, 1788, pp. 147–282.

Gambi L. 'La popolazione della Sicilia fra il 1374 e il 1376', *Quaderni di geografia umana per la Sicilia e per la Calabria*, 1 (1956), 3–10.

'I valori storici dei quadri ambientali', in R. Romano and C. Vivanti eds. *Storia d'Italia*, I, pp. 3–60.

Garufi C. A. *La Curia stratigoziale*, Messina, 1904.

'Patti agrari e comuni feudali di nuova fondazione in Sicilia. Dallo scorcio del secolo XI agli albori del Settecento. Studi storico-diplomatici', *ASS*, 3rd ser. 1 (1946), 31–113; 2 (1947), 7–131.

Gaudioso M. 'Per la storia del territorio di Lentini nel secondo Medio-Evo', *ASSO*, 2nd ser. 1 (1925), 40–89; 2 (1926), 227–394.

'Genesi e aspetti della "nobiltà civica" in Catania nel secolo XV', *Bollettino storico catanese*, 6 (1941), 29–67.

Natura giuridica delle autonomie cittadine nel 'Regnum Sicilie', Catania, 1952.

Sicilia feudale. La questione feudale in Francofonte, Catania, 1969.

La questione demaniale in Catania e nei 'casali' del Bosco etneo. Il Vescovo-barone, Catania, 1971.

La comunità ebraica di Catania nei secoli XIV e XV, Catania, 1974.

Genet J. P. and M. Le Mené eds. *Genèse de l'état moderne. Prélèvement et redistribution*, Paris, 1987.

Genuardi L. *Il parlamento siciliano*, Atti delle assemblee costituzionali italiane dal medio evo al 1831, ser. 1, I, Bologna, 1924.

Giannetti A. 'La strada dalla città al territorio: la riorganizzazione spaziale del Regno di Napoli nel Cinquecento', in C. De Seta ed. *Storia d'Italia: Annali*, VIII, pp. 241–85.

Giarrizzo G. 'La Sicilia dal Cinquecento all'Unità d'Italia', in V. D'Alessandro and G. Giarrizzo, *La Sicilia dal Vespro all'Unità d'Italia*, Storia d' Italia diretta da G. Galasso, XVI, Turin, 1989, pp. 97–793.

Gilissen J. 'La notion de la foire à la lumière comparative', in *La foire*, pp. 323–33.

Giménez Chornet V. 'Gobierno y control de los oficiales de la Camara de Sicilia (1424–1458)', in *Atti e comunicazioni del XIV Congresso di storia della Corona d'Aragona*, II, Cagliari, 1990, pp. 439–58.

Ginatempo M. and L. Sandri, *L'Italia delle città. Il popolamento urbano tra Medioevo e Rinascimento (secoli XIII–XVI)*, Florence, 1989.

Gioffrè D. 'Il commercio d'importazione genovese alla luce di registri del dazio 1495–1537', in *Studi in onore di Amintore Fanfani*, 5 vols., Milan, 1962, V, pp. 113–242.

Giorgetti G. *Contadini e proprietari nell'Italia moderna. Rapporti di produzione e contratti agrari dal secolo XVI a oggi*, 2nd rev. ed., Turin, 1974.

Girgensohn D. 'Dall'episcopato greco all'episcopato latino nell'Italia meridionale', in *La Chiesa greca in Italia dall'VIII al XVI secolo. Atti del Convegno storico interecclesiale (Bari 1969)*, 3 vols., Padua, 1973, I, pp. 25–43.

Giuffrida A. '"Lu quarteri di lu Cassaru". Note sul quartiere del Cassaro a Palermo nella prima metà del secolo XV', *MEFRM*, 83 (1971), 439–82.

'Il libro dei conti dell'Abate Angelo Senisio (1372–1381)', *BCSFLS*, 12 (1973), 151–66.

'Considerazioni sul consumo della carne a Palermo nei secolo XIV e XV', *MEFRM*, 87 (1975), 583–95.

'Aspetti e problemi del commercio dei panni in Sicilia dal XIV al XVI secolo', in M. Spallanzani ed. *Produzione commercio*, pp. 164–97.

'Aspetti della presenza genovese nei secoli XIV e XV', in Civico Istituto Colombiano, *Studi e testi, Saggi e documenti*, Genoa, 1978, I, pp. 265–93.

'La produzione dello zucchero in un opificio della piana di Carini nella seconda metà del sec. XV', in *La cultura materiale*, pp. 141–55.

'Itinerari di viaggi e trasporti', in R. Romeo ed. *Storia della Sicilia*, III, pp. 469–83.

Giuffrida V. 'Latifondi in Sicilia', in *Digesto italiano*, 24 vols., Turin, 1884–1921, XIV, pp. 31–51.

Giunta F. *Aragonesi e Catalani nel Mediterraneo*, 2 vols., Palermo, 1953–9.

Goitein S. D. 'Sicily and southern Italy in the Cairo Geniza documents', *ASSO*, 67 (1971), 9–33.

Goldberg P. J. 'Female migration to towns in the later Middle Ages', *Social history society newsletter*, 14 (1989), p. 10.

Goldthwaite R. A. 'I prezzi del grano a Firenze dal XIV al XVI secolo', *QS*, 28 (1975), 5–36.

Gras N. S. B. *The evolution of the English corn market from the twelfth to*

432 Bibliography

the eighteenth century, Harvard Economic Studies, 13, Cambridge, Mass., 1915.

Gregorio R. *Considerazioni sopra la storia di Sicilia dai tempi normanni sino ai presenti*, 6 vols., Palermo, 1805–16.

'Degli zuccheri siciliani', in Gregorio, *Discorsi attorno alla Sicilia*, Palermo, 1821.

Grendi E. 'Sulla "Teoria del sistema feudale" di Witold Kula', *QS*, 7 (1972), 735–54.

Grimaldi T. 'Palazzolo alla fine del XIV sec. (Due diplomi di re Martino)', *Studi acrensi*, 1 (1980–83), 49–100.

Grohmann A. 'Prime indagini sull'organizzazione fieristica siciliana nel Medio Evo e nell'Età Moderna, con particolare riferimento alla fiera di Sciacca', *Atti dell'Accademia pontaniana*, new ser. 18 (1968–9), 295–341.

Le fiere del Regno di Napoli in età aragonese, Naples, 1969.

Guarducci A. ed. *Sviluppo e sottosviluppo in Europa e fuori d'Europa dal secolo XIII alla Rivoluzione industriale*, Istituto Internazionale di Storia Economica 'F. Datini'. Pubblicazioni, 2nd ser., 10, Florence, 1983.

Guillou A. 'Il monachesimo in Italia meridionale e in Sicilia nel Medioevo', in *L'eremitismo in Occidente nei secoli XI e XII. Atti della II Settimana di studio (Mendola 1962)*, Milan, 1965, pp. 355–79.

'La soie sicilienne au Xe–XIe s.', in *Byzantino-Sicula II. Miscellanea di scritti in memoria di Giuseppe Rossi Taibbi*, Istituto siciliano di studi bizantini e neoellenici, 8, Palermo, 1975, pp. 285–8.

Hatcher J. *Plague, population and the English economy 1348–1530*, London, 1977.

Hay D. and J. Law, *Italy in the age of the Renaissance 1380–1530*, London–New York, 1989.

Heers J. *Gênes au XVe siècle. Activité économique et problèmes sociaux*, Affaires et gens d'affaires, 24, Paris, 1961.

'La mode et les marchés des draps de laine: Gênes et la montagne à la fin du Moyen Age', in M. Spallanzani ed. *Produzione commercio*, pp. 199–220.

Heers M.-L. 'Les Génois et le commerce de l'alun à la fin du Moyen Age', *Revue d'histoire économique et sociale*, 32 (1954), 30–53.

Herlihy D. 'Demography', in J. R. Strayer ed. *Dictionary of the Middle Ages*, New York, 1982 to date, IV, pp. 136–48.

Herlihy D. and C. Klapisch Zuber, *Tuscans and their families. A study of the Florentine Catasto of 1427*, New Haven–London, 1985.

Hibbert A. B. 'The economic policies of towns', in M. Postan, E. Rich and E. Miller eds. *Economic organization*, pp. 155–229.

Higounet-Nadal A. 'Le relèvement', in J. Dupâquier ed. *Histoire de la population française*, 4 vols., Paris, 1988, I, pp. 367–420.

Hillgarth J. N. *The Spanish kingdoms 1250–1516*, 2 vols., Oxford, 1976–8.

Hilton R. H. 'Rent and capital formation in feudal society', in *2nd International Conference of Economic History (Aix-en-Provence, 1962)*, 5 vols., Paris, 1965, II, pp. 33–68.

A medieval society. The West Midlands at the end of the thirteenth century, 1st ed. 1966; repr. Cambridge, 1983.

ed. *The transition from feudalism to capitalism*, London, 1978.

The decline of serfdom in medieval England, 2nd ed., London, 1983.

Hirschmann A. O. *National power and the structure of foreign trade*, Berkeley–Los Angeles, 1945.

'The rise and decline of development economics', in Hirschmann, *Essays in trespassing. Economics to politics and beyond*, Cambridge, 1981, pp. 1–24.

Hocquet J.-C. *Le sel et la fortune de Venise, II. Voiliers et commerce en Méditerranée 1200–1650*, Lille, 1979.

Le sel et la fortune de Venise, I. Production et monopole, 2nd rev. ed., Lille, 1982.

'Exploitation et appropriation des salines de la Méditerranée occidentale (1250–1350 env.)', in *XI Congresso di storia della Corona d'Aragona. La società mediterranea all'epoca del Vespro*, Palermo, 1984, pp. 219–48.

ed. *Le roi, le marchand et le sel*, Lille, 1987.

Hodgson G. M. *Economics and institutions. A manifesto for a modern institutional economics*, Oxford, 1988.

Hodson R. and R. L. Kaufman, 'Economic dualism: a critical review', *American sociological review*, 47 (1982), 727–39.

Hoshino H. *L'Arte della Lana in Firenze nel basso Medioevo. Il commercio della lana e il mercato dei panni fiorentini nei secoli XIII–XV*, Florence, 1980.

Hymer S. and S. Resnick, 'A model of an agrarian economy with nonagricultural activities', *American economic review*, 59 (1969), 493–506.

Ilera R. A. 'El comercio valenciano de exportación con Italia y Berbería a finales del siglo XIV', in *VIII Congreso de Historia de la Corona de Aragón*, 3 vols., Valencia, 1973, III, pp. 255–89.

Immagini di lavoro e vita contadina a San Piero Patti, Messina, 1981.

Jasny N. *The wheats of classical antiquity*, The Johns Hopkins University Studies in Historical and Political Science, ser. 62, 3, Baltimore, 1944.

Johns J. *The Muslims of Norman Sicily, c.1060–c.1194*, 2 vols., Ph.D. thesis, University of Oxford, 1983.

Jones E. L. 'Agricultural origins of industry', *Past and present*, 40 (1968), 58–71.

Jones P. 'Medieval agrarian society in its prime: Italy', in M. M. Postan ed. *The agrarian life of the Middle Ages*, 2nd ed., CEHE I, Cambridge, 1966, pp. 340–486.

'La storia economica. Dalla caduta dell'Impero romano al secolo XIV', in R. Romano and C. Vivanti eds. *Storia d'Italia*, II, pp. 1467–810.

'Economia e società nell'Italia medievale: la leggenda della borghesia', in R. Romano and C. Vivanti eds. *Storia d'Italia: Annali*, I, pp. 185–372.

Kaeuper R. W. *War, justice and public order. England and France in the later Middle Ages*, Oxford, 1988.

Kagan R. L. 'A golden age of litigation: Castile, 1500–1700', in J. Bossy ed.

434   Bibliography

Disputes and settlements. Law and human relations in the West, Cambridge, 1983, pp. 145–66.

Kanbur R. and J. McIntosh, 'Dual economies', in J. Eatwell, M. Milgate and P. Newman eds. *The new Palgrave. Economic development*, pp. 114–21.

Kellenbenz H. 'Rural industries in the West from the end of the Middle Ages to the eighteenth century', in P. Earle ed. *Essays in European economic history 1500–1800*, London, 1974, pp. 45–88.
'Wirtschaft und Gesellschaft Europas 1350–1650', in W. Fischer *et al. Handbuch der europäischen Wirtschafts- und Sozialgeschichte*, 6 vols., Stuttgart, 1980 to date, III, pp. 303–5.

Koenigsberger H. G. 'The parliament of Sicily and the Spanish Empire', in F. Giunta ed. *Mélanges Antonio Marongiu*, Brussels, 1968, pp. 81–96.
The practice of empire, Ithaca–New York, 1969.

Komlos J. and R. Landes, 'Anachronistic economics: grain storage in medieval England', *EcHR*, 2nd ser. 44 (1991), 36–45.

Kowaleski M. and J. M. Bennett, 'Crafts, gilds, and women in the Middle Ages: Fifty years after Marian K. Dale', *Signs: Journal of women in culture and society*, 14 (1989), 474–88.

Krekic B. *Dubrovnik (Raguse) et le Levant au moyen âge*, Documents et recherches, 5, Paris, 1961.

Kriedte P. 'Spätmittelalterliche Agrarkrise oder Krise des Feudalismus?', *Geschichte und Gesellschaft*, 7 (1981), 42–68.

Kriedte P., H. Medick and J. Schlumbohm, *Industrialization before industrialization. Rural industry in the genesis of capitalism*, Eng. trans. B. Schempp, Cambridge–Paris, 1981.

Küchler W. 'Länder- und Zentralfinanz des aragonesischen Staatenbundes im 15. Jahrhundert. Zur Rolle der spanischen und italienischen Länder in der Finanzpolitik der Krone', *Spanische Forschungen der Görresgesellschaft*, 1st ser. 28 (1975), 1–90.
Die Finanzen der Krone Aragon während des 15. Jahrhunderts (Alfons V und Johann II, Spanische Forschungen der Görresgesellschaft, 2nd ser. 22, Münster Westfalen, 1983.

Kula W. 'Il sottosviluppo economico in una prospettiva storica', *Annali della Fondazione Luigi Einaudi*, 3 (1969), 23–36.
Problemi e metodi di storia economica, Ital. trans. A. Zielinski, Milan, [1972].
An economic theory of the feudal system. Towards a model of the Polish economy 1500–1800, Eng. trans. L. Garner, London, 1976.
Les mésures et les hommes, French trans. J. Ritt, Paris, 1984.

Kussmaul A. *A general view of the rural economy of England, 1538–1840*, Cambridge, 1990.

Ladero Quesada M. A. 'Las ferias de Castilla. Siglos XII a XV', *Cuadernos de historia de España*, 67–8 (1982), 269–347.

La Lumia I. *I quattro Vicari. Studi di storia siciliana del XIV secolo*, Florence, 1867.
Studi di storia siciliana, 2 vols., Palermo, 1870.

La Mantia G. 'Su i più antichi capitoli della città di Palermo dal secolo XII al XIV e su le condizioni della città medesima negli anni 1354 al 1392', *ASS*, new ser. 40 (1915), 390–444.

'L'Università degli Studi di Catania e le pretensioni di Messina e Palermo dal secolo XV al XIX', *ASSO*, 2nd ser. 10 (1934), 300–16.

Lane F. C. 'Technology and productivity in seaborne transportation', in A. Vannini Marx ed. *Trasporti e sviluppo economico*, pp. 233–44.

Lane F. C. and R. C. Mueller, *Money and banking in medieval and Renaissance Venice, I. Coins and moneys of account*, Baltimore–London, 1985.

Langdon J. *Horses, oxen and technological innovation. The use of draught animals in English farming from 1066–1500*, Cambridge, 1986.

'Agricultural equipment', in G. Astill and A. Grant eds. *The countryside*, pp. 86–107.

Lapidus I. M. *Muslim cities in the later Middle Ages*, Cambridge, Mass., 1967.

Il lavoro contadino nei Nebrodi, Palermo, 1977.

Léonard E.-G. *Histoire de Jeanne Ire reine de Naples comtesse de Provence (1343–1382). La jeunesse de la reine Jeanne*, 3 vols., Monaco–Paris, 1932–7.

Leone A. 'Il Regno di Napoli e l'età aragonese', *Medioevo. Saggi e rassegne*, 7 (1982), 149–67.

Profili economici della Campania aragonese, Naples, 1983.

Leone S. 'Lineamenti di una storia delle corporazioni in Sicilia nei secoli XIV–XVII', *Archivio storico siracusano*, 2 (1956), 82–95.

Lepre A. *Storia del Mezzogiorno d'Italia*, 2 vols., Naples, 1986.

Le Roy Ladurie E. *Les paysans de Languedoc*, 2nd ed., 2 vols., Civilisations et sociétés, 42, Paris, 1966.

Leverotti F. 'Il consumo della carne a Massa all'inizio del XV secolo. Prime considerazioni', *Archeologia medievale*, 8 (1981), 227–38.

Lewis A. 'Economic development with unlimited supplies of labour', *The Manchester school of economic and social studies*, 22 (1954), 139–91.

Little I. M. D. *Economic development. Theory, policy and international relations*, New York, 1982.

López Rodríguez C. 'La estructura de los ingresos de la tesorería general de Alfonso el Magnanimo y la conquista de Italia (1424–47)', in *Atti e comunicazioni del XIV Congresso di storia della Corona d'Aragona*, V, Cagliari, 1990, pp. 313–40.

Lösch A. *The economics of location*, Eng. trans. W. H. Woglom, New Haven–London, 1954.

Luttrell A. T. ed. *Medieval Malta. Studies on Malta before the Knights*, London, 1975.

'Approaches to Medieval Malta', in Luttrell ed. *Medieval Malta*, pp. 1–70.

Luzzatto G. 'Capitalismo coloniale nel Trecento', in Luzzatto, *Studi di storia economica veneziana*, Padua, 1954, pp. 117–23.

Storia economica dell'età moderna e contemporanea, I, 4th rev. ed., Padua, 1955.

Breve storia economica dell'Italia medievale. Dalla caduta dell'Impero romano al principio del Cinquecento, 2nd ed., Turin, 1965.

Machlup F. 'Conceptual and causal relationships in the theory of economic integration in the twentieth century', in B. Ohlin *et al.* eds. *The international allocation of economic activity*, London, 1977, pp. 196–215.

Mack Smith D. 'The latifundia in modern Sicilian history', *Proceedings of the British Academy*, 55 (1965), 85–124.

MacKay A. *Money, prices and politics in fifteenth-century Castile*, London, 1981.

Macry P. *Mercato e società nel Regno di Napoli. Commercio del grano e politica economica nel Settecento*, Naples, 1974.

Maçzak A., H. Samsonowicz and P. Burke eds. *East-central Europe in transition from the fourteenth to the seventeenth century*, Cambridge–Paris, 1985.

Maggiore Perni F. *La popolazione di Sicilia e di Palermo dal X al XVIII secolo*, Palermo, 1892.

Mainoni P. 'I paratici a Milano in età visconteo-sforzesca: problemi e indirizzi di ricerca', *GISEM 1984–1989. Bollettino 1 (1990)*, 79–80.

Maire-Vigueur J. C. *Les pâturages de l'Eglise et la douane du bétail dans la Province du Patrimonio (XIV–XV siècles)*, Fonti e studi del Corpus membranarum italicarum, ser. I/II, Studi e ricerche, 18, Rome, 1981.

Mallett M. *The Florentine galleys in the fifteenth century*, Oxford, 1967.

Małowist M. 'The economic and social development of the Baltic countries', *EcHR*, 2nd ser. 12 (1959–60), 177–89.

'L'inégalité du développement économique en Europe au bas Moyen Age', in Małowist, *Croissance et régression en Europe, XIVe–XVIIe siècles. Recueil d'articles*, Paris, 1972, pp. 39–52.

Manca C. *Aspetti dell'espansione economica catalano-aragonese nel Mediterraneo occidentale. Il commercio internazionale del sale*, Biblioteca della rivista 'Economia e storia', 16, Milan, 1966.

Marino J. A. *Pastoral economics in the Kingdom of Naples*, Baltimore, 1988.

Marletta F. 'La costituzione e le prime vicende delle maestranze di Catania', *ASSO*, 1 (1904), 354–8; 2 (1905), 88–103, 224–33.

'L'arte della seta a Catania nei sec. XV–XVII', *ASSO*, 2nd ser. 2 (1926), 46–91.

Marrara D. 'Nobiltà civica e patriziato: una distinzione terminologica nel pensiero di alcuni autori italiani nell'età moderna', *Annali della Scuola Normale Superiore di Pisa: Lettere e Filosofia*, 3rd ser. 10 (1980), 219–32.

Martino C. 'La valle di Milazzo fra età angioina e aragonese (Appunti e problemi di topografia e storia dell'insediamento)', *Medioevo. Saggi e rassegne*, 4 (1979), 39–65.

Martino F. 'Una ignota pagina del Vespro: la compilazione dei falsi privilegi messinesi', *Quellen u. Forschungen aus Italienischen Archiven u. Bibliotheken*, forthcoming.

Maschke E. 'Die Wirtschaftspolitik Kaiser Friedrichs II. im Königreichs Sizilien', *Vierteljahrschrift für Sozial- und Wirtschaftsgeschichte*, 55 (1966), 289–328.

Mazzaoui M. F. *The Italian cotton industry in the later Middle Ages 1100–1600*, Cambridge, 1981.

Mazzarese Fardella E. 'Osservazioni sul suffeudo in Sicilia', *Rivista di storia del diritto italiano*, 34 (1961), 99–183.

I feudi comitali di Sicilia dai Normanni agli Aragonesi, Università di Palermo. Pubblicazioni a cura della Facoltà di Giurisprudenza, 36, Milan, 1974.

'L'aristocrazia siciliana nel secolo XIV e i suoi rapporti con le città demaniali: alla ricerca del potere', in R. Elze and G. Fasoli eds. *Aristocrazia e ceti popolari in Italia e in Germania*, Annali dell'Istituto storico italo-germanico, Quaderni 13, Bologna, 1984, pp. 177–93.

Melis F. *Aspetti della vita economica medievale (Studi nell'Archivio Datini di Prato)*, I, Siena, 1962.

'Werner Sombart e i problemi della navigazione nel Medio Evo', in G. Barbieri *et al. L'opera di Werner Sombart nel centenario della nascita*, Biblioteca della rivista 'Economia e storia', 8, Milan, 1964, pp. 85–149.

I vini italiani nel Medioevo, ed. A. Affortunati Parrini, Istituto Internazionale di Storia Economica 'F. Datini', Opere sparse di F. Melis, 7, Florence, 1984.

Mendels F. 'Proto-industralization: The first phase of the industrialization process', *JEH*, 32 (1972), 241–61.

'Seasons and regions in agriculture and industry during the process of industrialisation', in S. Pollard ed. *Region and Industrialisation. Studies in the role of the region in the economic history of the last two centuries*, Göttingen, 1980, pp. 177–95.

Merrington J. 'Town and country in the transition to capitalism', in R. H. Hilton ed. *Transition from feudalism to capitalism*, pp. 170–95.

I mestieri. Organizzazione tecniche linguaggi, Palermo, 1983.

Militi M. G. and C. M. Rugolo, 'Per una storia del patriziato cittadino in Messina (Problemi e ricerche sul secolo XV)', *ASM*, 3rd ser. 23–5 (1972–4), 113–65.

Miller E. 'The economic policies of governments. France and England', in M. M. Postan, E. Rich and Miller eds. *Economic organization*, pp. 338–40.

Millward R. 'The emergence of wage labour in early modern England', *Explorations in economic history*, 18 (1981), 21–39.

Milone F. *L'Italia nell'economia delle sue regioni*, Turin, 1955.

Sicilia. La natura e l'uomo, Turin, 1960.

Mineo E. I. 'Gli Speciale. Nicola viceré e l'affermazione politica della famiglia', *ASSO*, 79 (1983 [1986]), 287–371.

'Egemonia e radicamento della nobiltà militare catalana in Sicilia dopo il 1392: l'esempio dei Cruilles e dei Santapau', in M. Del Treppo ed. *Commercio, finanza, funzione pubblica. Stranieri in Sicilia e in Sardegna nei secoli XIII–XV*, Naples, 1989, pp. 89–127.

'Forme di successione familiare e di trasmissione patrimoniale nella Sicilia aragonese (secoli XIV–XV)', Ph.D. thesis, University of Palermo, 1989.

'Nazione, periferia, sottosviluppo. La Sicilia medievale di Henri Bresc', *RSI*, 101 (1990), 722–58.

Miskimin H. 'Monetary movements and market structure. Forces for contraction in fourteenth- and fifteenth-century England', *JEH*, 24 (1964), 470–90.

The economy of early Renaissance Europe 1300–1460, Cambridge, 1975.

Mokyr J. 'Growing-up and the industrial revolution in Europe', *Explorations in economic history*, 13 (1976), 371–96.

Mollat M. *Jacques Cœur ou l'esprit d'entreprise au XVe siècle*, Paris, 1988.

Motta G. 'Aspetti dell'economia siciliana alla fine del XIV secolo. Da una lettera di Manno d'Albizio a Francesco Datini', in *Studi in memoria di Federigo Melis*, II, pp. 507–27.

ed. *Studi dedicati a Carmelo Trasselli*, Soveria Mannelli, 1983.

Mueller R. 'Die wirtschaftliche Lage Italiens im Spätmittelalter', in F. Seibt and W. Eberhard eds. *Europa 1400*, pp. 221–32.

Nef J. U. 'Mining and metallurgy in medieval civilisation', in M. Postan and E. Rich eds. *Trade and industry*, pp. 429–92.

Nell E. J. 'Economic relationships in the decline of feudalism: an examination of economic interdependence and social change', *History and theory*, 6 (1966), 313–50.

Neveux H. *Vie et déclin d'une structure économique. Les grains du Cambrésis fin du XIVe-début du XVIIe siècle*, Paris, 1980.

Nicholas D. *The metamorphosis of a medieval city. Ghent in the age of the Arteveldes, 1302–1390*, Leiden, 1987.

Nicosia S. 'La coltivazione tradizionale del frumento nei latifondi del "Vallone"', in *La cultura materiale*, pp. 205–73.

Nigro G. *Gli uomini dell'Irco. Indagine sui consumi di carne nel basso Medioevo. Prato alla fine del 1300*, Florence, [1983].

North D. C. 'Location theory and regional economic growth', *Journal of political economy*, 63 (1955), 243–58.

'Transaction costs in history', *Journal of European economic history*, 14 (1985), 557–76.

North D. C. and R. P. Thomas, *The rise of the western world*, Cambridge, 1973.

Olgiati G. 'La Repubblica di Genova nella guerra di successione al regno di Napoli (1436–1442)', in *Atti e comunicazioni del XIV Congresso di storia della Corona d'Aragona*, I, Cagliari, 1990, pp. 687–707.

Ormrod D. *English grain exports and the structure of agrarian capitalism 1700–1760*, Hull, 1985.

Palliser D. M. 'Urban decay revisited', in J. A. F. Thomson ed. *Towns and townspeople in the fifteenth century*, Gloucester, 1988, pp. 1–21.

Palma J. G. 'Dependency', in J. Eatwell, M. Milgate and P. Newman eds. *The new Palgrave. Economic development*, pp. 91–7.

'Structuralism', in *ibid.*, pp. 316–22.

Palmeri N. *Opere edite ed inedite*, ed. C. Somma, Palermo, 1883.

Parker G. and L. M. Smith eds. *The general crisis of the seventeenth century*, London, 1978.

Penuti C. 'Il principe e le comunità soggette: il regime fiscale dalle "pattuizioni" al "buongoverno"', in A. De Maddalena and H. Kellenbenz eds. *Finanze e ragion di stato in Italia e in Germania nella prima Età moderna*, pp. 89–100.

Percy W. A. Jr. 'The revenues of the Kingdom of Sicily under Charles I of Anjou 1266–1285 and their relationship to the Vespers', Ph.D. thesis, University of Princeton, 1964.

'The earliest revolution against the "modern state": direct taxation in medieval Sicily and the Vespers', *Italian quarterly*, vol. 22, no. 84 (1981), 69–83.

'The indirect taxes of the medieval kingdom of Sicily', *Italian quarterly*, vol. 22, no. 85 (1981), 73–85.

Peri I. *Città e campagna in Sicilia, I. Dominazione normanna*, 2 vols., Atti, Accademia Scienze Lettere e Arti di Palermo, 4th ser. 13, Palermo, 1953–6.

'Rinaldo di Giovanni Lombardo "habitator terrae Policii"', in *Studi medievali in onore di Antonino De Stefano*, Palermo, 1956, pp. 429–506.

'La questione delle colonie "lombarde" in Sicilia', *Bollettino storico-bibliografico subalpino*, 57 (1959), 253–80.

Il villanaggio in Sicilia, Palermo, 1965.

'Economia agricola e crisi nella Sicilia medioevale. Interpretazioni e prospettive storiografiche', in *Storiografia e storia. Studi in onore di Eugenio Dupré Theseider*, 2 vols., Rome, 1974, I, pp. 95–104.

Uomini, città e campagne dall'XI al XIII secolo, Bari, 1978.

La Sicilia dopo il Vespro. Uomini, città e campagne 1282–1376, Bari, 1982.

Restaurazione e pacifico stato in Sicilia 1377–1501, Bari, 1988.

Perroy E. 'Social mobility among the French *noblesse* in the later Middle Ages', *Past and present*, 21 (1962), 25–38.

Persson K. G. 'Consumption, labour and leisure in the late Middle Ages', in D. Menjot ed. *Manger et boire au moyen âge*, 2 vols., Nice, 1984, I, pp. 211–23.

Pre-industrial economic growth. Social organization and technological progress in Europe, Oxford, 1988.

Pesez J. M. ed. *Brucato. Histoire et archéologie d'un habitat médiéval en Sicile*, 2 vols., Collection de l'École française de Rome, 78, Rome, 1984.

Petino A. 'L'arte ed il consolato della seta a Catania nei secoli XIV–XIX', *Bullettino storico catanese*, 6–7 (1942–3), 15–78.

Aspetti e momenti di politica granaria a Catania e in Sicilia nel Quattrocento, Catania, 1952.

Petralia G. *Banchieri e famiglie mercantili nel Mediterraneo aragonese. L'emigrazione dei pisani in Sicilia nel Quattrocento*, Biblioteca del 'Bollettino storico pisano', Collana storica, 34, Pisa, 1989.

Peyer H. C. 'Wollgewerbe, Viehzucht, Solddienst und Bevölkerungsentwicklung in Stand und Landschaft Freiburg i. Ue. vom 14. bis 16. Jh.', *Freiburger Geschichtsblätter*, 61 (1978 for 1977), 17–41.

Piaggia G. *Illustrazione di Milazzo e studi sulla morale e su' costumi dei villani del suo territorio*, Palermo, 1853.

Piccinni G. 'Note sull'alimentazione medievale', *Studi storici*, 23 (1982), 603–15.

Pinto G. *La Toscana nel tardo medio evo. Ambiente, economia rurale, società*, Florence, 1982.

Pipitone Federico G. *I Chiaromonti di Sicilia. Appunti e documenti*, Palermo, 1891.

Pirenne H. *Medieval cities, their origins, and the revival of trade*, Princeton, N.J., 1925.

Pisano Baudo S. *Storia di Lentini antica e moderna*, 3 vols., repr. Lentini, 1965–74.

Pispisa E. 'Il problema storico del Vespro', *ASM*, 3rd ser. 31 (1980), 57–82.

Messina nel Trecento. Politica economia società, Messina, 1980.

'Stratificazione sociale e potere politico a Messina nel Medioevo', *ASM*, 3rd ser. 32 (1981), 55–76.

Platania G. 'Sulle vicende della sericoltura in Sicilia', *ASSO*, 20 (1924), 242–75.

Polica S. 'Basso Medioevo e Rinascimento: "rifeudalizzazione" e "transizione"', *Bullettino dell'Istituto Storico Italiano per il Medio Evo e Archivio Muratoriano*, 88 (1979), 287–316.

Pontieri E. *Ricerche sulla crisi della monarchia siciliana nel secolo XIII*, 2nd rev. ed., Naples, 1950.

La Calabria a metà del secolo XV e la rivolta di Antonio Centelles, Naples, 1963.

Alfonso il Magnanimo re di Napoli 1433–1458, Naples, 1975.

Popkin S. L. *The rational peasant. The political economy of rural society in Vietnam*, Berkeley–Los Angeles–London, 1979.

Postan M. M. 'The fifteenth century', in Postan, *Essays on medieval agriculture and general problems of the medieval economy*, Cambridge, 1973, pp. 41–8.

'The trade of medieval Europe: the North', in Postan, *Medieval trade and finance*, Cambridge, 1973, pp. 92–231.

The medieval economy and society. An economic history of Britain in the Middle Ages, Harmondsworth, 1975.

Postan M. M. and E. E. Rich eds. *Trade and industry in the Middle Ages*, *CEHE*, II, Cambridge, 1952.

Postan M. M., E. E. Rich and E. Miller eds. *Economic organization and policies in the Middle Ages*, *CEHE*, III, Cambridge, 1963.

Powell J. M. 'Medieval monarchy and trade: the economic policy of Emperor Frederick II of Sicily', *Studi medievali*, 3rd ser. 3 (1962), 420–524.

Privitera S. *Storia di Siracusa antica e moderna*, 2 vols., Naples, 1878–9.

Pryor J. H. 'Foreign policy and economic policy: the Angevins of Sicily and the economic decline of southern Italy, 1266–1343', in L. O. Frappell ed. *Principalities, powers and estates: Studies in medieval and early modern government and society*, Adelaide, 1980, pp. 43–55.

Geography, technology, and war. Studies in the maritime history of the Mediterranean 649–1571, Cambridge, 1988.

Quattordio Moreschini A. ed. *Tre millenni di storia linguistica della Sicilia*, Biblioteca della società italiana di glottologia, 7, Pisa, 1984.

Ravallion M. *Markets and famines*, Oxford, 1987.

Rey M. *Le domaine du roi et les finances extraordinaires sous Charles VI (1388–1413)*, Paris, 1965.

Ribes Valiente M. L. 'La renta de la reina Maria en la ciudad de Siracusa (1456–1457)', in *Atti e comunicazioni del XIV Congresso di storia della Corona d'Aragona*, II, Cagliari, 1990, pp. 721–41.

Romano G. 'Messina nel Vespro siciliano e nelle relazioni siculo-angioine de' secoli XIII e XIV fino all'anno 1372', *Atti della Reale Accademia peloritana*, 14 (1899–1900), 187–242.

Romano R. 'La storia economica. Dal secolo XIV al Settecento', in Romano and C. Vivanti eds. *Storia d'Italia*, II, pp. 1811–1913.

Romano R. and U. Tucci eds. *Storia d'Italia: Annali*, VI, Turin, 1983.

'Premessa', in Romano and Tucci eds. *Storia d'Italia: Annali*, VI, pp. xix–xxxiii.

Romano R. and C. Vivanti eds. *Storia d'Italia*, 6 vols., Turin, 1972–6.

Storia d'Italia. Annali, I, Turin, 1978.

Romeo R. ed. *Storia della Sicilia*, 10 vols., Naples, 1979–81.

Ruddock A. A. *Italian merchants and shipping in Southampton, 1270–1600*, Southampton Record Series, 1, Southampton, 1951.

Rugolo C. M. 'L'organizzazione del lavoro nelle campagne siciliane del tardo Medioevo', *Quaderni medievali*, 15 (1983), 53–79.

'Maestri bottai in Sicilia nel secolo XV', *NRS* 69 (1985), 195–216.

Russell J. C. *Medieval regions and their cities*, Newton Abbott, 1972.

Ryder A. 'The evolution of imperial government in Naples under Alfonso V', in J. Hale, R. Highfield and B. Smalley eds. *Europe in the later Middle Ages*, London, 1965, pp. 332–57.

The kingdom of Naples under Alfonso the Magnanimous. The making of a modern state, Oxford, 1976.

'Cloth and credit: Aragonese war finance in the mid-fifteenth century', *War and society*, 2 (1984), 1–21.

Alfonso the Magnanimous King of Aragon, Naples, and Sicily 1396–1458, Oxford, 1990.

Salavert i Roca V. 'El problema estrategico del Mediterráneo occidental y la politica aragonese (siglos XIV y XV)', in *IV Congreso de Historia de la Corona de Aragón*, Palma de Mallorca, 1959, pp. 201–22.

Scalia G. 'Nuove considerazioni storiche e paleografiche sui documenti dell'Archivio capitolare di Catania per il ristabilimento della sede vescovile nel 1091', *ASSO*, 62 (1961), 5–53.

Scarlata M. 'Una famiglia della nobiltà siciliana nello spazio urbano e nel territorio tra XIII e XIV secolo', *Quaderni medievali*, 11 (1981), 67–83.

'Strutture urbane e habitat a Palermo fra XIII e XIV secolo. Un approccio al tema attraverso la lettura documentaria', *Schede medievali*, 8 (1985), 1–31.

'Mercati e fiere nella Sicilia aragonese', in *Mercati e consumi. Organizzazione e qualificazione del commercio in Italia dal XII al XX secolo*, 2 vols., Bologna, 1986, I, pp. 477–94.

Scaturro I. *Storia della città di Sciacca e dei comuni della contrada saccense fra il Belice e il Platani*, ed. G. Sacco, 2 vols., Naples, 1924–6.

Schofield R. S. 'Geographical distribution of wealth in England 1334–1649', *EcHR*, 2nd ser. 18 (1965), 483–510.

Scott T. *Freiburg and the Breisgau. Town–country relations in the age of Reformation and the Peasants' War*, Oxford, 1986.

'Economic conflict and co-operation on the Upper Rhine, 1450–1600', in E. I. Kouri and T. Scott eds. *Politics and society in Reformation Europe*, London, 1987, pp. 210–31.

Seibt F. and W. Eberhard eds. *Europa 1400. Die Krise des Spätmittelaters*, Stuttgart, 1984.

Sella D. *Crisis and continuity: the economy of Spanish Lombardy in the seventeenth century*, Cambridge, Mass.–London, 1979.

Sen A. *Poverty and famines. An essay on entitlement and deprivation*, Oxford, 1981.

Sereni E. 'Mercato nazionale e accumulazione capitalistica nell'Unità italiana', *Studi storici*, 1 (1959–60), 513–68.

'Da Marx a Lenin: la categoria di "formazione economico-sociale"', *Critica marxista*, 8 (1970), 29–79.

Singer H. 'Terms of trade and economic development', in J. Eatwell, M. Milgate and P. Newman eds. *The new Palgrave. Economic development*, pp. 323–8.

Slicher van Bath B. H. *The agrarian history of western Europe: AD 500–1850*, Eng. trans. O. Ordish, London, 1963.

'Les problèmes fondamentaux de la société pré-industrielle en Europe occidentale. Une orientation et une programme', *AAG Bijdragen*, 12 (1965), 3–46.

Smith A. *An inquiry into the nature and causes of the wealth of nations*, ed. E. Cannan, London, 1904.

Smith C. A. 'Regional economic systems: linking geographical models and socioeconomic problems', in Smith ed. *Regional analysis, I. Economic systems*, New York–San Francisco–London, 1976, pp. 3–63.

Sorrenti L. *Il patrimonio fondiario in Sicilia. Gestione delle terre e contratti agrari nei secoli XII–XV*, Milan, 1984.

Spahr R. 'Di un denaro inedito battuto nella zecca di Catania durante il regno di Maria d'Aragona (1377–1401)', *ASSO*, 2nd ser. 7 (1931), 76–80.

Spallanzani M. ed. *Produzione commercio e consumo dei panni di lana (nei secoli XII–XVIII)*, Istituto Internazionale di Storia Economica 'F. Datini', Prato, Pubblicazioni, 2nd ser., 2, Florence, 1976.

Spanò Bolani D. *Storia di Reggio di Calabria*, 2nd ed., 2 vols., Reggio Calabria, 1891.

Sprandel R. 'La production de fer au Moyen Age', *AESC*, 24 (1969), 305–21.

Spufford P. *Money and its use in medieval Europe*, Cambridge, 1988.

Starrabba R. 'Censimento della popolazione di Palermo fatto nel 1479', *Nuove effemeridi siciliane*, 3rd ser. 2 (1870), 269–72.

Il conte di Prades e la Sicilia (1477–1479), Palermo, 1872.

Stiglitz J. E. 'Rational peasants, efficient institutions, and a theory of rural

organization: Methodological remarks for development economics',
in P. Bardhan ed. *Economic theory*, pp. 19–29.

Stouff L. *Ravitaillement et alimentation en Provence aux XIVe et XVe
siècles*, Civilisations et sociétés, 20, Paris–La Haye, 1970.

Studi in memoria di Federigo Melis, 5 vols., Naples, 1978.

Tangheroni M. *Politica, commercio e agricoltura a Pisa nel Trecento*, Pisa,
1973.

*Aspetti del commercio dei cereali nei Paesi della Corona d'Aragona, I. La
Sardegna*, Pisa, 1981.

Thirsk J. 'The farming regions of England', in Thirsk ed. *The agrarian
history*, IV, pp. 1–112.

ed. *The agrarian history of England and Wales*, IV, Cambridge, 1967.

*Economic policy and projects. The development of a consumer society in
early modern England*, Oxford, 1978.

'Policies for retrenchment in seventeenth-century Europe. *A review
article*', *Comparative studies in society and history*, 22 (1980), 626–33,
637–8.

'Industries in the countryside', in Thirsk, *The rural economy of England.
Collected essays*, London 1984, pp. 217–33.

Tilly L. A. 'Food entitlement, famine and conflict', in R. I. Rotberg and
T. K. Rabb eds. *Hunger and history. The impact of changing food
production and consumption patterns on society*, Cambridge, 1985,
pp. 135–51.

Tits-Dieuaide M.-J. *La formation des prix céréaliers en Brabant et en
Flandre au XVe siècle*, Brussels, 1975.

Topolski J. 'L'influence du régime des réserves à corvée en Pologne sur le
développement du capitalisme (XVIe–XVIIIe siècles)', *Rivista di
storia dell'agricoltura*, 10 (1970), 267–76.

'Commerce des denrées agricoles et croissance économique de la zone
baltique aux XVIe et XVIIe siècles', *AESC*, 29 (1974), 425–35.

*La nascita del capitalismo in Europa. Crisi economica e accumulazione
originaria fra XIV e XVII secolo*, Ital. trans. G. Mizzau and M.
Petrusewicz Mizzau, Turin, 1979.

Torrisi N. 'Aspetti della crisi granaria siciliana nel sec. XVI', *ASSO*, 4th
ser. 10 (1957), 174–85.

Tramontana S. *Michele da Piazza e il potere baronale in Sicilia*, Messina–
Florence, 1963.

Antonello e la sua città, Palermo, 1981.

'La monarchia normanna e sveva', in A. Guillou *et al. Il Mezzogiorno dai
Bizantini a Federico II*, Storia d'Italia diretta da G. Galasso, III, Turin,
1983, pp. 435–768.

Trasselli C. *I privilegi di Messina e di Trapani (1160–1359), con una Appendice sui consolati trapanesi nel secolo XV*, Palermo, 1949.

'Ricerche su la popolazione di Sicilia nel secolo XV', *Atti dell'Accademia
di Scienze Lettere e Arti di Palermo*, 4th ser. 15 (1954–5), 213–71.

La questione sociale in Sicilia e la rivolta di Messina del 1464, Palermo,
1955.

'Produzione e commercio dello zucchero in Sicilia dal XIII al XIX secolo', *ES*, 2 (1955), 325–42.

'Nuovi documenti sui Peruzzi, Bardi e Acciaiuoli in Sicilia', *ES*, 3 (1956), 179–95.

'Prezzi dei panni a Palermo nel XIV secolo', *ibid.*, 88–90.

'Tessuti di lana siciliani a Palermo nel XIV secolo', *ibid.*, 303–16.

'Sul debito pubblico in Sicilia sotto Alfonso V d'Aragona', *Estudios de historia moderna*, 6 (1956–9), 71–112.

'Il mercato dei panni a Palermo nella prima metà del secolo XV', *ES*, 4 (1957), 140–66, 286–333.

'Sull'esportazione dei cereali dalla Sicilia negli anni 1402–7', *Annali della Facoltà di Economia e Commercio dell'Università di Palermo*, 11 (1957), 217–52; repr. in Trasselli, *Mediterraneo*, pp. 331–70.

Note per la storia dei banchi in Sicilia nel XIV secolo, Palermo, 1958.

Note per la storia dei banchi in Sicilia nel XV secolo, 2 vols., Palermo, 1959.

'Miniere siciliane dei secoli XV e XVI', *ES*, 11 (1964), 511–31.

'Sulla popolazione di Palermo nei secoli XIII–XIV', *ibid.*, 329–44.

'Ricerche sulla seta siciliana (sec. XIV–XVII)', *ES*, 12 (1965), 213–58.

'Villaggi deserti in Sicilia', *ES*, 13 (1966), 249–52.

Appunti di metrologia e numismatica siciliana per la scuola di Paleografia dell'Archivio di Stato di Palermo, Palermo, 1969.

'La siccità in Sicilia nel XVI secolo', *Rivista di storia dell'agricoltura*, 10 (1970), 20–47.

'Su le finanze siciliane da Bianca ai Viceré', in *IV Congreso de Historia de la Corona de Aragón*, 4 vols., Barcelona, 1970, II, pp. 51–97.

'Lineamenti di una storia dello zucchero siciliano', *ASSO*, 69 (1973), 27–55.

'Sui Biscaglini in Sicilia tra Quattro e Cinquecento', *MEFRM*, 85 (1973), 143–58.

Mediterraneo e Sicilia all'inizio dell'epoca moderna. (Ricerche quattro-centesche), Cosenza, 1977.

'Frumento e panni inglesi nella Sicilia del XV secolo', in Trasselli, *Mediterraneo*, pp. 289–329.

Da Ferdinando il Cattolico a Carlo V. L'esperienza siciliana, 1475–1525, 2 vols., Soveria Mannelli, 1982.

Storia dello zucchero siciliano, Storia economica di Sicilia, Testi e ricerche, 25, Caltanissetta–Roma, 1982.

Trifone R. *La legislazione angioina*, Naples, 1921.

Tucci U. 'La Sicilia nei Manuali di mercatura veneziani', in G. Motta ed. *Studi Trasselli*, pp. 639–50.

Tunzelmann, G. N. von 'Technical progress', in R. Floud and D. McCloskey eds. *The economic history of Britain since 1700, I. 1700–1860*, Cambridge, 1981, pp. 143–63.

Turnau I. 'The organization of the European textile industry from the thirteenth to the eighteenth century', *Journal of European economic history*, 17 (1988), 583–602.

Udovitch A. L., R. Lopez and H. Miskimin, 'From England to Egypt,

1350–1500', in M. A. Cook ed. *Studies in the economic history of the Middle East*, Oxford, 1970, pp. 93–128.

Unger R. W. *The ship in the medieval economy 600–1600*, London 1980.

Usher A. P. *The history of the grain trade in France 1400–1710*, Harvard Economic Studies, 9, Cambridge, Mass., 1913.

Van der Wee H. *The growth of the Antwerp market and the European economy, fourteenth–sixteenth centuries*, 3 vols., Université de Louvain, Receuil de travaux d'histoire et de philologie, 28–30, Louvain, 1963.

Van der Wee H. and T. Peeters, 'Un modèle dynamique de croissance interséculaire du commerce mondial (XIe–XVIIe siècles)', *AESC*, 25 (1970), 100–26.

Vannini Marx A. ed. *Trasporti e sviluppo economico. Secoli XIII–XVIII*, Istituto Internazionale di Storia Economica 'F. Datini'. Pubblicazioni, 2nd ser., 5, Florence, 1986.

Varvaro A. *Lingua e storia in Sicilia*, I, Palermo, 1981.

'Siciliano antico, siciliano letterario, siciliano moderno', in A. Quattordio Moreschini ed. *Tre millenni*, pp. 267–80.

Ventura D. 'Aspetti economico-sociali della schiavitù nella Sicilia medievale (1260–1498)', *Annali della Facoltà di Economia e Commercio dell'Università di Catania*, 24 (1978), 77–130.

Edilizia urbanistica ed aspetti di vita economica e sociale a Catania nel '400, Catania, 1984.

'Nella Sicilia del '400: terra e lavoro in alcuni contratti notarili del Catanese', in *Studi in onore di Antonio Petino, I. Momenti e problemi di storia economica*, Catania, 1984, pp. 103–35.

'Sul commercio siciliano di transito nel quadro delle relazioni commerciali di Venezia con le Fiandre (secoli XIV e XV)', *NRS*, 70 (1986), 15–32.

Verlinden C. 'L'esclavage en Sicile au bas moyen âge', *Bulletin de l'Institut historique belge de Rome*, 35 (1963), 13–113.

'Markets and fairs', in M. Postan, E. Rich and E. Miller eds. *Economic organization*, pp. 119–53.

'Les débuts de la production et de l'exportation du sucre à Madère. Quel rôle y jouèrent les Italiens?', in *Studi in memoria di Luigi Dal Pane*, Bologna, 1982, pp. 301–10.

Viazzo P. P. *Upland communities. Environment, population and social structure in the Alps since the sixteenth century*, Cambridge, 1989.

Vicens Vives J. *Fernando el Católico, principe de Aragón, rey de Sicilia (1458–1478)*, Madrid, 1952.

Villari R. *La rivolta antispagnola a Napoli. Le origini (1585–1647)*, Bari, 1976.

Ribelli e riformatori dal XVI al XVIII secolo, 2nd ed., Rome, 1983.

Volpes R. *Delle coniazioni non ufficiali, in Sicilia, durante il Regno di Federico III [IV] 'il semplice'*, Naples, 1958.

Vries J. de. *The Dutch rural economy in the Golden Age 1500–1700*, London, 1974.

The economy of Europe in an age of crisis, 1600–1750, Cambridge, 1976.

'Measuring the impact of climate on history: the search for appropriate methodologies', *Journal of interdisciplinary history*, 10 (1980), 599–630.

European urbanization 1500–1800, London, 1984.

Wallerstein I. *The modern world-system*, 3 vols., New York, 1974–89.

Weber M. *Economy and society*, ed. G. Roth and C. Wittich, New York, 1968.

Westermann E. ed. *Internationaler Ochsenhandel, 1350–1750*, Stuttgart, 1979.

Wickham C. *The mountains and the city. The Tuscan Appennines in the early Middle Ages*, Oxford, 1988.

Willan T. S. *The inland trade. Studies in English internal trade in the sixteenth and seventeenth centuries*, Manchester, 1976.

Wilson C. and G. Parker eds. *An introduction to the sources of European economic history 1500–1800*, London, 1977.

Wolffe B. P. *The royal demesne in English history: the Crown estate in the governance of the realm from the Conquest to 1509*, London, 1971.

Wrigley E. A. 'A simple model of London's importance in changing English society and economy, 1650–1750', *Past and present*, 37 (1967), 44–70.

Yver G. *Le commerce et les marchands dans l'Italie méridionale XIIIe et au XIVe siècle*, Paris, 1903.

Zangheri R. 'The historical relationship between agrarian and economic development in Italy', in E. L. Jones and S. J. Woolf eds. *Agrarian change and economic development: the historical problems*, London, 1969, pp. 23–39.

Index

Abruzzi, 25, 410
Abulafia, D., 10, 11, 20
Aci (Acireale), 46, 61n., 64, 130, 330,
  331n., 333n., 383; economy, 176,
  178, 179, 187, 205, 212, 214, 215,
  217; trade, 98, 105n., 108, 293
Acre, 178, 185
Adragna, 43
Adrano, 44, 130, 153, 215
Aeolian islands, see Lipari; Vulcano
Agliata, Battista, 251n.; Pietro, 337
Agnello, Giacomo, 367
agriculture, and credit markets, 144,
  166–7, 283–4, 276, 375;
  'Mediterranean', 164; profits, 171n.;
  and rate of urbanization, 72; slave
  labour, 296; see also contratti alla
  meta; land tenure; peasants;
  productivity
Agrigento, 27, 29, 321n., 334n., 335n.,
  355n., 356n., 358, 361–2, 366, 369n.,
  373n., 381; economy, 136n., 189,
  224–6, 235; grain exports, 138, 140,
  256, 274n; population, 42, 57n.,
  64–5, 67, 71; trade, 98, 102, 105n.,
  107n., 108, 121
Agrò, 47
Aidone, 44, 98, 186, 187, 326, 336n.
Aigues-Mortes, 235
Alagona, family, 92, 130, 318; Artale,
  55n., 91–4, 320, 351; Blasco II, 88,
  89; Blasco III, 127
Albanians, see settlement
Alcamo, 29, 43, 49n., 321n., 343n.,
  361, 367n.; economy, 136n., 172,
  173, 179n., 185, 187; trade, 98, 101,
  108
Alcara, 48, 335
Aleppo, 348

de Alexandro, Bartolomeo, 252n.
Alfonso V, king of Aragon, 82, 126,
  179, 203, 325, 391–2, 396n.; and
  aristocracy, 329–32, 334–5, 342–3,
  398; conquest of Naples, 85, 252–3,
  255, 380; policies (economic), 95,
  103, 105–7, 121, 122, 214, 230–1,
  234–5, 251, 258, 285n., 286, 306–7,
  374; policies (financial), 338, 342,
  380–2, 386, 389; policies (fiscal), 59,
  62n., 223, 228, 329, 355–7, 371,
  380–3, 400; and grain trade, 141–2,
  144n., 175, 271, 276–80, 283n.; and
  local communities, 127, 327–31, 334,
  359–60, 363–4, 367; see also Naples
Alghero, 106n.
Alì, 48, 127, 179n., 180n., 227–8
Allume, 234
Altavilla, 49n.
alum, 230–4; see also Chio; Pera;
  Phocea; Tolfa; Vulcano
Amalfi, 3, 185, 246, 250, 264n.
Amantea, 180n.
Amin, S., 14
Anca, 49
Ancona, 186, 202
Anfusum, 48
Angevins, and Sicily, 3, 4, 85, 247;
  taxation, 37, 50; urban policy, 349;
  warfare, 13, 55, 85, 86, 89, 125n.,
  247; see also Sicily; Vespers
Anidogli, 66
animal husbandry, 169–76, 188, 219,
  257, 346; and arable agriculture,
  174–5, 247, 259; specialized, 169,
  171–6, 181; see also livestock; meat;
  pasture; taxation; transhumance;
  and names of individual animals
Ansalone, Girolamo, 395

447

Antillo, 47
Antiochia, family, 315n., 318n.
Appennino Siculo, 26–7
Aragon, 200n.; aristocracy, 324–5;
crown of, 4, 17, 94, 95, 285, 401,
(taxation in), 384–90; *see also*
market structures; merchants
Aragona, Peri, 217; Vinciguerra, 55n.
de Aricio, Jacobus, 217
aristocracy, and economic
development, 14, 403, 405, 411–12;
economic strategies, 96, 134, 171,
178, 210, 214, 217–18, 260, 316,
317–22, 326, 333, 338, 345–7, 371,
399; income, 315–17, 325–6, 328–9,
339, 340–1, 346–7, 371; lesser, *see*
knights (*milites*); membership, 56,
283, 284, 322–5, 326, 344–5, 399;
and *mero e misto imperio*, 331–2,
394, 395, 399; seigneurial dues,
excise and taxes, 102, 121, 161n.,
318–21, 327–9, 332–3, 335, 346, 371;
and state, 88–9, 132, 317–22, 334–5,
338–45, 347, 369, 371, 379, 380,
395–9; and subjects, 326–31, 335–8,
343; taxation of, 40, 62n.; *see also*
Alfonso V; Aragon; Castile;
demesne; feudal lands; land;
Valencia
Assoro (Asaro), 44, 130, 172n., 260n.
Augusta, 45, 64–5, 130, 131, 361, 383;
economy, 176, 178, 212–18, 224,
226; trade, 98, 108
de Averna, Nicola, 252n.
Avola, 44, 57n., 153, 321n., 334n.,
361; economy, 214, 215, 217
Aymard, M., 11, 12, 184, 282, 404
Azores, 219

Balearic Islands, 225; *see also* Majorca
Balsamo, family, 218; Angelo, 215n.
Baltic, agricultural productivity, 163;
grain trade, 408; *see also* Eastern
Europe; grain; Poland
Bandadini, 66
banking, 284, 337
de Barbera, Giovanni, 258n.
Barberi, Gian Luca, 216
Barcelona, 249n., 384, 393;
manufacture, 211; trade, 106n., 190,
262, 303; *see also* Catalonia
Bardi, Florentine merchants, 230, 272;
see also merchants
barley, 50, 52, 120n., 138, 145n.

Barresi, Giovan Antonio, 252n.
Batticano, 193
Bavuso, 47, 205n.
Belice, *see* Platani river
Bellomo, family, 217, 218
de Benedictis, Cristofaro, 395n.
beryl, 236
Biancavilla, 66
Bisacquino, 43
Biscay, 229–30; *see also* iron
Bivona, 42, 105
Black Death, 139; consequences, 55–6,
80, 202; *see also* epidemics
Blanchard, I. S. W., 175
Blanche of Navarre, queen of Sicily,
393
Bloch, M., 315
Boccetta, 205n.
Bolo, 48
di Bonacquisto, Nicola, 232
Bonagia, 131, 179
Bonfilio, family, 218; Ludovico, 215n.
Bonfornello, 212
de Bonizia, Pietro, 252n.
borgesi, 253, 363–4, 370, 372
Borromei, Andrea di Lodovico, 252n.
de Brandino, Francesco, 252n.
Brenner, R., 21
Bresc, H., 11, 12–16, 20, 33, 36, 40,
60, 162, 174, 201, 270n., 274n., 276,
277n., 279, 281–3, 292, 294, 297n.
Brescia, 227
Bronte, 48
Brucato, 43, 86, 193, 212
Bruges, 230
Buccheri, 44, 335n., 336, 362
de Bufalis, Nicola, 205n.; Onofrio
205n.
bullion flows, 301, 302, 308–9, 386,
388–90; *see also* coinage
Burgio, 42, 336n.
Buscemi, 44, 57n., 153, 336n.
Butera, 44
Buxio, Enrico, 260n.

Cacalimata Grecine, 48
Caccamo, 45, 66, 231
Cadrà (Chadara), 44, 130
Cafagna, L., 8, 11
Caggi, 46
Cagliari, 106n., 187
Calabria, 25, 410; economy, 186, 187,
189, 201, 228; rebellion in, 128, 228,
235n., 254; and Sicily, 82–3, 105,

201, 205–6, 219, 245–67; trade, 53, 138, 140, 179, 180, 220, 230; and War of the Vespers, 85, 87–8, 138; *see also* Messina; Naples; Reggio Calabria; val Demone; Vespers
Calascibetta, 44, 108, 146n., 224, 369n., 370n., 373n.
Calatabiano, 46, 52, 334n., 369n.; economy, 214–18
Calatafimi, 43, 49n., 100
da Calci, Onofrio, 252n.
Calegra, 48
Calidoro, 46
Callura, 130
Caltabellotta, 42, 66, 90n., 224, 380; county of, 122n.; treaty of, 85
Caltagirone, 130n., 263n., 335n., 352, 355n., 357, 360–3, 366, 370n.; economy, 173, 189, 191, 193; population, 44, 54, 67, 71; trade, 98, 100, 105, 108, 120n.
Caltanissetta, 44, 108, 187, 230, 329n., 333n.; county of, 161n.
Caltavuturo, 42, 117, 193, 321n.
Calvaruso (Calabruso), 47
Camera reginale, 67, 131, 154, 252n., 304n., 343n., 361–3; trade, 98–9, 103, 105, 141n; *see also* demesne; Syracuse
Cammarata, 42, 57n., 224–6, 252n., 326, 332n., 333, 336n.; Monte di, 27
Campo, Pietro, 211
Campolo, Marino, 205
Capizzi, 45, 98, 101, 103, 173, 334n., 343n., 367
Capo Passero, 224
Capo San Vito, 27
Capri (val Demone), 49n.
captaincy, 127, 320, 357, 363, 367
Capua, 105–7, 264
Caracciolo, Francesco, 258n.
Cardona, family, 217; Artale, 259n.; Juan, 259
Carini, 43, 129, 212
Caronetto di Gerardino, 252n.
Caronia, 46, 259n.
Caronie, *see* Nebrodi mountains
Carradore, Giovanni, 205n.
Carrère, C., 303
Caruso, Antonio, 214n.
Casal di messer Nicola, 48
Casal del Vescovo, 48
Casale Giovanni Baroni, 49
Casale San Giorgio, 49

casali, 53; *see also* settlement
Casalvecchio, 47
Caspe, compromise of, 285, 325
Cassaro, 45
Castania, 47, 61n., 205n., 335n., 336
Castelbuono (Ypsigro), 46, 49n., 173, 193
Castellammare, 43, 121n., 140–1
castellany, 127
Castelluccio (Castel di Lucio), 46, 49n., 66
Castelmanfredi, 193
Castelvetrano, 43, 57n., 59–60, 131, 326, 335n.
Castiglione, 46, 130n., 191, 194, 321n., 332n., 370n.
Castile, aristocracy, 325; *comuneros*, 369
Castrogiovanni (Enna), 29, 117, 118, 125, 230, 334n., 343n., 355n., 356n., 360–4, 367, 370, 373n.; economy, 172, 187, 189, 190, 224–6, 230–4; population, 44, 54, 57n., 67, 152, 195; trade, 98, 105n., 108, 118
Castronovo, 42, 71, 98, 108, 136n., 283n., 326, 332–3, 355n., 363, 367, 381, 382
Castroreale, 45, 108, 127, 128n., 228n., 356n., 361, 368n., 369n; economy, 136n., 193, 205
'Catalan' party, 88, 92, 94, 130, 317–18; *see also* 'Latin' party
Catalonia, 357n., 378n., 384; aristocracy, 324–5; civil war, 63, 215n., 278, 383; political relations with Sicily, 94, 272; *remença* uprising in, 327, 338; trade, 93, 185, 186, 189, 225, 285, 303–4, 307–8, 396; urban society, 348; *see also* Barcelona; merchants
Catania, 18, 21, 32, 57n., 90, 91, 138, 146–8, 153, 164, 287, 335n., 355, 356n., 369n., 381; cloth market, 92–3, 94, 286, 297n.; district, 129–30, 148; economy, 173, 187, 189, 191, 194, 202, 205, 206, 214, 226; fairs, 108, 118, 250, 297n.; population, 44, 54, 57, 58, 62n., 63–7, 71, 74; rise of, 87, 88, 95, 130, 245, 248–50; social structure, 144n., 197, 249n., 351–2, 359, 360, 366, 373n.; trade, 94, 98–9, 102–5, 121, 229, 263, 277n., 286n., 293; and urban hierarchy, 70, 152,

Catania—(*cont.*)
154, 248–51; wine, 136n., 137n., 176, 178, 180; *see also* val di Noto
Catanzaro, 202, 252n.
Catona, 261
Cattafì, 48
cattle, 173; and sugar industry, 216–17; trade, 105, 106, 117, 118, 257–61, 293; *see also* animal husbandry; oxen
Cefalà (Chitala), 43, 66
Cefalù, 263n., 356n., 362, 364n.; population, 45, 54, 64, 69; trade, 98, 99, 103, 105n.; wine, 176, 178
Centelles Ventimiglia, Antonio, 258, 343n., 396n.
central places, 83, 150–1; *see also* urbanization
Cerami, 47
Cesarò, 47
Chamopetra (feudo), 105, 316
Charles I of Anjou, king of Sicily, 4, 135, 138, 182n., 188, 278, 291
Charles II of Anjou, king of Naples, 4
Charles V, emperor of Spain, 347, 387n., 398
Charles of Viana, 128n., 266, 393–7
cheese, 188, 226; *caciocavallo*, 174; consumption, 170, 293; prices, 170; trade, 16n., 106, 170, 174, 187, 259, 292–3, 301–2, 303
chestnuts, 257
Chiaromonte (Gulfi), 44, 49n., 325n.
Chiaromonte, family, 88–93, 102, 130, 139, 141, 247n., 318, 319, 359; Giacomo, 90; Manfredi, 90n., 93, 321n.; Simone, 91n.; *see also* Palermo
Chio, 231
de Chirino (Chirini), Giovanni, 203–4
de Chiros, Nicola, 205
Chiusa, 42, 55n.
Christaller, W., 150
Ciminna, 43
Cinamo, Bartolomeo, 259
Cisario, family, 318n.
cities, *see* central places; demesne; district; economic development; town–country relations; urban administration; urbanization
civic nobility (*nobiles*), 344, 345, 358–9, 360, 363–7, 372; economic activities, 134, 178, 205, 217–18, 346; and state revenue, 342, 370, 380; *see also* urban élite
climate, changes in, 169; and

'Mediterranean' agriculture, 164; and supply crises, 143; *see also* grain; rainfall; water supply
cloth, demand for, 77, 296–9; dyeing, 185; fibres, specialized cultivation of, 162, 185–8; imports, 182, 184, 199, 296–300, 301, 303, 309; industry, 9, 182–200; markets, 92–3, 118, 182–4, 196; prices, 198n., 287–9, 298–9; trade, 10, 12n., 13, 118, 171, 182; *see also* Catania; cotton; flax; fustian; hemp; Palermo; wool
Coeur, Jacques, 263, 264n.
coinage, counterfeit, 90–1, 265, 308; devaluation, 89, 92; feudal mints, 89–92; hoarding, 91, 236, 309; minting, 90, 246, 250, 389n.; *see also* bullion flows; currency
Collesano, 46, 49n., 212, 236; county of, 260
Cologne, 205n.
colonialism, *see* economic backwardness
Comiso, 45, 66, 193
Comito, Andrea, 205n.
communes, 124, 134
Compagno, Antonio, 203
Conca d'Oro, 27, 128–9
Condrò, 47
Constance of Hohenstaufen, queen of Aragon, 3
Constantinople, 176, 231
Conte Ranieri, 66, 382n.
Contessa Entellina, 66
contratti alla meta, 144, 171, 205; *see also* agriculture; land tenure; *meta*
copper, 236, 301
Corleone, 18, 29, 66, 137n., 179, 343n., 355, 356n., 366n., 367n., 369n.; population, 42, 64–5, 71, 195; trade, 98, 105n., 108
de Coronato, Agostino, 252n.; Andrea, 252n.; Battista, 252n.; Giovanni, 252n.; Pietro, 252n.
Corsica, 225
de Costanzo, Jacobus, 258n.
cotton, cloth, 118n., 184, 187, 188–9, 199; cultivation, 185–6, 316; trade, 106, 185–6, 301–2, 303; *see also* cloth
Crimea, bubonic plague from, 55
Crisafi, Nicola, 236
de Criscimanno, Andrea, 252n.
crisis, late medieval, 1, 21, 314–15, 401; seventeenth-century, 12, 403

Croce, B., 3–4, 13, 14, 20, 87, 240, 249, 254–5; *see also* Vespers
Crotone, 203, 260
Cruilles, family, 217; Joan, 127n.
currency, and exchange system, 89–92; standardization, 265; *see also* coinage; market structure
Cyprus, 185

Damascus, 348
Damiani, Giovanni, 251n.
Datini, Francesco, merchant, 94, 118; *see also* merchants
dearth, *see* grain
Del Treppo, M., 95, 303–4
demand, *see* cloth; income distribution
demesne, and aristocracy, 89, 91, 159, 319–22, 326, 327, 333–4, 339, 347, 350–2, 397; conflict in, 354–5, 361–5, 368–70, 372; district, 121, 131, 353; immigration, 64–5; and royal authority, 88, 320–2, 328, 334–5, 337–43, 347–74, 390–7, 400; social structure, 348–53, 357–70, 372–4, 399–401; taxation, 62n., 63, 353–7, 367–8, 376–8, 381–7; and toll franchises, 103–5, 411; urbanization of, 67, 407, 411; versus feudal lands, 105, 123, 378, 411; *see also borgesi; Camera reginale*; civic nobility; district; feudal lands; *massari; popolo*; taxation; town–country relations; urban administration
demography, *see* population
Denmark, 259
dependency, *see* economic backwardness
d'Este, Borso, 385n.
Dirillo, 45
dispute settlement, 326–8, 335–8
district, urban, 53, 124–33; *see also* Catania; demesne; Messina; Palermo; Randazzo; town–country relations
Dogana dei Paschi, 169; *see also* transhumance
Dogana delle pecore, 169, 175; *see also* transhumance
Donacby, 43
Doren, A., 3, 20
Doria, family, 272n.
Duro, Giacomo, 252n.; Simone, 252n.

Eastern Europe, economic
backwardness, 2; economic development, 22–3, 402; *see also* Baltic; European economy; Poland
economic backwardness, 14, 163, 182, 185; and foreign trade, 4, 5, 6–7, 10, 93, 270–91, 312–13; in Middle East, 219n.; and transition to capitalism, 2, 11, 12, 403–12; *see also* Eastern Europe; economic development; southern Italy
economic development, and cities, 3, 6, 7, 20, 23; and information, 81, 151, 288–9; and institutions, 10, 20, 22–3, 77, 79, 80–1, 122–3, 144–5, 158, 314–15, 405–9, 411–12; through organizational change, 76n.; and politics, 10, 13, 20–1, 240, 256–7, 276–80, 284–7; and taxation, 403, 410; theories of, 5, 11, 13, 16; *see also* aristocracy; economic backwardness; economic dualism; income distribution; market structure; peasants; property relations; trade
economic dualism, 5–10; 12, 84, 157–8, 218–22, 238–9, 241, 268–70; 402; *see also* economic backwardness; economic development; market structure
economic growth, 162–239; rates of, 237–8; *see also* productivity
Elba, 229
Eleanor of Sicily, queen of Aragon, 92
Egypt, sugar industry, 211; trade, 303, 308
England, 10, 80n., 87, 144n., 145, 163, 164, 188, 290
epidemics, 56, 68, 212, 256, 403; *see also* Black Death
Etna, 26, 27, 230
European economy, 1, 75, 76–9, 406; *see also* Eastern Europe

factionalism, 368, 374
fairs, international, 96, 107; local and regional, 96; new, 107–19; as evidence of trade, 113–19; *see also* trade; transaction costs
family structure, 349–50, 352–3, 358; *see also* population
Faro (Messina), 205n., 224
Favara, 42, 65, 224, 334n., 335n.
Favarotta, 369n.
Fazello, Tommaso, 236, 242

Federico III, king of Sicily, 88, 125, 247, 271-2, 347, 399; and *Camera reginale*, 67n.; policies, 121, 137, 165, 194, 278, 280, 377n.
Federico IV, king of Sicily, 89, 90, 91, 92, 94, 102, 202, 319, 320, 321n., 324
Ferdinand I, king of Aragon, 325, 327, 343
Ferdinand II, king of Spain, 123, 264; and grain trade, 277, 278, 280, 308; policies, 175, 259, 337-8, 347, 371, 383, 398
Ferla (Ferula), 44, 57n., 65, 153, 321n., 329n., 330, 335n., 336
Ferrante (Ferdinand I), king of Naples, 228, 254, 258, 263, 264, 383n., 396n.
Ferruleto, 251
de Fessina, Nicola, 252n.
feudal lands, and lords, 326-31, 335-8, 368-70, 371; taxation of, 62n., 63; and toll franchises, 103, 411; *see also* aristocracy; demesne
Ficarazzi, 211, 212, 219
Ficarra, 47, 108, 259n., 329n., 330, 332n., 333, 335n., 336
de Fide, Lorenzo, 232n.; Simone, 232
fiefs, *see* land market
fish, trade, 106
Fiumedinisi, 47, 335n.; economy, 214, 215, 227-8, 236
Fiumefreddo, 48, 214, 215, 217
Flanders, 93, 163, 188, 204, 205n., 229, 235
flax, 185, 186-7, 205, 256n., 257; trade, 301; *see also* cloth; linen
Florence, 11, 55, 145n., 157, 183, 188, 288n., 365; political relations with Sicily, 283-4; trade, 190, 235, 272, 285; *see also* merchants
Forza d'Agrò, 180n.
Francavilla, 27, 45, 57n., 67, 98, 102, 153, 179, 321n., 330, 334n.
Francavilla (*feudo*), 367
France, 80n., 87, 189, 235
Francofonte, 44, 55n., 108, 130, 335n.
Frederick II, king of Sicily, 3, 13, 37n., 86, 222; trade, 17, 116, 280, 308, 374
fur, trade, 118, 301
fustian, 183, 189, 200; *see also* cloth

Gadara, 48, 205n.
Gaeta, 105, 106, 107, 264, 271n., 309n.
Gaetani, Bernabò, 218; Pietro, 211, 214n., 217, 251n., 325n., 333, 399

Gagliano, 46, 335n., 336n.
Galasso, G., 403
Galati, 47, 109; 329n., 330, 333n., 336n.
Gallo, Alafranchino, 194
Galo, 48
Gangi, 27, 46, 173, 336n.
Garufi, 48
Genoa, 11, 183, 202; political relations with Sicily, 94, 285; trade, 10, 16n., 94, 186, 187, 202, 204, 215n., 229, 231, 232, 271-2, 285-6, 292, 300-3, 408; *see also* merchants
de Gentili, Marco, 252n.
Geraci, 46, 129, 316, 329, 336; economy, 173, 191, 193, 263n.
Germany, 189, 369
Gesso, 205n.
Giardinello, 193
Giarratana, 44, 49n., 57n., 153
Gibellina, 42
Gioeni, Bartolomeo, 252n.
Gioiosa Guardia, 47, 55n., 121n., 132, 334n.
de Giordano, Virgilio, 203
Giovanni di Alessandro, 205n.
Giovanni of Aragon, regent of Sicily, 88
Giuliana, 42
goats, trade, 257
gold, mines, 236; *see also* bullion flows
Gotto, family, 218; Andrea, 215n.
Gozo, 139, 261, 328n., 337
grain, measures, 120-2; per capita consumption, 52; prices, 61, 146-8, 170, 277-8, 287-9; Sicilian output, 52; specialized production, 13, 16, 29, 32, 68, 140, 141, 181; storage, 143-4, 291; supply crises, 56, 138, 139, 142-6, 149-50, 167, 252, 256, 278, 279, 308, 316, 337, 407; *see also* town–country relations; trade, 9, 12, 13, 128-32, 136-50, 187, 196, 256, 304, (arbitrage), 144, 291, (domestic to foreign), 272, 274-5, (excise), 87, 120, 139, (export), 93, 146, 168, 270-91, 303, 308, 407-8, (export to output ratio), 275, 282; yields, 163, 275, 291; *see also* agriculture; Alfonso V; Baltic; Greece; Poland; taxation; Turkey; val di Mazara
Graniti, 46
Gratteri, 47, 236
de Gravina, Carlo, 334

Greece, Greek, and grain trade, 272; monasteries, 245; population, 241; settlements, 33
Gregory XI, Pope, 57
Guastanella, 43
guilds, and cloth industries, 184, 196–7, 199–200, 360; legislation by, 133; monopolies, 156, 360; and urban society, 198–9, 358–60, 364, 366, 372; and women, 197
Gunder Frank, A., 14

harvests, 142–6; *see also* grain
hemp, cultivation, 52, 187–8; manufacture, 185, 187, 191, 220; *see also* cloth
Henry VI, German emperor, 243
Henry VII, German emperor, 247
historical records, 14–15, 16n., 18–19, 83
Hohenstaufen, dynasty, 3, 349, 358
horses, breeds, 262, 263; as draught animals, 164–5, 216n.; trade, 258n., 261–4
Hundred Years War, 85
Hungary, 259

Iblei mountains, 29
income distribution, changes in, (and demand), 77, 78, (consequences), 77, 159, 160, 183, 409n; *see also* economic development
iron, 27; mines, 227–30; trade, 106, 118n., 171, 228–30, 253, 254, 256, 301; toll, 228; *see also* Biscay; Elba
Ischia, 316; trade, 105, 106, 107, 235n., 264
Isnello, 47, 61n., 173, 329n., 331n., 334n.
Isola del Giglio, 106, 264
Ispica (Spaccaforno), 44
Itala, 48

James II, king of Aragon, 88, 137, 139, 347; and grain trade, 308; taxation by, 59, 375
jasper, quarries, 236
Jews, 128, 229n.; expulsion of, 195, 204, 337; and manufactures, 195, 200, 202, 204, 206, 252n.; taxation of, 67n., 337, 379, 380
Jones, P., 6–7, 9, 10, 11
Juan II, king of Aragon, 231, 263, 264n., 266, 286n., 332, 368, 370,

388–9, 393–6; and grain trade, 277n., 278, 280; taxation by, 63, 383
justiciary, office of, 88, 320; territory, 36–7, 125

knights (*milites*), 316, 322–3, 344–5, 346, 350–1, 352, 360; *see also* aristocracy
Koenigsberger, H. G., 400n.
Küchler, W., 387
Kula, W., 281–2

labour market, 173, 184, 219; female, 80n., 294–5; *see also* guilds
Ladislas, king of Naples, 251
land, market, 165, 323, 344–5; rent, 132, 168, 316, 325–6; tenure (*latifundium*), 13, 163, (*masseria*), 164, 166–8, 282, 291, 326, 346, (peasant freehold), 33, 151, 156, 165, 181–2, 282, 319, 338, 364; *see also* property rights
Languedoc, 68n.
Lanza, Perruccio, 330; Pietro, 333
latifundium, *see* land tenure
'Latin' party, 88, 92, 93, 318; *see also* 'Catalan' party
Lazio, 9, 25
lead, mines, 236
leather, manufacture, 173–4, 257; trade, 106, 118, 256, 259, 293, 301, 303, 304, 309
de Lello, Pietro, 252n.
Lenin, V.I., 22n.
Lentini, 67, 98, 103, 126, 130, 138, 334, 362, 369n., 376n.; economy, 135n., 174, 187, 191, 193, 224, 279; fairs, 109, 118, 173, 260, 333n.; population, 45, 64, 71, 152
da Lentini, Alaimo, 102
Leoga, 49n.
Leonor of Castile, queen of Portugal, 380
Lepre, A., 403
Levant, 4; trade, (European), 296, 302, 303, 304, 309, (Sicilian), 176, 221, 234, 243, 251, 253, 407
Librizzi, 47, 132
Licata, 130n., 355n., 356n., 361, 382n.; economy, 16n., 138, 215, 235, 274n.; population, 42, 74; trade, 99, 105n., 109
Licodia, 44, 332n., 369n.; fair, 109
Liguria, 292

Limina, 47, 61n., 66
linen, manufacture, 183–6, 190–1, 198,
    199; export, 190, 205; *see also* flax
Linguaglossa, 47, 130n., 370n.
Lipari, economy, 185, 186, 230, 231,
    232, 258n., 293; trade, 105, 106, 221,
    264, 266
Lisico, 49, 330
livestock, trade, 173, 228, 256, 257–64,
    293–4; *see also* animal husbandry;
    Denmark; Hungary; Poland
Locadi, 47
Lombardo, 66
Lombardy, 50, 82, 94, 186, 189, 405,
    409
London, 55, 157
Longi, 46
Lösch, A., 150
Louis of Hungary, king of Naples, 91n.
Louis III, king of Naples, 253n.
Lucca, 200, 232
Ludovico, king of Sicily, 88, 89n., 202,
    318, 319
Luzzatto, G., 4, 5, 8, 11

Madeira, 216, 217, 219
Madonie mountains, 27, 173, 185, 191,
    219, 220, 242, 260
Majorca, 273n., 307; *see also* Balearic
    Islands; merchants
Maletta, 66, 332n.
Maletta, family, 318n.
Malta, 328n., 330; economy, 179n.,
    186, 189, 190, 303; trade, 99, 101,
    105n., 131, 139, 178, 186
Maltese, Giorgio, 229n.
Mandanici, 48, 205n.
Manfred of Hohenstaufen, king of
    Sicily, 125
Maniaci, 66
manufacture, 76, 78–9, 168, 182; rural,
    207–10; *see also* Jews; *and names of
    individual commodities*
Marche, 5
Marco di Frescobaldo, 252n.
Marella, 205n.
Maria, queen of Sicily, 94, 320n., 324
Mariano di Giovanni, 252n.
market integration, and depopulation,
    78; in Europe, 76–7, 406; in Italy, 4,
    8, 11–12, 404–5; measurement of,
    158, 161; in Sicily, 70, 88, 92, 94,
    118, 121, 134, 135–6, 141–3, 148–50,
    152, 154, 158–9, 238, 291, 375, 402,

410–11; in southern Italy, 9, 13, 306,
    405, 410–12; *see also* market
    structures; peasants; region;
    specialization
market structures, and cloth industry,
    195–9; and distribution of
    population, 69–70, 73;
    fragmentation, 141, 178, 202, 247,
    272, 273; and institutions, 21–2, 96;
    and 'Mediterranean common
    market', 95, 106, 107, 307–8, 374;
    and patterns of urbanization, 72,
    150–7; regional, 83, 84, 129, 138,
    149–50, 154, 175–6, 250, 264–7; and
    the state, 81, 95–123, 411; and terms
    of trade, 187–9; and warfare, 87,
    88–95; *see also* currency; economic
    development; economic dualism;
    market integration; region;
    specialization; trade; Vespers
Markward von Anweiler, 102
Marquet, Pere, 252n.
Marsa, 224
Marsala, 29, 61n., 131, 137, 356n.,
    361, 367n., 383; economy, 130, 190,
    212, 224–6, 234; population, 42,
    64–5, 71, 74, 331n.; trade, 99, 102,
    109
Marseilles, 185, 186
Martin I, king of Aragon, 127n., 251,
    273, 324, 340, 341, 378n.
Martini, 48
Martino I, king of Sicily, 230, 257, 273,
    322, 324, 339, 340, 357, 391, 393;
    taxation by, 40, 50, 355, 375, 381n.;
    and trade, 102, 113–15, 116
Mascali, 47
massari, 144n., 166–7, 174–5, 276–7,
    279, 283, 345, 370, 372; *see also* land
Masse, 205n.
Matana, 49
Mazara, 29, 137, 140, 321n., 329n.,
    332n., 343n., 355n., 356n., 367n.,
    376n., 381, 382n., 383n.; economy,
    136n., 187, 203, 224, 234;
    population, 43, 69, 71, 74; trade, 99,
    102, 105n., 109
Mazarino, 44, 100
measurements, standardization of, 97,
    120–2; *see also* transaction costs
meat, consumption, 169, 170, 174, 175,
    176, 259, 293; prices, 170, 259;
    trade, 131, 301; *see also* animal
    husbandry; livestock

Melilli, 45, 225
merchants, Catalan, 92, 93, 94, 105–6,
196, 283, 285–6, 307–11, (hegemony
in crown of Aragon), 95, 307–8;
Florentine, 92, 204, 251–2n., 284,
286; Genoese, 92, 93, 94, 105–6,
196, 202, 243, 250, 283–6, 288,
308–11; Majorcan, 92; Messinese,
243–5, 311, 351; Palermitan, 118;
Pisan, 92, 251–2n., 283–4, 286;
Sicilian, 197, 244, 344; Venetian,
252n., 284, 309n.
Merco, 66
Messina, 18, 20, 61n., 117, 125, 251,
323, 332n., 334n., 349, 356n., 381,
393, 410; and Angevins, 85, 125,
139, 140; citizenship, 251; district,
100, 124–8, 130, 133, 135, 205, 241,
251; economy, 124–5, 134–5, 136n.,
174–80, 186–91, 194, 224–6, 228–30,
257, 302, (decline of), 87–8, 95,
244–8; fairs, 109, 118, 203, 251; food
supply, 53, 88, 124, 125–6, 138–40,
148, 149, 245–8, 272; immigration,
64, 206, 251, 255, 331n.; mint, 90,
246, 250; population, 40, 45, 52–9,
62n., 63, 67, 71; relations with
Calabria, 82–3, 87–8, 138, 139, 140,
179, 203, 228–9, 240–67, 296, 302;
and Sicilian independence, 128, 250,
395–7, 400; silk industry, 67, 200–7,
294, 295–6, 303; social structure,
345n., 348, 350–2, 358n., 360–5, 372,
396n.; *stratigoto*, 125, 127, 357;
taxation, 52, 128, 250n., 357; trade,
94, 133, 202, 204, 234, 243, 263,
266–7, 293, 297n., 302–3, 309n.;
trade privileges, 97, 99–102, 105,
106n., 128, 243–4, 247; and urban
hierarchy, 70, 74, 151–7, 242–3, 246;
see also Appennino siculo; Calabria;
merchants; parliament; val Demone;
Vespers
Mesta, 175; *see also* animal husbandry;
transhumance
meta, 131, 144, 146; *see also contratti
alla meta*
Mezzogiorno, see southern Italy
Mezzoiuso, 330
Migaido, 66
Migari, Giacomo, 232
migration, seasonal, 219–20, 242; to
Sicily, 33, 61, 68, 73, 195, 208, 209,
251, 256, 349, 365; within Sicily, 61,
64–5, 71–2, 331, 349; *see also*
Messina; Palermo; population;
serfdom
Milan, 11, 55, 157, 285; *see also*
Lombardy
Milazzo, 27, 61n., 85, 126, 355n., 357,
361, 366, 369n., 370n.; economy,
136n., 191; population, 45, 54, 64–5,
69, 331; relations with Messina, 52,
53, 125, 127, 138, 139–40; trade, 99,
103, 261
Militello, 44, 47, 109, 330, 333n.
millet, 52
mills, fulling, 184, 191, 193; grain, 62,
175; salt, 332n; wind, 226
Mineo, 45, 67, 152, 224, 369n.
mining, 222–37; *see also names of
individual minerals*
Miraballi, Giovanni, 204, 252n., 383n.
Mirto, 48, 49n.
Mirulla, family, 218; Giovanni, 228n.
Misilmeri, 129
Miskimin, H. A., 78, 183, 289
Mistretta, 45, 49n., 146n., 263n.,
343n., 355n., 356n., 360, 367, 370n;
economy, 173, 261, 334n.; trade, 99,
101, 103, 333
Modica (val di Mazara), 43
Modica (val di Noto), 32, 45, 49n.;
county, 66–7, 279n., 343n., 371;
economy, 186, 187, 193, 205, 225
Mohac, Manfredi, 352
Mola di Taormina, 46
Moncada, Gastone, 333; Guglielmo
Raimondo, 161n., 218
money, *see* coinage; currency
Monforte, 47, 52, 126, 127n., 205n.
Mongiuffi, 46
Monreale, 43, 66, 109, 129; archbishop
of, 89, 333n.
Montalbano, 47
' Monte Capodarso, 230
Monteliano, family, 318n.
Montemaggiore, 43, 66
Monterosso (Lupino), 45, 67
Monte San Giuliano (Erice), 18, 27,
131, 137, 334n., 343n., 356n., 361,
363, 370n.; economy, 206n., 224–5;
population, 42, 64; trade, 99, 102,
105n., 109
Monte Sara, 224
Moriella, 224
Morosini, Francesco, 252n.
Motta Camastra, 47, 109, 127

Motta d'Affermo (Sparto), 48, 49n.
Motta Sant'Anastasia (Motta di
Catania), 46, 130
Mozzicato, Pietro, 230–1
Mugana, 49
mules, trade, 261–4
Muleti, Giovanni, 205n.
Muro, 260n.
Murro, 224
Muslims, 173, 185, 200, 202, 241,
348–9; rebellion by, and
consequences, 13, 37n., 54, 86, 331,
349; status, 33; technological legacy,
13, 185n., 188, 195
Mussomeli, 42, 109, 193, 211, 224,
316n.
Muxaro, 43

de Nacerio, Ambrogio, 252n.
Naples, 3, 36, 53, 91n., 256n., 393,
410–11; kingdom of, 3–4, 254n.,
357n., (Aragonese conquest), 85,
252–3, 255, (and seventeenth-
century crisis), 403–12, (taxation),
223, 384–7, (trade with Sicily),
105–6, 258, 264–6, 285, 294, 304–8,
409–10, 412; trade with Sicily, 179,
180, 187, 229, 234, 235, 246, 254n.,
309n.; *see also* Alfonso V; Calabria;
southern Italy
Naro, 42, 67n., 68n., 129, 329n.,
355n., 356n., 369n., 381, 382;
economy, 189, 225–6; trade, 99, 101
Nasari, 49
Naso, 46, 109
Nebrodi mountains, 27, 172, 173, 219,
220, 241, 260
da Neocastro, Bartolomeo, 246
Netherlands, 163
Nicola da Monopoli, 252n.
Nicosia, 90, 321n., 332n., 343n., 355n.,
357, 361–2, 367n., 368n., 370, 373n.;
economy, 191, 193, 224–5;
population, 45, 54, 67, 71, 242;
trade, 99, 105n., 109, 117, 118, 173,
260
Normandy, 68n.
Normans, 2–3, 10-11, 13, 17, 200, 243,
349, 358
North, D. C., 96
North Africa, 82, 284n.; trade, 176,
185, 188, 200, 229, 258, 263n., 272,
292, 302, 303–4, 308–9, 408
northern Italy, 1, 3, 163

Noto, 18, 66, 129, 141n., 185, 321n.,
332n., 334n., 355, 356n., 359–60,
361–2, 369n.; economy, 173, 178,
187–94, 197, 214, 217, 224, 226;
population, 44, 67, 71; trade, 98,
100, 103, 109, 120n.; and urban
hierarchy, 70, 152, 249
Novara, 27, 47, 52, 127, 335n.

Occhiolà (Grammichele), 44
oil, linseed, 187; olive, 105, 122, 131,
219, 257
Oliveri, 48, 127, 334n.
Oriolis, Giovanni, 321n.
oxen, as draught animals, 163, 164–5;
see also cattle; livestock

Pages, Giovanni, 227
Pagliara, 48
Palagonia, 44, 61n., 330, 334
Palazzo Adriano, 43, 66, 187
Palazzolo, 44, 146n., 334n., 335n.,
369n.
Palermo, 15, 16, 18, 21, 27, 29, 50n.,
56, 68n., 89, 168, 175, 323, 325n.,
332n., 347n., 355n., 369n., 373n.,
381, 393, 395–7, 400; and
Chiaromonte, 93, 139, 141, 319;
cloth market, 93, 286, 287–9, 297–9;
district, 124, 128–9, 130, 133, 135;
economy, 173, 187, 189, 193, 194,
201–4, 210–19, 221, 234, 235, 259,
346; food supply, 88, 138, 140–1,
146–8, 256; immigration, 64, 65, 195,
349; mint, 90n., 91–2; population,
40, 42, 52–3, 55, 58, 62n., 63, 67, 71;
secrezia revenues, 55n., 249, 377–8;
social structure, 197, 347–51, 358n.,
359, 362–6; taxation, 52, 376n., 395;
trade, 94, 97–100, 103, 105, 110,
120–1, 135, 161n., 179–80, 254n.,
257, 261, 263, 273, 276n., 277, 286,
296, 300, 304–5, 306; and urban
hierarchy, 70, 74, 151–7, 242, 249,
299; *see also* val di Mazara;
merchants
Palizzi, family, 88, 89, 90n., 318, 351;
Matteo, 93
de Panfilia, Sebastiano, 252n.
Pantelleria, 100, 186, 337
Pantica, 225
Papacudi, 48
Paris, 50, 55, 157
de Parisio, Raimondo, 231, 232n.

parliament, 337n., 347, 390–2, 394; of
Messina, 391; of Syracuse, 141, 378
Partanna, 42, 336n.
Partinico, 212
Passaneto, 335n.
Passaneto, family, 318n.
pasture, 128, 164; and arable, 168, 169;
see also animal husbandry
Patellaro, 43
Paternò, 44, 130, 362, 369n.; economy,
187, 226n., 231
Patti, 45, 58, 64, 126, 131–2, 191, 195,
333n., 334n., 335n., 355n., 360,
361–2, 366; bishop of, 230;
economy, 172–9, 189, 206; trade,
100, 105, 110, 118, 261
peasants, economic strategies, 22,
76n., 77–9, 182, 199, 207–10,
219–20, 268–70, 282, 295, 411n.;
struggles by, 327, 369, 403, 410; *see
also* agriculture; economic
development; land tenure; serfdom
Pedro of Aragon, *infante*, 256n.
Pegolotti, Francesco, 176, 185
Pela, Giovanni, 232n.
Peloritani mountains, 27, 32, 219, 241
Pera, 231
Peralta, Antonio, 122n.; Guglielmo,
90n., 91
Perpignan, 91n., 235
Peruzzi, Florentine merchants, 272; *see
also* merchants
Peter III, king of Aragon, 3, 37, 50,
138, 176, 222–3, 246, 322; and grain
trade, 308
Peter IV, king of Aragon, 91n.
Petralia Soprana, Sottana, 46, 49n.,
173, 224, 332n., 334n.
Petraperzia, 44, 153, 252n., 260n., 326,
335n., 336n.
Pettineo, 46, 49n.
Philip II, emperor of Spain, 387n.
Phocea, 231
Piana dei Greci, 66
Piazza, 29, 44, 64–5, 70, 71, 118, 152,
283n., 334n., 355n., 361–3, 364n.,
367n., 369n., 370, 373n.; economy,
136n., 172, 175n., 193; trade, 98,
100, 102, 110, 117, 118, 173, 260,
333n.
da Piazza, Michele, 56, 92, 93, 202,
352
Pidadachi, 66
Piedmont, 5

Pietra d'Amico, 43
Pietro II, king of Sicily, 278, 321, 347n.
pigs, 172, 173, 266; trade, 257–60
piracy, 69, 128, 152, 253n.; *see also*
transaction costs
Piraino, 47
Pirenne, H., 6
Pisa, 88, 229; immigration to Sicily,
283–4; trade, 272, 292; *see also*
banking; merchants
pitch, trade, 106, 229, 257
Platamone, family, 217
Platani river, 27, 29
Playa, Giacomo, 382n.
plough, 164–5
Poland, 10, 11; trade, (grain), 276,
281–2, 290, (livestock), 259; *see also*
Baltic; Eastern Europe
Polizzi, 42, 57n., 65, 71, 129, 146n.,
195, 321n., 334n., 355n., 356n.,
362–3, 373n., 382n.; economy, 173,
178, 191, 193; trade, 100, 105n., 110,
121n.
Pollicino, Andrea, 252n.; Artale,
252n.; Faccio, 252n.; Ruggiero,
328n.
Pollina, 46, 49n., 173
Pontieri, E., 20
popolo, 357, 358, 360, 363–6, 372,
373–4
population, ceiling to, 220; decline,
economic consequences of, 76–8,
162; density, 50, 54; distribution, 36,
54, 60, 67, 69–70, 73, 150; increase,
80, (as index of economic growth),
25, 33, 73, 79–80, 405, 408, (and
social conflict), 336; Malthusian
theory of, 21, 162, 208; mobility, 70,
349; size, 5, 33–73, 162, 406; *see also*
family structure; migration; serfdom;
settlement; *and names of individual
valli*
porphyry, quarries, 236
Porto Pisano, 94n.
Postan, M. M., 77–8
Pozzallo, 279n.
Prefoglio, family, 318n.
'price scissors', 78, 175, 198, 288; *see
also* cheese; grain; meat
prices, *see* cheese; cloth; grain; meat
Prizzi, 43, 224
production relations, 77; *see also*
property rights
productivity, agricultural, 8, 163–8,

productivity, agricultural—(*cont.*)
    272, 290–1, 403–4; labour, 168; *see
    also* economic growth
property relations, 22; *see also*
    production relations; property rights
property rights, 79, 81, 163, 165,
    268n.; *see also* economic
    development; land tenure;
    production relations; property
    relations
proto-industry, *see* manufacture
Protonotaro, 48
Provence, 67n., 170n., 348
Puglia, 9, 258, 265, 291n., 410
Puleo, Cesare, 252n.; Nicola, 252n.

questione meridionale, *see* southern
    Italy

Racalmuto, 43, 49n., 326
Racalseni (*feudo*), 370
Raccuia, 47
Raffadali, 225
Ragusa (Bicino), 29, 45, 66, 334n.;
    economy, 187, 193, 194
Raia, 43
rainfall, 29, 32; *see also* climate; water
    supply
Rametta, 46, 52, 127
Randazzo, 18, 117, 124–5, 126, 130n.,
    228n., 241, 332n., 334n., 335n.,
    336n., 355n., 356n., 361, 364n., 368,
    372, 373n.; district, 131, 191;
    economy, 136n., 174, 178, 187, 189,
    191, 193, 194, 206n.; population, 45,
    54, 64, 67, 71, 195, 242; trade, 100,
    102, 103, 105, 110, 118, 121n., 125,
    173, 190, 206, 260, 261n.
da Rasignano, Simone, 251n.
Regalbuto (Racalbuto), 45, 61n., 110,
    130, 335n., 336n., 361
Reggio Calabria, 82, 246, 247, 253–4,
    255n.; trade, 105, 106, 203, 228,
    235n., 241, 264, 266; *see also*
    Calabria; Messina
region, 1, 9; definition, 80–1, 82;
    differentiation of, 23–74, 81; *see also*
    market structures; specialization
Regiovanni, 45
Rella, Nicola, 252n.
Resico, 48
Resuttano, 260n., 369n.
Ridolfi, Leonardo, 235n.
Rimasi, Cataldo, 252n.
Rindelli, Bernardo, 252n.; Pietro, 217,
    252n.

Risalaimi, 193
Risignolo, Matteo, 228n.
rivers, navigation of, 103; *see also*
    transport
Rizari, Federico, 356n.; Goffredo, 217
Robert of Anjou, king of Naples, 85,
    247
Roccella, 47, 110, 117n., 329n., 333n.
Romagna, 5
Roman Campagna, 169
Romania, 179n.
Romano, Giovanni, 218
Rome, trade, 180n., 294, 304–5
Rosso, Enrico, 266n.
Ruvetum, 224

Saccàno, family, 218; Giacomo, 258;
    Ludovico, 236; Pietro, 258
Salaparuta, 49n.
Salemi, 42, 71, 131, 137, 342n., 355n.,
    356n., 358, 361, 369n.; economy,
    172, 193; trade, 101, 110
Salerno, 3
Salice, 205n.
Salso, river, 29, 138
salt, 29, 130–1, 222–7; trade, 94, 106,
    223–6, 256; *see also* taxation
saltpetre, 234–5, 303
Salvatore, 47
Sambuca, 42
San Calogero di Augusta, 110; abbey,
    333n.
San Filippo di Argirò, 110, 130, 225,
    333n., 361
San Filippo lo Grande, 205n.
San Filippo del Piano, 49, 52
San Fratello, 47, 111, 259n., 260n.,
    329n., 330, 335n., 343n., 361
San Giovanni Gemini, 225
San Marco, *casali*, 47; county, 47,
    49n., 215, 259n., 329n., 331n.
San Martino, 48
San Martino delle Scale, monastery,
    194
San Mauro, 46, 49n., 335n.
San Michele, 205n.
San Miniato, 252n.
San Pantaleo, 224
San Pietro di Nocino, 47
San Pietro Patti, 47, 111, 193, 321n.,
    329n., 332n., 333n., 343n., 356n.
San Pietro di Raccuia, 335n.
San Salvatore Ficalia, 49
San Salvatore di Linguafaro,
    monastery, 251n.

San Todaro, 66, 130
San Vito lo Capo, 130
Sant'Andrea, monastery, 333n.
Sant'Andrea dell'Arcivescovo, 48, 214n., 333n.
Sant'Angelo di Brolo, 48, 107n., 330, 355n., 369n.
Sant'Angelo Muxaro, 225
Santa Lucia, 45, 127, 128n., 361, 369n.; economy, 52, 136n., 193, 205n., 211, 214, 215
Santa Maria di Messina, monastery, 246n.
Santa Maria di Valle Josaphat, monastery, 246n.
Santo Spirito, 43; abbey, 333n.
Santo Stefano di Briga, 205n.
Santo Stefano (Mistretta), 127n., 128n., 369n.
Santo Stefano (di Quisquina), 43, 61n., 335n.
Saponara, 47, 332n.
Sardinia, 1, 9, 25, 273; trade, 94, 223–5, 273n., 303
Savoca, 47, 66, 111, 179n., 330, 369n.
Savona, 272n.
Scaletta, 47, 64, 252
Sciacca, 29, 42, 64, 68n., 71, 90n., 283n., 355n., 361–2, 364, 367n., 368n., 381, 382n.; economy, 136n., 173, 186–90, 230, 235; trade, 101, 102, 107n., 111, 161n., (grain), 137, 139, 140, 256, 274n.
Scicli, 45, 66, 187, 193, 362
Scilla, 105, 106, 254n., 264
Scillato, 111, 117
Sclafani, 42, 329n.; county of, 117, 191, 193, 332n.
Sclafani, family, 89, 318; Matteo, 55n.
secrezie, income from, 55n., 248–9, 252, 253–4, 377–8, 382, 385; *see also* taxation
da Serbia, Giorgio, 252n.
Sereni, E., 8, 11, 404
serfdom, 33, 282, 318–19, 330–1, 349; consequences of, 10; and individual mobility, 151, 319, 331; and labour services, 132, 330; as result of foreign trade, 276; *see also* peasants
da Settimo, Cellino, 251n.
settlement, desertions, 55, 86, 316; new, 55n., 61, 66, 68, 346, 408; patterns, 37, 54, 95; records of, 57n.; *see also casali*; Greece; *and names of individual valli*

Sferracavallo, 129
Sforza, Corrado, 263; Gian Galeazzo, duke of Milan, 263
sheep, husbandry, 172, 174, 188; trade, 257, 259
shipping, 303–4, 305, 310–12; *see also* trade; transport
Sicaminò, 48, 224
Sicily, eastern, 16, 18, 19, 36–7, 54, 85, 89, 92, 94, 102, 168, 336, (cities), 70, 95, 251, (economy), 93, 138, 140, 171, 180, 181, 186, 187, 189, 202, 203, 215, 217–18, 272, 274–5, 293, 408, (trade), 100, 102, 120, 121; kingdom of, (and Aragonese), 18, 50, 85, 93, 122, 180, 250, 304, 324–5, 352–3, 358, 390–7, 400, (civil war), 56, 85, 88–9, 94, 317–22, (claims to), 3, 4, 322, 324, (independence), 250, 393–7; western, 16, 18, 19, 37, 54, 85, 88, 89, 92, 94, 346, (cities), 70, (economy), 138, 171, 173, 181, 194, 215–17, 274, 292, (trade), 93, 102, 120, 300–3.
Sicily *citra Salsum, see* Sicily, eastern
Sicily *ultra Salsum, see* Sicily, western
Siculiana, 66, 332n.
silk, industry, 118n., 183, 185, 196n., 200–2, 206–10, 408–9; production, 201–6, 238, 407; trade 9, 201, 202, 203–5, 294–6, 301, 303
silver, mines, 236; *see also* bullion flows
Simeto, river, 103n.
Sinagra, 48, 191, 373n.
Sinopoli, 254n., 260n.
slaves, trade, 296, 303, 309; *see also* agriculture
Smith, Adam, 6
Smith, C. A., 150
Solanto, 129, 332n.
Soler, Antonio, 228n.
Sorrenti, L., 345
Sorrento, 180n.
Sortino, 44, 101, 102, 214
southern Italy, economy, 1, 5, 7, 9, 10, 163, 243; and economic theory, 2, 11; and *questione meridionale*, 1, 4, 7, 10, 402–12; *see also* market integration; market structure; Naples
Spaccaforno, 49n., 329n.
Spagnolo, Antonio, 254n.
Spain, 2, 82, 188, 201, 205, 223

Spatafora, Federico, 260n.; Giacomo, 205n.; Guglielmo, 236; Rinaldo, 215n.
Speciale, Nicola, 327–8; Vassallo, 217, 395n.
specialization, 76–7, 80, 83–4, 176, 208–9, 306, 409; hindrances to, 4, 79, 96, 134, 136, 160–1, 406–7, 412; regional, 1, 9, 12, 17, 25, 75–161, 162–239, 240–67, 269, 402, 407; *see also* animal husbandry; cloth; economic development; fairs; grain; market integration; region; trade; wine
spelt, 52
Sperlinga, 48
Spinola, family, 272n.; Atellino, 231; Damiano, 231–2
de Spuches, family, 218
Staiti, family, 211, 218; Andrea, 215n.; Giovan Andrea, 205n.; Nicolò, 215n.; Pietro, 205n.
state, administration, 337–8; bureaucracy, 211; crisis, 87, 89, 102, 132; policies (economic), 95, 113, 116, 236–7, 290, 374–5; policies (financial), 340–3, 375–83, 387–90; and urban society, 349, 354, 366–8; *see also* aristocracy; captaincy; castellany; demesne; justiciary; taxation; transaction costs; *and names of individual kings of Sicily*
steel, *see* iron
de Succarrati, Pietro, 252n.
sugar, industry, 187, 210–22, 237–8, 259, 284, 295, 346, 407; trade, 106, 210, 215n., 294–5, 301, 303; *see also* Azores; cattle; Egypt; Madeira; taxation
sulphur, 29, 230, 232, 234–5
Sunyer, Francesch, 265n.
Sutera, 42, 111, 121n., 224–5, 321n., 335n., 355n., 369n., 381, 382
Syracuse, 18, 29, 67, 131, 185, 252n., 321n., 360, 361–3, 373n., 381; economy, 176, 178, 186, 187, 189, 190, 194, 212, 226, 257; population, 45, 57n., 64, 71; trade, 99, 101, 102, 103, 105n., 111, 121, 229, 284n., 297n.; and urban hierarchy, 70, 152, 154, 249; *see also* Camera reginale; parliament; val di Noto

Tano, 65, 66

Taormina, 46, 52, 127, 129, 130n., 355n., 356n., 361–2, 369n.; economy, 178, 179, 214, 215, 217, 218; trade, 100–1, 102, 105, 111, 125 tariffs, *see* trade
taxation, 36, 37, 40, 52, 59–60, 375–83, 385–6; and animal husbandry, 175; direct, (*colletta*), 57, 59, (*donativo*), 62–3, 383, 390, (*fodrum*), 50, 138, 172, 176, (*subsidium*), 37 (*subventio generalis*), 36–7, 40n.; exemption from, 128, 376n., 395–6; and grain trade, 87, 120, 122–3, 141, 160, 271, 276–81, 291, 341, 342, 376, 378; indirect, 96, 97, 115, 116, 356, 376, 381–3, 385–6, (*gabella del cannamele*), 214, 216, (*gabella di dogana, ius dohane*), 107, 161n., 333n., 355n., (*gabella tareni*), 249, (*tratta, ius exiturae*), 139, 271n., 273, 276–8, 280–1; intensity, 329, 337, 354, 355–7, 366–7, 376, 380, 383–90; limits to, 59, 354, 375–6; opposition to, 87, 329, 367, 380–1, 387, 390–3; and regional resources, 383–90; of salt, 222–3, 381; and warfare, 87, 95, 328, 371, 376, 380, 383, 390, 403, 410; *see also* Aragon; aristocracy; demesne; economic development; feudal lands; Jews; Naples; *secrezie*; trade; transaction costs; *and names of individual kings of Sicily*
Termini, 18, 27, 29, 42, 68n., 140–1, 242, 252n., 356n., 360; economy, 138, 139, 225; trade, 101, 102, 111, 333; *see also* Appennino siculo
Terra di Lavoro, 410
Terranova (Eraclea), 44, 152, 154, 321n.; economy, 138, 185, 186, 224–5; population, 54, 64–5, 69, 71, 74
Thomas, R. P., 96
del Tignoso, Bartolomeo, 252n.
timber, transport, 168; trade, 124–5, 256, 257
tin, 236, 301
Tindari, 111, 118, 126, 132
Tolfa, 230n., 231, 232
Torto, river, 26
Tortorici, 47, 111, 215, 228n., 328n., 335n.
town–country relations, 78, 80–1, 83, 124–33, 156, 159–60; and grain supply, 137, 147–8; and guilds, 197–8; *see also* demesne; district

trade, balance of, 91n.; 300–12; and depopulation, 78, 79, 158; long-distance, (composition of), 17, 268–9, (impact of), 4, 6, 10, 12, 16, 83–4, 243, 268–70, 281–2, 300, 312–13, 404, 407–10, (volume of), 12, 410, (and politics), 82, 87, 92–3, 250, 276–80, 284–7; and tariffs, 79, 81, 82, 116; and tariff franchises, 83, 96–120, 137, 160–1, 241, 264, 306–7, 410–11; terms of, 79, 287–9, 409; *see also* currency; economic development; fairs; market integration; merchants; shipping, specialization; state; transaction costs; transport

transaction costs, 81–2, 83, 96–7, ·115–16, 121–3, 158, 241, 269–70, 291, 306, 342, 406, 412; and warfare, 86; *see also* economic development; fairs; market structure; measurements; piracy; state; trade; Vespers; warfare

transhumance, 169, 173, 188, 334n.; *see also* animal husbandry; *Dogana dei Paschi*; *Dogana delle pecore*; *Mesta*

transport, 123, 180, 411; costs, 81, 82, 137, 226, 291; *see also* rivers

Trapani, 18, 29, 56, 70, 130–1, 137, 140, 188, 256n., 326n., 343n., 355n., 356n., 361–2, 366, 396; economy, 135n., 136n., 173, 178, 179, 189, 206n., 212, 224–6, 234, 309; population, 42, 57n., 59–60, 69, 71, 74; trade, 94, 99, 101, 102, 105n., 111, 130, 161n., 229, 261, 286n.

Trasselli, C., 13n., 33, 62, 336, 338

Trastámara, dynasty, 325; *see also* Alfonso V; Ferdinand I; Juan II; Pedro of Aragon

Tremestieri, 205n.

Tripi, 47, 127, 211, 325n., 329n., 333, 399; economy, 214, 215, 217; trade, 101, 102, 110, 111

Trocculi, 43

de Troia, Antonio, 203

Troina, 45, 321n., 356n., 382; economy, 136n., 263n.; trade, 101, 102, 112

Tropea, 94n., 180n., 228n.

Tuffa di Tommaso, 251n.

Tunis, 244

tunny, industry, 172n., 219, 226, 284, 346; trade, 294–5, 303

Turkey, grain exports, 408

Tusa, 46, 49n., 66

Tuscany, 1, 82, 106, 170n., 235, 258, 291, 292

Uberti, family, 318n.

Ucria, 46, 179n., 191, 335n., 336n.

Umbria, 5

Umiliati, order of, 194

underdevelopment, *see* economic backwardness

urban administration, membership of, 323; powers, 132, 156, 353; records, 18; *see also* demesne; town–country relations

urban élites, 132, 159, 171, 211, 322–4, 345, 348, 350–3, 354, 358, 378, 379, 391–7; *see also* civic nobility

urbanization, 71, 72, 83; and regional markets, 150–7; threshold, 72n., 73–4, 151; and urban networks, 53, 70–1, 150–7; *see also* central places; economic development; market structures; town–country relations

de Urrea, Lope Ximen, 265–6, 365n.

de Ursa, Gilbert, 217

usage rights, 131, 369–70; *see also* property rights

da Uzzano, Giovanni, 120

Valcorrente, 46

val Demone, 32, 125; economy, 68, 149, 172–3, 174, 181, 187, 189, 191, 201–3, 206, 207–9, 214, 215, 220, 236, 240–67, 294–5, 346, 407; land tenure in, 156, 165, 282, 319; population, 51, 52n., 57–60, 63, 66–8, 73, 407; relations with Calabria, 87, 173, 241–67; settlement patterns, 54, 86, 198n.; social conflict, 327, 331, 336, 338, 372; trade, 118, 121, 256; urban hierarchy, 130, 131, 154; *see also* Calabria; Messina

val di Mazara, 32, 86; economy, 68, 172, 174, 181, 185, 187, 189, 210, 214, 336, 407–8; population, 51, 52n., 57, 58, 60, 62, 66, 68, 73; settlement patterns, 54, 198n., 338; social conflict, 327, 331, 372; urban hierarchy, 70, 154; *see also* Palermo

val di Noto, 32, 86; economy, 173–4, 181, 185, 187, 189, 191, 206, 209, 214, 215, 218, 220, 346, 407, 409;

462   *Index*

val di Noto—(*cont.*)
  population, 51, 52n., , 57, 58, 60, 63,
    66, 68, 73, 195, 407; settlement
    patterns, 54, 198, 338; social conflict,
    327, 331, 336, 372; trade, 103, 121,
    297n.; urban hierarchy, 70, 130, 152,
    154; *see also Camera reginale*;
    Catania; Syracuse
Valencia, trade, 190, 229, 262, 273n.;
    kingdom of, 381, 386, (aristocracy),
    324–5
vallo, 32–3
Venetico, 46
Veneto, 50, 236
Venice, 11, 55, 157; trade, 10, 204,
    205n., 229, 235, 272, 284n.
Ventimiglia, family, 88, 89, 92, 315n.,
    318; Francesco I, 316, 345;
    Francesco II, 90, 320, 321n.;
    Francesco, 337n.; Giovanni, 329
Vespers, revolt of, 349,
    (consequences), 3–4, 13, 95; war of,
    3–4, 57, 94, 247, (consequences), 69,
    85–95, 152, 201, 240, 244–5, 246–8,
    254–6, 271–2, 285; *see also*
    Angevins; Croce, B.; Sicily; vicars;
    warfare
Vicari, 42, 212
vicars, (regents) of Sicily, 89, 322; *see
    also* Vespers
Vicens Vives, J., 394, 397
Villafranca, 66
de Villardita, Giovanni, 252n.
Villari, R., 403
Vindicari, 224

Visconti, dinasty, 57; Filippo Maria,
    duke of Milan, 263, 264n.; Gian
    Galeazzo, duke of Milan, 94
Vizzini, 45, 67, 101, 102, 130n.
Vulcano, 230

wages, 56, 167–8, 170, 171n., 216, 316,
    373
Wallerstein, I., 11, 14
warfare, consequences of, 55, 86, 95,
    246, 252–3; *see also* Vespers
water supply, 27, 131, 183–4, 185, 191,
    212, 215, 216–17, 337; *see also*
    climate; rainfall
Weber, M., 6
William I, king of Sicily, 243
wine, production, 131, 135, 162,
    176–81, 219, 316, 346, (specialized),
    135, 178–81; trade, (domestic), 105,
    122, 129, 130, 132, 134–6, 178, 257,
    346, (long-distance), 9, 106, 135n.,
    179, 180n., 301
woodlands, 27, 29
wool, manufacture, 183, 184, 191–6,
    198, 199, 230, 231, (*orbace*), 118n.,
    184, 191, 194, 198, 199; production,
    174, 188; trade, 188, 301; *see also*
    sheep

Yandicaturi, 66
Yver, G., 4

Zacchi, Michele, 232n.
Zangheri, R., 405
Zumbo, Jaime, 217
Zuppardino, 48

Past and Present Publications

General Editor: PAUL SLACK, *Exeter College, Oxford*

Family and Inheritance: Rural Society in Western Europe 1200–1800, edited by Jack Goody, Joan Thirsk and E. P. Thompson*

French Society and the Revolution, edited by Douglas Johnson

Peasants, Knights and Heretics: Studies in Medieval English Social History, edited by R. H. Hilton*

Towns in Societies: Essays in Economic History and Historical Sociology, edited by Philip Abrams and E. A. Wrigley*

Desolation of a City: Coventry and the Urban Crisis of the Late Middle Ages, Charles Phythian-Adams

Puritanism and Theatre: Thomas Middleton and Opposition Drama under the Early Stuarts, Margot Heinemann*

Lords and Peasants in a Changing Society: The Estates of the Bishopric of Worcester 680–1540, Christopher Dyer

Life, Marriage and Death in a Medieval Parish: Economy, Society and Demography in Halesowen 1270–1400, Zvi Razi

Biology, Medicine and Society 1840–1940, edited by Charles Webster

The Invention of Tradition, edited by Eric Hobsbawm and Terence Ranger*

Industrialization before Industrialization: Rural Industry and the Genesis of Capitalism, Peter Kriedte, Hans Medick and Jürgen Schlumbohm*†

The Republic in the Village: The People of the Var from the French Revolution to the Second Republic, Maurice Aghulhon†

Social Relations and Ideas: Essays in Honour of R. H. Hilton, edited by T. H. Aston, P. R. Coss, Christopher Dyer and Joan Thirsk

A Medieval Society: The West Midlands at the End of the Thirteenth Century, R. H. Hilton

Winstanley: 'The Law of Freedom' and Other Writings, edited by Christopher Hill

Crime in Seventeenth-Century England: A County Study, J. A. Sharpe†

The Crisis of Feudalism: Economy and Society in Eastern Normandy c. 1300–1500, Guy Bois†

The Development of the Family and Marriage in Europe, Jack Goody*

Disputes and Settlements: Law and Human Relations in the West, edited by John Bossy

Rebellion, Popular Protest and the Social Order in Early Modern England, edited by Paul Slack

Studies on Byzantine Literature of the Eleventh and Twelfth Centuries, Alexander Kazhdan in collaboration with Simon Franklin†

The English Rising of 1381, edited by R. H. Hilton and T. H. Aston*

Praise and Paradox: Merchants and Craftsmen in Elizabethan Popular Literature, Laura Caroline Stevenson

The Brenner Debate: Agrarian Class Structure and Economic Development in Pre-Industrial Europe, edited by T. H. Aston and C. H. E. Philpin*

Eternal Victory: Triumphal Rulership in Late Antiquity, Byzantium, and the Early Medieval West, Michael McCormick*†

East-Central Europe in Transition: From the Fourteenth to the Seventeenth Century, edited by Antoni Mączak, Henry Samsonowicz and Peter Burke†

Small Books and Pleasant Histories: Popular Fiction and its Readership in Seventeenth-Century England, Margaret Spufford*

Society, Politics and Culture: Studies in Early Modern England, Mervyn James*

Horses, Oxen and Technological Innovation: The Use of Draught Animals in English Farming 1066–1600, John Langdon

Nationalism and Popular Protest in Ireland, edited by C. H. E. Philpin

Rituals of Royalty: Power and Ceremonial in Traditional Societies, edited by David Cannadine and Simon Price*

The Margins of Society in Late Medieval Paris, Bronisław Geremek†

Landlords, Peasants and Politics in Medieval England, edited by T. H. Aston

Geography, Technology, and War: Studies in the Maritime History of the Mediterranean, 649–1572, John H. Pryor*

Church Courts, Sex and Marriage in England, 1570–1640, Martin Ingram*

Searches for an Imaginary Kingdom: The Legend of the Kingdom of Prester John, L. N. Gumilev

Crowds and History: Mass Phenomena in English Towns, 1780–1835, Mark Harrison

Concepts of Cleanliness: Changing Attitudes in France since the Middle Ages, Georges Vigarello†

The First Modern Society: Essays in English History in Honour of Lawrence Stone, edited by A. L. Beier, David Cannadine and James M. Rosenheim

The Europe of the Devout: The Catholic Reformation and the Formation of a New Society, Louis Châtellier†

English Rural Society, 1500–1800: Essays in Honour of Joan Thirsk, edited by John Chartres and David Hey

Lordship, Knighthood and Locality: A Study in English Society c. 1180–c. 1280, P. R. Coss

English and French Towns in Feudal Society: A Comparative Study, R. H. Hilton

An Island for Itself: Economic Development and Social Change in Late Medieval Sicily, Stephan R. Epstein

* Published also as a paperback
† Co-published with the Maison des Sciences de l'Homme, Paris

Printed in the United Kingdom
by Lightning Source UK Ltd.
9724900001B/1-18